INSIDE COMMODORE DOS

INSIDE COMMODORE DOS

by

Richard Immers, Ph.D.
Adrian Public Schools
Adrian, Michigan

and

Gerald G. Neufeld, Ph.D.
Brandon University
Brandon, Manitoba
Canada

Technical Illustrations by
Diane M. Corralejo

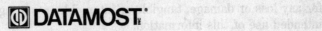

19821 Nordhoff Street, Northridge, CA 91324
(818) 709-1202

First Printing, July 1984
Second Printing, February 1985
Third Printing, May 1985
Fourth Printing, October 1985

RESTON PUBLISHING COMPANY, INC.
A Prentice-Hall Company
Reston, Virginia
ISBN 0-8359-3091-2

ACKNOWLEDGEMENTS

A manual like this one would not be possible without a great deal of technical assistance. Mike Todd's Disk File column in the *ICPUG Newsletter* proved to be an invaluable source of insight into the inner workings of Commodore's DOS. Raeto West's book, *Programming the PET/CBM*, was a constant companion. Jim Butterfield's numerous articles also provided valuable bits and pieces of information. Brad Templeton's POWER™ system and PAL™ assembler made the development of the programs in this manual a real joy. These packages are commercially available from Professional Software Inc. In addition, both the PAL disassembler and MICROMON were used as tools for disassembling the 1541 DOS.

We would also like to acknowledge the patience and forebearance of our families and friends. Without their support, producing this manual would have been considerably more difficult. Mike Louder of DATAMOST, Inc. also provided tremendous support for its production.

Finally, we would like to extend a special note of thanks to Dr. Tom MacNeil and Nancy Neufeld for their diligent work in proofreading this manual.

This manual was written on a Commodore computer system using the WordPro 4 Plus word processing system. The WordPro Plus™ Series is commercially available from Professional Software Inc. This sophisticated word processing system made editing and last minute revisions much easier.

TABLE OF CONTENTS

Ignorance is a precious thing.
Once lost, it can never be regained.

CHAPTER 1

INTRODUCTION

This manual is intended to supplement the documentation provided in the *1541 User's Manual*. Although this manual is primarily designed to meet the needs of the intermediate to advanced programmer, it will also be of interest to the novice Commodore user who wants to know more about how his 1541 disk drive works. This manual is not intended to replace the documentation provided by Commodore Business Machines, Inc. and the reader is assumed to be relatively familiar with the contents of the *1541 User's Manual*. For the sake of continuity and clarity, some of the information covered in the *1541 User's Manual* is also presented here. However, the majority of the information presented in this manual is original and is the result of intensive disassembly and annotation of the 1541's DOS by the authors. Some information is based on articles and notes published in a variety of publications as well as discussions with other knowledgeable disk experts.

This manual was not prepared with the assistance of Commodore Business Machines, Inc. Although we cannot guarantee the accuracy of all the information presented in this manual, the material has been thoroughly researched and tested.

There were several reasons for writing *Inside Commodore DOS*:

1. To correct errors and omissions in the *1541 User's Manual*.
2. To help you make more effective use of your disk drive.
3. To provide complete information on diskette formatting.
4. To provide complete information on the storage of files.
5. To allow you to read and write data in non-standard ways.
6. To help you make a backup copy of your "protected" diskettes.
7. To help you recover damaged diskettes.
8. To help you understand the operation of your disk drive.

Although this manual focuses primarily on the 1541 disk drive, much of the information also applies to other Commodore disk drives.

1.1 A Brief Word About the Programs

This book contains listings for 46 ready-to-use programs written in BASIC. These programs are copyrighted. They may NOT be used commercially, in whole or in part, period. Since many of the programs are long, typing them all in would be a time consuming, tedious task. Feel free to share your typing efforts with a friend who has also purchased a copy of this book. In return, we simply ask that you do not share a program with someone who does not own a legitimate copy of this book.

11

The programs in this book are disk utilities. They do not use flashy graphics or sound. Rather, they are extremely powerful tools. Remember, any tool can be dangerous if it is used improperly. Be sure that you know what you are doing before you use a given program. Always experiment with a program on a test diskette before you actually use it on one that contains valuable programs or data. Practice makes perfect.

Each program was individually tested on a variety of 1541 disk drives having a wide range of serial numbers. Moreover, each program always worked perfectly. Unfortunately, it is impossible to guarantee that a particular program will work with your model. If a given program does not seem to work properly, check your typing carefully. Any errors, especially in the DATA statements which contain a machine language program, will produce problems.

As a courtesy to the more advanced programmer, we have also included the source listings for each machine language routine. A source listing immediately follows a related BASIC program listing and has a file name ending in ".PAL". It is for use with the PAL assembler. *Note: If you are using a different assembler, you may have to make some minor changes.*

The programs in this book were designed to be not only useful and beneficial, but instructive as well. Many of them illustrate the "state of the art" in the use of Commodore's direct-access disk commands. Enjoy!

1.2 How to Type in the Programs

Program listings in books and magazines often suffer from two problems: typographical errors that occur when the program is retyped into a word processor and the readability of Commodore's control characters (e.g., the reverse field heart that means Clear Screen). To overcome these problems, the program listings for this book were created using a special "lister" program. This lister program took a working BASIC program and converted it into a WordPro™ file. At the same time, control characters were spelled out in words and surrounded by curly brackets. For example, a reverse field heart was converted to {CLR}. The table below summarizes the listing conventions, the corresponding control characters, and the proper key/keys to press on your C64 or VIC-20.

When You See	What It Represents	What You Type
{CLR}	Clear Screen	Hold down SHIFT and press CLR/HOME
{HOME}	Home Cursor	Press CLR/HOME
{DOWN}	Cursor Down	Press CRSR/DOWN
{UP}	Cursor Up	Hold down SHIFT and press CRSR/UP
{RIGHT}	Cursor Right	Press CRSR/RIGHT
{LEFT}	Cursor Left	Hold down SHIFT and press CRSR/LEFT
{RVS}	Reverse Field ON	Hold down CTRL and press 9
{ROFF}	Reverse Field OFF	Hold down CTRL and press 0

NOTE 1: When a number appears inside the curly brackets, it means you repeat the control character immediately to the left of the number that many times. For example:

{DOWN 5} means to press CRSR/DOWN five (5) times.

NOTE 2: All programs have been listed in a column 40 characters wide. Except where special characters have been spelled out between curly brackets, the lines are listed exactly as they appear on a Commodore 64 display. Spaces must be typed in as listed. Where necessary, count the character columns to determine the appropriate number of spaces.

Happy hunting and pecking!

CHAPTER 2

USING THE 1541'S DOS

2.1 The Purpose of a DOS

A disk operating system (DOS) is a machine language program that controls a disk drive. It does several different tasks:

1. Handling communications between a disk drive and a computer.
2. Carrying out housekeeping chores such as formatting a diskette.
3. Managing the storage of information on a diskette.
4. Reading and writing information onto a diskette's surface.

In many computer systems, a DOS is loaded into the main computer's memory from diskette when the computer is first switched on. In this type of system many of the tasks are carried out using the computer's microprocessor and RAM. Commodore uses a different approach. All of Commodore's disk drives are intelligent peripherals. They do not have to use the computer's resources; they have their own. For example, the 1541 disk drive contains its own 6502 microprocessor, 2K of RAM, two 6522 I/O chips, and a DOS program permanently stored in 15.8K of ROM.

The advantages of having an intelligent disk drive are:

1. The DOS does not use any of the computer's memory.
2. Some disk operations can be carried out independently from the CPU.
3. Disk operations do not slow down processing.
4. One disk drive can be shared among several computers.

The disadvantages of having an intelligent disk drive are:

1. It is very difficult to customize DOS routines.
2. You must replace the ROMs to convert to a new version of DOS.

2.2 Communicating with the 1541

Your Commodore 64 or VIC-20 can communicate with your 1541 disk drive in several ways:

1. Through the LOAD, SAVE, and VERIFY commands.
2. Through I/O using the command channel.
3. Through I/O using data communication channels.

15

Let's examine each of these in greater detail.

1. LOAD, SAVE, and VERIFY commands:

These BASIC commands are used to store and retrieve programs on the Commodore tape and disk drives. They are designed for ease of use, even by the novice. The BASIC interpreter in the computer interprets these commands and sends the disk drive the necessary information over the serial bus.

2. I/O using the command channel:

The command channel is used to send messages to the disk drive to carry out disk operations like: formatting a blank diskette, erasing an unwanted file, renaming a file, etc. These operations are often referred to as disk housekeeping. The command channel is also used to input messages, such as the current error status of the drive, generated by the DOS. For more details on how to use the command channel, see Section 2.4.

3. I/O using data communication channels:

The 1541 DOS supports a variety of kinds of files: program files, sequential files, relative files, user files, and direct-access files. The storage and retrieval of information in files is carried out using a data communication channel. Although this manual provides detailed information regarding how files are stored and organized, no attempt is made to teach you how to develop programs that make extensive use of file handling. We would encourage readers who are interested in file handling techniques to refer to Jim Butterfield's series of articles in *COMPUTE!*. The only I/O applications discussed in this manual are those relating to direct-access programming (see Chapter 5).

Since the rest of this manual makes extensive use of the command channel, let's examine it in some detail.

2.3 The Command Channel

The command channel (channel number 15) is an important communication link between your computer and the 1541 disk drive. It has several important functions. You can use it to:

1. Monitor the error status of the drive to ensure that everything is operating properly.
2. Send commands that direct the DOS to perform various housekeeping chores associated with disk handling.
3. Send commands that direct the DOS to read or write information to specific areas on a diskette.

This chapter focuses on the first two of these uses. Chapter 5 provides more detail on reading or writing to a diskette.

2.4 Using the Command Channel

Using the command channel is easy. Just follow these steps:

1. Establish communications using an OPEN statement.
2. Send commands to the DOS using a PRINT# statement.
3. Read DOS messages using a GET# or INPUT# statement.
4. Close the channel using a CLOSE statement when you are finished.

Let's go over each step to ensure that you know exactly what to do.

1. Establishing communications using an OPEN statement.

In order to establish a communication channel between your computer and your 1541 disk drive, you use an OPEN statement. An OPEN statement is a BASIC command which looks like this:

```
SYNTAX:  OPEN file#, device#, channel#

EXAMPLE: OPEN 15, 8, 15
```

where

file#   = the logical file number (1–127)

device#   = the device number (8 for a stock 1541)

channel#   = the channel number or secondary address (2-15)

NOTE: Channel numbers 0 & 1 are reserved for use by the DOS.
        Channel numbers 2-14 are data communications channels.
        Channel number 15 is the command channel.

The OPEN statement can be used either in immediate mode (typed and executed directly from the keyboard) or under program control (embedded in a program).

In the example above (OPEN 15, 8, 15) we opened logical file number 15 on the C64 to device number 8 (the disk drive) through channel 15 (the command channel).

2. Sending commands to the DOS using a PRINT# statement.

In order to send commands from your computer to the 1541, you use a PRINT# statement. A PRINT# statement is a BASIC command which looks like this:

```
SYNTAX:  PRINT# file#, "command"

EXAMPLE: PRINT#15, "NO:MY DISKETTE,MD"
```

where

file#   = the logical file number you used when you opened the command channel

command = the disk command to be sent to the DOS

NOTE: The statement is PRINT# not PRINT #. You *must not* put a space before the # sign. Spaces following the # sign are always optional. DO NOT use ?# as an abbreviation either. The correct abbreviation is pR(p then SHIFTED R).

In this example, the disk command is "N0:MY DISKETTE,MD". This command causes the DOS to prepare the blank diskette in the drive for first-time use.

Although there are many different disk commands, they fall into two groups:

1. Commands related to disk housekeeping.
2. Commands to read or write data to a diskette or the disk drive's RAM.

The disk housekeeping commands are discussed in the next part of this chapter. The commands relating to reading or writing data are discussed in Chapter 5 on Direct-Access Programming.

3. Reading DOS messages using a GET# or an INPUT# statement.

You may use either an INPUT# or a GET# statement to read the command channel and access any messages or data prepared for the computer by the DOS. Both INPUT# and GET# statements are BASIC commands. They look like this:

```
SYNTAX:   INPUT# file#, variable list
          GET# file#, variable list

EXAMPLE:  INPUT# 15, EN, EM$, ET, ES
          GET# 15, A$
```

where

file#   = the logical file number you used when you opened the command channel

variable list = one or more variable names separated by commas

NOTE: As was noted for PRINT# above, the BASIC statements are INPUT# and GET#, not INPUT # and GET #. You *must not* put a space before the # sign. Spaces following the # sign are always optional. Neither the INPUT# statement nor the GET# statement can be used in immediate mode (typed and executed directly from the keyboard). They must be included within a program.

The INPUT# command and the GET# command operate in much the same way as the more familiar INPUT and GET commands. INPUT# always reads as far as the next carriage return character while GET# reads a single byte of information. Generally, GET# is used in direct-access programming and INPUT# is used only for monitoring the drive's error status as indicated immediately below.

You can check the error status of your disk drive using the command channel. The DOS monitors every disk operation as it is carried out and prepares a status report indicating whether or not the operation was completed successfully. The report consists of an error code number, an English language message, and the track and sector where the problem, if any, was encountered. Here is a subroutine that checks the error status.

```
100 OPEN 15,8,15 : REM
   THE OPEN COMMAND CHANNEL
          . . .
500 INPUT#15,EN,EM$,ET,ES : REM
   INPUT THE ERROR STATUS
510 IF EN < 20 THEN RETURN : REM
   NO ERROR ENCOUNTERED
520 PRINT EN;EM$;ET;ES : REM
   PRINT THE ERROR STATUS ON SCREEN
530 CLOSE 15 : END : REM
   ABORT ON BAD STATUS
```

Line 100 opens the command channel. It is a good idea to open the command channel at the beginning of your program and leave it open until the end. Line 500 inputs the status report. The error code number is stored in EN, the message in EM$, the track in ET, and the sector in ES. Error codes less than 20 may be ignored (line 510). A complete list of the error codes and messages is contained in the back of your *1541 User's Manual*. A detailed explanation of the nature and cause of many of these errors is provided in Chapter 7 on Disk Protection.

4. CLOSE the command channel when you are done.

After you have finished using the command channel, it should be closed. Recall that the open command has three parameters: the logical file number, the device number, and the channel number. The close command has only one, the logical file number. It looks like this:

SYNTAX: CLOSE file#

EXAMPLE: CLOSE 15

where

file# = the logical file number you used when you opened the command channel

NOTE: Loading, running, or editing a program closes down all communication channels automatically. The command channel is closed properly in each instance. However, data channels are aborted rather than closed. When a data channel is aborted, the file is NOT CLOSED properly on the disk drive. You do not have to close the command channel after the issuance of every command. If you forget to close it, the worst that can happen is a ?FILE OPEN ERROR when you attempt to open it again. However, you should get into the habit of always closing a file when you are finished using it. You won't get into trouble leaving the command channel open, but you may lose an important data file if you leave a data communication channel open.

2.5 Disk Housekeeping

As your collection of programs grows, you will have to do some housekeeping to keep things in shape. Disk housekeeping chores include the following:

1. Preparing a blank diskette for first-time use.
2. Erasing the contents of a diskette currently in use.
3. Initializing a diskette.
4. Renaming a file.
5. Scratching or erasing a file.
6. Copying a file.

These operations are carried out by the DOS in response to commands sent to the drive using the command channel as indicated above. Once a disk housekeeping command is issued, the disk drive will carry out the task without further intervention by the computer. This means that you could edit or even RUN a program in RAM while the disk drive busily formats or validates a diskette. This is not really spooling. It occurs because the 1541 is an intelligent peripheral. The only thing that will cause your computer to wait for the disk drive to complete its task is your attempting to perform another disk operation. This includes closing the command channel.

Let's take a look at the disk commands used for housekeeping. *NOTE:* If you are using the DOS SUPPORT program that came on your 1541TEST/DEMO, the syntax for these disk commands is remarkably shorter. The > or @ keys are used to send a command to the disk drive. They take the place of the PRINT# statement. In addition, you do not have to open or close the command channel or embed the disk command in quotation marks. The DOS SUPPORT program will do this automatically for you. The DOS 5.1 syntax can be used only in immediate mode, however. It cannot be used in a program or a ?SYNTAX ERROR will result.

The New Command

When a fresh diskette is taken from its storage envelope, the 1541 cannot recognize it. The diskette must be formatted or newed prior to first-time use. Formatting or newing a diskette is performed by the DOS. The DOS proceeds to write concentric tracks made up of blocks/sectors to the diskette. In addition, a directory is set up, wherein the drive records information about all the files stored on the diskette. Chapter 3 provides a much more detailed account of this operation. The syntax for formatting a diskette is really quite simple:

```
SYNTAX:      OPEN 15, 8, 15
             PRINT#15, "NO:DISK NAME,ID"
             CLOSE 15

ALTERNATE:   PRINT#15, "N:DISK NAME,ID"

EXAMPLE:     OPEN 15, 8, 15
             PRINT#15, "NO:MY DISKETTE,MD"
             CLOSE 15

DOS 5.1:     >NO:DISK NAME,ID
             >N:DISK NAME,ID
```

The disk command, "N0:MY DISKETTE,MD", is sent to the drive by the PRINT#15 statement. The command has three parameters. The first parameter within quotes is N0:. The N stands for NEW. The 0 is a holdover from the dual drive system and indicates which drive. The 0 is optional on the 1541 and may be omitted. The colon terminates the DOS command. The second parameter is the disk name. It is limited to 16 characters in length. Generally these are alphanumeric characters. In the example above, we named the diskette: MY DISKETTE. The disk name is cosmetic and appears in the directory for reference purposes only. It is not written anywhere else on the diskette. The disk name is followed by a comma. The DOS looks or parses for this. After the comma are two alphanumeric characters for the disk ID. In the above example we selected MD as our disk identifier. The ID is written to every block or sector on the diskette. It is impossible to alter. The DOS repeatedly looks at the ID of a sector to be sure that you have not switched diskettes on it. Each diskette should be formatted with a unique ID. This will prevent the DOS from inadvertently overwriting programs on what appears to be an identical diskette.

A "full" new on a diskette takes roughly 2-3 minutes. There is a quicker way to erase a diskette that has already been used. This is accomplished by leaving off the disk ID. For example:

```
SYNTAX:        OPEN 15, 8, 15
               PRINT#15, "NO:DISK NAME"
               CLOSE 15

ALTERNATE: PRINT#15, "N:DISK NAME"

EXAMPLE:       OPEN 15, 8, 15
               PRINT#15, "NO:TEST DISKETTE"
               CLOSE 15

DOS 5.1:       >NO:DISK NAME
               >N:DISK NAME
```

Notice that no comma or ID follows the disk name. This command will work only on a diskette that has previously been formatted. It is referred to as a "short" new. A "short" new simply erases the first sector in the directory and writes an empty BAM (block availability map) to tell the DOS that we have a fresh diskette in use.

NOTE: A diskette that is plagued by read or write errors does not have to be pitched. Copy the files to another diskette first. Then do a "full" new on the offending diskette. This will erase and reformat the entire diskette. A "short" new rewrites only sectors 0 and 1 of track 18 and will not eliminate any read or write errors. See Chapter 8 about how to recover from both a "short" new and a "full" new.

The Initialize Command

Initialization has nothing to do with formatting. APPLE™ owners format a diskette by "initializing" it. This is NOT TRUE with Commodore. Initializing a diskette forces the DOS to read the disk ID and the contents of the BAM and store them in the drive's internal memory. The BAM establishes where the next available sector is for writing. Without it files would be overwritten. To initialize a diskette perform the following:

```
SYNTAX:      OPEN 15, 8, 15
             PRINT#15, "I0"
             CLOSE 15

ALTERNATE:   PRINT#15, "I"

DOS 5.1:     >I0
             >I
```

The I is short for INITIALIZE. The drive number can be ignored if you are using only
one 1541. The drive motor purrs for a few seconds and then settles down. It's that simple. It is a good habit to initialize a diskette each time you insert it into your 1541 drive.
This point cannot be overemphasized. Do it yourself. Do not rely upon the "autoinit"
feature of the drive. Initialization prevents the DOS from overwriting files in the event
that two diskettes with identical IDs are swapped. The drive cannot tell the difference
between two diskettes with identical IDs since it is the ID that the DOS uses to identify a diskette. Initialization also assures you that a diskette is properly seated in the
drive before use.

The 1541 drive has a built in autoinitialization feature. Once it encounters an error it
will retry a disk operation several times. Often it can recover from an error on its own.
If it fails, it gives up. Before doing so, though, it will do a "bump." On a bump the
read/write head is stepped outwards 45 tracks (slight overkill) to assure that it is on
track 1. The drive clatters when a protrusion on the stepper motor's drive pulley bumps
up against a mechanical stop. (It really isn't a melt down.) The head then steps inwards
to track 18 and the DOS awaits further instructions. Self initialization avoids this scenario.
Initialize every time you insert a diskette into the drive.

Initialization clears the error channel and turns off the flashing red LED. Unless, of
course, you are trying to initialize an unformatted diskette or forgot to put one in the
drive to begin with. Clearing the error channel destroys the error status the DOS
prepared for you. If error checking is important, retrieve the error message first; then
initialize the drive.

The Rename Command

Occasionally you will want to change the name of a file stored on a diskette. To rename
a file you first open the command channel and then send the rename command like this:

```
SYNTAX:      OPEN 15, 8, 15
             PRINT#15, "R0:NEW NAME=OLD NAME"
             CLOSE 15

ALTERNATE:   PRINT#15, "R:NEW NAME=OLD NAME"

EXAMPLE:     OPEN 15, 8, 15
             PRINT#15, "R0:DISPLAY T&S=DTS"
             CLOSE 15

DOS 5.1:     >R0:NEW NAME=OLD NAME
             >R:NEW NAME=OLD NAME
```

Again the syntax is exacting but simple to follow. The R0: means to rename on drive 0. It is short for RENAME0:. As before, the 0 is optional on the 1541. The next parameter is the new file name. A file name is generally alphanumeric in nature and 16 characters are allowed at the maximum. (Commas, colons, semicolons, and wild cards are not permitted. Cursor control and reverse video characters should be avoided.) The new file name is followed by an "=" sign. The last parameter is the existing or old file name. It must be spelled out exactly as it appears in the directory. Wild cards (*,?) are not allowed. If you make a typo on this parameter or the file does not appear in the directory, the rename command fails. No damage is done, so relax. In the above example our new file name is DISPLAY T&S. It replaces the old file name DTS. One final point. You cannot rename a file that is currently open for a read or write.

The Copy Command

The copy command allows you to easily backup an existing file on your diskette. There are three restrictions attached. First, the new file must have a different name. Second, the copy command will not work on a relative file. Third, you must have enough room on the diskette. The copy command looks like this:

```
SYNTAX:
  OPEN 15, 8, 15
  PRINT#15, "CO:BACKUP=0:ORIGINAL"
  CLOSE 15

ALTERNATE:
  PRINT#15, "C:BACKUP=ORIGINAL"

EXAMPLE:
  OPEN 15, 8, 15
  PRINT#15, "CO:MY PROGRAM B/U=0:MY PROGRAM"
  CLOSE 15

DOS 5.1:
  >CO:BACKUP=0:ORIGINAL
  >C:BACKUP=ORIGINAL
```

The C is short for COPY. The new file above is called MY PROGRAM B/U. It is a backup copy of a previous program called MY PROGRAM. Note that we must specify the drive number twice. Again this is a holdover from a dual drive configuration. The C does not appear twice, however. The same restrictions that apply to the rename command are also in effect here, i.e., 16 character file name limit, use of restricted characters, etc. The drive number is optional. See the alternate syntax to save a few keystrokes.

It is also possible to merge two or more sequential data files using the copy command. The syntax for this is as follows:

```
SYNTAX:
  OPEN 15, 8, 15
  PRINT#15, "CO:COMBINED=0:FILE1,0:FILE2,
    0:FILE3"
  CLOSE 15
```

```
ALTERNATE:
  PRINT#15, "C:COMBINED=FILE1,FILE2,FILE3"

EXAMPLE:
  OPEN 15, 8, 15
  PRINT#15, "CO:MAILFILE=O:NAME,O:ADDRESS,
    O:CITY"
  CLOSE 15

DOS 5.1:
  >CO:COMBINED=O:FILE1,O:FILE2,O:FILE3
  >C:COMBINED=FILE1,FILE2,FILE3
```

Our large file now consists of several files appended together. While this feature of the copy command is available, it is rarely used. Few programming techniques would require or ever utilize this feature. Note that this technique cannot be used to append a subroutine onto a BASIC program; the subroutine cannot be merged into the main program by the disk drive. You will need to use a programmer's aid like POWER™, SYSRES™, or BASIC AID™ for the C64 to do this.

The Scratch Command

To get rid of an unwanted file, we scratch it. The only exception is an unclosed file. An unclosed file is one that appears in the directory as having zero blocks and whose file type is preceded by an asterisk (*SEQ, *PRG, etc.). This will be explained below. To scratch a file, first remove the write protect tab and key in:

```
SYNTAX:      OPEN 15, 8, 15
             PRINT#15, "SO:FILE NAME"
             CLOSE 15

ALTERNATE:   PRINT#15, "S:FILE NAME"

EXAMPLE:     OPEN 15, 8, 15
             PRINT#15, "SO:TESTING 123"
             CLOSE 15

DOS 5.1:     >SO:FILE NAME
             >S:FILE NAME
```

The scratch command requires a single parameter, the file name, preceded by S or SCRATCH. As before, the drive number is optional.

There are some variations that incorporate wild cards. Wild cards in a file name are asterisks (*) or question marks (?). They should be used with utmost caution since more than one file can be scratched at a time.

```
EXAMPLE: OPEN 15, 8, 15
         PRINT#15, "SO:T*"
         CLOSE 15

DOS 5.1: >SO:T*
```

In the above example all files beginning with the letter T, regardless of file type, will be scratched. In the event that no file starts with the letter T, none will be affected. Careless use of a wild card can have catastrophic results. For example:

```
EXAMPLE: OPEN 15, 8, 15
         PRINT#15, "S0:*"
         CLOSE 15

DOS 5.1: >S0:*
```

The above command will scratch every file on the diskette. It is the equivalent of performing a short new on a diskette. Be careful!

The second wild card is the question mark. It is used to mask out characters that are not of importance. Suppose we want to scratch a number of files whose names are all eight characters long and end in .C64. We could not use .C64* to scratch them since the match falls at the end of the file name. However, we could use:

```
EXAMPLE: OPEN 15, 8, 15
         PRINT#15, "S0:????.C64"
         CLOSE 15

DOS 5.1: >S0:????.C64
```

Note that we used four question marks in the above example. An exact match of .C64 must occur on characters 5 through 8 of the file name. No match — no scratch. If we had 1541.C64 and C100.C64 on the disk, both would be scratched by the previous command. However, BACKUP.C64 would not be affected.

More than one wild card can be used within the same command. For example:

```
EXAMPLE: OPEN 15, 8, 15
         PRINT#15, "S0:T?ST*"
         CLOSE 15

DOS 5.1: >S0:T?ST*
```

This command would scratch files with these names: TEST, TASTY, TESTING123. The file TOAST would not be affected. Note that it makes no sense to send a command like this: "S0:T*ST???". The asterisk has priority over the question mark. All characters that appear after the asterisk are ignored.

A file type that begins with a * is unclosed: *SEQ, *PRG, etc. It was never closed properly. This can happen for a variety of reasons:

1. The diskette may have been at its physical capacity and a disk-full situation occurred during a save or write to a diskette.

2. A bad sector may have been encountered during a write to a diskette.

3. The file may have been left open following a write operation because you forgot to CLOSE the file, or you aborted the program by hitting either the RUN/STOP key or the RUN/STOP and the RESTORE keys.

4. Your program had a syntax error in it and the BASIC interpreter returned you to immediate mode.

(See Chapter 8 about how to recover an unclosed file.)

Whatever the cause, *an unclosed file should never be scratched!* Since the write operation was aborted, the internal organization of the diskette (i.e., the BAM), has been left in disarray. It does not match the actual file contents of the diskette. Any further attempt to write to that diskette will probably cause a loss of one or more files. Files can actually overlap one another now and you will be left with a poisoned diskette. The DOS does have a command to decorrupt itself. This is the validate command. When in doubt, validate your diskette!

The scratch command does not actually erase the file on your diskette. Rather it traces the file across the surface of the diskette and frees any sectors the file occupied. The file-type byte is also changed to a zero in the directory which indicates to the DOS that it is no longer active. *If you inadvertently scratch a file that you didn't mean to, stop right then and there!* You can recover it. Do not attempt to write to the diskette. The sectors just freed will be used on subsequent writes to the diskette. Once you write to the diskette, recovery is impossible. Chapter 8 on Getting Out of Trouble shows you how to recover a scratched file.

The Validate Command

This command tells the DOS to reconstruct its map which shows where information is stored on the diskette, so it conforms to the files listed in the directory. This is a simple way to decorrupt a damaged diskette. However, it is not a failsafe command as will be explained shortly. A validate command looks like this:

```
SYNTAX:      OPEN 15, 8, 15
             PRINT#15, "VO"
             CLOSE 15

ALTERNATE:   PRINT#15, "V"

DOS 5.1:     >VO
             >V
```

The V is an abbreviation for VALIDATE. As before, the 0 is optional for the 1541 drive.

What does a validate do? The DOS keeps a map that indicates which sectors on a diskette are currently in use. This map is stored on track 18, sector 0. It is referred to as the Block Availability Map or just the BAM for short. When the validate command is issued, all blocks are freed in the BAM on the diskette simulating a newly formatted blank diskette. The drive then picks up the first file in the directory and chains through the entire file. As sectors are picked up along the way, they are allocated in the BAM as currently in use. If the file is traced successfully, all blocks associated with it are put back into the BAM as in use. The next file is then picked up out of the directory and the process continues. When all files have been traced, the new BAM is written to the diskette and the internal count now matches the directory contents.

So far so good. Now let's see what happens to an unclosed file. When the DOS encounters an unclosed file in the directory during a validate command, all it does is change the file type byte in the directory entry to a 0 (scratched file). No attempt is made to trace the file. When the validate operation is complete, the unclosed file will no longer appear in a directory listing and any blocks associated with it will be free. This is what you want to happen. Now let's see what happens if you attempt to SCRATCH an unclosed file.

When you scratch a file, two things happen: the file-type byte in the directory for this file is set to 0 (scratched file) and the DOS traces through the chain of sectors that make up the file and marks each sector it encounters as available for use (free) in the BAM. This is just what you want to have happen for a normal file, but it can poison the diskette when you try it on an unclosed file. Here's why. The last sector of an unclosed file was never written out to the diskette. As a result, the second to the last sector points to a sector that is not really part of the file. The DOS doesn't realize this and continues to follow the "chain." If you are lucky, the "unwritten sector" will be a empty sector (never used since the disk was formatted). If this happens, the DOS will stop because pointers point to a non-existent track and sector (75,1). If you are unlucky, the "unwritten sector" will be part of a file that you scratched last week and the pointer will just happen to point into the middle of that very important file you just saved yesterday. When this happens, the DOS will merrily deallocate the remaining sectors in your file. The next write operation to the diskette will see this nice big open space and the new information will be saved right on top of your active file. Now the situation has gone from bad to worse and is in fact pathological — hence a poisoned disk. The only solution is to inspect each file first to ensure that it is not tainted and then copy it onto another diskette.

The validate routine is aborted if an error (an unreadable sector) is encountered. When it aborts, nothing radical occurs. The new BAM is not written to the disk until the validation process has been completed. Don't worry about the blank BAM getting you in trouble; the DOS will read the old one back in before it allows you to write to the disk. However, the diskette still remains corrupted with no quick remedy in sight. Chapter 8 on recovery deals with this and other disasters.

CHAPTER 3

DISKETTE FORMATTING

When you take a new floppy diskette out of the package, it is blank. Before the drive can store data onto it, it must be formatted. This is done by inserting the diskette into the drive and sending a NEW command to the DOS (see Section 2.5). During "formatting" or "newing," 35 concentric tracks are written to the diskette. Each track is made up of varying numbers of sectors/blocks where programs and data will eventually be stored. In addition to laying down empty blocks/sectors, the DOS creates a directory and a block availability map (BAM) and records them on track 18.

This chapter describes the formatting process and the tracks and sectors of a diskette. Chapter 4 describes the directory and the block availability map (BAM).

3.1 Layout of Tracks and Sectors

During the formatting (newing) process, the DOS divides the diskette into tracks and sectors. A track is a circular path on the diskette along which information is stored. Each track is concentric with the hole in the center of the diskette. There are a total of 35 tracks numbered from 1 to 35. Track 1 is the outermost track and track 35 is the innermost track. The read/write head may be positioned to any given track. The position of track 1 is determined by a mechanical stop that limits the outward movement of the read/write head. The other tracks are identified by their distance from track 1. The diagram below indicates the layout of the tracks on a formatted diskette.

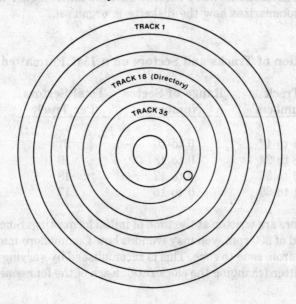

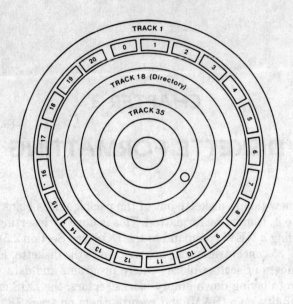

Although there are only 35 tracks, the stepper motor can position the read/write head to more than 70 different positions. This might seem to imply that additional tracks could be recorded on the surface of the diskette to increase its storage capacity. Unfortunately, the accuracy of the head positioning mechanism and the width of the path of magnetization produced by the read/write head makes the use of these "phantom" tracks unreliable. If you would like to experiment with this, the programs described in Chapter 9 allow you to experiment with stepping the head around.

Each track is divided into seventeen or more sectors (blocks). Each sector holds 256 bytes of data. (Some manufacturer's record data in 512 or 1024 byte sectors.) Whenever data is read from or written to a diskette, it is done one complete sector at a time.

On Commodore disk drives, the tracks are not divided into a fixed number of sectors. The number of sectors depends on the track number. The outer tracks (lower numbers) are longer and are divided into more sectors than the inner (higher numbered) tracks. The table below summarizes how the diskette is organized.

Organization of Tracks and Sectors on a 1541 Formatted Diskette

Zone	Track Numbers	Range of Sector Numbers	Total Sectors Per Track	Total Bytes Per Track
1	1 to 17	0 to 20	21	5376
2	18 to 24	0 to 18	19	4864
3	25 to 30	0 to 17	18	4608
4	31 to 35	0 to 16	17	4352

A total of 683 sectors are written at the time of initial formatting. Since the disk rotates at a constant speed of 300 rpm, you may wonder how Commodore manages to vary the number of sectors from zone to zone. This is accomplished by varying the rate at which data is read or written (changing the clock rate). Each of the four zones uses a different clock rate. This is accomplished by using a high speed clock and dividing the clock by N, where the value of N is determined by the zone. The table below summarizes the clock rates for each zone.

Zone	Tracks	Divisor	Clock Rate	Bits/Rotation
1	1 to 17	13	307,692 bits/sec	61,538.4
2	18 to 24	14	285,714 bits/sec	57,142.8
3	25 to 30	15	266,667 bits/sec	53,333.4
4	31 to 35	16	250,000 bits/sec	50,000.0

This scheme provides a recording density that varies from about 4000 bits/inch on the outer tracks to almost 6000 bits/inch on the inner tracks.

If all of the possible bits could be used for data alone, we would be able to store a total of 2,027,676 bits or 253,459 bytes on a diskette. Unfortunately, not all of these bytes can be used for data. The total storage capacity of a diskette formatted on the 1541 is 174,848 bytes. The need for space to store a directory to keep track of the location of the files on a diskette (see Chapter 4) further reduces us to an effective storage capacity of 169,984 bytes (256 bytes * 664 sectors).

3.2 Layout of a Sector

During the formatting (newing) process, the DOS creates and records onto the diskette all 683 sectors/blocks that will eventually be used for storing information. Each sector is comprised of two parts:

1. A header block that identifies the sector.
2. A data block that holds the 256 bytes of data.

The diagram below illustrates how these parts are arranged.

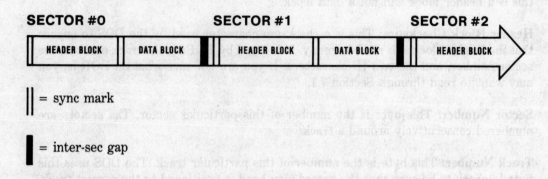

|| = sync mark

| = inter-sec gap

The sectors are recorded in numerical sequence along the circular track. Each sector consists of an identifying header block followed by a data block. The sectors are separated from each other by an inter-record gap. A special character called a SYNC MARK is used to mark the beginning of each header or data block.

A SYNC MARK is a very special character. It consists of 10 or more 1 bits in a row (normally 40 of them). This particular pattern of bits only occurs at the start of a header or data block. The hardware in the 1541 drive can detect this character and signal the DOS that a new data or header block is coming.

If you are puzzled about why several $FF characters in a row in the data block are not interpreted as a sync character, you may want to skip ahead to the section on Commodore's GCR encoding scheme in Chapter 7.

3.3 The Header Block

The header block of a sector allows the DOS to identify which track and sector is being read. It is composed of a sync mark, eight bytes of identifying information, and a header gap. The diagram below shows the layout of a header block.

SYNC MARK	HEADER BLOCK ID	HEADER BLOCK CHECKSUM	SECTOR NUMBER	TRACK NUMBER	ID CHARACTER NUMBER 2	ID CHARACTER NUMBER 1	$0F BYTE	$0F BYTE	HEADER GAP

NOTE: The header is recorded on disk exactly as indicated above. The diagram on page 54 of the *1541 User's Manual* is incorrect.

Let's examine the bytes that make up the header block:

Sync Mark: This consists of 10 or more 1 bits as described above. It warns the DOS that either a data block or a header block is coming.

Header Block ID: This is normally a $08 byte. It serves to indicate to the DOS that this is a header block and not a data block.

Header Block Checksum: This is a checksum character used by the DOS to ensure that the header block was read correctly. It is found by EORing the track number, the sector number, and the two ID characters. If you are not sure what an EOR is, you may want to read through Section 7.1.

Sector Number: This byte is the number of this particular sector. The sectors are numbered consecutively around a track.

Track Number: This byte is the number of this particular track. The DOS uses this byte to check to be sure that the record/play head is positioned to the correct track.

ID Character #2: This is the second ID character that you specified in the NEW command when the diskette was formatted (e.g., the 1 in "N0:GAMES,V1"). It is sometimes referred to as the ID HI. The DOS checks this byte against a master disk ID to ensure that you have not swapped diskettes.

ID Character #1: This is the first ID character that you specified in the NEW command when the diskette was formatted (e.g., the V in "N0:GAMES,V1"). It is sometimes referred to as the ID LO. The DOS checks this byte against a master disk ID to ensure that you have not swapped diskettes.

$0F Bytes: These bytes are used as padding (spacing) by the DOS during initial formatting. They are called "OFF" bytes. Once formatting is complete OFF bytes are never referenced again.

Header Gap: The header gap consists of eight $55 bytes. These eight bytes are used to provide breathing room between the header block and the data block. The DOS never reads these bytes. They allow the DOS time to set-up for reading the data block that follows. *NOTE:* The 4040 drive uses a nine byte header gap. This is one of the reasons why 1541 drives and 4040 drives are NOT WRITE COMPATIBLE! See Chapter 9 for more information.

NOTE: A header block is written *only* during the formatting process. It is never rewritten again, period.

3.4 The Data Block

The data block of a sector stores the 256 data bytes for this sector. It is composed of a sync mark, a data block ID character, the 256 bytes of data, a data block checksum byte, two off bytes, and an inter-sector gap. The diagram below depicts the layout of a data block.

SYNC MARK	DATA BLOCK ID	256 DATA BYTES	DATA BLOCK CHECKSUM	$00 BYTE	$00 BYTE	INTER-SECTOR GAP	SYNC MARK	HEADER BLOCK ID

Let's examine the bytes that make up the data block:

Sync mark: This consists of 10 or more 1 bits as previously described. It warns the DOS that either a data block or a header block is coming.

Data Block ID: This byte is normally a $07. It serves to indicate to the DOS that this is a data block and not a header block ($08).

256 Data Bytes: This is the actual data stored in the sector. See Chapter 4 about how Commodore uses the first two bytes as a forward track and sector pointer instead of actual data.

Data Block Checksum: This is a checksum character used by the DOS to ensure that the data block was read correctly. It is found by EORing all 256 data bytes together.

$00 Bytes: These two bytes are also called OFF bytes. They are used to pad a data block before it is written. They are not referenced again by the DOS.

33

Inter-sector Gap: This is also known as the "tail gap." Its purpose is to provide breathing room between the end of the data block and the start of the next sector. The length of the gap varies from zone to zone and from one drive to another (see the chart in Section 7.1). Between consectutive sectors the gap is normally 4 to 12 bytes long. The gap between the last sector on a track and sector zero is often longer — up to 100 bytes in length. The gap is designed to be long enough so that if you write a data block on a day when your drive is turning slightly faster than 300 rpm, you won't overwrite the start of the next sector. (Your drive may not be turning at exactly 300 rpm all the time because of fluctuations in the power supplied to your home or office, mechanical wear, belt slippage, changes in temperature, etc.) Note that the DOS never reads these bytes.

The entire data block (including the preceding sync mark) is rewritten each time data is recorded on a diskette.

This concludes our overview on how a diskette is formatted. Additional details about how bytes are encoded on the surface of a diskette are provided in Section 7.1. The actual recording process is described in Section 9.7.

CHAPTER 4

DISKETTE ORGANIZATION

4.1 Information Management

The information that is stored on a floppy disk is virtually useless unless it can be retrieved quickly. As a result, the organization and management of information is one of the most important tasks of the DOS. To do an efficient job of management, the DOS must be able to:

1. Keep track of which sectors contain data and which are still empty (available for use).

2. Assign names and storage locations to large blocks of related information (files).

3. Keep track of the sequence of sectors that were used to store a file.

The DOS stores most of this information in the directory on track 18, halfway between the outermost track (1) and the innermost track (35). Centering the directory serves to minimize head movement across the diskette and extends the life of both the drive and the media. The directory is subdivided into two areas—the map showing which sectors are in use and which are free (the Block Availability Map or BAM) and directory entries. The BAM resides solely on sector 0 of track 18. It informs the drive as to what sectors are currently in use and where subsequent writing to the diskette can safely take place. The remaining sectors (1-18) of track 18 contain directory entries (file names, file types, and pointers to where files are stored on the diskette).

4.2 The Directory You See

Let's examine the directory of the 1541TEST/DEMO diskette that came with your drive. Insert it in your drive and type on your keyboard:

```
LOAD "$0",8
```

then type

```
LIST
```

35

After a brief pause you should see the following on your screen:

```
0  "1541TEST/DEMO    " ZX  2A
13    "HOW TO USE"         PRG
5     "HOW PART TWO"       PRG
4     "VIC-20 WEDGE"       PRG
1     "C-64 WEDGE"         PRG
4     "DOS 5.1"            PRG
11    "COPY/ALL"           PRG
9     "PRINTER TEST"       PRG
4     "DISK ADDR CHANGE"   PRG
4     "DIR"                PRG
6     "VIEW BAM"           PRG
4     "CHECK DISK"         PRG
14    "DISPLAY T&S"        PRG
9     "PERFORMANCE TEST"   PRG
5     "SEQUENTIAL FILE"    PRG
13    "RANDOM FILE"        PRG
558 BLOCKS FREE.
```

The 0 refers to which drive was accessed. This is a holdover from the 4040 dual drive system. Next you see the diskette name — 1541TEST/DEMO. In the event that the diskette name is less than 16 characters in length, blank spaces are appended to the end of the name. This forced spacing is known as padding. Following the name of the diskette is the disk ID — ZX in this instance. These two characters are generally (but not always) the unique alphanumeric characters under which the diskette in question was formatted originally. The diskette name and ID are cosmetic in nature and appear in the directory for your reference purposes only. The 2A indicates the DOS version and format, 4040 in this instance — again a holdover. Next we see the active file entries on the diskette itself. Each directory entry has three fields:

1. The number of blocks/sectors the given file occupies.
2. The file name.
3. The file type.

Your demo diskette came with 15 active files on it. Moreover, they are all program files denoted by PRG. The last entry in the directory is the remaining number of available blocks/sectors left on the diskette for storage. It is the difference between 664 blocks available at the time of original formatting and the sum of the blocks of the active files (664 − 106 = 558).

What you see on your screen is not necessarily how the directory is stored on your diskette, however. Let's begin our look at the directory with the Block Availability Map (BAM).

4.3 The Block Availability Map (BAM)

The BAM is where the DOS keeps track of which sectors (blocks) on the diskette contain information (are in use) and which ones can be used for storing new information (are free). This map is stored on track 18, sector 0. Here is a hex dump of that sector on the 1541TEST/DEMO disk so we can examine it in detail.

1541TEST/DEMO

TRACK 18 — SECTOR 0

```
. 00:  12 01 41 00 15 FF FF 1F    ..A.....     BAM TRACK     1
. 08:  15 FF FF 1F 15 FF FF 1F    ........     BAM TRACKS   2-3
. 10:  15 FF FF 1F 15 FF FF 1F    ........     BAM TRACKS   4-5
. 18:  15 FF FF 1F 15 FF FF 1F    ........     BAM TRACKS   6-7
. 20:  15 FF FF 1F 15 FF FF 1F    ........     BAM TRACKS   8-9
. 28:  15 FF FF 1F 15 FF FF 1F    ........     BAM TRACKS 10-11
. 30:  15 FF FF 1F 15 FF FF 1F    ........     BAM TRACKS 12-13
. 38:  11 D7 5F 1F 00 00 00 00    .W......     BAM TRACKS 14-15
. 40:  00 00 00 00 00 00 00 00    ........     BAM TRACKS 16-17
. 48:  10 EC FF 07 00 00 00 00    ........     BAM TRACKS 18-19
. 50:  00 00 00 00 12 BF FF 07    .....?..     BAM TRACKS 20-21
. 58:  13 FF FF 07 13 FF FF 07    ........     BAM TRACKS 22-23
. 60:  13 FF FF 07 12 FF FF 03    ........     BAM TRACKS 24-25
. 68:  12 FF FF 03 12 FF FF 03    ........     BAM TRACKS 26-27
. 70:  12 FF FF 03 12 FF FF 03    ........     BAM TRACKS 28-29
. 78:  12 FF FF 03 11 FF FF 01    ........     BAM TRACKS 30-31
. 80:  11 FF FF 01 11 FF FF 01    ........     BAM TRACKS 32-33
. 88:  11 FF FF 01 11 FF FF 01    ........     BAM TRACKS 34-35
. 90:  31 35 34 31 54 45 53 54    1541TEST     DISK NAME
. 98:  2f 44 45 4D 4F A0 A0 A0    /DEMO
. A0:  A0 A0 5A 58 A0 32 41 A0      ZX 2A      DOS TYPE & DISK ID
. A8:  A0 A0 A0 00 00 00 00 00      .....      UNUSED
. B0:  00 00 00 00 00 00 00 00    ........
. B8:  00 00 00 00 00 00 00 00    ........
. C0:  00 00 00 00 00 00 00 00    ........
. C8:  00 00 00 00 00 00 00 00    ........
. D0:  00 00 00 00 00 00 00 00    ........
. D8:  00 00 00 00 00 00 00 00    ........
. E0:  00 00 00 00 00 00 00 00    ........
. E8:  00 00 00 00 00 00 00 00    ........
. F0:  00 00 00 00 00 00 00 00    ........
. F8:  00 00 00 00 00 00 00 00    ........
```

As indicated above, the BAM does not take up all 256 bytes on this sector. There are several other things stored here as well. The table below identifies the various parts. Note that the sector dump above uses hexadecimal notation while the table below gives the decimal equivalents.

Bytes	Contents	Purpose
0/1	18/1	Pointer to first sector of directory entries
2	65	ASCII character A indicating 1541/4040 format
3	0	Unused
4-143		Block Availability Map (BAM)
144-159		Diskette name padded with shifted spaces
160-161	160	Shifted spaces

162-163		Diskette ID	
164	160	Shifted space	
165-166	50/65	DOS version and format type (2A)	
167-170	160	Shifted spaces	
170-255	?	Unused	

In the BAM four bytes are used to describe the status of each track. As a result, the BAM takes up a total of 4 × 35 = 140 bytes (bytes 4-143 or $04-$8F). Let's examine the entry for track 14 to see what these four bytes mean. The entry for track 14 begins at byte 14 × 4 = 56 ($38). It looks like this:

```
. 38: 11 D7 5F 1F 00 00 00 00 .W...... BAM TRACKS 14-15
      ** ** ** **
```

The first byte for track 14 (location $38 = 56) indicates the number of blocks free on this track.

```
. 38: 11 D7 5F 1F 00 00 00 00 .W...... BAM TRACKS 14-15
      **
```

In this case there are $11 or 17 (1 * 16 + 1) blocks free.

When the DOS calculates the number of blocks free on a diskette, it sums this byte from each track's entry in the BAM. Let's do our own blocks free calculation to see how it is done. All we have to do is sum up the decimal values of every fourth byte starting with byte 4 like this:

ZONE	BYTE	TRACK	HEX VALUE	DECIMAL VALUE
1	4	1	$1F	21
	8	2	$1F	21
	12	3	$1F	21
	16	4	$1F	21
	20	5	$1F	21
	24	6	$1F	21
	28	7	$1F	21
	32	8	$1F	21
	36	9	$1F	21
	40	10	$1F	21
	44	11	$1F	21
	48	12	$1F	21
	52	13	$1F	21
	56	14	$11	17
	60	15	$00	0
	64	16	$00	0
	68	17	$00	0

2	72	18	$10	16
	76	19	$13	19
	80	20	$13	19
	84	21	$13	19
	88	22	$13	19
	92	23	$13	19
	96	24	$13	19
3	100	25	$12	18
	104	26	$12	18
	108	27	$12	18
	112	28	$12	18
	116	29	$12	18
	120	30	$12	18
4	124	31	$11	17
	128	32	$11	17
	132	33	$11	17
	136	34	$11	17
	140	35	$11	+ 17

574   BLOCKS FREE

Wait a minute! We calculated 574 blocks free but the directory shows 558. How do we explain this discrepancy? Easy. Remember that the DOS reserves track 18 for its own use. Therefore the blocks free on that particular track are not returned to us (574 − 16 = 558). Sixteen sectors on track 18 are still free, but available only to the DOS.

Now that you have seen how to calculate the number of blocks free on a diskette, let's get back to our analysis of track 14. The BAM entry looked like this:

```
. 38: 11 D7 5F 1F 00 00 00 00 .W...... BAM TRACKS 14-15
      ** ** ** **
```

The first byte was easy to interpret. The remaining three bytes are a bit trickier (no pun intended). They are a bit map showing the status of the sectors on a given track. Bit mapping is used to save space. If one byte were used for each of the 683 sectors, the BAM would take up three sectors (683 / 256). This would be inefficient. By using bit mapping, each byte describes the status of eight sectors. This way only three bytes are needed for each track. Let's examine the bit map for track 14 of our 1541 TEST/DEMO.

```
. 38: 11 D7 5F 1F 00 00 00 00 .W...... BAM TRACKS 14-15
      ** ** ** **
```

```
LOCATION        $39=57     $3A=58     $3B=59
BYTE VALUE       $D7        $5F        $1F
  BINARY       11010111   01011111   00011111 *

SECTOR                     111111      21111
NUMBER        76543210   54321098   xxx09876
```

```
* 1 = FREE
  0 = ALLOCATED
```

Sectors 0 to 7 are represented by the byte at location 57. Sectors 8 through 15 are stored in the byte at location 58. Finally, sectors 16 through 20 are depicted by the byte at location 59. When decoded, a bit that is high or a 1 indicates that a sector is not currently in use (free) and can be written to. A bit that is low or a 0 is currently in use (allocated) and will be overlooked by the DOS when writing subsequently takes place to the diskette. The third byte is always incomplete since a maximum of 21 sectors are written to any track. This particular byte is automatically adjusted by the DOS during initial formatting to indicate the proper number of sectors for this track. Three bytes are still used irregardless of the zone, however. If you count up the 1s in the bit map for track 14, you will find that there are 17 free sectors on track 14. This agrees with the blocks free count for the track stored at byte location $38 (56) in the BAM, i.e., $11 or 17 decimal.

To ensure that you understand how the bit mapping works, let's take a look at track 18. Since track 18 is used for storing the directory we would expect some allocation of sectors here. Byte 72 shows $10 or 16 sectors available here. They are bit mapped in bytes 73, 74, and 75 as follows:

```
. 48:  10 EC FF 07 00 00 00 00 ........   BAM TRACKS 18-19
       ** ** ** **


   LOCATION        $49=73      $4A=74      $4B=75
 BYTE VALUE         $EC         $FF         $07
    BINARY        11101100    11111111    00000111 *

    SECTOR                     111111       21111
    NUMBER        76543210    54321098    xxx09876


          *  1 = FREE
             0 = ALLOCATED
```

If you are still unsure of yourself, don't be too concerned. The DOS looks after the BAM. Let's move on and explore the actual directory entries themselves. Sectors 1 through 18 on track 18 are reserved specifically for them.

4.4 The Directory Entries

Recall that bytes 0 and 1 of track 18, sector 0 point to the next track and sector of the directory. In this particular instance, the BAM points to track 18, sector 1. Let's examine this sector in detail.

```
             1541TEST/DEMO

         TRACK 18 - SECTOR 01

. 00:  12 04 82 11 00 48 4F 57 .....HOW    FILE ENTRY #1
. 08:  20 54 4F 20 55 53 45 A0   TO USE
. 10:  A0 A0 A0 A0 A0 00 00 00    ...
```

```
.  18:   00 00 00 00 00 00 0D 00   ........
.  20:   00 00 82 11 03 48 4F 57   .....HOW      FILE ENTRY #2
.  28:   20 50 41 52 54 20 54 57    PART TW
.  30:   4F A0 A0 A0 A0 00 00 00   O      ...
.  38:   00 00 00 00 00 00 05 00   ........
.  40:   00 00 82 11 09 56 49 43   .....VIC      FILE ENTRY #3
.  48:   2D 32 30 20 57 45 44 47   -20 WEDG
.  50:   45 A0 A0 A0 A0 00 00 00   E      ...
.  58:   00 00 00 00 00 00 04 00   ........
.  60:   00 00 82 13 00 46 2D 36   .....C-6      FILE ENTRY #4
.  68:   34 20 57 45 44 47 45 A0   4 WEDGE.
.  70:   A0 A0 A0 A0 A0 00 00 00          ...
.  78:   00 00 00 00 00 00 01 00   ........
.  80:   00 00 82 13 01 44 4F 53   .....DOS      FILE ENTRY #5
.  88:   20 35 2E 31 A0 A0 A0 A0    5.1
.  90:   A0 A0 A0 A0 A0 00 00 00          ...
.  98:   00 00 00 00 00 00 04 00   ........
.  A0:   00 00 82 13 03 43 4F 50   .....COP      FILE ENTRY #6
.  A8:   59 2F 41 4C 4C A0 A0 A0   Y/ALL
.  B0:   A0 A0 A0 A0 A0 00 00 00          ...
.  B8:   00 00 00 00 00 00 0B 00   ........
.  C0:   00 00 82 13 09 50 52 49   .....PRI      FILE ENTRY #7
.  C8:   4E 54 45 52 20 54 45 53   NTER TES
.  D0:   54 A0 A0 A0 A0 00 00 00   T      ...
.  D8:   00 00 00 00 00 00 09 00   ........
.  E0:   00 00 82 10 00 44 49 53   .....DIS      FILE ENTRY #8
.  E8:   4B 20 41 44 44 52 20 43   K ADDR C
.  F0:   48 41 4E 47 45 00 00 00   HANGE...
.  F8:   00 00 00 00 00 00 04 00   ........
```

The contents of any directory sector can be tabled as follows:

Byte	Contents	Purpose
0		Track of the next directory block
1		Sector of the next directory block
2-31		File entry #1 in the directory block
32-33	0	Unused
34-63		File entry #2 in the directory block
64-65	0	Unused
66-95		File entry #3 in the directory block
96-97	0	Unused
98-127		File entry #4 in the directory block
128-129	0	Unused
130-159		File entry #5 in the directory block

160-161	0	Unused
162-191		File entry #6 in the directory block
192-193	0	Unused
194-223		File entry #7 in the directory block
224-225	0	Unused
226-255		File entry #8 in the directory block

Eight file entries are recorded per sector. Let's examine the contents of a single directory file entry.

```
. 00:  12 04 82 11 00 48 4F 57  .....HOW
       ** **
. 08:  20 54 4F 20 55 53 45 A0   TO USE
. 10:  A0 A0 A0 A0 A0 00 00 00      ...
. 18:  00 00 00 00 00 00 0D 00  ........
```

Because this is the first entry in the directory, bytes 0 and 1 are significant. They point to track 18, sector 4 (converts to 18). This indicates that there are further directory entries. You will note that the sectors are not sequential in nature, i.c., sector 1 does not point to sector 2, etc. Remember that the diskette itself is rotating at 300 rpm. Staggering the use of the sectors allows quicker access and fewer rotations of the drive mechanism and the media. Typically sectors are staggered in increments of 10. The directory track is staggered in increments of 3, however. The table below indicates the sequence in which a full directory containing 144 files is stored:

SECTOR FILLING SEQUENCE
FOR THE DIRECTORY

0 (BAM)
1, 4, 7, 10, 13, 16
2, 5, 8, 11, 14, 17
3, 6, 9, 12, 15, 18

When a diskette is initially formatted, sector 1 is set up with 8 null entries. As you store files on the diskette the directory grows. It soon becomes a long chain of directory sectors. The first two bytes in a sector point to the next directory sector in the chain (this is known as a forward pointer). But, what about the last sector in the chain? It has nothing to point to! In the last sector in the chain, there is no forward pointer; byte 0 contains a 0 ($00) and byte 1 contains a 255 ($FF) as indicated below. This indicates to the DOS that there are no more sectors in the directory.

```
. 00:  00 FF xx xx xx xx xx xx  ........
```

One final note about chaining. Commodore uses only forward pointers. A sector does not show where it came from, only where it is going. This makes recovery of corrupted files much more difficult, but more about that later.

Back to our example:

```
. 00: 12 04 82 11 00 48 4F 57  .....HOW
           **
. 08: 20 54 4F 20 55 53 45 A0   TO USE
. 10: A0 A0 A0 A0 A0 00 00 00       ...
. 18: 00 00 00 00 00 00 0D 00  ........
```

The first byte in the file entry is the file-type byte. In this instance we see an $82. This is interpreted by the DOS to mean that the file entry is a program. The following table outlines Commodores file types.

HEX	ASCII	FILE TYPE	DIRECTORY SHOWS
$00	0	Scratched	Does not appear
$80	128	Deleted	DEL
$81	129	Sequential	SEQ
$82	130	Program	PRG
$83	131	User	USR
$84	132	Relative	REL
$00	0	Unclosed deleted	Same as scratched
$01	1	Unclosed sequential	*SEQ
$02	2	Unclosed program	*PRG
$03	3	Unclosed user	*USR
$04	4	Unclosed relative	Cannot occur
$A0	160	Deleted @ replacement	DEL
$A1	161	Sequential @ replacement	SEQ
$A2	162	Program @ replacement	PRG
$A3	163	User @ replacement	USR
$A4	164	Relative @ replacement	Cannot occur
$C0	192	Locked deleted	DEL <
$C1	193	Locked sequential	SEQ <
$C2	194	Locked program	PRG <
$C3	195	Locked user	USR <
$C4	196	Locked relative	REL <

Note: It is possible to edit the file-type byte and get very unusual file types appearing in the directory (SR?< is one possibility). However, these file types have no practical use.

Enough esoterica for now. Let's get back to our example:

The next two bytes in the file entry are a pointer to where the first sector of that particular file is stored on the diskette.

43

```
.  00:  12 04 82 11 00 48 4F 57   .....HOW
                     ** **
.  08:  20 54 4F 20 55 53 45 A0    TO USE
.  10:  A0 A0 A0 A0 A0 00 00 00        ...
.  18:  00 00 00 00 00 00 0D 00   ........
```

This file starts on track 17 ($11), sector 0 ($00).

Next we have the file name.

```
.  00:  12 04 82 11 00 48 4F 57   .....HOW
                        ** ** **
.  08:  20 54 4F 20 55 53 45 A0    TO USE
        ** ** ** ** ** ** ** **
.  10:  A0 A0 A0 A0 A0 00 00 00        ...
        ** ** ** ** **
.  18:  00 00 00 00 00 00 0D 00   ........
```

In this case our file is named "HOW TO USE". Note that file names are padded out
to 16 characters with shifted spaces ($A0) just like the diskette name. The shifted spaces
do not show as part of the file name, however, when the directory is displayed.

```
.  00:  12 04 82 11 00 48 4F 57   .....HOW
.  08:  20 54 4F 20 55 53 45 A0    TO USE
.  10:  A0 A0 A0 A0 A0 00 00 00        ...
                        ** ** **
.  18:  00 00 00 00 00 00 0D 00   ........
```

The next three bytes are unused except for relative file entries. For a relative file bytes
$15 (21) and $16 (22) point to the first set of side sectors. Byte $17 (23) gives the record
size with which the relative file was created. This special file type will be examined in
detail later.

The next four bytes are always unused and therefore null ($00).

```
.  00:  12 04 82 11 00 48 4F 57   .....HOW
.  08:  20 54 4F 20 55 53 45 A0    TO USE
.  10:  A0 A0 A0 A0 A0 00 00 00        ...
.  18:  00 00 00 00 00 00 0D 00   ........
        ** ** ** **
```

The following two bytes are reserved for use by the DOS during the save and replace
operation (@ replacement). Their function can only be viewed by interrupting the drive
during a SAVE "@0:file name",8 routine. This is not recommended for obvious reasons.
(During an @ replacement the file-type byte is ORed with $20 first. A new copy of the
file is then written to the disk. Bytes 28 ($1C) and 29 ($1D) contain the track and sector
pointer to the start of the new replacement file. At the end of the @ operation the sectors that held the old file are marked as free in the BAM. The new track and sector

pointer is then moved from bytes 28 and 29 to bytes 3 ($03) and 4 ($04) respectively and bytes 28 and 29 are zeroed again. The proper file type is then restored at byte 2. See Chapter 9 about the bug in the @ replacement command.)

```
.  00:  12  04  82  11  00  48  4F  57    .....HOW
.  08:  20  54  4F  20  55  53  45  A0     TO USE
.  10:  A0  A0  A0  A0  A0  00  00  00        ...
.  18:  00  00  00  00  00  00  0D  00    ........
                                ** **
```

The final two bytes in a file entry are the number of blocks it occupies on the diskette. It is the sum of the leftmost byte (lo-byte) + the rightmost byte (hi-byte) * 256.

```
.  00:  12  04  82  11  00  48  4F  57    .....HOW
.  08:  20  54  4F  20  55  53  45  A0     TO USE
.  10:  A0  A0  A0  A0  A0  00  00  00        ...
.  18:  00  00  00  00  00  00  0D  00    ........
                                ** **
                                LO HI
```

In our example, the file is (13 + 0 * 256) = 13 blocks long.

To be sure you understand the file entries work let's break out the first sector of the test/demo directory to show each file entry. Remember that bytes 0 and 1 of each entry are unused with the exception of the first entry. Here they represent a forward track and sector chain and have nothing to do with that file in particular.

1541TEST/DEMO

TRACK 18 - SECTOR 01

DIRECTORY ENTRY 1

```
.  00:  12  04  82  11  00  48  4F  57    .....HOW    File type = $82 = PRG
.  08:  20  54  4F  20  55  53  45  A0     TO USE     Starts on 17/1 ($11/$00)
.  10:  A0  A0  A0  A0  A0  00  00  00        ...     Name: HOW TO USE
.  18:  00  00  00  00  00  00  0D  00    ........    File length: 13 BLOCKS
```

DIRECTORY ENTRY 2

```
.  20:  00  00  82  11  03  48  4F  57    .....HOW    File type = $82 = PRG
.  28:  20  50  41  52  54  20  54  57     PART TW    Starts on 17/3 ($11/$03)
.  30:  4F  A0  A0  A0  A0  00  00  00  O     ...     Name: HOW PART TWO
.  38:  00  00  00  00  00  00  05  00    ........    File length: 5 BLOCKS
```

45

DIRECTORY ENTRY 3

```
. 40:  00 00 82 11 09 56 49 43   .....VIC   File type = $82 = PRG
. 48:  2D 32 30 20 57 45 44 47   -20 WEDG   Starts on 17/9 ($11/09)
. 50:  45 A0 A0 A0 A0 00 00 00   E     ...  Name: VIC-20 WEDGE
. 58:  00 00 00 00 00 00 04 00   ........   File length: 4 BLOCKS
```

DIRECTORY ENTRY 4

```
. 60:  00 00 82 13 00 46 2D 36   .....C-6   File type = $82 = PRG
. 68:  34 20 57 45 44 47 45 A0   4 WEDGE    Starts on 19/0 ($13/$00)
. 70:  A0 A0 A0 A0 A0 00 00 00         ...  Name C-64 WEDGE
. 78:  00 00 00 00 00 00 01 00   ........   File length: 1 BLOCK
```

DIRECTORY ENTRY 5

```
. 80:  00 00 82 13 01 44 4F 53   .....DOS   File type = $82 = PRG
. 88:  20 35 2E 31 A0 A0 A0 A0    5.1       Starts on 19/1 ($13/$01)
. 90:  A0 A0 A0 A0 A0 00 00 00         ...  Name: DOS 5.1
. 98:  00 00 00 00 00 00 04 00   ........   File length: 4 BLOCKS
```

DIRECTORY ENTRY 6

```
. A0:  00 00 82 13 03 43 4F 50   .....COP   File type = $82 = PRG
. A8:  59 2F 41 4C 4C A0 A0 A0   Y/ALL      Starts on 19/3 ($13/03)
. B0:  A0 A0 A0 A0 A0 00 00 00         ...  Name: COPY/ALL
. B8:  00 00 00 00 00 00 0B 00   ........   File length: 11 BLOCKS
```

DIRECTORY ENTRY 7

```
. C0:  00 00 82 13 09 50 52 49   .....PRI   File type = $82 = PRG
. C8:  4E 54 45 52 20 54 45 53   NTER TES   Starts on 19/9 ($13/09)
. D0:  54 A0 A0 A0 A0 00 00 00   T     ...  Name: PRINTER TEST
. D8:  00 00 00 00 00 00 09 00   ........   File length: 9 BLOCKS
```

DIRECTORY ENTRY 8

```
. E0:  00 00 82 10 00 44 49 53   .....DIS   File type = $82 = PRG
. E8:  4B 20 41 44 44 52 20 43   K ADDR C   Starts on 16/0 ($10/00)
. F0:  48 41 4E 47 45 00 00 00   HANGE...   Name:DISK ADDR CHANGE
. F8:  00 00 00 00 00 00 04 00   ........   File length: 4 BLOCKS
```

We will end our tour of the directory by displaying the next sector (track 18, sector 4) which happens to end the directory chain ($00, $FF in bytes 0 and 1, respectively). Notice that only seven directory entries are present in this block. The last directory entry is a null entry. It will be converted into a valid entry when the directory is expanded.

1541TEST/DEMO

TRACK 18 - SECTOR 04

```
. 00:  00 FF 82 10 01 44 49 52   .....DIR   File type = $82 = PRG
. 08:  A0 A0 A0 A0 A0 A0 A0 A0              Starts on 16/1 ($10/01)
. 10:  A0 A0 A0 A0 A0 00 00 00      ...     Name: DIR
. 18:  00 00 00 00 00 00 04 00   ........   File length: 4 BLOCKS

. 20:  00 00 82 10 03 56 49 45   .....VIE   File type = $82 = PRG
. 28:  57 20 42 41 4D A0 A0 A0   W BAM      Starts on 16/3 ($10/03)
. 30:  A0 A0 A0 A0 A0 00 00 00      ...     Name: VIEW BAM
. 38:  00 00 00 00 00 00 06 00   ........   File length: 6 BLOCKS

. 40:  00 00 82 10 07 43 48 45   .....CHE   File type = $82 = PRG
. 48:  43 4B 20 44 49 53 4B A0   CK DISK    Starts on 16/7 ($10/07)
. 50:  A0 A0 A0 A0 A0 00 00 00      ...     Name: CHECK DISK
. 58:  00 00 00 00 00 00 04 00   ........   File length: 4 BLOCKS

. 60:  00 00 82 10 0F 44 49 53   .....DIS   File type = $82 = PRG
. 68:  50 4C 41 59 20 54 26 53   PLAY T&S   Starts on 16/15 ($10/$0F)
. 70:  A0 A0 A0 A0 A0 00 00 00      ...     Name: DISPLAY T&S
. 78:  00 00 00 00 00 00 0E 00   ........   File length: 14 BLOCKS

. 80:  00 00 82 14 02 50 45 52   .....PER   File type = $82 = PRG
. 88:  46 4F 52 4D 41 4E 43 45   FORMANCE   Starts on 20/2 ($14/$02)
. 90:  20 54 45 53 54 00 00 00   TEST...    Name: PERFORMANCE TEST
. 98:  00 00 00 00 00 00 09 00   ........   File length: 9 BLOCKS

. A0:  00 00 82 14 07 50 45 52   .....SEQ   File type = $82 = PRG
. A8:  55 45 4E 54 49 41 4C 20   UENTIAL    Starts on 20/7 ($14/$07)
. B0:  46 49 4C 45 A0 00 00 00   FILE ...   Name: SEQUENTIAL FILE
. B8:  00 00 00 00 00 00 05 00   ........   File length: 5 BLOCKS

. C0:  00 00 82 0F 01 52 41 4E   .....RAN   File type = $82 = PRG
. C8:  44 4F 4D 20 46 49 4C 45   DOM FILE   Starts on 15/1 ($0F/$01)
. D0:  A0 A0 A0 A0 A0 00 00 00      ...     Name: RANDOM FILE
. D8:  00 00 00 00 00 00 0D 00   ........   File length: 13 BLOCKS

. E0:  00 00 00 00 00 00 00 00   ........   NULL ENTRY
. E8:  00 00 00 00 00 00 00 00   ........
. F0:  00 00 00 00 00 00 00 00   ........
. F8:  00 00 00 00 00 00 00 00   ........
```

You will find four of the utilities listed in Appendix C particularly helpful in furthering your understanding of the organization of a diskette. The first program is DISPLAY TRACK & SECTOR. The hex dumps in this section were generated using this utility. A hex dump can be sent either to the screen or printer. When sent to the screen only half a page of the specified track and sector is displayed at one time to prevent scrolling. Bytes 0 – 127 ($00 – $7F) are displayed first followed by bytes 128 – 255 ($80 – $FF). Use this program for your own experimentation. The second program is DISPLAY A BLOCK AVAILABILITY MAP. It portrays the BAM in a two-dimensional representation. The diskette name, ID, DOS version, and blocks free are also displayed. The third program is VIRTUAL DIRECTORY. It displays a directory in its entirety including scratched files. Output can be directed to a printer by changing the OPEN 4, 3 statement in line 440 to OPEN 4,4. The last program, DISPLAY A CHAIN, traces a file chain. The chain of sectors may be viewed on the screen or sent to the printer.

The programming techniques that are used in these sample programs will be partially explained in later sections.

Now that we've seen how the directory is kept, let's look at how the different types of files are actually stored on a diskette. We'll start by looking at a program file.

4.5 Program File Storage

The most common type of file is a program file, PRG. It is designated by an $82 in the directory. Program file structure is quite simple. Diagrammatically, the first sector (block) in a program file looks like this.

TRACK LINK	SECTOR LINK	LOAD LO	LOAD HI	THE FIRST 252 BYTES OF YOUR PROGRAM

Byte	Purpose
0	Track of the next block in this file
1	Sector of the next block in this file
2	Lo-byte of the load address
3	Hi-byte of the load address
4-255	The first 252 bytes of the program

The first pair of bytes are the pointer to the track and sector of the next block in/the file. Technically, this is known as a "forward pointer." It points ahead to the next sector in the file. All Commodore files use this type of pointer.

The second pair of bytes is the "load address" of the file in lo-byte/hi-byte form. They indicate where the program is to be loaded into memory. A BASIC program that was saved from a C64 will have a $01 and a $08 in these two locations. This indicates that the program is to be loaded into memory starting at memory location $0801 (remember it is in lo-byte/hi-byte form). In decimal notation this is memory location 2049 — the start of BASIC on a C64.

Have you ever wondered about the significance of the ",1" in the command LOAD "name",8,1? It determines whether or not a program is "relocated" when it is loaded into memory. If you do not specify the ",1", the C64 will ignore the load address at the start of the file and load the program starting at memory location $0801 (2049). When the ",1" is present, the C64 (or VIC-20) will pay attention to the load address and load the program into memory starting at the location specified by bytes $02 and $03.

The remaining sectors, except the last one, look like this:

TRACK LINK	SECTOR LINK	THE NEXT 254 BYTES OF YOUR PROGRAM

Byte	Purpose
0	Track of the next block in this file
1	Sector of the next block in this file
2-255	The next 254 bytes of the program

The last block in a program file is special because:

1. It is the last sector.
2. It is usually only partially full.

To signal the DOS that this is the last block, the first byte is set to $00. The first byte is normally the track link. Since there is no track 0, the DOS knows that this is the last sector in the file. The second byte indicates the position of the last byte that is part of the program file. Any bytes beyond this position are garbage.

Diagrammatically, the last sector in a program file looks like this:

NULL $00	LAST BYTE	THE FINAL BYTES OF YOUR PROGRAM	GARBAGE

Byte	Purpose
0	Null byte to indicate that this is the last sector
1	Number of bytes to read from this sector (N)
2-N	The last (N−2) bytes of the program
(N+1)-255	Garbage

Let's examine the program file "DIR" on your 1541TEST/DEMO disk. DIR appears in the directory on track 18, sector 04. The directory entry looks like this:

TRACK 18 - SECTOR 04

```
. 00:  00 FF 82 10 01 44 49 52   .....DIR
. 08:  AO AO AO AO AO AO AO AO   ........
. 10:  AO AO AO AO AO 00 00 00   ........
. 18:  00 00 00 00 00 00 04 00   ........
```

From the entry we see that "DIR" starts at track 16 ($10), sector 01 ($01) and that the file is four blocks long (4 + 0 * 256).

```
. 00:  00 FF 82 10 01 44 49 52   .....DIR
            ** **
. 08:  AO AO AO AO AO AO AO AO   ........
. 10:  AO AO AO AO AO 00 00 00   ........
. 18:  00 00 00 00 00 00 04 00   ........
                          ** **
```

Let's look at the first block in this file.

TRACK 16 - SECTOR 01

```
. 00:  10 0B 01 04 0D 04 04 00   ........
. 08:  9F 32 2C 38 2C 31 35 00   .2,8,15.
. 10:  1E 04 05 00 99 22 93 22   ....."."
. 18:  3A 89 20 31 30 30 30 30   :. 10000
. 20:  00 2E 04 0A 00 9F 31 2C   ......1,
. 28:  38 2C 30 2C 22 24 30 22   8,0,"$0"
. 30:  00 3C 04 14 00 A1 23 31   .<....#1
. 38:  2C 41 24 2C 42 24 00 4A   ,A$,B$.J
. 40:  04 1E 00 A1 23 31 2C 41   ....#1,A
. 48:  24 2C 42 24 00 58 04 28   $,B$.X.(
. 50:  00 A1 23 31 2C 41 24 2C   ..#1,A$,
. 58:  42 24 00 60 04 32 00 43   B$...2.C
. 60:  B2 30 00 77 04 3C 00 8B   .0...<..
. 68:  20 41 24 B3 B1 22 22 20    A$.."" 
. 70:  A7 20 43 B2 C6 28 41 24   . C..(A$
. 78:  29 00 94 04 46 00 8B 20   )...F..
. 80:  42 24 B3 B1 22 22 20 A7   B$.."" .
. 88:  20 43 B2 43 AA C6 28 42    C.C..(B
. 90:  24 29 AC 32 35 36 00 AF   $).256..
. 98:  04 50 00 99 22 12 22 CA   .P..".".
. A0:  28 C4 28 43 29 2C 32 29   (.(C),2)
. A8:  3B A3 33 29 3B 22 92 22   ;.3);"."
. B0:  3B 00 C9 04 5A 00 A1 23   ;...Z..#
. B8:  31 2C 42 24 3A 8B 20 53   1,B$:. S
. C0:  54 B3 B1 30 20 A7 20 31   T..0 . 1
. C8:  30 30 30 00 DE 04 64 00   000.....
```

```
.  DO:  8B 20 42 24 B3 B1 C7 28   .  B$...(
.  D8:  33 34 29 20 A7 20 39 30 34)  .  90
.  EO:  00 00 05 6E 00 A1 23 31   ......#1
.  E8:  2C 42 24 3A 8B 20 42 24   ,B$:. B$
.  FO:  B3 B1 C7 28 33 34 29 A7   ...(34).
.  F8:  20 99 42 24 3B 3A 89 31   .B$;:.1
```

Not very recognizable is it? Remember this is C64 internal BASIC not a BASIC listing. Bytes 0 and 1 are of interest. They are the track and sector link that point to the next block in the program file. In this case, they point to track 16 ($10), sector 11 ($0B). Since this is the first data block of the file, bytes 2 and 3 are also important. They are the load address. We can see that the load address is $0401 or 1025 decimal. This file was written on a PET. (The start of BASIC memory on the C64 is at $0801. The VIC-20 begins at $1001, $1201, or $0401 depending ont he amount of external memory.) DIR will require a straight relocating load, i.e., LOAD "DIR",8. If you used a LOAD "DIR", 8,1 command, the program would be loaded into the screen RAM of the C64. *NOTE: If you load this program properly, you will NOT be able to get it to VERIFY correctly. The reason is that the internal BASIC links were changed when the program was relocated.*

```
.  OO:  10 0B 01 04 0D 04 04 00   ........
        ** ** ** **
```

Let's follow the forward chain to track 16, sector 11 and take a look at the start of the second block in our file.

TRACK 16 – SECTOR 11

```
.  OO:  10 02 31 30 00 1C 05 78   ..10....
.  O8:  00 A1 23 31 2C 42 24 3A   ..#1,B$:
.  1O:  8B 20 42 24 B2 C7 28 33   . B$..(3
```

Nothing much of interest here. Let's chain to track 16 ($10), sector 02 ($02) and take a look at the start of the next block.

TRACK 16 – SECTOR 02

```
.  OO:  10 OC B2 22 22 3A 99 22   ..."":."
.  O8:  3E 22 3B 00 1A 06 AB OF   >";.....
.  1O:  A1 42 24 3A 8B 42 24 B2   .B$:.B$.
```

Again, nothing much of interest. Chain to track 16 ($10), sector 12 ($0C).

```
           TRACK 16 - SECTOR 12

. 00:  00 68 8B 20 41 24 B2 22    ... A$."
. 08:  44 22 20 A7 20 31 30 00    D" . 10.
. 10:  2D 07 3C 28 8B 20 41 24    -.<(. A$
. 18:  B2 22 2E 22 20 B0 20 41    ."." . A
. 20:  24 B2 22 3E 22 20 B0 20    $.">" .
. 28:  41 24 B2 22 3E 22 20 A7    A$.">" .
. 30:  20 34 30 30 30 00 3E 07     4000.>.
. 38:  46 28 8B 20 41 24 B2 22    F(. A$."
. 40:  51 22 20 A7 20 80 00 52    Q" . ..R
. 48:  07 50 28 8B 20 41 24 B2    .P(. A$.
. 50:  22 53 22 20 A7 20 35 30    "S" . 50
. 58:  30 30 00 5E 07 F7 2A 89    00. ..*.
. 60:  20 31 30 31 30 30 00 00     10100..
. 68:  00 A0 00 A1 20 54 24 3A    .... T$:
. 70:  8B 20 54 24 B3 B1 22 22    . T$..""
. 78:  20 A7 20 8D 20 32 30 30    . . 200
```

~~~~~~

Now we're cooking. This is the last sector of the file. How can we tell? The track of the next block in the file is 0 ($00). But what about the sector link? It's a misnomer. The sector link in the last block is actually a byte count. It informs the DOS that only bytes 2 through 104 ($68) are important in this example. Recall that an end of file in BASIC is designated by three zeros in a row. An End-or-Identify (EOI) signal will be sent once byte 104 has been transferred across the serial bus. When the C64 receives this EOI signal, the status variable, ST, will be set to a value of 64. (Any further attempt to read a byte will cause the drive to time out.) Here's the tail end of our program. The three null bytes, ($00), at $66/7/8 are the last three bytes in our program file.

```
. 00:  00 68 8B 20 41 24 B2 22    ... A$."
. 08:  44 22 20 A7 20 31 30 00    D" . 10.
. 10:  2D 07 3C 28 8B 20 41 24    -.<(. A$
. 18:  B2 22 2E 22 20 B0 20 41    ."." . A
. 20:  24 B2 22 3E 22 20 B0 20    $.">" .
. 28:  41 24 B2 22 3E 22 20 A7    A$.">" .
. 30:  20 34 30 30 30 00 3E 07     4000.>.
. 38:  46 28 8B 20 41 24 B2 22    F(. A$."
. 40:  51 22 20 A7 20 80 00 52    Q" . ..R
. 48:  07 50 28 8B 20 41 24 B2    .P(. A$.
. 50:  22 53 22 20 A7 20 35 30    "S" . 50
. 58:  30 30 00 5E 07 F7 2A 89    00. ..*.
. 60:  20 31 30 31 30 30 00 00     10100..
. 68:  00 xx xx xx xx xx xx xx    .
```

~~~~~~

What about the rest of the block? Ignore it. It is garbage. The DOS does not zero out a buffer before it begins filling it with new information sent from the computer. As a result, the last block in a file, which is almost never filled with new information, is padded with whatever happened to be left in the buffer from a previous read or write operation. There are two exceptions to the rule, namely, the directory and relative files. A partial directory block is always padded with nulls ($00). Moreover, it always appears as a full block. Bytes 0 and 1 of the last directory block will contain a $00 and a $FF, respectively. Relative file structure will be explained shortly.

4.6 Sequential File Storage

The format of a sequential file is very straightforward. All the sectors, except the last one, look like this:

TRACK LINK	SECTOR LINK	254 BYTES OF DATA

Byte	Purpose
0	Track of the next block in this file
1	Sector of the next block in this file
2-255	254 bytes of data

The last block in a sequential file is special for two reasons:

1. It is the last sector.
2. It is usually only partially full.

To signal the DOS that this is the last block, the first byte is set to $00. The first byte is normally the track link. Since there is no track 0, the DOS knows that this is the last sector in the file. The second byte indicates the position of the last byte in the file. Any bytes beyond this position are garbage.

Diagrammatically, the last sector in the file looks like this:

NULL $00	LAST BYTE	THE FINAL DATA BYTES IN YOUR SEQUENTIAL FILE	GARBAGE

Byte	Purpose
0	Null byte to indicate this is the last sector
1	Position of the last byte in the file (N)
2-N	The last N−2 bytes of the sequential file
(N+1)-255	Garbage

No sequential files appear on the 1541TEST/DEMO. (The file named SEQUENTIAL FILE is a program file demonstrating the sequential access method.) The C-64 DISK BONUS PACK does come with one sequential file on it. The file named " DIRECTORY " appears as a SEQ when displaying the directory. " DIRECTORY " can be found at track 18, sector 01 on the C-64 DISK BONUS PACK. Let's take a peek at the directory entry for this file:

```
             TRACK 18 - SECTOR 01

. 20:  00 00 81 11 01 20 20 20   .....
. 28:  44 49 52 45 43 54 4F 52   DIRECTOR
. 30:  59 20 20 20 A0 00 00 00   Y    ...
. 38:  00 00 00 00 00 00 02 00   ........
```

" DIRECTORY " is the second file entry in the directory.

```
. 20:  00 00 81 11 01 20 20 20   .....
              ** ** **
. 28:  44 49 52 45 43 54 4F 52   DIRECTOR
. 30:  59 20 20 20 A0 00 00 00   Y    ...
. 38:  00 00 00 00 00 00 02 00   ........
                          **
```

A sequential file is designated by an $81 in the directory. The first block of this file is stored on track 17 ($11), sector 1 ($01). We also see that " DIRECTORY " is two blocks long (2 + 0 * 256). Let's take a look at the first half of the starting data block.

```
             TRACK 17 - SECTOR 01

. 00:  11 0B 43 36 34 20 53 54   ..C64 ST
. 08:  41 52 54 45 52 20 4B 49   ARTER KI
. 10:  54 20 20 20 36 34 20 20   T    64
. 18:  32 41 0D 31 35 34 31 20   2A.1541
. 20:  42 41 43 4B 55 50 0D 41   BACKUP.A
. 28:  4D 4F 52 54 20 54 41 42   MORT TAB
. 30:  4C 45 0D 41 52 52 4F 57   LE.ARROW
. 38:  0D 42 49 54 53 20 41 4E   .BITS AN
. 40:  44 20 42 59 54 45 53 0D   D BYTES.
. 48:  43 41 4C 45 4E 44 41 52   CALENDAR
. 50:  0D 43 48 41 4E 47 45 20   .CHANGE
. 58:  44 49 53 4B 0D 43 48 41   DISK.CHA
. 60:  52 20 42 4F 4F 54 0D 43   R BOOT.C
. 68:  4F 4C 4F 52 20 54 45 53   OLOR TES
. 70:  54 0D 43 4F 50 59 2D 41   T.COPY-A
. 78:  4C 4C 36 34 0D 44 45 4D   LL64.DEM
```

Bytes 0 and 1 are the track and sector link (forward pointer). They inform us that the next data block can be found at track 17, sector 11. The remaining 254 bytes are data. The sequential data that appear here are in fact the disk name (C64 STARTER KIT), the cosmetic disk ID (64), and the file names found on the C-64 DISK BONUS PACK. It is interesting to note that a carriage return character ($0D) was used as a delimiter to separate record entries. Next we see:

```
          TRACK 17 - SECTOR 11

. 00:  00 86 2D 20 59 41 4E 4B   ..- YANK
. 08:  45 45 0D 53 4F 55 4E 44   EE.SOUND
. 10:  20 2D 20 41 4C 49 45 4E    - ALIEN
. 18:  0D 53 4F 55 4E 44 20 2D   .SOUND -
. 20:  20 42 4F 4D 42 0D 53 4F    BOMB.SO
. 28:  55 4E 44 20 2D 20 43 4C   UND - CL
. 30:  41 50 0D 53 4F 55 4E 44   AP.SOUND
. 38:  20 2D 20 47 55 4E 46 49    - GUNFI
. 40:  52 45 0D 53 4F 55 4E 44   RE.SOUND
. 48:  20 2D 20 50 4F 4E 47 0D    - PONG.
. 50:  53 4F 55 4E 44 20 2D 20   SOUND -
. 58:  52 41 59 47 55 4E 0D 53   RAYGUN.S
. 60:  4F 55 4E 44 20 2D 20 53   OUND - S
. 68:  49 52 45 4E 0D 53 50 52   IREN.SPR
. 70:  49 54 45 20 42 4F 4F 54   ITE BOOT
. 78:  0D 53 55 50 45 52 4D 4F   .SUPERMO
. 80:  4E 36 34 2E 56 31 0D 59   N64.V1.Y
. 88:  54 53 50 52 49 54 45 53   TSPRITES
. 90:  A0 A0 A0 A0 A0 00 00 00   ........
. 98:  00 00 00 00 00 00 05 00   ........
. A0:  00 00 82 07 00 53 4E 4F   .....SNO
. A8:  4F 50 59 20 4D 41 54 48   OPY MATH
. B0:  A0 A0 A0 A0 A0 00 00 00   ........
. B8:  00 00 00 00 00 00 33 00   ......3.
. C0:  00 00 82 1D 00 41 4D 4F   .....AMO
. C8:  52 54 20 54 41 42 4C 45   RT TABLE
. D0:  A0 A0 A0 A0 A0 00 00 00   ........
. D8:  00 00 00 00 00 00 27 00   ......'.
. E0:  00 00 82 05 02 4D 4F 52   .....MOR
. E8:  54 47 41 47 45 A0 A0 A0   TGAGE...
. F0:  A0 A0 A0 A0 A0 00 00 00   ........
. F8:  00 00 00 00 00 00 2D 00   ......-.
```

We can see from the above data block that this is the last sector in the chain. Byte 0 contains a zero indicating no forward track. Byte 1 then is a byte count ($86=134). Byte 134 is the last byte in our data file. Recall that the status variable (ST) will be set to 64 on the C64 side after byte 134 has been read.

```
. 80:  4E 36 34 2E 56 31 0D xx   N64.V1.
```

55

The remainder of the block has been padded ($87–$FF). The padding is clearly recognizable this time around. It has no rhyme or reason but it is still interesting to say the least. A portion of the C-64 DISK BONUS PACK directory itself was used to pad the remainder of the data block in question.

```
. 80:  xx xx xx xx xx xx xx 59   N64.V1.Y
. 88:  54 53 50 52 49 54 45 53   TSPRITES
. 90:  A0 A0 A0 A0 A0 00 00 00   ........
. 98:  00 00 00 00 00 00 05 00   ........
. A0:  00 00 82 07 00 53 4E 4F   .....SNO
. A8:  4F 50 59 20 4D 41 54 48   OPY MATH
. B0:  A0 A0 A0 A0 A0 00 00 00   ........
. B8:  00 00 00 00 00 00 33 00   ......3.
. C0:  00 00 82 1D 00 41 4D 4F   .....AMO
. C8:  52 54 20 54 41 42 4C 45   RT TABLE
. D0:  A0 A0 A0 A0 A0 00 00 00   ........
. D8:  00 00 00 00 00 00 27 00   ......'.
. E0:  00 00 82 05 02 4D 4F 52   .....MOR
. E8:  54 47 41 47 45 A0 A0 A0   TGAGE...
. F0:  A0 A0 A0 A0 A0 00 00 00   ........
. F8:  00 00 00 00 00 00 2D 00   ......-.
```

4.7 Relative File Storage

Relative file types have the most elaborate internal structure. Relative files are often referred to as random access files. A relative file is actually two files in one:

1. A sequential data file with records of a fixed length.
2. A file of track and sector pointers called side sectors.

The sequential data file uses fixed length records so that the DOS can calculate where to find any given record. This makes it possible to position to a particular record and read or write it without disturbing the rest of the file. In the jargon of relative files, the length of one record in the sequential data file is known as the *record size*.

The complete file of track and sectors pointers is called the *side sector file*. The size of this file depends on the length of the sequential file. In general it is 1/120th the length of the sequential file (minimum length = 1 block; maximum length = 6 blocks). Each block in this file is known as a *side sector*. There are really two sets of track and sector pointers in this file. The larger set is a list of the track and sector numbers of the blocks used to store the sequential data file (its file chain). The other is a list of the track and sector numbers of the side sectors (the file chain of the side sector file).

The purpose of the side sector file is to allow the DOS to find any given record with remarkable efficiency. One disk read of a side sector is all that is required to locate the track and sector of the block where a particular record is stored. Two additional reads may then be required to retrieve a record itself if it spans two data blocks. This will be explained shortly when we examine records in more detail.

Remember that sequential data blocks have the following format:

Byte	Purpose
0	Track of the next block in this file
1	Sector of the next block in this file
2-255	254 bytes of data

Diagrammatically, each block (side sector) in the side sector file looks like this:

TRACK LINK	SECTOR LINK	SIDE SECTOR NUMBER	RECORD SIZE	TRACK/SECTOR LINKS FOR 6 SIDE SECTORS	TRACK/SECTOR LINKS FOR 120 DATA BLOCKS

Byte	Purpose
0	Track of the next side sector
1	Sector of the next side sector
2	Side sector number
3	Record length
4-15	Track and sector list of the side sector file

      4-5   Track and sector of side sector #0
      6-7   Track and sector of side sector #1
      8-9   Track and sector of side sector #2
      10-11 Track and sector of side sector #3
      12-13 Track and sector of side sector #4
      14-15 Track and sector of side sector #5

Byte	Purpose
16-256	Track and sector list of 120 data blocks

      16-17 Track and sector of data block #1
      18-19 Track and sector of data block #2
      20-21 Track and sector of data block #3

254-255 Track and sector of data block #120

To help you make some sense out of this, let's begin with the directory entry for a relative file. Here's the start of the directory of a diskette that has a relative file stored on it.

TRACK 18 - SECTOR 01

```
. 00:  00 FF 81 11 00 53 43 20   .....SC
. 08:  31 4D 41 47 20 46 49 4C   1MAG FIL
. 10:  45 A0 A0 A0 A0 00 00 00   E.......
. 18:  00 00 00 00 00 00 01 00   ........
. 20:  00 00 81 11 01 53 43 20   .....SC
. 28:  32 4D 41 47 20 46 49 4C   2MAG FIL
. 30:  45 A0 A0 A0 A0 00 00 00   E.......
. 38:  00 00 00 00 00 00 01 00   ........
. 40:  00 00 81 11 02 53 43 20   .....SC
. 48:  33 4D 41 47 20 46 49 4C   3MAG FIL
. 50:  45 A0 A0 A0 A0 00 00 00   E.......
. 58:  00 00 00 00 00 00 01 00   ........
. 60:  00 00 84 11 03 4D 41 47   .....MAG    Here's the entry
. 68:  20 46 49 4C 45 A0 A0 A0   FILE...     for the REL file:
. 70:  A0 A0 A0 A0 A0 11 0D 96   ........
. 78:  00 00 00 00 00 00 B4 01   ........
```

"MAG FILE" will serve as our demo throughout this section. Let's examine its directory entry in detail from track 18, sector 1.

```
. 60:  00 00 84 11 03 4D 41 47   .....MAG
       ** ** **
. 68:  20 46 49 4C 45 A0 A0 A0   FILE...     File type and T/S link
. 70:  A0 A0 A0 A0 A0 11 0D 96   ........
. 78:  00 00 00 00 00 00 B4 01   ........
```

From the directory entry we can see that "MAG FILE" is a relative file. A relative file is indicated by an $84 as the file type. The track and sector pointers in the directory reveal that "MAG FILE" starts at track 17 ($11), sector 03 ($03). This is the sequential data file portion of the relative file. It is the beginning of our data.

```
. 70:  A0 A0 A0 A0 A0 11 0D 96   ........
                      ** ** **       Side sector information
                                     Record length
```

Side sector information follows the file name. The first side sector begins at track 17 ($11), sector 13 ($0D). In addition, we see our record length ($96=150). Each record in our sequential data file is 150 bytes long. This is fixed throughout the entire data file.

```
. 78:  00 00 00 00 00 00 B4 01   ........
                         ** **        File length (lo/hi-byte)
```

Our sample relative file consumes a total of 436 blocks on the diskette (180 + 1 * 256). (There is still room for expansion.) We can determine the number of side sectors by simple divison. A side sector stores track and sector pointers for 120 data blocks of our sequential file. To determine the number of side sectors, simply divide the total number of blocks that appear in the directory entry by 120 and round up to the next higher integer:

$$436 / 120 = 3.6 \rightarrow 4$$

Four side sectors are needed to keep track of this much data. To figure out how many records currently exist requires a little more arithmetic. First we have to subtract the number of side sectors from the total number of blocks.

$$436 - 4 = 432$$

Now we can determine the total number of data bytes currently in use by our sequential file.

$$432 * 254 = 109728$$

Why 254 as a multiplier? Remember that the first two bytes of any data block are forward track and sector pointers (256 − 2 = 254). We finish our set of calculations by dividing this total by the fixed record length.

$$109728 / 150 = 731.52$$

A total of 731 records exist at the current time in "MAG FILE."

Let's examine the first side sector.

TRACK 17 − SECTOR 13   SIDE SECTOR #0

```
. 00:  OC 13 00 96 11 OD OC 13 ........  Forward pointer, SS #, size,
. 08:  06 10 13 OF 00 00 00 00 ........  and 6 pairs of side sector pointers
. 10:  11 03 11 OE 11 04 11 OF ........  120 pairs of data block
. 18:  11 05 11 10 11 06 11 11 ........  pointers
. 20:  11 07 11 12 11 08 11 13 ........
. 28:  11 09 11 14 11 OA 11 OB ........
. 30:  11 OC 10 00 10 OA 10 14 ........
. 38:  10 08 10 12 10 06 10 10 ........
. 40:  10 04 10 OE 10 02 10 OC ........
. 48:  10 01 10 OB 10 03 10 OD ........
. 50:  10 05 10 OF 10 07 10 11 ........
. 58:  10 09 10 13 OF 07 OF 11 ........
. 60:  OF 05 OF OF OF 03 OF OD ........
. 68:  OF 01 OF OB OF 00 OF OA ........
. 70:  OF 14 OF 08 OF 12 OF 06 ........
. 78:  OF 10 OF 04 OF OE OF 02 ........
. 80:  OF OC OF 09 OF 13 OE 07 ........
. 88:  OE 11 OE 05 OE OF OE 03 ........
```

```
. 90: OE OD OE 01 OE OB OE OO ........
. 98: OE OA OE 14 OE O8 OE 12 ........
. AO: OE O6 OE 10 OE O4 OE OE ........
. A8: OE O2 OE OC OE O9 OE 13 ........
. BO: OD 07 OD 11 OD O5 OD OF ........
. B8: OD O3 OD OD OD O1 OD OB ........
. CO: OD OO OD OA OD 14 OD O8 ........
. C8: OD 12 OD O6 OD 10 OD O4 ........
. DO: OD OE OD O2 OD OC OD O9 ........
. D8: OD 13 OC O7 OC 11 OC O5 ........
. EO: OC OF OC O3 OC OD OC O1 ........
. E8: OC OB OC OO OC OA OC 14 ........
. FO: OC O8 OC 12 OC O6 OC 10 ........
. F8: OC O4 OC OE OC O2 OC OC ........
```

Of primary interest are the first 16 bytes.

```
. OO: OC 13 OO 96 11 OD OC 13 ........
. O8: O6 10 13 OF OO OO OO OO ........
```

Bytes 0 and 1 show us that the next side sector resides at track 12 ($0C), sector 19 ($13).
Byte 2 informs us that this is side sector 0. A maximum of 6 side sectors are used by
any one relative file. This is determined solely by the physical storage capacity of the
diskette (664 blocks free after formatting divided by 120 track and sector pointers in
a side sector equals 5.53 side sectors). Side sectors are numbered from 0 to 5. Byte 3
shows us the record size again (150 bytes). Bytes 5-15 are the track and sector locations
of the six possible side sectors. They can be tabled as follows:

BYTE	SIDE SECTOR	TRACK - SECTOR
4- 5	0	17 ($11) - 13 ($0D)
6- 7	1	12 ($0C) - 19 ($13)
8- 9	2	6 ($06) - 16 ($10)
10-11	3	19 ($13) - 15 ($0F)
12-13	4	0 ($00) - 0 ($00)
14-15	5	0 ($00) - 0 ($00)

We can see from the table above that side sectors 4 and 5 have not yet been allocated.
Once our data file expands to encompass more than 480 and 600 sectors, respectively,
they will be allocated, provided there is room on the diskette.

The remaining 240 bytes are track and sector pointers to the first 120 blocks in the sequential file. From bytes 16 and 17 of side sector 0 we see that our data begins at track
17 ($11), sector 03 ($03). (This is the track and sector recorded in the directory itself.)
Track 17, sector 03 chains to track 17 ($11), sector 14 ($0E) which chains to track 17
($11), sector 4 ($04) and so on.

```
              TRACK  17  -  SECTOR  13            SIDE SECTOR #0

 .  10:  11  03  11  0E  11  04  11  0F   ........
         **  **
 .  18:  11  05  11  10  11  06  11  11   ........
 .  20:  11  07  11  12  11  08  11  13   ........
 .  28:  11  09  11  14  11  0A  11  0B   ........
 .  30:  11  0C  10  00  10  0A  10  14   ........
 .  38:  10  08  10  12  10  06  10  10   ........
 .  40:  10  04  10  0E  10  02  10  0C   ........
 .  48:  10  01  10  0B  10  03  10  0D   ........
 .  50:  10  05  10  0F  10  07  10  11   ........
 .  58:  10  09  10  13  0F  07  0F  11   ........
 .  60:  0F  05  0F  0F  0F  03  0F  0D   ........
 .  68:  0F  01  0F  0B  0F  00  0F  0A   ........
 .  70:  0F  14  0F  08  0F  12  0F  06   ........
 .  78:  0F  10  0F  04  0F  0E  0F  02   ........
 .  80:  0F  0C  0F  09  0F  13  0E  07   ........
 .  88:  0E  11  0E  05  0E  0F  0E  03   ........
 .  90:  0E  0D  0E  01  0E  0B  0E  00   ........
 .  98:  0E  0A  0E  14  0E  08  0E  12   ........
 .  A0:  0E  06  0E  10  0E  04  0E  0E   ........
 .  A8:  0E  02  0E  0C  0E  09  0E  13   ........
 .  B0:  0D  07  0D  11  0D  05  0D  0F   ........
 .  B8:  0D  03  0D  0D  0D  01  0D  0B   ........
 .  C0:  0D  00  0D  0A  0D  14  0D  08   ........
 .  C8:  0D  12  0D  06  0D  10  0D  04   ........
 .  D0:  0D  0E  0D  02  0D  0C  0D  09   ........
 .  D8:  0D  13  0C  07  0C  11  0C  05   ........
 .  E0:  0C  0F  0C  03  0C  0D  0C  01   ........
 .  E8:  0C  0B  0C  00  0C  0A  0C  14   ........
 .  F0:  0C  08  0C  12  0C  06  0C  10   ........
 .  F8:  0C  04  0C  0E  0C  02  0C  0C   ........
```

Let's trace the remaining side sectors now.

```
              TRACK  12  -  SECTOR  19            SIDE SECTOR #1

 .  00:  06  10  01  96  11  0D  0C  13   ........
 .  08:  06  10  13  0F  00  00  00  00   ........
 .  10:  0C  09  0B  13  0B  07  0B  11   ........
 .  18:  0B  05  0B  0F  0B  03  0B  0D   ........
 .  20:  0B  01  0B  0B  0B  00  0B  0A   ........
 .  28:  0B  14  0B  08  0B  12  0B  06   ........
 .  30:  0B  10  0B  04  0B  0E  0B  02   ........
 .  38:  0B  0C  0B  09  0A  13  0A  07   ........
 .  40:  0A  11  0A  05  0A  0F  0A  03   ........
 .  48:  0A  0D  0A  01  0A  0B  0A  00   ........
 .  50:  0A  0A  0A  14  0A  08  0A  12   ........
```

61

```
.  58:  0A 06 0A 10 0A 04 0A 0E  ........
.  60:  0A 02 0A 0C 0A 09 09 13  ........
.  68:  09 07 09 11 09 05 09 0F  ........
.  70:  09 03 09 0D 09 01 09 0B  ........
.  78:  09 00 09 0A 09 14 09 08  ........
.  80:  09 12 09 06 09 10 09 04  ........
.  88:  09 0E 09 02 09 0C 09 09  ........
.  90:  08 13 08 07 08 11 08 05  ........
.  98:  08 0F 08 03 08 0D 08 01  ........
.  A0:  08 0B 08 00 08 0A 08 14  ........
.  A8:  08 08 08 12 08 06 08 10  ........
.  B0:  08 04 08 0E 08 02 08 0C  ........
.  B8:  08 09 07 13 07 07 07 11  ........
.  C0:  07 05 07 0F 07 03 07 0D  ........
.  C8:  07 01 07 0B 07 00 07 0A  ........
.  D0:  07 14 07 08 07 12 07 06  ........
.  D8:  07 10 07 04 07 0E 07 02  ........
.  E0:  07 0C 07 09 06 13 06 07  ........
.  E8:  06 11 06 05 06 0F 06 03  ........
.  F0:  06 0D 06 01 06 0B 06 00  ........
.  F8:  06 0A 06 14 06 08 06 12  ........
```

Side sector 1 looks OK on this end.

TRACK 06 – SECTOR 16   **SIDE SECTOR #2**

```
.  00:  13 0F 02 96 11 0D 0C 13  ........
.  08:  06 10 13 0F 00 00 00 00  ........
.  10:  06 06 06 02 06 0C 06 04  ........
.  18:  06 0E 06 09 05 13 05 07  ........
.  20:  05 11 05 05 05 0F 05 03  ........
.  28:  05 0D 05 01 05 0B 05 00  ........
.  30:  05 0A 05 14 05 08 05 12  ........
.  38:  05 06 05 10 05 04 05 0E  ........
.  40:  05 02 05 0C 05 09 04 13  ........
.  48:  04 07 04 11 04 05 04 0F  ........
.  50:  04 03 04 0D 04 01 04 0B  ........
.  58:  04 00 04 0A 04 14 04 08  ........
.  60:  04 12 04 06 04 10 04 04  ........
.  68:  04 0E 04 02 04 0C 04 09  ........
.  70:  03 13 03 07 03 11 03 05  ........
.  78:  03 0F 03 03 03 0D 03 01  ........
.  80:  03 0B 03 00 03 0A 03 14  ........
.  88:  03 08 03 12 03 06 03 10  ........
.  90:  03 04 03 0E 03 02 03 0C  ........
.  98:  03 09 02 13 02 07 02 11  ........
.  A0:  02 05 02 0F 02 03 02 0D  ........
.  A8:  02 01 02 0B 02 00 02 0A  ........
.  B0:  02 14 02 08 02 12 02 06  ........
```

```
. B8:  02 10 02 04 02 0E 02 02    ........
. C0:  02 0C 02 09 01 13 01 07    ........
. C8:  01 11 01 05 01 0F 01 03    ........
. D0:  01 0D 01 01 01 0B 01 00    ........
. D8:  01 0A 01 14 01 08 01 12    ........
. E0:  01 06 01 10 01 04 01 0E    ........
. E8:  01 02 01 0C 01 09 13 0A    ........
. F0:  13 00 13 0B 13 01 13 0C    ........
. F8:  13 02 13 0D 13 03 13 0E    ........
```

Side sector 2 seems to be in order too.

TRACK 19 — SECTOR 15   SIDE SECTOR #3

```
. 00:  00 9F 03 96 11 0D 0C 13    ........
. 08:  06 10 13 0F 00 00 00 00    ........
. 10:  13 04 13 10 13 06 13 11    ........
. 18:  13 07 13 12 13 08 13 05    ........
. 20:  13 09 14 00 14 0A 14 01    ........
. 28:  14 0B 14 02 14 0C 14 03    ........
. 30:  14 0D 14 04 14 0E 14 05    ........
. 38:  14 0F 14 06 14 10 14 07    ........
. 40:  14 11 14 08 14 12 14 09    ........
. 48:  15 00 15 0A 15 01 15 0B    ........
. 50:  15 02 15 0C 15 03 15 0D    ........
. 58:  15 04 15 0E 15 05 15 0F    ........
. 60:  15 06 15 10 15 07 15 11    ........
. 68:  15 08 15 12 15 09 16 00    ........
. 70:  16 0A 16 01 16 0B 16 02    ........
. 78:  16 0C 16 03 16 0D 16 04    ........
. 80:  16 0E 16 05 16 0F 16 06    ........
. 88:  16 10 16 07 16 11 16 08    ........
. 90:  16 12 16 09 17 00 17 0A    ........
. 98:  17 01 17 0B 17 02 17 0C    ........
. A0:  00 00 00 00 00 00 00 00    ........
. A8:  00 00 00 00 00 00 00 00    ........
. B0:  00 00 00 00 00 00 00 00    ........
. B8:  00 00 00 00 00 00 00 00    ........
. C0:  00 00 00 00 00 00 00 00    ........
. C8:  00 00 00 00 00 00 00 00    ........
. D0:  00 00 00 00 00 00 00 00    ........
. D8:  00 00 00 00 00 00 00 00    ........
. E0:  00 00 00 00 00 00 00 00    ........
. E8:  00 00 00 00 00 00 00 00    ........
. F0:  00 00 00 00 00 00 00 00    ........
. F8:  00 00 00 00 00 00 00 00    ........
```

Hold it right there please. Bytes 0 and 1 should look familiar by now. Still thinking? (**Hint:** End of chain and a byte count.)

```
. 00: 00 9F 03 96 11 0D 0C 13 ........
      ** **
```

Byte 1 of side sector 3 shows a byte count of 159 ($9F). Recall that bytes 16-255 in a side sector are a list of track and sector pointers to 120 data blocks. As a result, bytes 158 and 159 must be interpreted together. They point to the last block in our sequential data file in this instance. The last block is stored on track 23 ($17), sector 12 ($0C). Notice too, that the remainder of the side sector is padded with nulls. The remaining 96 bytes are in limbo until our relative file is expanded. Bytes 160 and 161 will then point to the next track and sector of data and so on. When side sector 3 is full, a new side sector will be created. Bytes 0 and 1 of side sector 3 will then point to side sector 4. Bytes 12 and 13 in side sectors 0, 1, and 2 will also be updated to reflect the creation of side sector 4.

Now let's take a brief glance at the sequential file itself.

```
           TRACK 17 - SECTOR 03

. 00: 11 0E 4D 41 47 20 46 49  ..MAG FI
. 08: 4C 45 0D 20 37 30 39 0D  LE. 709.
. 10: 20 36 0D D4 49 54 4C 45   6..ITLE
. 18: 0D C3 4F 4D 50 55 54 45  ..OMPUTE
. 20: 52 0D CD 41 47 41 5A 49  R..AGAZI
. 28: 4E 45 0D C9 53 53 55 45  NE..SSUE
. 30: 0D D0 41 47 45 0D C3 4F  ..AGE..O
. 38: 4D 4D 45 4E 54 0D 0D 00  MMENT...
. 40: 00 00 00 00 00 00 00 00  ........
. 48: 00 00 00 00 00 00 00 00  ........
. 50: 00 00 00 00 00 00 00 00  ........
. 58: 00 00 00 00 00 00 00 00  ........
. 60: 00 00 00 00 00 00 00 00  ........
. 68: 00 00 00 00 00 00 00 00  ........
. 70: 00 00 00 00 00 00 00 00  ........
. 78: 00 00 00 00 00 00 00 00  ........
. 80: 00 00 00 00 00 00 00 00  ........
. 88: 00 00 00 00 00 00 00 00  ........
. 90: 00 00 00 00 00 00 00 00  ........
. 98: 20 31 35 30 20 0D 2E 0D   150 ...
. A0: 2E 0D 2E 0D 2E 0D 2E 0D  ........
. A8: 2E 0D 2E 0D 2E 0D 2E 0D  ........
. B0: 2E 0D 2E 0D 2E 0D 2E 0D  ........
. B8: 2E 0D 2E 0D 2E 0D 2E 0D  ........
. C0: 2E 0D 2E 0D 2E 0D 00 00  ........
. C8: 00 00 00 00 00 00 00 00  ........
. D0: 00 00 00 00 00 00 00 00  ........
```

```
.  D8:  00  00  00  00  00  00  00  00   ........
.  E0:  00  00  00  00  00  00  00  00   ........
.  E8:  00  00  00  00  00  00  00  00   ........
.  F0:  00  00  00  00  00  00  00  00   ........
.  F8:  00  00  00  00  00  00  00  00   ........
```

The block reveals a typical sequential file. Bytes 0 and 1 are the chain. The first data block links to track 17 ($11), sector 14 ($0E). The next 150 bytes (2 – 151) constitute our first record. Note that the unused bytes within a record are written as nulls ($00) by the DOS so the record is always a fixed length. The content of individual records will vary enormously. This is program dependent so the data block in question contains whatever data was specified by the program used. This particular record is from a free form data base. It was reserved to for management information by the main program and contains the following data:

1. The name of our relative file ("MAG FILE").
2. The number of active records (709).
3. The number of fields in use (6).
4. The field titles (TITLE, COMPUTER, MAGAZINE, ISSUE, PAGE, COMMENT).

In the sequential data file portion of a relative file, the record length (record size) is constant. In this case, the records are all 150 bytes long. Record number 2 begins at byte 152 ($98) and will extend on into the next data block. Two reads would be required to fetch the entire contents of this record. The first 104 bytes of the record will be found here, but the remaining 46 are in the next block of the file. Here they are.

TRACK 17 – SECTOR 14

```
.  00:  11  04  00  00  00  00  00  00   ........
.  08:  00  00  00  00  00  00  00  00   ........
.  10:  00  00  00  00  00  00  00  00   ........
.  18:  00  00  00  00  00  00  00  00   ........
.  20:  00  00  00  00  00  00  00  00   ........
.  28:  00  00  00  00  00  00  00  00   ........
.  30:  D3  4F  55  4E  44  20  D3  59   .OUND .Y
.  38:  4E  54  48  45  53  49  53  0D   NTHESIS.
.  40:  41  4C  4C  0D  C3  4F  4D  50   ALL..OMP
.  48:  55  54  45  0D  CA  41  4E  20   UTE..AN
.  50:  38  33  0D  32  36  0D  2E  0D   83.26...
.  58:  0D  2E  0D  2E  0D  2E  0D  2E   ........
.  60:  0D  2E  0D  2E  0D  2E  0D  2E   ........
.  68:  0D  2E  0D  2E  0D  2E  0D  2E   ........
.  70:  0D  00  00  00  00  00  00  00   ........
.  78:  00  00  00  00  00  00  00  00   ........
.  80:  00  00  00  00  00  00  00  00   ........
.  88:  00  00  00  00  00  00  00  00   ........
.  90:  00  00  00  00  00  00  00  00   ........
.  98:  00  00  00  00  00  00  00  00   ........
.  A0:  00  00  00  00  00  00  00  00   ........
```

```
. A8:  00 00 00 00 00 00 00 00  . . . . . . . .
. B0:  00 00 00 00 00 00 00 00  . . . . . . . .
. B8:  00 00 00 00 00 00 00 00  . . . . . . . .
. C0:  00 00 00 00 00 00 D7 52  . . . . . . . R
. C8:  49 54 49 4E 47 20 D4 52  ITING .R
. D0:  41 4E 53 50 4F 52 54 41  ANSPORTA
. D8:  42 4C 45 20 C2 41 53 49  BLE .ASI
. E0:  43 0D 41 4C 4C 0D C3 4F  C.ALL..O
. E8:  4D 50 55 54 45 0D CA 41  MPUTE..A
. F0:  4E 20 38 33 0D 33 36 0D  N 83.36.
. F8:  2E 0D 0D 2E 0D 2E 0D 2E  . . . . . . . .
```

Record number 2 is used again for management information by our data base. It simply contains the record length. One can see from the number of carriage returns ($0D) that while only 6 fields are in use, 21 were established by the main program. One can also see that a blank field from this data base is stored as a period ($2E = CHR$(46) = "."). Record number 3 begins at byte 48. It contains our first actual data. It would look like so:

Title: Sound Synthesis
Computer: All
Magazine: Compute (sic)
Issue: Jan 83
Page: 26
Comment: (none)

Just out of curiosity let's examine the last two sectors of our sequential file chain as reported in bytes 156-159 of side sector 3. Why two sectors? Our fixed length of 150 bytes dictates this. (A fixed record length of 1, 2, 127, or 254 would not span a given sector. The maximum length of a relative record is 254 bytes. 254 is the only number evenly divisible by these factors. A record length of 1 or 2 would be rather impractical.)

TRACK 23 - SECTOR 02

```
. 00:  17 0C 00 00 00 00 00 00  . . . . . . . .
. 08:  00 00 00 00 00 00 00 00  . . . . . . . .
. 10:  00 00 00 00 00 00 00 00  . . . . . . . .
. 18:  00 00 00 00 00 00 00 00  . . . . . . . .
. 20:  00 00 00 00 00 00 00 00  . . . . . . . .
. 28:  00 00 00 00 00 00 00 00  . . . . . . . .
. 30:  00 00 00 00 00 00 00 00  . . . . . . . .
. 38:  00 00 00 00 00 00 00 00  . . . . . . . .
. 40:  00 00 00 00 00 00 00 00  . . . . . . . .
. 48:  00 00 00 00 00 00 00 00  . . . . . . . .
. 50:  00 00 00 00 00 00 00 00  . . . . . . . .
. 58:  00 00 00 00 00 00 00 00  . . . . . . . .
. 60:  00 00 00 00 00 00 00 00  . . . . . . . .
. 68:  00 00 00 00 00 00 00 00  . . . . . . . .
. 70:  00 00 00 00 00 00 00 00  . . . . . . . .
. 78:  00 00 00 00 00 00 00 00  . . . . . . . .
```

```
. 80:  00 00 00 00 FF 00 00 00   ........
. 88:  00 00 00 00 00 00 00 00   ........
. 90:  00 00 00 00 00 00 00 00   ........
. 98:  00 00 00 00 00 00 00 00   ........
. A0:  00 00 00 00 00 00 00 00   ........
. A8:  00 00 00 00 00 00 00 00   ........
. B0:  00 00 00 00 00 00 00 00   ........
. B8:  00 00 00 00 00 00 00 00   ........
. C0:  00 00 00 00 00 00 00 00   ........
. C8:  00 00 00 00 00 00 00 00   ........
. D0:  00 00 00 00 00 00 00 00   ........
. D8:  00 00 00 00 00 00 00 00   ........
. E0:  00 00 00 00 00 00 00 00   ........
. E8:  00 00 00 00 00 00 00 00   ........
. F0:  00 00 00 00 00 00 00 00   ........
. F8:  00 00 00 00 00 00 00 00   ........
```

TRACK 23 - SECTOR 12

```
. 00:  00 B1 00 00 00 00 00 00   ........
. 08:  00 00 00 00 00 00 00 00   ........
. 10:  00 00 00 00 00 00 00 00   ........
. 18:  00 00 00 00 FF 00 00 00   ........
. 20:  00 00 00 00 00 00 00 00   ........
. 28:  00 00 00 00 00 00 00 00   ........
. 30:  00 00 00 00 00 00 00 00   ........
. 38:  00 00 00 00 00 00 00 00   ........
. 40:  00 00 00 00 00 00 00 00   ........
. 48:  00 00 00 00 00 00 00 00   ........
. 50:  00 00 00 00 00 00 00 00   ........
. 58:  00 00 00 00 00 00 00 00   ........
. 60:  00 00 00 00 00 00 00 00   ........
. 68:  00 00 00 00 00 00 00 00   ........
. 70:  00 00 00 00 00 00 00 00   ........
. 78:  00 00 00 00 00 00 00 00   ........
. 80:  00 00 00 00 00 00 00 00   ........
. 88:  00 00 00 00 00 00 00 00   ........
. 90:  00 00 00 00 00 00 00 00   ........
. 98:  00 00 00 00 00 00 00 00   ........
. A0:  00 00 00 00 00 00 00 00   ........
. A8:  00 00 00 00 00 00 00 00   ........
. B0:  00 00 FF 00 00 00 00 00   ........
. B8:  00 00 00 00 00 00 00 00   ........
. C0:  00 00 00 00 00 00 00 00   ........
. C8:  00 00 00 00 00 00 00 00   ........
. D0:  00 00 00 00 00 00 00 00   ........
. D8:  00 00 00 00 00 00 00 00   ........
. E0:  00 00 00 00 00 00 00 00   ........
. E8:  00 00 00 00 00 00 00 00   ........
. F0:  00 00 00 00 00 00 00 00   ........
. F8:  00 00 00 00 00 00 00 00   ........
```

An analysis of the preceding two sectors will all but end our discussion on relative file structure. Bytes 2-131 of track 23, sector 2 are the overflow of a previous record. Bytes 132-255 of this same track and bytes 2-27 of track 23, sector 12 make up the next record. This record is empty, as indicated by a 255 ($FF) in the first byte and nulls in the remaining bytes. Track 23, sector 12 has no forward chain and a byte count of 177 ($B1). Our last record in the relative file ends at byte 177 (28-177). What is interesting is the padding beyond this point:

```
. BO: xx xx FF 00 00 00 00 00 ........
. B8: 00 00 00 00 00 00 00 00 ........
. CO: 00 00 00 00 00 00 00 00 ........
. C8: 00 00 00 00 00 00 00 00 ........
. DO: 00 00 00 00 00 00 00 00 ........
. D8: 00 00 00 00 00 00 00 00 ........
. EO: 00 00 00 00 00 00 00 00 ........
. E8: 00 00 00 00 00 00 00 00 ........
. FO: 00 00 00 00 00 00 00 00 ........
. F8: 00 00 00 00 00 00 00 00 ........
```

We would expect to find all nulls ($00). Byte 178 ($B2), however, shows an $FF, i.e., the start of a new record. The DOS is one step ahead of the game when expansion time rolls around. A partial record has already been created in this instance. The DOS need only calculate the difference between 255 and the byte count to determine the number of nulls that must follow to complete the record:

255 – 177 = 78 bytes already in existence

It then takes the record size to figure out the padding needed:

Total Record Length – Bytes in Existence = Nulls to Go

150 – 78 = 72

Slick!

We will close our section on relative file structure by taking a brief look at how the computer, or you, can locate a particular relative record. Pick a number, any number. Record number 4 you say. No problem if you know the record length.

First we find the appropriate side sector.

4 – 1 = 3 previous records

3 * 150 fixed length = 450th starting byte (i.e., 0 – 449 previous bytes)

450 / 254 = 1.7716535

INT (1.7716535) + 1 = pointer set 2

Pointer set 2 / 120 sets of pointers in a side sector = 0.01666667

INT (0.01666667) = side sector 0

Where in side sector 0 is it? Easy.

Byte 14 + (pointer set 2 * 2 bytes in a pointer) = byte 18

Bytes 18 and 19 will contain the track and sector of our record.

Where in the actual data block is it? A piece of cake.

1.7716535 − INT(1.7716535) = remainder .7716535

2 (skip over bytes 0 and 1) + (.7716535 * 254 bytes of data) = byte 198

Still a disbeliever? Check it out yourself in the preceding hex dumps of track 17, sector 13 and track 17, sector 14.

4.8 User File Storage

A user file (USR) file is one that is designed by the user. This file type is designated by an $83 in the directory. Although a user file is a legal Commodore file type (USR), its use is quite rare. Using a USR file rather than a more common file type is for showmanship only.

A user file may have the structure of either a sequential file or a program file if it was created by the DOS. It may be structured entirely differently if it was created using direct-access techniques described in Chapter 5. Before you do something rash, remember that the DOS will expect to find the track and sector links in their normal places. If they are not there, all the blocks that make up your file will be earmarked as free in the BAM whenever the disk is validated!

4.9 Deleted File Storage

A deleted file (DEL) has a file-type byte of $80 in the directory. This is not a scratched file ($00), but an undocumented Commodore file type (DEL). It is extremely rare. Only one vendor has dared use a DEL file on a commercial product to date. It was not a functional file and was placed on the diskette to intimidate users as part of a low level protection scheme.

You cannot create a DEL file using an OPEN statement. You can only create a DEL file by changing the file-type byte of an existing file to $80 as described in the next section. Since a DEL file is really another file type in disguise, a DEL file may have the structure of either a sequential file or a program file. If it has the structure of a program file, it may be loaded using one of these commands:

```
LOAD "FILE NAME,DEL,R",8          (RELOCATED)

LOAD "FILE NAME,DEL,R",8,1        (NOT RELOCATED)
```

If a DEL file is structured like a sequential file, it may be opened in read mode using the following command:

```
OPEN 2,8,2,"FILE NAME,DEL,R"
```

4.10 Locked Files

Earlier in this chapter you may have been surprised to see locked files of various form in the table of legal file types. Locked file types are once again an undocumented feature of Commodore disk drives. A locked file cannot be scratched unless it is first unlocked. Unfortunately, the DOS does not support the locking or unlocking of a file. You have to do-it-yourself by editing the file-type byte in the directory entry for that file. The program EDIT TRACK & SECTOR listed in Appendix C allows you to do this. We will not describe the technique here. See the section on Unscratching a File in Chapter 8 for instructions on how to edit the file-type byte. Use the values from the table below, rather than those listed in Chapter 8, when locking or unlocking a file.

File Type	Normal		Locked	
Deleted	DEL	$80	DEL <	$C0
Sequential	SEQ	$81	SEQ <	$C1
Program	PRG	$82	PRG <	$C2
User	USR	$83	USR <	$C3
Relative	REL	$84	REL <	$C4

The DOS determines whether or not a file is locked by checking bit 6 of the file-type byte. If it is set (1), the file is locked. Even if a file has been locked, it may be renamed or copied using normal disk commands.

Conclusion

The material covered in this chapter is primarily of academic interest. However, do not attempt to recover a blown file unless you thoroughly understand the structure of the directory and how files are stored.

CHAPTER 5

DIRECT-ACCESS PROGRAMMING

5.1 Introduction to Direct-Access Programming

In Chapter 2 you learned how to use such DOS commands as NEW, SCRATCH, and VALIDATE, for diskette housekeeping. This chapter describes how to use another set of DOS commands known as direct-access commands. These commands are not commonly used in typical programming applications. However, they allow you to step beyond simple housekeeping chores to develop more powerful disk utility programs that do such things as:

Change a disk name or cosmetic ID.
Display a block availability map (the BAM).
Display a directory.
Display a track and sector.
Chain through a directory entry.
Edit a track and sector.
Recover an inadvertently scratched file.
Recover a damaged diskette.
Duplicate a diskette.
Copy a file.
Catalog a disk library.

As you grow with your 1541, the need for routines of this nature will become increasingly apparent, if it isn't already. This chapter illustrates the use of direct-access commands in simple programs. A basic understanding of the function of these commands is necessary to appreciate the routines found in subsequent chapters and Appendix C.

5.2 Beginning Direct-Access Programming

The 1541 DOS recognizes nine direct-access commands. These direct-access commands and their functions are listed below.

Direct-Access Command	Function
Block-Read (U1)	Read a data block into 1541 RAM.
Buffer-Pointer (B-P)	Set pointer to any byte in a disk buffer.
Block-Write (U2)	Write a data block from 1541 RAM to diskette.

Memory-Read (M-R)	Peek bytes out of 1541 RAM or ROM.
Memory-Write (M-W)	Poke bytes into 1541 RAM.
Block-Allocate (B-A)	Set bit in BAM to indicate a sector is in use.
Block-Free (B-F)	Set bit in BAM to indicate a sector is not in use.
Memory-Execute (M-E)	Execute a 6502 routine stored in 1541 RAM or ROM.
Block-Execute (B-E)	Load and execute a 6502 routine in 1541 RAM.

More often than not, direct-access commands complement one another in actual use. For example, a sector can be read from disk using a U1 command, examined using a B-P or M-R command, altered using a B-P or M-R command, and rewritten to disk using a U2 command.

The block-read (U1), buffer-pointer, and block-write (U2) comands are the easiest to comprehend and, as a result, the most widely used. The memory-read and memory-write commands represent a more sophisticated level of direct-access programming and are sometimes used in lieu of the buffer-pointer command. The block-allocate and block-free commands are used primarily for the maintenance of random access files. Random access files were the forerunner of relative files and are rarely used today. The memory-execute command is used at the guru level of disk programming and requires a rudimentary knowledge of both machine language and the innards of the 1541 to implement. The block-execute command, while documented by Commodore, is almost never used.

In order to use the commands mentioned above you will need to learn how to open a direct-access data channel. The format of a direct-access OPEN statement is:

```
SYNTAX:   OPEN file#, device#, channel#, "#"

EXAMPLE:  OPEN 2,8,2,"#"
          OPEN 1,8,14,"#"
```

where

file#   = the logical file number (1 to 127)

device#   = 8

channel#   = the secondary address of the associated open statement (2 to 14)

Opening a direct-access data channel establishes a communication link between the C64 and the 1541. In the first example, we opened logical file number 2 on the C64 side to device number 8 with a secondary address of 2 (channel number 2) on the 1541 side. The only time a channel number is ever referenced is as part of a direct-access command, e.g., a block-read command (U1). Data is always read from disk (GET# file#, INPUT# file#,) or written to disk (PRINT# file#,) by way of the logical file number of the direct-access OPEN statement NOT the channel number. The logical file number and the channel number do not have to match as they do in our first OPEN example. They are two separate entities. The logical file number which resides on the C64 side passes read or write commands to the channel number on the 1541 side. Any similarity between the logical file number and the channel number is for mnemonic purposes only. The second example is a perfectly legal direct-access OPEN statement. In this instance, we opened logical file number 1 (GET#1, PRINT#1,) to device number 8 with a secondary address of 14 (channel number 14) on the 1541 side. Whether or not you use mnemonic OPEN statements is strictly a matter of personal preference.

We will begin our tutorial on direct-access programming with a quick review of the 1541 format explained in Chapter 3. The table below outlines the range of track and sector numbers found on a diskette.

Zone	Track	Sector Range	Number of Sectors
1	1 - 17	0 - 20	21
2	18 - 24	0 - 18	19
3	25 - 30	0 - 17	18
4	31 - 35	0 - 16	17

NOTE: If you attempt to access a track less than 1, a track greater than 35, or a sector out of range for a given track, you will get a DOS error message number 66, ILLEGAL TRACK OR SECTOR.

5.3 Block-Read Command (U1)

The block-read command (U1) transfers the contents of a given track and sector to an area of disk RAM commonly referred to as a buffer or workspace. The format of a block-read command (U1) is:

SYNTAX:
```
  PRINT# file#, "U1"; channel#; drive#; track;
    sector
```

ALTERNATE:
```
  PRINT# file#, "U1:" channel#; drive#; track;
    sector
  PRINT# file#, "U1: channel#, drive#, track,
    sector"
```

EXAMPLE:
```
  PRINT#15,"U1";2;0;18;0
```

where

file#   = the logical file number of the command channel

channel#   = the secondary address of the associated open statement

drive#   = 0

track   = 1 to 35

sector   = 0 to the range for a given track

After a given track and sector has been transferred to a buffer with a block-read command (U1), the buffer pointer is automatically left in position 255. Bytes 0-255 of the buffer are now accessible from the starting position, i.e., byte 0. The GET# command is normally used to retrieve one byte at a time from the buffer by way of the logical file number of the direct-access OPEN statement. The GET# command is used rather than INPUT# because the data may contain null bytes, carriage returns and/or line feeds, commas, colons, or other control characters. When using the GET# command you must remember to test each incoming byte for equality with the null string "". A null byte must be converted to CHR$(0) or an ?ILLEGAL QUANTITY ERROR will result when you try to find the ASCII value of the byte. (The GET# command fails to make the necessary conversion for you.) The ASCII value of a byte is used to check for control characters. These characters are misinterpreted by the INPUT# command. The following example reads the block from track 18, sector 0 (the BAM) into disk RAM and prints the contents to the screen.

```
100 REM BLOCK-READ (U1)
110 OPEN 15,8,15
120 PRINT#15,"IO"
130 INPUT#15,EN$,EM$,ET$,ES$
140 IF EN$<>"00"GOTO 290
150 OPEN 2,8,2,"#"
160 PRINT#15,"U1";2;0;18;0
170 INPUT#15,EN$,EM$,ET$,ES$
180 IF EN$<>"00"GOTO 270
190 FOR I=0 TO 255
200 GET#2,B$
210 IF B$=""THEN B$=CHR$(0)
220 A=ASC(B$)
230 PRINT ST,I,A,
240 IF A>31 AND A<96 THEN PRINT B$,
250 PRINT
260 NEXT I
270 CLOSE 2
280 INPUT#15,EN$,EM$,ET$,ES$
290 CLOSE 15
300 END
```

Line Range	Description
110	Opens logical file number 15 (PRINT#15,) to device 8 with a secondary address of 15 (command channel).
120	Initializes drive 0.
130-140	Query the error channel.
150	Opens logical file number 2 (GET#2,) to device 8 with a secondary address of 2 (channel number 2) letting the 1541 assign a buffer area.
160	Reads the block from drive 0, track 18, sector 0 into channel 2 buffer area.
170-180	Query the error channel.
190	Begin loop to read 256 bytes.

200	Transfer a byte from channel 2 buffer area to C 64 memory by way of the GET# command (GET# logical file number not the channel number).
210	Test for equality with the null string "".
220	ASCII conversion of a byte.
230	Print the status variable (ST), our loop counter, and the ASCII value of the byte.
240	Print the byte if it's within normal ASCII range.
250	Terminate comma tabulation.
260	Increment loop counter.
270	Close logical file number 2.
280	Suppress the error light.
290	Close logical file number 15.
300	End.

An explanation of programming technique is in order here. Initialization (line 120) is done prior to opening a direct-access data channel (line 150). Initialization automatically shuts down all direct-access data channels (2 -14) that are open on the 1541 side. The command channel (15) is not affected. Logical files still remain open on the C64 side, however. Any attempt to access a data channel after initialization results in a 70, NO CHANNEL error. The DOS attempts to rewrite the BAM each time a direct-access channel is closed (line 270). If a diskette is either write protected or DOS protected, the BAM is not rewritten and the error light remains on until cleared. Fortunately, no damage has been done to the data on the diskette. The error light is quite distracting nevertheless. You can suppress the error light after closing a direct-access data channel simply by inputting the error number, message, track, and sector via the command channel (line 280).

The alternate formats of the block-read command (U1) in line 160 are:

`PRINT#15,"U1:"2;0;18;0`

`PRINT#15,"U1:2,0,18,0"`

Although the block-read command (U1) comes in three basic flavors, line 160 uses the preferred format. It will be used in demonstration programs throughout the chapter for consistency. Alternate formats will appear in passing.

Additionally, lines 210-220 are often combined into one BASIC statement for the sake of efficiency:

`A=ASC(B$+CHR$(0))`

Recall that lines 210-220 are necessary because the GET# command does not interpret nulls correctly.

5.4 Buffer-Pointer Command (B-P)

The buffer-pointer command allows access to any individual byte in a DOS buffer. Any byte from position 0 through 255 in the buffer may be read or overwritten. The format of a buffer-pointer command is:

SYNTAX:
  PRINT# file#, "B-P"; channel#; byte position

ALTERNATE:
  PRINT# file#, "B-P:" channel#; byte position
  PRINT# file#, "B-P: channel#, byte position"

EXAMPLE:
  PRINT#15,"B-P";2;144

where

file#   = the logical file number of the command channel

channel#   = the secondary address of the associated open statement

byte position = 0 to 255

The following program displays a disk name by reading only bytes 144 to 159 from track 18, sector 0.

```
100 REM BUFFER-POINTER
110 OPEN 15,8,15
120 PRINT#15,"IO"
130 INPUT#15,EN$,EM$,ET$,ES$
140 IF EN$<>"OO"GOTO 320
150 OPEN 2,8,2,"#"
160 PRINT#15,"U1";2;0;18;0
170 INPUT#15,EN$,EM$,ET$,ES$
180 IF EN$<>"OO"GOTO 300
190 PRINT#15,"B-P";2;144
200 FOR I=1 TO 16
210 GET#2,B$
220 IF B$=""THEN B$=CHR$(0)
230 A=ASC(B$)
240 IF A>127 THEN A=A-128
250 IF A<32 OR A>95 THEN A=63
260 IF A=34 THEN A=63
270 DN$=DN$+CHR$(A)
280 NEXT I
290 PRINT"{DOWN}DISK NAME: ";DN$
300 CLOSE 2
310 INPUT#15,EN$,EM$,ET$,ES$
320 CLOSE 15
330 END
```

Line Range	Description
190	Sets channel 2 pointer to position 144 in the buffer area.
200-280	Concatenate (build) the disk name one byte at a time by jamming it within printable ASCII range.

The alternate formats of the buffer-pointer command in line 190 are:

```
PRINT#15,"B-P:"2;144
```

```
PRINT#15,"B-P:2,144"
```

5.5 Block-Write Command (U2)

The block-write command (U2) writes the data from a DOS buffer to any given track and sector on a diskette. The format of a block-write command (U2) parallels that of a block-read command (U1). The format of a block-write command (U2) is:

```
SYNTAX:
  PRINT# file#, "U2"; channel#; drive#; track;
    sector
```

```
ALTERNATE:
  PRINT# file#, "U2:" channel#; drive#; track;
    sector
  PRINT# file#, "U2: channel#, drive#, track,
    sector"
```

```
EXAMPLE:
  PRINT#15,"U2";2;0;18;0
```

where

file#	= the logical file number of the command channel
channel#	= the secondary address of the associated open statement
drive#	= 0
track	= 1 to 35
sector	= 0 to the range for a given track

The entire contents of a buffer are written to disk during the execution of a block-write command (U2). The position of the buffer-pointer is irrelevant. It is not referred to by the DOS during the execution of a block-write command (U2).

The first program listed below allows a disk name to be changed using a block-write command (U2). The second example allows you to edit the cosmetic disk ID that appears in the BAM. *NOTE: This program does not change the formatting ID that is embedded in the header block of every sector.*

77

```
100 REM EDIT DISK NAME
110 FORI=1TO16
120 PAD$=PAD$+CHR$(160)
130 NEXTI
140 PRINT"{CLR}EDIT DISK NAME - 1541"
150 PRINT"{DOWN}REMOVE {RVS}WRITE PROTEC
T TAB{ROFF}"
160 PRINT"{DOWN}INSERT DISKETTE IN DRIVE
"
170 PRINT"{DOWN}PRESS {RVS}RETURN{ROFF}
TO CONTINUE"
180 GETC$:IFC$=""THEN180
190 IFC$<>CHR$(13)GOTO180
200 PRINT"OK"
210 OPEN15,8,15
220 PRINT#15,"I0"
230 INPUT#15,EN$,EM$,ET$,ES$
240 IFEN$="00"GOTO280
250 PRINT"{DOWN}"EN$", "EM$","ET$","ES$
260 CLOSE15
270 END
280 OPEN2,8,2,"#"
290 PRINT#15,"U1";2;0;18;0
300 INPUT#15,EN$,EM$,ET$,ES$
310 PRINT#15,"B-P";2;2
320 GET#2,B$
330 IFB$=""THENB$=CHR$(0)
340 DOS=ASC(B$)
350 IFDOS=65GOTO390
360 PRINT"{DOWN}73,CBM DOS V2.6 1541,00,
00"
370 PRINT"{DOWN}{RVS}FAILED{ROFF}"
380 GOTO720
390 PRINT#15,"B-P";2;144
400 FORI=1TO16
410 GET#2,B$
420 IFB$=""THENB$=CHR$(0)
430 A=ASC(B$)
440 IFA>127THENA=A-128
450 IFA<320RA>95THENA=63
460 IFA=34THENA=63
470 ODN$=ODN$+CHR$(A)
480 NEXTI
490 PRINT"{DOWN}OLD DISK NAME: ";ODN$
500 INPUT"{DOWN}NEW DISK NAME";NDN$
510 IFLEN(NDN$)<>0ANDLEN(NDN$)<17GOTO530

520 GOTO720
530 INPUT"{DOWN}ARE YOU SURE (Y/N)   Y{LE
FT 3}";Q$
```

```
540 IFQ$<>"Y"GOTO720
550 NDN$=LEFT$(NDN$+PAD$,16)
560 PRINT#15,"B-P";2;144
570 PRINT#2,NDN$;
580 PRINT#15,"U2";2;0;18;0
590 INPUT#15,EN$,EM$,ET$,ES$
600 IFEN$="00"GOTO640
610 PRINT"{DOWN}"EN$,  "EM$","ET$","ES$
620 PRINT"{DOWN}{RVS}FAILED{ROFF}"
630 GOTO720
640 CLOSE2
650 INPUT#15,EN$,EM$,ET$,ES$
660 PRINT#15,"IO"
670 INPUT#15,EN$,EM$,ET$,ES$
680 CLOSE15
690 PRINT"{DOWN}DONE!"
700 END
710 REM CLOSE
720 CLOSE2
730 INPUT#15,EN$,EM$,ET$,ES$
740 CLOSE15
750 END
```

Line Range	Description
280	Opens logical file number 2 (GET#2, PRINT#2,) to device 8 with a secondary address of 2 (channel number 2) letting the 1541 assign a buffer area.
310-380	Query DOS version.
550	Pad new diskette name.
560	Reset channel 2 pointer to position 144.
570	Overwrite existing disk name in channel 2 buffer area.
580	Write channel 2 buffer to drive 0, track 18, sector 0.
660	Update the BAM ($0700—$07FF) to reflect a disk name change.

The alternate formats of the block-write command (U2) in line 580 are:

```
PRINT#15,"U2:"2;0;18;0

PRINT#15,"U2:2,0,18,0"
```

```
100 REM EDIT DISK ID
110 PRINT"{CLR}EDIT DISK ID - 1541"
120 PRINT"{DOWN}REMOVE {RVS}WRITE PROTEC
T TAB{ROFF}"
```

```
130 PRINT"{DOWN}INSERT DISKETTE IN DRIVE
"
140 PRINT"{DOWN}PRESS {RVS}RETURN{ROFF}
TO CONTINUE"
150 GETC$:IFC$=""THEN150
160 IFC$<>CHR$(13)GOTO150
170 PRINT"OK"
180 OPEN15,8,15
190 PRINT#15,"IO"
200 INPUT#15,EN$,EM$,ET$,ES$
210 IFEN$="00"GOTO250
220 PRINT"{DOWN}"EN$", "EM$","ET$","ES$
230 CLOSE15
240 END
250 OPEN2,8,2,"#"
260 PRINT#15,"U1";2;0;18;0
270 INPUT#15,EN$,EM$,ET$,ES$
280 PRINT#15,"B-P";2;2
290 GET#2,B$
300 IFB$=""THENB$=CHR$(0)
310 DOS=ASC(B$)
320 IFDOS=65GOTO360
330 PRINT"{DOWN}73,CBM DOS V2.6 1541,00,
00"
340 PRINT"{DOWN}{RVS}FAILED{ROFF}"
350 GOTO690
360 PRINT#15,"B-P";2;162
370 FORI=1TO2
380 GET#2,B$
390 IFB$=""THENB$=CHR$(0)
400 A=ASC(B$)
410 IFA>127THENA=A-128
420 IFA<32ORA>95THENA=63
430 IFA=34THENA=63
440 ODI$=ODI$+CHR$(A)
450 NEXTI
460 PRINT"{DOWN}OLD DISK ID: ";ODI$
470 INPUT"{DOWN}NEW DISK ID";NDI$
480 IFLEN(NDI$)<>0ANDLEN(NDI$)<3GOTO500
490 GOTO690
500 INPUT"{DOWN}ARE YOU SURE (Y/N)   Y{LE
FT 3}";Q$
510 IFQ$<>"Y"GOTO690
520 NDI$=LEFT$(NDI$+CHR$(0),2)
530 PRINT#15,"B-P";2;162
540 PRINT#2,NDI$;
550 PRINT#15,"U2";2;0;18;0
560 INPUT#15,EN$,EM$,ET$,ES$
570 IFEN$="00"GOTO610
580 PRINT"{DOWN}"EN$", "EM$","ET$","ES$
```

```
590 PRINT"{DOWN}{RVS}FAILED{ROFF}"
600 GOTO690
610 CLOSE2
620 INPUT#15,EN$,EM$,ET$,ES$
630 PRINT#15,"I0"
640 INPUT#15,EN$,EM$,ET$,ES$
650 CLOSE15
660 PRINT"{DOWN}DONE!"
670 END
680 REM CLOSE
690 CLOSE2
700 INPUT#15,EN$,EM$,ET$,ES$
710 CLOSE15
720 END
```

The alternate formats of the block-write command (U2) in line 550 are:

```
PRINT#15,"U2:"2;0;18;0

PRINT#15,"U2:2,0,18,0"
```

That's enough about the block-write command (U2) for now.

5.6 Memory-Read Command (M-R)

The memory-read command allows you to read the contents of any area of the 1541's RAM or ROM. You must specify in the memory-read command the memory address of RAM or ROM that you want to read. The format of a memory-read command is:

```
SYNTAX:
  PRINT# file#, "M-R" CHR$(lo-byte) CHR$(hi-
    byte) CHR$(# of bytes)

ALTERNATE:
  PRINT# file#, "M-R:" CHR$(lo-byte) CHR$(hi-
    byte) CHR$(# of bytes)

EXAMPLE:
  PRINT#15,"M-R"CHR$(0)CHR$(3)
```

where

file#   = the logical file number of the command channel

lo-byte   = lo-byte of the memory address

hi-byte   = hi-byte of the memory address

# of bytes   = 1 to 255

The third parameter of the memory-read command, CHR$(# of bytes), is undocumented by Commodore. The use of the third parameter is always optional. The default is CHR$(1), i.e., 1 byte.

Typically a block-read command (U1) is issued prior to a memory-read command. A block-read command (U1) transfers the data that is recorded on a given track and sector to one of four pages (256 bytes) of RAM. A page of RAM is called a buffer. When you open a direct-access data channel to the 1541 with OPEN 2,8,2,"#", the DOS arbitrarily selects one buffer as a workspace for that channel. As long as you use the GET# file# command or the PRINT# file# command from the associated OPEN statement you do not need to know which buffer the DOS is using. The buffer in use is only important when you issue a memory-read command. You may tell the DOS which buffer area to use in the direct-access OPEN statement itself. The format for selecting a buffer is:

SYNTAX:
  OPEN file#, device#, channel#, "# buffer#"

EXAMPLE:
  OPEN 2,8,2,"#0"

where

buffer#   = 0 to 3

The table below shows how the buffer areas are organized in the 1541.

Buffer Number	Address	Example
	$0000 - $00FF	Not available (ZERO PAGE)
	$0100 - $01FF	Not available (STACK)
	$0200 - $02FF	Not available (COMMAND BUFFER)
0	$0300 - $03FF	OPEN 2,8,2,"#0"
1	$0400 - $04FF	OPEN 2,8,2,"#1"
2	$0500 - $05FF	OPEN 2,8,2,"#2"
3	$0600 - $06FF	OPEN 2,8,2,"#3"
	$0700 - $07FF	Not available (BAM)

NOTE: Two or more direct-access data channels cannot share the same buffer area. If you attempt to open a direct-access data channel to a buffer already in use a 70, a NO CHANNEL error will result.

The GET# command is used following a memory-read command to retrieve the contents of the buffer you selected. There is one major difference, however. Bytes are now fetched over the command channel not the logical file number of the "OPEN file#, device#, channel#, buffer#" statement. Bytes must still be tested for equality with the null string "" and converted to CHR$(0) if need be.

The next program selects buffer #0 ($0300 - $03FF) as a workspace and does a block-read of track 18, sector 0. Bytes are returned to the C64 side from buffer #0 with memory-read and GET# commands, and printed to the screen.

```
100 REM TWO PARAMETER MEMORY-READ
110 OPEN 15,8,15
120 PRINT#15,"IO"
130 INPUT#15,EN$,EM$,ET$,ES$
140 IF EN$<>"OO"GOTO 300
150 OPEN 2,8,2,"#0"
160 PRINT#15,"U1";2;0;18;0
170 INPUT#15,EN$,EM$,ET$,ES$
180 IF EN$<>"OO"GOTO 280
190 FOR I=0 TO 255
200 PRINT#15,"M-R"CHR$(I)CHR$(3)
210 GET#15,B$
220 IF B$=""THEN B$=CHR$(0)
230 A=ASC(B$)
240 PRINT I,A,
250 IF A>31 AND A<96 THEN PRINT B$,
260 PRINT
270 NEXT I
280 CLOSE 2
290 INPUT#15,EN$,EM$,ET$,ES$
300 CLOSE 15
310 END
```

Line Range	Description
150	Opens logical file number 2 to device 8 with a secondary address of 2 assigning buffer number 0 ($0300 - $03FF) as a workspace.
160	Reads the block from drive 0, track 18, sector 0 into channel 2 buffer area ($0300 - $03FF).
190	Begin loop to read 256 bytes ($0300 - $03FF).
200	Indexed memory-read command ($0300 - $03FF).
210	Transfer a byte from channel 2 buffer area to C64 memory via the command channel (GET#15,).

The alternate format of the standard memory-read command in line 200 is:

```
PRINT#15,"M-R:"CHR$(I)CHR$(3)
```

Please note that we deliberately omitted the third parameter of the memory-read command in the preceding example. The following example incorporates all three parameters of the memory-read command to read a disk name.

```
100 REM THREE PARAMETER MEMORY-READ
110 OPEN 15,8,15
120 PRINT#15,"I0"
130 INPUT#15,EN$,EM$,ET$,ES$
140 IF EN$<>"00"GOTO 320
150 OPEN 2,8,2,"#1"
160 PRINT#15,"U1";2;0;18;0
170 INPUT#15,EN$,EM$,ET$,ES$
180 IF EN$<>"00"GOTO 300
190 PRINT#15,"M-R"CHR$(144)CHR$(4)CHR$(1
6)
200 FOR I=1 TO 16
210 GET#15,B$
220 IF B$=""THEN B$=CHR$(0)
230 A=ASC(B$)
240 IF A>127 THEN A=A-128
250 IF A<32 OR A>95 THEN A=63
260 IF A=34 THEN A=63
270 DN$=DN$+CHR$(A)
280 NEXT I
290 PRINT"{DOWN}DISK NAME: ";DN$
300 CLOSE 2
310 INPUT#15,EN$,EM$,ET$,ES$
320 CLOSE 15
330 END
```

Line Range	Description
150	Opens logical file number 2 to device 8 with a secondary address of 2 assigning buffer number 1 ($0400 - $04FF) as a workspace.
160	Reads the block from drive 0, track 18, sector 0 into channel 2 buffer area ($0400 - $04FF).
190	Memory-read command ($0490 - $049F).
200	Begin loop to read 16 characters.
210	Transfer a byte from channel 2 buffer area to C64 memory over the command channel (GET#15,).

Inclusion of the third memory-read parameter means that we no longer have to issue a memory-read command to fetch each byte like we did in the first sample program. Instead, we establish a loop after the memory-read command to pull a byte in. (See lines

200-280 above.) The alternate format of the three parameter memory-read command in line 190 is:

```
PRINT#15,"M-R:"CHR$(144)CHR$(4)CHR$(16)
```

5.7 Memory-Write Command (M-W)

The memory-write command is the opposite of the memory-read command. Data is written to a DOS buffer via the command channel. The format of a memory-write command is:

```
SYNTAX:
  PRINT# file#, "M-W" CHR$(lo-byte) CHR$(hi-
    byte) CHR$(# of bytes) data

ALTERNATE:
  PRINT# file#, "M-W:" CHR$(lo-byte) CHR$(hi-
    byte) CHR$(# of bytes) data

EXAMPLE:
  PRINT#15,"M-W"CHR$(2)CHR$(5)CHR$(2)CHR$(1)
    CHR$(8)
  PRINT#15,"M-W"CHR$(2)CHR$(5)CHR$(2)CHR$(1)D$
```

where

file#   = the logical file number of the command channel

lo-byte   = lo-byte of the memory address

hi-byte   = hi-byte of the memory address

# of bytes = 1 to 34

data   = a string variable or a CHR$ iteration

A total of 34 data bytes may be written with each issuance of a memory-write command. Typically only 8, 16, or 32 data bytes are sent out at one time in a loop as our buffer size (256 bytes) is evenly divisible by these factors. At the most sophisticated level of disk programming, machine language programs can be poked into RAM inside the 1541 with a memory-write command and then executed. (See Chapter 7 for actual programs of this nature.) In practice, however, one encounters limited use of the memory-write command.

The following example demonstrates the use of the memory-write command. It allows you to change the load address of a program file. A routine of this nature would be used to aid in the disassembly of a program that normally loads into high memory (e.g., $8000-$BFFF) and is already occupied by a machine language monitor program (SUPERMON64) or ROM.

```
100 REM EDIT LOAD ADDRESS
110 H$="0123456789ABCDEF"
120 PRINT"{CLR}EDIT LOAD ADDRESS - 1541"

130 PRINT"{DOWN}REMOVE {RVS}WRITE PROTEC
T TAB{ROFF}"
140 PRINT"{DOWN}INSERT DISKETTE IN DRIVE
"
150 PRINT"{DOWN}PRESS {RVS}RETURN{ROFF}
TO CONTINUE"
160 GETC$:IFC$=""THEN160
170 IFC$<>CHR$(13)GOTO160
180 PRINT"OK"
190 OPEN15,8,15
200 PRINT#15,"IO"
210 INPUT#15,EN$,EM$,ET$,ES$
220 IFEN$="00"GOTO260
230 PRINT"{DOWN}"EN$","EM$","ET$","ES$
240 CLOSE15
250 END
260 PRINT#15,"M-R"CHR$(1)CHR$(1)
270 GET#15,DOS$
280 IFDOS$=""THENDOS$=CHR$(0)
290 DOS=ASC(DOS$)
300 IFDOS=65GOTO330
310 PRINT"{DOWN}73,CBM DOS V2.6 1541,00,
00"
320 GOTO910
330 INPUT"{DOWN}FILENAME";F$
340 IFLEN(F$)<>0ANDLEN(F$)<17GOTO360
350 GOTO920
360 OPEN2,8,2,"0:"+F$+",P,R"
370 INPUT#15,EN$,EM$,ET$,ES$
380 IFEN$="00"GOTO400
390 GOTO940
400 PRINT#15,"M-R"CHR$(24)CHR$(0)CHR$(2)

410 GET#15,T$
420 T=ASC(T$+CHR$(0))
430 GET#15,S$
440 S=ASC(S$+CHR$(0))
450 CLOSE2
460 INPUT#15,EN$,EM$,ET$,ES$
470 IFEN$="00"GOTO490
480 GOTO900
490 OPEN2,8,2,"#2"
500 PRINT#15,"U1";2;0;T;S
510 INPUT#15,EN$,EM$,ET$,ES$
520 IFEN$="00"GOTO540
530 GOTO900
```

```
540 PRINT#15,"M-R"CHR$(2)CHR$(5)CHR$(2)
550 GET#15,LOW$
560 LOW=ASC(LOW$+CHR$(0))
570 GET#15,HIGH$
580 HIGH=ASC(HIGH$+CHR$(0))
590 D=HIGH
600 GOSUB1010
610 OLA$=HD$
620 D=LOW
630 GOSUB1010
640 OLA$=OLA$+HD$
650 PRINT"{DOWN}OLD LOAD ADDRESS: ";OLA$

660 INPUT"{DOWN}NEW LOAD ADDRESS";NLA$
670 IFLEN(NLA$)=4GOTO690
680 GOTO960
690 INPUT"{DOWN}ARE YOU SURE (Y/N)   Y{LE
FT 3}";Q$
700 IFQ$<>"Y"GOTO960
710 HD$=RIGHT$(NLA$,2)
720 GOSUB1060
730 IFTME=1GOTO960
740 LOW=D
750 HD$=LEFT$(NLA$,2)
760 GOSUB1060
770 IFTME=1GOTO960
780 HIGH=D
790 PRINT#15,"M-W"CHR$(2)CHR$(5)CHR$(2)C
HR$(LOW)CHR$(HIGH)
800 PRINT#15,"U2";2;0;T;S
810 INPUT#15,EN$,EM$,ET$,ES$
820 IFEN$="00"GOTO840
830 GOTO940
840 CLOSE2
850 INPUT#15,EN$,EM$,ET$,ES$
860 CLOSE15
870 PRINT"{DOWN}DONE!"
880 END
890 REM CLOSE
900 PRINT"{DOWN}"EN$, "EM$","ET$","ES$
910 PRINT"{DOWN}{RVS}FAILED{ROFF}"
920 CLOSE15
930 END
940 PRINT"{DOWN}"EN$, "EM$","ET$","ES$
950 PRINT"{DOWN}{RVS}FAILED{ROFF}"
960 CLOSE2
970 INPUT#15,EN$,EM$,ET$,ES$
980 CLOSE15
990 END
1000 REM DECIMAL TO HEXADECIMAL
1010 H=INT(D/16)
```

```
1020 L=D-(H*16)
1030 HD$=MID$(H$,H+1,1)+MID$(H$,L+1,1)
1040 RETURN
1050 REM HEXADECIMAL TO DECIMAL
1060 TME=0
1070 H=0
1080 FORI=1TO16
1090 IFLEFT$(HD$,1)=MID$(H$,I,1)THENH=I:
I=16
1100 NEXTI
1110 IFH=0THENTME=1:GOTO1200
1120 H=H-1
1130 L=0
1140 FORI=1TO16
1150 IFRIGHT$(HD$,1)=MID$(H$,I,1)THENL=I
:I=16
1160 NEXTI
1170 IFL=0THENTME=1:GOTO1200
1180 L=L-1
1190 D=H*16+L
1200 RETURN
```

Line Range	Description
260-320	Query DOS version ($0101).
330-350	Input file name.
360-390	Opens logical file number 2 to device 8 with a secondary address of 2 for a program read.
400-440	Fetch file name track ($0018) and sector ($0019).
450	Close logical file number 2.
490	Reopens logical file number 2 to device 8 with a secondary address of 2 assigning buffer number 2 ($0500 - $05FF) as a workspace.
500	Reads the starting block of the filename from drive 0 as specified by $0018 and $0019 into channel 2 buffer area ($0500 - $05FF).
540	Three parameter memory-read command to fetch two byte load address ($0502 - $0503).
550	Fetch lo-byte of load address ($0502).
570	Fetch hi-byte of load address ($0503).
590-640	Decimal to hexadecimal conversion of load address.
660-700	Input new load address.
710-780	Hexadecimal to decimal conversion of new load address.
790	Memory-write of new two byte load address ($0502 - $0503).
800	Write channel 2 buffer ($0500 - $05FF) to drive 0, track ($0018), sector ($0019).

The alternate format of the memory-write command in line 790 is:

```
PRINT#15, "M-W:"CHR$(2)CHR$(5)CHR$(2)CHR$(LO)
  CHR$(HI)
```

5.8 Block-Allocate Command (B-A)

The block-allocate command allocates a sector in the BAM as in use. A sector is allocated by setting its associated bit low (0) on track 18, sector 0. (Review the coverage on bit mapping in Chapter 4 if necessary.) The DOS will not write to an allocated sector during a normal write operation such as a SAVE. However, an allocated sector can be overwritten with a block-write command (U2). Hence the origin of the term "direct-access." The format of a block-allocate command is:

```
SYNTAX:
  PRINT# file#, "B-A"; drive#; track; sector

ALTERNATE:
  PRINT# file#, "B-A:"; drive#; track; sector

EXAMPLE:
  PRINT#15, "B-A";0;1;7
```

where

file#   = the logical file number of the command channel

drive#   = 0

track   = 1 to 35

sector   = 0 to the range for a given track

The following program allocates every sector on a diskette. Run this program on a test diskette.

```
100 REM BLOCK-ALLOCATE
110 OPEN 15,8,15
120 PRINT#15,"IO"
130 INPUT#15,EN$,EM$,ET$,ES$
140 IF EN$<>"00"GOTO 310
150 OPEN 2,8,2,"#"
160 T=1
170 S=0
180 PRINT#15,"B-A";0;T;S
190 INPUT#15,EN$,EM$,ET$,ES$
```

```
200 IF EN$="00"GOTO 180
210 IF EN$<>"65"GOTO 330
220 BA=BA+1
230 PRINT T,S,BA
240 T=VAL(ET$)
250 IF T=0 GOTO 290
260 IF T=18 THEN T=19:S=0:GOTO 180
270 S=VAL(ES$)
280 GOTO 180
290 CLOSE 2
300 INPUT#15,EN$,EM$,ET$,ES$
310 CLOSE 15
320 END
330 PRINT"{DOWN}"EN$",  "EM$","ET$","ES$
340 CLOSE 2
350 INPUT#15,EN$,EM$,ET$,ES$
360 CLOSE 15
370 END
```

Line Range	Description
150	Open a direct-access channel.
160	Initialize track to 1.
170	Initialize sector to 0.
180	Block-allocate command.
190	Query error channel.
200	The track and sector were not allocated.
210	Something is amiss so bail out.
220	Counter representing the number of sectors allocated in line 170.
230	Print track, sector, counter.
240	The sector just allocated already was but the DOS returns the next available track in the error message (65, NO BLOCK, track, sector).
250	If the next available track is zero then all 683 blocks on the diskette have been allocated.
260	Don't allocate the directory.
270	The DOS returns the next available sector in the error message (65, NO BLOCK, track, sector).
280	Allocate the next available track and sector.
290	Close the direct-access channel.
330-370	Error handler.

The alternate format of the block-allocate command in line 180 is:

```
PRINT#15,"B-A:";0;T;S
```

The opening of a direct-access channel (line 150) is standard form. Why? Because the BAM is rewritten to a diskette when a direct-access data channel is closed (line 290).

In reality, though, the BAM is updated on the fly but very erratically. Thus, opening and closing a direct-access data channel is a good habit to get into. An ounce of prevention . . .

By the way, what happens when you try to save to a full disk? Error 72, DISK FULL right? Would you believe error 67, ILLEGAL TRACK OR SECTOR,36,01? Track 36? That's right. An error 72 only occurs during normal write mode (i.e., not a direct-access write) where at least 1 free block exists at the outset or the directory is at its physical limit, i.e., 144 active file entries.

A block remains allocated until a diskette is validated. Unless a given track and sector somehow chains to a directory entry its bit will be freed (1) during validation. (See the validate command in Chapter 2.) Caution must be taken to ensure that the block-allocate command does not allocate an unused sector in the directory. See line 260 above. Once a sector has been allocated in the directory, it is never deallocated by the DOS, even during a validate. An allocated directory sector can only be freed under software control.

The following program makes use of the block-allocate command to certify a formatted diskette. A worst-case binary pattern is written to any sector not currently in use. Bad sectors, if any, are allocated in the BAM. However, these bad sectors will be deallocated if the diskette is ever validated. (Sorry, but that's the nature of the beast.)

```
100 REM CERTIFY A DISKETTE - 1541
110 FORI=1TO32
120 NULL$=NULL$+CHR$(0)
130 WRITE$=WRITE$+CHR$(15)
140 NEXTI
150 DIMT%(681),S%(681)
160 PRINT"{CLR}              CERTIFY A DISK
ETTE"
170 PRINT"{DOWN}                  {RVS}WAR
NING{ROFF}"
180 PRINT"{DOWN}{RVS}RANDOM ACCESS{ROFF}
 AND {RVS}DEL{ROFF} FILES WILL BE LOST"
190 PRINT"REMOVE {RVS}WRITE PROTECT TAB{
ROFF}"
200 PRINT"{DOWN}INSERT DISKETTE IN DRIVE
"
210 PRINT"{DOWN}PRESS {RVS}RETURN{ROFF}
TO CONTINUE"
220 GETC$:IFC$=""THEN220
230 IFC$<>CHR$(13)GOTO220
240 PRINT"OK"
250 OPEN15,8,15
260 PRINT#15,"IO"
270 INPUT#15,EN$,EM$,ET$,ES$
280 IFEN$="OO"GOTO330
290 PRINT"{DOWN}"EN$", "EM$","ET$","ES$
300 CLOSE15
310 END
```

```
320 REM BAM
330 PRINT#15,"M-R"CHR$(0)CHR$(7)CHR$(192
)
340 FORI=0TO191
350 GET#15,B$
360 IFB$=""THENB$=CHR$(0)
370 BAM$=BAM$+B$
380 NEXTI
390 DOS=ASC(MID$(BAM$,3,1))
400 IFDOS=65GOTO460
410 CLOSE15
420 PRINT"{DOWN}73,CBM DOS V2.6 1541,00,
00"
430 PRINT"{DOWN}{RVS}FAILED{ROFF}"
440 END
450 REM BUFFER
460 I=0
470 FORJ=1TO8
480 PRINT#15,"M-W"CHR$(I)CHR$(4)CHR$(32)
WRITE$
490 I=I+32
500 NEXTJ
510 T=1
520 S=0
530 C=0
540 A=0
550 PRINT#15,"B-A";0;T;S
560 INPUT#15,EN$,EM$,ET$,ES$
570 IFEN$="00"GOTO620
580 T=VAL(ET$)
590 IFT=0ANDC=0GOTO760
600 IFT=0GOTO800
610 S=VAL(ES$)
620 T$=RIGHT$("0"+RIGHT$(STR$(T),LEN(STR
$(T))-1),2)
630 S$=RIGHT$("0"+RIGHT$(STR$(S),LEN(STR
$(S))-1),2)
640 C=C+1
650 IFC=1THENPRINT"{UP}    "
660 PRINT#15,"B-A";0;T;S
670 PRINT"{HOME}{DOWN 6}{RVS}CERTIFYING{
ROFF} TRACK ";T$;" - SECTOR ";S$
680 PRINT"{DOWN}NUMBER OF SECTORS CERTIF
IED    :";C
690 PRINT"{DOWN}NUMBER OF BAD SECTORS AL
LOCATED:";A
700 GOSUB1030
710 IFE=1GOTO550
720 A=A+1
730 T%(A)=T
```

```
740 S%(A)=S
750 GOTO550
760 CLOSE15
770 PRINT"{DOWN}ALL SECTORS HAVE BEEN AL
LOCATED"
780 PRINT"{DOWN}{RVS}FAILED{ROFF}"
790 END
800 I=0
810 FORJ=1TO6
820 PRINT#15,"M-W"CHR$(I)CHR$(4)CHR$(32)
MID$(BAM$,I+1,32)
830 I=I+32
840 NEXTJ
850 PRINT#15,"M-W"CHR$(192)CHR$(4)CHR$(3
2)NULL$
860 PRINT#15,"M-W"CHR$(224)CHR$(4)CHR$(3
2)NULL$
870 T=18
880 S=0
890 GOSUB1030
900 PRINT#15,"IO"
910 INPUT#15,EN$,EM$,ET$,ES$
920 IFA<>0GOTO960
930 CLOSE15
940 PRINT"{DOWN}NO BAD SECTORS!"
950 END
960 FORI=1TOA
970 PRINT#15,"B-A";0;T%(I);S%(I)
980 NEXTI
990 CLOSE15
1000 PRINT"{DOWN}DONE!"
1010 END
1020 REM SEEK
1030 JOB=176
1040 GOSUB1120
1050 IFE=1GOTO1080
1060 RETURN
1070 REM WRITE
1080 JOB=144
1090 GOSUB1120
1100 RETURN
1110 REM JOB QUEUE
1120 TRY=0
1130 PRINT#15,"M-W"CHR$(8)CHR$(0)CHR$(2)
CHR$(T)CHR$(S)
1140 PRINT#15,"M-W"CHR$(1)CHR$(0)CHR$(1)
CHR$(JOB)
1150 TRY=TRY+1
1160 PRINT#15,"M-R"CHR$(1)CHR$(0)
1170 GET#15,E$
```

```
1180 IFE$=""THENE$=CHR$(0)
1190 E=ASC(E$)
1200 IFTRY=500GOTO1220
1210 IFE>127GOTO1150
1220 RETURN
```

Line Range	Description
330-380	Store the BAM ($0700 - $07A0).
390-440	Query DOS version.
460-500	Write worst-case binary pattern to buffer at $0400.
510-540	Initialize track, sector, and counters.
550	Block-allocate command.
700	Write worst-case binary pattern at $0400 - $04FF to a deallocated track and sector.
710	Query error channel.
720-740	Error array.
800-890	Restore the BAM.
960-980	Allocate any bad sectors in error array.

The alternate format of the two block-allocate commands above are:

```
550 PRINT#15,"B-A:";0;T;S

970 PRINT#15,"B-A:";0;T%(I);S%(I)
```

Lines 330-380 and 800-890 compensate for a bug in the block-allocate command. (See Chapter 9 for the lowdown.) Lines 330-380 store an image of the BAM in C64 RAM. The BAM is restored in lines 800-890. Lines 1020-1230 will be explained in detail in Chapter 6 on intermediate disk programming techniques.

5.9 Block-Free Command (B-F)

The block-free command deallocates (frees) a sector in the BAM. A sector is deallocated by setting its associated bit high (1) on track 18, sector 0. The format of a block-free command is:

```
SYNTAX:
  PRINT# file#, "B-F"; drive#; track; sector

ALTERNATE:
  PRINT# file#, "B-F:"; drive#; track; sector

EXAMPLE:
  PRINT#15,"B-F";0;1;7
```

where

file#	= the logical file number of the command channel
drive#	= 0
track	= 1 to 35
sector	= 0 to the range for a given track

The following program deallocates every sector on a diskette. Run this program on a test diskette.

```
100 REM BLOCK-FREE
110 OPEN 15,8,15
120 PRINT#15,"I0"
130 INPUT#15,EN$,EM$,ET$,ES$
140 IF EN$<>"00"GOTO 260
150 OPEN 2,8,2,"#"
160 FOR T=1 TO 35
170 IF T=18 GOTO 240
180 NS=20+2*(T>17)+(T>24)+(T>30)
190 FOR S=0 TO NS
200 PRINT#15,"B-F";0;T;S
210 BF=BF+1
220 PRINT T,S,BF
230 NEXT S
240 NEXT T
250 CLOSE 2
260 INPUT#15,EN$,EM$,ET$,ES$
270 CLOSE 15
280 END
```

Line Range	Description
150	Open a direct-access channel.
160	Begin loop for tracks 1 to 35.
170	Don't deallocate the directory.
180	Calculate sector range.
190	Begin loop for sectors 0 to sector range.
200	Block-free command.
210	Counter to indicate number of blocks freed.
220	Print track, sector, counter.
250	Close the direct-access channel.

The alternate format of the block-free command in line 200 is:

```
PRINT#15,"B-F:";0;T;S
```

The opening and closing of a direct-access channel is essential if the block-free command is to work correctly. Experimentation in freeing a full diskette reveals that tracks 34 and 35 still remain allocated if this procedure is not followed.

5.10 Memory-Execute Command (M-E)

The memory-execute command is used to execute any standard ROM routine or, at the pinnacle of disk programming, a custom machine language program that has been poked into 1541 RAM. The format of a memory-execute command is:

```
SYNTAX:
  PRINT# file#, "M-E" CHR$(lo-byte) CHR$(hi-
    byte)

ALTERNATE:
  PRINT# file#, "M-E:" CHR$(lo-byte) CHR$(hi-
    byte)

EXAMPLE:
  PRINT#15,"M-E"CHR$(0)CHR$(6)
```

where

file#   = the logical file number of the command channel

lo-byte   = lo-byte of the RAM or ROM address

hi-byte   = hi-byte of the RAM or ROM address

Machine language programs are poked into 1541 RAM with the memory-write command. The following primitive program pokes a single RTS instruction to RAM and executes it.

```
100 REM MEMORY-EXECUTE
110 OPEN 15,8,15
120 PRINT#15,"M-W"CHR$(0)CHR$(6)CHR$(1)C
HR$(96)
130 PRINT#15,"M-E"CHR$(0)CHR$(6)
140 CLOSE15
150 END
```

Line Range	Description
120	Write 1 byte ($60) to RAM at $0600.
130	Execute RTS at $0600.

The alternate format of the memory-execute command in line 130 is:

```
PRINT#15,"M-E:"CHR$(0)CHR$(6)
```

More sophisticated coding is available in Chapter 7. In addition, refer to Chapter 9 for pertinent information about the execution of standard ROM routines.

5.11 Block-Execute Command (B-E)

The block-execute command is used to execute a machine language program that resides on diskette. A sector is read into a DOS buffer and executed in a manner similar to a LOAD and RUN on the C64. The format of a block-execute command is:

```
SYNTAX:
  PRINT# file#, "B-E"; channel#; drive#;
    track; sector

ALTERNATE:
  PRINT# file#, "B-E:"; channel#; drive#;
    track; sector
  PRINT# file#, "B-E: channel#, drive#,
    track, sector"

EXAMPLE:
  PRINT#15,"B-E";2;0;1;0
```

where

file#   = the logical file number of the command channel

channel#   = the secondary address of the associated open statement

drive#   = 0

track   = 1 to 35

sector   = 0 to the range for a given track

The block-execute command could be used in a diagnostic routine but it is difficult to visualize any other advantage that this command has over a normal memory-execute command. The following program demonstrates one of the few block-execute commands you will probably ever see. (lights, camera, action!) Run this program using a test diskette.

```
100 REM BLOCK-EXECUTE
110 OPEN 15,8,15
120 PRINT#15,"I0"
130 INPUT#15,EN$,EM$,ET$,ES$
140 IF EN$<>"00"GOTO 250
```

```
150 OPEN 2,8,2,"#3"
160 PRINT#15,"U1";2;0;1;0
170 INPUT#15,EN$,EM$,ET$,ES$
180 IF EN$<>"00"GOTO 220
190 PRINT#15,"M-W"CHR$(0)CHR$(6)CHR$(1)C
HR$(96)
200 PRINT#15,"U2";2;0;1;0
210 PRINT#15,"M-W"CHR$(0)CHR$(6)CHR$(1)C
HR$(0)
220 PRINT#15,"B-E";2;0;1;0
230 CLOSE 2
240 INPUT#15,EN$,EM$,ET$,ES$
250 CLOSE 15
260 END
```

Line Range	Description
150	Open a direct-access channel specifying buffer number 1 ($0600 - $06FF).
160	Block-read of track 1, sector 0 ($0600 - $06FF).
190	Write 1 byte ($60) to RAM at $0600.
200	Block-write to track 1, sector 0 ($0600 - $06FF).
210	Just to keep us honest.
220	Block-execute of track 1, sector 0 ($0600 - $06FF).

The alternate formats of the block-execute command in line 220 are:

```
PRINT#15,"B-E:";2;0;1;0

PRINT#15,"B-E:2,0,1,0"
```

5.12 Direct-Access Entomology

We will conclude our discussion of the disk utility command set by pointing out just a few of the DOS V2.6 direct-access anomalies we've found to date.

Block-Read (B-R)

Throughout the preceding section we relied solely upon the use of the U1 command to read a sector and not the traditional block-read command (B-R). Why? The block-read command (B-R) is unreliable, period. When the contents of a buffer are accessed with the GET# command — surprise, surprise! The number of bytes returned is a function of the number of the track you accessed. For example, a block-read (B-R) of any sector on track 15 will return only 15 bytes before sending an erroneous End-Or-Identify (EOI). The C64 status variable (ST) is set to 64 and any further attempt to access the buffer merely returns the same sequence of bytes over and over and over again. Moreover, the byte in position 0 can only be accessed when the buffer-pointer is reset to position 0 in line 190. See for yourself.

```
100 REM BLOCK-READ (B-R)
110 OPEN 15,8,15
120 PRINT#15,"IO"
130 INPUT#15,EN$,EM$,ET$,ES$
140 IF EN$<>"00"GOTO 300
150 OPEN 2,8,2,"#"
160 PRINT#15,"B-R";2;0;18;0
170 INPUT#15,EN$,EM$,ET$,ES$
180 IF EN$<>"00"GOTO 280
190 PRINT#15,"B-P";2;0
200 FOR I=0 TO 255
210 GET#2,B$
220 IF B$=""THEN B$=CHR$(0)
230 A=ASC(B$)
240 PRINT ST,I,A,
250 IF A>31 AND A<96 THEN PRINT B$,
260 PRINT
270 NEXT I
280 CLOSE 2
290 INPUT#15,EN$,EM$,ET$,ES$
300 CLOSE 15
310 END
```

What's even more problematic is the situation that occurs when you do a block-read (B-R) of a track and sector that was rewritten by the block-write command (B-W) which is discussed below. The EOI occurs in connection with the ASCII value of the 0th byte of the sector that was read. Byte 0 contains the value of the buffer-pointer position at the time the block was written with a block-write command (B-W). The forward track reference that was originally there, has been destroyed. The ASCII value of the 0th byte determines how many characters you can access before the EOI occurs. Run the block-read (B-R) program listed above against track 1, sector 0 after you've done the block-write (B-W) experiment listed below on a test disk. Change the track number in line 160 from an 18 to a 1 like this:

```
160 PRINT#15,"B-R";2;0;1;0
```

After further experimentation on your own, you should have little trouble understanding why the U1 command replaces the block-read command (B-R). Not only do user manuals continue to promote the use of the block-read command (B-R), but they also either ignore the U1 command altogether or simply mention it in passing without even a hint on how to use it.

Block-Write (B-W)

Recall that we also neglected to mention the block-write command (B-W) which we replaced with the U2 command. When you write a block with the block-write command (B-W) a different kind of dilemma occurs. Bytes 1 through 255 of the buffer are recorded on diskette correctly but the last position of the buffer-pointer is written to the 0th byte of the sector (the location of the forward track pointer). If it's any consolation, the data is still intact. Too bad the link has been destroyed. Run the following block-write program on a test diskette.

```
100 REM BLOCK-WRITE (B-W)
110 OPEN 15,8,15
120 PRINT#15,"I0"
130 INPUT#15,EN$,EM$,ET$,ES$
140 IF EN$<>"00"GOTO 260
150 OPEN 2,8,2,"#"
160 PRINT#15,"U1";2;0;1;0
170 INPUT#15,EN$,EM$,ET$,ES$
180 IF EN$<>"00"GOTO 240
190 FOR I=0 TO 255
200 PRINT#2,CHR$(I);
210 NEXT I
220 PRINT#15,"B-P";2;6
230 PRINT#15,"B-W";2;0;1;0
240 CLOSE 2
250 INPUT#15,EN$,EM$,ET$,ES$
260 CLOSE 15
270 END
```

Now run the original block-read (U1) program that we wrote using this diskette. Be sure to change the track in line 160 from an 18 to a 1 as follows:

```
160 PRINT#15,"U1";2;0;1;0
```

If all goes according to our diabolical plan, byte 0 will contain a 5 which is exactly where our buffer-pointer ended up. We arbitrarily set it to position 6 in line 220 above and 256 bytes later it wraps around to position 5. (Remember that bytes are numbered from 0 to 255 in a buffer area.)

Now change the U1 to a B-R in line 160 and run the program again. This time, only 5 bytes can be accessed before an EOI signal is returned.

UJ and UI-

Commodore has traditionally had a warm reset buried somewhere in ROM on every piece of hardware they have manufactured to date. The UJ command is to the 1541 what a SYS 64738 is to the C64, a warm reset. Or rather, that is what it's supposed to be. The issuance of a UJ command is supposed to reset the 1541. Instead, it hangs the 1541.

Press the RUN/STOP key and RESTORE key in tandem to regain control of the C64 after typing in this one liner in immediate mode.

```
OPEN 15,8,15,"UJ" : CLOSE15
```

Use U: in place of UJ.

The same thing is true for the UI- command although Commodore can't really be held responsible here. The UI- command was implemented to set the 1541 to VIC-20 speed, not to take the C64 out to lunch.

U3 - U9

The *VIC-1541 User's Manual* outlines 7 USER commands that perform a jump to a particular location in RAM. These USER commands and their respective jump addresses are:

User Number	Jump Address
U3 (UC)	$0500
U4 (UD)	$0503
U5 (UE)	$0506
U6 (UF)	$0509
U7 (UG)	$050C
U8 (UH)	$050F
U9 (UI)	$FFFA

These jump locations are not quite as mystifying as they appear at first glance. Let's modify our simplistic memory-execute program.

```
100 REM U3
110 OPEN 15,8,15
120 PRINT#15,"M-W"CHR$(O)CHR$(5)CHR$(1)C
HR$(96)
130 PRINT#15,"U3"
140 CLOSE15
150 END
```

One should be able to discern that any of the first six USER commands, U3 - U8, could double for a memory-execute command. It is very difficult to understand why Commodore included six jumps to the $0500 page (buffer number 2). Moreover, the U9 command jumps to $FFA which is a word table pointing to the NMI vector. U9 is an alternate reset that bypasses the power-on diagonstics.

CHAPTER 6

INTERMEDIATE
DIRECT-ACCESS PROGRAMMING

NOTE: This chapter is not intended for beginners. The reader is assumed to be relatively familiar with the direct-access programming commands described in Chapter 5.

The intermediate level of direct-access programming involves passing requests directly to the Floppy Disk Controller (FDC) via the job queue. Normally a 1541 command is initiated on the C64 side (e.g., SAVE, a block-read (U1), etc.). The command is interpreted by the 1541's 6502 Interface Processor (IP) as a set of simple operations called jobs. (This is analogous to the way the BASIC interpreter works inside the C64.) These jobs are poked into an area of 1541 RAM called the job queue. Every 10 milliseconds the job queue is scanned by the Floppy Disk Controller (FDC). If a job request is found the FDC executes it. The complete set of jobs that the FDC can perform are as follows:

1. Read a sector.
2. Write a sector.
3. Verify a sector.
4. Seek a track.
5. Bump the head to track number 1.
6. Jump to a machine language routine in a buffer.
7. Execute a machine language routine in a buffer.

The hexadecimal and decimal equivalents for each job request as seen by the FDC are:

Job Code	Description
$80 (128)	READ
$90 (144)	WRITE
$A0 (160)	VERIFY
$B0 (176)	SEEK
$C0 (192)	BUMP
$D0 (208)	JUMP
$E0 (224)	EXECUTE

If the FDC finds a job request in the job queue, it attempts to carry it out. Once the job is complete or aborted the FDC replaces the job code with an error code. The error codes returned by the FDC to the IP are listed below. The IP error codes and their respective error messages are what you see when you read the error channel.

FDC Code	IP Code	Error Message
$01 (1)	0	OK
$02 (2)	20	READ ERROR (header block not found)
$03 (3)	21	READ ERROR (no sync character)
$04 (4)	22	READ ERROR (data block not present)
$05 (5)	23	READ ERROR (checksum error in data block)
$07 (7)	25	WRITE ERROR (write-verify error)
$08 (8)	26	WRITE PROTECT ON
$09 (9)	27	READ ERROR (checksum error in header block)
$0B (11)	29	READ ERROR (disk ID mismatch)

A more detailed description of each of these error messages can be found in Chapter 7.

Suppose that we want to read the contents of a given track and sector. The command initiated on the C64 side is parsed by the IP. If the syntax is correct, it is broken down into a job code, a track, and a sector. Depending upon what buffer has been assigned, the job code is poked into the corresponding job queue table location. The track and sector for the job are poked into the corresponding header table locations. The buffers and their corresponding job queue and header table addresses are outlined below:

Buffer	Address	Job	Track	Sector
	$0000 - $00FF	Not available (ZERO PAGE)		
	$0100 - $01FF	Not available (STACK)		
	$0200 - $03FF	Not available (COMMAND BUFFER)		
#0	$0300 - $03FF	$0000	$0006	$0007
#1	$0400 - $04FF	$0001	$0008	$0009
#2	$0500 - $05FF	$0002	$000A	$000B
#3	$0600 - $06FF	$0003	$000C	$000D
	$0700 - $07FF	Not available (BAM)		

For example, a block-read command (U1) issued by the C64 to read the contents of track 18, sector 0 into buffer number 0 ($0300-$03FF) is checked for a syntax error and then broken down by the IP. In time, the FDC will find an $80 (128) at address $0000 in the job queue table, a $12 (18) at address $0006 in the header table, and a $00 (0) at address $0007 in the header table. Armed with that information, the FDC will attempt to seek (find) the track and read the sector. Upon successful completion of the read, the contents of the sector will be transferred to buffer number 0 ($0300-$03FF) and a $01 (1) will be returned by the FDC to address $0000. (If the job request could not be completed for some reason, the job request would be aborted and the corresponding error code would be stored at address $0000 instead.) Interrogation of the error channel will transfer the IP counterpart of the FDC error code, the English message, the track number, and the sector number to the C64 side. If the job request was successful (00, OK,00,00), the contents of the track and sector could then be retrieved from the buffer at $0300 – $03FF using a GET# command as described in the previous chapter.

What happens, though, if we bypass the drive's parser routine and attempt to work the FDC directly ourselves? We thought you'd never ask. Grand and glorious schemes become possibilities, and that's what intermediate direct-access programming is all about. Armed with a lookup table of job codes, a map of the 1541's buffer areas, a track, a sector, and a lookup table of error codes, the FDC is at your beck and call. Tired of those horrendous grating noises when your drive errs out? Well wish no more. The drive does not do a bump (the root of all evil) to reinitialize when you are working the job queue directly. What more could you ask for? We know. The code, right?

The following program works the job queue directly to read the block from track 18, sector 0 into buffer number 0 ($0300 – $03FF) and prints the contents to the screen. Sound vaguely familiar? It should. It's a modification of the first program we wrote under beginning direct-access programming.

```
100 REM JOB QUEUE READ
110 OPEN 15,8,15
120 PRINT#15,"I0"
130 INPUT#15,EN$,EM$,ET$,ES$
140 IF EN$<>"00"GOTO 340
150 REM SEEK
160 T=18
170 S=0
180 JOB=176
190 GOSUB 370
200 IF E<>1 GOTO 340
210 REM READ
220 JOB=128
230 GOSUB 370
240 IF E<>1 GOTO 340
250 FOR I=0 TO 255
260 PRINT#15,"M-R"CHR$(I)CHR$(3)
270 GET#15,B$
280 IF B$=""THEN B$=CHR$(0)
290 A=ASC(B$)
300 PRINT ST,I,A,
310 IF A>31 AND A<96 THEN PRINT B$,
320 PRINT
330 NEXT I
340 CLOSE 15
350 END
360 REM JOB QUEUE
370 TRY=0
380 PRINT#15,"M-W"CHR$(6)CHR$(0)CHR$(2)C
HR$(T)CHR$(S)
390 PRINT#15,"M-W"CHR$(0)CHR$(0)CHR$(1)C
```

```
HR$(JOB)
400 TRY=TRY+1
410 PRINT#15,"M-R"CHR$(0)CHR$(0)
420 GET#15,E$
430 IF E$=""THEN E$=CHR$(0)
440 E=ASC(E$)
450 IF TRY=500 GOTO 470
460 IF E>127 GOTO 400
470 RETURN
```

Line Range	Description
Main Program	
110	Open the command channel.
120-140	Initialize drive.
160	Initialize track to 18.
170	Initialize sector to 0.
180-190	SEEK track 18.
200	Query FDC error code.
220-230	READ sector 0 on track 18 into buffer number 0 ($0300-$03FF).
240	Query FDC error code.
250	Begin loop to read 256 bytes ($0300-$03FF).
260	Two parameter memory-read.
270	Transfer a byte from buffer number 0 to C64 memory by way of the command channel (GET#15,).
280	Test for equality with the null string "".
290	ASCII conversion of a byte.
300	Print the status variable (ST), our loop counter, and the ASCII value of the byte.
310	Print the byte if it's within printable ASCII range.
320	Terminate comma tabulation.
330	Increment loop counter.
340	Close the command channel.
350	End.
Subroutine	
370	Initialize try counter.
380	Stuff the track and sector numbers into buffer number 0's header table ($0006-$0007).
390	Stuff job code number into buffer number 0's job queue table ($0000).
400-460	Wait for FDC to complete the job.
470	Return with FDC error code in hand.

The good news is that working the job queue is not quite as complex as it at first appears. The subroutine in lines 370-470 is the very heart of the matter. We simply stuff our track and sector into the header table, our job code into the job queue table, and wait until the FDC has completed the operation.

Keep in mind that this example was using buffer number 0 ($0300-$03FF). The corresponding header table and job queue table addresses were $0006 for the track, $0007 for the sector, and $0000 for the job code. Please note that every job code is greater than 127. (Bit 7 is deliberately set high (1).) Recall that when the FDC has completed a job, the job code is replaced with an error code. All error codes are less than 128. (Bit 7 is deliberately set low (0).) Line 460 waits until bit 7 of the job code is set low (0) by the FDC. If bit 7 is high (1), the FDC is still working so we must continue to wait (line 410).

Error handling is a bit out of the ordinary too but not all that hard to comprehend either. An FDC error code of 1 means the job was completed successfully. Any other number indicates an error.

You will also note a simple hierarchy of jobs in the program listing. Before we can read a sector (line 220) we must always find the track first (line 180). Now are you ready for this one? Initialization is not necessary at all when working the job queue directly. Lines 120-140 were included as a force of habit. Applications like reading damaged or DOS protected diskettes may dictate that we do not initialize. Now for the bad news.

WARNING

Read this passage carefully. Then read it again for good measure. Experience is a hard teacher — test first, lesson afterward.

1. You must remember at all times when working the job queue that you have directly bypassed the parser routine. This is extremely dangerous because you have in effect killed all protection built into the 1541 itself. Let us explain. If by some poor misfortune you elect to do a read on track 99, the FDC doesn't know any better and takes off in search of track 99. You can physically lock the read/write head if it accidentally steps beyond its normal boundaries, i.e., a track less than 1 or a track greater than 35. No damage is done to the 1541 itself but if the power-on sequence doesn't return the head to center you will have to disassemble the drive and reposition the head manually. Exceeding the sector range for a given track is no problem, however. The drive will eventually give up trying to find a sector out of range and report an FDC error 2 (an IP 20 error). Tracks are a pain in the stepper motor, however.

2. You must keep your header table locations and your job queue table locations straight in relation to the buffer number you are working. If they are not in agreement, the drive will go off into never-never land. The FDC will either attempt to work a nonexistent job code or seek a track and sector out of bounds. Remember the FDC will do exactly what you tell it to do. You are at the helm at all times. At the minimum, you will have to power off the drive to regain control. Again, no physical damage has been done to the 1541 but you may have to reposition the read/write head yourself. We know from experience.

3. You should always monitor the job yourself. The try counter in line 450 is a stopgap measure. Five hundred wait cycles seems like an exaggerated figure here. However, you must give the drive adequate time to find a desired track and settle down before performing a job. If for some reason it cannot complete the job, it usually aborts and returns an error code on its own. If it doesn't, something is amiss and a try counter may trap it. (You might have to power off the drive to restore the status quo.) A try counter is a little like workman's compensation. Don't work the job queue without it.

Now, read these three paragraphs a second time.

The following program works the job queue directly to read track 18, sector 0 into buffer number 1 ($0400-$04FF). The disk name is returned with a three parameter memory-read of bytes 144-159 ($0490-$049F). It's another oldie but goodie.

```
100 REM JOB QUEUE READ - DISK NAME
110 OPEN 15,8,15
120 PRINT#15,"IO"
130 INPUT#15,EN$,EM$,ET$,ES$
140 IF EN$<>"00"GOTO 360
150 REM SEEK
160 T=18
170 S=0
180 JOB=176
190 GOSUB 390
200 IF E<>1 GOTO 360
210 REM READ
220 JOB=128
230 GOSUB 390
240 IF E<>1 GOTO 360
250 PRINT#15,"M-R"CHR$(144)CHR$(4)CHR$(1
6)
260 FOR I=1 TO 16
270 GET#15,B$
280 IF B$=""THEN B$=CHR$(0)
290 A=ASC(B$)
300 IF A>127 THEN A=A-128
310 IF A<32 OR A>95 THEN A=63
320 IF A=34 THEN A=63
330 DN$=DN$+CHR$(A)
340 NEXT I
350 PRINT"{DOWN}DISK NAME: ";DN$
360 CLOSE 15
370 END
380 REM JOB QUEUE
390 TRY=0
400 PRINT#15,"M-W"CHR$(8)CHR$(0)CHR$(2)C
HR$(T)CHR$(S)
410 PRINT#15,"M-W"CHR$(1)CHR$(0)CHR$(1)C
```

```
HR$(JOB)
420 TRY=TRY+1
430 PRINT#15,"M-R"CHR$(1)CHR$(0)
440 GET#15,E$
450 IF E$="" THEN E$=CHR$(0)
460 E=ASC(E$)
470 IF TRY=500 GOTO 490
480 IF E>127 GOTO 420
490 RETURN
```

Line Range	Description
120-140	Force of habit.
160	Initialize track to 18.
170	Initialize sector to 0.
180-190	SEEK track 18.
200	Query FDC error code.
220-230	READ sector 0 on track 18 into buffer number 1 ($0400-$04FF).
240	Query FDC error code.
250	Three parameter memory-read ($0490-$049F).
260-340	Concatenate the disk name one byte at a time by jamming it within printable ASCII range.
390	Initialize try counter.
400	Stuff the track and sector number into buffer number 1's header table ($0008-$0009).
410	Stuff the job code number into buffer number 1's job queue table ($0001).
420-480	Wait for FDC to complete the job.
490	Return with FDC error code in hand.

Not much new here except the buffer in use. Let's review the key memory addresses for working buffer number 1 ($0400-$04FF):

```
BUFFER NUMBER 1    = $0400 - $04FF
TRACK NUMBER       = $0008 (HEADER TABLE)
SECTOR NUMBER      = $0009 (HEADER TABLE)
JOB CODE           = $0001 (JOB QUEUE TABLE)
```

While we're at it, we might as well review the order of jobs for the sake of posterity. First SEEK a track. Then READ a sector.

The next program incorporates four FDC job codes, namely a SEEK, a READ, a WRITE, and indirectly a VERIFY. This routine is a modification of the edit disk name program found in the previous chapter. Keep in mind that we are working buffer number 2 here ($0500-$05FF). The header table addresses are $000A for the track and $000B for the sector. The job codes themselves will be poked into location $0002 in the job queue table.

```
100 REM JOB QUEUE READ/WRITE - EDIT DISK
 NAME
110 FOR I=1 TO 16
120 PAD$=PAD$+CHR$(160)
130 NEXT I
140 PRINT"{CLR}EDIT DISK NAME - 1541"
150 PRINT"{DOWN}REMOVE {RVS}WRITE PROTEC
T TAB{ROFF}"
160 PRINT"{DOWN}INSERT DISKETTE IN DRIVE
"
170 PRINT"{DOWN}PRESS {RVS}RETURN{ROFF}
TO CONTINUE"
180 GET C$:IF C$=""THEN 180
190 IF C$<>CHR$(13)GOTO 180
200 PRINT"OK"
210 OPEN 15,8,15
220 PRINT#15,"IO"
230 INPUT#15,EN$,EM$,ET$,ES$
240 IF EN$="00"GOTO 290
250 PRINT"{DOWN}"EN$","EM$","ET$","ES$
260 CLOSE 15
270 END
280 REM SEEK
290 T=18
300 S=0
310 JOB=176
320 GOSUB 660
330 REM READ
340 JOB=128
350 GOSUB 660
360 PRINT#15,"M-R"CHR$(144)CHR$(5)CHR$(1
6)
370 FOR I=1 TO 16
380 GET#15,B$
390 IF B$=""THEN B$=CHR$(0)
400 A=ASC(B$)
410 IF A>127 THEN A=A-128
420 IF A<32 OR A>95 THEN A=63
430 IF A=34 THEN A=63
440 ODN$=ODN$+CHR$(A)
450 NEXT I
460 PRINT"{DOWN}OLD DISK NAME: ";ODN$
470 INPUT"{DOWN}NEW DISK NAME";NDN$
480 IF LEN(NDN$)<>0 AND LEN(NDN$)<17 GOT
O 500
490 GOTO 630
500 INPUT"{DOWN}ARE YOU SURE (Y/N)  Y{LE
FT 3}";Q$
510 IF Q$<>"Y"GOTO 630
520 NDN$=LEFT$(NDN$+PAD$,16)
```

```
530 PRINT#15,"M-W"CHR$(144)CHR$(5)CHR$(1
6)NDN$
540 REM WRITE
550 JOB=144
560 GOSUB 660
570 PRINT#15,"IO"
580 INPUT#15,EN$,EM$,ET$,ES$
590 CLOSE 15
600 PRINT"{DOWN}DONE!"
610 END
620 REM CLOSE
630 CLOSE 15
640 END
650 REM JOB QUEUE
660 TRY=0
670 PRINT#15,"M-W"CHR$(10)CHR$(0)CHR$(2)
CHR$(T)CHR$(S)
680 PRINT#15,"M-W"CHR$(2)CHR$(0)CHR$(1)C
HR$(JOB)
690 TRY=TRY+1
700 PRINT#15,"M-R"CHR$(2)CHR$(0)
710 GET#15,E$
720 IF E$=""THEN E$=CHR$(0)
730 E=ASC(E$)
740 IF TRY=500 GOTO 780
750 IF E>127 GOTO 690
760 IF E=1 THEN RETURN
770 REM ERROR HANDLER
780 ET$=RIGHT$(STR$(T),LEN(STR$(T))-1)
790 IF T<10 THEN ET$="0"+ET$
800 ES$=RIGHT$(STR$(S),LEN(STR$(S))-1)
810 IF S<10 THEN ES$="0"+ES$
820 IF E>1 AND E<12 THEN EN$=RIGHT$(STR$
(E+18),2):GOTO 840
830 EN$="02":EM$="?TIME OUT":GOTO 860
840 IF E=7 OR E=8 THEN EM$="WRITE ERROR"
:GOTO 860
850 EM$="READ ERROR"
860 PRINT"{DOWN}"EN$", "EM$","ET$","ES$
870 PRINT"{DOWN}{RVS}FAILED{ROFF}"
880 CLOSE 15
890 END
```

Line Range	Description
290-320	SEEK track 18.
340-350	READ contents of sector 0 from track 18 into buffer number 2 ($0500-$05FF).
550-560	WRITE buffer number 2 ($0500-$05FF) to track 18, sector 0.
770-890	Error handler.

Lines 100 to 530 should be self explanatory by now. Lines 540-560 are equivalent to a block-write command (U2). To write a sector via the job queue we stuff the track and sector in the header table and a $90 (144) into the job queue table and let her rip.

The error handler, however, is of interest. The conversion from FDC code to IP code is quite easy. We simply add 18 to the FDC error code (line 820). Note that we try to restrict all errors within a range of 20 to 29. An FDC error code of 0 or greater than 11 is indicative that something went radically wrong. Line 820 arbitrarily reports a ?TIME OUT in this situation. Speaking from experience, the job just plainly didn't get done. A time out occurs very rarely, unless of course, one is inspecting a damaged or DOS-protected diskette.

Line 840 is another highlight. An FDC WRITE ($90) automatically flips to an FDC VERIFY ($A0) to compare the contents of the buffer against the sector just written. Kind of neat, isn't it? If the buffer and the sector do not match, we see an FDC error 7, i.e., an IP error number 25, WRITE ERROR. Since a VERIFY is done automatically by the FDC, we will not elaborate any further on this particular job code.

The job code for a BUMP is a $C0 (192). Why anybody would ever want to implement this job request is beyond us.

A subtle difference exists between the remaining two job codes, a JUMP ($D0) and an EXECUTE ($E0). A JUMP executes a machine language routine poked into RAM. No more, no less. Like a BUMP job, it is seldom used. The program that moves the read/write head in Chapter 9 is the only place where we have ever found a practical use for it.

An EXECUTE ($E0) is the Rolls Royce of job codes, however. Before a machine language routine is executed, the FDC makes sure that:

1. The drive is up to speed.
2. The read/write head is on the right track.
3. The read/write head has settled.

The FDC cannot be interrupted when performing an EXECUTE job. Once the FDC starts to EXECUTE the machine language routine, control is not returned to the IP until the routine is completed. A runaway routine cannot be debugged even with BRK instructions. You must power down the 1541 and try to second guess the side effects of the routine to determine what went wrong.

NOTE: The FDC does not automatically return an error code when the routine is completed. It is the programmer's responsibility to change the job code in the job queue table from an EXECUTE ($E0) to an $01 at the end of the routine. If this is not done, the FDC will find the same EXECUTE request on its next scan of the job queue and re-run the routine. Infinite regression!

Most of the programs in Chapter 7 make use of the EXECUTE job code in one form or another. Therefore, example programs will be given there.

CHAPTER 7

DOS PROTECTION

7.1 Commodore's Data Encoding Scheme

Before we can enter the netherworld of DOS protection you have to possess a thorough
understanding of how the 1541 records a sector on a diskette. Any given sector is divided into two contiguous parts, a header block and a data block. For clarity sake let's
review the parts of a sector discussed in Chapter 3.

Header Block (16 8-bit bytes)

Number of Bytes	Description
–	Sync Character
1	Header Block Identifier ($08)
1	Header Block Checksum
1	Sector Number
1	Track Number
1	ID LO
1	ID HI
2	Off Bytes ($0F)
8	Header Gap ($55)

Data Block (260 8-bit bytes)

Number of Bytes	Description
–	Sync Character
1	Data Block Identifier ($07)
256	Data Bytes
1	Data Block Checksum
2	Off Bytes ($00)
Variable	Tail Gap ($55)

The 1541 writes a track on the surface of a diskette as one continuous bit stream. There
are no demagnetized zones between sectors on a track to delineate where one sector
ends and another one begins. Instead, Commodore relies upon synchronization characters

for reference marks. A DOS 2.6 sync mark can be defined as five 8-bit $FF's written in succession to disk. Note that a sync mark is recorded at the front end of each header block and each data block. To differentiate a sync mark from a normal data byte, the 1541 writes to diskette in two modes, a sync mode and a normal write mode.

To appreciate the uniqueness of a sync mark we must first look at how a normal data byte is recorded. During normal write mode each 8-bit byte is encoded into 10 bits before it is written to disk. Commodore calls this encoding scheme *binary to GCR (Group Code Recording) conversion*. The conversion technique itself is quite straightforward. Each 8-bit byte is separated into two 4-bit nybbles, a high nybble and a low nybble. For example, the binary representation of $12 (18) is %00010010. The breakdown of this 8-bit byte into its two 4-bit nybbles is depicted below:

Hexadecimal	Binary	High Nybble	Low Nybble
$12 (18)	00010010	0001xxxx	xxxx0010

Mathematically speaking, a 4-bit nybble can be decoded into any one of 16 different decimal values ranging from 0 (all bits turned off) to 15 (all bits turned on) as follows:

Bit Number	3	2	1	0
Power of 2	3	2	1	0
Weight	8	4	2	1

Hence, the 1541's GCR lookup table contains just sixteen 4-bit nybble equivalencies:

Hexadecimal	Binary	GCR
$0 (0)	0000	01010
$1 (1)	0001	01011
$2 (2)	0010	10010
$3 (3)	0011	10011
$4 (4)	0100	01110
$5 (5)	0101	01111
$6 (6)	0110	10110
$7 (7)	0111	10111
$8 (8)	1000	01001
$9 (9)	1001	11001
$A (10)	1010	11010
$B (11)	1011	11011
$C (12)	1100	01101
$D (13)	1101	11101
$E (14)	1110	11110
$F (15)	1111	10101

Using the binary to GCR lookup table above, let's walk through the necessary steps to convert a $12 (18) to GCR form.

STEP 1. Hexadecimal to Binary Conversion

$12 (18) = 00010010

STEP 2. High Nybble to GCR Conversion

0001xxxx = $1 (1) = 01011

STEP 3. Low Nybble to GCR Conversion

xxxx0010 = $2 (2) = 10010

STEP 4. GCR Concatenation

01011 + 10010 = 0101110010

Two things should stand out when scrutinizing the 1541's binary to GCR lookup table.

1. No combination of any two 5-bit GCR bytes will ever yield 10 consecutive on bits (1s) which is used as the sync mark. Binary to GCR conversion eliminates all likelihood that a permutation of normal data bytes can ever be mistaken by the read/write electronics for a sync mark.

2. No more than two consecutive off bits (0s) appear in any given 10-bit GCR byte or combination of GCR bytes. This latter constraint was imposed for accuracy when clocking bits back into the 1541 during a read. (See Chapter 9 for additional information.)

This brings us full circle to what actually differentiates a sync mark from a normal data byte. Simply put, a sync mark is 10 or more on bits (1s) recorded in succession. Only one normal data byte, an $FF (%11111111), can even begin to fill the shoes of a sync mark. During normal write mode, however, an $FF would take the following GCR form, 1010110101. Enter sync mode. When the 1541 writes an $FF in sync mode *no binary to GCR conversion is done*. A single $FF is only eight consecutive on bits and falls short of the ten consecutive on bits needed to create a sync character. To remedy this, Commodore writes five consecutive 8-bit $FFs to disk. This records 40 on bits (1s) in succession. the overkill is intentional on the DOS's part. Commodore is trying to guarantee that the 1541 will never have any trouble finding a sync mark during subsequent reads/writes to a diskette.

Four 8-bit data bytes are converted to four 10-bit GCR bytes at a time by the 1541 DOS. RAM is only an 8-bit storage device though. This hardware limitation prevents a 10-bit GCR byte from being stored in a single memory location. Four 10-bit GCR bytes total 40 bits — a number evenly divisible by our overriding 8-bit constraint. Commodore subdivides the 40 GCR bits into five 8-bit bytes to solve this dilemma. This explains why four 8-bit data bytes are converted to GCR form at a time. The following step by step example demonstrates how this bit manipulation is performed by the DOS.

STEP 1. Four 8-bit Data Bytes
$08 $10 $00 $12

STEP 2. Hexadecimal to Binary Conversion
    1. Binary Equivalents

       $08 $10 $00 $12
       00001000 00010000 00000000 00010010

STEP 3. Binary to GCR Conversion
    1. Four 8-bit Data Bytes

       00001000 00010000 00000000 00010010

    2. High and Low Nybbles

       0000 1000 0001 0000 0000 0000 0001 0010

    3. High and Low Nybble GCR Equivalents

       01010 01001 01011 01010 01010 01010 01011 10010

    4. Four 10-bit GCR Bytes

       0101001001 0101101010 0101001010 0101110010

STEP 4. 10-bit GCR to 8-bit GCR Conversion
    1. Concatenate Four 10-bit GCR Bytes

       01010010010101101010010100101010100101110010

    2. Five 8-bit Subdivisions

       01010010 01010110 10100101 00101001 01110010

STEP 5. Binary to Hexadecimal Conversion
    1. Hexadecimal Equivalents

       01010010 01010110 10100101 00101001 01110010
       $52 $56 $A5 $29 $72

STEP 6. Four 8-bit Data Bytes are Recorded as Five 8-bit GCR Bytes

$08 $10 $00 $12   are recorded as $52 $56 $A5 $29 $72

Four normal 8-bit bytes are always written to diskette as five 8-bit GCR bytes by the DOS. The 1541 converts these same five 8-bit GCR bytes back to four normal 8-bit bytes during a read. The steps outlined above still apply but they are performed in the reverse order. (The appendix contains various mathematical conversion routines for your use.)

In light of the above discussion, we need to recalculate the number of bytes that are actually recorded in a sector. We stated in Chapter 3 that a header block was comprised of eight 8-bit bytes excluding the header gap. This is recorded on the diskette as ten 8-bit GCR bytes. The formula for determining the actual number of bytes that are recorded is:

Number of 8-bit GCR Bytes Recorded = (Number of 8-bit Data Bytes/4) * 5

Similarly, a data block consisting of 260 8-bit bytes is written to disk as 325 8-bit GCR bytes. Lest we forget, each sync mark is five 8-bit bytes. We must also remember to add in the header gap which is held constant at eight bytes. (Header gap bytes ($55) are not converted to GCR form and serve only to separate the header block from the data block.) An entire sector is recorded as 353 bytes not 256 data bytes.

	Data Bytes	GCR Bytes
Sync Character ($FF)	5 *	5
Header Block	8	10
Header Gap ($55)	8 *	8
Sync Character ($FF)	5 *	5
Data Block	260	325

* No binary to GCR conversion.

We deliberately excluded the inter-sector (tail) gap in calculating the number of bytes in a given sector. Why? Because the tail gap is never referenced again by the DOS once formatting is complete. During formatting the Floppy Disk Controller (FDC) erases a track by writing 10240 overlapping 8-bit $FFs. Once a track has been erased the FDC writes 2400 8-bit $FFs (%11111111) followed by 2400 8-bit $55s (%01010101). The intent is to wrap around the circumference of the track with a clearly discernable on/off pattern of bytes. The FDC then counts to see how many sync ($FF) and nonsync ($55) bytes were actually written to the track. From this count the FDC subtracts the total number of bytes that the entire range of sectors in a given zone will use. The remainder is then divided by the number of sectors in that zone to determine the size of the tail gap. The algorithm is analogous to cutting a pie. The tail gap varies not only between tracks due to a decrease in both circumference and the sector range but between disk drives as well, due to varying motor speeds. A stopgap measure is incorporated into the algorithm for the latter reason. If a tail gap is not computed to be at least four bytes in length formatting will fail and an error will be reported. In general, the length of the tail gaps fall into the ranges tabled below:

Zone	Tracks	Number of Sectors	Variable Tail Gap
1	1 - 17	21	4 - 7
2	18 - 24	19	9 - 12
3	25 - 30	18	5 - 8
4	31 - 35	17	4 - 8

Note that the values given above do not apply to the highest numbered sector on a track. The gap between this sector and sector 0 is usually much longer. We have seen tail gaps in excess of 100 bytes here.

Also note that a header block is never rewritten after formatting is complete. The data block of a sector, including the sync character, is completely rewritten every time data is written to that sector. The eight byte header gap is counted off by the DOS to determine where to start writing the data block.

7.2 Checksums

The only remaining concern we have at this time is how we compute a checksum. Unlike tape storage where a program file is recorded twice in succession, data is recorded on diskette only once. In other words, there is no cyclic redundancy. Checksum comes to the rescue. A single byte checksum or hashtotal is used by the DOS to determine whether or not an error occurred during a read of a header block or a data block. A checksum is derived by Exclusive-ORing (EOR) bytes together. Two bytes are EORed together at one time by comparing their respective bits. The four possible EOR bit combinations are shown in the following truth table.

EOR Truth Table

0 EOR 0 = 0
0 EOR 1 = 1
1 EOR 0 = 1
1 EOR 1 = 0

A header block checksum is the EOR of: the sector number, the track number, the ID LO, and the ID HI. (These four bytes serve to differentiate sectors from one another on a diskette.) A data block checksum is the EOR of all 256 8-bit data bytes in a sector. Recall that a data block normally consists of a forward track and sector pointer plus 254 data bytes. Please note that bytes are EORed by the DOS prior to their GCR conversion.

The following example demonstrates how a header block checksum is calculated. The algorithm for calculating a data block checksum is identical, only longer.

	Hexadecimal	Binary
Sector Number	$00 (0)	00000000
Track Number	$12 (18)	00010010
ID LO	$58 (88)	01011000
ID HI	$5A (90)	01011010

STEP 1. Initialization
        EOR $00 (0) With Sector Number

$$\begin{array}{r} \$00 = 00000000 \\ \text{Sector Number (\$00)} = \underline{00000000} \\ \\ 00000000 \end{array}$$

STEP 2. EOR With Track Number

$$\begin{array}{r} 00000000 \\ \text{Track Number (\$12)} = \underline{00010010} \\ \\ 00010010 \end{array}$$

STEP 3. EOR With ID LO

$$00010010$$
$$\text{ID LO (\$58)} = \underline{01011000}$$

$$01001010$$

STEP 4. EOR With ID HI

$$01001010$$
$$\text{ID HI (\$5A)} = \underline{01011010}$$

$$00010000$$

STEP 5. Binary to Hexadecimal Conversion

00010000

$10 (16)

The checksum for $00, $12, $58, and $5A is thus $10 (16). This checksum just happens
to be the header block checksum for track 18, sector 0 on the 1541TEST/DEMO. In addition, the binary to GCR conversion tour presented earlier was for the first four bytes
($08 $10 $00 $12) of the same header block.

7.3 Description of DOS Error Messages

In Chapter 6 we presented a table of FDC and IP error codes. The following table outlines
the order in which errors are evaluated by the DOS during a read and a write,
respectively.

READ ERRORS

FDC Job Request	FDC Error Code	IP Error Code	Error Message
SEEK	$03 (3)	21	No Sync Character
SEEK	$02 (2)	20	Header Block Not Found
SEEK	$09 (9)	27	Checksum Error in Header Block
SEEK	$0B (11)	29	Disk ID Mismatch
READ	$02 (2)	20	Header Block Not Found
READ	$04 (4)	22	Data Block Not Present
READ	$05 (5)	23	Checksum Error in Data Block
READ	$01 (1)	0	OK

WRITE ERRORS

FDC Job Request	FDC Error Code	IP Error Code	Error Message
WRITE	– –	73	DOS Mismatch
WRITE	$0B (11)	29	Disk ID Mismatch
WRITE	$08 (8)	26	Write Protect On
WRITE	$07 (7)	25	Write-Verify Error
VERIFY	$01 (1)	0	OK

Each error is described in greater detail below.

21 READ ERROR (NO SYNC CHARACTER)

The FDC could not find a sync mark (10 or more consecutive on bits) on a given track within a prescribed 20 millisecond time limit. A time out has occurred.

20 READ ERROR (HEADER BLOCK NOT FOUND)

The FDC could not find a GCR header block identifier ($52) after 90 attempts. The FDC did a seek to a track and found a sync character. The FDC then read the first GCR byte immediately following it. This GCR byte was compared against a GCR $52 ($08). The comparison failed and the try counter was decremented. The FDC waited for another sync character and tried again. Ninety attempts were made.

27 READ ERROR (CHECKSUM ERROR IN HEADER BLOCK)

The FDC found a header block on that track. This header block was read into RAM and the GCR bytes were converted back to their original binary form. The FDC then EORed the sector number, the track number, the ID LO, and the ID HI together. This independent checksum was EORed against the actual checksum found in the header block itself. If the result of the EOR was not equal zero, the checksums were not equal. The comparison failed and the FDC returned a $09 to the error handler.

29 READ ERROR (DISK ID MISMATCH)

The IDs recorded in the header block found above did not match the master copy of the disk id's stored in $0012 and $0013. These zero page memory addresses are normally updated from track 18 during initialization of a diskette. Note that they also can be updated by a seek to a track from the job queue.

20 READ ERROR (HEADER BLOCK NOT FOUND)

A GCR image of the header was created using the sector number, the track number, and the master disk IDs. The FDC attempted to find a header on this track that matched the GCR image in RAM for that sector. Ninety attempts were made before this error was reported.

22 READ ERROR (DATA BLOCK NOT PRESENT)

The header block for a given track and sector passed the previous five tests with flying colors. The FDC found the data block sync mark and read the next 325 GCR bytes into RAM. These GCR bytes were converted back into 260 8-bit binary bytes. The first decoded 8-bit byte was compared against a preset data block identifier at $0047 and failed to match. Note this zero page memory address normally contains a $07.

23 READ ERROR (CHECKSUM ERROR IN DATA BLOCK)

An independent checksum was calculated for the 256 byte data block converted above. This checksum did not match the actual checksum read from the diskette.

00, OK,00,00

Nothing wrong here.

73 DOS MISMATCH (CBM DOS V2.6 1541)

An attempt was made to write to a diskette with a non-compatible format. The DOS version stored at location $0101 was not a $41. This memory address is normally updated during initialization by reading byte 2 from track 18, sector 0.

29 READ ERROR (DISK ID MISMATCH)

Same as 29 READ ERROR above but conflicting id's were found during a write attempt rather than a read. Repeated occurrance of this error on a standard diskette is indicative of a seating problem or a slow-burning alignment problem.

26 WRITE PROTECT ON

An attempt was made to write to a diskette while the write protect switch is depressed. Remove the write protect tab from the write protect notch.

25 WRITE-VERIFY ERROR

The contents of the data just written to a sector did not match the data in RAM when they were read back. This was probably caused by a flaw on the surface of the diskette. The end result was an unclosed file. Validate the diskette to decorrupt the BAM. (See Chapter 2.)

00, OK,00,00

Looking good.

7.4 Analyzing a Protected Diskette

Bad sectoring is central to any disk protection scheme. In a nutshell, disk protection involves the deliberate corruption of a given track or sector. The authenticity of a diskette is often determined by a short loader program that reads the corrupted track or sector. In essence the FDC or IP error code is a password allowing access to the run time module. As a result the loader is extremely protected. If it can be cracked the program is generally freed from its bonds. This is easier said than done though. A loader is usually rendered indecipherable (Coda Obscura) through an autostart feature, the use of unimplemented 6502 op codes, encryption, or compilation. Frankly speaking, it's much easier to go after the whole disk. The following passages will introduce you to the black art of bit copying.

The appendix contains four routines written specifically to assist in the interrogation of a diskette. They are:

1. Interrogate Formatting IDs
2. Interrogate a Track
3. Shake, Rattle, and Roll
4. Interrogate a Diskette

These four programs tend to complement one another quite well in actual use. Their uses and limitations are discussed below.

INTERROGATE FORMATTING ID'S returns the embedded disk ID for each track using a SEEK. Recall that working the job queue prevents the dreaded BUMP. A seek to a track is deemed successful by the FDC if at least one intact sector can be found. The header of said sector is stored in zero page from $0016–$001A. The ASCII equivalents of the ID HI ($0016) and ID LO ($0017) are read and printed to the CRT if the SEEK was good. At a glance one can determine if a protected diskette has a blown track or if it has been formatted with multiple ID's. This latter scheme is less commonly used to date. This program will not report the integrity of each individual sector. We have other routines for that task.

There is one severe drawback to this program as it stands. Occasionally the FDC gets hung up on a track. The SEEK may continue to attempt to find a sync mark without timing out. (You must power off the 1541 to recover from this situation.) Experimentation in interrogating unformatted diskettes has produced the same effect. We surmise that the track in question was passed over during high-speed duplication. The FDC may in fact be homing in on a residual bit pattern left over from the manufacturer's certification process. The program has a built-in fail-safe mechanism for this very reason. Please take note: Lines 110-140 establish an active track array. All tracks are presumed active at the onset (line 130). Line 240 tests the integrity of the track prior to a seek. If a track is inactive (its flag equals 0) the track is bypassed and the program will work from start to finish. Should the need arise simply patch in a line that reads:

145 T(track number)=0

145 T(17)=0, for example.

If it's any comfort at all, a loader cannot check the integrity of said track either. The sole function of such a track is to discourage prying eyes.

122

INTERROGATE A TRACK scans a single track using the job queue. The track is found with a SEEK and then the integrity of each sector is verified with a READ. IP error codes are returned to the screen. No BUMP occurs. The routine may occasionally provide erroneous information. This is a major shortcoming of a READ from the queue. Certain errors are returned clean as a whistle (22, 23, 27). A partially formatted track (mid-track 21 error) or a smattering of 20 errors tend to throw the FDC into an absolute tizzy. Make note of this. Repeated runs of the same track often return a different error pattern. Errors tend to accumulate when a BUMP is overridden. Solution? See the following paragraph.

SHAKE, RATTLE, AND ROLL also scans a single track by using a U1 command rather than a direct READ from the job queue. The track is still found by a SEEK, however, to prevent 29 errors in the event that multiple formatting played a part in the protection scheme. A 29 error is not an error *per se*. It is merely a stumbling block. A U1 without a SEEK to a multiple-formatted diskette will report a DISK ID MISMATCH. Information can be stored on a track with a different ID. A loader will retrieve it by the same method we're using here. Errors will force a BUMP so use discretion. Please note that a full track of 21 errors, 23 errors, or 27 errors does not need to be read with this routine. After you analyze a track, write the errors down and file your notes away for archival needs. Your 1541 will love you for it.

INTERROGATE A DISKETTE is the lazy man's routine. It scans an entire diskette reporting only bad sectors to the screen. The program is essentially INTERROGATE A TRACK in a loop. Note that you may have to patch around a track to map the entire diskette. See the example patch above.

7.5 Duplicating a Protection Scheme

The following table represents the state of the error. The rank order in which errors tend to crop up on copy protected diskettes are as follows:

1. 21 ERROR (FULL TRACK)
2. 23 ERROR (SINGLE SECTOR)
3. 23 ERROR (FULL TRACK)
4. 20 ERROR (SINGLE SECTOR)
5. 27 ERROR (FULL TRACK)
6. 29 ERROR (MULTIPLE FORMATTING)
7. 22 ERROR (SINGLE SECTOR)
8. 21 ERROR (PARTIAL TRACK)

Historically speaking, the 21 error (full track) and the 29 error appeared on the scene concurrently. At the present time, a full track 21 error and a single sector 23 error are the predominant errors used to corrupt a diskette. These same two errors are also the easiest to duplicate. The last entry, partial formatting of a track, is the new kid on the block.

The following 13 programs can be used to duplicate a multitude of errors on a diskette. They are:

File Name	Error Number	Error Range
21 ERROR	21	FULL TRACK
DESTROY A SECTOR	20, 21	SINGLE SECTOR
23A ERROR	23	SINGLE SECTOR
23B ERROR	23	*SINGLE SECTOR
23M ERROR	23	FULL TRACK
20 ERROR	20	SINGLE SECTOR
20M ERROR	20	FULL TRACK
27M ERROR	27	FULL TRACK
22A ERROR	22	SINGLE SECTOR
22B ERROR	22	*SINGLE SECTOR
FORMAT A DISKETTE	29	MULTIPLE FORMATTING ID'S
BACKUP	—	SINGLE DRIVE BACKUP
COPY	—	SINGLE FILE COPY

* Creates an exact duplicate of a bad sector.

Source listings for the machine language routines in these programs are included as a courtesy to the more advanced reader. The BASIC drivers themselves are nondescript and will not be explained in depth. It is assummed that the reader has digested the sections on beginning and intermediate direct-access programming in Chapters 5 and 6. Algorithms will be briefly mentioned along with any new techniques and/or limitations that apply.

7.6 How to Create 21 Errors on a Full Track

Limitations: None.

Parameters: Track number.

FULL TRACK 21 ERROR

```
100 REM 21 ERROR - 1541
110 PRINT"{CLR}21 ERROR - 1541"
120 PRINT"{DOWN}INSERT CLONE IN DRIVE"
130 INPUT"{DOWN}DESTROY TRACK";T
140 IFT<10RT>35THENEND
150 INPUT"{DOWN}ARE YOU SURE  Y{LEFT 3}"
;Q$
160 IFQ$<>"Y"THENEND
170 OPEN15,8,15
180 PRINT#15,"I0"
```

```
190 INPUT#15,EN$,EM$,ET$,ES$
200 IFEN$="00"GOTO250
210 PRINT"{DOWN}"EN$", "EM$", "ET$", "ES$
220 CLOSE15
230 END
240 REM SEEK
250 JOB=176
260 GOSUB400
270 FORI=0TO23
280 READD
290 D$=D$+CHR$(D)
300 NEXTI
310 PRINT#15,"M-W"CHR$(0)CHR$(4)CHR$(24)
D$
320 REM EXECUTE
330 PRINT"{DOWN}{RVS}DESTROYING{ROFF} TR
ACK";T
340 JOB=224
350 GOSUB400
360 PRINT"{DOWN}DONE!"
370 CLOSE15
380 END
390 REM JOB QUEUE
400 TRY=0
410 PRINT#15,"M-W"CHR$(8)CHR$(0)CHR$(2)C
HR$(T)CHR$(0)
420 PRINT#15,"M-W"CHR$(1)CHR$(0)CHR$(1)C
HR$(JOB)
430 TRY=TRY+1
440 PRINT#15,"M-R"CHR$(1)CHR$(0)
450 GET#15,E$
460 IFE$=""THENE$=CHR$(0)
470 E=ASC(E$)
480 IFTRY=500GOTO510
490 IFE>127GOTO430
500 RETURN
510 CLOSE15
520 PRINT"{DOWN}{RVS}FAILED{ROFF}"
530 END
540 REM 21 ERROR
550 DATA  32,163,253,169, 85,141,  1, 28

560 DATA 162,255,160, 48, 32,201,253, 32

570 DATA   0,254,169,  1, 76,105,249,234
```

```
100 REM 21.PAL
110 REM
120 OPEN2,8,2,"@0:21.B,P,W"
130 REM
140 SYS40960
150 ;
160 .OPT P,02
170 ;
180 *= $0500
190 ;
200 JSR $FDA3 ; ENABLE WRITE
210 LDA #$55  ; NON SYNC BYTE
220 STA $1C01
230 LDX #$FF
240 LDY #$48
250 JSR $FDC9 ; WRITE 18432 NON SYNC BYT
ES
260 JSR $FE00 ; ENABLE READ
270 LDA #$01
280 JMP $F969
```

Full Track 21 Error Source Annotation

This routine borrows from FORMT ($FAC7). Prior to formatting a track, the FDC erases it with sync marks ($FDA3). Experimentation has shown that an RTS from this ROM entry point would create a track of all 20 errors. Thus we are forced to trace the FORMT routine a little farther. The subroutine WRTNUM ($FDC3) writes either sync or non-sync bytes. By entering six bytes into this routine we can establish the number of bytes it writes. A JSR to $FE00 is necessary to re-enable read mode. Otherwise the write head is left on and it will erase everything in its path. Note that we LDA #$01, the FDC error code for OK, and JMP to the error handler at $F969 to exit.

7.7 How to Create a 21 Error on a Single Sector

Limitations: Preceding sector must be intact (See the annotation below).

Parameters: Track and sector number.

DESTROY A SECTOR

```
100 REM DESTROY A SECTOR - 1541
110 DIMD$(7)
120 PRINT"{CLR}DESTROY A SECTOR - 1541"
130 PRINT"{DOWN}INSERT CLONE IN DRIVE"
140 INPUT"{DOWN}DESTROY TRACK AND SECTOR
  (T,S)";T,S
150 IFT<1ORT>35THENEND
```

```
160 NS=20+2*(T>17)+(T>24)+(T>30)
170 IFS<0ORS>NSTHENEND
180 INPUT"{DOWN}ARE YOU SURE  Y{LEFT 3}"
;Q$
190 IFQ$<>"Y"THENEND
200 OPEN15,8,15
210 PRINT#15,"I0"
220 INPUT#15,EN$,EM$,ET$,ES$
230 IFEN$="00"GOTO280
240 PRINT"{DOWN}"EN$","EM$","ET$","ES$
250 CLOSE15
260 END
270 REM SEEK
280 IFS=0THENS=NS:GOTO300
290 S=S-1
300 JOB=176
310 GOSUB570
320 REM READ
330 JOB=128
340 GOSUB570
350 FORJ=0TO7
360 FORI=0TO7
370 READD
380 D$(J)=D$(J)+CHR$(D)
390 NEXTI
400 NEXTJ
410 I=0
420 FORJ=0TO7
430 PRINT#15,"M-W"CHR$(I)CHR$(5)CHR$(8)D
$(J)
440 I=I+8
450 NEXTJ
460 REM EXECUTE
470 PRINT#15,"M-W"CHR$(2)CHR$(0)CHR$(1)C
HR$(224)
480 PRINT#15,"M-R"CHR$(2)CHR$(0)
490 GET#15,E$
500 IFE$=""THENE$=CHR$(0)
510 E=ASC(E$)
520 IFE>127GOTO480
530 CLOSE15
540 PRINT"{DOWN}DONE!"
550 END
560 REM JOB QUEUE
570 TRY=0
580 PRINT#15,"M-W"CHR$(8)CHR$(0)CHR$(4)C
HR$(T)CHR$(S)CHR$(T)CHR$(S)
590 PRINT#15,"M-W"CHR$(1)CHR$(0)CHR$(1)C
HR$(JOB)
600 TRY=TRY+1
```

```
610 PRINT#15, "M-R"CHR$(1)CHR$(0)
620 GET#15, E$
630 IFE$=""THENE$=CHR$(0)
640 E=ASC(E$)
650 IFTRY=500GOTO680
660 IFE>127GOTO600
670 IFE=1THENRETURN
680 CLOSE15
690 PRINT"{DOWN}{RVS}FAILED{ROFF}"
700 END
710 REM DESTROY A SECTOR
720 DATA 32, 16,245, 32, 86,245,162,  0
730 DATA 80,254,184,202,208,250,162, 69
740 DATA 80,254,184,202,208,250,169,255
750 DATA141,  3, 28,173, 12, 28, 41, 31
760 DATA  9,192,141, 12, 28,162,  0,169
770 DATA 85, 80,254,184,141,  1, 28,202
780 DATA208,247, 80,254, 32,  0,254,169
790 DATA  1, 76,105,249,234,234,234,234
```

SINGLE SECTOR 21 ERROR SOURCE LISTING

```
100 REM DAS.PAL
110 REM
120 OPEN2,8,2,"@0:DAS.B,P,W"
130 REM
140 SYS40960
150 ;
160 .OPT P,O2
170 ;
180 *= $0500
190 ;
200 JSR $F510 ; FIND HEADER
210 JSR $F556 ; FIND SYNC
220 ;
230 ;* WAIT OUT DATA *
240 ;
250 LDX #$00
260 READ1 BVC READ1
270 CLV
280 DEX
290 BNE READ1
300 ;
310 LDX #$45
320 READ2 BVC READ2
330 CLV
340 DEX
350 BNE READ2
360 ;
370 LDA #$FF ; DATA DIRECTION OUT
```

```
380 STA $1C03
390 LDA $1C0C; ENABLE WRITE MODE
400 AND #$1F
410 ORA #$C0
420 STA $1C0C
430 ;
440 LDX #$00
450 LDA #$55
460 WRITE1 BVC WRITE1
470 CLV
480 STA $1C01
490 DEX
500 BNE WRITE1
510 ;
520 WRITE2 BVC WRITE2
530 ;
540 JSR $FE00 ; ENABLE READ MODE
550 ;
560 LDA #$01
570 JMP $F969
```

Single Sector 21 Error Source Annotation

This routine finds the preceding sector and syncs up to its data block (lines 200-210). Lines 250-350 wait out 325 GCR bytes. We flip to write in lines 370-420 and write out 256 non-sync bytes. This overwrites both sync marks of the sector that was input. This routine will create a 20 error on a single sector as it stands. By serendipity, it has a unique side effect. If two consecutive sectors are destroyed we get a 21 error on both of them. The FDC times out trying to find one or the other or both. Caution must be used when spanning a sector range. To duplicate the following scheme we must destroy sector 0 first followed by sectors 20, 19, and 18 respectively.

Sector	Error Number
0	21
1 - 17	OK
18 - 20	21

Repeat. This routine will not create a 21 error on a single sector *per se*. Two consecutive sectors must be destroyed.

7.8 How to Create a 23 Error on a Single Sector

Limitations: None.

Parameters: Track and sector number.

```
100 REM 23A ERROR - 1541
110 DIMD$(11)
120 PRINT"{CLR}23 ERROR - 1541"
130 PRINT"{DOWN}INSERT CLONE IN DRIVE"
140 INPUT"{DOWN}DESTROY TRACK AND SECTOR
 (T,S)";T,S
150 IFT<10RT>35THENEND
160 NS=20+2*(T>17)+(T>24)+(T>30)
170 IFS<00RS>NSTHENEND
180 INPUT"{DOWN}ARE YOU SURE   Y{LEFT 3}"
;Q$
190 IFQ$<>"Y"THENEND
200 OPEN15,8,15
210 PRINT#15,"IO"
220 INPUT#15,EN$,EM$,ET$,ES$
230 IFEN$="00"GOTO280
240 PRINT"{DOWN}"EN$", "EM$","ET$","ES$
250 CLOSE15
260 END
270 REM SEEK
280 JOB=176
290 GOSUB550
300 REM READ
310 JOB=128
320 GOSUB550
330 FORJ=OTO11
340 FORI=OTO7
350 READD
360 D$(J)=D$(J)+CHR$(D)
370 NEXTI
380 NEXTJ
390 I=0
400 FORJ=OTO11
410 PRINT#15,"M-W"CHR$(I)CHR$(5)CHR$(8)D
$(J)
420 I=I+8
430 NEXTJ
440 REM EXECUTE
450 PRINT#15,"M-W"CHR$(2)CHR$(0)CHR$(1)C
HR$(224)
460 PRINT#15,"M-R"CHR$(2)CHR$(0)
470 GET#15,E$
480 IFE$=""THENE$=CHR$(0)
490 E=ASC(E$)
500 IFE>127GOTO460
510 CLOSE15
520 PRINT"{DOWN}DONE!"
530 END
```

```
540 REM JOB QUEUE
550 TRY=0
560 PRINT#15,"M-W"CHR$(8)CHR$(0)CHR$(4)C
HR$(T)CHR$(S)CHR$(T)CHR$(S)
570 PRINT#15,"M-W"CHR$(1)CHR$(0)CHR$(1)C
HR$(JOB)
580 TRY=TRY+1
590 PRINT#15,"M-R"CHR$(1)CHR$(0)
600 GET#15,E$
610 IFE$=""THENE$=CHR$(0)
620 E=ASC(E$)
630 IFTRY=500GOTO660
640 IFE>127GOTO580
650 RETURN
660 CLOSE15
670 PRINT"{DOWN}{RVS}FAILED{ROFF}"
680 END
690 REM 23 ERROR
700 DATA 169,  4,133, 49,165, 58,170,232

710 DATA 138,133, 58, 32,143,247, 32, 16

720 DATA 245,162,  8, 80,254,184,202,208

730 DATA 250,169,255,141,  3, 28,173, 12

740 DATA  28, 41, 31,  9,192,141, 12, 28

750 DATA 169,255,162,  5,141,  1, 28,184

760 DATA  80,254,184,202,208,250,160,187

770 DATA 185,  0,  1, 80,254,184,141,  1

780 DATA  28,200,208,244,185,  0,  4, 80

790 DATA 254,184,141,  1, 28,200,208,244

800 DATA  80,254, 32,  0,254,169,  5,133

810 DATA  49,169,  1, 76,105,249,234,234
```

SINGLE SECTOR 23 ERROR SOURCE LISTING

```
100 REM 23A.PAL
110 REM
120 OPEN2,8,2,"@0:23A.B,P,W"
130 REM
140 SYS40960
150 ;
```

```
160 .OPT P,02
170 ;
180 *= $0500
190 ;
200 LDA #$04
210 STA $31
220 ;
230 LDA $3A
240 TAX
250 INX                        ; INCREMENT
CHECKSUM
260 TXA
270 STA $3A
280 ;
290 JSR $F78F                  ; CONVERT TO
 GCR
300 JSR $F510                  ; FIND HEADER
#
310 ;
320 LDX #$08
330 WAITGAP BVC WAITGAP        ; WAIT OUT G
AP
340 CLV
350 DEX
360 BNE WAITGAP
370 ;
380 LDA #$FF                   ; ENABLE WRI
TE
390 STA $1C03
400 LDA $1C0C
410 AND #$1F
420 ORA #$C0
430 STA $1C0C
440 LDA #$FF
450 LDX #$05
460 STA $1C01
470 CLV
480 WRITESYNC BVC WRITESYNC
490 CLV
500 DEX
510 BNE WRITESYNC
520 ;
530 LDY #$BB
540 OVERFLOW LDA $0100,Y       ; WRITE OUT
OVERFLOW BUFFER
550 WAIT1 BVC WAIT1
560 CLV
570 STA $1C01
580 INY
590 BNE OVERFLOW
```

```
600 BUFFER LDA $0400,Y        ; WRITE OUT
BUFFER
610 WAIT2 BVC WAIT2
620 CLV
630 STA $1C01
640 INY
650 BNE BUFFER
660 WAIT3 BVC WAIT3
670 ;
680 JSR $FE00                 ; ENABLE REA
D
690 ;
700 LDA #$05
710 STA $31
720 LDA #$01
730 JMP $F969
```

Single Sector 23 Error Source Annotation

This routine borrows from WRIGHT ($F56E). Our entry point is 12 bytes into the routine. This bypasses the write protect test and the computation of the checksum. The driver routine reads the sector into $0400-$04FF. Lines 200-210 of the source listing set the indirect buffer pointer to this workspace. The checksum is next incremented at $003A. Buffer number 1 is converted to GCR form. Recall that 260 data bytes are converted into 325 8-bit GCR bytes. More than one buffer is used to store the GCR image. The first 69 GCR bytes are stored in an overflow buffer at $01BB-$01FF. The remaining 256 bytes are found at $0400-$04FF. We sync up to the appropriate sector in line 300, count off the eight byte header gap, and flip to write mode. Five $FFs are then written to disk (the sync mark) followed first by the overflow buffer and then the regular buffer. We restore the indirect buffer pointer at $0031 to a $05 and jump to the error handler with a $01 in hand.

7.9 How to Duplicate a 23 Error on a Single Sector

Limitations: None (Requires disk swapping).

Parameters: Track and sector number.

DUPLICATE A SINGLE SECTOR 23 ERROR

```
100 REM DUPLICATE A 23 ERROR - 1541
110 DIMD$(10)
120 PRINT"{CLR}DUPLICATE A 23 ERROR - 15
41"
130 PRINT"{DOWN}INSERT MASTER DISKETTE I
N DRIVE"
140 INPUT"{DOWN}READ TRACK AND SECTOR (T
,S)";T,S
150 IFT<10RT>35THENEND
```

```
160 NS=20+2*(T>17)+(T>24)+(T>30)
170 IFS<0ORS>NSTHENEND
180 INPUT"{DOWN}ARE YOU SURE   Y{LEFT 3}"
;Q$
190 IFQ$<>"Y"THENEND
200 OPEN15,8,15
210 PRINT#15,"IO"
220 INPUT#15,EN$,EM$,ET$,ES$
230 IFEN$="00"GOTO280
240 PRINT"{DOWN}"EN$,  "EM$","ET$","ES$
250 CLOSE15
260 END
270 REM SEEK
280 JOB=176
290 GOSUB650
300 REM READ
310 JOB=128
320 GOSUB650
330 CLOSE15
340 PRINT"{DOWN}INSERT CLONE IN DRIVE"
350 PRINT"{DOWN}PRESS {RVS}RETURN{ROFF}
TO CONTINUE"
360 GETC$:IFC$=""THEN360
370 IFC$<>CHR$(13)GOTO360
380 PRINT"OK"
390 OPEN15,8,15
400 REM SEEK
410 JOB=176
420 GOSUB650
430 FORJ=0TO10
440 FORI=0TO7
450 READD
460 D$(J)=D$(J)+CHR$(D)
470 NEXTI
480 NEXTJ
490 I=0
500 FORJ=0TO10
510 PRINT#15,"M-W"CHR$(I)CHR$(5)CHR$(8)D
$(J)
520 I=I+8
530 NEXTJ
540 REM EXECUTE
550 PRINT#15,"M-W"CHR$(2)CHR$(0)CHR$(1)C
HR$(224)
560 PRINT#15,"M-R"CHR$(2)CHR$(0)
570 GET#15,E$
580 IFE$=""THENE$=CHR$(0)
590 E=ASC(E$)
600 IFE>127GOTO560
610 CLOSE15
```

```
620 PRINT"{DOWN}DONE!"
630 END
640 REM JOB QUEUE
650 TRY=0
660 PRINT#15,"M-W"CHR$(8)CHR$(0)CHR$(4)C
HR$(T)CHR$(S)CHR$(T)CHR$(S)
670 PRINT#15,"M-W"CHR$(1)CHR$(0)CHR$(1)C
HR$(JOB)
680 TRY=TRY+1
690 PRINT#15,"M-R"CHR$(1)CHR$(0)
700 GET#15,E$
710 IFE$=""THENE$=CHR$(0)
720 E=ASC(E$)
730 IFTRY=500GOTO760
740 IFE>127GOTO680
750 RETURN
760 PRINT"{DOWN}FAILED"
770 CLOSE15
780 END
790 REM DUPLICATE A SECTOR
800 DATA 169,   4,133, 49, 32,143,247, 32

810 DATA  16,245,162,  8, 80,254,184,202

820 DATA 208,250,169,255,141,  3, 28,173

830 DATA  12, 28, 41, 31,  9,192,141, 12

840 DATA  28,169,255,162,  5,141,  1, 28

850 DATA 184, 80,254,184,202,208,250,160

860 DATA 187,185,  0,  1, 80,254,184,141

870 DATA   1, 28,200,208,244,185,  0,  4

880 DATA  80,254,184,141,  1, 28,200,208

890 DATA 244, 80,254, 32,  0,254,169,  5

900 DATA 133, 49,169,  1, 76,105,249,234
```

DUPLICATE A SINGLE SECTOR 23 ERROR SOURCE LISTING

```
100 REM 23B.PAL
110 REM
120 OPEN2,8,2,"@0:23B.B,P,W"
130 REM
140 SYS40960
150 ;
```

```
160 .OPT P,02
170 ;
180 *= $0500
190 ;
200 LDA #$04
210 STA $31
220 ;
230 JSR $F78F                    ; CONVERT TO
  GCR
240 JSR $F510                    ; FIND HEADER
#
250 ;
260 LDX #$08
270 WAITGAP BVC WAITGAP          ; WAIT OUT G
AP
280 CLV
290 DEX
300 BNE WAITGAP
310 ;
320 LDA #$FF                     ; ENABLE WRI
TE
330 STA $1C03
340 LDA $1C0C
350 AND #$1F
360 ORA #$C0
370 STA $1C0C
380 LDA #$FF
390 LDX #$05
400 STA $1C01
410 CLV
420 WRITESYNC BVC WRITESYNC
430 CLV
440 DEX
450 BNE WRITESYNC
460 ;
470 LDY #$BB
480 OVERFLOW LDA $0100,Y         ; WRITE OUT
OVERFLOW BUFFER
490 WAIT1 BVC WAIT1
500 CLV
510 STA $1C01
520 INY
530 BNE OVERFLOW
540 BUFFER LDA $0400,Y           ; WRITE OUT
BUFFER
550 WAIT2 BVC WAIT2
560 CLV
570 STA $1C01
580 INY
590 BNE BUFFER
```

136

```
600 WAIT3 BVC WAIT3
610 ;
620 JSR $FE00                          ; ENABLE REA
D
630 ;
640 LDA #$05
650 STA $31
660 LDA #$01
670 JMP $F969
```

Duplicate a Single Sector 23 Error Source Annotation

Identical to the 23A.PAL file with one exception. The checksum is left intact after a
corrupted data block is read from the master using the job queue. The sector is stored
at $0400-$04FF and the checksum at $003A. The checksum is not recalculated or in-
cremented. The entire sector and its checksum are rewritten to the clone.

7.10 How to Create 23 Errors on a Full Track

Limitations: None.

Parameters: Track number.

FULL TRACK 23 ERROR

```
100 REM 23M ERROR - 1541
110 DIMD$(11)
120 PRINT"{CLR}MULTIPLE 23 ERROR - 1541"

130 PRINT"{DOWN}INSERT CLONE IN DRIVE"
140 INPUT"{DOWN}DESTROY TRACK";T
150 IFT<1ORT>35THENEND
160 INPUT"{DOWN}ARE YOU SURE  Y{LEFT 3}"
;Q$
170 IFQ$<>"Y"THENEND
180 OPEN15,8,15
190 PRINT#15,"IO"
200 INPUT#15,EN$,EM$,ET$,ES$
210 IFEN$="00"GOTO260
220 PRINT"{DOWN}"EN$", "EM$","ET$","ES$
230 CLOSE15
240 END
250 REM SEEK
260 JOB=176
270 GOSUB580
280 NS=20+2*(T>17)+(T>24)+(T>30)
290 FORS=0TONS
300 REM READ
310 JOB=128
```

```
320 GOSUB580
330 IFS>0GOTO460
340 FORJ=0TO11
350 FORI=0TO7
360 READD
370 D$(J)=D$(J)+CHR$(D)
380 NEXTI
390 NEXTJ
400 I=0
410 FORJ=0TO11
420 PRINT#15,"M-W"CHR$(I)CHR$(5)CHR$(8)D
$(J)
430 I=I+8
440 NEXTJ
450 REM EXECUTE
460 PRINT"{HOME}{DOWN 8}{RVS}DESTROYING{
ROFF} TRACK"T"- SECTOR"S
470 PRINT#15,"M-W"CHR$(2)CHR$(0)CHR$(1)C
HR$(224)
480 PRINT#15,"M-R"CHR$(2)CHR$(0)
490 GET#15,E$
500 IFE$=""THENE$=CHR$(0)
510 E=ASC(E$)
520 IFE>127GOTO480
530 NEXTS
540 CLOSE15
550 PRINT"{HOME}{DOWN 8}DONE!
         "
560 END
570 REM JOB QUEUE
580 TRY=0
590 PRINT#15,"M-W"CHR$(8)CHR$(0)CHR$(4)C
HR$(T)CHR$(S)CHR$(T)CHR$(S)
600 PRINT#15,"M-W"CHR$(1)CHR$(0)CHR$(1)C
HR$(JOB)
610 TRY=TRY+1
620 PRINT#15,"M-R"CHR$(1)CHR$(0)
630 GET#15,E$
640 IFE$=""THENE$=CHR$(0)
650 E=ASC(E$)
660 IFTRY=500GOTO690
670 IFE>127GOTO610
680 RETURN
690 CLOSE15
700 PRINT"{DOWN}{RVS}FAILED{ROFF}"
710 END
720 REM 23 ERROR
730 DATA 169,   4,133, 49,165, 58,170,232

740 DATA 138,133, 58, 32,143,247, 32, 16
```

```
750 DATA 245,162,  8, 80,254,184,202,208

760 DATA 250,169,255,141,  3, 28,173, 12

770 DATA  28, 41, 31,  9,192,141, 12, 28

780 DATA 169,255,162,  5,141,  1, 28,184

790 DATA  80,254,184,202,208,250,160,187

800 DATA 185,  0,  1, 80,254,184,141,  1

810 DATA  28,200,208,244,185,  0,  4, 80

820 DATA 254,184,141,  1, 28,200,208,244

830 DATA  80,254, 32,  0,254,169,  5,133

840 DATA  49,169,  1,133,  2, 76,117,249
```

FULL TRACK 23 ERROR SOURCE LISTING

```
100 REM 23M.PAL
110 REM
120 OPEN2,8,2,"@0:23M.B,P,W"
130 REM
140 SYS40960
150 ;
160 .OPT P,02
170 ;
180 *= $0500
190 ;
200 LDA #$04
210 STA $31
220 ;
230 LDA $3A
240 TAX
250 INX                    ; INCREMENT CHE
CKSUM
260 TXA
270 STA $3A
280 ;
290 JSR $F78F              ; CONVERT TO GC
R
300 JSR $F510              ; FIND HEADER
310 ;
320 LDX #$08
330 WAITGAP BVC WAITGAP    ; WAIT OUT GAP
340 CLV
350 DEX
```

```
360 BNE WAITGAP
370 ;
380 LDA #$FF                    ; ENABLE WRITE
390 STA $1C03
400 LDA $1C0C
410 AND #$1F
420 ORA #$C0
430 STA $1C0C
440 LDA #$FF
450 LDX #$05
460 STA $1C01
470 CLV
480 WRITESYNC BVC WRITESYNC
490 CLV
500 DEX
510 BNE WRITESYNC
520 ;
530 LDY #$BB
540 OVERFLOW LDA $0100,Y ; WRITE OUT OVE
RFLOW BUFFER
550 WAIT1 BVC WAIT1
560 CLV
570 STA $1C01
580 INY
590 BNE OVERFLOW
600 BUFFER LDA $0400,Y     ; WRITE OUT BUF
FER
610 WAIT2 BVC WAIT2
620 CLV
630 STA $1C01
640 INY
650 BNE BUFFER
660 WAIT3 BVC WAIT3
670 ;
680 JSR $FE00                   ; ENABLE READ
690 ;
700 LDA #$05
710 STA $31
720 LDA #$01
730 STA $02
740 JMP $F975
```

Full Track 23 Error Source Annotation

See the annotation for 23A.PAL. The BASIC driver loops to do all sectors on a given track.

7.11 How to Create a 20 Error on a Single Sector

Limitations: Preceding sector must be intact.
         (See the annotation for a single sector 21 error)

Parameters: Track and sector number.

SINGLE SECTOR 20 ERROR

```
100 REM 20 ERROR - 1541
110 DIMD$(11)
120 PRINT"{CLR}20 ERROR - 1541"
130 PRINT"{DOWN}INSERT CLONE IN DRIVE"
140 INPUT"{DOWN}DESTROY TRACK AND SECTOR
 (T,S)";T,S
150 IFT<1ORT>35THENEND
160 NS=20+2*(T>17)+(T>24)+(T>30)
170 IFS<0ORS>NSTHENEND
180 INPUT"{DOWN}ARE YOU SURE   Y{LEFT 3}"
;Q$
190 IFQ$<>"Y"THENEND
200 OPEN15,8,15
210 PRINT#15,"IO"
220 INPUT#15,EN$,EM$,ET$,ES$
230 IFEN$="00"GOTO280
240 PRINT"{DOWN}"EN$,  "EM$","ET$","ES$
250 CLOSE15
260 END
270 REM SEEK
280 IFS=0THENS=NS:GOTO300
290 S=S-1
300 JOB=176
310 GOSUB570
320 REM READ
330 JOB=128
340 GOSUB570
350 FORJ=0TO11
360 FORI=0TO7
370 READD
380 D$(J)=D$(J)+CHR$(D)
390 NEXTI
400 NEXTJ
410 I=0
420 FORJ=0TO11
430 PRINT#15,"M-W"CHR$(I)CHR$(5)CHR$(8)D
$(J)
440 I=I+8
450 NEXTJ
460 REM EXECUTE
470 PRINT#15,"M-W"CHR$(2)CHR$(0)CHR$(1)C
HR$(224)
```

```
480 PRINT#15,"M-R"CHR$(2)CHR$(0)
490 GET#15,E$
500 IFE$=""THENE$=CHR$(0)
510 E=ASC(E$)
520 IFE>127GOTO480
530 CLOSE15
540 PRINT"{DOWN}DONE!"
550 END
560 REM JOB QUEUE
570 TRY=0
580 PRINT#15,"M-W"CHR$(8)CHR$(0)CHR$(4)C
HR$(T)CHR$(S)CHR$(T)CHR$(S)
590 PRINT#15,"M-W"CHR$(1)CHR$(0)CHR$(1)C
HR$(JOB)
600 TRY=TRY+1
610 PRINT#15,"M-R"CHR$(1)CHR$(0)
620 GET#15,E$
630 IFE$=""THENE$=CHR$(0)
640 E=ASC(E$)
650 IFTRY=500GOTO680
660 IFE>127GOTO600
670 IFE=1THENRETURN
680 CLOSE15
690 PRINT"{DOWN}{RVS}FAILED{ROFF}"
700 END
710 REM 20 ERROR
720 DATA   32, 16,245, 32, 86,245,160, 20

730 DATA  165, 25,201, 18,144, 12,136,136

740 DATA  201, 25,144,  6,136,201, 31,144

750 DATA    1,136,230, 24,197, 24,144,  6

760 DATA  240,  4,169,  0,133, 25,169,  0

770 DATA   69, 22, 69, 23, 69, 24, 69, 25

780 DATA  133, 26, 32, 52,249, 32, 86,245

790 DATA  169,255,141,  3, 28,173, 12, 28

800 DATA   41, 31,  9,192,141, 12, 28,162

810 DATA    0,181, 36, 80,254,184,141,  1

820 DATA   28,232,224,  8,208,243, 80,254

830 DATA   32,  0,254,169,  1, 76,105,249
```

SINGLE SECTOR 20 ERROR SOURCE LISTING

```
100 REM 20.PAL
110 REM
120 OPEN2,8,2,"@0:20.B,P,W"
130 REM
140 SYS40960
150 ;
160 .OPT P,02
170 ;
180 *= $0500
190 ;
200 JSR $F510              ; FIND HEADER BLOC
K
210 JSR $F556              ; FIND DATA BLOCK
220 ;
230 LDY #$14
240 LDA $19
250 CMP ##$12
260 BCC ZONE
270 DEY
280 DEY
290 CMP ##$19
300 BCC ZONE
310 DEY
320 CMP ##$1F
330 BCC ZONE
340 DEY
350 ZONE INC $18
360 CMP $18
370 BCC HEADER
380 BEQ HEADER
390 LDA #$00
400 STA $19
410 ;
420 HEADER LDA #$00
430 EOR $16
440 EOR $17
450 EOR $18
460 EOR $19
470 STA $1A
480 ;
490 JSR $F934              ; CREATE NEW HEADER
# IMAGE
500 JSR $F556              ; FIND HEADER BLOC
K
510 LDA ##$FF              ; WRITE MODE
520 STA $1C03
530 LDA $1C0C
540 AND ##$1F
```

143

```
550 ORA #$CO
560 STA $1COC
570 LDX #$00
580 WRITE LDA $0024,X
590 WAIT1 BVC WAIT1
600 CLV
610 STA $1C01
620 INX
630 CPX #$08
640 BNE WRITE
650 WAIT2 BVC WAIT2
660 ;
670 JSR $FE00          ; READ MODE
680 ;
690 LDA #$01
700 JMP $F969
```

Single Sector 20 Error Source Annotation

This routine represents a halfhearted attempt to rewrite a header. It is dependent upon the preceding sector being intact. Lines 200-210 sync up to the preceding header and data block. Lines 230-400 calculate the next sector in the zone. A header image for the sector is created in RAM at $0024-$002C. We sync up one more time which positions us to the start of the header block we want to destroy. We flip to write mode and rewrite the header. We are coming in just a shade too slow and create enough noise at the end of the sync mark to destroy the actual header block identifier. (Tweaking the internal clock reveals that the header was completely rewritten.) If the tail gap was a constant length our task would be analogous to rewriting a sector where the FDC syncs up to a header block, reads the header, and counts off eight bytes. We would similarly sync up to a data block, count off 325 GCR bytes, then count off the tail gap, and flip to write mode. However, it is virtually impossible to gauge the length of the tail gap, so we're stuck. Rest assured, though. It still gets the job done.

7.12 How to Create 20 Errors on a Full Track

Limitations: None.

Parameters: Track number.

FULL TRACK 20 ERROR

```
100 REM 20M ERROR - 1541
110 DIMD$(24)
120 PRINT"{CLR}MULTIPLE 20 ERROR - 1541"

130 PRINT"{DOWN}INSERT CLONE IN DRIVE"
140 INPUT"{DOWN}DESTROY TRACK";T
150 IFT<10RT>35THENEND
160 INPUT"{DOWN}ARE YOU SURE   Y{LEFT 3}"
;Q$
```

```
170 IFQ$<>"Y"THENEND
180 OPEN15,8,15
190 PRINT#15,"IO"
200 INPUT#15,EN$,EM$,ET$,ES$
210 IFEN$="00"GOTO260
220 PRINT"{DOWN}"EN$, "EM$", "ET$", "ES$
230 CLOSE15
240 END
250 REM SEEK
260 NS=20+2*(T>17)+(T>24)+(T>30)
270 S=NS
280 JOB=176
290 GOSUB580
300 FORI=0TO23
310 READD
320 D$=D$+CHR$(D)
330 I$=I$+CHR$(0)
340 NEXTI
350 PRINT#15,"M-W"CHR$(0)CHR$(6)CHR$(24)
D$
360 REM EXECUTE
370 PRINT"{DOWN}{RVS}DESTROYING{ROFF} TR
ACK";T
380 JOB=224
390 GOSUB580
400 PRINT#15,"M-W"CHR$(0)CHR$(6)CHR$(24)
I$
410 FORJ=0TO24
420 FORI=0TO7
430 READD
440 D$(J)=D$(J)+CHR$(D)
450 NEXTI
460 NEXTJ
470 I=0
480 FORJ=0TO24
490 PRINT#15,"M-W"CHR$(I)CHR$(4)CHR$(8)D
$(J)
500 I=I+8
510 NEXTJ
520 REM EXECUTE
530 PRINT#15,"M-E"CHR$(0)CHR$(4)
540 CLOSE15
550 PRINT"{DOWN}DONE!"
560 END
570 REM JOB QUEUE
580 TRY=0
590 PRINT#15,"M-W"CHR$(12)CHR$(0)CHR$(2)
CHR$(T)CHR$(S)
600 PRINT#15,"M-W"CHR$(3)CHR$(0)CHR$(1)C
HR$(JOB)
```

```
610 TRY=TRY+1
620 PRINT#15, "M-R"CHR$(3)CHR$(0)
630 GET#15,E$
640 IFE$=""THENE$=CHR$(0)
650 E=ASC(E$)
660 IFTRY=500GOTO690
670 IFE>127GOTO610
680 RETURN
690 CLOSE15
700 PRINT"{DOWN}{RVS}FAILED{ROFF}"
710 END
720 REM 21 ERROR
730 DATA  32,163,253,169, 85,141,  1, 28

740 DATA 162,255,160, 48, 32,201,253, 32

750 DATA   0,254,169,  1, 76,105,249,234

760 REM 20M ERROR
770 DATA169,  0,133,127,166, 12,134, 81
780 DATA134,128,166, 13,232,134, 67,169
790 DATA  1,141, 32,  6,169,  8,141, 38
800 DATA  6,169,  0,141, 40,  6, 32,  0
810 DATA193,162,  0,169,  9,157,  0,  3
820 DATA232,232,173, 40,  6,157,  0,  3
830 DATA232,165, 81,157,  0,  3,232,169
840 DATA  0,157,  0,  3,232,157,  0,  3
850 DATA232,169, 15,157,  0,  3,232,157
860 DATA  0,  3,232,169,  0, 93,250,  2
870 DATA 93,251,  2, 93,252,  2, 93,253
880 DATA  2,157,249,  2,238, 40,  6,173
890 DATA 40,  6,197, 67,208,189,138, 72
900 DATA169, 75,141,  0,  5,162,  1,138
910 DATA157,  0,  5,232,208,250,169,  0
920 DATA133, 48,169,  3,133, 49, 32, 48
930 DATA254,104,168,136, 32,229,253, 32
940 DATA245,253,169,  5,133, 49, 32,233
950 DATA245,133, 58, 32,143,247,169, 35
960 DATA133, 81,169,169,141,  0,  6,169
970 DATA  5,141,  1,  6,169,133,141,  2
980 DATA  6,169, 49,141,  3,  6,169, 76
990 DATA141,  4,  6,169,170,141,  5,  6
1000 DATA169,252,141,  6,  6,169,224,133

1010 DATA  3,165,  3, 48,252, 76,148,193
```

```
100 REM 20M.PAL
110 REM
120 OPEN2,8,2,"@0:20M.B,P,W"
130 REM
140 SYS40960
150 ;
160 .OPT P,O2
170 ;
180 *= $0400
190 ;
200 ;* INITIALIZATION *
210 ;
220 LDA #$00
230 STA $7F
240 LDX $0C
250 STX $51
260 STX $80
270 LDX $0D
280 INX
290 STX $43
300 LDA #$01
310 STA $0620
320 LDA #$08          ; TAIL GAP
330 STA $0626
340 LDA #$00
350 STA $0628         ; SECTOR COUNTER
360 ;
370 JSR $C100         ; LED ON
380 ;
390 ;* CREATE HEADERS *
400 ;
410 LDX #$00
420 HEADER LDA #$09 ; HBID
430 STA $0300,X
440 INX
450 INX               ; CHECKSUM
460 LDA $0628
470 STA $0300,X       ; SECTOR
480 INX
490 LDA $51
500 STA $0300,X       ; TRACK
510 INX
520 LDA #$00
530 STA $0300,X       ; IDL
540 INX
550 STA $0300,X       ; IDH
560 INX
570 LDA #$0F
```

```
580 STA $0300,X        ; GAP
590 INX
600 STA $0300,X        ; GAP
610 INX
620 ;
630 LDA #$00           ; COMPUTE CHECKSUM
640 EOR $02FA,X
650 EOR $02FB,X
660 EOR $02FC,X
670 EOR $02FD,X
680 STA $02F9,X
690 ;
700 INC $0628
710 LDA $0628
720 CMP $43
730 BNE HEADER
740 ;
750 TXA
760 PHA
770 ;
780 ;* CREATE DATA *
790 ;
800 LDA #$4B           ; 1541 FORMAT
810 STA $0500
820 LDX #$01           ; 1541 FORMAT
830 TXA
840 DATA STA $0500,X
850 INX
860 BNE DATA
870 ;
880 ;* CONVERT TO GCR *
890 ;
900 LDA #$00
910 STA $30
920 LDA #$03
930 STA $31
940 JSR $FE30
950 PLA
960 TAY
970 DEY
980 JSR $FDE5
990 JSR $FDF5
1000 LDA #$05
1010 STA $31
1020 JSR $F5E9
1030 STA $3A
1040 JSR $F78F
1050 ;
1060 ;* JUMP INSTRUCTION *
1070 ;
```

148

```
1080 LDA #$23
1090 STA $51
1100 ;
1110 LDA #$A9
1120 STA $0600
1130 LDA #$05
1140 STA $0601
1150 LDA #$85
1160 STA $0602
1170 LDA #$31
1180 STA $0603
1190 LDA #$4C
1200 STA $0604
1210 LDA #$AA
1220 STA $0605
1230 LDA #$FC
1240 STA $0606
1250 ;
1260 LDA #$E0
1270 STA $03
1280 ;
1290 WAIT LDA $03
1300 BMI WAIT
1310 ;
1320 JMP $C194
```

Full Track 20 Error Source Annotation

This routine has a real surprise in store. Initialization in lines 220-290 sets the drive number to 0 ($007F) rather than rely on a default. The track is read from the header table location $000C and stored at $0051. (Recall that the driver set up the header table.) This memory location normally contains an $FF at powerup to let the drive know that formatting has not yet begun. We must reset it to the active track, or the drive will do a BUMP to track one to start the format. Similarly, we read the sector range from $000D, incremented this number to obtain a sector total for the track, and stored it at $0043. Line 300 is our try counter. Normally the drive makes 10 attempts to format a single track. We either get it right the first time or give up. (The driver erases the track as a safeguard.) We cannot allow the FDC to reattempt to format the track because it will bypass our machine language routine and re-enter the standard ROM routine. Lines 310-330 arbitrarily sets the tail gap to eight bytes in length. This avoids duplicating 245 bytes of code from $FB1D to $FC12. RAM is at a dire premium and we have neither the overhead nor the desire.

Next we turn on the LED for cosmetic purposes (line 370) and build our header table and a dummy data block (lines 410-860). We incremented the data block identifier in line 420. Binary to GCR conversion is done in lines 900-1040. Now for the jump instruction. First we reset the track number to 35 (lines 1080-1090) to let the FDC think that this is the last track of a normal format. Why? We will be passing control to a standard ROM routine in a minute and will let the FDC execute it. In other words, we are going to work the 6502 in both IP and FDC modes. Formatting is done as a single job; one

149

track at a time. When a track is formatted the FDC looks at $0051 to see if 35 tracks have been done. If not, it increments $0051 and does the next track as another discrete job. The IP is going to wait for the FDC to reformat the track and then retake control. We store the indirect buffer pointer to our data block buffer and a jump to $FCAA at $0600. This ensures that the data block will not be lost in the ensuing shuffle. We then set up the job queue for an execute of buffer number 3 ($0600) and away we go. The IP monitors the FDC while it is reformatting the track. (Not only that, but the FDC will verify the track to ensure that it was reformatted incorrectly!) When bit seven of the job code ($E0) goes low, the IP wrestles control away from the FDC and jumps to ENDCMD ($C194) to terminate the routine. DOS ist gut!

7.13 How to Create 27 Errors on a Full Track

Limitations: None.

Parameters: Track number.

FULL TRACK 27 ERROR

```
100 REM 27M ERROR - 1541
110 DIMD$(25)
120 PRINT"{CLR}MULTIPLE 27 ERROR - 1541"

130 PRINT"{DOWN}INSERT CLONE IN DRIVE"
140 INPUT"{DOWN}DESTROY TRACK";T
150 IFT<10RT>35THENEND
160 INPUT"{DOWN}ARE YOU SURE  Y{LEFT 3}"
;Q$
170 IFQ$<>"Y"THENEND
180 OPEN15,8,15
190 PRINT#15,"IO"
200 INPUT#15,EN$,EM$,ET$,ES$
210 IFEN$="00"GOTO260
220 PRINT"{DOWN}"EN$", "EM$","ET$","ES$
230 CLOSE15
240 END
250 REM SEEK
260 NS=20+2*(T>17)+(T>24)+(T>30)
270 S=NS
280 JOB=176
290 GOSUB580
300 FORI=0TO23
310 READD
320 D$=D$+CHR$(D)
330 I$=I$+CHR$(0)
340 NEXTI
350 PRINT#15,"M-W"CHR$(0)CHR$(6)CHR$(24)
D$
360 REM EXECUTE
```

```
370 PRINT"{DOWN}{RVS}DESTROYING{ROFF} TR
ACK";T
380 JOB=224
390 GOSUB580
400 PRINT#15,"M-W"CHR$(0)CHR$(6)CHR$(24)
I$
410 FORJ=0TO25
420 FORI=0TO7
430 READD
440 D$(J)=D$(J)+CHR$(D)
450 NEXTI
460 NEXTJ
470 I=0
480 FORJ=0TO25
490 PRINT#15,"M-W"CHR$(I)CHR$(4)CHR$(8)D
$(J)
500 I=I+8
510 NEXTJ
520 REM EXECUTE
530 PRINT#15,"M-E"CHR$(0)CHR$(4)
540 CLOSE15
550 PRINT"{DOWN}DONE!"
560 END
570 REM JOB QUEUE
580 TRY=0
590 PRINT#15,"M-W"CHR$(12)CHR$(0)CHR$(2)
CHR$(T)CHR$(S)
600 PRINT#15,"M-W"CHR$(3)CHR$(0)CHR$(1)C
HR$(JOB)
610 TRY=TRY+1
620 PRINT#15,"M-R"CHR$(3)CHR$(0)
630 GET#15,E$
640 IFE$=""THENE$=CHR$(0)
650 E=ASC(E$)
660 IFTRY=500GOTO690
670 IFE>127GOTO610
680 RETURN
690 CLOSE15
700 PRINT"{DOWN}{RVS}FAILED{ROFF}"
710 END
720 REM 21 ERROR
730 DATA   32,163,253,169, 85,141,  1, 28

740 DATA 162,255,160, 48, 32,201,253, 32

750 DATA    0,254,169,  1, 76,105,249,234

760 REM 27M ERROR
770 DATA169,   0,133,127,166, 12,134, 81
780 DATA134,128,166, 13,232,134, 67,169
```

```
790 DATA   1,141, 32,   6,169,   8,141, 38
800 DATA   6,169,  0,141, 40,   6, 32,   0
810 DATA193,162,   0,169,   8,157,   0,   3
820 DATA232,232,173, 40,   6,157,   0,   3
830 DATA232,165, 81,157,   0,   3,232,169
840 DATA   0,157,   0,   3,232,157,   0,   3
850 DATA232,169, 15,157,   0,   3,232,157
860 DATA   0,   3,232,169,   0, 93,250,   2
870 DATA 93,251,   2, 93,252,   2, 93,253
880 DATA   2,157,249,   2,254,249,   2,238
890 DATA 40,   6,173, 40,   6,197, 67,208
900 DATA186,138, 72,169, 75,141,   0,   5
910 DATA162,   1,138,157,   0,   5,232,208
920 DATA250,169,   0,133, 48,169,   3,133
930 DATA 49, 32, 48,254,104,168,136, 32
940 DATA229,253, 32,245,253,169,   5,133
950 DATA 49, 32,233,245,133, 58, 32,143
960 DATA247,169, 35,133, 81,169,169,141
970 DATA   0,   6,169,   5,141,   1,   6,169
980 DATA133,141,   2,   6,169, 49,141,   3
990 DATA   6,169, 76,141,   4,   6,169,170
1000 DATA141,   5,   6,169,252,141,   6,   6

1010 DATA169,224,133,   3,165,   3, 48,252

1020 DATA 76,148,193,234,234,234,234,234
```

FULL TRACK 27 SOURCE LISTING

```
100 REM 27M.PAL
110 REM
120 OPEN2,8,2,"@0:27M.B,P,W"
130 REM
140 SYS40960
150 ;
160 .OPT P,02
170 ;
180 *= $0400
190 ;
200 ;* INITIALIZATION *
210 ;
220 LDA #$00
230 STA $7F
240 LDX $0C
250 STX $51
260 STX $80
270 LDX $0D
280 INX
290 STX $43
300 LDA #$01
```

```
310 STA $0620
320 LDA #$08            ; TAIL GAP
330 STA $0626
340 LDA #$00
350 STA $0628           ; SECTOR COUNTER
360 ;
370 JSR $C100           ; LED ON
380 ;
390 ;* CREATE HEADERS *
400 ;
410 LDX #$00
420 HEADER # LDA #$08 ; HBID
430 STA $0300,X
440 INX
450 INX                 ; CHECKSUM
460 LDA $0628
470 STA $0300,X         ; SECTOR
480 INX
490 LDA $51
500 STA $0300,X         ; TRACK
510 INX
520 LDA #$00
530 STA $0300,X         ; IDL
540 INX
550 STA $0300,X         ; IDH
560 INX
570 LDA #$0F
580 STA $0300,X         ; GAP
590 INX
600 STA $0300,X         ; GAP
610 INX
620 ;
630 LDA #$00            ; COMPUTE CHECKSUM
640 EOR $02FA,X
650 EOR $02FB,X
660 EOR $02FC,X
670 EOR $02FD,X
680 STA $02F9,X
690 ;
700 INC $02F9,X         ; INCREMENT CHECKSUM

710 ;
720 INC $0628
730 LDA $0628
740 CMP $43
750 BNE HEADER
760 ;
770 TXA
780 PHA
790 ;
```

```
800 ;* CREATE DATA *
810 ;
820 LDA #$4B              ; 1541 FORMAT
830 STA $0500
840 LDX #$01              ; 1541 FORMAT
850 TXA
860 DATA STA $0500,X
870 INX
880 BNE DATA
890 ;
900 ;* CONVERT TO GCR *
910 ;
920 LDA #$00
930 STA $30
940 LDA #$03
950 STA $31
960 JSR $FE30
970 PLA
980 TAY
990 DEY
1000 JSR $FDE5
1010 JSR $FDF5
1020 LDA #$05
1030 STA $31
1040 JSR $F5E9
1050 STA $3A
1060 JSR $F78F
1070 ;
1080 ;* JUMP INSTRUCTION *
1090 ;
1100 LDA #$23
1110 STA $51
1120 ;
1130 LDA #$A9
1140 STA $0600
1150 LDA #$05
1160 STA $0601
1170 LDA #$85
1180 STA $0602
1190 LDA #$31
1200 STA $0603
1210 LDA #$4C
1220 STA $0604
1230 LDA #$AA
1240 STA $0605
1250 LDA #$FC
1260 STA $0606
1270 ;
1280 LDA #$E0
1290 STA $03
```

```
1300 ;
1310 WAIT LDA $03
1320 BMI WAIT
1330 ;
1340 JMP $C194
```

Full Track 27 Error Source Annotation

See the annotation for 20M.PAL. The only major difference is in line 700 above. Note the header block identifier ($08) in line 420 is left alone.

7.14 How to Create a 22 Error on a Single Sector

Limitations: None.

Parameters: Track and sector number.

SINGLE SECTOR 22 ERROR

```
100 REM 22A ERROR - 1541
110 PRINT"{CLR}22A ERROR - 1541"
120 PRINT"{DOWN}INSERT CLONE IN DRIVE"
130 INPUT"{DOWN}DESTROY TRACK AND SECTOR
 (T,S)";T,S
140 IFT<1ORT>35THENEND
150 NS=20+2*(T>17)+(T>24)+(T>30)
160 IFS<OORS>NSTHENEND
170 INPUT"{DOWN}ARE YOU SURE  Y{LEFT 3}"
;Q$
180 IFQ$<>"Y"THENEND
190 OPEN15,8,15
200 PRINT#15,"IO"
210 INPUT#15,EN$,EM$,ET$,ES$
220 IFEN$="00"GOTO270
230 PRINT"{DOWN}"EN$,  "EM$","ET$","ES$
240 CLOSE15
250 END
260 REM SEEK
270 JOB=176
280 GOSUB440
290 IFE<>1GOTO550
300 REM READ
310 JOB=128
320 GOSUB440
330 IFE<>1ANDE<>4ANDE<>5GOTO550
340 PRINT#15,"M-W"CHR$(71)CHR$(O)CHR$(1)
CHR$(6)
350 REM WRITE
360 JOB=144
```

```
370 GOSUB440
380 PRINT#15,"M-W"CHR$(71)CHR$(0)CHR$(1)
CHR$(7)
390 IFE<>1GOTO550
400 CLOSE15
410 PRINT"{DOWN}DONE!"
420 END
430 REM JOB QUEUE
440 TRY=0
450 PRINT#15,"M-W"CHR$(8)CHR$(0)CHR$(2)C
HR$(T)CHR$(S)
460 PRINT#15,"M-W"CHR$(1)CHR$(0)CHR$(1)C
HR$(JOB)
470 TRY=TRY+1
480 PRINT#15,"M-R"CHR$(1)CHR$(0)
490 GET#15,E$
500 IFE$=""THENE$=CHR$(0)
510 E=ASC(E$)
520 IFTRY=500GOTO540
530 IFE>127GOTO470
540 RETURN
550 CLOSE15
560 PRINT"{DOWN}{RVS}FAILED{ROFF}"
570 END
```

SINGLE SECTOR 22 ERROR SOURCE LISTING

None. Line 340 in the program creates a single sector 22 error by decrementing the data block identifier. Line 380 restores the status quo.

7.15 How to Duplicate a 22 Error on a Single Sector

Limitations: None (requires disk swapping).

Parameters: Track and sector number.

DUPLICATE A SINGLE SECTOR 22 ERROR

```
100 REM DUPLICATE A 22 ERROR - 1541
110 PRINT"{CLR}DUPLICATE A 22 ERROR - 15
41"
120 PRINT"{DOWN}INSERT MASTER IN DRIVE"
130 INPUT"{DOWN}TRACK AND SECTOR (T,S)";
T,S
140 IFT<1ORT>35THENEND
150 NS=20+2*(T>17)+(T>24)+(T>30)
160 IFS<0ORS>NSTHENEND
170 INPUT"{DOWN}ARE YOU SURE   Y{LEFT 3}"
;Q$
```

```
180 IFQ$<>"Y"THENEND
190 OPEN15,8,15
200 PRINT#15,"IO"
210 INPUT#15,EN$,EM$,ET$,ES$
220 IFEN$="00"GOTO270
230 PRINT"{DOWN}"EN$", "EM$","ET$","ES$
240 CLOSE15
250 END
260 REM SEEK
270 JOB=176
280 GOSUB550
290 REM READ
300 JOB=128
310 GOSUB550
320 PRINT#15,"M-R"CHR$(56)CHR$(0)
330 GET#15,D$
340 IFD$=""THEND$=CHR$(0)
350 CLOSE15
360 PRINT"{DOWN}REMOVE MASTER FROM DRIVE
"
370 PRINT"INSERT CLONE IN DRIVE"
380 PRINT"PRESS {RVS}RETURN{ROFF} TO CON
TINUE"
390 GETC$:IFC$=""THEN390
400 IFC$<>CHR$(13)GOTO390
410 PRINT"OK"
420 OPEN15,8,15
430 REM SEEK
440 JOB=176
450 GOSUB550
460 PRINT#15,"M-W"CHR$(71)CHR$(0)CHR$(1)
D$
470 REM WRITE
480 JOB=144
490 GOSUB550
500 PRINT#15,"M-W"CHR$(71)CHR$(0)CHR$(1)
CHR$(7)
510 CLOSE15
520 PRINT"{DOWN}DONE!"
530 END
540 REM JOB QUEUE
550 TRY=0
560 PRINT#15,"M-W"CHR$(8)CHR$(0)CHR$(2)C
HR$(T)CHR$(S)
570 PRINT#15,"M-W"CHR$(1)CHR$(0)CHR$(1)C
HR$(JOB)
580 TRY=TRY+1
590 PRINT#15,"M-R"CHR$(1)CHR$(0)
600 GET#15,E$
610 IFE$=""THENE$=CHR$(0)
```

```
620 E=ASC(E$)
630 IFTRY=500GOTO660
640 IFE>127GOTO580
650 RETURN
660 PRINT#15,"M-W"CHR$(71)CHR$(0)CHR$(1)
CHR$(7)
670 CLOSE15
680 PRINT"{DOWN}{RVS}FAILED{ROFF}"
690 END
```

DUPLICATE A SINGLE SECTOR 22 ERROR SOURCE LISTING

None. Line 320 in the program reads the data block identifier from the master. Lines 460-490 duplicate the error on the clone. Line 500 puts our house back in order.

7.16 How to Format a Diskette with Multiple IDs

Limitations: None (requires disk swapping).

Parameters: None.

MULTIPLE ID FORMATTING

```
100 REM FORMAT A DISKETTE - 1541
110 DIMT(35),H$(35),L$(35)
120 PRINT"{CLR}FORMAT A DISKETTE - 1541"

130 PRINT"{DOWN}INSERT {RVS}MASTER{ROFF}
 IN DRIVE"
140 GOSUB910
150 PRINT"{DOWN}{RVS}FETCHING{ROFF} FORM
ATTING ID"
160 OPEN15,8,15
170 FORI=1TO35
180 T(I)=1
190 NEXTI
200 JOB=176
210 FORT=1TO35
220 IFT(T)=0GOTO340
230 GOSUB970
240 IFE=1GOTO280
250 H$(T)=CHR$(0)
260 L$(T)=CHR$(0)
270 GOTO340
280 PRINT#15,"M-R"CHR$(22)CHR$(0)
290 GET#15,H$(T)
300 IFH$(T)=""THENH$(T)=CHR$(0)
310 PRINT#15,"M-R"CHR$(23)CHR$(0)
320 GET#15,L$(T)
```

158

```
330 IFL$(T)=""THENL$(T)=CHR$(0)
340 NEXTT
350 T=18
360 GOSUB970
370 CLOSE15
380 PRINT"{CLR}FORMAT A DISKETTE - 1541"

390 PRINT"{DOWN}INSERT {RVS}BLANK{ROFF}
IN DRIVE"
400 GOSUB910
410 OPEN15,8,15
420 FORJ=0TO6
430 FORI=0TO7
440 READD
450 D$(J)=D$(J)+CHR$(D)
460 NEXTI
470 NEXTJ
480 I=0
490 FORJ=0TO6
500 PRINT#15,"M-W"CHR$(I)CHR$(4)CHR$(8)D
$(J)
510 I=I+8
520 NEXTJ
530 FORI=1TO35
540 PRINT#15,"M-W"CHR$(49+I)CHR$(4)CHR$(
1)L$(I)
550 PRINT#15,"M-W"CHR$(84+I)CHR$(4)CHR$(
1)H$(I)
560 NEXTI
570 REM EXECUTE
580 PRINT"{DOWN}{RVS}FORMATTING{ROFF} DI
SKETTE"
590 PRINT#15,"M-E"CHR$(0)CHR$(4)
600 INPUT#15,EN$,EM$,ET$,ES$
610 T=18
620 S=0
630 JOB=176
640 GOSUB970
650 JOB=128
660 GOSUB970
670 PRINT#15,"M-W"CHR$(0)CHR$(4)CHR$(3)C
HR$(18)CHR$(1)CHR$(65)
680 JOB=144
690 GOSUB970
700 S=1
710 JOB=128
720 GOSUB970
730 PRINT#15,"M-W"CHR$(0)CHR$(4)CHR$(2)C
HR$(0)CHR$(255)
740 JOB=144
750 GOSUB970
```

```
760 CLOSE15
770 OPEN15,8,15
780 PRINT#15,"NO:1541 FORMAT"
790 INPUT#15,EN$,EM$,ET$,ES$
800 S=0
810 JOB=128
820 GOSUB970
830 PRINT#15,"M-W"CHR$(162)CHR$(4)CHR$(2
)CHR$(50)CHR$(54)
840 JOB=144
850 GOSUB970
860 PRINT#15,"M-W"CHR$(162)CHR$(7)CHR$(2
)CHR$(50)CHR$(54)
870 CLOSE15
880 PRINT"{DOWN}DONE!"
890 END
900 REM DELAY
910 PRINT"{DOWN}PRESS {RVS}RETURN{ROFF}
TO CONTINUE"
920 GETC$:IFC$=""THEN920
930 IFC$<>CHR$(13)GOTO920
940 PRINT"OK"
950 RETURN
960 REM JOB QUEUE
970 TRY=0
980 PRINT#15,"M-W"CHR$(8)CHR$(0)CHR$(2)C
HR$(T)CHR$(S)
990 PRINT#15,"M-W"CHR$(1)CHR$(0)CHR$(1)C
HR$(JOB)
1000 TRY=TRY+1
1010 PRINT#15,"M-R"CHR$(1)CHR$(0)
1020 GET#15,E$
1030 IFE$=""THENE$=CHR$(0)
1040 E=ASC(E$)
1050 IFTRY=500GOTO1070
1060 IFE>127GOTO1000
1070 RETURN
1080 REM NEW
1090 DATA169,  0,133,127, 32,  0,193,169

1100 DATA 76,141,  0,  6,169,199,141,  1

1110 DATA  6,169,250,141,  2,  6,169,224

1120 DATA133,  3,164, 81,185, 49,  4,133

1130 DATA 19,185, 84,  4,133, 18,192, 35

1140 DATA208,240,165,  3, 48,252, 76,148

1150 DATA193,234,234,234,234,234,234,234
```

MULTIPLE ID FORMATTING SOURCE LISTING

```
100 REM FAD.PAL
110 REM
120 OPEN2,8,2,"@0:FAD.B,P,W"
130 REM
140 SYS40960
150 ;
160 .OPT P,02
170 ;
180 *= $0400
190 IDL = $0431
200 IDH = IDL+35
210 ;
220 LDA #$00
230 STA $7F        ; DRIVE NUMBER
240 ;
250 JSR $C100      ; LED
260 ;
270 LDA #$4C       ; JUMP TO $FAC7
280 STA $0600
290 LDA #$C7
300 STA $0601
310 LDA #$FA
320 STA $0602
330 ;
340 LDA #$E0
350 STA $03
360 ;
370 TABLE LDY $51 ; TRACK NUMBER
380 ;
390 LDA IDL,Y      ; ID LO
400 STA $13
410 ;
420 LDA IDH,Y      ; ID HI
430 STA $12
440 ;
450 CPY #$23       ; TRACK 35
460 BNE TABLE
470 ;
480 WAIT LDA $03
490 BMI WAIT
500 ;
510 JMP $C194
```

Multiple ID Formatting Source Annotation

This is a modification of the standard formatting routine, NEW ($EE0D). Embedded IDs are read from each track on the master and tabled in 1541 RAM starting at $0431 by the driver. The appropriate ID for each track is stored as the master disk ID ($12/3) by the IP before control is passed to the FDC to format a track. After a track is format- ted, the IP retakes control, finds the next ID in the table, stores it at $12/3, and passes control back to the FDC. Because we do not have a N0:DISK NAME,ID command in the command buffer, we cannot use the later portions of the standard formatting routine to create the BAM and directory. Lines 670-780 of the driver clean up afterward.

7.17 How to Backup a DOS Protected Diskette

Limitations: Does not recreate any bad sectors. Requires six passes to backup a diskette (see the annotation below).

Parameters: A formatted diskette.

1541 BACKUP

```
100 REM 1541 BACKUP
110 POKE56,33
120 CLR
130 FORI-1TO144
140 READD
150 POKE49151+I,D
160 NEXTI
170 DIMT(35)
180 FORI=1TO35
190 T(I)=1
200 NEXTI
210 READSRW,ERW
220 PRINT"{CLR}1541 BACKUP"
230 PRINT"{DOWN}INSERT MASTER IN DRIVE"
240 GOSUB1110
250 OPEN15,8,15
260 RW=8448
270 FORI=1TO126
280 POKE8447+I,0
290 NEXTI
300 RAM=8704
310 POKE252,34
320 C=0
330 REM SEEK
340 FORT=SRWTOERW
350 NS=20+2*(T>17)+(T>24)+(T>30)
360 IFT(T)=0GOTO410
370 JOB=176
380 GOSUB1190
390 IFE=1GOTO470
400 T(T)=0
410 RW=RW+(NS+1)
420 RAM=RAM+(256*(NS+1))
```

```
430 POKE252, (RAM/256)
440 R=R+(NS+1)
450 GOTO620
460 REM READ
470 FORS=0TONS
480 GOSUB1300
490 PRINT"{HOME}{DOWN 7}{RVS}READING{ROF
F} TRACK "T$" - SECTOR "S$
500 JOB=128
510 GOSUB1190
520 IFE=1GOTO550
530 R=R+1
540 IFE<>4ANDE<>5GOTO580
550 SYS49165
560 C=1
570 POKERW,1
580 RW=RW+1
590 RAM=RAM+256
600 POKE252, (RAM/256)
610 NEXTS
620 NEXTT
630 CLOSE15
640 IFC=0GOTO1010
650 PRINT"{CLR}1541 BACKUP"
660 PRINT"{DOWN}INSERT CLONE IN DRIVE"
670 GOSUB1110
680 OPEN15,8,15
690 RW=8448
700 RAM=8704
710 POKE252,34
720 REM SEEK
730 FORT=SRWTOERW
740 NS=20+2*(T>17)+(T>24)+(T>30)
750 JOB=176
760 GOSUB1190
770 IFE=1GOTO820
780 RAM=RAM+(256*(NS+1))
790 W=W+(NS+1)
800 GOTO990
810 REM WRITE
820 IFT(T)=1GOTO870
830 RW=RW+(NS+1)
840 RAM=RAM+(256*(NS+1))
850 POKE252, (RAM/256)
860 GOTO990
870 FORS=0TONS
880 IFPEEK(RW)=0GOTO950
890 GOSUB1300
900 PRINT"{HOME}{DOWN 7}{RVS}WRITING{ROF
F} TRACK "T$" - SECTOR "S$
```

```
910 SYS49228
920 JOB=144
930 GOSUB1190
940 IFE<>1THENW=W+1
950 RW=RW+1
960 RAM=RAM+256
970 POKE252,(RAM/256)
980 NEXTS
990 NEXTT
1000 CLOSE15
1010 IFERW<>35GOTO210
1020 PRINT"{HOME}{DOWN 2}READ ERRORS :"R
"          "
1030 PRINT"{DOWN}WRITE ERRORS:"W
  "
1040 PRINT"   "
1050 PRINT"DONE!"
1060 PRINT"                              "

1070 POKE56,160
1080 CLR
1090 END
1100 REM DELAY
1110 PRINT"{DOWN}PRESS {RVS}RETURN{ROFF}
 TO CONTINUE"
1120 IFC=0ANDSRW<>1GOTO1160
1130 GETC$: IFC$<>""THEN1130
1140 GETC$: IFC$=""THEN1140
1150 IFC$<>CHR$(13)GOTO1140
1160 PRINT"OK"
1170 RETURN
1180 REM JOB QUEUE
1190 TRY=0
1200 PRINT#15,"M-W"CHR$(8)CHR$(0)CHR$(2)
CHR$(T)CHR$(S)
1210 PRINT#15,"M-W"CHR$(1)CHR$(0)CHR$(1)
CHR$(JOB)
1220 TRY=TRY+1
1230 PRINT#15,"M-R"CHR$(1)CHR$(0)
1240 GET#15,E$
1250 E=ASC(E$+CHR$(0))
1260 IFTRY=500GOTO1280
1270 IFE>127GOTO1220
1280 RETURN
1290 REM STR$(T,S)
1300 T$=RIGHT$("0"+RIGHT$(STR$(T),LEN(ST
R$(T))-1),2)
1310 S$=RIGHT$("0"+RIGHT$(STR$(S),LEN(ST
R$(S))-1),2)
1320 RETURN
1330 REM $C000
```

```
1340 DATA 77, 45, 82,   0,   4,255,128, 77

1350 DATA 45, 87,   0,   4, 32,169,   0,133

1360 DATA251,141,   3,192, 32, 34,192,169

1370 DATA128,133,251,141,   3,192, 32, 34

1380 DATA192, 96,162, 15, 32,201,255,162

1390 DATA  0,189,   0,192, 32,210,255,232

1400 DATA224,   7,208,245, 32,204,255,162

1410 DATA 15, 32,198,255,160,   0, 32,207

1420 DATA255,145,251,200,192,129,208,246

1430 DATA 32,204,255, 96,169,   0,141, 10

1440 DATA192,240, 11,173, 10,192, 24,105

1450 DATA 32,141, 10,192,240, 47,162, 15

1460 DATA 32,201,255,162,   0,189,   7,192

1470 DATA 32,210,255,232,224,   6,208,245

1480 DATA173, 10,192,133,251,160,   0,177

1490 DATA251, 32,210,255,200,192, 32,208

1500 DATA246,169, 13, 32,210,255, 32,204

1510 DATA255,169,   0,240,198, 96,234,234

1520 REM TRACK
1530 DATA1,6,7,12,13,17,18,24,25,30,31,3
5
```

1541 BACKUP SOURCE LISTING

```
100 REM BACKUP.PAL
110 REM
120 OPEN 2,8,2,"@0:M.B,P,W"
130 REM
140 SYS40960
150 ;
160 .OPT P,02
170 ;
```

```
180 ; M-R / M-W ROUTINES
190 ;
200 *= $C000
210 ;
220 ; RAM LOCATIONS USED
230 ; -------------------
240 POINT = $00FB ;POINTER TO READ/WRITE
 PAGE
250 ;
260 ; ROM ROUTINES USED
270 ; -----------------
280 CHKOUT = $FFC9 ;OPEN CHANNEL FOR OUT
PUT
290 CHROUT = $FFD2 ;OUTPUT A CHARACTER
300 CLRCHN = $FFCC ;CLEAR ALL CHANNELS
310 CHKIN =  $FFC6 ;OPEN CHANNEL FOR INP
UT
320 CHRIN =  $FFCF ; INPUT A CHARACTER
330 ;
340 ; DISK M-R & M-W COMMANDS
350 ;
360 MR .ASC "M-R"
370 .BYTE $00,$04,$FF,$80
380 ;
390 MW .ASC "M-W"
400 TEMP .BYTE $00,$04,$20
410 ;
420 ;*---------------------------*
430 ;*   READ FROM DISK ROUTINES *
440 ;*---------------------------*
450 ; M-R ENTRY POINT
460 ; ---------------------
470 LDA #$00
480 STA POINT   ;POINT TO FIRST HALF
490 STA MR+3    ;ASK FOR FIRST HALF
500 JSR READIT  ;READ FIRST HALF
510 ;
520 LDA #$80
530 STA POINT   ;POINT TO SECOND HALF
540 STA MR+3    ;ASK FOR SECOND HALF
550 JSR READIT  ;READ SECOND HALF
560 ;
570 RTS         ;RETURN TO BASIC
580 ;
590 ; SUBROUTINE TO READ IN HALF PAGE
600 ; -------------------------------
610 READIT LDX #$0F ;PREPARE CHANNEL 15
FOR OUTPUT
620 JSR CHKOUT
630 ;
```

```
640 LDX #$00
650 LOOP1 LDA MR,X ;SEND M-R COMMAND
660 JSR CHROUT
670 INX
680 CPX #$07
690 BNE LOOP1
700 ;
710 JSR CLRCHN ; CLEAR THE CHANNEL
720 ;
730 LDX #$0F ;PREPARE CHANNEL 15 FOR INP
UT
740 JSR CHKIN
750 ;
760 LDY #$00
770 LOOP2 JSR CHRIN
780 STA (POINT),Y
790 INY
800 CPY #$81
810 BNE LOOP2
820 ;
830 JSR CLRCHN ; CLEAR THE CHANNEL
840 RTS ;END OF READ HALF PAGE
850 ;
860 ;*---------------------------*
870 ;*   SEND TO DISK ROUTINES   *
880 ;*---------------------------*
890 ; FIRST M-W ENTRY POINT
900 ; ----------------------
910 MRITE LDA #$00 ;INITIALIZE PART PAGE
  POINTER
920 STA TEMP
930 BEQ ENTER
940 ;
950 LOOP3 LDA TEMP
960 CLC
970 ADC #$20
980 STA TEMP
990 BEQ DONE
1000 ;
1010 ENTER LDX #$0F ;PREPARE CHANNEL 15
FOR OUTPUT
1020 JSR CHKOUT
1030 ;
1040 LDX #$00
1050 LOOP4 LDA MW,X ;SEND "M-W LO HI $20
"
1060 JSR CHROUT
1070 INX
1080 CPX #$06
1090 BNE LOOP4
```

```
1100 ;
1110 LDA TEMP ;POINT TO START OF PART PA
GE
1120 STA POINT
1130 ;
1140 LDY #$00
1150 ;
1160 LOOP5 LDA (POINT),Y ;SEND 32 CHARAC
TERS
1170 JSR CHROUT
1180 INY
1190 CPY #$20
1200 BNE LOOP5    ;NOT DONE 32 YET
1210 ;
1220 LDA #$0D     ;CARRIAGE RETURN
1230 JSR CHROUT
1240 JSR CLRCHN ;CLEAR THE CHANNEL
1250 ;
1260 LDA #$00
1270 BEQ LOOP3  ;ALWAYS TO DO NEXT PART
1280 ;
1290 DONE RTS    ;BACK TO BASIC
```

1541 Backup Source Annotation

The BASIC driver reads a sector from the master diskette into 1541 RAM using the job queue. The contents of the RAM are transferred into the C64 with a machine language memory-read. After a pass is complete, the clone is inserted into the drive. A machine language memory-write command is then used to transfer the bytes back to 1541 RAM. The BASIC drive writes the buffer out to the diskette using the job queue. The above routine illustrates how to do memory-read and memory-write commands in machine language. It is interesting to note that reading 256 bytes from 1541 RAM appears to take amost ten times as long as writing 256 bytes to 1541 RAM. However, the C64 internal clock is not reliable at all while performing I/O to the disk drive. Bypassing a bad track can be done anywhere between lines 200-340 if necessary. Any of the previous 11 routines may be used to recreate any errors that you found on the master diskette after a backup is made.

7.18 How to Copy a File

Limitations: 125 blocks in length
          Will not copy a relative file
          Wild cards are not permitted

Parameters: File name and file type.

```
100 REM 1541 COPY
110 POKE56,16
120 CLR
130 POKE251,0
140 POKE252,16
150 POKE253,0
160 POKE254,16
170 FORI=1TO72
180 READD
190 POKE49151+I,D
200 NEXTI
210 PRINT"{CLR}1541 COPY"
220 PRINT"{DOWN}INSERT MASTER IN DRIVE"
230 GOSUB750
240 GOSUB810
250 INPUT"{DOWN}FILENAME";F$
260 IFLEN(F$)<>0ANDLEN(F$)<17GOTO280
270 GOTO1000
280 INPUT"{DOWN}FILE TYPE (DSPU)  P{LEFT
 3}";T$
290 IFT$="D"ORT$="S"ORT$="P"ORT$="U"GOTO
310
300 GOTO1000
310 RW$="R"
320 GOSUB890
330 SYS49152
340 CLOSE2
350 INPUT#15,EN$,EM$,ET$,ES$
360 IFEN$="00"GOTO380
370 GOTO850
380 CLOSE15
390 PRINT"{DOWN}INSERT CLONE IN DRIVE"
400 GOSUB750
410 GOSUB810
420 PRINT#15,"M-R"CHR$(1)CHR$(1)
430 GET#15,D$
440 D=ASC(D$+CHR$(0))
450 IFD=65GOTO490
460 PRINT"{DOWN}73,CBM DOS V2.6 1541,00,
00"
470 GOTO710
480 PRINT#15,"M-R"CHR$(250)CHR$(2)CHR$(3
)
490 GET#15,L$
500 L=ASC(L$+CHR$(0))
510 GET#15,B$
520 GET#15,H$
530 H=ASC(H$+CHR$(0))
```

```
540 C=L+(H*256)
550 S=PEEK(252)+((PEEK(253)-16)*256)
560 B=INT((S/254)+.5)
570 IFC-B>=0GOTO600
580 PRINT"{DOWN}72,DISK FULL,00,00"
590 GOTO710
600 RW$="W"
610 GOSUB890
620 SYS49182
630 CLOSE2
640 INPUT#15,EN$,EM$,ET$,ES$
650 PRINT"{DOWN}DONE!"
660 CLOSE15
670 POKE56,160
680 CLR
690 END
700 REM CLOSE
710 CLOSE15
720 PRINT"{DOWN}{RVS}FAILED{ROFF}"
730 GOTO670
740 REM DELAY
750 PRINT"{DOWN}PRESS {RVS}RETURN{ROFF}
TO CONTINUE"
760 GETC$:IFC$=""THEN760
770 IFC$<>CHR$(13)GOTO760
780 PRINT"OK"
790 RETURN
800 REM INITIALIZATION
810 OPEN15,8,15
820 PRINT#15,"IO"
830 INPUT#15,EN$,EM$,ET$,ES$
840 IFEN$="00"THENRETURN
850 PRINT"{DOWN}"EN$", "EM$","ET$","ES$
860 CLOSE15
870 GOTO670
880 REM FILE NOT FOUND - FILE EXISTS
890 OPEN2,8,2,"0:"+F$+","+T$+","+RW$
900 INPUT#15,EN$,EM$,ET$,ES$
910 IFEN$="00"THENRETURN
920 CLOSE2
930 PRINT"{DOWN}"EN$", "EM$","ET$","ES$
940 PRINT"{DOWN}{RVS}FAILED{ROFF}"
950 INPUT#15,EN$,EM$,ET$,ES$
960 CLOSE15
970 GOTO670
980 REM LOAD - SAVE
990 DATA162,  2, 32,198,255,160,  0, 32
1000 DATA228,255,145,251, 32,183,255, 41

1010 DATA 64,208,  8,200,208,241,230,252
```

170

```
1020 DATA 76,  5,192,132,251, 32,204,255

1030 DATA 96,162,  2, 32,201,255,160,  0

1040 DATA177,253, 32,210,255,196,251,240

1050 DATA  8,200,208,244,230,254, 76, 38

1060 DATA192,165,254,197,252,208,242,132

1070 DATA253, 32,204,255, 96,234,234,234
```

COPY A FILE SOURCE LISTING

```
100 REM COPY.PAL
110 REM
120 OPEN2,8,2,"@0:COPY.B,P,W"
130 REM
140 SYS40960
150 ;
160 .OPT P,02
170 ;
180 *= $C000
190 ;
200 ; LOAD
210 ;
220 LDX #$02
230 JSR $FFC6            ; OPEN2,8,2
240 ;
250 LOAD LDY #$00
260 READ JSR $FFE4       ; IN
270 STA ($FB),Y
280 JSR $FFB7            ; READST
290 AND #64
300 BNE READY
310 INY
320 BNE READ
330 INC $FC
340 JMP LOAD
350 ;
360 READY STY $FB
370 JSR $FFCC            ; CLOSE2
380 RTS
390 ;
400 ; SAVE
410 ;
420 LDX #$02
430 JSR $FFC9            ; OPEN2,8,2
440 ;
450 SAVE LDY #$00
```

```
460 WRITE LDA ($FD),Y
470 JSR $FFD2            ; OUT
480 CPY $FB
490 BEQ BREAK
500 CONT INY
510 BNE WRITE
520 INC $FE
530 JMP SAVE
540 ;
550 BREAK LDA $FE
560 CMP $FC
570 BNE CONT
580 ;
590 STY $FD
600 JSR $FFCC            ; CLOSE2
610 RTS
```

Copy a File Source Annotation

This routine emulates a LOAD and SAVE from machine language.

Conclusion

In conclusion, we hope that this chapter has taken some of the mystery out of DOS protection schemes. We encourage serious readers to study the program listings carefully. The programming techniques employed are perhaps the most sophisticated applications of Commodore's direct-access commands that you will ever see.

CHAPTER 8

GETTING OUT OF TROUBLE

The best way to get out of trouble is to stay out of trouble in the first place! It is much easier to recover a lost file by digging out an archival copy than trying to recover it from a blown diskette. Need we remind you? BACKUP! BACKUP! BACKUP!

However, since we feel that Murphy was a rash optimist, the likelihood of you always finding that backup copy is minimal, unless of course, you manage to recover that file on the diskette. Then, and only then, will the archival copy magically appear right where you thought you left it.

Since you are reading this chapter, you probably have a problem and are in desperate need of help. Please read on.

8.1 Unscratching a File

Inadvertently scratching a file is by far the most common problem. As long as you have not written any new information to the diskette since you scratched that file, it can be recovered. Recall that when a file is scratched, it is not erased from the diskette. Only two things have happened:

1. The file-type byte in the directory entry is set to $00.
2. The sectors associated with that file are freed in the BAM.

To unscratch a file, all you have to do is change the file-type byte back to its original value and VALIDATE the diskette to re-allocate the sectors.

The programs VIRTUAL DIRECTORY and EDIT TRACK & SECTOR, which are listed in Appendix C, help you to do this. Here's how you should use these programs to recover a scratched file.

STEP 1. Load and run the VIRTUAL DIRECTORY program on the diskette. The directory will be displayed in groups of eight entries. Scratched files are highlighted in reverse video. Each group constitutes a different sector on track 18. Count the groups to determine which group the scratched entry is in. Note not only which group the scratched entry is in, but also whether it is in the first half or the last half of the group. (One of the first four file entries or one of the last four.)

Consult the table below to determine the number of the sector containing the entry.

Group - Sector	Group - Sector	Group - Sector
1 - 18,1	7 - 18,2	13 - 18,3
2 - 18,4	8 - 18,5	14 - 18,6
3 - 18,7	9 - 18,8	15 - 18,9
4 - 18,10	10 - 18,11	16 - 18,12
5 - 18,13	11 - 18,14	17 - 18,15
6 - 18,16	12 - 18,17	18 - 18,18

STEP 2. Load and run the EDIT TRACK & SECTOR program on the diskette with the scratched file. When asked for the track and sector, enter track 18 and the sector number you read from the table. When prompted for the starting byte, enter 00 if the scratched file entry was one of the first four files in the group. Enter an 80 if the scratched file was displayed among the last four in the group.

STEP 3. When the hex dump of the half-sector is displayed, cursor over to the third column of hexadecimal numbers on the display. Next locate the name of the file in the ASCII display on the right-hand side of the screen. Move the cursor down until it is on the same line as the start of the file name. If you have done things correctly you should be on a row labeled with a $00, $20, $40, $60, $80, $A0, $C0, or $E0. The byte under the cursor should be a 00. This is the file-type byte. The 00 indicates a scratched file. Type over the 00 value with the value that corresponds to the correct file type as indicated below.

File Type	Value
PRG	82
SEQ	81
REL	84
USR	83
DEL	80

STEP 4. Hold down the SHIFT key and press the CLR/HOME key. This will terminate the edit mode. When asked whether to rewrite this track and sector, press Y and the modified sector will be written to the diskette in a few seconds.

STEP 5. Load and list the directory to see if the file name now appears. If it does not, you made a mistake and things may have gone from bad to worse. Hopefully, the file will be listed.

STEP 6. VALIDATE the diskette by entering in direct mode:

`OPEN 15,8,15,"V0":CLOSE15`

If the drive stops and the error light is not flashing, everything has gone according to plan and the file has been recovered successfully. (If the VALIDATE command failed, see sections 8.2 and 8.3.)

NOTE: It is a good idea to practice these steps on a test diskette before you attempt to recover your lost Accounts Receivable! To do this: SAVE a file to disk, SCRATCH it, and follow the steps outlined above.

8.2 Recovering a Soft Error

In Chapter 7 we described in detail the read/write DOS errors. We did not, however, categorize these errors by type. Read/write errors fall into two categories: "hard" errors and "soft" errors. A hard error is one that cannot be recovered, period. Hard errors are errors that occur in a header block. Recall that a header block is never rewritten after initial formatting. Since a header block cannot be rewritten, the data in a sector containing a hard error is unrecoverable. (Unfortunately, this also means that the forward pointer has been lost and, for all intents and purposes, the remainder of the file as well.) Soft errors are errors that occur in a data block. Since data blocks can be rewritten, soft errors can sometimes be recovered if the diskette itself is not flawed or physically damaged. The table below indicates whether a read/write error is a hard or soft error.

Soft Errors	Hard Errors
22 Read Error	20 Read Error
23 Read Error	21 Read Error
	27 Read Error
	29 Read Error

Appendix C contains two programs that are useful in trying to recover a sector that has a soft error. However, recovery cannot be guaranteed in all cases. These two programs are RECOVER TRACK & SECTOR and LAZARUS. The first program attempts to rewrite a damaged sector. LAZARUS will attempt to resurrect an entire diskette. The latter program returns a status report of the number of read errors encountered. It also reports the number of write errors that occurred. A write error indicates that a soft error encountered along the way was actually a hard error in disguise. Sorry about that.

8.3 Recovering a Hard Error

A hard error does not necessarily mean that an entire file is unrecoverable. In all honesty, though, the technique that we are about to describe is a shot in the dark. Before you attempt the steps outlined below ask yourself the following question. Are you experiencing errors on other diskettes in your library? If you answered yes to this question, the cause of these errors may be in the disk drive itself. Your 1541 may be out of alignment and a trip to your nearest Commodore dealer is in order. If the problem occurs on only one diskette read on.

NOTE: This section does not apply to relative files. Refer to section 8.4 instead.

WARNING: The technique we are about to describe here is not for the faint-hearted. Consult with your physician before attempting this exercise.

STEP 1. Load and run the VALIDATE A DISKETTE program contained in Appendix C. This program emulates the VALIDATE command from BASIC. It will chain through each active file entry in the directory and highlight a bad file without aborting.

STEP 2. Load and run FIND A FILE. This program will return the track and sector locations of where the file resides in the directory as well as where it starts on the diskette. The directory track and sector is extraneous information for our present purpose. Note only the starting track and sector.

STEP 3. Load and run DISPLAY A CHAIN. This program requires you to input a track and sector. Input the starting track and sector obtained in step 2. The program will chain through all forward track and sectors on the diskette from this entry point until an error is encountered. (If the error is a soft error, STOP! Do not pass GO. Go directly to section 8.2.) Ignore the sector where the error was encountered. The file is virtually lost from that point on. (Recall that the link has been destroyed.) Make note of the last successful track and sector displayed.

STEP 4. Load and run EDIT TRACK & SECTOR. You will want to input the track and sector obtained in step 3. The starting byte is always 00. Change the first two bytes to 00 and FF, respectively. Rewrite the sector when prompted to do so. You have in effect severed the forward track and sector link described in Chapter 4. This allows you to manipulate the front end of the file. It is the only portion of the file that is clearly intact.

If it is a BASIC PRG file, the internal BASIC links have been destroyed. You can restore the links on the C64 with a machine language monitor or on the diskette with the EDIT TRACK & SECTOR program. If you do not restore the BASIC links, the C64 will crash as soon as you attempt to edit the last line of the program. Using EDIT TRACK & SECTOR, call up the sector that was just rewritten. You will have to inspect both half-pages of the block. Look for the last 00 byte in the page. Change the two bytes that immediately follow it to a 00 00 also. Note the position of the last 00 byte edited in hexadecimal. If you are in the second-half of the block, rewrite the sector and then recall the first-half. Change the forward sector pointer to the hexadecimal position of the last 00 byte you changed. Rewrite the sector a final time. You will now be able to load, list, and edit the program. Hopefully, you will remember to save it to a different diskette this time.

If it was a SEQ file, the recovered data is intact. You will have to read it into C64 RAM and rewrite it to another file. If you do not know how to manipulate a sequential file contact someone who does.

8.4 Recovering a Relative File

The only realistic way to recover a REL file is to open it for a read and copy it record by record into a sequential file. The program to do this should not abort when an error is encountered. Simply skip over the record and go on. This way only the records that reside, in whole or in part, on the damaged sector are not recovered. If you do not know how to do this, take your diskette to an experienced programmer and see if he/she can assist you.

8.5 Recovering an Entire Diskette

NOTE: This section applies only to a diskette that cannot be initialized.

Chapter 7 contains a program called 1541 BACKUP (section 7.15). Run this program to make a backup of your blown diskette. After you have made a backup, load and list the directory. If the directory appears normal, you will want to validate the backup. If the validate command fails, inspect and copy each intact file to a new diskette. Some files may be lost in the process.

If the directory cannot be displayed in its entirety, a hard error was encountered on track 18 during the backup operation. The sector containing the hard error could not be copied. As a result, the directory on the backup is corrupt. Load and run DISPLAY A CHAIN on the backup. Attempt to follow the chain starting at track 18, sector 1. The display will indicate the location of the uncopyable sector by aborting. Run EDIT TRACK & SECTOR on the backup to relink the directory around this sector. Refer to the table in section 8.1 to determine which sector normally follows the one in question. Keep in mind that eight files will be lost by this action. If all goes well you should be able to list the directory now. Inspect and copy all remaining files to a new diskette.

8.6 Recovering a Physically Damaged Diskette

If your diskette has sustained physical damage all is not lost. The most common forms of physical damage are a warped jacket or environmental contamination. In either case, the solution is to don a pair of plastic gloves, carefully slit open the protective jacket, remove the plastic disk, wash it if necessary, and insert it into another jacket. Obtaining a new jacket may mean destroying a perfectly good diskette, though. *NOTE:* Some brands of head cleaners come with a reusable jacket that is just right for this job.

Be sure to keep your fingers off the recording surface at all times! Handle the plastic disk only by the edges or the central hub ring. Also make a mental note as to which side faces up. (The reinforcing ring is usually affixed to this side.)

If the plastic disk is gummy, you will want to wash it carefully. Use a small amount of photographer's wetting agent to keep the water from leaving a residue. Allow the plastic disk to air dry.

Once you have inserted the plastic disk inside a new jacket, attempt to initialize it. If you cannot initialize it, try turning the diskette over. You may have the wrong side up.

If the diskette can be initialized, make a backup NOW!

8.7 Recovering an Unclosed File

An unclosed file is one whose file type is preceded by an asterisk in a directory listing (e.g., *SEQ, *PRG). Such files cannot be read normally. However, there is an undocumented read mode that will allow you to read an unclosed file. This is the M mode. The M stands for MODIFY. The way to open a file for a read normally looks like this:

```
SYNTAX:
  OPEN 2, 8, 2, "file name,S,R"          (SEQ file)
  OPEN 2, 8, 2, "file name,P,R"          (PRG file)
```

To read an unclosed file substitute, an M for the R in the OPEN statement like this:

```
SYNTAX:
  OPEN 2, 8, 2, "file name,S,M"          (SEQ file)
  OPEN 2, 8, 2, "file name,P,M"          (PRG file)
```

The file can now be read into the C64 and stored in RAM. There is one problem, though. You will have to display the incoming data bytes because an EOI will not be returned by the disk drive. Note that the last sector written to the diskette will contain an erroneous forward track and sector pointer. As a result, there is no realistic way to determine when you have read beyond the actual contents of the unclosed file itself. Watch the incoming data bytes carefully. Your read program should have an embedded breakpoint. When you think you've captured all of the data bytes, rewrite them to another diskette.

Once you have the data safely stored on another diskette, use the techniques described at the end of Section 8.3 to restore the internal BASIC links if it was a PRG file.

Don't forget to VALIDATE the diskette which has the unclosed file in the directory while you're at it. Recall that scratching an unclosed file poisons the BAM.

8.8 Recovering from a Short New

If you have inadvertently performed a short NEW on a diskette, there is more hope than you think. Recall that a short NEW only zeros out the BAM and sector 1 from track 18. Run the EDIT TRACK & SECTOR program on the diskette in question. Call up track 18, sector 1 and change the forward track and sector pointer from a 00, FF to a 12, 04.

Next, load and list the directory. If your diskette contained more than eight active files, all but the first eight files will be displayed on the screen. (The first eight files have been lost for now.) Do not attempt to VALIDATE the diskette because the directory sectors will not be reallocated. Copy all of the remaining files onto a new diskette.

If the first eight files are very important, you can attempt to recover them as well. However, it will not be easy! You must find the starting track and sector locations of these files yourself through a process of elimination. Begin by making a grid with a space for each sector on the diskette like this:

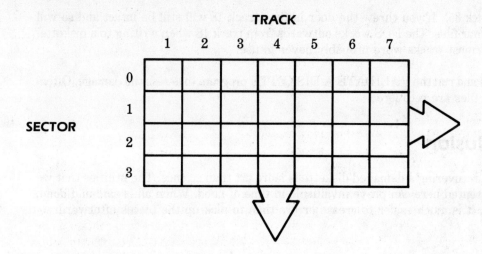

Next, VALIDATE the original diskette and then load and run the program DISPLAY A BLOCK AVAILABILITY MAP listed in Appendix C. Working from the display on the CRT, indicate on your chart which sectors are in use by other files. Once you have done this, you should see a blank area centered around track 18. This is where you lost files reside.

Now, load and run the DISPLAY A CHAIN program. The first file probably starts on track 17, sector 0. Record the chain displayed to the screen on your chart. Once you have recorded the first chain, begin looking for the next one. It probably begins on an open space on track 17 or, if the first chain was a long one, on track 19, sector 0. Work outward from track 18 until you have located all eight missing files.

Once you have the starting track and sector locations for the files, use the EDIT TRACK & SECTOR program to reconstruct track 18, sector 1. The tables and hex dumps from Chapter 4 can be used as a guide. Be sure to substitute the starting track and sector locations that you found and *not* the ones in this manual.

Now copy the eight files onto another disk. Once this is done, take a break and meditate on the virtues of archival backups!

8.9 Recovering from a Full New

If you are reading this section in desperation, relax. It is already too late. However, if it dawns on you in the future that you are holding a blank diskette in your hand while the master that you were going to backup is being reformatted, don't PANIC! Attempt to regain your composure and pop the drive door open. At this point you don't care what the 1541 User's Manual says about opening the drive door when the red activity indicator is on. You are losing one full track every time you hear the stepper motor click.

Next attempt to make a backup copy of the diskette using the 1541 BACKUP program listed on page 162. (Please, try to remember which diskette you want to format this time.) Recall that formatting works from the outermost track (track 1) to the innermost track (track 35). If you threw the door in time track 18 will still be intact and so will most of your files. The DOS works outwards from track 18 when writing to a diskette. The outermost tracks were probably never in use.

Now load and run the VALIDATE A DISKETTE program to assess the damage. Oftentimes all files are recovered.

Conclusion

In short, recovering a damaged diskette is more art than science. The utilities that we have presented here can prove invaluable in time of need. When all is said and done, however, it is much easier to create errors than to pick up the pieces afterward.

CHAPTER 9

OVERVIEW OF THE 1541 DOS

9.1 Introduction to 1541 DOS

Recall that in Chapter 2 we stated that the 1541 is an intelligent peripheral. It contains its own 6502 microprocessor, 2K of RAM, I/O chips, and the DOS program which is permanently stored in 15.8K of ROM. The diagram below illustrates how the RAM, ROM, and I/O chips are arranged.

	2K of RAM		Input-Output Chips	
$0000	Job queue, constants, pointers & work area	$1800	6522 VIA CHIP Main I/O to computer	$180F
$0100	Stacks, work areas and overflow buffer			
$0200	Command buffer & work	$1C00	6522 VIA CHIP Main I/O to disk	$1C0F
$0300	Data buffer #0			
$0400	Data buffer #1			
$0500	Data buffer #2		DOS in 15.8K of ROM	
$0600	Data buffer #3	$C100	Communications and file management	$F259
$0700	Buffer for BAM		Disk controller routines	
$0800		$FFFF		

9.2 The Hard Working 6502

The 1541 disk drive is a new addition to Commodore's line of disk drives. Commodore's earlier drives, the 2040, 4040, 8050 and 8250 had three microprocessors: a 6502 to handle communications with the computer, a 6504 to act as a disk controller, and a 6532 to translate between normal 8-bit characters and the 10-bit GCR code that is actually written on the diskette. The 1541 has only one 6502 to do everything.

The 6502 in the 1541 alternates between two modes of operation: Interface Processor (IP) mode and Floppy Disk Controller (FDC) mode. The 6502 switches to its FDC mode approximately every 10 milliseconds. The switch is made in response to an interrupt (IRQ) generated by one of the 6522 timers. The main IRQ handling routine checks to see if the IRQ was generated by the timer. If it was, the 6502 begins to execute the FDC routines. Once in FDC mode the interrupt signal is disabled and the 6502 remains in FDC mode until any jobs it has to do are completed. If the interrupt signal was not disabled, it might disrupt a read or write job.

9.3 Major IP Routines

One of the difficulties in using the detailed ROM maps in Appendix B is locating the routine you want. This section summarizes the major IP routines and their entry points to help you find your way around.

a) Initialization

When the disk drive is first switched on, the RESET line is held low. This causes the 6502 to do an indirect JMP via the vector at $FFFC to the initialization procedure at $EAA0. The main features of the initialization process are shown below.

OVERVIEW OF INITIALIZATION

$EAA0	Test zero page RAM
$EAC9	Do checksum test of ROM's
$EAF0	Test remainder of RAM
$EB22	Initialize I/O chips
$EB4B	Set up buffer tables
$EB87	Set up buffer pointers
$EBC2	JSR to inititialize FDC
$EBDA	Initialize serial bus

b) Main IP Idle Loop

Whenever the drive is inactive and the 6502 is in IP mode, the 6502 executes the code from $EBE7 to $EC9D looking for something to do.

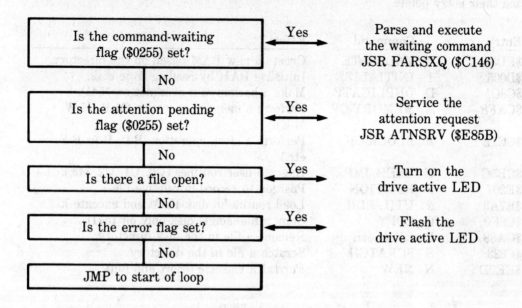

c) Computer—Disk Drive Communications

The routines that handle communication on the serial bus are localized in one small area of ROM, from $E853 to $EA6E. The entry points for the major routines are summarized below.

Entry	Routine	Function
$E853	ATNIRQ	An IRQ is generated when the computer sets the ATN line of the serial bus low. Branch to here from IRQ handler to set attention pending flag.
$E85B	ATNSRV	Service an ATN signal on the serial bus
$E909	TALK	Send data out on the serial bus
$E9C9	ACPTR	Accept one byte of data from the serial bus
$EA2E	LISTEN	Accept incoming data bytes from the serial bus

d) Execution of Disk Commands

When the computer sends the 1541 a disk command, such as NEW, VERIFY, or SCRATCH, the command is stored temporarily in the command buffer ($0200-$0229) and the command pending flag ($0255) is set. The next time the 6502 works its way though the IP idle loop ($EBE7-$EC9D) it finds that the command pending flag has been set. It then does a JSR to the PARSXQ routine ($C146) to parse and execute the command. The parser first checks the command table ($FE89-94) to see if this is a valid command. Next it checks the syntax of the command. If the command is correct, a JMP is made to the appropriate ROM routine. The table below summarizes the various disk commands and their entry points.

Entry	Command	Effect
$ED84	V VALIDATE	Create a new BAM based on the directory.
$D005	I INITIALIZE	Initialize BAM by reading from disk.
$C8C1	D DUPLICATE	Make a backup of a disk (not on 1541).
$CAF8	M MEMORY-OP	Perform a memory operation (M-R, M-W, M-E).
$CC1B	B BLOCK-OP	Perform a block operation (B-P, B-A, B-F, etc.).
$CB5C	U USER JMP	Execute user routines (U0, U1, U2, etc.).
$E207	P POSITION	Position to record in relative file.
$E7A3	& UTIL LDR	Load routine in disk RAM and execute it.
$C8F0	C COPY	Copy a file (single disk only on 1541).
$CA88	R RENAME	Rename a file in the disk directory.
$C823	S SCRATCH	Scratch a file in the directory.
$EE0D	N NEW	Format a diskette (short and full).

For more details on these routines see Appendix B.

If no errors are encountered during the execution of a command, the routine is terminated with a JMP to the ENDCMD ($C194). If errors are encountered, .A is loaded with an error code, and the routine is aborted with a JMP to the command level error processing routine at $E645.

e) File Management

File management is a major function of the interface processor. As a result, there are many ROM routines that deal directly or indirectly with the management of files, the directory and the BAM. A few of the major entry points are summarized below.

Entry	Routine	Function of File Management Routine
$C5AC	SRCHST	Search directory for valid or deleted entry.
$CBB4	OPNBLK	OPEN a direct access buffer.
$CE0E	FNDREL	Find a record in a relative file.
$D156	RDBYT	Read byte from a file. Get next sector if needed.
$D19D	WRTBYT	Write byte to file. Write sector if full.
$D50E	SETJOB	Set up read or write job for FDC.
$D6E4	ADDFIL	Add a file to the directory.
$D7B4	OPEN	OPEN a channel for read, write, load, or save.
$DAC0	CLOSE	Close the file associated with given channel#.
$DBA5	CLSDIR	Close directory entry for a write file.
$DC46	OPNRCH	OPEN a channel to read using double buffering.

$DCDA	OPNWCH	OPEN a channel to write using double buffering.
$DFD0	NXTREC	Set up next record for a relative file.
$E31F	ADDREL	Add a new sector to a relative file.
$E44E	NEWSS	Add new side sectors to relative file.
$E4FC	ERRTAB	IP mode error message table.
$E645	CMDER2	IP mode error handler.
$EA6E	PEZRO	Display error diagnostics by flashing LED.
$EAA8	DSKINT	Initialize IP side of disk.
$EC9E	STDIR	Convert directory to pseudo program and load.
$EF5C	WFREE	Mark given sector as free in the BAM.
$EF90	WUSED	Mark given sector as in use in the BAM.
$F11E	NXTTS	Finds next available sector from the BAM.

9.4 Using the IP Routines

The interface processor routines in the 1541's ROM are relatively easy to use. They can be executed by using the command channel to send the disk drive the appropriate memory-execute (M-E) command.

Before you try to use one of the IP routines you should:

1. Use the ROM maps in this chapter to locate a routine.
2. Use the tools given in Section 9.13 to make a copy of that area of ROM.
3. Disassemble the routine.
4. Study the disassembly (use the ROM analysis in Appendix B as a guide) to determine any setup that is necessary.

NOTE: You cannot use the memory-execute (M-E) technique described in this section when you are using any routine that involves reading from or writing to a diskette.
The reason for this restriction is that memory-execute commands are carried out while the processor is in the IP mode. In this mode, the processor is interrupted every 10 milliseconds by an IRQ and switches into FDC mode. Any read or write operation will be interrupted if this occurs. See Section 9.6 for the technique to use if you want to use a routine that reads from or writes to the diskette.

Once you are sure that the routine performs the operation you want and what setup is needed, you are ready to design your program. Your program will normally have three parts:

1. A Setup Section

   This section normally consists of one or more memory-write (M-W) commands to poke any required setup values into the 1541's RAM memory.

2. A Section to Execute the Routine

   This section normally consists of one memory-execute (M-E) command to force the 1541's microprocessor to execute the ROM routine.

3. An Information Retrieval Section

This section normally consists of one or more memory-read (M-R) commands to peek the results of the routine out of the 1541's RAM for use by your program.

Let's take a look at a typical application of this technique.

Suppose we were writing a data base management program. One thing we would like to build into our program is a check to be sure that we can never produce an unclosed file (*SEQ). This would happen if the user entered too much data and completely filled the disk. We can't rely on checking the drive's error channel in this situation because the DOS sends the disk full error too late; the damage is already done. We are going to have to have some independent method of finding the number of blocks free on the diskette before we write out the file.

Since we know that a directory listing shows the number of blocks free, we'll start by looking for some routines that deal with the directory. The chart of ROM routines that deal with file management in Section 9.3 (e) has one entry that looks promising: STDIR ($EC9E), convert directory to pseudo program and load. We now turn to Appendix B and look up this routine. Scanning through this routine doesn't turn up an algorithm that appears to calculate the number of blocks free and we're back to square one. What about the initialize routine? From the chart on the execution of disk commands in Section 9.3 (d) we find that this routine starts at $D005. Back to Appendix B. Eureka! At $D075 we find the routine NFCALC. A bit of disassembly indicates that this routine probably needs very little setup to calculate the number of blocks free and that it stores the lo-byte of the count in NDBL ($02FA) and the hi-byte in NDBH ($02FC). Before we set up an elaborate program, let's check out these RAM locations using a test program like this:

```
10 OPEN 15,8,15,"I"
20 GOSUB 120:REM CHECK DISK STATUS
30 OPEN 1,8,5,"@0:TEST FILE,S,W"
40 GOSUB 120:REM CHECK DISK STATUS
50 FOR K=1 TO 300
60 PRINT#1,"THIS IS TEST RECORD NUMBER";
K
70 PRINT K;:GOSUB 170:REM CHECK BLOCKS F
REE
80 NEXT
90 CLOSE 1:CLOSE15:END
100 :
110 REM SUB TO CHECK DISK STATUS
120 INPUT E,E$,T,S
130 PRINT E;E$;T;S
140 RETURN
150 :
160 REM SUB TO READ BLOCKS FREE
170 PRINT#15,"M-R"CHR$(250)CHR$(2)CHR$(3
)
180 GET#15,X$:NL=ASC(X$+CHR$(0))
```

```
190 GET#15,X$:REM JUNK
200 GET#15,X$:NH=ASC(X$+CHR$(0))
210 PRINT "BLOCKS FREE=" 256*NH+NL
220 RETURN
```

After trying our test program, we find our problem is solved. As we write out our records the DOS automatically updates the count in NDBL and NDBH to reflect the number of blocks left. We don't really need to execute a ROM routine after all. A memory-read command is all we need. The moral? A bit of time spent studying and testing can really simplify your life.

Since the "blocks free" example really didn't illustrate the use of an IP routine, let's try again. This time we are interested in converting normal bytes into their GCR equivalents to see what is actually written out to the disk. After snooping through the IP tables in Section 9.3 without any luck, we try the FDC tables in Section 9.5. We find what we need in 9.5 (c): PUT4GB ($F6D0), convert four data bytes into five GCR bytes. In checking Appendix B we find that, although this is nominally an FDC routine, it does not involve reading from, or writing to, a diskette. This means we can use the memory-execute technique.

After a bit of disassembly we know what set-up is required:

1. The routine expects to find four normal bytes stored in RAM from $52-$55.

2. The pointer at $30/31 should point to the start of where the five GCR bytes that result from the conversion are to be stored. We'll use $0300-$0304.

3. The GCR pointer at $34 should be $00.

4. The entry point for the routine is definitely $F6D0.

Now that we know what we have to do, let's set up the program.

First, we'll start by inputting the four bytes we want to convert and storing them in disk RAM from $52 (82) to $55 (85) using a memory-write command (M-W). Second, we will use memory-write (M-W) commands to set the pointers at $30 (to 0), $31 (to 3), and $34 (to 0). Third, we'll execute the routine using a memory-execute (M-E) command. Finally, we will peek the results from $0300-4 of the disk RAM using a memory-read (M-R) command and five GET# statements. Here's what the program looks like:

```
100 REM CONVERT BINARY TO GCR
110 PRINT"{CLR}ENTER FOUR BYTES (DECIMAL
){DOWN}"
120 B$(0)="0":B$(1)="1":FORK=0TO7:P(K)=2
^K:NEXT
130 FORK=0TO7:P(K)=2^K:NEXT
140 OPEN 15,8,15
150 :
160 REM INPUT BYTES & STORE IN DISK RAM
($52/5)
170 FOR K=0TO3
180 PRINT"BYTE#"K"=";:INPUT X
```

187

```
190 IF   X<O OR X>255 GOTO 180
200 PRINT"{UP}"TAB(18);:GOSUB430
210 PRINT#15, "M-W"CHR$(82+K)CHR$(0)CHR$(
1)CHR$(X)
220 NEXT
230 :
240 REM SET UP POINTER TO STORAGE AREA (
$30/31)
250 PRINT#15, "M-W"CHR$(48)CHR$(0)CHR$(2)
CHR$(0)CHR$(3)
260 :
270 REM SET UP GCR POINTER ($34)
280 PRINT#15, "M-W"CHR$(52)CHR$(0)CHR$(1)
CHR$(0)
290 :
300 REM EXECUTE PUT4GB ($F6D0) IPC ROUTI
NE
310 PRINT#15, "M-E"CHR$(208)CHR$(246)
320 :
330 REM PEEK OUT AND DISPLAY RESULTS
340 PRINT#15, "M-R"CHR$(00)CHR$(3)CHR$(5)

350 PRINT"{DOWN}THE FIVE EQUIVALENT GCR
BYTES ARE:{DOWN}"
360 FOR K=1 TO 5
370 GET#15, X$:X=ASC(X$+CHR$(0))
380 PRINT"BYTE#"K"="X;TAB(18);:GOSUB430
390 NEXT
400 CLOSE 15:END
410 :
420 SUB TO DISPLAY BINARY EQUIVALENTS
430 PRINT"%";
440 FOR L=7TO0STEP-1
450 T=INT(X/2^L)
460 X=X-T*P(L)
470 PRINTB$(T);
480 NEXT:PRINT:RETURN
```

Many of the other IP ROM routines are just as easy to use. However, be careful because some are tricky. Some expect to find a particular command in the command buffer. These are tough to use because the memory-execute command will wipe out any set-up you have done in the command buffer area. In these cases you will have to store a short machine language routine in the disk RAM that sets up the proper command in the buffer before it JMP's to the IP routine. When you execute the routine, it should overwrite the M-E command in the buffer with the command you want there. Happy sleuthing!

9.5 Major FDC Routines

One of the difficulties in finding an FDC routine to do the job you want is finding your way through the detailed ROM maps in Appendix B. This section summarizes the major FDC routines and their entry points.

a) Initialization

When the disk drive is first switched on, the reset line is pulsed lo. This causes the 6502 to RESET and it does an indirect JMP via the vector at $FFFC to the initialization procedure at $EAA0. As part of the set up procedure, the variables and I/O chips for the FDC are initialized by the CNTINT routine ($F259-AF).

b) Main FDC Idle Loop

Every 10 milliseconds the 6522 timer generates an interrupt (IRQ) and the 6502 begins to execute the main FDC loop looking for something to do. The main features of this loop are summarized below.

OVERVIEW OF MAIN FDC LOOP ($F2B0)

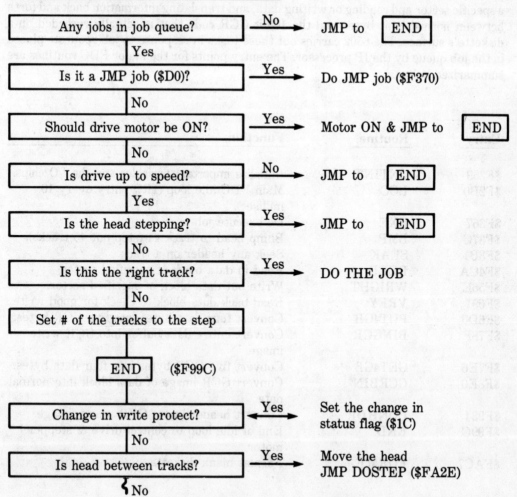

189

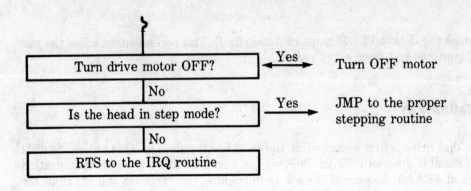

At the end of this loop, or when the job has been completed, the timer interrupt is re-enabled and the 6502 leaves FDC mode.

c) Major FDC Entry Points

When in FDC mode the 6502 executes routines that directly control the operation of the disk drive. These include: turning the drive motor ON or OFF, controlling the stepper motor that moves the head from track to track, formatting a blank diskette, locating a specific sector and reading or writing data, and translating information back and forth between normal 8-bit bytes and the 10-bit GCR code that is actually recorded on a diskette's surface. The 6502 carries out these tasks in response to job requests placed in the job queue by the IP processor. The entry points for the major FDC routines are summarized below.

Entry	Routine	Function
$F259	CNTINT	Initialize important variables and the I/O chips.
$F2B0	LCC	Main FDC idle loop (IRQ entry every 10 millisec).
$F367	EXE	Do execute job.
$F37C	BMP	Bump head to track #1 (step out 45 tracks).
$F3B1	SEAK	Seek any header on a track.
$F4CA	REED	Read in data block of specified sector.
$F56E	WRIGHT	Write out data block of specified sector.
$F691	VRFY	Read back data block to check for good write.
$F6D0	PUT4GB	Convert four data bytes into five GCR bytes.
$F78F	BINGCR	Convert entire data buffer into GCR write image.
$F7E6	GET4GB	Convert five GCR bytes into four data bytes.
$F8E0	GCRBIN	Convert GCR image of data block into normal data.
$F934	CONHDR	Convert header into a GCR search image.
$F99C	END	End of idle loop to control drive & stepper motor.
$FAC7	FORMT	Format blank diskette.

Since the read, write and format routines are of particular interest, let's look at them in more detail.

d) Read Data Block of Specified Sector

Before the read job code ($80) is placed in the job queue, the IP puts the desired track and sector numbers into the header table as indicated below.

Job queue location	Use buffer #	address	Track # address	Sector # address
$0000	0	$0300-FF	$0006	$0007
$0001	1	$0400-FF	$0008	$0009
$0002	2	$0500-FF	$000A	$000B
$0003	3	$0600-FF	$000C	$000D
$0004	4	$0700-FF	$000E	$000F
$0005	5	NO RAM	$0010	$0011

Once the track and sector values are in place, the IP puts the read job code into the job queue in the location that corresponds to the data buffer where the data is to be stored. The next time the 6502 is in FDC mode it finds the job request. If necessary, it turns on the drive motor, waits for it to get up to speed, and moves the head to the proper track. It then executes the read routine outlined below:

OVERVIEW OF THE FDC READ ROUTINE

$F4D1	Find correct sector
$F4D4	Read data: first 256 into the data buffer and the rest into the overflow buffer
$F4ED	Convert GCR to normal
$F4F0	Check data block ID
$F4FB	Check data checksum
$F505	Exit, read was OK

e) Write Data Block of Specified Sector

Before the write job code ($90) is placed in the job queue, the IP puts the desired track and sector numbers into the header table as indicated below.

Job queue location	Use buffer #	address	Track # address	Sector # address
$0000	0	$0300-FF	$0006	$0007
$0001	1	$0400-FF	$0008	$0009
$0002	2	$0500-FF	$000A	$000B
$0003	3	$0600-FF	$000C	$000D
$0004	4	$0700-FF	$000E	$000F
$0005	5	NO RAM	$0010	$0011

Once the track and sector values are in place, the IP puts the write job code into the job queue in the location that corresponds to the data buffer containing the data to be written. The next time the 6502 is in FDC mode it finds the job request. If necessary, it turns on the drive motor, waits for it to get up to speed, and moves the head to the proper track. It then executes the write routine outlined below:

OVERVIEW OF THE FDC WRITE ROUTINE

$F575	Calculate checksum.
$F57A	Test if write protect on.
$F586	Convert buffer to GCR.
$F589	Find correct sector.
$F58C	Wait out header gap.
$F594	Switch to write mode and write out five $FF's as sync.
$F5B1	Write out overflow buffer.
$F5BF	Write out data buffer.
$F5CC	Switch to read mode.
$F5D9	Convert GCR back to 8-bit.
$F5DC	Change job code to VERIFY.
$F5E6	Go back to verify it.

f) Format a Blank Diskette

The IP format routine at $C8C6 sets up a JMP $FAC7 instruction at $0600 and then puts an EXECUTE job code ($E0) into the job queue ($0003). On its next pass through the idle loop the FDC finds the execute job code, executes the code at $0600, and jumps to the formatting routine outlined below.

192

$FAC7	Check if this is first entry. If not, branch to $FAF5.
$FACB	Do bump to track #1 (CLUNK!)
$FAE3	Initialize error count and bytes around track. Exit.
$FAF5	Check if on right track.
$FB00	Check for write protect tab.
$FB0C	Erase track with sync.
$FB0F	Write half of track with sync and other half with non-sync.
$FB35	Time sync & non-sync parts.
$FB7D	Compare times and calculate how long tail gaps should be.
$FC36	Create images of headers.
$FC86	Create dummy data block.
$FC8E	Convert headers to GCR.
$FC9E	Convert data block to GCR.
$FCAA	Write out sectors in sequence.
$FD24	Go to read mode and verify.
$FD8B	All sectors OK; do next track.
$FD96	All tracks done; exit.

9.6 Using the FDC Routines

Some of the floppy disk controller routines in the 1541's ROM are relatively easy to use. Others are much more difficult.

The easy ones are those that do not involve reading or writing to a diskette. An example of this type of routine would be the GET4GB ($F7E6) routine that converts 5 GCR bytes into 4 normal 8-bit binary bytes. These routines can be executed by using the techniques described in Section 9.4.

The tough ones are those that involve reading or writing to a diskette. To illustrate how to do this, we'll try something interesting. How about developing a routine that allows us to move the head anywhere on a diskette (say track 5) and read the next header (or whatever) that passes over the read/write head.

First we have to find out how to move the head around. A quick check of the map of the I/O chips at the end of Appendix A tells us that the stepper motor that moves the head is controlled by bits 0 and 1 of DSKCNT ($1C00). Cycling these two bits causes the head to move. Hmm... Cycling the bits must mean: 00-01-10-11-00 versus 11-10-01-00-11. Time out for a bit of testing. Here's our program:

```
100 REM MOVE THE 1541'S HEAD
110 PRINT"{CLR}{DOWN}COMMANDS: U=UP D=DO
WN Q=QUIT"
120 OPEN 15,8,15,"I"
130 PRINT#15,"M-R"CHR$(0)CHR$(28)
140 GET#15,X$:X=ASC(X$+CHR$(0))
150 BI=X AND 3
160 PRINT"{HOME}{DOWN 3}BI="BI
170 GET A$
180 IF A$="U"THEN BI=BI+1
190 IF A$="D"THEN BI=BI-1
200 IF A$="Q"THEN CLOSE 15:END
210 BI=BI AND 3
220 R=(X AND 252)OR BI
230 PRINT#15,"M-W"CHR$(0)CHR$(28)CHR$(1)
CHR$(R)
240 GOTO 130
```

After much peeking through the drive door with a flashlight we discover that our program actually does make the head move. When we press "U" the head moves closer to the center (higher track numbers) and when we press "D" the head moves outward (lower track numbers). We've got it! Quick let's write it down before we forget.

To move the head, cycle bits 0 and 1 of $1C00

```
00 → 01 → 10 → 11 → 00    head moves inwards
 0     1     2     3     0

11 → 10 → 01 → 00 → 11    head moves outwards
 3     2     1     0     3
```

The only problem that remains is to find out how much the head moves each time. Hmm... If we read from a track and then peek at $1C00... Time for more testing:

```
10 REM CHECK PHASE FOR ALL TRACKS
20 OPEN 15,8,15,"I"
```

```
30 OPEN 1,8,5,"#"
40 FOR TR=1 TO 35
50 PRINT#15,"U1:5 0"TR;0
60 PRINT#15,"M-R"CHR$(0)CHR$(28)
70 GET#15,X$:X=ASC(X$+CHR$(0))
80 PRINT TR;X AND 3
90 NEXT
100 CLOSE1:CLOSE15
```

When we run this test program, we get a very interesting table:

1	0	2	2	3	0	4	2	5	0	6	2	7	0
8	2	9	0	10	2	11	0	12	2	13	0	14	2
15	0	16	2	17	0	18	2	19	0	20	2	21	0
22	2	23	0	24	2	25	0	26	2	27	0	28	2
29	0	30	2	31	0	32	2	33	0	34	2	35	0

The phase of the stepper motor is always even (0 or 2) when the head is on a track. Therefore, the head must be moving half a track at a time. Very interesting indeed!

Now that we can move the head around, we want to find out how to read something. But before we go rummaging through the ROM's, wasn't there something about the clock rate being different for each zone? Ah, here it is. Bits 5 and 6 of $1C00 set the recording density. Let's see. Bit 5 represents 32 and bit 6, 64. Let's change one line of our last test program and try again. Here's the new line:

```
80 PRINT TR;X AND 96
```

When we run our revised program, we get another interesting table.

1	96	2	96	3	96	4	96	5	96	6	96	7	96
8	96	9	96	10	96	11	96	12	96 ·	13	96	14	96
15	96	16	96	17	96	18	64	19	64	20	64	21	64
22	64	23	64	24	64	25	32	26	32	27	32	28	32
29	32	30	32	31	0	32	0	33	0	34	0	35	0

By George, we've got it.

	$1C00			
Zone	Tracks	Bit 6	Bit 5	Number
1	1-17	1	1	96
2	18-24	1	0	64
3	25-30	0	1	32
4	31-35	0	0	0

Let's do some digging in those ROM's now. A quick scan through the table of Major FDC Entry Points in Section 9.5 (c) turns up SEAK ($F3B1), seek any header on the track. A check of the detailed analysis in Appendix B looks promising. A careful study of a disassembly of the routine indicates that this is just what we were looking for. And, we don't have to do much setup either. Here's all the information we need:

1. The entry point is $F3B1.
2. JOB ($45) should be $30 so the branch at $F3E6 is taken.
3. JOBN ($3F) should contain the correct buffer number so the error handler routine at $F969 works properly.

Now comes the tricky part. Since the routine involves reading from or writing to a diskette, we cannot execute the routine using a memory-execute command. We have to use a two step process:

1. Use a memory-write command to store a machine language routine (it does the set-up and then a JMP to $F969) into the start of one of the buffers (we'll use buffer –0 at $0300).
2. Force the 6502, while in FDC mode, to execute our routine by putting a JUMP or EXECUTE job code in the appropriate spot in the job queue (we'll put a JUMP code into $0000).

The program listed below puts it all together for us. It may appear a bit intimidating at first. But, if you are interested in exploring the innards of your drive it is one of the most powerful tools presented in this manual. It allows you to move the head anywhere you want and read the next header passing over the read/write head. The screen display shows you where the head is, what track and sector was read, and describes any read errors that were encountered.

```
100 PRINT"{CLR}{DOWN}    MOVE THE 1541'S
READ/WRITE HEAD"
110 PRINT"{DOWN 2}INSERT TEST DISK"
120 PRINT"{DOWN 2}PRESS {RVS}RETURN{ROFF
} WHEN READY"
130 :
140 REM  MACHINE CODE ROUTINE TO READ A
HEADER
150 REM  RESIDES AT $0300 (BUFFER #0)
160 :
170 DATA 169,48:     :REM LDA #$30
180 DATA 133,69:     :REM STA $45
190 DATA 169,00:     :REM LDA #$00
200 DATA 133,63:     :REM STA $3F
210 DATA 76,177,243 :REM JMP $F3B1
220 :
230 D$(0)="00":D$(1)="01":D$(2)="10":D$(
3)="11"
240 DIM FD$(16)
250 FD$(0)="                          "
260 FD$(1)="01 ALL OK                 "
270 FD$(2)="02 HEADER BLOCK NOT FOUND"
280 FD$(3)="03 NO SYNC CHARACTER      "
290 FD$(9)="09 HEADER BLOCK CHKSUM ER"
300 T=18:N1$="?":N2$="?":TR=255
310 GET A$:IF A$<>CHR$(13) GOTO 310
320 :
```

```
330 OPEN 15,8,15,"I"
340 :
350 REM DIG OUT MASTER DISK ID
360 :
370 PRINT#15,"M-R"CHR$(18)CHR$(0)CHR$(2)

380 GET#15,I1$:IFI1$=""THENI1$=CHR$(0)
390 GET#15,I2$:IFI2$=""THENI2$=CHR$(0)
400 :
410 PRINT"{CLR}"
420 :
430 REM READ THE DISK CONTROLLER PORT
440 :
450 PRINT#15,"M-R"CHR$(0)CHR$(28)
460 GET#15,A$: IF A$=""THEN A$=CHR$(0)
470 A=ASC(A$)
480 CV=3 AND A
490 A=(159ANDA)OR(96+32*((T>17)+(T>24)+(
T>30)))
500 PRINT#15,"M-W"CHR$(0)CHR$(28)CHR$(1)
CHR$(A OR 4)
510 :
520 REM DISPLAY VALUES
530 :
540 PRINT"{HOME}{DOWN}    MOVE THE 1541'S
 READ/WRITE HEAD"
550 PRINT"{DOWN}CURRENT PHASE ="CV
560 PRINT"BITS 1 & 0 OF $1C00 ARE "D$(CV
)
570 PRINT"{DOWN}MASTER DISK ID: "I1$;I2$
580 PRINT"{DOWN}TRACK # FROM STEPPER:"T"
{LEFT}      "
590 PRINT"{DOWN}FDC ERROR:"FD$(E)
600 T$=STR$(TR):S$=STR$(SE): IF E<>1 THEN
 T$="??":N1$="?":N2$="?":S$="??"
610 PRINT"{DOWN}TRACK # AS READ:   "RIGHT
$(T$,2)
620 PRINT"SECTOR # AS READ: "RIGHT$(S$,2
)
630 PRINT"ID OF TRACK READ: "N1$;N2$
640 PRINT"{DOWN 2}COMMANDS:"
650 PRINT"{DOWN}  F1 = MOVE HEAD OUT (LO
WER TRACK #)
660 PRINT"   F3 = MOVE HEAD IN (HIGHER TR
ACK #)
670 PRINT"   F5 = ATTEMPT TO READ TRACK #
 & ID"
680 PRINT"   F7 = TERMINATE PROGRAM"
690 PRINT"    I = INITIALIZE (TO TRACK 18
)"
700 P=PEEK(197)
```

```
710 IF P=3 GOTO 910
720 IF P=4 AND T>1 THEN C=-1:GOTO 800
730 IF P=5 AND T<35 THEN C=1:GOTO 800
740 IF P=6 GOTO 990
750 IF P=33 THEN PRINT#15,"I":T=18:E=0:A
=214:GOTO480
760 GOTO 450
770 :
780 REM CHANGE PHASE IN RESPONSE TO COMM
AND
790 :
800 CV=(CV + C)AND3
810 T=T+C*.5:IFT<1 THENT=1
820 IFT>36THENT=36
830 B=A AND 252
840 C=B+CV
850 PRINT#15,"M-W"CHR$(0)CHR$(28)CHR$(1)
CHR$(C)
860 E=0
870 GOTO 450
880 :
890 REM TERMINATE PROGRAM (DRIVE OFF)
900 :
910 PRINT#15,"M-W"CHR$(0)CHR$(28)CHR$(1)
CHR$(240)
920 FOR K=1TO10:GETA$:NEXT
930 CLOSE 15:END
940 :
950 REM ATTEMPT TO READ ANY HEADER
960 :
970 REM READ & SEND MACHINE CODE ROUTINE

980 :
990 RESTORE:C$=""
1000 FOR K=1 TO 11:READ X:C$=C$+CHR$(X):
NEXT
1010 PRINT#15,"M-W"CHR$(0)CHR$(3)CHR$(11
)C$
1020 :
1030 REM PUT JMP JOB IN THE JOB QUEUE
1040 :
1050 PRINT#15,"M-W"CHR$(0)CHR$(0)CHR$(1)
CHR$(208)
1060 :
1070 REM WAIT FOR JOB TO FINISH
1080 :
1090 PRINT#15,"M-R"CHR$(0)CHR$(0)
1100 GET#15,E$:E=ASC(E$+CHR$(0))
1110 IF E>127 GOTO 790
1120 :
```

```
1130 REM "E" IS FDC ERROR CODE RETURNED
1140 IF E<>1 GOTO 450
1150 :
1160 REM CLEAN READ SO DIG OUT ID, TRAK
& SECT
1170 :
1180 PRINT#15,"M-R"CHR$(22)CHR$(O)CHR$(4
)
1190 GET#15,N1$
1200 GET#15,N2$
1210 GET#15,X$:TR=ASC(X$+CHR$(O))
1220 GET#15,X$:SE=ASC(X$+CHR$(O))
1230 GOTO 450
```

Although this program allows you to move the head and read data in half-track increments, you can't double the capacity of your drive by using all 70 "tracks." The magnetic path produced by the read/write head is just too wide. However, it may be possible to devise a protection scheme in which the "protected information" is recorded when the head is in an "odd phase" (1 or 3). Crosstalk from the two odd-phase tracks, though, would make the diskette unreadable except by a specialized routine like this.

9.7 The Recording Process

A floppy diskette consists of a circular piece of plastic. It is coated on both sides with a thin layer of magnetic particles, usually particles of iron oxide. Each particle is made up of a large number of extremely small atomic magnets called "magnetic domains." When a floppy diskette is new, these magnetic domains are oriented randomly and the surface is unmagnetized.

The record/play head consists of a coil of wire wrapped around a ring of iron or other magnetic material. A small segment of the ring is missing. This is the "gap." The gap is the part that comes in contact with the surface of the diskette. Magnified many times, the head looks something like this:

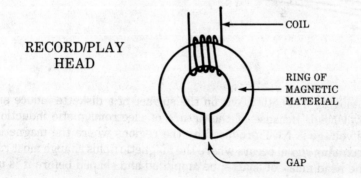

RECORD/PLAY HEAD — COIL — RING OF MAGNETIC MATERIAL — GAP

Write Mode:

In write mode an electric current passes through the coil. The current causes the head to become an electromagnet whose strength and polarity depends on the amount and direction of the electric current. The gap in the ring interrupts the magnetic field and causes it to flare outwards. If the gap is in contact with the surface of the floppy diskette, some of the magnetic domains on the surface shift position and line up with the magnetic field of the head. Some of these magnetic domains retain their new orientation even after leaving the vicinity of the gap, i.e., the surface of the diskette has become magnetized.

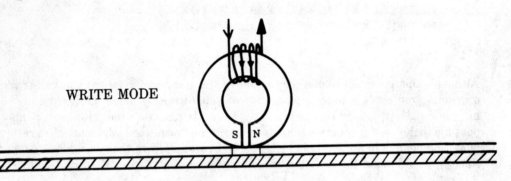

WRITE MODE

The amount and direction of the current flowing through the coil determines the strength and polarity of the electromagnet. The more current, the stronger the electromagnet, and the greater the magnetization of the surface of the diskette. In audio recording, the amount of current flowing through the coil fluctuates to match the changing audio signal. In digital recording, there are only two possible currents, full current in one direction or full current in the other direction. When data is recorded onto the surface of a floppy diskette, the track becomes a series of bar magnets laid end to end.

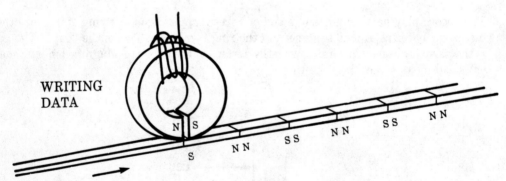

WRITING DATA

Read mode:

In read mode the moving magnetic areas on the surface of a diskette induce an electrical voltage in the head. Because of the nature of electromagnetic induction, the maximum induced voltage is NOT produced by the regions where the magnetic field is greatest. The maximum signal occurs where the magnetic fields change most rapidly. The signal from the head must, of course, be amplified and shaped before it is usable.

Writing data to a diskette:

When data is being recorded onto a floppy diskette, the data is "clocked out" at a fixed rate. This permits an interesting recording scheme. The direction of the current flowing through the head changes only when a "1" bit is to be recorded. Zeros are represented by the absence of a transition at a particular location. The diagram below represents what is actually recorded on a diskette.

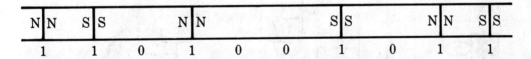

Note that the data recorded onto a diskette is not divided into bytes. There is just one continuous stream of bits. In order to know where to begin to read or write bits, we need some special identifying mark. This is the function of the SYNC mark, a string of 10 or more 1's in a row. The GCR code (see Chapter 7) is designed so that no combination of bytes can produce more than eight "1" bits in a row. This guarantees the uniqueness of the sync mark.

The 1541 records between 4000 and 6000 magnetic zones (bits) per inch. Since the diskette rotates at a constant angular velocity (300 rpm), you may wonder how Commodore manages to get more bits on the outer tracks than the inner ones. The 1541 manages this bit of magic by clocking out the data at different rates depending on the track. On the longer outer tracks, the data is clocked out faster than for an inner track (see table in Chapter 3). However, the increase in clock rate is not really proportional to the increase in track length. This means that the outer tracks have a bit density of only 4300 bits/inch while the inner tracks are recorded at 6000 bits/inch. If the clock were not increased for the outer tracks, the bit density on the outermost track would fall to about 3500 bits/inch.

Reading data from a diskette:

When data is being read from a floppy diskette, the data is "clocked in" at a fixed rate. A magnetic transition is interpreted as a "1" bit. The lack of a signal when data is expected is interpreted as a "0" bit. Since the speed of the drive is not absolutely constant, we can run into problems if there are too many "0" (no signal) bits in a row. Commodore's GCR code is designed so that no GCR byte, or combination of GCR bytes, ever contains more than two consecutive "0" bits. As a further precaution, the clock is zeroed (cleared) every time a "1" bit is read. This re-synchronizes the clock to the bit stream and prevents small fluctuations in the speed of the drive from causing read errors.

9.8 Block Diagram of the 1541

This block diagram of the 1541 electronics emphasizes the components involved in reading and writing data.

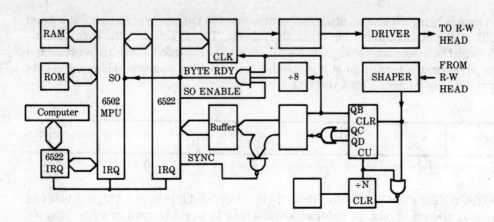

The divide-by-N counter determines the actual rate at which bits are read or written. For tracks 1-17 the clock divisor is 13, for tracks 18-24 it is 14, for tracks 25-30 it is 15, and for tracks 31-35 it is 16.

9.9 Writing Data to a Diskette

The diagrams below highlight the important components and waveforms involved in the writing of a GCR encoded data byte to disk.

WRITE MODE

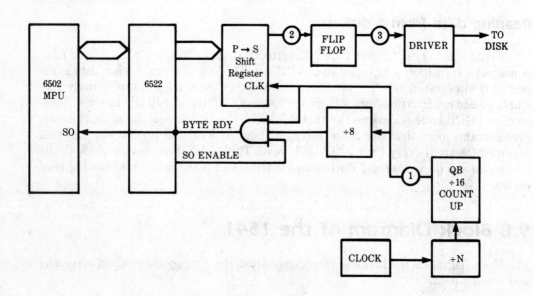

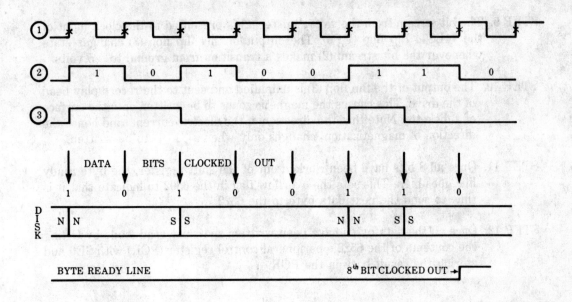

To help clarify the recording process let's follow a byte of data (10100110) as it is written to a diskette.

STEP 1. The 6502 converts the header block ID ($07), the 256 data bytes, the data block checksum, and two null bytes into 325 GCR encoded bytes.

STEP 2. The head is positioned to the appropriate track and the clock divisor is set to the correct value for this track.

STEP 3. The track is read until the correct sector header block is found. Wait out the header gap.

STEP 4. Switch to write mode by ANDing the contents of the 6522's peripheral control register (PCR) with $1F, ORing the result with $C0, and storing the final result back in the PCR.

STEP 5. Write out five $FF characters as the data block sync mark.

STEP 6. Transfer the first 8-bit byte of the GCR encoded data to the data lines (D0-D7) of the 6522 PIA.

STEP 7. Since Port A of the 6522 is configured as an output port, the data appears on the Port A lines PA0 to PA7. This transfers the byte to the 74LS165 (UD3) parallel to serial shift register.

STEP 8. The bits are clocked out of the shift register (2) whenever the QB line (1) of the 74LS193 hexadecimal counter (UF4) makes a transition from ground to +5 volts.

203

STEP 9. The bit stream from the shift register (2) is presented to the clock input of the 74LS74 flip flop (UF6). The output of this flip flop (3) changes state whenever the bit stream (2) makes a transition from ground to +5 volts.

STEP 10. The output of the flip flop (3) is amplified and sent to the record/play head of the drive. This causes the magnetic zones to be written onto the surface of a diskette. Note that the direction of the electric current, and hence the direction of magnetization, changes only when a "1" is to be written.

STEP 11. Once all 8 bits have been clocked out of the shift register, the byte ready line goes high. This sets the overflow flag in the 6502 to indicate that it is time to send the next data byte to the 6522.

STEP 12. Once all the data bytes have been written, switch to read mode by ORing the contents of the 6522's peripheral control register (PCR) with $E0 and storing the result back in the PCR.

9.10 Reading Data From a Diskette

The diagrams below highlight the important components and waveforms involved in reading a GCR encoded byte of data.

1541 BLOCK DIAGRAM
READ MODE

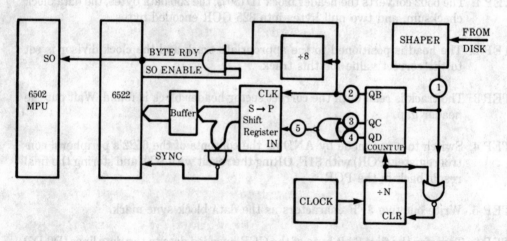

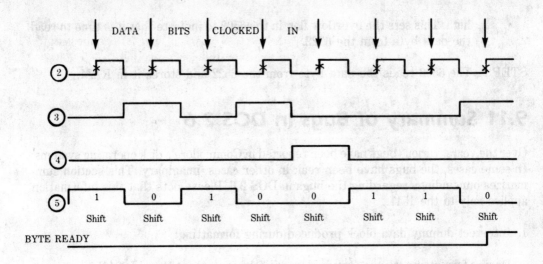

DATA BITS CLOCKED IN

② ③ ④ ⑤ 1 0 1 0 0 1 1 0

Shift Shift Shift Shift Shift Shift Shift Shift

BYTE READY

To help clarify the reading process let's follow a byte of data as it is read from a diskette.

STEP 1. The head is positioned to the appropriate track and the clock divisor is set to the correct value for this track.

STEP 2. The track is read until the correct sector header block is found.

STEP 3. Wait for the sync mark at the start of the data block.

STEP 4. As the track passes over the record/play head a stream of weak electrical pulses is induced in the head. A pulse is induced whenever the magnetic field changes its orientation. The pulse is amplified and shaped (1).

STEP 5. The stream of pulses from the shaper circuitry (1) is fed to the CLEAR input of the 74LS193 hexadecimal counter (UF4) and to the 74LS02 (UE5) NOR gate. Whenever a pulse occurs, the hexadecimal counter (UF4) and the divide by N counter (UE7) are cleared to a count of zero. This ensures that the clock is always synchronized with the incoming stream of pulses.

STEP 6. Once the hexadecimal counter has been cleared, it begins to count up the clock pulses it receives from the divide by 16 counter. QA (not shown) is the 1's bit of the counter. QB (2) is the 2's bit of the counter. QC (3) and QD (4) are the 4's and 8's bits, respectively.

STEP 7. On each ground to +5 volt transition of QB (2), a bit is shifted into the 74LS164 serial to parallel shift register (UD2). The bit that is shifted in (5) is found by NORing the QC (3) and QD (4) lines of the counter. Note that whenever a pulse clears the divide by 16 counter, the next bit is read as a "1." If the counter has not been cleared before the next ground to +5 volt transition of QB (2), the next bit is read as a "0."

STEP 8. Once 8 bits have been clocked into the shift register, the byte ready line goes high. This sets the overflow flag in the 6502 to indicate that it is time to read the data byte from the 6522.

STEP 9. The 6502 reads the data byte from the 6522 and stores it in RAM.

9.11 Summary of Bugs in DOS 2.6

Over the years, various bugs have been reported in Commodore's disk operating systems. In some cases, the bugs have been real; in other cases, imaginary. This section summarizes our findings regarding the bugs in DOS 2.6. Please note that this information applies only to the 1541.

1. Incorrect dummy data block produced during formatting:

   During formatting, all the Commodore disk drives (except the old 2040's) write out a dummy data block for each track and sector. On all the drives, except the 1541, this dummy data block consists of 256 null bytes ($00). On the 1541 the dummy data block consists of one $4B character followed by 255 $01 bytes. This is caused by an unnecessary INX instruction at $FC86. If this byte were replaced by a NOP ($EA), the normal dummy data block would be produced.

   The difference in the dummy data blocks does not cause any real problems and provides an easy way to identify a diskette formatted on the 1541.

2. The save and replace command "@0":

   Over the years numerous writers have advised Commodore owners not to use the save and replace command because it contained a bug. Our study of the ROM routines and a lot of testing has convinced us that the bug in the replace command is a myth. There are, however, two situations in which the use of the @ replacement command can cause problems:

a) Replacing an unclosed file, *SEQ, *PRG, etc:

   When you replace a file, the new file is written to diskette first. Then the DOS proceeds to trace through the file chain of the old file and marks the sectors it finds as available-for-use in the BAM. If the old file was unclosed, the track and sector links may be incorrect and some of the blocks in a different active file on the diskette may be freed (see a more detailed description of what happens in Section 2.5 on scratching a file). If this happens, subsequent writing to the diskette will overwrite the data in this file. This is the most likely cause of user complaints about a bug in the save and replace command on the 2040 and 4040 drives. The code at $C835 prevents this from happening on the 1541 drive.

b) Not enough space on disk:

   When a file is replaced, the new file is written to diskette before the old file is scratched. If there is not enough space on the disk for the new copy of the file, the process aborts. When this occurs, the error light will come on (72, DISK FULL). Usually, this makes people wonder if something went wrong; so they VERIFY to be sure the file has been saved correctly. The file verifies as OK. A check of the directory indicates no unclosed files. However, the file may appear somewhat shorter than before. This did not occur because your program has been compacted. Rather, it was truncated by the DOS. It isn't all there! We hope you have a backup handy. If not, you may still be able to recover your file. A printout of the BAM and some quick work on editing the directory entry's starting track and sector are in order. (See Chapter 8.) The sectors shown as unallocated (free) in the BAM hold the only complete copy of your program, the original version that is. The latter portions of the @ replacement version of your program have been stored in disk WOM (Write Only Memory) by the DOS. Bye, bye.

3. The Block-Read (B-R) command:

This command has been replaced by the U1 command and with good reason. The B-R command has two serious bugs that make it unusable on the 1541. The use of this command is NOT RECOMMENDED! See Chapter 5 for the gory details.

4. The Block-Write (B-W) command:

This command has been replaced by the U2 command and with good reason too. The B-W command is also unusable on the 1541. The use of this command is NOT RECOMMENDED either. Chapter 5 again gives the scoop.

5. The Block-Allocate (B-A) command:

Although this command seems to work correctly on other Commodore drives, it does not work properly on the 1541. This command really has two functions:

a) To allocate a free sector in the BAM:

When the track and sector specified in the block-allocate command is free (not in use) in the BAM, the block allocate command should allocate the block in the BAM. The B-A command appears to do this correctly on the 1541.

b) Find the next available track & sector:

If the track and sector specified in the block-allocate command is already allocated (in use) in the BAM, the block allocate command should not change the BAM in any way. It should return a 65, NO BLOCK error and report the track and sector of the next available block in the BAM. This feature of the B-A command was included to allow the programmer who is creating his own random access files to determine the next free block that he/she can use.

This feature of the B-A command does not work correctly on the 1541! The command does return the track and sector of a free block all right, but with a difference!

1. It occasionally returns a sector on track 18. This should not happen because track 18 is reserved for the directory.

207

2. It ALLOCATES ALL THE BLOCKS on the track that it returns in the error message in the BAM.

Because of these bugs, the use of the B-A command on the 1541 is NOT RECOMMENDED. However, the CERTIFY A DISKETTE program listed in Chapter 5 does work. The reason for this is that this program stores a duplicate copy of the BAM in C64 RAM which is later rewritten to the diskette. This technique repairs the damage done by the B-A command.

6. UJ: or U: command:

Commodore disk drives have traditionally used one or both of these commands to enable the user to reset the drive (just as though the drive were turned OFF and then ON again). Neither command works correctly on the 1541 drive. The drive goes on a trip to never-never land and must be turned OFF and then ON again to recover from one of these commands. The command "U;" is the one to use to reset the 1541.

7. UI- command:

The 1541 manual indicates that this command is used to set the disk drive to operate correctly with the VIC-20. Current 1541's work with a VIC-20, period.

Summary

Despite its flaws, the DOS in the 1541 is a remarkably efficient peripheral. The DOS programs for most other microcomputers are vastly inferior to DOS 2.6; a little faster maybe, but not as smart. The support of relative file structures, read ahead buffering, and the underlying principles of asynchronous I/O make the 1541 an outstanding bargain in the world of microcomputing. These features are normally found only in multiuser or multiprocess operating systems.

9.12 Write Incompatability with 4040

Programs or data stored on a diskette formatted on a 1541 disk drive can be READ using a 2040 or 4040 disk drive. Conversely, a 1541 disk drive can READ a diskette formatted on either a 2040 or 4040 disk drive. However, *these drives are not completely write compatible.*

This write-incompatibility problem appears to be caused by two things:

1. Differences in the header gap length.
2. Alignment problems (particularly with the 1541).

Let's consider the differences in the header gap length first.

Differences in Header Gap Length

The 2040 and 4040 drives use a header gap that is nine GCR bytes long while the 1541 uses a header gap that is only eight non-GCR bytes long. On this basis we would expect the header gaps to be 90 and 64 bits long respectively. However, when we use a bit-grabber to view the gap we find that the actual header gaps as recorded on disk are 100 bits for the 4040 and 92 bits for the 1541. In read mode, this makes no difference. After reading the header bytes to check that this is the correct sector, all the drives simply wait for the next sync mark. The number of bytes in the header gap does not matter. Once the sync mark is over, the first character in the data block is read. This is the data block ID character. If it is not a $07, the DOS reports a 22 READ ERROR (data block not found).

In write mode, however, the length of the header gap is important. After reading the header bytes to check that this is the correct sector, all the drives count off the bytes that make up the header gap. Once the correct number of bytes have been read, the drive flips to write mode and begins writing out the data block sync character. Since this is reputed to be an important aspect of the write incompatibility problem, let's examine what happens in some detail.

The last part of the header gap and the start of the data block sync mark in a sector of a diskette that has just been formatted on a 1541 disk drive looks something like this:

```
                 Sync mark
1541    xxxxxxxxxx1111111111111111111111111111111111111→ 92 bits
```

The last part of the header gap and the start of the data block sync mark in a sector of a diskette that has just been formatted on a 4040 disk drive looks something like this:

```
                                             Sync mark
4040    xxxxxxxxxxxxxxxxxxxxxxxxxxxxxxxxxxxxxx111111111111→ 100 bits
```

When a sector of a diskette that was ORIGINALLY FORMATTED ON A 4040/2040 disk drive is REWRITTEN ON A 1541, the result is as follows:

```
Original                                     Sync mark
4040    xxxxxxxxxxxxxxxxxxxxxxxxxxxxxxxxxxxxxx 111111111111→
Rewrite                 Sync mark
1541        xxxxxxxxxx-11111111111111111111111111111111111111→
                        Sync mark
Result      xxxxxxxxxx-111111111111111111111111111111111111111→
```

NOTE: The "-" marks when the drive switches into write mode. A transient current appears to flow through the record/play head during this time interval.

The original sync mark on the diskette has been completely overwritten by the new one. This sector can be read cleanly on any drive. It appears that a 1541 drive should be able to write data onto a diskette that was originally formatted on a 4040 drive *without causing any problems*.

When a sector of a diskette that was *originally formatted* on a 1541 disk drive is *rewritten* on a 4040/2040, the result is as follows:

```
Original                   Sync mark
1541          xxxxxxxxxx1111111111111111111111111111111111111➤
Rewrite                             Sync mark
4040          xxxxxxxxxxxxxxxxxx-1111111111111111111111111111111➤
                        Pseudo-sync      Sync mark
Result        xxxxxxxxxx1111111-11111111111111111111111111111111➤
```

NOTE: The "·" marks when the drive switches into write mode. A transient current appears to flow through the record/play head during this time interval.

In this case, the original sync mark on the diskette has NOT been completely overwritten by the new one. The start of the old sync mark is still there. What actually gets recorded at the start of the "new" sync mark depends on the speed of the drives, the polarity of the magnetic field used to record the original "1" at that spot on the diskette, and any transients that flow through the head as it switches into write mode.

Before you read this next section, be sure that you understand Section 9.7 on the Recording Process.

Let's take a look at an "exploded" view of that spot just before the new sync character is written. Remember, a "1" is not recorded as magnetization in a particular direction. It is simply a change in the direction. Now that you've got that straight, here is what that spot might look like.

Original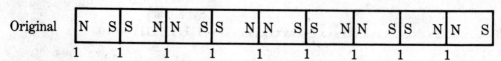

Everything appears normal. Now let's write that sync mark.

Original by a 1541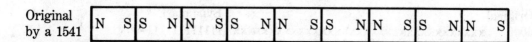

Replacement sync mark written by a 4040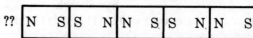

?? = effects of transient currents

Result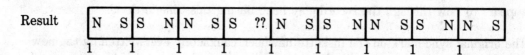

Everything worked out just fine. We have a clean sync mark and the sector can be read cleanly by either drive. However, suppose our 74LS74 flip-flop (UF6) had been in the opposite state or the speed of this drive did not exactly match this new one. What would happen? Take a look.

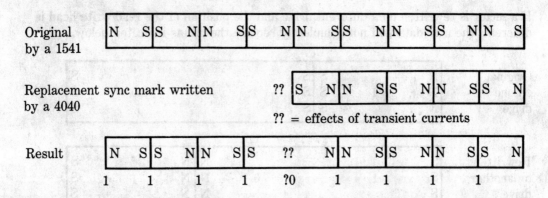

Argh! Potential problems. Because the magnetic polarity of the new "1" happened to match the polarity of the existing zone, we appear to have just created a double-length magnetic zone. If we have, this will be interpreted as a "0" bit. From a study of the bits actually recorded on disk, this appears to happen every time! If there are more than 10 preceeding "1" bits, this single "0" will be interpreted as the end of the sync mark and the drive will interpret the rest of the sync bits as data. Since this will definitely NOT be decoded as a $07 byte, the drive errs out with a 22 READ ERROR.

Since the header gaps only differ in length by 8 bits, we should always have only seven 1's in the pseudo-sync. An examination of the bits recorded on the disk seems to support this conclusion. As a further test we did some testing using recently aligned drives. We found surprisingly few errors when we use a 4040 disk drive to rewrite all non-directory sectors on a 1541 formatted disk. On a freshly formatted diskette, we found no errors at all after rewriting over 2400 sectors. If the sectors of the 1541 diskette had been rewritten several times using a 1541 before they were rewritten on a 4040, we did start to find a few errors. However, the error count was low. Usually less than two errors when rewriting all 640 sectors and these tended to occur in two specific areas: on tracks 25 or 26 or on tracks 31 or 32. These findings lead us to conclude that the differences in header gap length is NOT the cause of write compatibility problems between the 1541 and 4040 disk drives.

If for some reason you want to reduce the difference in header gap further when writing onto a 1541 formatted diskette using a 4040 drive, enter the following magic incantation in either program or immediate mode.

```
OPEN 15,8,15
PRINT#15, "M-W"CHR$(157)CHR$(16)CHR$(1)CHR$(8)
CLOSE 15
```

This will change the header gap length of the 4040 drive from 9 to 8 GCR bytes (actual length = 90 bits). You can now write to the 1541 diskette with little fear of damage. However, you must remember to reset your 4040 drive (turn it off or issue a UJ command) before you insert one of your 4040 formatted diskettes. Otherwise, a magnetic plague will develop among your 4040 formatted diskettes. Don't say you weren't warned!

Head Positioning Problems

Since we encountered so few errors using properly aligned drives, we feel that most of the reported problems of incompatibilities are the result of head positioning errors.

If a sector is rewritten on a different drive and the position of the read/write head is different, the new data will not completely replace the old as indicated below.

Original on one drive	N			S	S					S
	N	1		S	S	1			0	S
	N			S	S					S

Rewritten on another drive	S				N	N				S
	S	1		0	N	N		1		S
	S				N	N				S

Original	N	1	S	S	1			0		S

Rewritten by another drive	S				N	N				S
	S	1		0	N	N		1		S
	S				N	N				S

When this sector is read on the original drive, the head will pick up both the new signal and the old signal. The relative strengths of these two signals depend on the amount of the original signal remaining. If the two drives are sufficiently different, the read signal will be garbled and produce an abundance of 22 and 23 READ ERROR's.

Summary

In conclusion, although there is a difference in header gap size between the 1541 and the 4040 drives, this does NOT appear to be the cause of write incompatibility problems. Most complaints about the write incompatibilities of various disk drives are probably due to problems in head positioning. Further evidence for this is the fact that some schools are experiencing similar difficulties when students use several different 1541 drives for saving programs on a single diskette.

9.13 TOOLS FOR EXPLORATION

To make your exploration of the 1541 easier we have developed two programs to assist you.

a) Disk peek program

   This program allows you to look at a hex dump of any area of the 1541's RAM or ROM. This is a very useful tool for examining the contents of the 1541's RAM.

b) Create a file program

   This program allows you to read out any area of the 1541's RAM or ROM and store the contents into a program file with any load address you choose. You can then load the file into your 64's memory and examine it using an extended machine language monitor such as SUPERMON.

NOTE: Line 160 contains a special character #184 repeated 21 times. This character can be typed by holding down the Commodore logo key in the lower left corner and pressing the U key.

1541 DISK PEEK

```
100 REM 1541 DISK PEEK
110 REM BY GERALD NEUFELD
120 CO=0:C2=2:C7=7:CA=10:F=15:CG=16:HO=4
8:HX=127
130 Z$=CHR$(0):N$=""
140 M$=" {RVS}      PRESS:   P TO PAUSE    Q
 TO QUIT    {ROFF}"
150 PRINT"{CLR}"TAB(9)"PEEK OF 1541'S ME
MORY"
160 PRINTTAB(9)"{#184 21}"
170 PRINTTAB(4)"  COPYRIGHT: G. NEUFELD,
 1983"
180 PRINT"{DOWN}            ONE MOMENT PLEAS
E ...."
190 DIM HX$(255),H$(15)
191 FOR K=0 TO 9:H$(K)=CHR$(48+K):NEXT:F
ORK=1TO15:H$(K)=CHR$(55+K):NEXT
200 FORJ=0TOF:FORK=0TOF:HX$(J*16+K)=H$(J
)+H$(K):NEXT:NEXT
210 PRINT"{HOME}{DOWN 2}"M$
220 PRINT"{DOWN} INPUT START ADDRESS IN
 HEXADECIMAL"
230 OPEN 15,8,15
240 PRINT"{DOWN} $0000":PRINT"{UP}";
250 INPUT H$
260 HL=CO:HH=CO:FORK=1TO2:C=ASC(MID$(H$,
K))-HO:IFC>CATHENC=C-C7
270 IF C<CO OR C>F THENPRINT"{UP 2}";:GO
TO240
280 D=ASC(MID$(H$,K+2))-HO:IFD>CATHEND=D
-C7
290 IF D<CO OR D>F THENPRINT"{UP 2}";:GO
TO240
300 HH=HH+C*CG^(C2-K):HL=HL+D*CG^(C2-K):
NEXTK
310 PRINT"{UP}"TAB(6);
320 PRINT#15,"M-R"CHR$(HL)CHR$(HH)CHR$(8
)
330 O$="":FOR K=COTOC7:GET#15,A$:IF A$=N
$THENA$=Z$
340 A=ASC(A$):E=AANDHX:E$=".":IFE>31ANDE
<97THENE$=CHR$(E)
350 O$=O$+E$:PRINT" "HX$(ASC(A$));:NEXT:
```

```
PRINT" {RVS}"O$
360 FL=0:HL=HL+8:IFHL>255THENHL=HL-256:H
H=HH+1:FL=1:PRINTM$
370 IF HL=128 THEN FL=1:PRINTM$
380 PRINT" $"HX$(HH)HX$(HL);:IFFL=1THENP
RINT:PRINT"{UP}";:GOTO250
390 GET A$:IF A$=""GOTO 320
400 IF A$="P"THENPRINT:PRINT"{UP}";:GOTO
250
410 CLOSE15
```

CREATE A FILE

```
10 PRINT"{CLR}{DOWN}"TAB(6)"DISK ROM TO
FILE"
20 INPUT"{DOWN}START AT LOCATION (HEX)
C100{LEFT 6}";A$
30 Z$=A$:GOSUB280:S=Z:IF ZF=1 GOTO 20
40 PRINT"{UP}"TAB(31)Z
50 INPUT"{DOWN}QUIT AT LOCATION (HEX)  F
FFF{LEFT 6}";A$
60 Z$=A$:GOSUB280:Q=Z:IF ZF=1 GOTO 50
70 PRINT"{UP}"TAB(31)Z
80 INPUT"{DOWN}SAVE IN FILE NAMED  ROM 1
541{LEFT 10}";F$
90 INPUT"{DOWN}WITH LOAD ADDRESS OF (HEX
)  1100{LEFT 6}";A$
100 Z$=A$:GOSUB280:L=Z:IF ZF=1 GOTO 90
110 PRINT"{UP}"TAB(31)Z
120 OPEN15,8,15,"IO"
130 OPEN 1,8,5,"@0:"+F$+",P,W"
140 INPUT#15,EN,EM$,ET,ES
150 IF EN>19 THEN PRINT"{DOWN}DISK ERROR
"EN;EM$;ET;ES:CLOSE1:CLOSE15:STOP
160 PRINT"{DOWN 2}"
170 LH=INT(L/256):LL=L-256*LH
180 PRINT#1,CHR$(LL);CHR$(LH);
190 FOR K=S TO Q
200 KH=INT(K/256):KL=K-256*KH
210 PRINT#15,"M-R"CHR$(KL)CHR$(KH)
220 GET#15,A$:IF A$="" THEN A$=CHR$(0)
230 PRINT#1,A$;
240 PRINT"{UP}WORKING ON"K
250 NEXT
260 CLOSE1:CLOSE15:END
270 :
280 Z=0:ZF=0
290 IF LEN(Z$)>4 THEN ZF=1:PRINT"{DOWN}{
RVS}HEX STRING TOO LONG":RETURN
300 IF LEN(Z$)<4 THEN ZF=1:PRINT"{DOWN}{
```

```
RVS}HEX STRING TOO SHORT":RETURN
310 FOR K=1 TO 4
320 ZN=ASC(MID$(Z$,K))-48:IF ZN>9 THEN Z
N=ZN-7
330 IF ZN<0 OR ZN>15 THEN ZF=1:PRINT"{DO
WN}{RVS}BAD HEX CHARACTER":RETURN
340 Z = Z + ZN * 16^(4-K)
350 NEXT
360 RETURN
```

HAVE FUN!

Late News

In early 1984 Commodore began shipping the 1541 disk drives that contained a new $E000-$FFFF ROM. The part numbers of these ROMs are: original 901229-03 revised 901229-05. The changes in the new ROM are:

$E683 $E68B	Eliminate JSR TO ITTERR($EA4E) to solve stack overflow problems.
$E780 to $E7A1	Eliminate power-on boot of the utility loader to solve possible problems during initialization.
$E9DC	Insert JMP to patch at $FF20.
$EAA4	Insert JMP to patch at $EF10.
$EBDB/DD/E0/E2	Change initialization of the serial bus.
$FEE6	New ROM checksum.
$FF10	New patch to change the initialization of the serial bus during the power-up routine DSKINT.
$FF20	New patch to the serial bus listen routine ACPTR.

The ROM in the SX-64 has an additional change. The header block gap at $F58D has been changed from $08 to $09 to eliminate the difference in header gap size between the 4040 and SX-64.

APPENDIX A
1541 RAM VARIABLE DEFINITIONS

```
-----------------------------------------------------------------
                    JOB QUEUE: $0000-$0005
The job queue is used to tell the disk controller what
disk operations to perform. A disk command such as LOAD,
SAVE, SCRATCH, etc. is interpreted by the drive's 6502
(while in its normal mode) and broken down into a set of
simple operations (jobs) such as: read track 9 sector 18
into data buffer #2, write the data in buffer #3 out to
track 12 sector 5, etc. The track and sector information
required for the job is placed into the header table and
the JOB CODE corresponding to the job to be done is put
in the job queue. The job code's position in the queue
indicates which data buffer (if any) is to be used and
where the track and sector information is stored in the
header table. When the 6502 is next in its floppy disk
controller mode (it switches every 10 milliseconds), it
scans the job queue looking for jobs to do. If it finds
one, it carries it out making use of the track and sector
information in the header table. Once the job is done,
or aborted, the disk controller replaces the job code
with an error code that indicates the job status.
-----------------------------------------------------------------
        JOB CODES                    ERROR CODES
-------------------------    ------------------------------------
  $80 READ a sector          $01 job completed successfully!
  $90 WRITE a sector         $02 header block not found
  $A0 VERIFY a sector        $03 no SYNC character
  $B0 SEEK any sector        $04 data block not found
  $C0 BUMP (move) head       $05 data block checksum error
      to track #1            $07 verify error after write
  $D0 JUMP to machine        $08 write protect error
      code in buffer         $09 header block checksum error
  $E0 EXECUTE code in        $0A data block too long
      buffer once up to      $0B ID mismatch error
      speed & head ready     $10 byte decoding error
-----------------------------------------------------------------
ADDRESS| NAME |          JOB QUEUE DEFINITIONS
-----------------------------------------------------------------
$0000  | JOBS | Use buffer #0 ($0300+), find T/S in $06/7
$0001  |      | Use buffer #1 ($0400+), find T/S in $08/9
$0002  |      | Use buffer #2 ($0500+), find T/S in $0A/B
$0003  |      | Use buffer #3 ($0600+), find T/S in $0C/D
$0004  |      | Use buffer #4 ($0700+), find T/S in $0E/F
$0005  |      | Use buffer #5 (no RAM), find T/S in $10/1
-----------------------------------------------------------------
                   HEADER TABLE: $0006-$0011
This is the area that specifies which tracks and sectors
are to be used for the jobs in the job queue. Tracks and
sectors are not needed for BUMP or JUMP jobs.
-----------------------------------------------------------------
ADDRESS  | NAME |         HEADER TABLE DEFINITIONS
-----------------------------------------------------------------
$0006/7  | HDRS | Track/sector for job in $0000 (buffer 0)
$0008/9  |      | Track/sector for job in $0001 (buffer 1)
$000A/B  |      | Track/sector for job in $0002 (buffer 2)
$000C/D  |      | Track/sector for job in $0003 (buffer 3)
$000E/F  |      | Track/sector for job in $0004 (buffer 4)
$0010/1  |      | Track/sector for job in $0005 (buffer 5)
-----------------------------------------------------------------
```

ADDRESS	NAME	1541 RAM VARIABLE DEFINITIONS
$0012	DSKID	Master copy of disk ID. This is the ID specified when the disk was formatted. It is updated whenever a SEEK job is performed (see ROM patch $EF25). The initialize command performs a seek and therefore updates the master ID. 　　$0012　first ID character 　　$0013　second ID character
$0014/5		Unused - Disk ID for drive #1
$0016	HEADER	Image of the most recent header read. The characters appear here in the same sequence that Commodore's manual says they are recorded onto the disk surface. 　　$0016　first ID character 　　$0017　second ID character 　　$0018　track number 　　$0019　sector number 　　$001A　header checksum NOTE: They are actually recorded onto disk in the opposite sequence.
$001B	ACTJOB	Not used
$001C	WPSW	Flag to indicate that there has been a change in the write protect status.
$001D		UNUSED　(WPSW for drive #1)
$001E	LWPT	last state of the write protect switch
$001F		UNUSED　(LWPT for drive #1) Set to $01 on power-up
$0020	DRVST	disk drive status 　bit　　meaning 　---　　------- 　　4　　shut down drv motor? 1=yes 0=no 　　5　　drive motor　　　1=on 0=off 　　6　　head stepping　　1=on 0=off 　　7　　drive ready?　　1=no 0=yes
$0021		UNUSED　(DRVST for drive #1)
$0022	DRVTRK	Track currently under R/W head
$0023		UNUSED　(DRVTRK for drive #1)
$0024- $002D	STAB	Work area for doing interconversions of binary data and its GCR write images
$002E/F	SAVPNT	Temporary storage of pointers
$0030/1	BUFPNT	Pointer to currently active buffer
$0032/3	HDRPNT	Pointer to active values in header table
$0034	GCRPNT	Pointer to last character converted
$0035	GCRERR	Not used
$0036	BYTCNT	Byte counter for GCR/binary conversions
$0037	BITCNT	Not used
$0038	BID	Data block ID character ($07)
$0039	HBID	Header block ID character ($08)
$003A	CHKSUM	Storage of data or header checksum

ADDRESS	NAME	1541 RAM VARIABLE DEFINITIONS
$003B	HINIB	Unused
$003C	BYTE	Unused
$003D	DRIVE	Always $00 on 1541
$003E	CDRIVE	Currently active drive ($FF if inactive)
$003F	JOBN	Position of last job in job queue (0-5)
$0040	TRACC	Byte counter for GCR/binary conversions
$0041	NXTJOB	Position of next job in job queue (0-5)
$0042	NXTRK	Next track to move head to
$0043	SECTR	Sector counter. Used by format routine
$0044	WORK	Temporary workspace
$0045	JOB	Temporary storage of job code
$0046	CTRACK	Unused
$0047	DBID	Data block ID code. Set on reset to $07. This may be changed to write or read data blocks with different data block ID codes. However, the first nybble of the data block ID code should always be a zero ($0-). Otherwise, the controller will have difficulty detecting the end of the sync mark and the start of DBID. If you try to read a sector whose DBID is different from the value stored here, the disk controller will put an error code of $04 in the job queue and the drive will report a #22 error (DATA BLOCK NOT FOUND).
$0048	ACLTIM	Timer for acceleration of head
$0049	SAVSP	Temporary save of the stack pointer
$004A	STEPS	The number of steps to move the head to get to the desired track. To move the head over 1 track, requires XX steps. Values between 0 and 127 move the head out (to lower track numbers). Values over 128 move the head (256-value) steps in (to higher track numbers)
$004B	TMP	Temporary storage
$004C	CSECT	Last sector read
$004D	NEXTS	Next sector to service
$004E	NXTBF	Hi byte of a pointer to the next buffer of GCR bytes to be changed into binary. The GCR bytes in the overflow buffer are translated first. This points to the buffer that holds the rest of them.
$004F	NXTPNT	Lo byte of a pointer to the next GCR byte location that is to be translated
$0050	GCRFLG	Flag to indicate whether the data in the currently active buffer has been left in binary (0) or GCR (1) form.
$0051	FTNUM	Used by the formatting routine to store the number of the track currently being formatted. Set on reset to $FF.

ADDRESS	NAME	1541 RAM VARIABLE DEFINITIONS
$0052/5	BTAB	Staging area for the four binary bytes being converted to GCR by PUT4BG($F6D0) or from GCR by GET4GB($F7E6).
$0056/D	GTAB	Staging area for the five GCR bytes being converted from binary by PUT4BG ($F6D0) or to binary by GET4GB($F7E6).
$005E	AS	Number of steps to use to accelerate or decelerate when stepping the head ($04)
$005F	AF	Acceleration/deceleration factor ($04)
$0060	ACLSTP	Number of steps left to accelerate or decelerate when stepping the head
$0061	RSTEPS	Number of steps left to step the head in fast stepping (run) mode.
$0062/3	NXTST	Pointer to the appropriate head stepping routine. Normally $FA05 (not stepping)
$0064	MINSTP	Minimum number of steps for the head to move to make the use of fast stepping mode useful($C8). If fewer steps needed, use the slow stepping mode.
$0065/6	VNMI	Pointer to start of NMI routine ($EB2E). Set on power up or drive reset.
$0067	NMIFLG	Flag to indicate whether NMI in progress
$0068	AUTOFG	Flag to enable (0) or disable (1) the auto initialization of a disk (read BAM) if ID mismatch detected.
$0069	SECINC	Sector increment for use by SEQ routine. Set on reset to ($0A).
$006A	REVCNT	Counter for error recovery (number of attempts so far) Set on reset to $05
$006B/C	USRJMP	Pointer to the start of the user jump table($FFF6). Set on power up or reset.
$006D/E	BMPNT	Pointer to the start of the bit map ($0400). Set when a disk is initialized.
$006F	T0=TEMP	Temporary work area ($6F on reset)
$0070	T1	Temporary work area
$0071	T2	Temporary work area
$0072	T3	Temporary work area ($FF on reset)
$0073	T4	Temporary work area
$0074		Temporary work area
$0075/6	IP	Indirect pointer variable ($0100) Set on power up or reset.
$0077	LSNADR	Listener address ($28 on reset)
$0078	TLKADR	Talker address ($48 on reset)
$0079	LSNACT	Active listener flag
$007A	TLKACT	Active talker flag
$007B	ADRSED	Addressed flag
$007C	ATNPND	Attention pending flag
$007D	ATNMOD	6502 in attention mode
$007E	PRGTRK	Last program accessed
$007F	DRVNUM	Current drive number (always 0 in 1541)
$0080	TRACK	Current track number ($00 after use)
$0081	SECTOR	Current sector number ($00 after use)
$0082	LINDX	Logical index (current channel#)

ADDRESS	NAME	1541 RAM VARIABLE DEFINITIONS
$0083	SA	Current secondary address
$0084	ORGSA	Original secondary address
$0085	DATA	Temporary data byte
$0086	R0	Temporary result
$0087	R1	Temporary result
$0088	R2	Temporary result
$0089	R3	Temporary result
$008A	R4	Temporary result
$008B/E	RESULT	Result area ($008B-$008E)
$008F/3	ACCUM	Accumulator ($008F-0093)
$0094/5	DIRBUF	Directory buffer ($0094-0095) $05/$02
$0096	ICMD	IEEE command in (not used on 1541)
$0097	MYPA	MY PA flag $00
$0098	CONT	Bit counter for serial $00
		--
		Buffer byte pointers
		These pointers (one for each buffer) are
		used to point at the next byte in the
		buffer to be used. The B-P command sets
		these pointers.
		--
$0099/A	BUFTAB	Points to next byte in buffer #0 ($0300)
$009B/C		Points to next byte in buffer #1 ($0400)
$009D/E		Points to next byte in buffer #2 ($0500)
$009F/0		Points to next byte in buffer #3 ($0600)
$00A1/2		Points to next byte in buffer #4 ($0700)
$00A3/4		Points to next byte in CMD buffer($0200)
$00A5/6		Points to next byte in ERR buffer($02D6)
		--
$00A7/D	BUF0	Table of channel#'s assigned to each of the buffers. $FF is inactive buffer.
$00AE/4	BUF1	Table of channel#'s assigned to each of the buffers. $FF is inactive buffer.
$00B5/A	RECL	Table of lo bytes of record numbers for each buffer
$00BB/0	RECH	Table of hi bytes of record numbers for each buffer
$00C1/6	NR	Table of next record numbers for buffers
$00C7/C	RS	Table of record size for each buffer
$00CD/2	SS	Table of side sectors for each buffer
$00D3	F1PTR	File stream 1 pointer
$00D4	RECPTR	Pointer to start of record
$00D5	SSNUM	Number of side sector
$00D6	SSIND	Index to side sector
$00D7	RELPTR	Relative file pointer to track
$00D8/C	ENTSEC	Sector of directory entries
$00DD/1	ENTIND	Index of directory entries
$00E2/6	FILDRV	Default flag, drive # (all 0 on 1541)
$00E7/B	PATTYP	Pattern, replace, closed-flags, type
$00EC/1	FILTYP	Channel file type
$00F2/7	CHNRDY	Channel status
$00F8	EIOFLG	Temporary for EOI
$00F9	JOBNUM	Current job number

ADDRESS	NAME	1541 RAM VARIABLE DEFINITIONS
$00FA/E	LRUTBL	Least recently used table
$00FF/0	NODRV	No drive flag for drives 0 and 1
$0101/2	DSKVER	DOS version taken from track 18 sector 0 for drives 0 and 1
$0103	ZPEND	Unused

```
---------------------------------------------
              STACK AREA  $0104-$01FF
---------------------------------------------
```

ADDRESS	NAME	1541 RAM VARIABLE DEFINITIONS
$0200- $0229	CMDBUF	Command buffer ($0200-$0229) Disk commands such as: N0:GAMES #1,G1 that are sent to the disk drive from the computer over the serial bus are stored here. The command is parsed to locate special characters such as : , Once the command has been interpreted, ROM routines are executed to do it.
$022A	CMDNUM	Command code number
$022B/D	LINTAB	SA:LINDX table ($022B-$023D) This table indicates the current status of each data channel (secondary address) Each position represents one channel, channel 0=$022B; 1=$022C; 2=$022D; etc. Possible channel status values are: $FF - inactive $81 - open for write $41 - read/write $01 - open for read
$022E/3	CHNDAT	Channel data byte ($023E-$0243) The most recent byte read or written for each channel
$0244/9	LSTCHR	Channel last character pointer Points to the last character read or written in the buffer for each channel
$024A	TYPE	Active file type
$024B	STRSIZ	Length of the string
$024C	TEMPSA	Temporary secondary address
$024D	CMD	Temporary job command
$024E	LSTSEC	Work area for finding best sector to do
$024F/0	BUFUSE	Buffer allocation
$0251/2	MDIRTY	BAM dirty flag (drives 0/1)
$0253	ENTFND	Directory entry found flag
$0254	DIRLST	Directory listing flag
$0255	CMDWAT	Command waiting flag
$0256	LINUSE	LINDX use word
$0257	LBUSED	Last buffer used
$0258	REC	Record size. Used by directory routines
$0259	TRKSS	Side sector track. Used by dir routines
$025A	SECSS	Side sector sector. Used by dir routines
$025B/F	LSTJOB	Last job by buffer ($025B/C/D/E/F)
$0260/5	DSEC	Sector of directory entry by buffer
$0266/B	DIND	Index of directory entry by buffer
$026C	ERWORD	Error word for recovery
$026D	ERLED	Error LED mask for flashing
$026E	PRGDRV	Last program drive
$026F	PRGSEC	Last program sector

ADDRESS	NAME	1541 RAM VARIABLE DEFINITIONS
$0270	WLINDX	Write LINDX
$0271	RLINDX	Read LINDX
$0272/3	NBTEMP	# blocks temp
$0274	CMDSIZ	Command string size
$0275	CHAR	Character under the parser
$0276	LIMIT	PTR limit in comparison
$0277	F1CNT	File stream 1 count
$0278	F2CNT	File stream 2 count
$0279	F2PTR	File stream 2 pointer

		PARSER TABLES ($027A-$0289)

$027A/F	FILTBL	Table of filename pointers
$0280/4	FILTRK	First file link (Track)
$0285/9	FILSEC	First file link (Sector)

$028A	PATFLG	Pattern presence flag
$028B	IMAGE	File stream image
$028C	DRVCNT	Number of drive searches
$028D	DRVFLG	Drive search flag
$028E	LSTDRV	Last drive w/o error. Used as the default drive number.
$028F	FOUND	Found flag in directory searches
$0290	DIRSEC	Directory sector
$0291	DELSEC	Sector of first available entry
$0292	DELIND	Index of first available entry
$0293	LSTBUF	=0 if last block
$0294	INDEX	Current index in buffer
$0295	FILCNT	Counter of file entries
$0296	TYPFLG	Match by type of flag
$0297	MODE	Active file mode (R,W)
$0298	JOBRTN	Job return flag
$0299	EPTR	Pointer for recovery
$029A	TOFF	Total track offset
$029B/C	UBAM	Last BAM update pointer
$029D/0	TBAM	Track # of BAM image (drive 0/1)
$02A1/0	BAM	BAM images ($02A1-02B0)

		OUTPUT BUFFERS ($02B1-$02F8)

$02B1/4	NAMBUF	Directory buffer ($02B1-$02D4)
$02D5/8	ERRBUF	Error message buffer ($02D5-$02F8)

$02F9	WBAM	Don't write BAM flag. Set to 0 at start and end of any disk command.
$02FA/B	NDBL	# of disk blocks free (lo byte 0/1)
$02FC/D	NDBH	# of disk blocks free (hi byte 0/1)
$02FE/F	PHASE	Current phase of head stepper motor

ADDRESS	NAME	1541 RAM VARIABLE DEFINITIONS
		DATA BUFFERS ($0300-$07FF)
		--
$0300	BUF0	Data buffer #0 ($0300-$03FF)
$0400	BUF1	Data buffer #1 ($0400-$04FF)
$0500	BUF2	Data buffer #2 ($0500-$05FF)
$0600	BUF3	Data buffer #3 ($0600-$06FF)
$0700	BUF4	Data buffer #4 ($0700-$07FF) BAM ONLY!

ADDRESS	NAME	1541 I/O DEFINITIONS
		SERIAL I/O 6522 ($1800-$180F)
		--
$1800	PB	DATA PORT B - Serial data I/O
		--
		BITS FOR SERIAL HANDSHAKE
	DATIN	Bit 0 - $01 Data in line
	DATOUT	Bit 1 - $02 Data out line
	CLKIN	Bit 2 - $04 Clock in line
	CLKOUT	Bit 3 - $08 Clock out line
	ATNA	Bit 4 - $10 Attention acknowledge line
	ATN	Bit 7 - $80 Attention in line
		--
$1801	PA1	DATA PORT A - Unused
$1802	DDRB1	DATA DIRECTION FOR PORT B
$1803	DDRA1	DATA DIRECTION FOR PORT A - Unused
$1804	T1LC1	TIMER 1 LOW COUNTER
$1805	T1HC1	TIMER 1 HIGH COUNTER
$1806	T1LL2	TIMER 1 LOW LATCH
$1807	T1HL2	TIMER 1 HIGH LATCH
$1808	T2LC1	TIMER 2 LOW COUNTER
$1809	T2HC1	TIMER 2 HIGH COUNTER
$180A	SR1	SHIFT REGISTER
$180B	ACR1	AUXILIARY CONTROL REGISTER
$180C	PCR1	PERIPHERAL CONTROL REGISTER
$180D	IFR1	INTERRUPT FLAG REGISTER
$180E	IER1	INTERRUPT ENABLE REGISTER
		DISK CONTROLLER 6522 ($1C00-$1C0F)
		--
$1C00	DSKCNT	DATA PORT B - Disk controller I/O
		--
		Bit 0 - $01 Bits 0 & 1 are cycled to
		Bit 1 - $02 step the head
		Bit 2 - $04 Motor on (1) or off (0)
		Bit 3 - $08 Drive active LED on/off
		Bit 4 - $10 Write protect sense
		Bit 5 - $20 Density select (0)
		Bit 6 - $40 Density select (1)
		Bit 7 - $80 SYNC detect line
		--

ADDRESS	NAME	1541 I/O DEFINITIONS
$1C01	DATA2	DATA PORT A - GCR data I/O to diskette
$1C02	DDRB2	DATA DIRECTION FOR PORT B
$1C03	DDRA2	DATA DIRECTION FOR PORT A
$1C04	T1LC2	TIMER 1 LOW COUNTER
$1C05	T1HC2	TIMER 1 HIGH COUNTER
$1C06	T1LL2	TIMER 1 LOW LATCH
$1C07	T1HL2	TIMER 1 HIGH LATCH
$1C08	T2LC2	TIMER 2 LOW COUNTER
$1C09	T2HC2	TIMER 2 HIGH COUNTER
$1C0A	SR2	SHIFT REGISTER
$1C0B	ACR2	AUXILIARY CONTROL REGISTER
$1C0C	PCR2	PERIPHERAL CONTROL REGISTER
$1C0D	IFR2	INTERRUPT FLAG REGISTER
$1C0E	IER2	INTERRUPT ENABLE REGISTER

APPENDIX B
ANALYSIS OF THE 1541's ROM

Here be dragons and ogres!
Travelers, walk not alone.

NAME	ADDRESS	DESCRIPTION OF WHAT ROM ROUTINE DOES
SETLDA	$C100	Turn on drive-active LED: Set bit 3 of DSKCNT ($1C00) to turn on LED for the current drive (DRVNUM; $7F).
LEDSON	$C118	Turn on drive-active LED: Set bit 3 of DSKCNT ($1C00) to turn on drive active LED for drive 0.
ERROFF	$C123	Turn off error LED: Store $00 in ERWORD ($026C) and in ERLED ($026D) to clear any error status and turn off drive-active/error LED.
ERRON	$C12C	Turn on error LED: Store $80 in ERWORD ($026C) to ensure LED will continue to flash and set bit 3 of DSKCNT to turn the LED on using the LED mask from LEDMSK ($FECA).
PARSXQ	$C146	Parse string in command buffer: Clear the "don't write BAM" flag, WBAM ($02F9) and move the drive number of the last successful job from LSTDRV ($028E) ($028E) to DRVNUM ($7F). This makes the last used drive the default drive.
	$C150	JSR to OKERR ($E6BC) to clear any errors and move the OK error message into the error buffer.
	$C153	Check if the command's secondary address (ORGSA; $84) was $0F (command channel).
	$C15D	If it was not $0F, exit with a JMP to OPEN ($D7B4).
PS5	$C160	If the secondary address was $0F, JSR to CMDSET ($C2B3) to interpret the command and set up the necessary variables and registers (on return .Y=0).
	$C163	Move first character of command from the command buffer ($0200) to CHAR ($0275).
PS10	$C16A	Search the command table (CMDTBL; $FE89) for this character. If not found, exit by loading .A with a #$31 (BAD COMMAND) and jumping to the command level error handler (CMDERR; $C1C8).
PS20	$C17A	If found, store the command's position in the table (the command number) into CMDNUM ($022A). Check if this command must be parsed by comparing the command number with $09. If parsing is required (NEW, RENAME, SCRATCH, COPY, & LOAD),
	$C181	JSR to TAGCMD ($C1EE) to set tables, pointers and patterns.

NAME	ADDRESS	DESCRIPTION OF WHAT ROM ROUTINE DOES
PS30	$C184	Move the address of the appropriate ROM routine from the tables, CJUMPL ($FE95) and CJUMPH ($FEA1) into $6F/$70 (TEMP). Exit with an indirect JMP to the routine via the vector at TEMP ($6F).
ENDCMD	$C194	Terminate command successfully: Clear the "don't write BAM" flag, WBAM ($02F9). Load .A with the error status from ERWORD ($026C). If non-zero, an error has occurred so exit with a JMP to CMDERR ($C1C8).
SCREND	$C1A3	If command completed with no errors, set TRACK ($80), SECTOR ($81), and the pointer into the command buffer, CB($A3) to $00. JSR to ERRMSG ($E6C7) and ERROFF ($C123) to clear any error status.
SCREN1	$C1AD	Move current drive number from DRVNUM ($7F) to last used drive number, LSTDRV ($028E). Set the drive-busy flag, NODRV ($FF) to $00 to indicate that the drive is inactive. JSR to CLRCB ($C1BD) to zero the command buffer. JMP to FREICH ($D4DA) to clear the internal channel.
CLRCB	$C1BD	Clear the command buffer ($0200-$0228): Erase any old command information by overwriting the old command with $00.
CMDERR	$C1C8	Command level error handling: Set TRACK ($80) and SECTOR ($81) to $00 and JMP to CMDER2 ($E645).
SIMPRS	$C1D1	Simple parser: Initialize .X and the file table pointer FILTBL ($027A) to $00. Load .A with a $3A (:) and JSR to PARSE ($C268) to scan the command string for a colon.
	$C1DB	On return Z=1 if ":" found and .Y points to its position in the command. If not found, leave FILTAB=$00 and exit. If ":" was found, set FILTAB=(":" position - 1) and exit. All exits are with a JMP to SETANY ($C368) to set the drive number.
PRSCLN	$C1E5	Find colon (:) in command string: Load .X and .Y with $00 and .A with $3A (:) and JMP to PARSE ($C268).
		Tag command string, set up CMD structure and file stream pointers:

NAME	ADDRESS	DESCRIPTION OF WHAT ROM ROUTINE DOES
		COMMAND STRUCTURE (Bit mapped) ------------------ The disk commands, RENAME, SCRATCH, NEW, and LOAD, are analyzed by this routine to determine the command structure. As the command is parsed, bits in IMAGE ($028B) are set or cleared to indicate the presence or absence of various parts of the command. Once the command has been analyzed, its structure image is checked against the correct structure for that command given in STRUCT($FEA5+)

Bit	Name	Meaning
7	P1	Wild cards present (Y=1)
6	G1	More than one file implied (Y=1)
5	D1	Drive # specified (not default)
4	N1	Filename1 given
3	P2	Wild cards present (Y=1)
2	G2	More than one file implied (Y=1)
1	D2	Drive # specified (not default)
0	N2	Filename2 given

NOTE: Bits 7-4 refer to file #1
      Bits 3-0 refer to file #2

NAME	ADDRESS	DESCRIPTION OF WHAT ROM ROUTINE DOES
TAGCMD	$C1EE	JSR to PRSCLN ($C1E5) to locate the position of the colon (:) that is a necessary part of all these commands. e.g. R0:NEWNAME=OLDNAME (Rename)
TC25	$C1F3	If no colon was found, load .A with $34 to indicate a bad command and exit with a JMP to CMDERR ($C1C8).
TC30	$C1F8	If a colon was found, set FILTAB to the colon position - 1.
	$C1FD	Check if a comma was found before the colon (.X > 0 on return from PARSE).
	$C1FE	If a comma was found, the syntax is bad so exit via TC25 ($C1F3).
TC35	$C200	Load .A with $3D (=) and JSR to PARSE ($C268). On return .X=0 indicates that no wild-card characters (? or *) were found. If any were found, set bit 6 (G1) of IMAGE ($028B) to indicate that the command applies to more than one file.
TC40	$C20A	In all cases, set bit 5 (D1) of IMAGE to indicate that a drive # is present and set bit 0 (N2) to indicate that a second file name is given (fixed later)

NAME	ADDRESS	DESCRIPTION OF WHAT ROM ROUTINE DOES
	$C20F	Increment .X and use it to set the lengths of filenames 1 and 2, F1CNT and F2CNT ($0277/8). Filename 2 will default to the same length as filename 1.
	$C216	Check if PARSE found any wild cards by loading PATFLG ($028A). If any found, set bit 7 (P1) of IMAGE ($028B).
	$C223	Set pattern flag, PATFLG ($028A) to $00 to prepare for parsing the rest of the command.
TC50	$C228	Check if there is any command left to parse by checking the value of .Y set by PARSE. If .Y=0, nothing left so branch to TC75 ($C254) to check structure.
	$C22B	Store value from .Y in filetable, FILTBL ($027A),X. Set the pointer to the start of filename #2, F2PNT ($0279) from the current value of F1CNT ($0277).
	$C234	Load .A with $8D (shifted CR) and JSR to PARSE ($C268) to parse the rest of the command. On return increment .X so it points to the end of the string and put the value into F2CNT ($0278). Decrement the value of .X to restore its former value.
	$C23E	Check if any wild cards were found by PARSE in filename 2 by checking the pattern flag, PATFLG ($028A). If any were found, set 3 (P2) of IMAGE ($028B).
TC60	$C245	Check if there was a second filename by checking if .X = F1CNT. If second file name is only 1 chr long, branch to TC70.
	$C24A	Set bit 2 to indicate that the command implies more than one second file name.
TC70	$C24C	Set bit 1 to indicate that a second drive is specified and bit 0 to indicate that a second file name is given. EOR this with IMAGE (clears bit 0) and store the result back into IMAGE ($028B).
TC75	$C254	Check IMAGE against the entry for that command (CMD number from CMDNUM, $022A) in the structure table, STRUCT ($FEA5+) If match, syntax is OK; exit with an RTS
TC80	$C260	Store IMAGE in ERWORD ($026C). Load .A with a $30 to indicate a bad syntax and exit with a JMP to CMDERR ($C1C8).

NAME	ADDRESS	DESCRIPTION OF WHAT ROM ROUTINE DOES
		Parse string: On entry, .A contains the character to be found in the string, .Y points to the the character in the string where the scan is to start, and .X points into the file table, FILTAB,X. The routine scans the string for special characters "*", "?", and "," as well as the desired character. In scanning the string .Y is used as a pointer to the character in the command string being examined and .X is a pointer into the file table, FILTAB ($027B+) for storing the positions (.Y value) of the start & end of file names that are found. When a wild card (* or ?) is found, the pattern flag PATFLG ($028A) is incremented. When a comma is found, its position is noted in the file table, FILTAB and a check is made to ensure that not too many file names are present. When the special character is found or the end of the command is reached, the routine ends. If no wild cards have been found, the pattern type, PATTYP,X is set to $80. Otherwise it is left unchanged. On exit, .Y=0 and the Z flag =0 if the desired character has not been found. If it has been found, .Y = the position of the character and the Z flag is set.
PARSE	$C268	Store the desired character in CHAR ($0275).
PR10	$C26B	Start of loop using .Y as a counter to scan the command string. If .Y is greater than or equal to the length of the command string, CMDSIZE ($0274), branch to PR30 ($C29E).
	$C270	Load command string character into .A and increment .Y counter. Check if it is the desired character. If it is, branch to PR35 ($C2A0).
	$C278	Check if it is a wild card ("*" or "?"). If not, branch to PR25 ($C283).
PR20	$C280	Increment the pattern flag, PATFLG ($028A) to count the # of wild cards.
PR25	$C283	Check if it is a comma (","). If not, branch back to PR10 to get next command string character.

NAME	ADDRESS	DESCRIPTION OF WHAT ROM ROUTINE DOES
	$C287	Transfer character count from .Y to .A and store in the file table, FILTAB+1,X ($027B,X) to indicate where the file name ends. Load .A with the pattern flag PATFLG and AND it with $7F. If the result is zero (no wild cards found), branch to PR28.
	$C292	Wild cards were present, so store $80 in PATTYP,X ($E7,X) to indicate this. Also store $80 into PATFLG to zero the count of wild cards but indicate that there are wild cards in the string.
PR28	$C299	Increment .X (counts number of files & points into FILTAB) and compare it to $04 (the maximum number of file names allowed in a command string). If the maximum has not been exceeded, branch back to PR10 to continue the scan.
PR30	$C29E	Load .Y with $00 to indicate that the desired character was not found.
PR35	$C2A0	Store a copy of the command size, CMDSIZ ($0274) into the file table, FILTAB+1,X ($027B,X). Load the pattern flag, PATFLG and AND it with $7F. If the result is 0, no wild cards have been found so branch to PR40.
	$C2AD	Wild cards were present, so store $80 in PATTYP,X ($E7,X) to indicate this.
PR40	$C2B1	Transfer character count from .Y to .A. This sets the Z flag if the desired character has not been found.
		--
		Initialize command tables & pointers Find length of command string and zero all variables and pointers.
CMDSET	$C2B3	Load .Y from BUFTAB+CBPTR ($A3). This is the length of the command that was sent from the computer. If .Y=0, branch to CS08 ($C2CB).
	$C2B7	Decrement .Y and if .Y=0, branch to CS07 ($C2CA).
	$C2BA	Load .A with the character from the command buffer, CMDBUF,Y ($0200,Y) and see if it is a carriage return ($0D). If it is, branch to CS08 ($C2CB).
	$C2C1	Decrement .Y and load the next character from the command buffer. If this is a carriage return ($0D), branch to CS08 ($C2CB). If not, increment .Y
CS07	$C2CA	Increment .Y pointer into command buffer

NAME	ADDRESS	DESCRIPTION OF WHAT ROM ROUTINE DOES
CS08	$C2CB	Store length of command (.Y) in CMDSIZ ($027B). Compare length (.Y) with the maximum allowable length ($2A) to set the carry flag. Load .Y with $FF. If command length was OK, branch to CMDRST.
	$C2D4	Command over-size so set command number ($022A) to $FF, load .A with $32 to indicate a TOO LONG ERROR and exit with a JMP to CMDERR ($C1C8).
CMDRST	$C2DC	Zero all important variables & pointers: BUFTAB+CBPTR ($A3) REC ($0258) FILTBL ($027A-7F) TYPE ($024A) ENTSEC ($00D8-DC) TYPFLG ($0296) ENTIND ($00DD-E1) F1PTR ($00D3) FILDRV ($00E2-E6) F2PTR ($0279) PATTYP ($00E7-EB) PATFLG ($028A) FILTRK ($0280-84) ERWORD ($026C) FILSEC ($0285-89)
ONEDRV	$C312	Set first drive & table pointers: Change pointer to end of the first file name (F1CNT; $0277) to point to the end of the second file name (use value from F2CNT; $0278). Store $01 in F2CNT and in F2PTR ($0279) to clear these variables
ALLDRS	$C320	Set up all drives from F2CNT: Load .Y with last drive used from LSTDRV ($028E) and .X with $00.
AD10	$C325	Save .X into F1PTR ($D3). Load .A from FILTAB,X ($027A,X) so it points to the start of the Xth file specified in the command string.
	$C32A	JSR to SETDRV ($C33C) to set drive #. On return .Y contains the drive number specified in the command or the default. NOTE: Bits represent drives (If bit 7 set, use default. Bit 0 = drive #0/1)
	$C32D	Recover .X pointer from F1PTR. Store .A in FILTAB,X ($027A,X). Move drive # from .Y to .A and store in FILDRV,X ($027A,X)
	$C335	Increment .X pointer and compare it to F2CNT ($0278) to see if any more files were specified. If more, branch back to AD10 to do the next one. If not, RTS
SETDRV	$C33C	Set drive # from text or default to 0 On entry and exit .A is an index into the command buffer. On entry .Y is the default drive #. On exit it is the drive specified or the default drive.

NAME	ADDRESS	DESCRIPTION OF WHAT ROM ROUTINE DOES
	$C33C	Move pointer into command buffer from .A to .X
	$C33D	Load .Y with $00 to ensure that the 1541's default drive is ALWAYS DRIVE #0
	$C33F	Load .A with $3A (:) to prepare to hunt for a colon (drive # is just before :).
	$C341	Check for colon in command string at CMDBUF+1,X ($0201,X). Picks up syntax: X#:FILENAME as in S0:JUNK If found, branch to SD40.
	$C346	Check for colon in command string at CMDBUF,X ($0200,X). Picks up default drive syntax as in S:JUNK If colon NOT found, branch to SD40.
	$C34B	Colon found so increment pointer (.X) so it points to the first character in the filename.
SD20	$C34C	Transfer .Y to .A to set up the default drive
SD22	$C34D	AND .A with $01 to ensure drive number in ASCII form ($30 or $31) is converted to $00 or $01.
SD24	$C34F	Transfer .A to .Y to restore drive #. Transfer .X to .A to restore index into command string and exit with an RTS.

		Set drive # from command string with the syntax: X#:FILENAME. On entry .X points to the # in the command string.
SD40	$C352	Load .A with the drive number (in ASCII) from CMDBUF,X ($0200,X).
	$C355	Increment .X twice so it points to the first character in the file name.
	$C357	Compare .A (drive number) to $30 (dr#0). If equal, branch back to SD22 ($C34D)
	$C35B	Compare .A (drive number) to $31 (dr#1). If equal, branch back to SD22 ($C34D) If not equal, must be default drive so branch back to SD20 ($C34C).

		Set drive # from command string with the syntax: X#,FILE or xx=FILE.
SD50	$C361	Transfer the drive number from .Y to .A.
	$C362	OR .A with $80 to set the default drive bit and then AND the result with $81 to mask off any odd bits. Branch back to SD24 ($C34F) to terminate routine.

		Set drive # from any configuration:
SETANY	$C368	Set IMAGE ($028B) to $00.
	$C36D	Load .Y from FILTBL ($027A).
SA05	$C370	Load .A with the (CB),Y character from the command string and JSR to TST0V1 to test for a "0" or "1".

NAME	ADDRESS	DESCRIPTION OF WHAT ROM ROUTINE DOES
	$C371	On return .A contains $00 or $01 if the drive was specified. If not specified, .A is $80 or $81. If the drive number was given, branch to SA20 ($C388).
	$C377	Increment the pointer into the command string (.Y). Compare the pointer value to the command length (CMDSIZ; $0274) to see if we are at the end. If we are, branch to SA10 ($C383).
	$C37D	If not "0" or "1", set the pointer (.Y) to the end of the command less one (so it points to the last character before the RETURN to pick up things like V0) and loop back to SA05 ($C370).
SA10	$C383	Decrement IMAGE (becomes $FF) to flag a default drive status and load .A with a $00 to ensure default to 0 on the 1541.
SA20	$C388	AND the drive number in .A with $01, and store the result in the current drive number, DRVNUM ($7F).
	$C38C	Exit with a JMP to SETLDS ($C100) to turn on the drive active light.

		Toggle drive number:
TOGDRV	$C38F	Load .A with current drive number from DRVNUM ($7F). EOR it with $01 to flip bit #0, AND it with $01 to mask off the bits 1-7, and store the result back in DRVNUM ($7F).

		Set pointers to one file stream and check type:
FS1SET	$C398	Zero .Y and load .A with the pointer to the end of file name 1 (F1CNT; $0277).
	$C39D	Compare .A to the pointer to the end of file name 2 (F2CNT; $0278). If equal, there is no second file so branch to FS15 ($C3B8).
	$C3A2	Decrement F2CNT and load .Y with its value. Load .A with the pointer to the filetype in the command string from FILTAB,Y ($027A,Y). Transfer this value to .Y and use it to load the file type into .A from the command string (CB),Y.
	$C3AC	Load .Y with $04 (the number of file types less 1).
FS10	$C3B0	Loop to compare the file type in .A to the list of possible file types,TYPLST,Y When a match occurs, branch to FS15 ($C3B8). If no match found this time, decrement .Y and, if there are any file types left, loop back to FS10. NOTE: if no match occurs, file assumed to be DEL.

NAME	ADDRESS	DESCRIPTION OF WHAT ROM ROUTINE DOES
FS15	$C3B8	Transfer file type from .Y to .A and store in TYPFLG ($0296).
TST0V1	$C3BD	Test if character in .A is ASCII 0 or 1: Compare .A to ASCII "0" ($30) and then to ASCII "1" ($31). If a match in either case, branch to T0V1. OR .A with $80 to set bit 7 to indicate no match was found.
T0V1	$C3C7	AND .A with $81 to convert ASCII to HEX and preserve bit 7.
OPTSCH	$C3CA	Determine optimal search for LOOKUP and FINFIL: Zero TEMP ($6F) and DRVFLG ($028D) and push $00 onto the stack. Load .X with value from F2CNT ($0278). Note: TEMP is the drive mask.
OS10	$C3D5	Pull .A from the stack and OR it with the value in TEMP ($6F). Push the result back onto the stack. Load .A with $01 and store this value in TEMP. Decrement .X (pointer into file table). If no files left (.X=$FF), branch to $OS30.
	$C3E0	Load .A with the drive for the file from FILDRV,X ($E2,X). If this file uses the default drive (bit 7 set), branch to OS15. Do two ASL's on TEMP ($6F).
OS15	$C3E8	Do one LSR on .A. If drive number in .A was 1, the carry bit is set so branch back to OS10.
	$C3EB	Since drive number was 0, do one ASL on TEMP ($6F) and branch back to OS10.
OS30	$C3EF	Pull .A from the stack and transfer this value to .X. Use this value as an index and load .A with a value from the search table, SCHTBL-1,X ($C43F,X). Push this value onto the stack, AND it with $03, and store the result in DRVCNT ($028C). Pull the original value off the stack and do an ASL. If bit 7 is not set, branch to OS40.
	$C3FE	If bit 7 was set, load A. with the value from FILDRV ($E2).
OS35	$C400	AND .A with $01 and store the result in DRVNUM ($7F). Load .A with DRVCNT ($028C) and if $00, only one drive is addressed so branch to OS60.
	$C409	JSR to AUTOI ($C63D) to check the drive status and initialize it if necessary. On return, branch to OS70 if the drive is ready (.A=0).
OS45	$C41B	Drive is not ready so load .A with $74 to indicate the drive is not ready and JSR to CMDERR ($C1C8).

NAME	ADDRESS	DESCRIPTION OF WHAT ROM ROUTINE DOES
OS50	$C420	JSR to TOGDRV ($C38F) to switch drives and JSR to AUTOI ($C63D) to check this drive's status and init it if necessary. On return, save the processor status on the stack. JSR to TOGDRV to switch back to the first drive. On return, pull the status back off the stack. If the second drive is active, branch to OS70.
	$C42D	Since second drive is not active, set DRVCNT ($020C) to $00 to indicate only one drive addressed and branch to OS70.
OS60	$C434	JSR to AUTOI ($C63D) to check the drive status and initialize it if necessary. On return, branch to OS45 if the drive is NOT ready (.A<>0).
OS70	$C439	Teminate routine with a JMP to SETLDS ($C100) to turn on the drive active LEDs
OS45	$C43C	Do a ROL on the value in .A and JMP to OS35 ($C400).
SCHTBL	$C440	Search Table BYTES $00, $80, $41 BYTES $01, $01, $01, $01 BYTES $81, $81, $81, $81 BYTES $42, $42, $42, $42
		Look up all files in command string in the directory and fill tables with info.
LOOKUP	$C44F	JSR to OPTSCH to find optimal search pattern and turn on drive active LEDs.
LK05	$C452	Store $00 in DELIND ($0292), to indicate that we are NOT looking for a deleted or unused directory entry. But, for one or more specific file names. JSR to SRCHST ($C5AC) to start the search process.
	$C45A	On return, branch to LK25 if a valid file name was found (Z flag =0)
LK10	$C45C	Since no file name was found, decrement DRVCNT ($028C), the number of drive searches to be made. If any more left (DRVCNT >= 0), branch to LK15.
	$C461	Since there are no more drive searches to be done, exit with an RTS.
LK15	$C462	Store $01 in DRVFLG ($028D) and JSR to TOGDRV ($C38F) to switch drives. JSR to SETLDS ($C100) to turn on the other LED. Then JMP back to LK05 to begin the search on the other drive.
LK20	$C470	JSR to SEARCH ($C617) to read the next valid file name in the directory.
	$C473	On return, branch to LK30 to abandon the search if a valid file name was NOT found (Z flag = 1).

NAME	ADDRESS	DESCRIPTION OF WHAT ROM ROUTINE DOES
LK25	$C475	JSR to COMPAR ($C4D8) to compare the list of files found with list of those required. On return, FOUND ($028F) is 0 if all files have NOT been found.
	$C478	Load .A with the value from FOUND. If not all the files have been found yet, branch to LK26 to continue the search.
	$C47D	All files have been found so exit from the routine with an RTS.
LK26	$C47E	Load .A with the value from ENTFND ($0253) to check if the most recent compare found a match. If not (.A=$FF), branch to LK20 to search directory for another valid file name. If a match was found, branch back to LK25 to try again.
LK30	$C485	Load .A with the value from FOUND. If not all the files have been found yet, branch to LK10 to continue the search.
	$C48A	All files found so exit with an RTS.
		--
		Find next file name matching any file in stream & return with entry stuffed into tables:
FFRE	$C48B	JSR to SRRE ($C604) to set up and read in the next block of directory entries.
	$C48E	If no files found, branch to FF10.
	$C490	If files were found, branch to FF25.
		--
FF15	$C492	Store $01 in DRVFLG ($028D) and JSR to TOGDRV ($C38F) to switch to the other drive. JSR to SETLDS ($C100) to turn on the new drive active light.
		Find starting entry in the directory:
FFST	$C49D	Store $00 in DELIND ($0292), to indicate that we are NOT looking for a deleted or unused directory entry. But, for one or more specific file names. JSR to SRCHST ($C5AC) to start the search process.
	$C4A5	On return, branch to FF25 if a valid file name was found (Z flag =0)
	$C4A7	Store .A value in FOUND ($028F).
FF10	$C4AA	Load .A from FOUND ($028F). If non-zero, all files found so branch to FF40 & exit
	$C4AF	Since there is nothing more on this drive, decrement DRVCNT by 1. If any more drives left, branch to FF15 to try the other drive. If none left, do an RTS
		--
		Continue scan of directory:
FNDFIL	$C4B5	JSR to SEARCH ($C617) to retrieve the next valid file name from the directory.

NAME	ADDRESS	DESCRIPTION OF WHAT ROM ROUTINE DOES
	$C4B8	On return, branch to FF10 if no more entries available on this drive.
FF25	$C4BA	JSR to COMPAR ($C4D8) to see if any of the names found match the ones needed.
	$C4BD	On return, load .X from ENTFND ($0253). If a match on a name was found (.X<128), branch to FF30 to check the file type. If no match found (.X>127), load .A with the value from FOUND($028F) to check if all files have been found. If not(.A=0), branch back to FNDFIL to load another name from the directory.
	$C4C7	If .A<>0, all files have been found so branch to FF40 and exit with an RTS.
FF30	$C4C9	Check the file type flag, TYPFLG($0296). If it is $00, there is no file type restriction so branch to FF40 and exit.
	$C4CE	Load the file pattern type from PATTYP,X ($E7,X), AND it with the file type mask #$07, and compare it to the value in TYPFLG ($0296). If the file types do not match, branch back to FNDFIL to continue the search.
FF40	$C4D7	Terminate the routine with an RTS.
		--
		Compare all file names in command list with each valid entry in directory. Any matches are tabulated.
COMPAR	$C4D8	Set the found-entry flag, ENTFND ($0253) to $FF and zero the pattern flag PATFLG ($028A). JSR to CMPCHK ($C589) to check the file table for unfound files. If there are unfound files (Z flag = 1), branch to CP10 to begin comparing.
CP02	$C4E6	Terminate routine with an RTS.
CP05	$C4E7	JSR to CC10 ($C594) to set F2PTR ($0279) to point to the next file needed on this drive. On return, branch to CP02 to exit if no more files needed on this drive.
CP10	$C4EC	Load .A with the current drive number from DRVNUM ($7F) and EOR it with the drive number specified for the file, FILDRV,X ($E2,X). LSR the result. If the carry flag is clear, the drive number is correct for this file so branch to CP20 to find the name in the directory list.
	$C4F3	AND the value in .A with $40 to check if we are to use the default drive (NOTE: $40 rather than $80 because of the LSR). If we can not use the default drive, branch back to CP05 to set up the next file name on our list of files needed.

NAME	ADDRESS	DESCRIPTION OF WHAT ROM ROUTINE DOES
	$C4F7	Compare DRVCNT ($028C) with $02. If equal, don't use default drive so branch back to CP05.
CP20	$C4FE	At this point we have a match on the drive numbers so check the directory entries to see if we can match a name. Load .A with the pointer to the position of the required file name from FILTBL,X ($027A,X) and transfer this value to .X.
	$C502	JSR to FNDLMT to find the end of the command string. On return, load the pointer into the directory buffer (.Y) with $03 (so it points past the file type, track and sector) and JMP to CP33.
CP30	$C50A	Compare the .Xth character in the command string (the required filename) with the .Yth character in the directory buffer (the directory entry). If equal, branch to CP32 to set up for the next character.
	$C511	No exact match so check if the command buffer character is a "?" which will match any character. If not, branch to to CP05 to try the next file name.
	$C515	Compare the character we just used from the directory buffer with $A0 to see if we've reached the end of the name. If we have, branch to CP05 to try the next file name.
CP32	$C51B	Increment .X and .Y
CP33	$C51D	Compare .X with the length of the command string, LIMIT ($0276). If we are at the end, branch to CP34.
	$C522	Check if the new character in the file name, CMDBUF,X ($0200,X) is a "*". If it is, it matches everything so branch to CP40 to tabulate this match.
	$C529	If not a "*", branch to CP30 to keep on matching.
CP34	$C52B	Compare .Y to $13 to see if we are at the end of the name in the directory. If we are, branch to CP40 to tabulate.
	$C52F	If not at the limit, check the character in the directory entry name. If it isn't an $A0, we did not get to the end of the name so branch back to CP05 to try again
CP40	$C535	The filenames match so keep track of it by storing the pointer to the entry from F2PNT ($0279) into ENTFND ($0253).
	$C53B	Get the file type pattern ($80,$81,etc) from PATTYP,X ($E7,X), AND it with $80, and store it in PSTFLG.

NAME	ADDRESS	DESCRIPTION OF WHAT ROM ROUTINE DOES
	$C542	Get the pointer to the directory entry from INDEX ($0294) and store it in the entry index, ENTIND,X ($DD,X).
	$C547	Get the sector on track 18 on which the entry is stored from SECTOR ($81) and store it in, ENTSEC,X ($D8,X).
	$C54B	Zero .Y and load .A with the file type of this directory entry from (DIRBUF),Y ($94),Y. Increment .Y. Save the type on the stack. AND the type with $40 to see if this is a locked file type, and store the result in TEMP ($6F). Pull the file type off the stack and AND it with $DF ($FF-$20). If the result is > 127 (the replacement bit not set), branch to CP42
CP42	$C55A	OR the result with $20.
	$C55C	AND the result with $27 and OR it with the value stored in TEMP ($6F) and store the final result back in TEMP.
	$C562	Load .A with $80, AND .A with the file pattern type from PATTYP,X ($E7,X), OR the result with the value in TEMP ($6F), and store the final result back in PATTYP,X.
	$C56A	Load .A with the file's drive number from FILDRV,X ($E2,X). AND it with $80 to preserve the default drive bit, OR it with the current drive number, DRVNUM ($7F) and store the result back into FILDRV,X ($E2,X).
	$C572	Move the file's first track link from (DIRBUF),Y(.Y=1) to FILTRK,X ($0280) and increment .Y.
	$C578	Move the file's first sector link from (DIRBUF),Y(.Y=2) to FILSEC,X ($0285).
	$C57D	Check the current record length, REC ($0258). If NOT $00, branch to CMPCHK.
	$C582	Set .Y to $15 and move the file entry's record size from (DIRBUF),Y to REC.
CMPCHK	$C589	Check table for unfound files Set all-files-found flag, FOUND ($028F) to $FF. Move the number of files to test from F2CNT ($0278) to F2PTR ($0279).
CC10	$C594	Decrement the file count, F2PTR ($0279). If any files left, branch to CC15. If none left, exit with an RTS.
CC15	$C59A	Load .X with the number of the file to test from F2PTR. Load .A with the file's pattern type from PATTYP,X ($E7,X). If file has not been found yet (bit 7 is still set) abort search by branching to CC20.

NAME	ADDRESS	DESCRIPTION OF WHAT ROM ROUTINE DOES
CC20	$C5A6	Load .A with the file's first track link from FILTRK,X ($0280,X). If non-zero, the file has been found, so branch back to CC10 to test the next file. Load .A with $00 and store it in the all-files-found flag, FOUND ($028F) to indicate that all files have NOT been found and exit with an RTS.
SRCHST	$C5AC	Initiate search of directory: Returns with valid entry (DELIND=0) or with the first deleted entry (DELIND=1) Load .Y with $00 and store it in DELSEC. ($0291). Decrement .Y to $FF and store it in the found-an-entry flag, ENTFND ($0253).
	$C5B5	To start search at the beginning of the directory, set TRACK ($80) to $12 (#18) (from $FE79) and SECTOR ($81) to $01. Also store $01 in last-sector-in-file flag, LSTBUF ($0293).
	$C5C1	JSR to OPNIRD ($D475) to open the internal channel (SA=16) for a read and to read in the first one or two sectors in the file whose T/S link is given in TRACK ($80) and SECTOR ($81).
SR10	$C5C4	Test LSTBUF ($0293) to see if we have exhausted the last sector in the directory file. If not (LSTBUF <> $00), branch to SR15.
	$C5C9	Exit with an RTS.
SR15	$C5CA	Set the file count, FILCNT ($0295) to $07 to indicate that there are 8 entries (0-7) left to examine in the buffer.
	$C5CF	Load .A with $00 and JSR to DRDBYT to read the first byte in the sector (the track link). On return store this value into LSTBUF ($0293). This sets LSTBUF to $00 if there are no more blocks left in in the directory file.
SR20	$C5D7	JSR to GETPNT ($D4E8) to set the directory pointer, DIRBUF ($94/5) to the data that was just read into the active buffer, BUFTAB,X ($99/A,X).

NOTE: DIRBUF does NOT point to the start of the data buffer ($0300, $0400,...). It points to the first data byte ($0302, $0402,...). As the entries are examined, it is update to point to the start of the entry ($0x02, $0x22, $0x42,...).

NAME	ADDRESS	DESCRIPTION OF WHAT ROM ROUTINE DOES
	$C5DA	Decrement the entry count, FILCNT and load .Y with $00 to begin examination of the first directory entry.
	$C5DF	Test the entry's file type in (DIRBUF),Y If non-zero, this is NOT a deleted or blank entry so branch to SR30.
	$C5E3	Process a scratched or blank entry Test DELSEC ($0291) to see if a deleted entry has already been found. If it has (DELSEC <> $00), branch to SEARCH($C617)
	$C5E8	This is first deleted entry so JSR to CURBLK ($DE3B) to set up the current sector in SECTOR ($81). Save the sector number in DELSEC ($0291).
	$C5F0	Load .A with the low byte of the pointer to the start of this entry (its position in the data buffer) from DIRBUF ($94). Load .X with the current value of DELIND ($0292). This sets the Z flag to 1 if only valid entries are desired. Store the pointer in .A into DELIND.
	$C5F8	If the Z flag is set, we need valid entries, not deleted ones, so branch to SEARCH to continue the search.
	$C5FA	We wanted a deleted entry and we found one so terminate routine with an RTS.
SR30	$C5FB	We have found a valid entry. Check if we are looking for one by comparing DELIND ($0292) to $01. If not equal, we want a valid entry so branch to SR50.
	$C602	If DELIND = 1, we want a deleted entry, not a valid one, so branch to SEARCH to continue the quest!

SRRE	$C604	Re-enter the directory search: Set TRACK ($80) to $12 (#18) from $FE85 Set SECTOR ($81) from the last directory sector used, DIRSEC ($0290).
	$C60E	JSR to OPNIRD ($D475) to open the internal channel (SA=16) for a read and to read in the first one or two sectors in the file whose T/S link is given in TRACK ($80) and SECTOR ($81).
	$C611	Load .A with the pointer INDEX ($0294) that points to the start of the last entry we were examining and JSR to SETPNT ($D4C8) to set the DIRPNT ($94/5) to point to the start of the entry.

NAME	ADDRESS	DESCRIPTION OF WHAT ROM ROUTINE DOES
SEARCH	$C617	Continue search of entries: Set found-entry flag, ENTFND ($0253) to $FF. Load .A with number of entries left in the buffer from FILCNT ($0295). If none left, branch to SR40 to get the next buffer of directory entries.
	$C621	There is at least one more entry left in this buffer so load .A with $20 (the # of characters in each entry) and JSR to INCPTR ($D1C6) to set DIRPTR ($94/5) to point to the start of the next entry. JMP to SR20 ($C5D7) to process it.
SR40	$C629	Get next buffer of entries: JSR to NXTBUF ($D44D) to read in the next directory sector and JMP to SR10 to begin processing it.
SR50	$C62F	We have found a valid entry so save how far we got and return. Save low byte of the pointer to the entry, from DIRBUF ($94) in INDEX ($0294).
	$C634	JSR to CURBLK ($DE3B) to store the sector we are checking in SECTOR ($81).
	$C637	Save the current sector number from SECTOR ($81) in DIRSEC ($0290) and RTS.

AUTOI	$C63C	Check drive for active diskette, init if needed. Return no drive status. Test auto-initialization flag, AUTOFG ($68). If AUTOFG <> 0, auto-init is disabled so branch to AUTO2 ($C669).
	$C641	Load .X with the current drive number from DRVNUM ($7F). Test whether the diskette has been changed by doing an LSR on the write-protect-change flag for the current drive, WPSW,X ($1C/D). If the carry flag, C, is clear, the disk has not been changed so branch to AUTO2.
	$C647	Load .A with $FF. Store this value as the job return code in JOBRTN ($0298).
	$C64C	JSR to ITRIAL ($D00E) to do a SEEK to the current drive to determine if a diskette is present.
	$C64F	Load .Y with $FF (default to true).
	$C651	Compare the value in return job code in .A with $02. If equal, NO SYNC was found so branch to AUTO1 to abort.
	$C655	Compare the value in return job code in .A with $03. If equal, NO HEADER was found so branch to AUTO1 to abort.
	$C659	Compare the value in return job code in .A with $0F. If equal, NO DRIVE was found so branch to AUTO1 to abort.
	$C65D	Seems OK so load .Y with $00.

NAME	ADDRESS	DESCRIPTION OF WHAT ROM ROUTINE DOES
AUTO1	$C65F	Load .X with the current drive number DRVNUM ($7F). Transfer the value of .Y into .A ($00 if OK;$FF if BAD) and store in the current drive status, NODRV,X ($FF,X). If status is bad (not $00), branch to AUTO2 to abort.
	$C666	JSR to INITDR ($D042) to initialize the current drive.
AUTO2	$C669	Load .A with the current no-drive status and terminate routine with an RTS. NOTE: Z flag set if all is OK.

		Transfer filename from CMD to buffer: On entry, .A=string size; .X=starting index in command string; .Y=buffer #
TRNAME	$C66E	Save .A (string size) on the stack.
	$C66F	JSR to FNDLMT ($C6A6) to find the limit of the string in the command buffer that is pointed to by .X.
	$C672	JSR to TRCMBF ($C688) to transfer the command buffer contents from .X to LIMIT to the data buffer whose number is in .Y
	$C675	Restore the string size into .A from the stack. Set the carry flag and subtract the maximum string size, STRSIZ ($024B).
	$C67A	Transfer the result from .A to .X. If the result is 0 or negative, the string does not need padding so branch to TN20.
	$C67F	String is short and needs to be padded so load .A with $A0.
TN10	$C681	Loop to pad the string in the directory buffer with .X $A0's.
TN20	$C687	Terminate routine with an RTS.

		Transfer CMD buffer to another buffer: .X=index to first chr in command buffer LIMIT=index to last chr+1 in CMD buffer .Y=buffer#. Uses current buffer pointer.
TRCMBF	$C688	Multiply .Y by 2 (TYA;ASL;TAY).
	$C68B	Use current buffer pointers, BUFTAB,Y ($99/A,Y) to set the directory buffer pointers, DIRBUF ($94/5).
		Zero .Y (index into directory buffer)
TR10	$C697	Move character from CMDBUF,X ($0200,X) to (DIRBUF),Y ;($94),Y.
	$C69C	Increment .Y. If .Y equals $00, branch to TR20 to abort.
	$C69F	Increment .X. If .X < LIMIT ($0276) branch back to TR10 to do next character
TR20	$C6A5	Terminate routine with an RTS.

NAME	ADDRESS	DESCRIPTION OF WHAT ROM ROUTINE DOES
		Find the limit(end) of the string in the command buffer that is pointed to by X
FNDLMT	$C6A6	Zero the string size, STRSIZ ($024B). Transfer the starting pointer from .X to .A and save it on the stack.
FL05	$C6AD	Load .A with the Xth command string character, CMDBUF,X ($0200,X).
	$C6B0	Compare the character to a ",". If they match, we're at the end. Branch to FL10.
	$C6B4	Compare the character to a "=". If they match, we're at the end. Branch to FL10.
	$C6B8	Increment STRSIZ ($024B) and .X
	$C6BC	Check if the string size, STRSIZ, has reached the maximum size of $0F (#15). If it has, branch to FL10 to quit.
	$C6C3	Compare .X to the pointer to the end of the command string, CMDSIZ ($0274). If we're NOT at the end. Branch to FL05.
FL10	$C6C8	Store the .X value (the last character plus 1) into LIMIT ($0276).
	$C6CB	Pull the original .X value off the stack into .A and transfer it to .X
	$C6CD	Terminate routine with an RTS.
		Get file entry from directory: (called by STDIR and GETDIR)
GETNAM	$C6CE	Save secondary address, SA ($83) on the stack.
	$C6D1	Save the current channel#, LINDX ($82) on the stack.
	$C6D4	JSR to GNSUB ($C6DE) to get a directory entry using the internal read channel SA=$11(#17).
	$C6D7	Pull the original SA and LINDX values from the stack and reset these variables
	$C6DD	Terminate the routine with an RTS.
		Get file entry subroutine:
GNSUB	$C6DE	Set current secondary address, SA ($83) to $11 (internal read secondary address)
	$C6E2	JSR to FNDRCH ($D0EB) to find an unused read channel.
	$C6E5	JSR to GETPNT ($D4E8) to set the directory buffer pointer, DIRBUF ($94/5) from the pointer to the currently active buffer using values from BUFTAB ($30/1).
	$C6E8	Test the found entry flag, ENTFLG($0253) to see if there are more files. If there are more (ENTFLG > 127), branch to GN05.
	$C6ED	No more entries so test DRVFLG ($028D) to see if we have the other drive to do. If DRVFLG <> 0, branch to GN050 to do the other drive.

NAME	ADDRESS	DESCRIPTION OF WHAT ROM ROUTINE DOES
	$C6F2	JSR to MSGFRE ($C806) to send the BLOCKS FREE message.
	$C6F5	Clear carry bit and exit with an RTS.

GN05	$C6F7	Test drive flag, DRVFLG ($028D). If $00, branch to GN10.
GN050	$C6FC	Decrement drive flag, DRVFLG ($028D). If not $00, branch to GN051 to do a new directory.
	$C701	Decrement drive flag, DRVFLG ($028D).
	$C704	JSR to TOGDRV ($C38F) to switch drives.
	$C707	JSR to MSGFRE ($C806) to send the BLOCKS FREE message.
	$C70A	Set the carry flag and exit with a JMP to TOGDRV ($C38F) to switch drives.
GN051	$C70E	Load .A with $00 and zero the hi byte of the number of blocks counter, NBTEMP+1 ($0273) and the drive flag DRVFLG($028D)
	$C716	JSR to NEWDIR ($C7B7) to begin a new directory listing.
	$C719	Set the carry flag and exit with an RTS.
GN10	$C71B	Load .X with $18 (#24), the length of an entry in a directory listing e.g. 114 "PROGRAM FILENAME" PRG
	$C71D	Load .Y with $1D, the position of the hi byte of the # of blocks in the file.
	$C71F	Load .A with the hi byte of the # of blocks in the file. Store this into the hi byte of the block counter, NBTEMP+1 ($0273). If zero, branch to GN12.
	$C726	Load .X with $16 (#22) the directory length less 2.
GN12	$C728	Decrement Y so it points to the position of the lo byte of the # of blocks in the file.
	$C729	Load .A with the lo byte of the # of blocks in the file. Store this into the lo byte of the block counter, NBTEMP ($0272).
	$C72E	Compare .X to $16 (#22) the directory length less 2. If they are equal, branch to GN14.
	$C732	Compare .A (the lo byte of the blocks) with $0A (#10). If .A<10 branch to GN14
	$C736	Decrement .X (we will need less padding since # of blocks is at least 2 digits.
	$C737	Compare .A (the lo byte of the blocks) with $64 (#100). If A<100 branch to GN14
	$C73B	Decrement .X (we will need less padding since # of blocks is at least 3 digits.

NAME	ADDRESS	DESCRIPTION OF WHAT ROM ROUTINE DOES
GN14	$C73C	JSR to BLKNB ($C7AC) to clear the name buffer for the next entry. On return Y=0
	$C73F	Load .A with the file type from the directory buffer (DIRBUF),Y and save the file type onto the stack.
	$C742	Do an ASL of the value in .A to set the carry bit if this is a valid file that has not been closed. (see BCS $C764)
	$C743	If .A<128, branch to GN15.

NOTE: The branch at $C742 and the code following is what
      produces the PRG<, SEQ<, etc. file types. Note that
      these file types are LOCKED and can't be SCRATCHED!
      The locking and unlocking of files is NOT supported
      by any Commodore DOS. To lock a file, change its
      file type in its directory entry from $80, $81, etc
      to $C0, $C1, etc. Reverse the process for unlocking

NAME	ADDRESS	DESCRIPTION OF WHAT ROM ROUTINE DOES
	$C745	Load .A with a $3C (a "<").
	$C747	Store this value into the name buffer NAMBUF+1,X ($02B1,X).

NAME	ADDRESS	DESCRIPTION OF WHAT ROM ROUTINE DOES
GN15	$C74A	Pull the file type off the stack and AND it with $0F to mask off the higher bits. Transfer it to .Y to use as an index.
	$C74E	Move last character in file type name from TP2LST,Y ($FEC5,Y) to the name buffer, NAMBUF,X ($02B1,X).
	$C754	Decrement .X
	$C755	Move middle character in file type name from TP1LST,Y ($FEC0,Y) to the name buffer, NAMBUF,X ($02B1,X).
	$C75B	Decrement .X
	$C75C	Move first character in file type name from TYPLST,Y ($FEBB,Y) to the name buffer, NAMBUF,X ($02B1,X).
	$C762	Decrement .X twice
	$C764	If carry bit is set (indicates valid entry; see $C742) branch to GN20.
	$C766	Load .A with $2A (a "*") to indicate an improperly closed file.
	$C768	Store the "*" in NAMBUF+1,X ($02B1,X).
GN20	$C76B	Store a shifted space, $A0 in the buffer (between name & type) and decrement .X
	$C771	Load .Y with $12 (#18) so it points to the end of the name in the dir buffer.
GN22	$C773	Loop to transfer the 16 characters in the file name from the directory buffer to the name buffer.
	$C77E	Load .A with $22 (a '"')
	$C780	Store quotation mark before the name.

NAME	ADDRESS	DESCRIPTION OF WHAT ROM ROUTINE DOES
GN30	$C783	Loop to scan up the name looking for a quote mark($22) or a shifted space($A0). When either character is found or the end of the name is reached, store a $22 (quote mark) at that location. Then AND any remaining characters in the name with $7F to clear bit 7 for each one.
GN40	$C7A7	JSR to FNDFIL ($C4B5) to find the next entry. On return, set the carry bit.
GN45	$C7AB	Terminate the routine with an RTS.

		Blank the name buffer:
BLKNB	$C7AC	Load .Y with $1B, the length of the name buffer, and .A with $20, a space.
BLKNB1	$C7B0	Loop to store $20's in all locations in the name buffer, NAMBUF ($02B1-CB)
	$C7B6	Terminate the routine with an RTS.

		New directory in listing
NEWDIR	$C7B7	JSR to BAM2X ($F119) to set BAM pointer in buffer 0/1 tables and leave in .X
	$C7BA	JSR to REDBAM ($F0DF) to read in the BAM to $0700-FF if not already present.
	$C7BD	JSR to BLKNB ($C7AC) to blank the name buffer, NAMBUF ($02B1-CB).
	$C7C0	Set TEMP ($6F) to $FF
	$C7C4	Set NBTEMP ($0272) to the current drive number from DRVNUM ($7F)
	$C7C9	Set NBTEMP+1 ($0273) to $00
	$C7CE	Load .X with the position of the read BAM job in the queue from JOBNUM ($F9).
	$C7D0	Set high byte of the pointer to the directory buffer, DIRBUF ($94/5) using a value (3,4,5,6,7,7) from BUFIND,X($FEE0)
	$C7D5	Set low byte of the pointer to the directory buffer, DIRBUF ($94/5) using the value ($90) from DSKNAM ($FE88). DIRBUF now points to the start of the disk name in the BAM buffer ($0x90)
	$C7DA	Load .Y with $16 (#22), the name length.
ND10	$C7DC	Load .A with character, (DIRBUF),Y and test if it is a shifted blank ($A0). If not, branch to ND20.
	$C7E2	Since it is not a shifted blank, load .A with a $31 (ASCII "1") for version #1.
	$C7E4	BYTE $2C here causes branch to ND20.
ND15	$C7E5	Load .A with character, (DIRBUF),Y and test if it is a shifted blank ($A0). If not, branch to ND20.
	$C7EB	Since it is not a shifted blank, load .A with a $20 (ASCII space).
ND20	$C7ED	Store the character in .A into the name buffer, NAMBUF+2,Y ($02B3,Y).

NAME	ADDRESS	DESCRIPTION OF WHAT ROM ROUTINE DOES
	$C7F1	If more characters left (.Y>=0) branch back to ND15.
	$C7F3	Store a $12 (RVS on) in NAMBUF ($02B1)
	$C7F8	Store a $22 (quote) in NAMBUF+1 ($02B2)
	$C7FD	Store a $22 (quote) in NAMBUF+18 ($02C3)
	$C800	Store a $20 (space) in NAMBUF+19 ($02C4)
	$C805	Terminate routine with an RTS.

		Set up message "BLOCKS FREE"
MSGFRE	$C806	JSR to BLKNB ($C7AC) to clear the name buffer.
	$C809	Load .Y with $0B (message length -1).
	$C80B	Loop using .Y as index to move message from FREMSG,Y ($C817,Y) to NAMBUF,Y ($02B1,Y).
	$C814	Terminate routine with a JMP to NUMFRE ($EF4D) to calculate the number free.

FREMSG	$C817	Message "BLOCKS FREE"

- * - * - SCRATCH ONE OR MORE FILES - * - * -

NAME	ADDRESS	DESCRIPTION OF WHAT ROM ROUTINE DOES
SCRTCH	$C823	JSR to FS1SET ($C398) to set up for one file stream.
	$C826	JSR to ALLDRS ($C320) to all drives needed based on F2CNT.
	$C829	JSR to OPTSCH ($C3CA) to determine best sequence of drives to use.
	$C82C	Zero file counter, R0 ($86)
	$C830	JSR to FFST ($C49D) to find the first directory entry. If not successful, branch to SC30.

NOTE: THE FOLLOWING CODE PREVENTS FREEING THE SECTORS OF AN UNCLOSED FILE.

NAME	ADDRESS	DESCRIPTION OF WHAT ROM ROUTINE DOES
SC15	$C835	JSR to TSTCHN ($DDB7) to test for active files from index table.
	$C838	If file active (carry clear), branch to SC25.

NOTE: THE FOLLOWING CODE PREVENTS THE SCRATCHING OF A LOCKED FILE (BIT 6 OF THE FILE TYPE SET).

NAME	ADDRESS	DESCRIPTION OF WHAT ROM ROUTINE DOES
	$C83A	Load .Y with $00.
	$C83C	Load .A with file type from (DIRBUF),Y ($94,Y).
	$C83E	AND the file type with $40 to test if it is a locked file (bit 6 of filetype set)
	$C840	If a locked file, branch to SC25.

	$C842	JSR to DELDIR ($C8B6) to delete the directory entry. Stores $00 as the file type and rewrite the sector on disk.

NAME	ADDRESS	DESCRIPTION OF WHAT ROM ROUTINE DOES
	$C845	Load .Y with $13 (#19).
	$C847	Test whether this is a relative file by loading .A with 19th character of the entry (the track of the side-sector pointer for a REL file) from (DIRBUF),Y
	$C849	If $00, not a REL file so branch to SC17
	$C84B	Store track pointer into TRACK ($80).
	$C84D	Increment .Y and move sector pointer from (DIRBUF),Y into SECTOR ($81).
	$C852	JSR to DELFIL ($C87D) to free the side sectors by updating and writing the BAM

NOTE: THE FOLLOWING CODE PREVENTS FREEING THE SECTORS
OF A FILE IF ITS REPLACEMENT WAS INCOMPLETE (BIT 5 SET).

NAME	ADDRESS	DESCRIPTION OF WHAT ROM ROUTINE DOES
SC17	$C855	Load .X with the directory entry counter ENTFND ($0253) and .A with $20.
	$C85A	AND .A with the file pattern type in PATTYP,X ($E7,X) to check if this is an opened but unclosed file.
	$C85C	If unclosed file, branch to SC20.
	$C85E	Move initial track link from FILTRK,X ($0280,X) into TRACK ($80).
	$C863	Move initial sector link from FILSEC,X ($0285,X) into SECTOR ($81).
	$C868	JSR to DELFIL ($C87D) to free the file blocks by updating and writing the BAM
SC20	$C86B	Increment the file counter, R0 ($86).
SC25	$C86D	JSR to FFRE ($C48B) to match the next filename in the command string.
	$C870	If a match found, branch to SC15
SC30	$C872	All done. Store number of files that have been scratched, R0 ($86) into TRACK ($80)
	$C876	Load .A with $01 and .Y with $00
	$C87A	Exit with a JMP to SCREND ($C1A3)
		Delete file by links:
DELFIL	$C87D	JSR to FRETS ($EF5F) to mark the first file block as free in the BAM.
	$C880	JSR to OPNIRD ($D475) to open the internal read channel (SA=17) and read in the first one or two blocks.
	$C883	JSR to BAM2X ($F119) to set BAM pointers in the buffer tables.
	$C886	Load .A from BUF0,X ($A7,X) and compare it to $FF to see if buffer inactive. If inactive (.A=$FF), branch to DEL2 Load write BAM flag, WBAM ($02F9), OR it with $40 to set bit 6 and store it back in WBAM to indicate both buffers active.

NAME	ADDRESS	DESCRIPTION OF WHAT ROM ROUTINE DOES
DEL2	$C894	Zero .A and JSR to SETPNT($D4C8) to set pointers to the currently active buffer.
	$C899	JSR to RDBYT ($D156) to direct read one byte (the track link from the buffer)
	$C89C	Store track link into TRACK ($80)
	$C89E	JSR to RDBYT ($D156) to direct read one byte (the sector link from the buffer)
	$C8A1	Store sector link into SECTOR ($81)
	$C8A3	Test track link. If not $00 (not final sector in this file), branch to DEL1
	$C8A7	JSR to MAPOUT ($EEF4) write out the BAM.
	$C8AA	Exit with a JMP to FRECHN ($D227) to free the internal read channel.
DEL1	$C8AD	JSR to FRETS($EF5F) to de-allocate(free) specified in TRACK ($80) & SECTOR ($81) in the BAM.
	$C8B0	JSR to NXTBUF ($D44D) to read in the next block in the file (use T/S link).
	$C8B3	JMP to DEL2 to de-allocate the new block
DELDIR	$C8B6	Delete the directory entry: Load .Y with $00 (will point to the 0th character in the entry; the file type).
	$C8B8	Set the file type, (DIRBUF),Y; ($94),Y to $00 to indicate a scratched file.
	$C8BB	JSR to WRTOUT ($DE5E) to write out the directory block.
	$C8BE	Exit with a JMP to WATJOB ($D599) to wait for the write job to be completed.

```
    *   DUPLICATE DISK  *   NOT AVAILABLE ON THE 1541
```

| | $C8C1 | Load .A with a $31 to indicate a bad command and JMP to CMDERR ($C1C8). |

```
    - * - * -    FORMAT DISKETTE ROUTINE     - * - * -
```

This routine sets up a jump instruction in buffer 0 that points to the code used by the disk controller to do the formatting. It then puts an exectute job code in the job queue. The routine then waits while the disk controller actually does the formatting.

FORMAT	$C8C6	Store JMP $FABB ($4C,$BB,$FA) at the start of buffer 0 ($0600/1/2).
	$C8D5	Load .A with $03 and JSR to SETH ($D6D3) to set up header of active buffer to the values in TRACK ($80) and SECTOR ($81).
	$C8DA	Load drive number, DRVNUM ($7F), EOR it with $E0 (execute job code) and store the result in the job queue ($0003).

NAME	ADDRESS	DESCRIPTION OF WHAT ROM ROUTINE DOES
FMT105	$C8E0	Load .A from the job queue ($0003). If .A > 127, the job has not been finished yet so branch back to FMT105.
	$C8E4	Compare .A with $02. if .A < 2, the job was completed OK so branch to FMT110.
	$C8E8	Error code returned by disk controller indicates a problem so load .A with $03 and .X with $00 and exit with a JMP to ERROR ($E60A).
FMT110	$C8EF	Job completed satisfactorily so exit with an RTS.

- * - * -   COPY DISK FILES ROUTINE   - * - * -

NAME	ADDRESS	DESCRIPTION OF WHAT ROM ROUTINE DOES
DSKCPY	$C8F0	Store $E0 in BUFUSE ($024F) to kill the BAM buffer.
	$C8F5	JSR to CLNBAM ($F0D1) to set track and sector links in BAM to $00.
	$C8F8	JSR to BAM2X ($F119) to return the BAM LINDX in .X.
	$C8FB	Store $FF in BUF0,X ($A7,X) to mark the BAM as out-of-memory.
	$C8FF	Store $0F in LINUSE ($0256) to free all LINDXs.
	$C904	JSR to PRSCLN ($C1E5) to parse the command string and find the colon.
	$C907	If colon found (Z flag =0), branch to DX0000.
	$C909	Colon not found in command string so command must be CX=Y. This command is not supported on the 1541 so exit with a JMP to DUPLCT ($C8C1).
DX0000	$C90C	JSR to TC30 ($C1F8) to parse the command string.
DX0005	$C90F	JSR to ALLDRS ($C320) to put the drive numbers into the file table.
	$C912	Load .A with the command pattern image as determined by the parser from IMAGE ($028B). AND the image with %01010101 ($55). If the result is not $00, the command must be a concatenate or normal copy so branch to DX0020.
	$C919	Check for pattern matching in the name (as in c1:game=0:*) by loading .X from FILTBL ($027A) and then loading .A from the command string, CMDBUF,X ($0200,X).
	$C91F	The value in .A is compared to $2A ("*") If there is no match, there is no wild so branch to DX0020.
DX0010	$C923	Load .A with the $30 to indicate a syntax error and JMP to CMDERR ($C1C8).

NAME	ADDRESS	DESCRIPTION OF WHAT ROM ROUTINE DOES
DX0020	$C928	Load .A with the command pattern image as determined by the parser from IMAGE ($028B). AND the image with %11011001 ($D9). If the result is not $00, the syntax is bad so branch to DX0010 and abort.
	$C92F	JMP to COPY ($C952) to do the file copy. syntax error and JMP to CMDERR ($C1C8).
PUPS1	$C932	Subroutine used to set up for copying entire disk (C1=0). Not used on 1541.
		Copy file(s) to one file:
COPY	$C952	JSR to LOOKUP ($C44F) to look up the file(s) listed in the command string in the directory.
	$C955	Load .A with the number of filenames in the command string from F2CNT($0278) and compare it with $03. If fewer than three files, this is not a concatenate so branch to COP10 ($C9A1).
	$C95C	Load .A with the first file drive number from FILDRV ($E2) and compare it to the second drive number in FILDRV+1 ($E3). If not equal, this is not a concatenate so branch to COP10 ($C9A1).
	$C962	Load .A with the index to the first file entry from ENTIND ($DD) and compare it to the second file's index in ENTIND+1 ($DE). If not equal, this is not a concatenate so branch to COP10 ($C9A1).
	$C968	Load .A with the first file's sector link from ENTSEC ($D8) and compare it to the second file's link in ENTSEC+1 ($D9). If not equal, this is not a concatenate so branch to COP10 ($C9A1).
		CONCATENATE FILES
	$C96E	JSR to CHKIN ($CACC) to check if input file exists.
	$C971	Set F2PTR ($0279) to $01 and JSR to OPIRFL ($C9FA) to open the internal read channel, read in the directory file, and locate the named file.
	$C979	JSR to TYPFIL ($D125) to determine the file type. If $00, a scratched file so branch to COP01 (file type mismatch).
	$C97E	Compare the file type to $02. If not equal, it is not a deleted program file so branch to COP05 to continue.
COP01	$C982	Bad file name. Load .A with $64 to indicate a file type mismatch and JSR to CMDERR ($C1C8).

NAME	ADDRESS	DESCRIPTION OF WHAT ROM ROUTINE DOES
COP05	$C987	Set secondary address, SA ($83) to $12 (#18, the internal write channel)
	$C98B	Move the active buffer pointer from LINTAB+IRSA ($023C) to LINTAB+IWSA ($023D).
	$C991	Deactivate the internal read channel by storing $FF in LINTAB+IRSA ($023C).
	$C996	JSR to APPEND ($DA2A) to copy first file
	$C999	Load .X with $02 and JSR to CY10 ($C9B9) to copy second file behind the first.
	$C99E	Exit routine with a JMP to ENDCMD ($C194)

COPY   FILE

NAME	ADDRESS	DESCRIPTION OF WHAT ROM ROUTINE DOES
COP10	$C9A1	JSR to CY ($C9A7) to do copy.
	$C9A3	Exit routine with a JMP to ENDCMD ($C194)

NAME	ADDRESS	DESCRIPTION OF WHAT ROM ROUTINE DOES
CY	$C9A7	JSR to CHKIO ($CAE7) to check if file exists.
	$C9AA	Get drive number from FILDRV ($E2), AND it with $01 (mask off default bit), and store it in DRVNUM ($7F).
	$C9B0	JSR to OPNIWR ($D486) to open internal write channel.
	$C9B3	JSR to ADDFIL ($D6E4) to add the new file name to the directory and rewrite the directory.
	$C9B6	Load .X with pointer from F1CNT ($0277).
CY10	$C9B9	Store .X in F2CNT ($0278).
	$C9BC	JSR to OPIRFL ($C9FA) to open internal read channel and read in one or two blocks of the directory.
	$C9BF	Set secondary address, SA ($83) to $11, to set up the internal read channel.
	$C9C3	JSR to FNDRCH ($D0EB) to find an unused read channel.
	$C9C6	JSR to TYPFIL ($D125) to determine if the file is a relative file.
	$C9C9	If not a relative file (Z flag not set on return), branch to CY10A.
	$C9CB	JSR to CYEXT ($CA53) to open copy the relative file records.
CY10A	$C9CE	Store $08 (EOI signal) into EOIFLG ($F8).
	$C9D2	JMP to CY20.
CY15	$C9D5	JSR to PIBYTE ($CF9B) to write out last byte to disk.
CY20	$C9D8	JSR to GIBYTE ($CA35) to get a byte from the internal read channel.
	$C9DB	Load .A with $80 (the last record flag) and JSR to TSTFLG ($DDA6) to see if this is the last record.

NAME	ADDRESS	DESCRIPTION OF WHAT ROM ROUTINE DOES
	$C9E0	On return if Z flag is set (test failed; this is not the last record) branch to CY15 to do some more. Last record done so JSR to TYPFIL($D125) to get file type.
	$C9E5	On return if Z flag is set branch to CY30 to do some more.
	$C9E7	JSR to PIBYTE ($CF9B) to write out last byte to disk.
CY30	$C9EA	Check if there are more files to copy by loading .X from F2PTR ($0279), incrementing it by 1, and comparing it to F2CNT ($0278). If the carry bit is clear, there are more files to copy so branch back to CY10.
	$C9F3	Since no more files to copy, set the SA ($83) to $12 (internal write channel) and JMP to CLSCHN ($DB02) to close the copy channel and file.
OPIRFL	$C9FA	Open internal read channel to read file: Load .X with the file pointer F2PTR ($0279) and use this as an index to load .A with the drive number of the file to be read from FILDRV,X ($E2,X). AND this drive number with $01 to mask off the default drive bit, and store the value in DRVNUM ($7F) to set the drive number.
	$CA03	Set the current TRACK ($80) to 18 ($12), the directory track.
	$CA08	Set the current SECTOR($81) to the sector containing the directory entry for this file from ENTSEC,X ($D8,X). the directory track.
	$CA0C	JSR to OPNIRD ($D475) to open the internal read channel to read the directory.
	$CA0F	Load .X with the file pointer F2PTR ($0279) and use this as an index to load .A with the pointer to the start of the entry from ENTIND,X ($DD,X).
	$CA14	JSR to SETPNT ($D4C8) to set the track sector pointers from the entry.
	$CA17	Load .X with the file pointer F2PTR ($0279) and use this as an index to load .A with the file's pattern mask from PATTYP,X ($E7,X). AND this value with $07 (the file type mask) and use it to set the file type in TYPE ($024A).
	$CA21	Set the record length, REC ($0258) to $00 since this is not a relative file.
	$CA26	JSR to OPREAD ($D9A0) to open a read channel.

NAME	ADDRESS	DESCRIPTION OF WHAT ROM ROUTINE DOES
	$CA29	Load .Y with $01 and JSR to TYPFIL ($D125) to get the file type.
	$CA2E	If Z flag set on return (indicates that this is not a relative file) branch to OPIR10.
	$CA30	Increment .Y by 1.
OPIR10	$CA31	Transfer the value in .Y into .A
	$CA32	Exit with a JMP to SETPNT ($D4C8) to set the track & sector pointers from the directory entry.
		--
GIBYTE	$CA35	Get byte from internal read channel: Set the secondary address, SA ($83) to $11 (#17) the internal read channel.
		--
GCBYTE	$CA39	Get byte from any channel: JSR to GBYTE ($D39B) to get the next byte from the read channel.
	$CA3C	Store the byte in DATA ($85).
	$CA3E	Load .X with the logical file index LINDX ($82) and use this as an index to load .A with the channel status flag, CHNRDY,X
	$CA42	EOR .A with $08, the not EOI send code and store the result in EOIFLG ($F8).
	$CA46	If .A <> $00 (EOI was sent!), branch to GIB20 and exit.
	$CA48	JSR to TYPFIL ($D125) to get the file type. If Z flag set on return (indicates this is not a relative file), branch to GIB20 and exit.
	$CA4D	Load .A with $80 (the last record flag) and JSR to SETFLG ($DD97).
GIB20	$CA52	Terminate routine with an RTS.
		--
CYEXT	$CA53	Copy relative records: JSR to SETDRN ($D1D3) to set drive #.
	$CA56	JSR to SSEND ($E1CB) to position side sector and BUFTAB to the end of the last record.
	$CA59	Save side sector index, SSIND ($D6) and the side sector number, SSNUM ($D5) onto the stack.
	$CA5F	Set the secondary address, SA ($83) to $12, the internal write channel.
	$CA63	JSR to FNDWCH ($D107) to find an unused write channel.
	$CA66	JSR to SETDRN ($D1D3) to set drive #.
	$CA69	JSR to SSEND ($E1CB) to position side sector and BUFTAB to the end of the last record.

NAME	ADDRESS	DESCRIPTION OF WHAT ROM ROUTINE DOES
	$CA6C	JSR to POSBUF ($E2C9) to position the proper data blocks into the buffers.
	$CA6F	Set R1 ($87) to the current value of the side sector index, SSIND ($D6).
	$CA73	Set R0 ($86) to the current value of the side sector number, SSNUM ($D5).
	$CA77	Zero R2 ($88) and the low bytes of the record pointer RECPTR ($D4) and the relative file pointer ($D7).
	$CA7F	Restore the original values of the side side sector number, SSNUM ($D5) and the sector index, SSIND ($D6) from the stack
	$CA85	Terminate the routine with a JMP to ADDR1 ($E33B).

RENAME FILE IN THE DIRECTORY

NAME	ADDRESS	DESCRIPTION OF WHAT ROM ROUTINE DOES
RENAME	$CA88	JSR to ALLDRS ($C320) to set up all the drives given in the command string.
	$CA8B	Load .A with the drive specified for the second file from FILDRV+1 ($E3), AND it with $01 to mask off the default drive bit, and store the result back in FILDRV+1 ($E3).
	$CA91	Compare the second drive number (in .A) with the first one in FILDRV ($E2). If equal, branch to RN10.
	$CA95	OR the drive number in .A with $80 to set bit 7. This will force a search of both drives for the named file.
RN10	$CA97	Store the value in .A into FILDRV ($E2)
	$CA99	JSR to LOOKUP ($C44F) to look up both file names in the directory.
	$CA9C	JSR to CHKIO ($CAE7) to check for the existance of the files named.
	$CA9F	Load the value from FILDRV+1 ($E3), AND it with $01 to mask off the default drive bit, and use the result to set the currently active drive, DRVNUM ($7F).
	$CAA5	Set the active sector number, SECTOR ($81) using the directory sector in which the second file name was found (from ENTSEC+1; $D9).
	$CAA9	JSR to RDAB ($DE57) to read the directory sector specified in TRACK($80) and SECTOR ($81).
	$CAAC	JSR to WATJOB ($D599) to wait for the job to be completed.
	$CAAF	Load .A with the pointer to the entry in the buffer from ENTIND+1 ($DE), add $03 (so it points to the first character in the file name), and JSR to SETPNT($D4C8) to set the pointers to the file name.

NAME	ADDRESS	DESCRIPTION OF WHAT ROM ROUTINE DOES
	$CAB7	JSR to GETACT ($DF93) to store the active buffer number in .A.
	$CABA	Transfer the buffer number to .Y, load .X from the file table FILTBL ($027A), .A with $10 (the number of characters in a file name) and JSR to TRNAME($C66E) to transfer the file name from the command string to the buffer containing the file entry.
	$CAC3	JSR to WRTOUT ($DE5E) to write out the revised directory sector.
	$CAC6	JSR to WATJOB ($D599) to wait for the job to be completed.
	$CAC9	Terminate the routine with a JMP to ENDCMD ($C194).
CHKIN	$CACC	Check existance of input file: Load .A with the first file type from PATTYP+1 ($E8), AND it with the file type mask ($07) and store it in TYPE ($024A).
	$CAD3	Load .X from F2CNT ($0278).
CK10	$CAD6	Decrement .X by 1 and compare it with the value of F1CNT ($0277).
	$CADA	If the carry is clear, the file has been found so branch to CK10.
	$CADC	Load .A with the file's track link from FILTRK,X ($0280,X). If link is NOT $00, branch to CK10.
	$CAE1	Since the file has not been found, load .A with $62 and exit with a JMP to CMDERR ($C1C8).
CK20	$CAE6	Terminate routine with an RTS.
CHKIO	$CAE7	Check existance of I/O file: JSR to CHKIN ($CACC) to check for the existance of the input file.
CK25	$CAEA	Load .A with the file's track link from FILTRK,X ($0280,X). If link equals $00, branch to CK30.
	$CAEF	The file already exists so load .A with $62 and exit with a JMP to CMDERR($C1C8)
CK30	$CAF4	Decrement .X (file counter). If more files exist, branch back to CK25. CMDERR ($C1C8).
	$CAF7	Terminate routine with an RTS.
MEMORY ACCESS COMMANDS (M-R, M-W, AND M-E)		
MEM	$CAF8	Check that the second character in the command is a "-" by: loading .A with the character from CMDBUF+1 ($0201), and comparing it with $2D ("-"). If not equal, branch to MEMERR ($CB4B).

NAME	ADDRESS	DESCRIPTION OF WHAT ROM ROUTINE DOES
	$CAFF	Set up address specified in command by moving the characters from CMDBUF+3 ($0202) and CMDBUF+4 ($0203) to TEMP ($6F) and TEMP+1 ($70).
	$CB09	Set .Y to $00.
	$CB0B	Load .A with the third character of the command (R,W,E) from CMDBUF+2 ($0202).
	$CB0E	Compare .A with "R". If equal, branch to MEMRD ($CB20).
	$CB12	JSR to KILLP ($F258) to kill protection. NOTE: this does nothing on the 1541!
	$CB15	Compare .A with "W". If equal, branch to MEMWRT ($CB50).
	$CB19	Compare .A with "E". If NOT equal, branch to MEMERR ($CB4B).
MEMEX	$CB1D	Do indirect jump using the pointer set up in TEMP ($006F).
MEMRD	$CB20	Load .A with the contents of (TEMP),Y ($6F),Y and store the value in DATA($85)
	$CB24	Compare the command string length,CMDSIZ ($0274), with $06. If it is less than or equal to 6 (normally 5), branch to M30.

```
---------------------------------------------------------------
            NOTE: PREVIOUSLY UNDOCUMENTED COMMAND!!
---------------------------------------------------------------
    PRINT#15,"M-R";CHR$(LO);CHR$(HI);CHR$(HOW MANY)
---------------------------------------------------------------
```

NAME	ADDRESS	DESCRIPTION OF WHAT ROM ROUTINE DOES
MRMULT	$CB2B	Multi-byte memory read: Load .X with the 6th character in the command string from CMDBUF+5 ($0205).
	$CB2E	Decrement .X (now $00 if only one to read).
	$CB2F	If the result is $00, all done so branch to M30.
	$CB31	Transfer the value in .X to .A and clear the carry flag.
	$CB33	Add the lo byte of the memory pointer in TEMP ($6F). This value is the lo byte of the last character to be sent.
	$CB35	Increment the lo byte pointer in TEMP ($6F) so it points to the second memory location to be read.
	$CB37	Store the value in .A into LSTCHR+ERRCHN ($0249).
	$CB3A	Load .A with the current value of TEMP ($6A), the lo byte of the second memory location to be read and store this value in CB+2 ($A5).
	$CB3E	Load .A with the current value of TEMP+1 ($70), the hi byte of the second memory location to be read and store this value in CB+3 ($A6).

NAME	ADDRESS	DESCRIPTION OF WHAT ROM ROUTINE DOES
	$CB42	Continue memory read with a JMP to GE20 ($D443).
M30	$CB45	JSR to FNDRCH ($D0EB) to find an unused read channel.
	$CB48	Terminate memory read with a JMP to GE15 ($D43A).
MEMERR	$CB4B	Load .A with $31 to indicate a bad command and JMP to CMDERR ($C1C8).
MEMWRT	$CB50	Move byte from CMDBUF+6,Y ($0206,Y) to memory at TEMP,Y ($BF,Y).
	$CB55	Increment .Y and compare .Y with the number of bytes to do, CMDBUF+5 ($0205).
	$CB59	If more to do, branch back to M10.
	$CB5B	Terminate memory write with an RTS.
USER COMMANDS		NOTE: U0 restores pointer to JMP table
USER	$CB5C	User jump commands: Load .Y with the second byte of the command string from CMDBUF+1 ($0201).
	$CB5F	Compare .Y to $30. If not equal, this is NOT a U0 command so branch to US10.
USRINT	$CB63	Restore normal user jump address ($FFEA) storing $EA in USRJMP ($6B) and $FF in USRJMP+1 ($6C).
	$CB6B	Terminate routine with an RTS.
US10	$CB6C	JSR to USREXC ($CB72) to execute the code according to the jump table.
	$CB6F	Terminate routine with a JMP to ENDCMD ($C194).
USREXC	$CB72	Decrement .Y, transfer the value to .A, AND it with $0F to convert it to hex, multiply it by two (ASL), and transfer the result back into .Y.
	$CB78	Transfer the lo byte of the user jump address from the table at (USRJMP),Y to IP ($75).
	$CB7C	Increment .Y by 1.
	$CB7D	Transfer the hi byte of the user jump address from the table at (USRJMP),Y to IP+1 ($76).
	$CB81	Do an indirect jump to the user code through the vector at IP ($0076).
OPNBLK	$CB84	Open direct access buffer in response to an OPEN "#" command: Use the previous drive number, LSTDRV ($028E) to set the current drive number DRVNUM ($7F).
	$CB89	Save the current secondary address, SA ($83) on the stack.

NAME	ADDRESS	DESCRIPTION OF WHAT ROM ROUTINE DOES
	$CB8C	JSR to AUTOI ($C63D) to initialize the disk. This is necessary for proper channel assignment.
	$CB8F	Restore the original secondary address, SA ($83) by pulling it off the stack.
	$CB92	Load .X with the command string length CMDSIZ ($0274). Decrement .X by 1.
	$CB96	If .X not equal to zero, a specific buffer number has been requested(e.g.#1) so branch to OB10.
	$CB98	No specific buffer requested so get any available buffer by loading .A with $01 and doing a JSR to GETRCH ($D1E2).
	$CB9D	On return, JMP to OB30.
OB05	$CBA0	Load .A with $70 to indicate that no channel is available and JMP to CMDERR ($C1C8).
OB10	$CBA5	Specific buffer requested so load .Y with $01 and JSR to BP05 ($CC7C) to check the block parameters.
	$CBAA	Load .X with the number of the buffer requested from FILSEC ($0285) and check it against $05 (the highest numbered buffer available). If too large, branch to OB05 and abort the command.
	$CBB1	Set TEMP ($6F) and TEMP+1 ($70) to $00 and set the carry flag.
OB15	$CBB8	Loop to shift a 1 into the bit position in TEMP or TEMP+1 that corresponds to the buffer requested. For example: TEMP+1(00000000) TEMP(0000001)=buffer 0 TEMP+1(00000000) TEMP(0000100)=buffer 2 TEMP+1(00000001) TEMP(0000000)=buffer 8
	$CBBF	Load .A with the value in TEMP ($6F) and AND it with the value in BUFUSE ($024F) which indicates which buffers are already in use. If the result is NOT $00, the buffer requested is already in use so branch to OB05 to abort.
	$CBC6	Load .A with the value in TEMP+1 ($70) and AND it with the value in BUFUSE+1 ($0250) which indicates which buffers are already in use. If the result is NOT $00, the buffer requested is already in use so branch to OB05 to abort.
	$CBCD	Mark the buffer requested as in use by ORing the value in TEMP with the value in BUFUSE and the value in TEMP+1 with the value in BUFUSE+1.
	$CBDD	Set up the channel by loading .A with $00 and doing a JSR to GETRCH ($D1E2) to find an unused read channel.
	$CBE2	Load .X with the current channel# from LINDX ($82).

NAME	ADDRESS	DESCRIPTION OF WHAT ROM ROUTINE DOES
	$CBE4	Use .X as an index to move the sector link from FILSEC($0285) to BUF0,X($A7,X)
	$CBE9	Transfer the sector link from .A to .X.
	$CBEA	Use .X as an index to move the current drive number from DRVNUM($7F) to JOBS,X ($00,X) and to LSTJOB,X ($025B,X).
OB30	$CBF1	Load .X with the current secondary address, SA ($83).
	$CBF3	Load .A with the current value from the logical index table, LINTAB,X ($022B,X). OR this value with $40 to indicate that it is read/write mode and store the result back in LINTAB,X.
	$CBFB	Load .Y with the current channel#, LINDX ($82).
	$CBFD	Load .A with $FF and store this value as the channel's last character pointer LSTCHR,Y ($0244,Y).
	$CC02	Load .A with $89 and store this value in CHNRDY,Y ($00F2,Y) to indicate that the channel is a random access one and is ready.
	$CC07	Load .A with the channel number from BUF0,Y ($00A7,Y) and store it in CHNDAT,Y($023E,Y) as the first character
	$CC0D	Multiply the sector value in .A by 2 and transfer the result into .X
	$CC0F	Set the buffer table value BUFTAB,X ($99,X) to $01.
	$CC13	Set the file type value FILTYP,Y ($EC,Y) to $0E to indicate a direct access file type.
	$CC18	Terminate routine with a JMP to ENDCMD ($C1C4).

BLOCK COMMANDS   (B-A;B-F;B-R;B-W;B-E;B-P)

NAME	ADDRESS	DESCRIPTION OF WHAT ROM ROUTINE DOES
BLOCK	$CC1B	Block commands: Zero .X and .Y. Load .A with $2D ("-") and JSR to PARSE ($C268) to locate the sub-command (separated from the command with a "-").
	$CC24	On return branch to BLK40 if Z flag is not set ("-" was found).
BLK10	$CC26	Load .A with $31 to indicate a bad command and JMP to CMDERR ($C1C8).
BLK30	$CC2B	Load .A with $30 to indicate a bad syntax and JMP to CMDERR ($C1C8).
BLK40	$CC30	Transfer the value in .X to .A. If not $00, branch to BLK30.
	$CC33	Load .X with $05 (the number of block commands - 1).

NAME	ADDRESS	DESCRIPTION OF WHAT ROM ROUTINE DOES
	$CC35	Load .A with the first character in the sub-command from CMDBUF,Y ($0200,Y).
BLK50	$CC38	Loop to compare the first character in the sub-command with the characters in the command table BCTAB,X ($CC5D,X). If a match is found, branch to BLK60. If NO MATCH is found, branch to BLK10.
BLK60	$CC42	Transfer the pointer to the command in the command table from .X to .A. OR this value with $80 and store it as the command number in CMDNUM ($022A).
	$CC48	JSR to BLKPAR ($CC6F) to parse the block parameters.
	$CC4B	Load .A with the command number from CMDNUM ($022A), multiply it by 2 (ASL), and transfer the result into .X.
	$CC50	Use .X as an index into the jump table BCJMP,X ($CC63) to set up a jump vector to the ROM routine at TEMP ($6F/70).
	$CC5A	Do an indirect JMP to the appropriate ROM routine via the vector at TEMP($6F).
	$CC5D	Block sub-command table ($CC5D-$CC62) .BYTE "AFRWEP"
	$CC63	Block jump table ($CC63-$CC6E) $CC63/4 $03,$CD BLOCK-ALLOCATE $CD03 $CC65/6 $F5,$CC BLOCK-FREE $CCF5 $CC67/8 $56,$CD BLOCK-READ $CD56 $CC69/A $73,$CD BLOCK-WRITE $CD73 $CC6B/C $A3,$CD BLOCK-EXECUTE $CDA3 $CC6D/E $BD,$CD BLOCK-POINTER $CDBD
BLKPAR	$CC6F	Parse the block parameters: Zero .X and .Y. Load .A with $3A (":") and JSR to PARSE ($C268) to find the colon, if any.
	$CC78	On return branch to BP05 if Z flag is not set (":" found; .Y= ":"-position+1)
	$CC7A	Load .Y with $03 (start of parameters)
BP05	$CC7C	Load .A with the .Yth character from the command string.
	$CC7F	Compare the character in .A with $20, (a space). If equal, branch to BP10.
	$CC83	Compare the character in .A with $29, (a skip chr). If equal, branch to BP10.
	$CC87	Compare the character in .A with $2C, (a comma). If NOT equal, branch to BP20.
BP10	$CC8B	Increment .Y. Compare .Y to the length of the command string in CMDSIZ ($0274). If more left, branch back to BP05.
	$CC91	If no more, exit with an RTS.

NAME	ADDRESS	DESCRIPTION OF WHAT ROM ROUTINE DOES
BP20	$CC92	JSR to ASCHEX ($CCA1) to convert ASCII values into hex and store the results in tables.
	$CC95	Increment the number of parameters processed F1CNT ($0277).
	$CC98	Load .Y with the value in F2PTR ($0279)
	$CC9B	Compare the value in .X (the original value of F1CNT ($0277) to $04 (the maximun number of files - 1). If the value in .X <= $04, branch to BP10.
	$CC9F	If .X was > $04, the syntax is bad so branch to BLK30 ($CC2B).

		Convert ASCII to HEX and store the converted values in the FILTRK ($0280) and FILSEC ($0285) tables:
		On entry: .Y = pointer into CMD buffer
ASCHEX	$CCA1	Zero TEMP($6F), TEMP+1($70), and TEMP+3 ($72) as a work area.
	$CCA9	Load .X with $FF.
AH10	$CCAB	Load .A with the command string byte from CMDBUF,Y.
	$CCAE	Test if the character in .A is numeric by comparing it to $40. If non-numeric, branch to AH20.
	$CCB2	Test if the character in .A is ASCII by comparing it to $30. If it is not an ASCII digit, branch to AH20.
	$CCB6	AND the ASCII digit with $0F to mask off the higher order bits and save this new value on the stack.
	$CCB9	Shift the values already in the table one position (TEMP+1 goes into TEMP+2; TEMP goes into TEMP+1).
	$CCC1	Pull the new value off the stack and store it in TEMP.
	$CCC4	Increment .Y and compare it to the command length stored in CMDSIZ ($0274). If more command left, branch back to AH10.
		Convert the values in the TEMP table into a single hex byte:
AH20	$CCCA	Save the .Y pointer to the command string into F2PTR ($0279), clear the the carry flag, and load .A with $00.
AH30	$CCD0	Increment .X by 1 (index into TEMP).
	$CCD1	Compare .X to $03 to see if we're done yet. If done, branch to AH40.
	$CCD5	Load .Y from TEMP,Y ($6F,Y).
AH35	$CCD7	Decrement .Y by 1. If Y<0 branch to AH30
	$CCDA	Add (with carry) the value from DECTAB,X ($CCF2,X) to .A. This adds 1, 10 or 100. If there is no carry, branch to AH35.

NAME	ADDRESS	DESCRIPTION OF WHAT ROM ROUTINE DOES
	$CCDF	Since there is a carry, clear the carry, increment TEMP+3, and branch back to AH35.
AH40	$CCE4	Save the contents of .A (the hex number) onto the stack.
	$CCE5	Load .X with the command segment counter from F1CNT ($0277).
	$CCE8	Load .A with the carry bit (thousands) from TEMP+3 ($72) and store it in the table, FILTRK,X ($0280,X).
	$CCED	Pull the hex number off the stack and store it in the table, FILSEC,X($0285,X)
	$CCF1	Terminate routine with an RTS.
DECTAB		The decimal conversion table:
	$CCF2	Byte $01 = 1
	$CCF3	Byte $0A = 10
	$CCF4	Byte $64 = 100
BLKFRE	$CCF5	Free (de-allocate) block in the BAM: JSR to BLKTST ($CDF5) to test for legal block and set up track & sector.
	$CCF8	JSR to FRETS ($EF5F) to free the block in the BAM and mark the BAM as changed.
	$CCFB	Terminate routine with a JMP to ENDCMD ($C194).
	$CCFE	Unused code: LDA #$01 / STA WBAM($02F9)
BLKALC	$CD03	Allocate a sector (block) in the BAM: JSR to BLKTST ($CDF5) to test for legal block and set up track & sector.
	$CD06	Load .A with the current sector pointer, SECTOR ($81) and save this on the stack.
	$CD09	JSR to GETSEC ($F1FA) to set the BAM and find the next available sector on this track.
	$CD0C	If Z flag is set on return to indicate that the desired sector is in use and there is no greater sector available on this track, branch to BA15.
	$CD0E	Pull the requested sector from the stack and compare it to the current contents of SECTOR ($81). If not equal, the requested sector is already in use so branch to BA30.
	$CD13	Requested sector is available so JSR to WUSED ($EF90) to allocate the sector in the BAM and terminate the command with a JMP to ENDCMD ($C194).
BA15	$CD19	Pull the desired sector off the stack. It is of no further use since that sector is already in use.

NAME	ADDRESS	DESCRIPTION OF WHAT ROM ROUTINE DOES
BA20	$CD1A	Set the desired sector, SECTOR ($81) to $00, increment the desired track, TRACK ($80) by 1, and check if we have reached the maximum track count of 35 (taken from MAXTRK $FECB). If we have gone all the way, branch to BA40.
	$CD27	JSR to GETSEC ($F1FA) to set the BAM and find the next available sector on this track.
	$CD2A	If Z flag is set on return, no greater sector is available on this track so branch back to BA20 to try another track
BA30	$CD2C	Requested block is not available so load .A with $65 to indicate NO BLOCK ERROR and JMP to CMDER2 ($E645).
BA40	$CD31	No free sectors are available so load .A with $65 to indicate NO BLOCK ERROR and JMP to CMDERR ($C1C8).
BLKRD2	$CD36	B-R Sub to test parameters: JSR to BKOTST ($CDF2) to test block parameters and set track & sector.
	$CD39	JMP to DRTRD ($D460) to read block
GETSIM	$CD3C	B-R Sub to get byte w/o increment: JSR to GETPRE ($D12F) set parameters.
	$CD3F	Load .A with the value in (BUFTAB,X), ($99,X).
	$CD41	Terminate routine with an RTS.
BLKRD3	$CD42	B-R Sub to do read: JSR to BLKRD2 ($CD36) to test parameters
	$CD45	Zero .A and JSR to SETPNT ($D4C8) to set the track and sector pointers.
	$CD4A	JSR to GETSIM ($CD3C) to read block. On return .Y is the LINDX.
	$CD4D	Store the byte in .A into LSTCHR,Y ($0244,Y) as the last character.
	$CD50	Store $89 in CHNRDT,Y($F2,Y) to indicate that it is a random access channel and is now ready.
	$CD55	Exit routine with an RTS.
BLKRD	$CD56	Block read a sector: JSR to BLKRD3 ($CD42) to set up to read the requested sector.
	$CD59	JSR to RNGET1 ($D3EC) to read in the sector.
	$CD5C	Terminate routine with a JMP to ENDCMD ($C194).

NAME	ADDRESS	DESCRIPTION OF WHAT ROM ROUTINE DOES
		U1: Block read of a sector:
		--
		NOTE: The only real difference between a B-R command and a U1 (preferred) is that the U1 command move the last byte into the data buffer and stores $FF as the last byte read.
		--
UBLKRD	$CD5F	JSR to BLKPAR ($CC6F) to parse the block parameters.
	$CD62	JSR to BLKRD3 ($CD42) to set up to read the requested sector.
	$CD65	Move the last character read from LSTCHR,Y ($0244,Y) to CHNDAT,Y ($023E,Y)
	$CD6B	Store $FF in LSTCHR,Y ($0244,Y) as the last character to be read.
	$CD70	Terminate routine with a JMP to ENDCMD ($C194) which ends with an RTS.
		--
		Block-write of a sector:
BLKWT	$CD73	JSR to BKOTST ($CDF2) to test the buffer and block parameters and set up the drive, track, and sector pointers.
	$CD76	JSR to GETPNT ($D4E8) to read the active buffer pointers. On exit, .A points into the buffer.
	$CD79	Transfer .A to .Y and decrement .Y.
	$CD7B	If the value in .A is greater than $02, branch to BW10
	$CD7F	Load .Y with $01.
BW10	$CD81	Load .A with $00.
	$CD83	JSR to SETPNT ($D4C8) to set the buffer pointers.
	$CD86	Transfer the value in .Y to .A and JSR to PUTBYT ($CFF1) to put the byte in .A into the active buffer of LINDX.
	$CD8A	Transfer the value of .X to .A and save it on the stack.
BW20	$CD8C	JSR to DRTWRT ($D464) to write out the block.
	$CD8F	Pop the value off the stack and transfer it back into .X.
	$CD91	JSR to RNGET2 ($D3EE) to set the channel ready status and last character.
	$CD94	Terminate routine with a JMP to ENDCMD ($C194) which ends with an RTS.
		--
		U2: Block write of a sector:
UBLKWT	$CD97	JSR to BLKPAR ($CC6F) to parse the block parameters.
	$CD9A	JSR to BKOTST ($CDF2) to test the buffer and block parameters and set up the drive, track, and sector pointers.

NAME	ADDRESS	DESCRIPTION OF WHAT ROM ROUTINE DOES
	$CD9D	JSR to DRTWRT ($D464) to write out the block.
	$CDA0	Terminate routine with a JMP to ENDCMD ($C194) which ends with an RTS.
BLKEXC	$CDA3	Block execute a sector: JSR to KILLP ($F258) to kill the disk protection. Does nothing on the 1541!
	$CDA6	JSR to BLKRD2 ($CC6F) to read the sector
	$CDA9	Store $00 in TEMP ($6F) as the lo byte of the JMP address)
	$CDAD	Load .X from JOBNUM ($F9) and use it as an index to load the hi byte of the JMP address from BUFIND,X ($FEE0,X) and store it in TEMP+1 ($70).
	$CDB4	JSR to BE10 ($CDBA) to execute the block.
	$CDB7	Terminate routine with a JMP to ENDCMD ($C194) which ends with an RTS.
BE10	$CDBA	JMP (TEMP) Used by block execute.
BLKPTR	$CDBD	Set the buffer pointer: JSR to BUFTST ($CDD2) to test for allocated buffer.
	$CDC0	Load the buffer number of the channel requested from JUBNUM ($F9), multiply it by two (ASL), and transfer the result into .X. Load .A with the new buffer pointer value from FILSEC+1 ($0286) and store it in the buffer table BUFTAB,X ($99,X).
	$CDC9	JSR to GETPRE ($D12F) to set up pointers
	$CDCC	JSR to RNGET2 ($D3EE) to ready the channel for I/O.
	$CDCF	Terminate routine with a JMP to ENDCMD ($C194) which ends with an RTS.
BUFTST	$CDD2	Test whether a buffer has been allocated for the secondary address given in SA. Load .X with the file stream 1 pointer, F1PTR ($D3) and then increment the original pointer F1PTR ($D3).
	$CDD6	Load .A with that file's secondary address from FILSEC,X ($0285,X).
	$CDD9	Transfer the secondary address to .Y. Decrement it by 2 (to eliminate the reserved secondary addresses 0 and 1) and compare the result with $0C (#12). If the original SA was between 2 and 14, it passes the test so branch to BT20.
BT15	$CDE0	Load .A with $70 to indicate no channel is available and JMP to CMDERR ($C1C8).

NAME	ADDRESS	DESCRIPTION OF WHAT ROM ROUTINE DOES
BT20	$CDE5	Store the original secondary address (in .A) into SA ($83) as the active SA.
	$CDE7	JSR to FNDRCH ($D0EB) to find an unused read channel. If none available, branch to BT15.
	$CDEC	JSR to GETACT ($DF93) to get the active buffer number. On return, store the active buffer number in JOBNUM ($F9). read channel. If none available, branch
	$CDF1	Terminate routine with an RTS.
		Test all block parameters: buffer allocated and legal block. If OK, set up drive, track, and sector values.
BKOTST	$CDF2	JSR to BUFTST($CDD2) to test if buffer is allocated for this secondary address.
		Set the drive number, track, and sector values requested for a block operation and test to see that these are valid.
BLKTST	$CDF5	Load .X with the channel number from F1PTR ($D3)
	$CDF7	Load .A with the drive number desired from FILSEC,X($0285,X), AND it with $01 to mask off the default drive bit, and store the result as the current drive number, DRVNUM ($7F).
	$CDFE	Move the desired sector from FILSEC+2,X ($0287,X) to SECTOR ($81).
	$CE03	Move the desired track from FILSEC+1,X ($0286,X) to TRACK ($80).
	$CE08	JSR to TSCHK ($D55F) to test whether the track and sector values are legal.
	$CE0B	JMP to SETLDS to turn on drive active LED. Do RTS from there.

FIND RELATIVE FILE

INPUTS: (ALL 1 BYTE)		OUTPUTS: (ALL 1 BYTE)
RECL	- record # (lo byte)	SSNUM - side sector #
RECH	- record # (hi byte)	SSIND - index into SS
RS	- record size	RELPTR - pointer into
RECPTR	- pointer into record	sector

NAME	ADDRESS	DESCRIPTION OF WHAT ROM ROUTINE DOES
FNDREL	$CE0E	JSR to MULPLY($CE2C) to find total bytes TOTAL = REC# x RS + RECPTR
	$CE11	JSR to DIV254 to divide by 254. The result is the record's location (in sectors) from the start of the file.
	$CE14	Save the remainder (in .A) into RELPTR ($D7). This points into the last sector.
	$CE18	JSR to DIV120 to divide by 120. The result points into the side sector file.

NAME	ADDRESS	DESCRIPTION OF WHAT ROM ROUTINE DOES
	$CE1B	Increment the pointer into the sector, RELPTR ($D7) by two to bypass the two link bytes at the start of the sector.
	$CE1F	Move the quotient of the division by 120 from RESULT ($8B) to SSNUM ($D5).
	$CE23	Load .A with the remainder of the division from ACCUM+1 ($90), multiply it by two (ASL) because each side sector pointer occupies two bytes (t & s), add $10 (#16) to skip the initial link table in the sector, and store the resulting side sector index (points into the sector holding the side sectors) into SSIND ($D6).
	$CE2B	Terminate routine with an RTS.

		Calculate a record's location in bytes.
		TOTAL = REC# x RS + RECPTR
MULPLY	$CE2C	JSR to ZERRES ($CED9) to zero the RESULT area ($8B-$8D).
	$CE31	Zero ACCUM+3 ($92).
	$CE33	Load .X with the LINDX ($82) and use it to move the lo byte of the record number from RECL,X ($B5) to ACCUM+1 ($90).
	$CE37	Move the hi byte of the record number from RECH,X ($BB) to ACCUM+2 ($91).
	$CE3B	If the hi byte of the record number is not $00, branch to MUL25.
	$CE3D	If the lo byte of the record number is $00, branch to MUL50 to adjust for record #0 (the first record).
MUL25	$CE41	Load .A with the lo byte of the record size from ACCUM+1 ($90), set the carry flag, subtract $01, and store the result back in ACCUM+1. If the carry flag is still set, branch to MULT50.
	$CE4A	Decrement the hi byte of the record size in ACCUM+2 ($91).
MUL50	$CE4C	Copy the record size from RS,X ($C7,X) to TEMP ($6F).
MUL100	$CE50	Do an LSR on TEMP ($6F). If the carry flag is clear, branch to MUL200 (no add this time).
	$CE54	JSR to ADDRES ($CEED) to add.
		RESULT = RESULT + ACCUM+1,2,3
MUL200	$CE57	JSR to ACCX2 ($CEE5) to multiply the ACCUM+1,2,3 by two.
	$CE5A	Test TEMP to see if done, if not branch back to MUL100.
	$CE5E	Add the byte pointer to the result.
MUL400	$CE6D	Terminate routine with an RTS.

NAME	ADDRESS	DESCRIPTION OF WHAT ROM ROUTINE DOES

DIVIDE ROUTINE:

RESULT ($8B) = QUOTIENT   ACCUM+1 ($90) = REMAINDER

		Divide by 254 entry point:
DIV254	$CE6E	Load .A with $FE (#254)
	$CE70	Byte $2C (skip over next instruction)
		Divide by 120 entry point:
DIV120	$CE71	Load .A with $78 (#120)
	$CE73	Store divisor into TEMP ($6F).
	$CE75	Swap ACCUM+1,2,3 with RESULT,1,2
	$CE84	JSR to ZERRES ($CED9) to zero RESULT,1,2
DIV150	$CE87	Zero .X
DIV200	$CE89	Divide by 256 by moving the value in ACCUM+1,X ($90,X) to ACCUM,X ($8F,X).
	$CE8D	Increment .X. If .X is not 4 yet, branch back to DIV200.
	$CE92	Zero the hi byte, ACCUM+3 ($92). Check if this is a divide by 120 by testing bit 7 of TEMP. If it is a divide by 254, branch to DIV300.
	$CE9A	Do an ASL of ACCUM ($8F) to set the carry flag if ACCUM > 127. Push the processor status on the stack to save the carry flag. Do an LSR on ACCUM to restore its original value. Pull the processor status back off the stack and JSR to ACC200 ($CEE6) to multiply the value in the ACCUM,1,2 by two so that we have, in effect, divided by 128. <div align="center">X/128 = 2 * X/256</div>
DIV300	$CEA3	JSR to ADDRES ($CEED) to add the ACCUM to the RESULT.
	$CEA6	JSR to ACCX2 ($CEE5) to multiply the ACCUM by two.
	$CEA9	Check if this is a divide by 120 by testing bit 7 of TEMP. If it is a divide by 254, branch to DIV400.
	$CEAD	JSR to ACCX4 ($CEE2) to multiply the ACCUM by four. A= 4 * (2 * A) = 8 * A
DIV400	$CEB0	Add in the remainder from ACCUM ($8F) to ACCUM+1. If a carry is produced, increment ACCUM+2 and, if necessary, ACCUM+3.
DIV500	$CEBF	Test if remainder is less than 256 by ORing ACCUM+3 and ACCUM+2. If the result is not zero, the remainder is too large so branch to DIV to crunch some more.
	$CEC5	Test if remainder is less than divisor subtracting the divisor, TEMP ($6F) from the remainder in ACCUM+1 ($90). If the remainder is smaller, branch to DIV600.
	$CED0	Since the remainder is too large, add 1 to the RESULT.

NAME	ADDRESS	DESCRIPTION OF WHAT ROM ROUTINE DOES
DIV600	$CED6	Store the new, smaller remainder in ACCUM+1 ($90).
	$CED8	Terminate routine with an RTS.
ZERRES	$CED9	Zero the RESULT area: Load .A with $00 and store in RESULT ($8B), RESULT+1($8C), and RESULT+2($8D).
	$CEE1	Terminate routine with an RTS.
ACCX4	$CEE2	Multiply ACCUM by 4: JSR ACCX2 ($CEE5)
ACCX2	$CEE5	Multiply ACCUM by 2: Clear the carry flag.
ACC200	$CEE6	Do a ROL on ACCUM+1($90), ACCUM+2($91), and ACCUM+2($92).
	$CEEC	Terminate routine with an RTS.
ADDRES	$CEED	Add ACCUM to RESULT: Load .X with $FD.
ADD100	$CEF0	Add RESULT+3,X ($8E,X) and ACCUM+4,X ($93) and store the result in RESULT+3.
	$CEF6	Increment .X. If not $00 yet, branch back to ADD100.
	$CEF9	Terminate routine with an RTS.
LRUINT	$CEFA	Initialize LRU (least recently used) table: Load .X with $00.
LRUILP	$CEFC	Transfer .X to .A. Store the value in .A into LRUTBL,X ($FA,X).
	$CEFF	Increment .X and compare it to $04, the command channel number. If not yet equal, branch back to LRUILP.
	$CF04	Load .A with $06, the BAM logical index for the floating BAM, and store this value into LRUTBL,X ($FA,X).
	$CF08	Terminate routine with an RTS.
LRUUPD	$CF09	Update LRU (least recently used) table: Load .Y with $04, the command channel number. Load .X from LINDX ($82) the current channel number.
LRULP1	$CF0D	Load .A with the value from LRUTBL,Y ($00FA,Y). Store the current channel number (from .X) into LRUTBL,Y.
	$CF12	Compare the value in .A with the current channel number in LINDX ($82). If they are equal, branch to LRUEXT to exit.
	$CF16	Decrement .Y the channel counter. If no more channels to do (Y<0) branch to LRUINT ($CEFA) since no match was found.
	$CF19	Transfer .A to .X and JMP to LRULP1 .A into LRUTBL,X ($FA,X).
LRUEXT	$CF1D	Terminate routine with an RTS.

NAME	ADDRESS	DESCRIPTION OF WHAT ROM ROUTINE DOES
		Double buffer: Switch the active and inactive buffers.
DBLBUF	$CF1E	JSR to LRUUPD ($CF09) to update the LRU (least recently used) table.
	$CF21	JSR to GETINA ($DFB7) to get the LINDX channel's inactive buffer number (in .A)
	$CF24	On return, if there is an inactive buffer, branch to DBL15.
	$CF26	There is no inactive buffer so make one! JSR to SETDRN ($D1D3) to set the drive number to the one in LSTJOB.
	$CF29	JSR to GETBUF ($D28E) to get a free buffer number. If no buffers available, branch to DBL30 and abort.
	$CF2E	JSR to PUTINA ($DFC2) to store the new buffer number as the inactive buffer.
	$CF31	Save the current values of TRACK ($80) and SECTOR ($81) on the stack.
	$CF37	Load .A with $01 and JSR to DRDBYT ($D4F6) to direct read .A bytes. Store the byte read as the current SECTOR($81)
	$CF3E	Load .A with $00 and JSR to DRDBYT ($D4F6) to direct read .A bytes. Store the byte read as the current TRACK($80).
	$CF45	If the TRACK byte was $00 (last sector in the file), branch to DBL10.
	$CF47	JSR to TYPFIL ($D125) to determine the file type we are working on. If it is a relative file, branch to DBL05.
	$CF4C	JSR to TSTWRT ($DDAB) to see if we are writing this file or just reading it. If just reading, branch to DBL05 to read ahead.
	$CF51	We are writing so JSR to TGLBUF ($CF8C) to toggle the buffers. On return, JMP to DBL08.
DBL05	$CF57	JSR to TGLBUF ($CF8C) to toggle the inactive and inactive buffers.
	$CF5A	JSR to RDAB ($DE57) to read in the next sector of the file (into active buffer).
DBL08	$CF5D	Pull the old SECTOR($81) and TRACK($80) values from the stack and restore them.
	$CF63	JMP to DBL20.
DBL10	$CF66	Pull the old SECTOR($81) and TRACK($80) values from the stack and restore them.
DBL15	$CF6C	JSR to TGLBUF ($CF8C) to toggle the inactive and active buffers.
DBL20	$CF6F	JSR to GETACT ($DF93) to get the active buffer number (in .A). Transfer the active buffer number into .X and JMP to WATJOB ($D599) to wait until job is done

NAME	ADDRESS	DESCRIPTION OF WHAT ROM ROUTINE DOES
DBL30	$CF76	No buffers to steal so load .A with $70 to indicate a NO CHANNEL error and JMP to CMDERR ($C1C8).
DBSET	$CF7B	Set up double buffering: JSR to LRUUPD ($CF09) to update the LRU (least recently used) table.
	$CF7E	JSR to GETINA ($DFB7) to get the number of the inactive buffer (in .A).
	$CF81	If there is an inactive buffer, branch to DBS10 to exit.
	$CF83	JSR to GETBUF ($DF93) to find an unused buffer. If no buffers available, branch to DBL30 ($CF76) to abort.
	$CF88	JSR to PUTINA ($DFC2) to set the buffer found as the inactive buffer.
DBS10	$CF8B	Terminate routine with an RTS.
TGLBUF	$CF8C	Toggle the inactive & active buffers: Input: LINDX = current channel # Load .X with the channel number from LINDX ($82) and use it as an index to load .A with the buffer number from BUF0,X ($A7). EOR this number with $80 to change its active/inactive state and store the modified value back in BUF0,X.
	$CF94	Load .A with the buffer number from BUF1,X ($AE). EOR this number with $80 to change its active/inactive state and store the modified value back in BUF1,X.
	$CF9A	Terminate routine with an RTS.
PIBYTE	$CF9B	Write byte to internal write channel: Load .X with $12 (#18) the secondary address of the internal write channel and use it to set the current secondary address SA ($83).
	$CF9F	JSR to FNDWCH ($D107) to find an unused write channel.
	$CFA2	JSR to SETLED ($C100) to turn on the drive active LED.
	$CFA5	JSR to TYPFIL ($D125) to determine the current file type. If NOT a relative file, branch to PBYTE ($CFAF).
	$CFAA	Load .A with $20 (the overflow flag bit) and JSR to CLRFLG ($DD9D) to clear the overflow flag.
PBYTE	$CFAF	Write byte to any channel: Load .A with the current secondary address from SA ($83). Compare the SA with $0F (#15) to see if we are using the command channel. If SA=$0F, this is the command channel so branch to L42 ($CFD8). If not, branch to L40 ($CFBF).

NAME	ADDRESS	DESCRIPTION OF WHAT ROM ROUTINE DOES
PUT	$CFB7	Main routine to write to a channel: Check if this is the command channel or a data channel by loading the original secondary address from ORGSA ($84), ANDing it with $8F, and comparing the result with $0F (#15). If less than 15, this is a data channel so branch to L42.
L40	$CFBF	JSR to TYPFIL ($D125) to determine the file type. If we are NOT working on a sequential file, branch to L41.
	$CFC4	Since this is a sequential file, load .A with the data byte from DATA ($85) and JMP to WRTBYT ($D19D) to write the byte to the channel.
L41	$CFC9	If Z flag not set, we are writing to a true random access file (USR) so branch to L46.
	$CFCB	We are writing to a relative (REL) file so JMP to WRTREL ($E0AB).
L46	$CFCE	Since this is a USR file, load .A with the data byte from DATA ($85) and JSR to PUTBYT ($CFF1) to write it to the channel.
	$CFD3	To prepare to write the next byte: load .Y with the channel number from LINDX ($82) and JMP to RNGET2 ($D3EE).
L42	$CFD8	Since this is the command channel, set LINDX ($82) to $04 (the command channel number).
	$CFDC	Test if command buffer is full by doing a JSR to GETPNT ($D4E8) to get the position of the last byte written and comparing it to $2A. If they are equal, the buffer is full so branch to L50.
	$CFE3	Since there is space, load .A with the command message byte from DATA ($85) and JSR to PUTBYT ($CFF1) to write it to the command channel.
L50	$CFE8	Test if this is the last byte of the message by checking the EOIFLG ($F8). If it is zero, this is the last byte so branch to L45.
	$CFEC	Terminate command with an RTS.
L45	$CFED	Increment CMDWAT ($0255) to set the command-waiting flag.
	$CFF0	Terminate command with an RTS.
PUTBYT	$CFF1	Put byte in .A into the active buffer of the channel in LINDX: Save byte in .A onto the stack.
	$CFF2	JSR to GETACT ($DF93) to get the active buffer number (in .A). If there is an active buffer, branch to PUTB1.

NAME	ADDRESS	DESCRIPTION OF WHAT ROM ROUTINE DOES
PUTB1	$CFF7	No active buffer so pull the data byte off the stack, load .A with $61 to indicate a FILE NOT OPEN error, and JMP to CMDERR ($C1C8).
	$CFFD	Multiply the buffer number by 2 (ASL) and transfer this value to .X
	$CFFF	Pull the data byte off the stack and store it in the buffer at (BUFTAB,X) ($99,X).
	$D002	Increment the buffer pointer BUFTAB,X NOTE: Z flag is set if this data byte was stored in the last position in the buffer!
	$D004	Terminate routine with an RTS.

INITIALIZE   DRIVE(S)

NAME	ADDRESS	DESCRIPTION OF WHAT ROM ROUTINE DOES
INTDRV	$D005	Initialize drive(s): (Disk command) JSR to SIMPRS ($C1D1) to parse the disk command.
	$D008	JSR to INITDR ($D042) to initialize the drive(s).
ID20	$D00B	Terminate command with a JMP to ENDCMD ($C194).

NAME	ADDRESS	DESCRIPTION OF WHAT ROM ROUTINE DOES
ITRIAL	$D00E	Initialize drive given in DRVNUM: JSR to BAM2A ($F10F) to get the current BAM pointer in .A.
	$D011	Transfer the BAM pointer to .Y and use it as an index to load the BAM LINDX from BUF0,Y ($A7,Y) into .X. If there is a valid buffer number for the BAM (not $FF), branch to IT30.
	$D018	No buffer so we had better get one! Save the BAM pointer in .A on the stack and JSR to GETBUF ($D28E) to find an unused buffer. If a buffer is available, branch to IT20.
	$D01F	No buffer available so load .A with $70 to indicate a NO CHANNEL error and JSR to CMDER3 ($E648).
IT20	$D024	Pull the BAM pointer from the stack and transfer it to .Y. Transfer the new buffer number from .X to .A, OR it with $80 (to indicate an inactive status), and store the result in BUF0,Y ($00A7,Y) to allocate the buffer.
IT30	$D02C	Transfer the buffer number from .X to .A, AND it with $0F to mask off the inactive status bit, and store it in JOBNUM ($F9).
	$D031	Set SECTOR ($81) to $00 and TRACK ($80) to $12 (#18) to prepare to read the BAM.

NAME	ADDRESS	DESCRIPTION OF WHAT ROM ROUTINE DOES
	$D03A	JSR to SETH ($D6D3) to set up the seek image of the BAM header.
	$D03D	Load .A with $B0 (the job code for a SEEK) and JMP to DOJOB ($D58C) to do the seek to track 18. Does an RTS when done.

		Initialize drive:
INITDR	$D042	JSR to CLNBAM ($F0D1) to zero the track numbers for the BAM.
	$D045	JSR to CLDCHN ($D313) to allocate a channel for the BAM.
	$D048	JSR to ITRIAL ($D00E) to allocate a buffer for the BAM and seek track 18.
	$D04D	Store $00 in MDIRTY,X ($0251) to indicate that the BAM for drive .X is NOT DIRTY (BAM in memory matches BAM on the diskette).
	$D052	Set the master ID for the diskette in DSKID,X ($12/3 for drive 0) from the track 18 header values ($16/17) read during the seek to track 18.
	$D05D	JSR to DOREAD ($D586) to read the BAM into the buffer.
	$D060	Load the disk version(#65 for 4040/1541) from the $0X02 position in the BAM and store it in DSKVER,X($0101,drive number)
	$D06F	Zero WPSW,X ($1C,X) to clear the write protect switch and NODRV,X ($FF,X) to clear the drive-not-active flag.
NFCALC	$D075	Count the number of free blocks in BAM JSR to SETBPT ($EF3A) to set the bit map pointer and read in the BAM if necessary
	$D078	Initialize .Y to $04 and zero .A and .X (.X will be the hi byte of the count).
NUMF1	$D07D	Clear carry and add (BMPNT),Y; ($6D),Y to the value in .A. If no carry, branch to NUMF2.
	$D082	Increment .X (the hi byte of the count).
NUMF2	$D083	Increment .Y four times so it points to the start of the next track byte in the BAM. Compare .Y to $48 (the directory track location). If .Y=$48, branch to NUMF2 to skip the directory track.
	$D08B	Compare .Y to $90 to see if we are done. If there is more to do, branch to NUMF1.
	$D08F	All done. Save the lo byte of the count on the stack and transfer the hi byte from .X to .A. Load .X with the current drive number from DRVNUM ($7F) and store the hi byte of the count (in .A) into NDBH,X ($02FC,X). Pull the lo byte of the count off the stack and save it in NDBL,X ($02FA,X).

NAME	ADDRESS	DESCRIPTION OF WHAT ROM ROUTINE DOES
	$D09A	Terminate routine with an RTS.
STRRD	$D09B	Start reading ahead: Use the values in TRACK and SECTOR to read a data block. Use the track and sector pointers to set up the next one. JSR to SETHDR ($D6D0) to set up the header image using TRACK ($80) and SECTOR ($81) values.
	$D09E	JSR to RDBUF ($D0C3) to read the first block into the data buffer.
	$D0A1	JSR to WATJOB ($D599) to wait for the read job to be completed.
	$D0A4	JSR to GETBYT ($D137) to get the first byte from the data buffer (track link) and store it in TRACK ($80).
	$D0A9	JSR to GETBYT ($D137) to get the second byte from the data buffer (sector link) and store it in SECTOR ($81).
	$D0AE	Terminate routine with an RTS.
STRDBL	$D0AF	Start double buffering: (reading ahead) JSR to STRRD ($D09B) to read in a data block and set up the next one.
	$D0B2	Check the current TRACK ($80) value. If not $00, we are not at the end of the file so branch to STR1.
	$D0B6	Terminate routine with an RTS.
STR1	$D0B7	JSR to DBLBUF ($CF1E) to set up buffers and pointers for double buffering and set TRACK and SECTOR for the next block.
	$D0BA	JSR to SETHDR ($D6D0) to set up the header image using TRACK ($80) and SECTOR ($81) values.
	$D0BD	JSR to RDBUF ($D0C3) to read the next block into the data buffer.
	$D0C0	JMP to DBLBUF ($CF1E) to set up buffers and pointers for double buffering and set TRACK and SECTOR for the next block.
RDBUF	$D0C3	Start a read job of TRACK and SECTOR Load .A with $80, the job code for a read, and branch to STRTIT ($D0C9).
WRTBUF	$D0C7	Start a write job of TRACK and SECTOR Load .A with $90, the job code for a write.
STRTIT	$D0C9	Store command desired (in .A) as the current command in CMD ($024D).
	$D0CC	JSR to GETACT ($DF93) to get the active buffer number (in .A). Transfer the active buffer number into .X.

NAME	ADDRESS	DESCRIPTION OF WHAT ROM ROUTINE DOES
	$D0D0	JSR to SETLJB ($D506) to set up drive number (from the last job), check for legal track & sector, and, if all OK, do the job. On return .A=job number and .X=buffer number.
	$D0D3	Transfer buffer number from .X to .A and save it on the stack. Multiply the buffer number by two (ASL) and transfer the result into .X and use it as an index to store $00 in the buffer table pointer BUFTAB,X ($99,X)
	$D0DB	JSR to TYPFIL ($D125) to get the file type. Compare the file type to $04. If this is not a sequential file, branch to WRTC1.
	$D0E2	Since this is a sequential file, increment the lo byte of the block count in NBKL,X ($B5,X) and, if necessary, the hi byte in NBKH,X ($BB,X).
WRTC1	$D0E8	Pull the original buffer number off the stack and transfer it back into .X.
	$D0EA	Terminate routine with an RTS.

FNDRCH	$D0EB	Find the assigned read channel: Compare the current secondary address from SA ($83) with $13 (#19) the highest allowable secondary address+1. If too large, branch to FNDC20.
	$D0F1	AND the secondary address with $0F NOTE: This masks off the high order bits of the internal channel sec adr's: Internal read $11 (17) -> $01 Internal write $12 (18) -> $02
FNDC20	$D0F3	Compare the sec addr in .A with $0F(15), the command channel sec addr. If they are not equal, branch to FNDC25.
	$D0F7	Load .A with $10, the sec addr error value.
FNDC25	$D0F9	Transfer the sec addr from .A to .X, set the carry flag, and load the channel number from LINTAB,X ($022B,X). If bit 7 is set, no channel has been assigned for this sec addr, so branch to FNDC30 to exit (with carry bit set).
	$D100	AND the current channel number with $0F and store the result as the current channel number in LINDX ($82). Transfer the channel number into .X and clear the carry bit.
FNDC30	$D106	Terminate routine with an RTS.

NAME	ADDRESS	DESCRIPTION OF WHAT ROM ROUTINE DOES
FNDWCH	$D107	Find the assigned write channel: Compare the current secondary address from SA ($83) with $13 (#19) the highest allowable secondary address+1. If too large, branch to FNDW13.
	$D10D	AND the secondary address with $0F NOTE: This masks off the high order bits of the internal channel sec adr's: Internal read $11 (17) -> $01 Internal write $12 (18) -> $02
FNDW13	$D10F	Transfer the sec addr from .A to .X, and load the channel number assigned to this sec addr from LINTAB,X ($022B,X).
	$D113	Transfer this channel number to .Y.
	$D114	Do an ASL of the channel number in .A.
	$D115	If a channel has been assigned for this sec addr (bit 7 of LINTAB,X is not set) branch to FNDW15.
	$D117	If no channel assigned has been assigned for this secondary address (bit 6 also set), branch to FNDW20 and abort.
FNDW10	$D119	Transfer the original sec addr from .Y to .A, AND it with $0F to mask off any high order bits, and store it in LINDX ($82) as the currently active channel. Transfer the channel number to .X, clear the carry flag, and terminate with RTS.
FNDW15	$D121	If bit 6 of LINTAB,X is set (indicates an inactive channel), branch to FNDW10.
FNDW20	$D123	Abort by setting the carry flag and terminate the routine with an RTS.
		--
TYPFIL	$D125	Get current file type: Load .X with the current channel number from LINDX ($82).
	$D127	Load .A with the file type from the file type table, FILTYP,X ($EC,X).
	$D129	Divide the file type by 2 (LSR), AND it with $07 to mask off higher order bits, and compare the result with $04 (set the Z flag if it is a REL file!).
	$D12E	Terminate the routine with an RTS.
		--
GETPRE	$D12F	Set buffer pointers: JSR to GETACT ($DF93) to get the active buffer number (in .A).
	$D132	Multiply the buffer number by 2 (ASL) and transfer the result into .X.
	$D134	Load .Y with the current channel number from LINDX ($82).
	$D136	Terminate the routine with an RTS.
		--

NAME	ADDRESS	DESCRIPTION OF WHAT ROM ROUTINE DOES
GETBYT	$D137	Read one byte from the active buffer: If last data byte in buffer, set Z flag. JSR to GETPRE to set buffer pointers.
	$D13A	Load .A with the pointer to the last character read from LSTCHR,Y ($0244,Y).
	$D13D	If pointer is zero, branch to GETB1.
	$D13F	Load the data byte from (BUFTAB,X) ($99,X) and save it on the stack.
	$D142	Load the pointer from BUFTAB,X ($99,X) and compare it to the pointer to the last character read in LSTCHR,Y. If the pointers are not equal, branch to GETB2.
	$D149	Store $FF in BUFTAB,X ($99,X)
GETB2	$D14D	Pull the data byte off the stack and increment BUFTAB,X ($99,X). This will set the Z flag if this is the last byte.
	$D150	Terminate routine with an RTS.
GETB1	$D151	Load the data byte from (BUFTAB,X) ($99,X).
	$D153	Increment BUFTAB,X ($99,X).
	$D155	Terminate routine with an RTS.
RDBYT	$D156	Read byte from file: The next file will be read if necessary and CHNRDY($F2) will be set to EOI if we have read the last character in file. JSR to GETBYT to read a byte from the active buffer. On return, if Z flag is not set, we did not read the last byte in the buffer so branch to RD3 and RTS.
	$D162	We read the last byte so load .A with $80, the EOI flag.
RD01	$D164	Store the channel status (in .A) into CHNRDY,Y ($00F2,Y).
	$D167	Load .A with the byte from DATA ($85).
	$D169	Exit from routine with an RTS.
RD1	$D16A	JSR to DBLBUF ($CF1E) to begin double buffering.
	$D16D	Load .A with $00 and JSR to SETPNT ($D4C8) to set up the buffer pointers
	$D172	JSR to GETBYT ($D137) to read the first byte from the active buffer (track link)
	$D175	Compare the track link to $00. If it is $00, there is no next block so branch to RD4.
	$D179	There is another block in this file so store the track link in TRACK ($80).
	$D17B	JSR to GETBYT ($D137) to read the next byte from the active buffer (sector link) and store it in SECTOR ($81).
	$D180	JSR to DBLBUF ($CF1E) to begin double buffering.

NAME	ADDRESS	DESCRIPTION OF WHAT ROM ROUTINE DOES
	$D183	JSR to SETDRN ($D1D3) to set up the drive number.
	$D186	JSR to SETHDR ($D6D0) to set up the next header image.
	$D189	JSR to RDBUF ($D0C3) to read in the next block in the file.
	$D18C	JSR to DBLBUF ($CF1E) to toggle the active & inactive buffers & read ahead.
	$D18F	Load .A with the byte from DATA ($85).
RD3	$D191	Exit from routine with an RTS.
RD4	$D192	JSR to GETBYTE ($D137) to get the next byte.
	$D195	Load .Y with the current channel number from LINDX ($82) and store the new character as the pointer to the last character read from the data buffer LSTCHR,Y ($0244,Y).
	$D19A	Load .A with the byte from DATA ($85).
	$D19C	Exit from routine with an RTS.
		--
		Write character to the active channel: If this fills the buffer, write the data buffer out to disk.
WRTBYT	$D19D	JSR to PUTBYT ($CFF1) to write the byte to the active channel.
	$D1A0	If Z flag is set on return, the buffer is full so branch to WRT0.
	$D1A2	Exit from routine with an RTS.
WRT0	$D1A3	JSR to SETDRN ($D1D3) to set the current drive number from the one in LSTJOB.
	$D1A6	JSR to NXTTS ($F11E) to get the next available track and sector.
	$D1A9	Load .A with $00 and JSR to SETPNT ($D4C8) to set up the buffer pointers.
	$D1AB	Load .A with the next available track from TRACK ($80) and JSR to PUTBYT ($CFF1) to store the track link.
	$D1B3	Load .A with the next available sector from SECTOR ($81) and JSR to PUTBYT ($CFF1) to store the sector link.
	$D1B8	JSR to WRTBUF ($D0C7) to write out the buffer to disk.
	$D1BB	JSR to DBLBUF ($CF1E) to toggle the active and inactive buffers and set up the next inactive buffer.
	$D1BE	JSR to SETHDR ($D6D0) to set up the header image for the next block.
	$D1C1	Load .A with $02 (to bypass the track and sector link) and JMP to SETPNT to set up the pointers to the next buffer.

NAME	ADDRESS	DESCRIPTION OF WHAT ROM ROUTINE DOES
INCPTR	$D1C6	Increment the pointer of the active buffer by .A
		Store the value from .A in TEMP ($6F).
	$D1C8	JSR to GETPNT ($D4E8) to get the active buffer pointer (in .A).
	$D1CB	Clear the carry flag and add the value from TEMP ($6F). Store the result into BUFTAB,X ($99,X) and into DIRBUF ($94).
	$D1D2	Terminate routine with an RTS.
SETDRN	$D1D3	Set drive number: Sets DRVNUM to the same drive as was used on the last job for the active buffer. JSR to GETACT ($D4E8) to get the active buffer number (in .A).
	$D1D6	Transfer the buffer number to .X and use it as an index to load the last job number from LSTJOB,X ($025B) into .A.
	$D1DA	AND the job number with $01 to mask off all but the drive number bit and store the result as the current drive number in DRVNUM ($7F).
	$D1DE	Terminate routine with an RTS.
GETWCH	$D1DF	Open a new write channel: .A = number of buffers needed The routine allocates a buffer number and sets the logical file index, LINDX. Set the carry flag to indicate that we want a write channel.
	$D1E0	Branch to GETR2.
GETRCH	$D1E2	Open a new read channel: .A = number of buffers needed The routine allocates a buffer number and sets the channel#, LINDX. Clear the carry flag to indicate that we want a read channel.
GETR2	$D1E3	Save the processor status (the carry flag) onto the stack.
	$D1E4	Save the number of buffer needed (in .A) into TEMP ($6F).
	$D1E6	JSR to FRECHN ($D227) to free any channels associated with this secondary address.
	$D1E9	JSR to FNDLNX ($D37F) to find the next free logical index (channel) to use and allocate it.
	$D1EC	Store the new channel number in LINDX as the current channel number.
	$D1EE	Load .X with the current secondary address from SA ($83).

NAME	ADDRESS	DESCRIPTION OF WHAT ROM ROUTINE DOES
	$D1F0	Pull the processor status off the stack and if carry flag is clear (read), branch to GETR55.
GETR52	$D1F3	OR the channel number in .A with $80 to set bit 7 to indicate a write file.
GETR55	$D1F5	Store the channel number (in .A) into the logical index table, LINTAB,X ($022B,X). NOTE: Bit 7 set for a write channel
	$D1F8	AND the channel number in .A with $3F to mask off the write channel bit and transfer the result to .Y.
	$D1FB	De-allocate any buffers associated with this channel by storing $FF in BUF0,Y ($00A7,Y), in BUF1,Y ($00AE,Y), and in SS,Y ($00CD,Y).
GETR3	$D206	Decrement the value in TEMP ($6F). This is the number of buffers to allocate. If there are no more to allocate ($FF), branch to GETR4 and exit.
	$D20A	JSR to GETBUF ($D28E) to allocate a new buffer. If a buffer was allocated, branch to GETR5.
GETERR	$D20F	No buffers available, so JSR to RELBUF ($D25A) to release any buffers allocated
	$D212	Load .A with $70 to indicate a NO CHANNEL error and JMP to CMDERR ($C1C8).
GETR5	$D217	Store the buffer number (in .A) into BUF0,Y ($00A7,Y).
	$D21A	Decrement the value in TEMP ($6F). This is the number of buffers to allocate. If there are no more to allocate ($FF), branch to GETR4 and exit.
	$D21E	JSR to GETBUF ($D28E) to allocate a new buffer. If a buffer was NOT allocated, branch to GETERR and abort.
	$D223	Store the buffer number (in .A) into BUF1,Y ($00AE,Y).
GETR4	$D226	Terminate routine with an RTS.
		Free channel associated with SA Read and write channels are freed. The command channel is not freed.
FRECHN	$D227	Load .A with the secondary address from SA ($83). Compare it with $0F (#15), the command channel secondary address. If the secondary address is not $0F, branch to FRECO.
	$D22D	Since we are not to free the command channel, simply exit with an RTS.
		Free data channel associated with SA:
FRECO	$D22E	Load .X with the secondary address from SA ($83).

NAME	ADDRESS	DESCRIPTION OF WHAT ROM ROUTINE DOES
	$D230	Load .A with the channel number associated with this secondary address from LINTAB,X ($022B,X). If it is $FF, there is no associated channel so branch to FRE25 and exit.
	$D237	AND the channel number with $3F to mask off the higher order bits and store the result as the current channel in LINDX ($82).
	$D23B	Free the channel by storing $FF into LINTAB,X ($022B,X).
	$D240	Load .X with the channel number from LINDX ($82) and store $00 as the channel status (free) in CHNRDY,X ($F2,Y).
	$D246	JSR to RELBUF ($D25A) to release buffers
RELINX	$D249	Load .X with the channel number from LINDX ($82) and .A with $01.
REL15	$D24D	Decrement .X, the channel number. If it is $FF (no lower channel numbers), branch to REL10.
	$D250	Do an ASL on the value in .A. Note that the bit set shifts left one position each time through the loop.
	$D251	If .A <> 0, branch to REL15 (always).
REL10	$D253	OR the value in the accumulator with LINUSE ($0256) to free the channel (bit = 1 for free; bit = 0 for used). Store the resulting value back in LINUSE ($0256).
FRE25	$D259	Terminate routine with an RTS.
		--
		Release buffers associated with channel:
RELBUF	$D25A	Load .X with the channel number from LINDX ($82).
	$D25C	Load .A with the buffer number for this channel from BUF0,X ($A7,X). Compare the buffer number with $FF (free). If it is already free, branch to REL1.
	$D262	Save the buffer number on the stack and store $FF into BUF0,X ($A7,X) to free this buffer.
	$D267	Pull the buffer number off the stack and JSR to FREBUF ($D2F3) to free the buffer
REL1	$D26B	Load .X with the channel number from LINDX ($82).
	$D26D	Load .A with the buffer number for this channel from BUF1,X ($AE,X). Compare the buffer number with $FF (free). If it is already free, branch to REL2.
	$D273	Save the buffer number on the stack and store $FF into BUF1,X ($AE,X) to free this buffer.
	$D278	Pull the buffer number off the stack and JSR to FREBUF ($D2F3) to free the buffer

NAME	ADDRESS	DESCRIPTION OF WHAT ROM ROUTINE DOES
REL2	$D27C	Load .X with the channel number from LINDX ($82).
	$D27E	Load .A with the side sector for this channel from SS,X ($CD,X). Compare the side sector with $FF (free). If it is already free, branch to REL3.
	$D284	Save the side sector on the stack and store $FF into SS,X ($CD,X) to free the side sector pointer.
	$D289	Pull the side sector off the stack and JSR to FREBUF ($D2F3) to free any buffer
REL3	$D28D	Terminate routine with an RTS.
GETBUF	$D28E	Get a free buffer number: .Y=channel # If successful, initialize JOBS & LSTJOB and return with buffer number in .A. If not successful, .A = $FF; N flag set.
	$D28E	Save channel number by transferring it from .Y to .A and pushing it on the stack.
	$D290	Load .Y with $01 and JSR to FNDBUF ($D2BA) to find a free buffer (# in .X). If one is found, branch to GBF1.
	$D297	Decrement .Y and JSR to FNDBUF ($D2BA) to find a free buffer (# in .X). If one found, branch to GBF1.
	$D29D	Can't find a free one so let's try to steal one! JSR to STLBUF ($D339) to try to steal an inactive one. On return, buffer # in .A so transfer it to .X. If we didn't get one, branch to GBF2.
GBF1	$D2A3	Wait till any job using JOBS,X ($00,X) is completed.
	$D2A7	Clear the job queue by setting JOBS,X ($00,X) and LSTJOB,X ($025B,X) to the current drive number using the value from DRVNUM ($7F).
	$D2AE	Transfer the buffer number from .X to .A multiply it by two (ASL), and transfer the result to .Y.
	$D2B1	Store a $02 on BUFTAB,Y ($0099,Y) so the pointer points beyond the track and sector link.
GBF2	$D2B6	Restore the original .Y value from the stack.
	$D2B8	Transfer the buffer number from .X to .A to set the N flag if not successful.
	$D2B9	Terminate routine with an RTS.

NAME	ADDRESS	DESCRIPTION OF WHAT ROM ROUTINE DOES
		Find a free buffer and set BUFUSE:
		On entry: .Y = index into BUFUSE
		Y=0 buffers 0-7; Y=1 buffers 8-15
		If successful, .X = buffer number
		If not successful, .X = $FF; N flag set
FNDBUF	$D2BA	Load .X with $07 (for bit test)
FB1	$D2BC	Load .A with BUFUSE,Y ($024F,X). Each bit indicates whether a buffer is free (1) or in use (0). AND this value in .A with the bit mask, BMASK,X ($EFE9,X). Each of these masks has just one bit set. If the result of the AND is $00, we have found a free buffer so branch to FB2.
	$D2C4	Decrement .X to try next buffer. If any left, branch back to FB1.
	$D2C7	No more buffers to try (.X=$FF) so exit with an RTS.
FB2	$D2C8	Found a free buffer so let's grab it! Load .A with the value in BUFUSE,Y ($024F,Y), EOR it with the bit map for the free buffer, BMASK,X ($EFE9,X), and store the result back in BUFUSE,Y.
	$D2D1	Transfer the buffer number from .X to .A and if .Y is $00, branch to FB3.
	$D2D5	Since .Y is $01 (never happens on the 1541), we have to add 8 to the buffer number. So: Clear the carry flag and add $08 to the buffer number in .A.
FB3	$D2D8	Transfer the buffer number from .A to .X
FRI20	$D2D9	Terminate routine with an RTS.
		--
		Free the inactive buffer:
FREIAC	$D2DA	Load .X with the current channel number from LINDX ($82).
	$D2DC	Load .A with the buffer number from BUF0,X ($A7,X). If bit 7 is set, branch to FRI10.
	$D2E0	Transfer the channel number from .X to .A, clear the carry flag, add $07 (the maximum number of channels +1), and transfer the result back into .X. This is the alternate buffer for this channel
	$D2E5	Load .A with the buffer number from BUF0,X ($A7,X). If bit 7 is NOT set, this buffer is active too so exit to FRI20 (above).
FRI10	$D2E9	Compare the buffer number to $FF. If it is $FF, the buffer is free already so exit to FRI20 (above).
	$D2ED	Save the buffer number on the stack.
	$D2EE	Free the buffer by storing $FF into BUF0,X ($A7,X).
	$D2F2	Pull the buffer number off the stack.

NAME	ADDRESS	DESCRIPTION OF WHAT ROM ROUTINE DOES
FREBUF	$D2F3	Free buffer in BUFUSE: AND the buffer number with $0F to mask off any higher order bits, transfer the result into .Y and increment .Y by 1.
FREB1	$D2F7 $D2F9	Load .X with $10 (#16) 2 * 8 bits Loop to ROR BUFUSE+1 ($0250) and BUFUSE ($024F) 16 times. Use .Y to count down to 0. When .Y is zero, the bit that corresponds to the buffer we want is in the carry flag so we clear the carry bit to free that buffer. We then keep looping until .X has counted down all the way from $10 to $FF. When .X reaches $FF, the bits are all back in the right places, so exit with an RTS.
CLRCHN	$D307	Clear all channels except the CMD one: Set the current secondary address in SA ($83) to $0E (#14)
CLRC1	$D30B	JSR to FRECHN ($D227) to free the channel whose secondary address is SA
	$D30E	Decrement the value in SA ($83). If it is not $00, branch back to CLRC1.
	$D312	Terminate routine with an RTS.
CLDCHN	$D313	Close all channels except the CMD one: Set the current secondary address in SA ($83) to $0E (#14)
CLSD	$D317	Load .X with the secondary address from SA ($83) and use it as an index to load .A with the channel number from LINTAB,X ($022B,X). Compare the channel number with $FF; if equal, no channel has been assigned so branch to CLD2.
	$D320	AND the channel number with $3F to mask off the higher order bits and store the result in LINDX ($82) as the current channel number.
	$D324	JSR to GETACT to get the active buffer number for this channel (returned in .A)
	$D327	Transfer the buffer number to .X and use it load .A with the last job number for this buffer from LSTJOB,X ($025B,X).
	$D32B	AND the last job number with $01 and compare it with the current drive number in DRVNUM ($7F). If not equal, branch to CLD2.
	$D331	JSR to FRECHN ($D227) to free this channel.
	$D334	Decrement the secondary address in SA ($83) and if there are more to do (not $FF yet), branch back to CLSD
	$D338	Terminate routine with an RTS.

NAME	ADDRESS	DESCRIPTION OF WHAT ROM ROUTINE DOES
		Steal an inactive buffer:
		Scan the least recently used table and steal the first inactive buffer found. Returns the stolen buffer number in .A
STLBUF	$D339	Save the value in T0 ($6F) on the stack and zero .Y (the index to LRUTBL).
STL05	$D33E	Load .X (the channel index) with the value from LRUTBL,Y ($FA,Y).
	$D340	Load .A with the buffer status for this channel from BUF0,X ($A7,X). If this buffer is active (status < 128), branch to STL10.
	$D344	Compare the status to $FF (unused). If not equal, it's inactive so branch to STL30 to steal it!
STL10	$D348	Transfer the channel number from .X to .A, clear the carry flag, add $07 (the maximum number of channels +1), and transfer the result back into .X. Note .X now points to the alternative buffer for this channel.
	$D34D	Load .A with the buffer status for this channel from BUF0,X ($A7,X). If this buffer is active (status < 128), branch to STL30.
STL20	$D355	Increment .Y and compare the new value with #$05 (the maximum number of channels + 1). If there are still some channels left to check, branch to STL05
	$D35A	No luck stealing a buffer so load .X with $FF (indicates failure) and branch to STL60 to exit.
STL30	$D35E	Store the channel number (in .X) into T0 ($6F) temporarily.
	$D360	AND the buffer number in .A with $3F to mask off any higher order bits and transfer the result to .X.
STL40	$D363	Check if the buffer is being used for a job currently underway by loading .A with the job queue byte for the buffer from JOBS,X ($00,X). If bit 7 is set, a job is in progress so branch back to STL40 to wait for completion.
	$D367	Compare the job queue value with $02 to see if any errors occurred. If there were no errors (job queue was $01), branch to STL50 to steal the buffer.
	$D36B	No luck so load .X with the value we save into T0 ($6F) and compare it to $07 (the maximum number of channels+1).
	$D36F	If .X < $07 we still need to check the alternative buffer for this channel so branch to STL10.

NAME	ADDRESS	DESCRIPTION OF WHAT ROM ROUTINE DOES
	$D371	If .X >= $07, we were checking the alternative channel so branch back to STL20 to check the next channel.
STL50	$D373	We've found an inactive buffer, now to steal it! Load .Y with the channel number from T0 ($6F) and store $FF into BUF0,Y ($A7,Y) to steal it.
STL60	$D37A	Pull the original value of T0 off the stack and restore it. Transfer the buffer number from .X to .A (sets the N flag if not successful) and terminate routine with an RTS.
FNDLDX	$D37F	Find free LINDX and allocate in LINUSE Load .Y with $00 and .A with $01.
FND10	$D383	Test whether the same bit is set in LINUSE ($0256) and the accumulator. If a bit is set in LINUSE, the corresponding channel is free. If the test indicates a free channel, branch to FND30.
	$D388	Increment .Y (the counter) and do an ASL on the value in the accumulator to shift the test bit one place left. If more tests are needed, branch to FND10.
	$D38E	No channel found so load .A with $70 to to indicate a NO CHANNEL error and JMP to CMDERR ($C1C8).
FND30	$D391	EOR the bit mask (in .A) with $FF to flip the bits, AND the flipped mask with LINUSE to clear the appropriate bit, and store the result back in LINUSE ($0256).
	$D399	Transfer the channel number (LINDX) from .Y to .A and exit with an RTS.
GBYTE	$D39B	Get next byte from a channel: JSR to FNDRCH ($D0EB) to find an unused read channel.
	$D39E	JSR to SETLDS ($C100) to turn on the drive active light.
	$D3A1	JSR to GET ($D3AA) to get one byte from any type of file.
	$D3A4	Load .X with the current channel number from LINDX ($82) and load .A with the data byte from CHNDAT,X ($023E).
	$D3A9	Terminate routine with an RTS.
GET	$D3AA	Get next byte from any type of file: Load .X with the current channel number from LINDX ($82) JSR to TYPFIL ($D125) to determine the file type. If Z flag not set on return, this is not a relative file so branch to GET00.

NAME	ADDRESS	DESCRIPTION OF WHAT ROM ROUTINE DOES
	$D3B1	It is a relative file so JMP to RDREL ($E120) to do this type.
GET00	$D3B4	Test if the current secondary address from SA ($83) is $0F (the CMD channel). If it is, branch to GETERC ($D414).
	$D3BA	Test if the last character we sent on this channel was an EOI by checking if the channel status in CHNRDY,X ($F2,X) is $08. If the last character was NOT an EOI, branch to GET1.
	$D3C0	Last character was EOI so JSR to TYPFIL ($D125) to determine the file type.
	$D3C3	If the file type is NOT $07, a random access file, branch to GET0.
	$D3C7	This is a direct access file so we will leave it active. Store an $89 (random access file ready) as the channel status in CHNRDY,X ($F2,X) and exit with a JMP to RNDGET ($D3DE) to get the next character ready.
GET0	$D3CE	Last character sent was EOI so set the channel status as NOT READY by storing a $00 in CHNRDY,X ($F2,X).
	$D3D2	Terminate routine with an RTS.
GET1	$D3D3	Test if this is a LOAD by testing if the secondary address in SA ($83) is a $00. If it is a LOAD, branch to GET6.
GET2	$D3D7	It's not a LOAD. Maybe it's a random access file. JSR to TYPFIL ($D125) to determine the file type. If the file type is less than $04, it is NOT a random access file, so branch to SEQGET.
RNDGET	$D3DE	It is a random access file so JSR to GETPRE ($D12F) to set up the right pointers in .X and .Y.
	$D3E1	Load the pointer to the data byte into .A from BUFTAB,X ($99,X). Compare this value to the pointer to the last character pointer in LSTCHR,Y ($0244,Y) to see if we are up to the last one yet. If not, branch to RNGET1.
	$D3E8	We're at the last character so wrap the pointer around to the start again by storing $00 in BUFTAB,X ($99,X).
RNGET1	$D3EC	Increment BUFTAB,X ($99,X) to point to the next character.
RNGET2	$D3EE	Load .A with the data byte from BUFTAB,X ($99,X).
RNGET4	$D3F0	Save the data byte in CHNDAT,Y ($023E,Y)
	$D3F3	Load the pointer from BUFTAB,X and compare it to the value in LSTCHR,Y ($0244,Y) to see if this is the last character we're supposed to get. If NOT, branch to RNGET3.

NAME	ADDRESS	DESCRIPTION OF WHAT ROM ROUTINE DOES
	$D3FA	Since this is the last character, set the channel status in CHNRDY,Y to $00 to indicate an EOI (end of information).
RNGET3	$D3FF	Terminate routine with an RTS.
SEQGET	$D400	JSR to RDBYT ($D156) to read the next data byte.
GET3	$D403	Load .X with the channel number from LINDX ($82) and store the data byte in CHNDAT,X ($00F2,X).
	$D408	Terminate routine with an RTS.
GET6	$D409	Seems to be a LOAD. Test if it is a directory listing by seeing if DIRLST ($0254) is a $00. If it is, this is not a directory listing so branch to SEQGET.
	$D40E	It is a directory listing so JSR to GETDIR ($ED67) to get a byte from the directory and then JMP to GET3.

		Get byte from the error channel:
GETERC	$D414	JSR to GETPNT ($D4E8) to read the active buffer pointer. If the buffer number is NOT $D4, lo byte of the pointer to one byte below error buffer, branch to GE10.
	$D41B	Check if DIRBUF+1 ($95) equals $02, the hi byte of the pointer to the error buffer. If not, branch to GE10.
	$D421	Store a $0D (#13; RETURN) in DATA ($85) and JSR to ERROFF ($C123) to turn off the error LED.
	$D428	Load .A with $00 and JSR to ERRTS0 ($E6C1) to transfer the error message to the error buffer.
	$D42D	Decrement CB+2 ($A5) so this pointer points to the start of the message, load .A with $80 (EOI out status), and branch (always!) to GE30.
GE10	$D433	JSR to GETBYT ($D137) to read a byte of the error message. Store the byte in DATA ($85) and, if not $00, branch to GE20.
GE15	$D43A	Load .A with $D4, the lo byte of the pointer to one byte below the error buffer and JSR to SETPNT ($D4C8) to set the pointers to the error buffer.
	$D43F	Store the hi byte of the pointer to the error buffer ($02) into BUFTAB+1,X ($9A,X).
GE20	$D443	Load .A with $88, the channel status byte for ready-to-talk.
GE30	$D445	Store the value in .A as the error channel status in CHNRDY+ERRCHN ($F7).

NAME	ADDRESS	DESCRIPTION OF WHAT ROM ROUTINE DOES
	$D447	Load .A with the byte from DATA ($85) and store it as the channel data byte for the error channel in CHNDAT+ERRCHN ($0243).
	$D44C	Terminate routine with an RTS.
NXTBUF	$D44D	Read in the next block of a file by following the track and sector link. Set an EOF (end of file) indicator if the track link (first byte) is $00. JSR to GETACT ($DF93) to get the active buffer number (in .A). Multiply the buffer number by 2 (ASL) and transfer it to .X.
	$D452	Store a $00 in BUFTAB,X ($99,X) to set the buffer pointer to the first byte.
	$D456	Check first byte (track link) in the buffer, (BUFTAB,X). If it is zero, there are no more blocks to get so branch to NXTB1.
	$D45A	Decrement the buffer pointer, BUFTAB,X ($99,X) by 1 so it is $FF and JSR to RDBYT ($D156). This forces a read of the next sector because we set the pointer to the end of the current buffer.
NXTB1	$D45F	Terminate routine with an RTS.
DRTRD	$D460	Direct block read: Load .A with $80, the job code for read and branch to DRT.
DRTWRT	$D464	Direct block write: Load .A with $90, the job code for write
DRT	$D466	OR the job code in .A with the current drive number in DRVNUM ($7F) and store the result in CMD ($024D).
	$D46B	Load .A with the number of the buffer to use for the job from JOBNUM ($F9) and JSR to SETH ($D6D3) to set up the header image for the job.
	$D470	Load .X with the number of the buffer to use for the job from JOBNUM ($F9) and JMP to DOIT2 ($D593) to do the job.
OPNIRD	$D475	Open internal read channel: (SA=17) Use this entry point for PRG files. Load .A with $01 (program file type)
OPNTYP	$D477	Open internal read channel (.A=any type) Use this entry point for any file type. Store file type (.A) into TYPE ($024A)
	$D47A	Store $11 (#17) as the current secondary address in SA ($83).

NAME	ADDRESS	DESCRIPTION OF WHAT ROM ROUTINE DOES
	$D47E	JSR to OPNRCH ($DC46) to open a read channel.
	$D481	Set .A to $02 and JMP to SETPNT ($D4C8) to set the buffer pointer to point past the track and sector link.
OPNIWR	$D486	Open internal write channel (SA=18) Store $12 (#18) as the current secondary address in SA ($83).
	$D48A	JMP to OPNWCH ($DCDA) to open the write channel.
NXDRBK	$D48D	Allocate the next directory block: JSR to CURBLK ($DE3B) set the TRACK ($80) and SECTOR ($81) values from the current header.
	$D490	Set TEMP ($6F) to $01 and save the current value of SECINC ($69), the sector increment used for sequential files, on the stack.
	$D497	Set the sector increment, SECINC ($69) to $03, the increment used for the directory track.
	$D49B	JSR to NXTDS ($F12D) to determine the next available track and sector.
	$D49E	Restore the original sector increment in SECINC ($69) from the stack.
	$D4A1	Set .A to $00 and JSR to SETPNT ($D4C8) to set the pointer to the first byte in the active buffer (track byte).
	$D4A6	Load .A with the next track from TRACK ($80) and JSR to PUTBYT ($CFF1) to store the track link in the buffer.
	$D4AB	Load .A with the next sector from SECTOR ($81) and JSR to PUTBYT ($CFF1) to store the sector link in the buffer.
	$D4B0	JSR to WRTBUF ($D0C7) to write the buffer out to disk.
	$D4B3	JSR to WATJOB ($D599) to wait until the write job is complete.
	$D4B6	Set .A to $00 and JSR to SETPNT ($D4C8) to set the pointer to the first byte in the active buffer (track byte).
NXDB1	$D4BB	Loop to zero the entire buffer.
	$D4C0	JSR to PUTBYT ($CFF1) to store $00 as the next track link.
	$D4C3	Load .A with $FF and JMP to PUTBYT ($CFF1) to store $FF as the sector link.
SETPNT	$D4C8	Set up pointer into active data buffer On entry: .A contains new pointer value Save the new pointer (in .A) into TEMP ($6F) and JSR to GETACT ($DF93) to find the active buffer number (in .A).

NAME	ADDRESS	DESCRIPTION OF WHAT ROM ROUTINE DOES
	$D4CD	Multiply the buffer number by 2 (ASL) and transfer the result into .X.
	$D4CF	Move the high byte of the buffer pointer from BUFTAB+1,X ($9A,X) to DIRBUF+1($95)
	$D4D3	Load the new buffer pointer value from TEMP ($6F) into .A. Store this new value into BUFTAB,X ($99,X) and DIRBUF ($94).
	$D4D9	Terminate routine with an RTS.
FREICH	$D4DA	Free both internal channels: (SA=17&18) Set SA ($83) to $11 (#17) the internal read channel and JSR to FRECHN ($D227) to free the internal read channel.
	$D4E1	Set SA ($83) to $12 (#18) the internal write channel and JMP to FRECHN ($D227) to free the internal write channel.
GETPNT	$D4E8	Get the active buffer pointer: JSR to GETACT ($DF93) to get the active buffer number (in .A).
SETDIR	$D4EB	Multiply the buffer number by two (ASL) and transfer the result into .X.
	$D4ED	Move the hi byte of the buffer pointer from BUFTAB+1,X ($9A,X) into the hi byte of the directory buffer pointer DIRBUF+1 ($95).
	$D4F1	Move the lo byte of the buffer pointer from BUFTAB,X ($99,X) into the lo byte of the directory buffer pointer DIRBUF ($94). (.A = lo byte of the pointer)
	$D4F5	Terminate routine with an RTS.
DRDBYT	$D4F6	Direct read of a byte: (.A = position) On entry:.A = position of byte in buffer On exit:.A = data byte desired Store lo byte of pointer to desired byte (in .A) into TEMP+2 ($71).
	$D4F8	JSR to GETACT ($DF93) to get the active buffer number (in .A).
	$D4FB	Transfer buffer number into .X and load .A with the hi byte of the active buffer pointer from BUFIND,X ($FEE0,X). Store this value into TEMP+3 ($72). This creates a pointer to the byte in $71/72.
	$D501	Zero .Y and load .A with the desired byte from (TEMP+2),Y; ($71),Y.
	$D505	Terminate routine with an RTS.
SETLJB	$D506	Set up job using last job's drive: NOTE: For this entry, job code is in CMD and .X is buffer number (job #) Load .A with previous job number from LSTJOB,X ($025B,X), AND the job number with $01 to leave just the drive number

NAME	ADDRESS	DESCRIPTION OF WHAT ROM ROUTINE DOES
		bits, and OR the result with the new job code on CMD ($024D). The resulting new job code is in .A.
		Set up new job: NOTE: For this entry, job code is in .A and .X is buffer number (job #)
SETJOB	$D50E	Save new job code on the stack and store the number of the buffer to use (.X) in JOBNUM ($F9).
	$D511	Transfer the buffer number from .X to .A, multiply it by 2 (ASL) and transfer it back into .X.
	$D514	Move the desired sector from HDRS+1,X ($07,X) into CMD ($024D).
	$D519	Load .A with the desired track from HDRS,X ($06,X). If it is $00, branch to TSERR ($D54A).
	$D51D	Compare the desired track (in .A) with the maximum track number from MAXTRK ($FED7). If it is too large, branch to TSERR ($D54A).
	$D522	Transfer the desired track number from .A to .X.
	$D523	Pull the job code off the stack and immediately push it back onto the stack.
	$D525	AND the job code in .A with $F0 to mask off the drive bits and compare it to $90 (the job code for a write). If this is not a write job, branch to SJB1.
	$D52B	Pull the job code off the stack and immediately push it back onto the stack.
	$D52D	Do an LSR on the job code in .A to find the drive to use. If it is drive 1, branch to SJB2.
	$D530	Use drive 0 so load DOS version from DSKVER ($0101) and branch to SJB3.
SJB2	$D535	Use drive 1 so load DOS version from DSKVER+1 ($0102).
SJB3	$D538	If DOS version is $00 (no number), it is OK, so branch to SJB4.

		NOTE: On the 1541 the DOS version code (normally 65) is stored in ROM, not in RAM as on the 4040. This means you can not soft set a DOS version number on the 1541! However, a DOS version number of $00 is OK.

NAME	ADDRESS	DESCRIPTION OF WHAT ROM ROUTINE DOES
	$D53A	Compare the DOS version number with the 1541 DOS version number ($65) from VERNUM ($FED5). If the version numbers do not match, branch to VNERR ($D572).
SJB4	$D53F (	Transfer the desired track number from .X to .A and JSR to MAXSEX ($F24B) to calculate the maximum sector number+1 for this track (returned in .A). Compare this value with the desired sector number in CMD. If the desired sector number is legal, branch to SJB1.
TSERR	$D54A	Track and/or sector number is illegal so JSR to HED2TS ($D552) to store the values in TRACK ($80) and SECTOR ($81).
TSER1	$D54D	Load .A with $66 to indicate a bad track and sector and JMP to CMDER2 ($E645).
HED2TS	$D552	Set desired track and sector values: Load .A with the number of the buffer to use for this job from JOBNUM ($F9). Multiply the buffer number by 2 (ASL) and transfer it to .X.
	$F556	Move the desired track number from HDRS,X ($06,X) to TRACK ($80).
	$F55A	Move the desired sector number from HDRS+1,X ($07,X) to SECTOR ($81).
	$F55E	Terminate routine with an RTS.
TSCHK	$D55F	Check for bad track and sector values: Load .A from TRACK ($80). If the track is $00, branch back to TSER1 ($D54D).
	$D563	Compare the track to the maximum track number allowed, MAXTRK ($FED7). If too large, branch back to TSER1.
	$D568	JSR to MAXSEC ($F24B) to calculate the maximum sector number allowed on this track. If too large, branch to TSER1.
	$D571	Terminate routine with an RTS.
VNERR	$D572	Bad DOS version number: JSR to HED2TS ($D552) to store the values in TRACK ($80) and SECTOR ($81).
	$D575	Load .A with $73 to indicate a bad DOS version number and JMP to CMDER2 ($E645)
SJB1	$D57A	Conclude job set up: Load .X with the number of the buffer to use for the job from JOBNUM ($F9).
	$D57C	Pull the job code off the stack.
	$D57D	Store the job code as the current command in CMD ($024D), in the job queue at JOBS,X ($00,X) to activate the disk controller, and in LSTJOB,X.

NAME	ADDRESS	DESCRIPTION OF WHAT ROM ROUTINE DOES
	$D585	Terminate routine with an RTS.
DOREAD	$D586	Do a read job; return when done OK: Load .A with $80, the read job code and branch to DOJOB.
DOWRIT DOJOB	$D58A $D58C	Do a write job; return when done OK: Load .A with $90, the write job ccde. OR the job code with the current drive number in DFVNUM ($7F).
	$D58E	Load .X with the number of the buffer to use for the job from JOBNUM ($F9).
DOIT DOIT2	$D590 $D593 $D596	Store complete job code in CMD ($024D). Lcad .A with job code from CMD ($024D). JSR to SETJOB ($D50E) to start job.
WATJOB	$D599	Wait until job is completed: JSR to TSTJOB ($D5A6) to check if job is done yet (error code returned in .A).
	$D59C $D59E $D59F	If job not done yet, branch to WATJOB. Save error ccde on the stack. Set job completed flag, JOBRTN ($0298), to $00.
	$D5A4 $D5A5	Recover error code from stack (in .A). Terminate routine with an RTS.
TSTJOB	$D5A6	Test if job done yet: If not done, return. If done OK, then return. If not OK, redo the job. Load .A with value from the job queue, JOBS,X ($00,X).
	$D5A8	If .A > 127, job not done yet so branch to NOTYET to exit with carry flag set.
	$D5AA	If .A < 2, job was completed with no errors so branch to OK to exit with the carry flag clear.
	$D5AE	Compare the error code to $08. If it is $08, a fatal write protect error has occured so branch to TJ10 and abort.
	$D5B2	Compare the error code to $0B. If it is $0B, a fatal ID mismatch error has occured so branch to TJ10 and abort.
	$D5B6	Compare the error code to $0F. If it is NOT $0F, a non-fatal error has occured so branch to RECOV and try again. NOTE: an error code of $0F means a fatal drive-not-available error has occured.
TJ10	$D5BA	Test bit 7 of the job return flag, JOBRTN ($0298). If it is set, the disk has been initialized and this is the first attempt to carry out the job, so branch to OK to return with the carry flag clear.

NAME	ADDRESS	DESCRIPTION OF WHAT ROM ROUTINE DOES
	$D5BF	JMP to QUIT2 ($D63F) to try to recover.
OK	$D5C2	Clear the carry flag and terminate the routine with an RTS.
NOTYET	$D5C4	Set the carry flag and terminate the routine with an RTS.
RECOV	$D5C6	Save .Y value and the current drive number from DRVNUM ($7F) on the stack.
	$D5CB	Load the job code for the last job from LSTJOB,X ($025B,X), AND it with $01 to mask off the non-drive bits, and store the result as the current drive number in DRVNUM ($7F).
	$D5D2	Transfer the drive number from .A to .Y and move the LED error mask from LEDMSK,Y ($FECA,Y) to ERLED ($026D)
	$D5D9	JSR to DOREC ($D6A6) to do last job recovery. On return, if the error code (in .A) is $01, it worked so branch to REC01.
	$D5E0	Retry didn't work, JMP to REC95 ($D66D)
REC01	$D5E3	Load .A with the original job code from LSTJOB,X ($025B,X), AND it with $F0 to mask off the drive number bits, and save it on the stack.
	$D5E9	Check if the job code was $90 (a write job). If not, branch to REC0.
	$D5ED	This is a write job. OR the current drive number from DRVNUM ($7F) with $B8 (the job code for a sector seek) and store the result in LSTJOB,X ($025B,X). This replaces the original write job with a seek job during recovery.
REC0	$D5F4	See if the head is on track by checking bit 6 of REVCNT (6A). If this bit is set, the head is on track so branch to REC5.
		Head nct on track so zero the offset table pointer, EPTR ($0299) and the total offset TOFF ($029A).
REC1	$D600	Load .Y with the offset table pointer EPTR ($0299) and .A with the total offset TOFF ($029A).
	$D606	Set the carry flag and subtract the offset OFFSET,Y ($FEDB) from the total offset in .A. Store the result as the new total offset in TOFF ($029A).
	$D60D	Load .A with the head offset from OFFSET,Y and JSR to HEDOFF ($D676) to move the head so it is on track.
	$D613	Increment the cffset table pointer and JSR to DOREC ($D6A6) to attempt to recover. On return, if the error code in .A < $02, the recovery worked so branch to REC3.

NAME	ADDRESS	DESCRIPTION OF WHAT ROM ROUTINE DOES
	$D61D	That try at recovery did not work so increment the offset table pointer by 1 and load .A with the offset from OFFSET,Y ($FEDB,Y). If the value loaded is not $00, branch to REC1 to try again.
REC3	$D625	One more try on the offset. Load .A with the total offset from TOFF ($029A) and JSR to HEDOFF ($D676). If no error on return, branch to REC9.
REC5	$D631	Check bit 7 of the error recover count REVCNT ($6A). If this bit is clear, branch to REC7 to do a bump to track 1.
QUIT	$D635	Pull the original job code off the stack. If it is NOT $90 (a write job) branch to QUIT2.
	$D63A	For write jobs only, OR the job code in .A with the drive number from DRVNUM and put the result in LSTJOB,X ($025B,X) to restore the original value.
QUIT2	$D63F	Load .A with the error code from JOBS,X ($00,X) and abort with a JSR to ERROR ($E60A).
REC7	$D644	Pull the job code off the stack (in .A).
REC5	$D645	Check bit 7 of the job return flag JOBRTN ($0298). If this bit is set, branch to REC95 to exit with job error. Push the job code back onto the stack.
	$D64B	Do a bump to track 1 by loading .A with $C0 (BUMP job code), ORing it with the current drive number from DRVNUM ($7F), and storing the result in the job queue at JOBS,X ($00,X).
REC8	$D651	Wait for current job to be completed.
	$D655	JSR to DOREC ($D6A6) to try one more time. On return, if the error code (.A) is not $01 (no error), give up in disgust and branch to QUIT.
REC9	$D65C	Pull the original job code off the stack and compare it to $90 (the job code for a write job). If this isn't a write job, branch to REC95.
	$D661	OR the job code (in .A) with the drive number from DRVNUM ($7F) and store the value in LSTJOB,X.
	$D666	JSR to DOREC ($D6A6) to try one last time. On return, if the error code (.A) is not $01 (no error), give up in disgust and branch to QUIT2.
REC95	$D66D	Pull the original drive number off the stack and store it in DRVNUM ($7F).
	$D670	Pull the original .Y value off the stack and restore .Y.

NAME	ADDRESS	DESCRIPTION OF WHAT ROM ROUTINE DOES
	$D672	Load .A with the error code from JOBS,X ($00,X), clear the carry flag, and exit with an RTS.

		Adjust head offset:
		On entry: .A = OFFSET
HEDOFF	$D676	If .A=0, no offset required so branch to HOF3.
	$D67A	If .A > 127, head needs to be stepped inward so branch to HOF2.
HOF1	$D67C	We want to move head outward 1 track so: load .Y with $01 and JSR to MOVHED ($D693) to move the head.
	$D681	On return, set the carry flag and subtract $01 from the value in .A. If the result is not $00, the head has not finished so branch back to HOF1.
	$D686	If the head is finished moving, branch to HOF3.
HOF2	$D688	We want to move head inward 1 track so: load .Y with $FF and JSR to MOVHED ($D693) to move the head.
	$D68D	On return, clear the carry flag and add $01 to the value in .A. If the result is not $00, the head has not finished so branch back to HOF2.
HOF3	$D692	Terminate routine with an RTS.

		Step head inward or outward 1 track:
MCVHED	$D693	Save the value in .A onto the stack.
	$D694	Transfer the number of steps to move (phase) from .Y into .A.
	$D695	Load .Y with the current drive number from DRVNUM ($7F).
	$D697	Store the phase into PHASE,Y ($02FE,Y).
MH10	$D69A	Compare the phase in .A with the value in PHASE,Y ($02FE,Y). If they are equal, the controller has not yet moved the head so branch back to MH10.
	$D69F	Store $00 in PHASE,Y ($02FE,Y) so head won't move any more.
	$D6A4	Pull original value of .A off the stack.
	$D6A5	Terminate routine with an RTS.

DOREC	$D6A6	Load .A with the retry counter, REVCNT ($6A), AND it with $3F to mask off the high order bits, and transfer the result into .Y.
DOREC1	$D6AB	Load .A with the error LED mask from ERLED ($026D), EOR it with the disk controller port B, DSKCNT ($1C00) and store it back in DSKCNT ($1C00) to turn the drive light OFF.

NAME	ADDRESS	DESCRIPTION OF WHAT ROM ROUTINE DOES
	$D6B4	Restart the last job by moving the job code from LSTJOB,X ($025B,X) to the job queue at JOBS,X ($00,X).
DOREC2	$D6B9	Loop to wait until the value in the job queue at JOBS,X ($00,X) is less than 127 (indicates job has been completed). Test to see if the error code returned is $01 (successful). If everything was OK, branch to DOREC3.
	$D6C1	It didn't work. Decrement the error counter in .Y and, if .Y has not counted down to $00 yet, branch to DOREC1 and keep trying.
DOREC3	$D6C4	Save the error code onto the stack.
	$D6C5	Load .A with the error LED mask from ERLED ($026D), OR it with the disk controller port B, DSKCNT ($1C00) and store it back in DSKCNT ($1C00) to turn the drive light back ON.
	$D6CE	Pull the error code back off the stack.
	$D6CF	Terminate routine with an RTS.
		--
		Set up the header for the active buffer: Uses values in TRACK, SECTOR, & DSKID.
SETHDR	$D6D0	JSR to GETACT ($DF93) to get the number of the active buffer (returned in .A).
	$D6D3	Multiply the number of the active buffer (in .A) by 2 (ASL) and transfer the result into .Y.
	$D6D5	Move the track number from TRACK ($80) to HDRS,Y ($0006,Y).
	$D6DA	Move the sector number from SECTOR ($81) to HDRS+1,Y ($0007,Y).
	$D6DF	Load .A with the current drive number from DRVNUM ($7F), multiply it by 2(ASL) and transfer the result to .X. NOTE: this last bunch of code really does nothing. On the 4040 it is done in preparation for moving the ID characters. However, this is not done here on the 1541!
	$D6E3	Terminate routine with an RTS.
		--
		Add new filename to the directory:
ADDFIL	$D6E4	Save the following variables onto the stack: SA ($83), LINDX ($82), SECTOR ($81), and TRACK ($80).
	$D6F0	Set the current secondary address, SA ($83) to $11 (#17), the internal read channel.
	$D6F4	JSR to CURBLK ($DE3B) to find a read channel and set TRACK ($80) and SECTOR ($81) from the most recently read header

NAME	ADDRESS	DESCRIPTION OF WHAT ROM ROUTINE DOES
	$D6F7	Save the file type, TYPE ($024A) of the file to be added onto the stack.
	$D6FB	Load .A with the drive number for the new file, and it with $01, and store the result as the current drive, DRVNUM($7F)
	$D701	Load .X with the last job number from JOBNUM ($F9).
	$D706	EOR the drive number in .A with the last job code from LSTJOB,X ($025B,X), divide the result by 2 (LSR), and check if the carry flag is clear. If it is, the new file uses the same drive as the last job so there is no need to change the drive and we can branch to AF08.
	$D709	Store $01 in DELIND ($0292) to indicate that we are searching for a deleted entry and JSR to SRCHST ($C5AC). On return, if .A=0, all directory sectors are full so branch to AF15 to start a new sector. If .A<>0, we have found a spot to put the new entry so branch to AF20.
AF08	$D715	Since we have used this drive before, some of the directory information is in memory. Check if DELSEC ($0291) is $00. If it is, we didn't locate a deleted entry the last time we read in the directory so branch to AF10.
	$D71A	Since DELSEC is not $00, it is the number of the sector containing the first available directory entry. See if this sector is currently in memory by comparing this sector number with the one in SECTOR ($81). If they are equal, the sector is in memory so branch to AF20.
	$D71E	Since the desired sector is not in memory, set SECTOR ($81) to the desired sector number and JSR to DRTRD ($D460) to read in the sector. Now branch to AF20.
AF10	$D726	Store $01 in DELIND ($0292) to indicate that we are looking for a deleted entry and JSR to SEARCH ($C617) to find the first deleted or empty directory entry.
	$D72E	On return, if .A is not equal to $00, a deleted or empty entry was found so branch to AF20.
AF15	$D730	No empty entries so we have to start a new sector so JSR to NXDRBK ($D48D) to find us the next available sector.

NAME	ADDRESS	DESCRIPTION OF WHAT ROM ROUTINE DOES
	$D733	Move the new sector number from SECTOR ($81) to DELSEC ($0291) and set DELIND ($0292) to $02.
AF20	$D73D	Load .A with the pointer that points to first character in the directory entry, DELIND($0292), and JSR to SETPNT($D4C8) to set the pointers to this entry.
	$D743	Pull the file type off the stack and store it back in TYPE ($024A).
	$D747	Compare the file type to $04 (REL type). If this is not a relative file, branch to AF25.
	$D74B	Since it is a REL file, OR the file type (in .A) with $80 to set bit 7.
AF25	$D74D	JSR to PUTBYT ($CFF1) to store the file type (in .A) into the buffer.
	$D750	Pull the file's track link off the stack, store it in FILTRK ($0280), and JSR to PUTBYT ($CFF1) to store the track link in the buffer.
	$D757	Pull the file's sector link off the stack, store it in FILSEC ($0285), and JSR to PUTBYT ($CFF1) to store the sector link in the buffer.
	$D75E	JSR to GETACT ($DF93) to get the active buffer number (in .A) and transfer the value to .Y
	$D762	Load .X with the file table pointer from FILTAB ($027A).
	$D766	Load .A with $10 (#16) and JSR to TRNAME ($C66E) to transfer the file name to the buffer.
	$D76D	Loop to fill directory entry with $00's from (DIRBUF),16 to (DIRBUF),27.
	$D776	Check the value in TYPE ($024A) to see if this is a relative file. If not, branch to AF50.
	$D77D	For REL files only: Load .Y with $10.
	$D77F	Move the side-sector track number from TRKSS ($0259) to (DIRBUF),Y. Increment Y
	$D785	Move the side-sector sector number from SECSS ($025A) to (DIRBUF),Y. Increment Y
	$D78B	Move the record length from REC ($0258) to (DIRBUF),Y.
AF50	$D790	JSR to DRTWRT ($D464) to write out the directory sector.
	$D793	Pull the original value of LINDX off the stack, store it back in LINDX ($82), and transfer the value into .X.
	$D797	Pull the original value of SA off the stack, store it back in SA ($83).

NAME	ADDRESS	DESCRIPTION OF WHAT ROM ROUTINE DOES
	$D79A	Load .A with the number of the directory sector containing the new entry from DELSEC ($0291) and store it in ENTSEC ($D8) and in DSEC,X ($0260,X).
	$D7A5	Load .A with the pointer to the start of the new entry from DELIND ($0292) and store it in DIND,X ($0266,X).
	$D7AA	Load .A with the file type of the new entry from TYPE ($024A) and store it in PATTYP ($E7).
	$D7AF	Load .A with the current drive number from DRVNUM ($7F) and store it in FILDRV ($E2).
	$D7B3	Terminate routine with an RTS.

		Open a channel from serial bus: The open, load, or save command is parsed. A channel is allocated and the directory is searched for the filename specified in the command.
OPEN	$D7B4	Move the current secondary address from SA ($83) to TEMPSA ($024C).
	$D7B9	JSR to CMDSET ($C2B3) to set the command string pointers. On return, store the .X value in CMDNUM ($022A).
	$D7BC	Load .X with the first character in the command string CMDBUF ($0200). Load .A with the secondary address from TEMPSA ($024C). If the secondary address is not $00, this is not a load so branch to OP021.
	$D7C7	Compare the value in .X with $2A ("*") to check if the command is "load the last referenced program". If not $2A, branch to OP021.
	$D7CB	Appears to be "load last". Check by loading .A with the last program's track link from PRGTRK ($7E). If .A=0, there is no last program so branch to OP0415 to initialize drive 0.
OP02	$D7CF	Seems OK, let's load last program. Store the program's track link (in .A) into TRACK ($80).
	$D7D1	Move the program's drive number from PRGDRV ($026E) to DRVNUM ($7F).
	$D7D8	Store $82 (program) as the file type in PATTYP ($E7).
	$D7DC	Move the program's sector link from PRGSEC ($026F) into SECTOR ($81).
•	$D7E1	JSR to SETLDS ($C100) to turn on the drive active LED.
	$D7E4	JSR to OPNRCH ($DC46) to open a read channel.

NAME	ADDRESS	DESCRIPTION OF WHAT ROM ROUTINE DOES
	$D7E7	Load .A with $04 (2 * program type), OR it with the drive number in DRVNUM ($7F)
ENDRD	$D7EB	Load .X with the number of the active buffer from LINDX ($82).
	$D7ED	Store the value in .A as the file type in FILTYP,Y ($00EC,Y).
	$D7F0	Terminate routine with a JMP to ENDCMD ($C194).
OP021	$D7F3	Compare the byte in .X (the first in the command string) with $24 ("$") to check if we are to load the directory. If it is NOT "$", branch to OP041.
	$D7F7	We want the directory. But, should we load it or just open it as a SEQ file? Check the secondary address in TEMPSA (024C). If it is not $00, branch to OP04 to open it as a SEQ file.
	$D7FC	JMP to LOADIR ($DA55) to load the directory.
OP04	$D7FF	Open the directory as a SEQ file. JSR to SIMPRS ($C1D1) to parse the command string.
	$D802	Move the directory's track link from DIRTRK ($FE85) into TRACK ($80).
	$D807	Zero the desired sector, SECTOR ($81)
	$D80B	JSR to OPNRCH ($DC46) to open the read channel.
	$D80E	Load .A with the current drive number from DRVNUM ($7F) and OR it with $02 (2 * the SEQ file type).
	$D812	Terminate routine with a JMP to ENDRD ($D7EB).
OP041	$D815	Compare the byte in .X (the first in the command string) with $23 ("#") to check if this is to be a direct access channel If it is NOT "#", branch to OP042.
	$D819	Continue routine with a JMP to OPNBLK ($CB84).
OP0415	$D81C	Set the file type flag TYPFLG ($0296) to $02 (program file).
	$D821	Zero the current drive number DRVNUM ($7F) and the last job drive number LSTDRV ($028E).
	$D828	JSR to INITDR ($D042) to initialize drive #0.
OP042	$D82B	JSR to PRSCLN ($C1E5) to parse the command string to find the colon.
	$D82E	If none found, branch to OP049
	$D830	Zero .X and branch to OP20 (always).

NAME	ADDRESS	DESCRIPTION OF WHAT ROM ROUTINE DOES
OP049	$D834	Transfer the byte in .X to .A. If the byte is $00, branch to OP10.
OP05	$D837	Oops, trouble! Load .A with $30 to indicate a BAD SYNTAX error and JMP to CMDERR ($C1C8).
OP10	$D83C	Decrement .Y so it points to the ":" If .Y=0, first character is a ":" so branch to OP20.
	$D83F	Decrement .Y so it points to the byte just before the ":".
OP20	$D840	Store the pointer to the file name (in .Y) into FILTBL ($027A).
	$D843	Load .A with $8D (shifted return) and JSR to PARSE ($C268) to parse the rest of the command string.
	$D848	Increment .X (file count) and store the result into F2CNT ($0278).
	$D84C	JSR to ONEDRV ($C312) to set up one drive and the necessary pointers.
	$D84F	JSR to OPTSCH ($C3CA) to determine the optimal search pattern.
	$D852	JSR to FFST ($C49D) to search the disk directory for the file entry.
	$D857	Zero the record length, REC ($0258), MODE ($0297) (read mode), and the file type, TYPE ($024A) (deleted file).
	$D861	Test the value of F1CNT ($0277). If it is $00, there are NO wild cards in the filename so branch to OP40.
	$D866	JSR to CKTM ($DA09) to set the file type and mode.
	$D869	Test the value of F1CNT ($0277). If it is $01, there is only one wild card in the filename so branch to OP40.
	$D86F	Compare .Y to $04. If .Y=$04, this is a relative file so branch to OP60 to set the record size.
	$D873	JSR to CKTM ($DA09) to set the file type and mode.
OP40	$D876	Restore the original secondary address into SA ($83) using the value from TEMPSA ($024C).
	$D87B	Test the secondary address, if it is greater or equal to $02, this is not a load or save so branch to OP45.
	$D87F	This is a load or save. Set MODE ($0297) (0=read; 1=write) using the secondary address (0=load; 1=save).
	$D882	Set the write BAM flag, WBAM ($02F9) to $40 to flag that BAM is dirty.

NAME	ADDRESS	DESCRIPTION OF WHAT ROM ROUTINE DOES
	$D887	Load .A with the file type, TYPE ($024A) If it is not $00 (deleted file type), branch to OP50. NOTE: load & save of files have TYPE set to $00 in $D857.
	$D88C	Set file type, TYPE ($024A) to $02 (program file type).
OP45	$D891	Load .A with the file type, TYPE ($024A) If it is not $00 (scratched file type), branch to OP50.
	$D896	Load the file type as given in the directory from PATTYP ($E7), AND it with $07 (file type mask), and store the result as the file type in TYPE ($024A)
	$D89D	Test the file's first track link in FILTRK ($0280). If it is not $00, the file exists so branch to OP50.
	$D8A2	The file doesn't exist, set TYPE ($024A) to $01 (the default value; a SEQ file).
OP50	$D8A7	Check MODE ($0297). If it is $01, it is write mode so branch to OP75 to write.
	$D8AE	JMP to OP90 ($D940) to open to read or load.
OP60	$D8B1	Handle relative file: Load .Y with the pointer from FILTBL,X.
	$D8B4	Load .A with the file's record size as given in the directory from CMDBUF,Y and store it in REC ($0258).
	$D8BA	Test if the file's track link in FILTRK ($0280) is $00. If it is NOT $00, the file is present so branch to OP40 to read it.
	$D8BF	Set the MODE ($0297) to $01 (write mode) and branch to OP40 (always).
OF75	$D8C6	Load .A with the file's type as given in the directory from PATTYP ($E7), AND it with $80 to determine if it is a deleted file, and transfer the result to .X. If it is not a deleted file, branch to OP81
OP77	$D8CD	Open to write. Load .A with $20 and test if any bits in .A and the file type in PATTYP ($E7) match. If not, branch to OP80.
	$D8D3	JSR to DELDIR ($C8B6) to delete the directory entry and write out the revised sector.
	$D8D6	JMP to OPWRIT ($D9E3) to open the channel to write.
OP80	$D8D9	Load .A with the entry's track link from FILTRK ($0280). If it is not $00, there is an existing file so branch to OP81.

NAME	ADDRESS	DESCRIPTION OF WHAT ROM ROUTINE DOES
	$D8DE	File not found but that's OK. JMP to OPWRIT ($D9E3) to open a write channel.
OP81	$D8E1	Load .A with CMDBUF ($0200), the first byte of the command string. If it equals $40 ("@"), branch to OP82. NCTE: THIS IS WHERE REPLACE FILE COMMAND IS DETECTED!
	$D8E8	Transfer .X value into .A. If it is not $00, branch to OP815.
	$D8EB	Load .A with $63 to indicate a FILE EXISTS ERROR and JMP to CMDERR ($C1C8).
OP815	$D8F0	Load .A with $33 to indicate a bad filename and JMP to CMDERR ($C1C8).
		REPLACE FILE ROUTINE * MAY HAVE BUG!
OP82	$D8F5	Load the file type of the directory entry from PATTYP ($E7), AND it with the file type mask $07, and compare the result with the command string file type in TYPE ($024A). If the file types do not match, branch to OP115 to abort.
	$D8FE	Compare the file type (in .A) with $04. If it is $04, this is a relative file so branch to OP115 to abort.
	$D902	JSR to OPNWCH ($DCDA) to open the write channel.
	$D905	Move the active buffer number from LINDX ($82) to WLINDX ($0270).
	$D90A	Set the secondary address, SA ($83) to $11 (#17) the internal read channel.
	$D90E	JSR to FNDRCH ($D0EB) to find an unused read channel.
	$D911	Load .A with the current value of the pointer into the directory buffer, INDEX ($0294) and JSR to SETPNT ($D4C8) to set the buffer pointers to point to the INDEXth byte. NOTE: at this point INDEX points to the first byte in the entry, the file type.
	$D917	Zero .Y. Then load .A with the file type from (DIRBUF),Y; ($94),Y, OR the file type with $20 (set the replace bit), and store the result back in (DIRBUF),Y.
	$D91F	Load .Y with $1A (#26) and move the new track link from TRACK($80) to (DIRBUF),Y
	$D925	Increment .Y and move the new sector link from SECTOR ($81) to (DIRBUF),Y.
	$D92A	Load .X with the active buffer number from WLINDX ($0270).
	$D92D	Load .A with the sector of the directory entry ENTSEC ($D8) and copy it into DSEC,X ($0260,X).

NAME	ADDRESS	DESCRIPTION OF WHAT ROM ROUTINE DOES
	$D932	Load .A with the pointer to the start of the directory entry ENTIND ($DD) and copy it into DIND,X ($0266,X).
	$D937	JSR to CURBLK ($DE3B) to set TRACK ($80) and SECTOR ($81) from header of most recently read header.
	$D93A	JSR to DRTWRT ($D464) to do direct block write of directory block to disk.
	$D93D	JMP to OPFIN ($D9EF) to finish opening the file.
OP90	$D940	Test the directory entry's track link in FILTRK ($0280). If it is NOT $00, the file exists so branch to OP100.
OP95	$D945	Load .A with $62 to indicate a FILE NOT FOUND error and JMP to CMDERR ($C1C8).
OP100	$D94A	Compare the value in MODE ($0297) to $03 (open to modify). If MODE=$03 branch to OP110.
	$D951	Check bit 5 of the directory entry's file type. If this bit is set, it flags a file that is already opened (or not closed properly). If the bit is NOT SET, branch to OP110 and carry on.
	$D957	Load .A with $60 to indicate a FILE OPEN error and JMP to CMDERR ($C1C8).
OP110	$D95C	Load .A with the directory entry's file type from PATTYP ($E7), AND it with $07 to mask off higher order bits, and compare it with the file type specified in the command string from TYPE ($024A). If the file types match, branch to OP120
OP115	$D965	Load .A with $64 to indicate a FILE TYPE MISMATCH error and JMP to CMDERR ($C1C8)
OP120	$D96A	Load .Y with $00 and use it to zero F2PTR ($0279).
	$D96F	Load .X with the mode from MODE ($0297) If MODE is not $02 (open to append), branch to OP125.
	$D976	Compare the file type (in .A) with $04. If it is $04, this is a relative file so branch to OP115.
	$D97A	This applies only to opening to append. Load .A with the file type from (DIRBUF),Y ;($94),Y, AND it with $4F, and store it back in (DIRBUF),Y.
	$D980	Save the secondary address from SA ($83) onto the stack and set SA ($83) to $11 (#17, the internal read channel).
	$D987	JSR to CURBLK ($DE3B) to set TRACK ($80) and SECTOR ($81) from header of most recently read header.

NAME	ADDRESS	DESCRIPTION OF WHAT ROM ROUTINE DOES
	$D98A	JSR to DRTWRT ($D464) to do direct block write of directory block to disk.
	$D98D	Pull original secondary address off the stack and restore it in SA ($83).
OP125	$D990	JSR to OPREAD ($D9A0) to open the file for a read.
	$D993	Check if MODE ($0297) is $02 (append). If it isn't $02, branch to OPFIN ($D9EF)
	$D99A	JSR to APPEND ($DA2A) to read to the end of the file.
	$D99D	JMP to ENDCMD ($C194) to terminate.
OPREAD	$D9A0	Open a file to read: Copy the relative file values from the directory entry (DIRBUF),Y; ($94),Y into their RAM variable locations: Track for side sector to TRKSS ($0259) Sector for side sector to SECSS ($025A)
	$D9AE	Load .A with the record size from the directory entry. Load .X with the size from the command string, REC ($0258).
	$D9B3	Store the value in .A into REC ($0258).
	$D9B6	Transfer the value from .X into .A. If the command string size is $00, branch to OP130 (defaults to entry size).
	$D9B9	Compare the two record lengths. If they are equal, branch to OP130.
	$D9BE	Record lengths do not match, load .A with $50 to indicate a READ PAST END OF FILE error and JSR to CMDERR ($C1C8).
OP130	$D9C3	Load .X with the pointer F2PTR ($0279).
	$D9C6	Copy the track link from FILTRK,X ($0280,X) to TRACK ($80).
	$D9CB	Copy the sector link from FILSEC,X ($0285,X) to SECTOR ($81).
	$D9D0	JSR to OPNRCH ($DC46) to open a read channel.
	$D9D3	Load .Y with the active buffer number from LINDX ($82).
	$D9D5	Load .X with the pointer F2PTR ($0279).
	$D9D8	Copy the directory sector containing the entry from ENTSEC,X ($D8,X) to DSEC,Y ($0260,Y).
	$D9DF	Copy the pointer to the entry in the directory sector from ENTIND,X ($DD,X) to DIND,Y ($0266,Y).
	$D9E2	Terminate the routine with an RTS.

NAME	ADDRESS	DESCRIPTION OF WHAT ROM ROUTINE DOES
OPWRIT	$D9E3	Open a file to write: Load .A with the drive number for the file from FILDRV ($E2), AND it with $01 to mask off non-drive bits, and store the result as the current drive in DRVNUM ($7F).
	$D9E9	JSR to OPNWCH ($DCDA) to open a write channel.
	$D9EC	JSR to ADDFIL ($D6E4) to add the entry to the directory.
OPFIN	$D9EF	If the secondary address is greater than $01, it is a not a program file so branch to OPF1.
	$D9F5	JSR to GETHDR ($DE3E) to set up TRACK and SECTOR values from the last header read.
	$D9F8	Copy the track link from TRACK ($80) to PRGTRK ($7E).
	$D9FC	Copy the file drive from DRVNUM ($7F) to PRGDRV ($026E).
	$DA01	Copy the sector link from SECTOR ($81) to PRGSEC ($026F).
OPF1	$DA06	Terminate routine with a JMP to ENDSAV ($C199).

CKTM	$DA09	Check mode or file type: Load .Y with the pointer from FILTBL,X. Load .A with the mode or file type from the command string, CMDBUF,Y. Load .Y with $04, the number of modes.
CKM1	$DA11	Loop to compare mode requested with the table of modes, MODLST,Y ($FEB2,Y). If no match is found, branch to CKM2. If a match is found, fall through. VALID MODES: 0 = R (READ) 　　　　　　　1 = W (WRITE) 　　　　　　　2 = A (APPEND) 　　　　　　　3 = M (MODIFY)
	$DA19	Store .Y counter (0-3) in MODE ($0297)
CKM2	$DA1C	Loop to compare type requested with the table of types, TPLST,Y ($FEB6,Y). If no match is found, branch to CKT2. If a match is found, fall through. VALID TYPES: 0 = D (DELETED) 　　　　　　　1 = S (SEQUENTIAL) 　　　　　　　2 = P (PROGRAM) 　　　　　　　3 = U (USER) 　　　　　　　4 = R (RELATIVE)
	$DA26	Store .Y counter (0-3) in TYPE ($024A)
CKT2	$DA29	Terminate the routine with an RTS.

NAME	ADDRESS	DESCRIPTION OF WHAT ROM ROUTINE DOES
APPEND	$DA2A	Append information to the end of a file Reads through old file to end. JSR to GCBYTE ($CA39) to get a byte from the data channel.
	$DA2D	Test if we are at the end of file. If not, loop back to APPEND.
	$DA34	JSR to RDLNK ($DE95) to set TRACK ($80) and SECTOR ($81) from the track and sector links in the last block. NOTE: TRACK will be $00 and SECTOR will be a pointer to the end of the file.
	$DA37	Load .X with the end of file pointer from SECTOR ($81), increment it by 1, and transfer the result to .A. If the new value of the pointer is not $00, there is space left at the end of this sector so branch to AP30.
	$DA3D	No space left in this sector so JSR to WRT0 ($D1A3) to get the next sector. Load .A with $02 so it points to the start of the data area for this new sector.
AP30	$DA42	JSR to SETPNT ($D4C8) to set the active buffer pointers.
	$DA45	Load .X with the active buffer number from LINDX ($82) and store $01 (channel ready at the end of file) in the channel status flag CHNRDY,X ($F2,X).
	$DA4B	Load .X with the sec. address SA ($83). Load .A with $80, OR it with the active buffer number in LINDX ($82), and store the result in LINTAB,X ($022B,X) to indicate that this is now a write file.
	$DA54	Terminate the routine with an RTS.

LOADIR	$DA55	Load the directory ($): Store $0C (load) as the command code in CMDNUM ($022A).
	$DA5A	Load .A with $00 (load only drive #0)
	$DA5C	Load .X with the command length from CMDSIZ ($0274) and decrement the length in .X by 1. If the result is $00, branch to LD02 to load complete directory for drive 0.
LD01	$DA62	Decrement the length in .X by 1. If the result is still not $00, this must be a selective load by name so branch to LD03
	$DA65	Load .A with the second character in the command string from CMDBUF+1 ($0201) and JSR to TST0V1 ($C3BD) to test if the character is an ASCII "0" or "1". If not, branch to LD03 to load by name.
LD02	$DA6D	Store the drive number desired (in .A) into FILDRV ($E2).

NAME	ADDRESS	DESCRIPTION OF WHAT ROM ROUTINE DOES
	$DA6F	Increment F1CNT ($0277), F2CNT ($0278), and FILTBL ($027A).
	$DA78	Store $80 in PATTYP ($E7) to represent the file type.
	$DA7C	Store $2A ("*") as the first two bytes in the command string CMDBUF ($0200) and CMDBUF+1 ($0201)
	$DA84	Branch always to LD10.
LD03	$DA86	JSR to PRSCLN ($C2DC) to find the colon in the command string. If no colon is found, branch to LD05.
	$DA8B	Colon found so JSR to CMDRST ($C2DC) to zero all command string variables.
	$DA8E	Load .Y with $03.
LD05	$DA90	Decrement .Y twice and store the result in FILTBL ($027A).
	$DA95	JSR to TC35 ($C200) to parse and set up the tables.
	$DA98	JSR to FS1SET ($C398) to set pointers to file name and check type.
	$DA9B	JSR to ALLDRS ($C320) to set up all drives required.
LD10	$DA9E	JSR to OPTSCH ($C3CA) to determine the best drive search pattern.
	$DAA1	JSR to NEWDIR ($C7B7) to read in BAM and set up disk name, ID, etc as first line in directory.
	$DAA4	JSR to FFST ($C49D) to find file start entry.
LD20	$DAA7	JSR to STDIR ($EC9E) to start the directory loading function.
	$DAAA	JSR to GETBYT ($D137) to read first byte from the buffer.
	$DAAD	Load .X with the active buffer number from LINDX ($82).
	$DAAF	Store the first byte (in .A) into CHNDAT,X ($023E,X).
	$DAB2	Load .A with the current drive number from DRVNUM ($7F) and use this value to set the last job drive LSTDRV ($028E).
	$DAB7	OR the drive number in .A with $04 and store the result as the file type in FILTYP,X ($EC,X).
	$DABB	Zero BUFTAB+CBPTR ($A3). Note: CBPTR is the command buffer pointer ($0A).
	$DABF	Terminate the routine with an RTS.

		Close the file related to the specified secondary address:
CLOSE	$DAC0	Zero the write BAM flag, WBAM ($02F9).
	$DAC5	If secondary address, SA ($83) is not zero (directory load), branch to CLS10

NAME	ADDRESS	DESCRIPTION OF WHAT ROM ROUTINE DOES
	$DAC9	Close directory: Zero the directory listing flag DIRLST ($0254) and JSR to FRECHN ($D227) to free the channel.
CLS05	$DAD1	JMP to FREICH ($D4DA) to free the internal channel and terminate routine.
CLS10	$DAD4	If secondary address (in .A) is $0F(#15) branch to CLSALL to close all files.
	$DAD8	JSR to CLSCHN ($DB02) to close channel.
	$DADB	If secondary address in SA ($83) is $01 (save), branch to CLS05 to close the internal channel and exit.
	$DAE1	Check the error status in ERWORD ($026C) If status is not $00, the last command produced an error so branch to CLS15.
	$DAE6	JMP to ENDCMD ($C194) to end command.
CLS15	$DAE9	Error so JMP to SCREN1 ($C1AD)
-----	------	---
		Close all files: (when CMD closed)
CLSALL	$DAEC	Set secondary address, SA ($83) to $0E.
CLS20	$DAF0	JSR to CLSCHN ($DB02) to close channel.
	$DAF3	Decrement SA ($83). If more secondary addresses to do (SA>=0) loop to CLS20.
	$DAF7	Check the error status in ERWORD ($026C) If status is not $00, the last command produced an error so branch to CLS25.
	$DAFC	JMP to ENDCMD ($C194) to end command.
CLS25	$DAFF	Error so JMP to SCREN1 ($C1AD)
-----	------	---
		Close file with specified sec. address
CLSCHN	$DB02	Load .X with the secondary address from SA ($83).
	$DB04	Load .A with the channel status from LINTAB,X ($022B,X). If the status is not $FF (closed), branch to CLSC28.
	$DB09	Channel already closed so terminate routine with an RTS.
CLSC28	$DB0C	AND the channel status (in .A) with $0F to leave only the buffer number and store the result in LINDX ($82).
	$DB10	JSR to TYPFIL ($D125) to determine the file type (returned in .A).
	$DB13	If file type is $07 (direct channel) branch to CLSC30.
	$DB17	If file type is $04 (relative file) branch to CLSREL.
	$DB1B	JSR to FNDWCH ($D107) to find an unused write channel. If none found, branch to CLSC31
	$DB20	JSR to CLSWRT ($DB62) to close off sequential write.
	$DB23	JSR to CLSDIR ($DBA5) to close directory

NAME	ADDRESS	DESCRIPTION OF WHAT ROM ROUTINE DOES
CLSC30	$DB26	JSR to MAPOUT ($EEF4) to write out BAM.
CLSC31	$DB29	JMP to FRECHN ($D227) to free channel and terminate the command.

		Sub to close relative file:
CLSREL	$DB2C	JSR to SCRUB ($DDF1) to write out BAM if it is dirty (RAM version modified).
	$DB2F	JSR to DBLBUF ($CF1E) to set up double buffering and read ahead.
	$DB32	JSR to SSEND ($E1CB) to position side sector & buffer table pointer to the end of the last record.
	$DB35	Load .X with the side sector number from SSNUM ($D5), store this byte in T4($73), and increment T4 by 1.
	$DB3B	Zero T1 ($70) and T2 ($71).
	$DB41	Load .A with the pointer to the side sector value in the directory buffer from SSIND ($D6), set the carry flag, subtract $0E (the side sector offset-2), and store the result in T3 ($72).
	$DB48	JSR to SSCALC ($DF51) to calculate the number of side sector blocks needed.
	$DB4B	Load .X with the active buffer number from LINDX ($82).
	$DB4D	Move the lo byte of the number of side sector blocks from T1 ($70) to NBKL,X ($B5,X) and the hi byte from T2 ($71) to NBKH,X ($BB,X).
	$DB55	Load .A with $40 (the dirty flag for a relative record flag) and JSR to TSTFLG ($DDA6) to test if relative record must be written out. If not, branch to CLSR1.
	$DB5C	JSR to CLSDIR ($DBA5) to close the directory file.
CLSR1	$DB5F	JMP to FRECHN ($D227) to clear the channel and terminate routine.

		Close a sequential file write channel:
CLSWRT	$DB62	Load .X with the active buffer number from LINDX ($82).
	$DB64	Load .A with the number of bytes written in this sector from NBKL,X ($B5,X) and OR .A with the number of data blocks written from NBKL,X ($B5,X). If the result is not $00, at least one block of the file has been written so branch to CLSW10.
	$DB6A	No blocks have been written so JSR to GETPNT ($D4E8) to get the pointer into the data buffer (returned in .A). If this value is greater than two, at least one byte has been written so branch to CLSW10.

NAME	ADDRESS	DESCRIPTION OF WHAT ROM ROUTINE DOES
	$DB71	No bytes have been written so load .A with $0D (carriage return) and JSR to PUTBYT ($CFF1) to write it out to the data buffer.
CLSW10	$DB76	JSR to GETPNT ($D4E8) to get the pointer into the data buffer (returned in .A). If the pointer value is not $02, the buffer is not empty so branch to CLSW20.
	$DB7D	Since we have an empty buffer, JSR to DBLBUF ($CF1E) to switch buffers.
	$DB80	Load .X with the active buffer number from LINDX ($82).
	$DB82	Load .A with the number of bytes written in this sector from NBKL,X ($B5,X). If this value is not equal to $00, branch to CLSW15.
	$DB86	Decrement the number of data blocks written in NBKH,X ($BB,X) by 1.
CLSW15	$DB88	Decrement the number of bytes written in this sector, NBKL,X ($B5,X) by 1.
	$DB8A	Load .A with $00.
CLSW20	$DB8C	Set the carry flag, subtract $01 from the number of bytes written in this sector (.A), and save the result on the stack.
	$DB90	Load .A with $00 and JSR to SETPNT ($D4C8) to set the buffer pointers to the first byte in the data buffer (the track link).
	$DB95	JSR to PUTBYT ($CFF1) to write $00 out as the track link.
	$DB98	Pull the bytes written from the stack.
	$DB99	JSR to PUTBYT ($CFF1) to write out the bytes in this sector as the sector link.
	$DB9C	JSR to WRTBUF ($D0C7) to write the data buffer out to disk.
	$DB9F	JSR to WATJOB ($D599) to wait for the write job to be completed.
	$DBA2	JMP to DBLBUF ($CF1E) to make sure that both buffers are OK.
	------	---
CLSDIR	$DBA5	Close directory after writing file: Load .X with the active buffer number from LINDX ($82). Save this value into WLINDX ($0270).
	$DBAA	Save the current secondary address from SA ($83) onto the stack.
	$DBAD	Copy the sector of the directory entry for the file from DSEC,X ($0260,X) into SECTOR ($81).
	$DBB2	Copy the pointer to the directory entry for the file from DIND,X ($0266,X) into INDEX ($0294).

NAME	ADDRESS	DESCRIPTION OF WHAT ROM ROUTINE DOES
	$DBB8	Load .A with the file type from FILTYP,X ($EC,X), AND it with $01 to mask off the non-drive bits, and store the result as the current drive number in DRVNUM ($7F)
	$DBBE	Ccpy the directory track number (#18) from DIRTRK ($FE85) into TRACK ($80).
	$DBC3	JSR to GETACT ($DF93) to get the active buffer number (returned in .A).
	$DBC6	Save the active buffer number onto the stack and into JOBNUM ($F9).
	$DBC9	JSR to DIRTRD ($D460) to read in the directory sector containing the entry.
	$DBCC	Load .Y with $00.
	$DBCE	Load .A with the hi byte of the pointer to the active buffer from BUFIND,X ($FEE0,X) and store it in R0+1 ($87).
	$DBD3	Complete the pointer into the directory buffer by copying the lo byte of the pointer from INDEX ($0294) to R0 ($86).
	$DBD8	Load .A with the file type from the directory entry (R0),Y, AND it with $20, and checking if the result is $00. If it is $00, this is NCT a replace so branch to CLSD5.

NOTE: Here is where we do the directory
      entry when a file is replaced.
 - * - * - Possible bugs! - * - * -

NAME	ADDRESS	DESCRIPTION OF WHAT ROM ROUTINE DOES
	$DBDE	JSR to TYPFIL ($D125) to determine the file type (returned in .A).
	$DBE1	If file type is $04 (a relative file) branch to CLSD6.
	$DBE5	Load .A with the file type from R0,Y, AND it with $8F to mask off the replace bit, and store the result back in R0,Y.
	$DBEB	Increment .Y. The pointer at (R0),Y now points to the old track link.
	$DBEC	Copy the old track link from (R0),Y to into TRACK ($80).
	$DBF0	Store the .Y value into TEMP+2 ($71).
	$DBF2	Load .Y with $1B (#27). The pointer at (R0),Y now points to the replacement sector link.
	$DBF4	Load .A with the replacement sector link from (R0),Y and save it on the stack.
	$DBF7	Decrement .Y. The pointer at (R0),Y now points to the replacement track link.
	$DBF8	Load .A with the replacement track link. If this link is NOT $00, branch to CLSD4
	$DBFC	Trouble! Replacement track link should never be $00. So put replacement track link in TRACK ($80).

NAME	ADDRESS	DESCRIPTION OF WHAT ROM ROUTINE DOES
	$DBFE	Pull replacement sector link off the stack and put it in SECTOR ($81).
	$DC01	Load .A with $67 to indicate a SYSTEM TRACK OR SECTOR error and JMP to CMDER2 ($E645).
CLSD4	$DC06	Push the replacement track link onto the stack.
	$DC07	Load .A with $00. Zero the replacement track link in the entry (R0),Y.
	$DC0B	Increment .Y.
	$DC0C	Zero replacement sector link in (R0),Y.
	$DC0E	Pull the replacement track link off the stack.
	$DC0F	Load .Y with the original pointer value from TEMP+2 ($71). Note: pointer at (R0),Y now points to the second byte of the entry, the track link.
	$DC11	Store the replacement track link as the final track link in (R0),Y.
	$DC13	Increment .Y. Note: the pointer at (R0),Y now points to the third byte of the entry, the sector link.
	$DC14	Move the old sector link from (R0),Y to SECTOR ($81).
	$DC18	Pull the replacement sector link off the stack and store it as the final sector link in (R0),Y.
	$DC1B	JSR to DELFIL ($C87D) to delete the old file from the BAM by following the track and sector links.
	$DC1E	JSR to CLSD6 ($DC29) to finish closing.
CLSD5	$DC21	Load .A with the file type from (R0),Y, AND it with $0F to mask off any high order bits, OR it with $80 to set the closed bit, and store the result back in (R0),Y.
CLSD6	$DC29	Load .X with the active buffer number that was saved into WLINDX ($0270).
	$DC2C	Load .Y with $1B (#27). The pointer at (R0),Y now points to the low byte of the number of blocks in the file.
	$DC2E	Copy the lo byte of the number of blocks from NBKL,X ($B5,X) to (R0),Y.
	$DC32	Increment .Y.
	$DC33	Copy the hi byte of the number of blocks from NBKH,X ($BB,X) to (R0),Y.
	$DC37	Pull the original buffer number off the stack and transfer it into .X.
	$DC39	Load .A with $90 (write job code) and OR it with the drive number in DRVNUM($7F).
	$DC3D	JSR to DOIT ($D590) to write out the revised directory sector.

NAME	ADDRESS	DESCRIPTION OF WHAT ROM ROUTINE DOES
	$DC40	Pull the original secondary address off the stack and transfer it into SA ($83).
	$DC43	JMP to FNDWCH ($D107) to exit.

		Open read channel with two buffers: Sets secondary address in LINTAB and initializes all pointers, including the ones for a relative file.
OPNRCH	$DC46	Load .A with $01 and JSR to GETRCH ($D1E2) to set up one read channel
	$DC4B	JSR to INITP ($DCB6) to clear pointers.
	$DC4E	Load .A with the file type and save this value on the stack.
	$DC52	Multiply the file type in .A by 2 (ASL), OR it with the current drive in DRVNUM ($7F) and store it in FILTYP,X to set the file type.
	$DC57	JSR to STRRD ($D09B) to read the first one or two blocks in the file.
	$DC5A	Load .X with the active buffer number from LINDX ($82).
	$DC5C	Load .A with the current track number from TRACK ($80). If the track number is not $00 (not the last block in the file), branch to CR10.
	$DC60	Load .A with the current sector number from SECTOR ($81). Since TRACK=$00, this is the pointer to the last character in the file. Store this value in LSTCHR,X ($0244,X).
OR10	$DC65	Pull the original file type off the stack. If this is not a relative file, branch to OR30.
	$DC6A	Load .Y with the secondary address from SA ($83). Load the channel type from LINTAB,Y ($022B,Y), OR it with $40 to mark it as a READ/WRITE file, and store the channel type back in LINTAB,Y.
	$DC74	Copy the record size from REC ($0258) into RS,X ($C7,X).
	$DC79	JSR to GETBUF ($D28E) to set up a buffer for the side sectors. If a buffer is available, branch to OR20.
	$DC7E	Since no buffer is available for the side sectors, abort with a JMP to GBERR ($D20F).
OR20	$DC81	Load .X with the active buffer number (side sector buffer) from LINDX ($82).
	$DC83	Store the side sector buffer number in SS,X ($CD,X).
	$DC85	Copy the side sector track link from TRKSS ($0259) into TRACK ($80).

NAME	ADDRESS	DESCRIPTION OF WHAT ROM ROUTINE DOES
	$DC8A	Copy the side sector sector link from SECSS ($025A) into SECTOR ($81).
	$DC8F	JSR to SETH ($D6D3) to set up the side sector header image.
	$DC92	JSR to RDSS ($DE73) to read in the side sector block.
	$DC95	JSR to WATJOB ($D599) to wait for the job to be completed.
OROW	$DC98	Load .X with the active buffer number (side sector buffer) from LINDX ($82).
	$DC9A	Set the next record pointer in the side sector buffer NR,X ($C1,X) to $02.
	$DCA0	Load .A with $00 and JSR to SETPNT ($D4C8) to set the buffer pointers to the start of the side sector buffer.
	$DCA3	JSR to RD4C ($E153) to set up the first record.
	$DCA6	JMP to GETHDR ($DE3E) to restore the track and sector pointers and exit.
OR30	$DCA9	JSR to RDBYT ($D156) to read a byte.
	$DCAC	Load .X with the active buffer number (side sector buffer) from LINDX ($82).
	$DCAE	Store the data byte (in .A) into CHNDAT,X ($023E,X).
	$DCB1	Store $88 (ready to talk) as the channel status in CHNRDY,X ($F2,X).
	$DCB5	Terminate routine with an RTS.

INITP	$DCB6	Initialize variables for open channel: Load .X with the active buffer number from LINDX ($82).
	$DCB8	Load buffer number from BUF0,X ($A7,X), multiply it by two (ASL), and transfer the result into .Y.
	$DCBC	Store $02 into the buffer pointer BUFTAB,Y ($0099,Y) so it points to the first data byte in the buffer.
	$DCC1	Load .A with the alternative-buffer number from BUF1,X ($AE,X), OR it with $80 to set the buffer-inactive bit, and store the result back in BUF1,X.
	$DCC7	Multiply the buffer number (in .A) by two (ASL) and transfer the result to .Y.
	$DCC9	Store $02 into the buffer pointer BUFTAB,Y ($0099,Y) so it points to the first data byte in the buffer.
	$DCCE	Zero the lo and hi bytes of the number of blocks written, NBKL,X ($B5,X) and NBKH,X ($BB,X).
	$DCD4	Zero the last data byte LSTCHR,X ($0244),X.
	$DCD9	Terminate routine with an RTS.

NAME	ADDRESS	DESCRIPTION OF WHAT ROM ROUTINE DOES
OPNWCH	$DCDA	Open write channel with two buffers: JSR to INTTS ($F1A9) to get the first track and sector.
	$DCDD	Load .A with $01 and JSR to GETWCH ($D1DF) to get one buffer for writing.
	$DCE2	JSR to SETHDR ($D6D0) to set up header image.
	$DCE5	JSR to INITP ($DCB6) to set up pointers.
	$DCE8	Load .X with the active buffer number from LINDX ($82).
	$DCEA	Load .A with the file type from TYPE ($024A) and save it onto the stack.
	$DCEE	Multiply the file type in .A by two (ASL), OR it with the drive number from DRVNUM ($7F), and store the result as the file type in FILTYP,X ($EC,X).
	$DCF3	Pull the original file type off the stack and if this is a relative file (type = $04), branch to OW10.
	$DCF8	Since this is not a relative file, set channel status, CHNRDY,X ($F2,X) to $01 (active listener).
	$DCFC	Terminate routine with an RTS.
OW10	$DCFD	Load .Y with the secondary address from SA ($83).
	$DCFF	Load .A with the buffer type from LINTAB,Y ($022B,Y), AND it with $3F to mask off higher order bits, OR it with $40 to flag this as a READ/WRITE file, and store the result back in LINTAB,Y.
	$DD09	Copy record size from REC ($0258) into RS,X ($C7,X).
	$DD0E	JSR to GETBUF ($D28E) to get a new buffer for storing the side sectors. If a buffer is available, branch to OW20
	$DD13	No buffer available so abort with a JMP to GBERR ($D20F).
OW20	$DD16	Load .X with the active buffer number from LINDX ($82).
	$DD18	Store the new side sector buffer number into SS,X ($CD,X).
	$DD1A	JSR to CLRBUF ($DEC1) to clear the side sector buffer.
	$DD1D	JSR to NXTTS ($F11E) to find the next available track and sector.
	$DD20	Copy the new track link from TRACK ($80) to TRKSS ($0259).
	$DD25	Copy the new sector link from SECTOR ($81) to SECSS ($025A).
	$DD2A	Load .X with the active buffer number from LINDX ($82).

NAME	ADDRESS	DESCRIPTION OF WHAT ROM ROUTINE DOES
	$DD2C	Load .A with the side sector buffer number from SS,X ($CD,X).
	$DD2E	JSR to SETH ($D6D3) to set up the header
	$DD31	Load .A with $00 and JSR to SETSSP ($DEE9) to set the buffer pointers using the current SS pointer (in .A)
	$DD36	Load .A with $00 and JSR to PUTSS ($DD8D) to set a null side sector link.
	$DD3B	Load .A with $11 (the side sector offset plus 1) and JSR to PUTSS ($DD8D) to set the last character.
	$DD40	Load .A with $00 and JSR to PUTSS ($DD8D) to set this side sector number.
	$DD45	Load .A with the record size from REC ($0258) and JSR to PUTSS ($DD8D) to set the record size.
	$DD4B	Load .A with the file track link from TRACK ($80) and JSR to PUTSS ($DD8D) to set the track link.
	$DD50	Load .A with the file sector link from SECTOR ($81) and JSR to PUTSS ($DD8D) to set the sector link.
	$DD55	Load .A with the side sector offset ($10) and JSR to PUTSS ($DD8D) to set the side sector offset.
	$DD5A	JSR to GETHDR ($DE3E) to get the track and sector of the first side sector.
	$DD5D	Load .A with the SS track link from TRACK ($80) and JSR to PUTSS ($DD8D) to set the SS track link.
	$DD62	Load .A with the SS sector link from SECTOR ($81) and JSR to PUTSS ($DD8D) to set the SS sector link.
	$DD67	JSR to WRTSS ($DE6C) to write out the side sector block.
	$DD6A	JSR to WATJOB ($D599) to wait for the write job to be completed.
	$DD6D	Load .A with $02 and JSR to SETPNT ($D4C8) to set the pointer into the data buffer to the start of the data.
	$DD72	Load .X with the active buffer number from LINDX ($82).
	$DD74	Set the carry flag, load .A with $00, subtract the record size from RS,X ($C7,X), and store the result in NR,X ($C1,X) to set NR for a null buffer.
	$DD7B	JSR to NULBUF ($E2E2) to set null records in the active buffer.
	$DD7E	JSR to NULLNK ($DE19) to set track link to $00 and sector link to last non-zero character.
	$DD81	JSR to WRTOUT ($DE5E) to write out the null record block.

NAME	ADDRESS	DESCRIPTION OF WHAT ROM ROUTINE DOES
	$DD84	JSR to WATJOB ($D599) to wait for the write job to be completed.
	$DD87	JSR to MAPOUT ($EEF4) to write out the BAM.
	$DD8A	JMP to OROW ($DC98) finish opening the channel.
PUTSS	$DD8D	Put byte into the side sector: Push byte in .A onto the stack.
	$DD8E	Load .X with the active buffer number from LINDX ($82).
	$DD90	Load .A with the side sector buffer number from SS,X ($CD,X).
	$DD92	JMP to PUTB1 ($CFFD).
SCFLG	$DD95	Set/Clear flag: If carry flag clear, branch to CLRFLG
SETFLG	$DD97	Set flag: Load .X with the active buffer number from LINDX ($82).
	$DD99	OR the byte in .A with the file type in FILTYP,X ($EC,X).
	$DD9B	If result is not $00, branch to CLRF10.
CLRFLG	$DD9D	Clear flag: Load .X with the active buffer number from LINDX ($82).
	$DD9F	EOR the byte in .A with $FF to flip all the bits.
	$DDA1	AND the byte in .A with the file type in FILTYP,X ($EC,X).
CLRF10	$DDA3	Store the result in .A, as the new file type in FILTYP,X ($EC,X).
	$DDA5	Terminate routine with an RTS.
TSTFLG	$DDA6	Test flag: Load .X with the active buffer number from LINDX ($82).
	$DDA8	AND the byte in .A with the file type in FILTYP,X ($EC,X).
	$DDAA	Terminate routine with an RTS.
TSTWRT	$DDAB	Test if this is a write job: JSR to GETACT ($DF93) to get the active buffer number (returned in .A).
	$DDAE	Transfer the buffer number to .X.
	$DDAF	Load .A with the last job code from LSTJOB,X ($025B), AND the job code with $F0 to mask off the drive bits, and compare the result with $90 (write job code). This sets the Z flag if this is a write job.

NAME	ADDRESS	DESCRIPTION OF WHAT ROM ROUTINE DOES
	$DDB6	Terminate routine with an RTS.
		--
		Test for active files in LINDX tables:
		C=0 if file active X=ENTFND; Y=LINDX
		C=1 if file inactive X=18
TSTCHN	$DDB7	Load .X with $00 (secondary address)
TSTC20	$DDB9	Save .X value into TEMP+2 ($71).
	$DDBB	Load .A with the buffer number for this secondary address from LINTAB,X (022B,X) If the buffer number is NOT $FF, branch to TSTC40 for further testing.
TSTC30	$DDC2	Restore .X value from TEMP+2 ($71) and increment it by 1. If the resulting .X value is less than $10 (the maximum sec. address - 2), loop back to TSTC20.
TSTRTS	$DDC9	Terminate routine with an RTS.
TSTC40	$DDCA	Save .X value into TEMP+2 ($71).
	$DDCC	AND the buffer number in .A with $3F to mask off the higher order bits and transfer the result into .Y.
	$DDCF	Load .A with the file type for this secondary address from FILTYP,Y ($EC,Y), AND it with $01 to mask off the non-drive bits, and store the result in TEMP+1 ($70).
	$DDD6	Load .X with the index entry found from ENTFND ($0253).
	$DDD9	Load .A with the drive number for this secondary address from FILDRV,X ($E2,X), AND it with $01 to mask off the non-drive bits, and compare the result with the drive number in TEMP+1 ($70). If the drives do not match, branch to TSTC30.
	$DDE1	Drive numbers match, now check if the directory entries match by comparing the entry sector in DSEC,Y($026C,Y) with the one in ENTSEC,X ($D8,X). If they do not match, branch to TSTC30.
	$DDE8	Drive numbers are match, now check if the directory entries match by comparing the entry index in DIND,Y ($0266,Y) with the one in ENTIND,X ($DD,X). If they do not match, branch to TSTC30.
	$DDEF	Clear the carry flag to indicate that all tests passed and active file found.
	$DDF0	Terminate routine with an RTS.
		--
		Write out buffer if dirty:
		NOTE: a buffer is dirty if the copy in RAM has been modified so it does not match the copy on disk.
SCRUB	$DDF1	JSR to GAFLGS ($DF9E) to get active buffer number and set in LBUSED.

NAME	ADDRESS	DESCRIPTION OF WHAT ROM ROUTINE DOES
	$DDF4	If V flag not set, buffer is not dirty so branch to SCR1.
	$DDF6	JSR to WRTOUT ($DE5E) to write out the buffer to disk.
	$DDF9	JSR to WATJOB ($D599) to wait for the job to be completed.
SCR1	$DDFC	Terminate routine with an RTS.
		--
SETLNK	$DDFD	Put TRACK and SECTOR into header: JSR to SET00 ($DE2B) to set up pointer to header.
	$DE02	Move desired track from TRACK ($80) to (DIRBUF),Y; ($94),Y. Increment .Y
	$DE05	Move desired sector from SECTOR ($81) to (DIRBUF),Y; ($94),Y.
	$DE09	Terminate routine with a JMP to SDIRTY ($E105) to flag the buffer as dirty.
		--
GETLNK	$DE0C	Set TRACK & SECTOR from link in buffer: JSR to SET00 ($DE2B) to set up pointer to header.
	$DE0F	Move track link from (DIRBUF),Y;($94),Y to TRACK ($80). Increment .Y.
	$DE14	Move sector link from (DIRBUF),Y ($94),Y to SECTOR ($80).
	$DE18	Terminate routine with an RTS.
		--
NULLNK	$DE19	Set track link to $00 and sector link to the last non-zero character in buffer. JSR to SET00 ($DE2B) to set up pointer to header.
	$DE1C	Store $00 as track link in (DIRBUF),Y ($94),Y. Increment .Y.
	$DE21	Load .X with the active buffer number from LINDX ($82).
	$DE23	Load .A with the pointer into the data buffer from NR,X ($C1,X), decrement it by 1, and store the result as the sector link in (DIRBUF),Y; ($94),Y.
	$DE2A	Terminate routine with an RTS.
		--
SET00	$DE2B	Set up pointer to active buffer: JSR to GETACT ($DF93) to get the active buffer number (returned in .A).
	$DE2E	Multiply the buffer number (in .A) by two (ASL) and transfer the result to .X.
	$DE30	Move the hi byte of the buffer pointer from BUFTAB+1,X ($9A,X) to DIRBUF+1($95)
	$DE34	Store $00 as the lo byte of the buffer pointer in DIRBUF ($94).
	$DE38	Zero .Y and exit routine with an RTS.

NAME	ADDRESS	DESCRIPTION OF WHAT ROM ROUTINE DOES
CURBLK	$DE3B	Set TRACK & SECTOR from header: JSR to FNDRCH ($D0EB) to find an unused read channel.
GETHDR	$DE3E	JSR to GETACT ($DF93) to get the active buffer number (returned in .A).
	$DE41	Store the buffer number in JOBNUM ($F9)
	$DE43	Multiply the buffer number (in .A) by two (ASL) and transfer the result to .Y.
	$DE45	Move the track number from the header table, HDRS,X ($0006,Y) to TRACK ($80).
	$DE4A	Move the sector number from the header table, HDRS+1,X ($0007,Y) to SECTOR($81).
	$DE4F	Terminate routine with an RTS.

WRTAB	$DE50	Do read and write jobs: Store $90(write job code) in CMD($024D) and branch to SJ10 (always).
RDAB	$DE57	Store $80(read job code) in CMD($024D) and branch to SJ10 (always).
WRTOUT	$DE5E	Store $90(write job code) in CMD($024D) and branch to SJ20 (always).
RDIN	$DE65	Store $80(read job code) in CMD($024D) and branch to SJ20 (always).
WRTSS	$DE6C	Store $90(write job code) in CMD($024D) and branch to RDS5 (always).
RDSS	$DE73	Load .A with $80(read job code)
RDS5	$DE75	Store job code (in .A) into CMD($024D).
	$DE78	Load .X with the active buffer number from LINDX ($82).
	$DE7A	Load .A with the side sector buffer number from SS,X ($CD,X) and tranfer it to .X. If the SS buffer number < 127, branch to SJ30.
SJ10	$DE7F	JSR to SETHDR ($D6D0) to set header from TRACK and SECTOR.
	$DE82	JSR to GETACT to get the active buffer number (returned in .A).
	$DE85	Transfer the buffer number to .X.
	$DE86	Copy the drive number from DRVNUM ($7F) to LSTJOB,X ($025B,X).
SJ20	$DE8B	JSR to CDIRTY ($E115) to clear the dirty buffer flag.
	$DE8E	JSR to GETACT ($DF93) to get the active buffer number (returned in .A).
	$DE91	Transfer the buffer number to .X.
	$DE92	Continue routine with JMP to SETLJB ($D506) to set last used buffer.

RDLNK	$DE95	Set TRACK & SECTOR from link in buffer: Load .A with $00 and JSR to SETPNT ($D4C8) to set the buffer pointer to the first byte in the buffer (track link).

NAME	ADDRESS	DESCRIPTION OF WHAT ROM ROUTINE DOES
	$DE9A	JSR to GETBYT ($D137) to read the track link. Store the link in TRACK ($80).
	$DE9F	JSR to GETBYT ($D137) to read the sector link. Store the link in SECTOR ($81).
	$DEA4	Terminate routine with an RTS.
		Move bytes from one buffer to another: On entry: .A = number of bytes to move .Y = from buffer # .X = to buffer #
BOTOB0	$DEA5	Save number of bytes to move (in .A) onto the stack.
	$DEA6	Zero TEMP ($6F) and TEMP+2 ($71).
	$DEAC	Move the hi byte cf the from buffer pointer from BUFIND,Y ($FEE0,Y) to TEMP+1 ($70).
	$DEB1	Move the hi byte of the to buffer pointer from BUFIND,X ($FEE0,X) to TEMP+3 ($72).
	$DEB6	Pull the number-of-bytes-to-move from the stack, transfer it into .Y, and decrement .Y by 1 (0th byte is #1).
B02	$DEB9	Loop using .Y as a count-down index to transfer bytes from (TEMP)Y to (TEMP+2)Y
	$DEC0	Terminate routine with an RTS.
		Clear buffer: (buffer # in .A)
CLRBUF	$DEC1	Transfer buffer number from .A to .Y.
	$DEC2	Move the hi byte of the from buffer pointer from BUFIND,Y ($FEE0,Y) to TEMP+1 ($70).
	$DEC7	Zero TEMP ($6F) and .Y
CB10	$DECC	Loop to fill buffer with $00's.
	$DED1	Terminate routine with an RTS.
		Set side sector pointer to $00:
SSSET	$DED2	Zero .A and JSR to SSDIR ($DEDC) to set DIRBUF with current SS pointer.
	$DED7	Load .Y with $02. Load .A with the side sector pointer from (DIRBUF),Y; ($94),Y.
	$DEDB	Terminate routine with an RTS.
		Use SS pointer to set DIRBUF: On entry: .A = lo byte
SSDIR	$DEDC	Store lo byte (in .A) into DIRBUF ($94).
	$DEDE	Load .X with the active buffer number from LINDX ($82).
	$DEE0	Load .A with the side sector buffer number from SS,X ($CD,X).
	$DEE2	Transfer SS buffer number to .X.
	$DEE3	Copy hi byte of buffer pointer from BUFIND ($FEE0) to DIRBUF+1 ($95).
	$DEE8	Terminate routine with an RTS.

NAME	ADDRESS	DESCRIPTION OF WHAT ROM ROUTINE DOES
		Use SS pointer to set DIRBUF & BUFTAB:
		On entry: .A = lo byte
SETSSP	$DEE9	Save lo byte (in .A) onto the stack.
	$DEEA	JSR to SSDIR ($DEDC) to set DIRBUF from current SS pointer.
	$DEED	On return, .A contains the hi byte of the SS buffer pointer. Save the hi byte onto the stack.
	$DEEE	Transfer the SS buffer number from .X to .A, multiply it by two (ASL), and transfer it back into .X.
	$DEF1	Pull hi byte of SS buffer pointer off the stack and store it in BUFTAB+1,X ($9A,X).
	$DEF4	Pull lo byte of SS buffer pointer off the stack and store it in BUFTAB,X ($99,X).
	$DEF7	Terminate routine with an RTS.
		Use SSNUM & SSIND to set SS & BUFTAB:
		On return V = 0 all OK
		V = 1 out of range
SSPOS	$DEF8	JSR to SSTEST ($DF66) to test if SSNUM & SSIND are resident and within range.
	$DEFB	If N flag set, out of range so branch to SSP10.
	$DEFD	If V flag clear, it is in residence so branch to SSP20.
	$DEFF	Since V flag set, maybe in range and maybe not. Do another test: Load .X with the active buffer number from LINDX ($82).
	$DF01	Load .A with the side sector buffer number from SS,X ($CD,X).
	$DF03	JSR to IBRD ($DF1B) to read in the SS.
	$DF06	JSR to SSTEST ($DF66) to test again.
	$DF09	If N flag clear, it is in range so branch to SSP20.
SSP10	$DF0B	Out of range so JSR to SSEND ($E1CB) to set SS & BUFTAB to end of last record.
	$DF0E	BIT with ER1 ($FECE) to set flags and terminate routine with an RTS.
SSP20	$DF12	Load .A with the SS pointer from SSIND ($D6).
	$DF14	JSR to SETSSP ($DEE9) to set DIRBUF and BUFTAB.
	$DF17	BIT with ER0 ($FECD) to set flags and terminate routine with an RTS.
		Indirect block read/write: On entry: .A = buffer number for R/W .X = active buffer (LINDX) (DIRBUF),Y points to T&S to be R/W
IBRD	$DF1B	Store buffer number (.A) in JOBNUM ($F9)

NAME	ADDRESS	DESCRIPTION OF WHAT ROM ROUTINE DOES
	$DF1D	Load .A with $80 (read job code) and branch to IBOP.
IBWT	$DF21	Store buffer number (.A) in JOBNUM ($F9)
	$DF23	Load .A with $90 (write job code)
IBOP	$DF25	Push the job code onto the stack.
	$DF26	Load .A with the file's drive number from FILTYP,X ($EC,X), AND it with $01 to mask off the non-drive bits, and use it to set the drive, DRVNUM ($7F)
	$DF2C	Pull the job code off the stack, OR it with the drive number in DRVNUM ($7F), and store the result in CMD ($024D).
	$DF32	Move the track number from (DIRBUF),Y ($94),Y to TRACK ($80). Increment .Y
	$DF37	Move the sector number from (DIRBUF),Y ($94),Y to SECTOR ($81).
	$DF3B	Load .A with the buffer number from JOBNUM ($F9) and JSR to SETH ($D6D3) to set up the header.
	$DF40	Load .X with the buffer number from JOBNUM ($F9) and JMP to DOIT2 ($D593) to do the job.

		Get side sector pointers:
GSSPNT	$DF45	Load .X with the active buffer number from LINDX ($82).
	$DF47	Load .A with the side sector buffer number from SS,X ($CD,X)
	$DF49	JMP to SETDIR($D4EB) to set the DIRBUF pointers.

		Calculate side sectors:
SCAL1	$DF4C	Load .A with $78, the number of side sector pointers in a buffer.
	$DF4E	JSR to ADDT12 ($DF5C) to add the number of side sectors needed * 120.
SSCALC	$DF51	Decrement .X. If .X >= $00, branch to SCAL1.
	$DF54	Load .A with the number of SS indices needed from T3 ($72) and multiply it by 2 (ASL) since two bytes (track & sec) are needed for each index.
	$DF57	JSR to ADDT12 to add .A to T1 & T2.
	$DF5A	Load .A with the number of SS blocks needed from T4 ($73)
ADDT12	$DF5C	Clear the carry flag.
	$DF5D	Add the contents of T1 ($70) to the contents of the accumulator and store the result back in T1 ($70).

NAME	ADDRESS	DESCRIPTION OF WHAT ROM ROUTINE DOES
ADDRTS	$DF61 $DF63 $DF65	If carry is clear, branch to ADDRTS. Increment the value in T2 ($71). Terminate routine with an RTS.

Test SSNUM & SSIND for range & residence
Flag meanings on exit:

	N	Range	V	Residence	
	0	OK	0	YES	ER0
	0	MAYBE	1	NO	ER1
	1	BAD	0	YES	ER2
	1	BAD	1	NO	ER3

NAME	ADDRESS	DESCRIPTION OF WHAT ROM ROUTINE DOES
SSTEST	$DF66	JSR to SSSET ($DED2) to set the pointer to $00 and get the SS number (in .A).
	$DF69	Compare the SS number in .A with the one in SSNUM ($D5). If they are not equal, branch to ST20.
	$DF6D	Load .Y with the pointer into the SS buffer from SSIND ($D6)
	$DF6F	Load .A from (DIRBUF),Y; ($94),Y. If this value is $00, the proper side sector is not present so branch to ST10.
	$DF73	BIT ER0 ($FECD) to clear the N and V flags. All OK so exit with an RTS.
ST10	$DF77	Definitely out of range so BIT with E2 ($FECF) and exit with an RTS.
ST20	$DF7B	Load .A with the SS number from SSNUM ($D5) and compare it with $06, the number of side sector links. If the value in SSNUM > $06, branch to ST30.
	$DF81	Multiply the SS number in .A by 2 (ASL) and transfer the result into .Y.
	$DF83	Load .A with $04, and store this value in DIRBUF ($94), lo byte of the pointer.
	$DF87	Load .A with the value from (DIRBUF),Y ($94),Y. If this value is not $00, branch to ST40.
ST30	$DF8B	Way out of range so BIT with E3 ($FED0) and exit with an RTS.
ST40	$DF8F	Not in residence and range is unknown so BIT with E1 ($FECE) and exit with RTS

Get active buffer number:
 On exit: .A = active buffer number
          .X = LINDX
       Flag N = 1 if no active buffer

NAME	ADDRESS	DESCRIPTION OF WHAT ROM ROUTINE DOES
GETACT	$DF93	Load .X with the current buffer number from LINDX ($82).
	$DF95	Load .A with the buffer number from BUF0,X ($A7,X). If bit 7 is not set, this buffer is active so branch to GA1.

NAME	ADDRESS	DESCRIPTION OF WHAT ROM ROUTINE DOES
	$DF99	Load .A with the buffer number from BUF1,X ($AE,X).
GA1	$DF9B	AND the buffer number with $BF to strip the dirty bit.
	$DF9D	Terminate routine with an RTS.
		Get active buffer & set LBUSED: On exit: .A = active buffer number .X = LINDX Flag N = 1 if no active buffer Flag V = 1 if buffer is dirty
GAFLGS	$DF9E	Load .X with the current buffer number from LINDX ($82).
GA2	$DFA0	Save buffer number into LBUSED ($0257).
	$DFA3	Load .A with the buffer number from BUF0,X ($A7,X). If bit 7 is not set, this buffer is active so branch to GA3.
	$DFA7	Transfer the buffer number from .X to .A, clear the carry flag, add $07 (the maximum number of channels + 1), and store the result in LBUSED ($0257).
	$DFAE	Load .A with the buffer number from BUF1,X ($AE,X).
GA3	$DFB0	Store the buffer number in T1 ($70).
	$DFB2	AND the buffer number with $1F and BIT the result with T1 ($70) to set the N and V flags.
	$DFB6	Terminate routine with an RTS.
		Get a channel's inactive buffer number: On entry: LINDX = channel number On exit: .A = buffer # or $FF if none
GETINA	$DFB7	Load .X with the channel number from LINDX ($82).
	$DFB9	Load .A with the buffer number from BUF0,X ($A7,X). If bit 7 is set, this buffer is inactive so branch to GI10.
	$DFBD	Load .A with the buffer number from BUF1,X ($AE,X).
GI10	$DFBF	Compare the buffer number with $FF to set the Z flag if inactive buffer found.
	$DFC1	Terminate routine with an RTS.
		Set the inactive buffer's buffer number: On entry: .A = buffer number
PUTINA	$DFC2	Load .X with the channel number from LINDX ($82).
	$DFC4	OR the buffer number in .A with $80 to set the inactive buffer bit.
	$DFC6	Load .Y with the buffer number from BUF0,X ($A7,X). If bit 7 is clear, the other buffer is the inactive one so branch to PI1.

NAME	ADDRESS	DESCRIPTION OF WHAT ROM ROUTINE DOES
	$DFCA	This buffer is inactive so store new buffer number in BUF0,X ($A7,X).
	$DFCC	Exit with an RTS.
PI1	$DFCD	This buffer is inactive so store new buffer number in BUF1,X ($AE,X).
	$DFCF	Exit with an RTS.
NXTREC	$DFD0	Set up next relative record: Load .A with $20 (overflow flag) and JSR to CLRFLG ($DD9D) to clear the record overflow flag.
	$DFD5	Load .A with $80 (last record flag) and JSR to TSTFLG ($DDA6) to test if we are out beyond the last record. If not, branch to NXTR40.
	$DFDC	Load .X with the current channel number from LINDX ($82).
	$DFDE	Increment the lo byte of the record counter in RECL,X ($B5,X). If the result is not $00, branch to NXTR15.
	$DFE2	Increment the hi byte of the record counter in RECH,X ($BB,X).
NXTR15	$DFE4	Load .X with the current channel number from LINDX ($82).
	$DFE6	Load .A with the pointer to the next record from NR,X ($C1,X).
	$DFE8	If the next record pointer is $00, there is no next record so branch to NXTR45.
	$DFEA	JSR to GETPNT ($D4E8) to get the buffer pointer.
	$DFED	Load .X with the current channel number from LINDX ($82).
	$DFEF	Compare the buffer pointer in .A with the pointer in NR,X ($C1,X). If BT<NR then branch to NXTR20.
	$DFF3	Not in this buffer, must be in the next one so JSR to NRBUF ($E03C) to set up the next one.
NXTR20	$DFF6	Load .X with the current channel number from LINDX ($82).
	$DFF8	Load .A with the pointer to the next record from NR,X ($C1,X).
	$DFFA	JSR to SETPNT ($D4C8) to advance to the next record.
	$DFFD	Load .A with the first byte of the record from (BUFTAB,X) ($99,X).
	$DFFF	Save the first data byte into DATA ($85)
	$E001	Load .A with $20 (overflow flag) and JSR to CLRFLG ($DD9D) to clear the record overflow flag.
	$E006	JSR to ADDNR ($E304) to advance the NR pointer.

NAME	ADDRESS	DESCRIPTION OF WHAT ROM ROUTINE DOES
NXOUT	$E009	Save the new value of NR (in .A) onto the stack. If the carry flag is clear, we have NOT crossed a block boundary so branch to NXTR30.
	$E00C	Load .A with $00 and JSR to DRDBYT ($D4F6) to read the track link of the data block. If the track link is not $00, this is not the last block so branch to NXTR30.
	$E013	Pull the new NR value off the stack and compare it to $02. If it equals $02, branch to NXTR50.
NXTR45	$E018	Load .A with $80 (last record flag) and JSR to SETFLG ($DD97) to set this flag.
NXTR40	$E01D	JSR to GETPRE ($D12F) to get pointers.
	$E020	Move the data byte from BUFTAB,X ($99,X) to LSTCHR ($0244).
	$E025	Store $0D (carriage return) in DATA($85)
	$E029	Terminate routine with an RTS.
NXTR50	$E02A	JSR to NXTR35 ($E035) to store NR value
	$E02D	Load .X with the channel number from LINDX ($82). Store $00 in NR,X ($C1,X).
	$E033	Terminate routine with an RTS.
NXTR30	$E034	Pull the new NR value off the stack.
NXTR35	$E035	Load .X with the channel number from LINDX ($82). Store the byte in .A into NR,X ($C1,X).
	$E039	Terminate routine with a JMP to SETLST ($E16E) to set the pointer to the last character.

NRBUF	$E03C	Set up next record in buffer: JSR to SETDRN ($D1D3) to set drive number to agree with the last job.
	$E03F	JSR to RDLNK ($DE95) to set TRACK and SECTOR from the track & sector link.
	$E042	JSR to GAFLGS ($DF9E) to test if the current buffer is dirty (changed). If V flag clear, it is clean; branch to NRBU50 so we don't write it out.
	$E047	JSR to WRTOUT ($DE5E) to write it out.
	$E04A	JSR to DBLBUF ($CF1E) to toggle the active and inactive buffers.
	$E04D	Load .A with $02 and JSR to SETPNT ($D4C8) to set the pointer to point to the first data byte in the new sector.
	$E052	JSR to TSTWRT ($DDAB) to test if the last job was a write. If it was not a write job, branch to NRBU20 ($E07B) since buffer is OK.

NAME	ADDRESS	DESCRIPTION OF WHAT ROM ROUTINE DOES
	$E057	JSR to RDAB ($DE57) to read in needed buffer.
	$E05A	JSR to WATJOB ($D599) to wait for the read job to be completed.
NRBU50	$E05D	JSR to DBLBUF ($CF1E) to toggle the active and inactive buffers.
	$E060	JSR to TSTWRT ($DDAB) to test if the last job was a write. If it was not a write job, branch to NRBU70.
	$E065	JSR to RDAB ($DE57) to read in needed buffer.
	$E068	JSR to WATJOB ($D599) to wait for the read job to be completed.
NRBU70	$E06B	JSR to RDLNK ($DE95) to set TRACK and SECTOR from the track & sector link.
	$E06E	Load .A with the track link from TRACK ($80). If track link is $00, this is the last block with no double buffering needed so branch to NRBU20.
	$E072	JSR to DBLBUF ($CF1E) to toggle the active and inactive buffers.
	$E075	JSR to RDAB ($DE5E) to start a read job for the inactive buffer.
	$E078	JSR to DBLBUF ($CF1E) to toggle the active and inactive buffers.
NRBU20	$E07B	Terminate routine with an RTS.

NAME	ADDRESS	DESCRIPTION OF WHAT ROM ROUTINE DOES
		Put relative record into buffer:
RELPUT	$E07C	JSR to SDIRTY ($E105) to flag buffer as dirty (RAM version changed).
	$E07F	JSR to GETACT ($DF93) to get active buffer number (returned in .A).
	$E082	Multiply the buffer number (in .A) by two (ASL) and transfer the result to .X.
	$E084	Copy the data byte from DATA ($85) into the buffer at (BUFTAB,X) ($99,X).
	$E088	Load .Y with the lo byte of the pointer BUFTAB,X and increment the pointer in .Y by 1. If the new pointer value is NOT $00, branch to RELP05.
	$E08D	Load .Y with the channel number from LINDX ($82).
	$E08F	Load .A with the next record pointer from NR,Y. If this value is $00, branch to RELP07.
RELP06	$E094	Load .Y with $02.
RELP05	$E096	Transfer the contents of .Y to .A.
	$E097	Load .Y with the channel number from LINDX ($82).
	$E099	Compare the contents of .A to NR,Y ($C1,Y) to test if NR = pointer. If they are not equal, NR is not a pointer so branch to RELP10 to set new pointer.

NAME	ADDRESS	DESCRIPTION OF WHAT ROM ROUTINE DOES
RELP07	$E09E	Load .A with $20 (the overflow flag) and JMP to SETFLG ($DD97) to set the overflow flag and exit.
RELP10	$E0A3	Increment the lo byte of the pointer BUFTAB,X ($99,X). If the result is not $00, we don't need the next buffer so branch to RELP20.
	$E0A7	JSR to NRBUF($E03C) to get next buffer.
RELP20	$E0AA	Terminate routine with an RTS.

		Write out relative records:
WRTREL	$E0AB	Load .A with $A0 (last record flag + overflow flag) and JSR to TSTFLG ($DDA6) to check for last record & overflow.
	$E0B0	If Z flag clear, some flag is set so branch to WR50.
WR10	$E0B2	Load .A with the byte from DATA ($85) and JSR to RELPUT ($E07C) to put the data into the buffer.
WR20	$E0B7	Load .A with the EOIFLG ($F8). If it equals $00, an EOI was NOT sent so branch to WR40.
	$E0BB	Terminate routine with an RTS.
WR30	$E0BC	Load .A with $20 (overflow flag) and JSR to TSTFLG ($DDA6) to test for an overflow error.
	$E0C1	If Z set, no error so branch to WR40.
	$E0C3	Overflow error so load .A with $51 (recover flag) and store it in ERWORD ($026C) to flag the error.
WR40	$E0C8	JSR to CLREC ($E0F3) to clear the rest of the record.
	$E0CB	JSR to RD40 ($E153) to set up for the next record.
	$E0CE	Load .A from ERWORD ($026C). If it is $00, no errors so branch to WR45.
	$E0D3	Abort with a JMP to CMDERR ($C1C8)
WR45	$E0D6	Terminate with a JMP to OKERR ($E6BC).
WR50	$E0D9	AND the error flag in .A with $80 (the last record flag). If the result is not $00, the last record flag was set so branch to WR60 to add to file.
	$E0DD	Load .A with the EOIFLG ($F8). If this is $00, an EOI was not sent so branch to WR30.
WR51	$E0E1	Terminate routine with an RTS.
WR60	$E0E2	Load .A with the data byte from DATA ($85) and push it onto the stack.

NAME	ADDRESS	DESCRIPTION OF WHAT ROM ROUTINE DOES
	$E0E5	JSR to ADDREL ($E31C) to add to the relative file.
	$E0E9	Pull the data byte off the stack and put it back in DATA ($85).
	$E0EB	Load .A with $80 (last record flag) and JSR to CLRFLG ($DD9D) to clear the flag.
	$E0F0	JMP to WR10.

		Clear rest of relative record:
CLREC	$E0F3	Load .A with $20 (overflow flag) and JSR to TSTFLG ($DDA6) to test the flag.
	$E0F8	If Z flag not set, overflow has occured so branch to CLR10 to exit.
	$E0FA	Set DATA ($85) to $00 and JSR to RELPUT ($E07C) to put a null byte in the buffer
	$E101	Loop with a JMP to CLREC ($E0F3).
CLR10	$E104	Terminate routine with an RTS.

		Set buffer dirty flag:
SDIRTY	$E105	Load .A with $40 (dirty flag).
	$E107	JSR to SETFLG ($DD97) to set flag.
	$E10A	JSR to GAFLGS ($DF9E) to get active buffer number in .A and set flags.
	$E10D	OR the contents of .A with $40 to set the dirty flag.
	$E10F	Load .X with the number of the last buffer used from LBUSED ($0257).
	$E112	Store the content of .A as the buffer number in BUF0,X ($A7,X).
	$E114	Terminate routine with an RTS.

		Clear buffer dirty flag:
CDIRTY	$E115	JSR to GAFLGS ($DF9E) to get active buffer number and set flags.
	$E118	AND the contents of .A with $BF to clear the dirty flag.
	$E11A	Load .X with the number of the last buffer used from LBUSED ($0257).
	$E11D	Store the content of .A as the buffer number in BUF0,X ($A7,X).
	$E11F	Terminate routine with an RTS.

		Read relative record:
RDREL	$E120	Load .A with $80 (last record flag) and JSR to TSTFLG ($DDA6) to test the flag.
	$E125	If Z flag not set, last record error has occured so branch to RD05.
RD10	$E127	JSR to GETPRE ($D12F) to set pointers to existing buffer.
	$E12A	Load .A with the lo byte of the buffer pointer from BUFTAB,X ($99,X).

NAME	ADDRESS	DESCRIPTION OF WHAT ROM ROUTINE DOES
	$E12C	Compare this value to the contents of LSTCHR,Y ($0244). If they are equal, branch to RD40 because we want the next record not the last one.
	$E131	Increment the buffer pointer in BUFTAB,X ($99,X). If the result is not equal to $00, we don't need the next buffer so branch to RD20.
	$E135	JSR to NRBUF ($E03C) to read in the next buffer of relative records.
RD15	$E138	JSR to GETPRE ($D12F) to set pointers to existing buffer.
RD20	$E13B	Load .A with the data byte from (BUFTAB,X); ($99,X).
RD25	$E13D	Store the data byte in CHNDAT,Y($023E,Y)
	$E140	Load .A with $89 (random access - ready) and store this as the channel status in CHNRDY,Y ($F2,Y).
	$E145	Load the pointer from BUFTAB,X ($99,Y) and compare it to the pointer to the last character in the record from LSTCHR,Y ($0244,Y). If they are equal, branch to RD30 to send EOI.
	$E14C	Terminate routine with an RTS.
RD30	$E14D	Load .A with $81 (random access - EOI) and store this as the channel status in CHNRDY,Y ($F2,Y).
	$E152	Terminate routine with an RTS.
RD40	$E153	JSR to NXTREC ($DFD0) to get the next record.
	$E156	JSR to GETPRE ($D12F) to set pointers to existing buffer.
	$E159	Load .A with the byte from DATA ($85).
	$E15B	JMP to RD25 to carry on.
RD05	$E15E	No record error so load .X with the channel number from LINDX ($82).
	$E160	Store $0D (carriage return) as the data byte in CHNDAT,X ($023E,X).
	$E165	Load .A with $81 (random access - EOI) and store this as the channel status in CHNRDY,Y ($F2,Y).
	$E169	Load .A with $50 (no record error) and abort with a JMP to CMDERR ($C1C8).
		--
		Set pointer to last character in record:
SETLST	$E16E	Load .X with the channel number from LINDX ($82)
	$E170	Copy the next record pointer from NR,X ($C1,X) into R1 ($87).

NAME	ADDRESS	DESCRIPTION OF WHAT ROM ROUTINE DOES
	$E174	Decrement the pointer in R1 ($87) by 1 and compare the result to $02, the pointer to the first data byte in the sector. If the pointer does not equal $02, branch to SETL01.
	$E17A	Store $FF into R1 ($87) so it points to the last byte in a sector.
SETL01	$E17E	Copy the record size from RS,X ($C7,X) into R2 ($88).
	$E182	JSR to GETPNT ($D4E8) to get the pointer into the active buffer (returned in .A) Compare this value with the pointer in R1 ($87). If R1 >= .A branch to SETL10.
	$E18D	JSR to DBLBUF ($CF1E) to toggle the active and inactive buffers.
	$E190	JSR to FNDLST ($E1B2) to find the last character. On return, if carry is clear, branch to SETL05.
	$E195	Load .X with the channel number from LINDX ($82).
	$E197	Store the character in .A into LSTCHR,X ($0244,X).
	$E19A	JMP to DBLBUF ($CF1E) to toggle the active and inactive buffers and exit.
SETL05	$E19D	JSR to DBLBUF ($CF1E) to toggle the active and inactive buffers.
	$E1A0	Store $FF into R1 ($87) so it points to the last byte in a sector.
SETL10	$E1A4	JSR to FNDLST ($E1B2) to find the last non-zero character in the record. On return, if carry set, branch to SETL40.
	$E1A9	JSR to GETPNT ($D4E8) to get the pointer into the active buffer (returned in .A)
SETL40	$E1AC	Load .X with the channel number from LINDX ($82).
	$E1AE	Store the character in .A into LSTCHR,X ($0244,X).
	$E1B1	Terminate routine with an RTS.

FNDLST	$E1B2	Find last non-zero character in record: JSR to SET00 ($DE2B) to set up pointer to start of buffer.
	$E1B5	Load .Y with the offset to start at from R1 ($87).
FNDL10	$E1B7	Load .A with the data byte from the buffer at (DIRBUF),Y; ($94),Y. If the data byte is not $00, branch to FNDL20.
	$E1BB	Decrement the pointer in .Y. If the resulting pointer is less than or equal to $02, branch to FNDL30 since the start of the record is not in here.

NAME	ADDRESS	DESCRIPTION OF WHAT ROM ROUTINE DOES
	$E1C0	Decrement the record size in R2 ($88). If R2 has not counted down to $00 yet, branch FNDL10.
FNDL30	$E1C4	Decrement the record size in R2 ($88). Clear the carry flag to indicate that the record was not found here and exit from the routine with an RTS.
FNDL20	$E1C8	Found the last non-zero character so transfer the pointer from .Y to .A.
	$E1C9	Set the carry flag to indicate it was found here and terminate with an RTS.
SSEND	$E1CE	Set SS & BUFTAB to end of last record: JSR to SSSET ($DED2) to set the SS pointer to $00.
	$E1CE	Store the side sector number returned in .A into SSNUM ($D5).
	$E1D0	Set the lo byte of the pointer in DIRBUF ($94) to $04.
	$E1D4	Load .Y with $A0 (the side sector offset less 6) and branch to SE20 (always).
SE10	$E1D8	Decrement pointer in .Y by 2. If the result is less than $00, branch to BREAK
SE20	$E1DC	Look for the last SS number by loading .A from (DIRBUF),Y; ($94),Y. If the byte is $00, we have not found it yet so branch back to SE10.
	$E1E0	Transfer the pointer in .Y into .A.
	$E1E1	Multiply the pointer in .A by 2 (ASL) and compare the result to the side sector number in SSNUM ($D5). If they are equal, this is the last SS number so branch to SE30.
	$E1E6	Store the SS number in .A into SSNUM ($D5).
	$E1E8	Load .X with the channel number from LINDX ($82).
	$E1EA	Load .A with the side sector from SS,X ($CD,X) and JSR to IBRD ($DF1B) to do an indirect block read of the last side sector.
SE30	$E1EF	Zero .Y and set the lo byte of the pointer in DIRBUF ($94) to $00.
	$E1F3	Load .A with track link from (DIRBUF),Y ($94),Y. If the link is not $00, branch to BREAK.
	$E1F7	Increment .Y
	$E1F8	Load .A with sector link from (DIRBUF),Y ($94),Y. This points to the last good byte in the buffer. Transfer the pointer to .Y, decrement it by 1, store it in SSIND ($D6), and transfer it back to .A.

NAME	ADDRESS	DESCRIPTION OF WHAT ROM ROUTINE DOES
	$E1FF	JMP to SETSSP ($DEE9) to set DIRBUF and BUFTAB with current SS pointer.
BREAK	$E202	Load .A with $67 to indicate a SYSTEM TRACK OR SECTOR error and JSR to CMDERR2 ($E645).

RECORD COMMAND   Position pointer to given record

NAME	ADDRESS	DESCRIPTION OF WHAT ROM ROUTINE DOES
RECORD	$E207	Note: set to last record if out of range JSR to CMDSET ($C2B3) to initialize the pointers and tables.
	$E20A	Load .A with the second character in the command from CMDBUF+1 ($0201) and use it to set the secondary address in SA ($83)
	$E20F	JSR to FNDRCH ($D0EB) to find an unused read channel.
	$E212	If carry flag clear, channel found so branch to R20.
	$E214	Load .A with $70 to indicate a NO CHANNEL error and JSR to CMDERR ($C1C8).
R20	$E219	Load .A with $A0 (last record flag plus overflow flag) and JSR to CLRFLG ($DD9D) to clear these flags.
	$E21E	JSR to TYPFIL ($D125) to determine the file type. If the Z flag is set, it is a relative file so branch to R30.
	$E223	Load .A with $64 to indicate a FILE TYPE MISMATCH error and JSR to CMDERR ($C1C8)
R30	$E228	Load .A with the file type from FILTYP,X ($EC,X), AND the type with $01 to mask off the non-drive bits, and store the result as the drive # in DRVNUM ($7F).
	$E22E	Load .A with the third character in the command from CMDBUF+2 ($0202) and use it to set the lo byte of the record number in RECL,X ($B5,X).
	$E233	Load .A with the fourth character in the command from CMDBUF+3 ($0203) and use it to set the hi byte of the record number in RECH,X ($BB,X).
	$E238	Load .X with the channel number from LINDX ($82).
	$E23A	Store $89 (random access - ready) as the channel status in CHNRDY,X ($F2,X).
	$E23E	Load .A with the fifth character in the command from CMDBUF+4 ($0204). This is the byte pointer into the record. If the byte pointer is $00, branch to R40.
	$E243	Set the carry flag and subtract $01 from the byte pointer. If the result is $00, branch to R40.

NAME	ADDRESS	DESCRIPTION OF WHAT ROM ROUTINE DOES
	$E248	Compare the adjusted byte pointer to the record size in RS,X ($C7,X). If the byte pointer is within the record, branch to R40.
	$E24C	Load .A with $51 (record overflow) and store it in ERWORD ($026C). Zero .A.
R40	$E253	Store the byte pointer (in .A) into RECPTR ($D4).
	$E255	JSR to FNDREL ($CE0E) to calculate the side sector pointers.
	$E258	JSR to SSPOS ($DEF8) to set the side sector pointers. If V flag is clear, we have not attempted to go beyond the last record so branch to R50.
	$E25D	Load .A with $80 (last record flag) and JSR to SETFLG ($DD97) to set the flag.
	$E262	JMP to RD05 ($E15E) to set pointers to the last record.
R50	$E265	JSR to POSITN ($E275) to position to the desired record.
	$E268	Load .A with $80 (last record flag) and JSR to TSTFLG ($DDA6) to test if this flag has been set. If not, branch to R60 to exit.
	$E26F	JMP to RD05 ($E15E) to set pointers to the last record.
R60	$E272	JMP to ENDCMD ($C194) to terminate.
------	-------	--
		Position to record: Moves relative record into active buffer and the next block into inactive buffer.
POSITN	$E275	JSR to POSBUF ($E29C) to position data blocks into buffers.
	$E278	Load .A with the pointer from RELPNT ($D7) and JSR to SETPNT ($D4C8) to set up the buffer pointers.
	$E27D	Load .X with the channel number from LINDX ($82).
	$E27F	Load .A with the record size from RS,X (C7,X) and set the carry flag.
	$E282	Subtract the pointer in RECPNT ($D4) from the record size in .A to find the offset. If offset > $00, branch to P2.
	$E286	Trouble! JMP to BREAK ($E202).
P2	$E289	Clear the carry flag and add the pointer in RELPNT ($D7). If there is no carry, branch to P30.
	$E28E	Add another $01 and set the carry flag.
P30	$E291	JSR to NXOUT ($E009) to set up the next record.

NAME	ADDRESS	DESCRIPTION OF WHAT ROM ROUTINE DOES
	$E294	JMP to RD15 ($E138) to complete set up.

		- * - * - UNUSED CODE - * - * -
	$E297	Load .A with $51 (record overflow) and JSR to CMDERR ($C1C8).

		Position proper data blocks into buffers
POSBUF	$E29C	Save the lo byte of the DIRBUF ($94/5) pointer into R3 ($89).
	$E2A0	Save the hi byte of the DIRBUF ($94/5) pointer into R4 ($8A).
	$E2A4	JSR to BHERE ($E2D0) to check if desired block is in the buffer. If not, branch to P10 to read it in.
	$E2A9	Terminate routine with an RTS.
P10	$E2AA	JSR to SCRUB ($DDF1) to clean the buffer
	$E2AD	JSR to GETLNK ($DE0C) to set TRACK and SECTOR from the link.
	$E2B0	If TRACK ($80) is $00, there is no next track so branch to P80.
	$E2B4	JSR to BHERE ($E2D0) to check if desired block is in the buffer. If not, branch to P75 to read it in.
	$E2B9	JSR to DBLBUF ($CF1E) to toggle the active and inactive buffers.
	$E2BC	JMP to FREIAC ($D2DA) to free the inactive buffer.
P75	$E2BF	JSR to FREIAC ($D2DA) to free the inactive buffer.
P80	$E2C2	Load .Y with $00.
	$E2C4	Move the desired track from (R3),Y ($89),Y into TRACK ($80). Increment .Y
	$E2C9	Move the desired sector from (R3),Y ($89),Y into SECTOR ($81).
	$E2CD	JMP to STRDBL ($D0AF) to read in the desired block and the next one too.

		Check if desired block is in buffer:
BHERE	$E2D0	JSR to GETHDR ($DE3E) to set TRACK and SECTOR from the header.
BHERE2	$E2D3	Load .Y with $00
	$E2D5	Compare the desired track from (R3),Y ($89),Y with the value in TRACK ($80). If they are equal, branch to BH10 to compare the sectors.
	$E2D9	No match (Z=0) so exit with an RTS
BH10	$E2DC	Increment .Y.
	$E2DD	Compare the desired sector from (R3),Y ($89),Y with the value in SECTOR ($81). This sets Z=1 if they are equal.
	$E2E1	Terminate routine with an RTS.

NAME	ADDRESS	DESCRIPTION OF WHAT ROM ROUTINE DOES
NULBUF	$E2E2	Set null records in active buffer: JSR to SET00 ($DE2B) to set pointers to start of data buffer.
	$E2E5	Loop to fill data buffer with $00's from $xx02 to $xxFF.
	$E2EE	JSR to ADDNR ($E304) to calculate the position of the next record (in .A).
NB20	$E2F1	Store the new pointer value in NR,X ($C1,X).
	$E2F3	Transfer the next record pointer to .Y.
	$E2F4	Store $FF as the first character in the next reccrd at (DIRBUF),Y; ($94),Y.
	$E2F8	JSR to ADDNR ($E304) to calculate the position of the next record (in .A).
	$E2FB	If carry flag is clear, we haven't done all the records in this block yet so branch to NB20.
	$E2FD	If the Z flag is not set, branch to NB30
	$E2FF	Store $00 into NR,X ($C1,X) to flag the last record.
NB30	$E303	Terminate routine with an RTS.
		--
		Add record size & next record pointer: On exit: C=1 if crossed buffer boundary
ADDNR	$E304	Load .X with the channel number from LINDX ($82).
	$E306	Load .A with the next record pointer from NR,X ($C1,X) and set the carry flag
	$E309	If NR pointer is $00 branch to AN05.
	$E30B	Clear the carry flag and add the record size from RS,X ($C7,X).
	$E30E	If carry clear, branch to AN10.
	$E310	If result is not $00, branch to AN05.
	$E312	Load .A with $02 (bypass link)
	$E314	BIT with ER00 ($FECC) to set flags.
	$E317	Terminate routine with an RTS
AN05	$E318	Add $01 to the contents of .A to adjust for the link and set the carry flag.
AN10	$E31B	Terminate routine with an RTS
		--
		Add blocks to a relative file:
ADDREL	$E31C	JSR to SETDRN ($D1D3) to set drive #.
	$E31F	JSR to SSEND ($E1CB) to set up end of file.
	$E322	JSR to POSBUF ($E29C) to position the proper data blocks into the buffers.
	$E325	JSR to DBSET ($CF7C) to set up double buffering.
	$E328	Copy side sector index from SSIND ($D6) into R1 ($87).
	$E32C	Copy side sector number from SSNUM ($D5) into R0 ($86).

NAME	ADDRESS	DESCRIPTION OF WHAT ROM ROUTINE DOES
	$E330	Set R2 ($88) to $00 to clear the flag fcr one block.
	$E334	Set RECPTR ($D4) to $00 to clear this for calculations.
	$E338	JSR to FNDREL ($CE0E) to calculate the side sector pointers.
ADDR1	$E33B	JSR to NUMFRE ($EF4D) to calculate the number of blocks free.
	$E33E	Load .Y with the channel number from LINDX ($82).
	$E340	Load .X with the record size from RS,Y ($C7,Y), decrement the size by 1, and transfer the result into .A.
	$E344	Clear the carry flag and add the record pointer, RELPTR ($D7) to the record size in .A.
	$E347	If no carry results, there is no span to the next block so branch to AR10.
	$E349	Increment the SS pointer, SSIND ($D6) twice. If the result is not zero, branch to AR10.
	$E34F	Increment the side sector number, SSNUM (D5) by 1 and store $10 (the side sector offset) into SSIND ($D6) since we are starting a new block.
AR10	$E355	Load .A with the SS index from R1, clear the carry flag, add $02, and JSR to SETSSP ($DEE9) to set DIRBUF & BUFTAB.
	$E35D	Load the side sector number from SSNUM ($D5) and compare it with $06, the number of side sector links. If SSNUM is less than or equal to $06, the range is valid so branch to AR25.
AR20	$E363	Load .A with $52 to indicate a TOO BIG RELATIVE FILE error and JSR to CMDERR ($C1C8).
AR25	$E368	Load .A with the side sector index from SSIND ($D6) and set the carry flag.
	$E36B	Subtract the SS index from R1 ($87). If the result is positive, branch to AR30.
	$E36F	Subtract $0F (the side sector index offset less 1) and clear the carry flag.
AR30	$E372	Store the number of side sector indicies (in .A) into T3 ($72).
	$E374	Load .A with the SS number from SSNUM ($D5). Subtract the SS number from R0 ($86) to find the number of side sectors needed. Store the number needed into T4 ($73).
	$E37A	Zero T1 ($70) and T2 ($71) to serve as a results accumulator.

NAME	ADDRESS	DESCRIPTION OF WHAT ROM ROUTINE DOES
	$E380	Transfer the number of side sectors needed from .A to .X and JSR to SSCALC ($DF51) to calculate the number of blocks needed.
	$E384	Load .A with the hi byte of the number needed from T2 ($71). If the hi byte is not $00, branch to AR35.
	$E388	Load .X with the lo byte of the number needed from T1 ($70). Decrement .X by 1. If the result is not $00, branch to AR35
	$E38D	Increment R2 ($88) by 1.
AR35	$E38F	Check if there are enough blocks left: Compare the hi byte of the number of blocks needed (in .A) with the hi byte of the number of blocks free in NBTEMP+1 ($0273). If there are more than enough, branch to AR40. If there are NOT enough, branch to AR20. If we have just enough, we had better check the lo byte.
	$E396	Load .A with the lo byte of the number free from NBTEMP ($0272) and compare it with the lo byte of the number needed in T1 ($70). If there are not enough, branch to AR20 to abort.
AR40	$E39D	Load .A with $01 and JSR to DRDBYT ($D4F6) to read the sector link.
	$E3A2	Clear the carry flag and add $01 to .A to give the NR.
	$E3A5	Load .X with the channel number from LINDX ($82).
	$E3A7	Store the NR value (in .A) into NR,X ($C1,X).
	$E3A9	JSR to NXTTS ($F11E) to get the next available track and sector.
	$E3AC	JSR to SETLNK ($DDFD) to set the track and sector link in the current block.
	$E3AF	Load .A with the add-1-block flag from R2 ($88). If the flag is set, branch to AR50.
	$E3B3	JSR to WRTOUT ($DE5E) to write the current block to disk.
AR45	$E3B6	JSR to DBLBUF ($CF1E) to switch buffers.
	$E3B9	JSR to SETHDR ($D6D0) to set header from TRACK and SECTOR.
	$E3BC	JSR to NXTTS ($F11E) to get the next available track and sector.
	$E3BF	JSR to SETLNK ($DDFD) to set the track and sector link in the current block.
	$E3C2	JSR to NULBUF ($E2E2) to clean out the buffer
	$E3C5	JMP to AR55 ($E3D4).
AR50	$E3C8	JSR to DBLBUF ($CF1E) to switch buffers.

NAME	ADDRESS	DESCRIPTION OF WHAT ROM ROUTINE DOES
	$E3CB	JSR to SETHDR ($D6D0) to set header from TRACK and SECTOR.
	$E3CE	JSR to NULBUF ($E2E2) to clean out the buffer
	$E3D1	JSR to NULLNK ($DE19) to set link for the last block.
AR55	$E3D4	JSR to WRTOUT ($DE5E) to write the current block to disk.
	$E3D7	JSR to GETLNK ($DE0C) to set TRACK and SECTOR from the track & sector link.
	$E3DA	Save the value of TRACK ($80) and SECTOR ($81) onto the stack.
	$E3E0	JSR to GETHDR ($DE3E) to set TRACK and SECTOR from the last sector read.
	$E3E3	Save the value of TRACK ($80) and SECTOR ($81) onto the stack.
	$E3E9	JSR to GSSPNT ($DF45) to calculate the side sector pointer (returned in .A)
	$E3EC	Transfer the pointer in .A to .X. If the pointer value is not $00, we don't need another side sector so branch to AR60.
	$E3EF	JSR to NEWSS ($E44E) to get another side sector.
	$E3F2	Load .A with $10, side sector offset, and JSR to SETSSP ($DEE9) to set the side sector pointer.
	$E3F7	Increment the side sector count in R0 ($86) by 1.
AR60	$E3F9	Pull this sector's track off the stack and JSR to PUTSS ($DD8D) to write it into the side sector buffer.
	$E3FD	Pull this sector's sector off the stack and JSR to PUTSS ($DD8D) to write it into the side sector buffer.
	$E401	Pull this sector's sector link off the stack and store it in SECTOR ($81).
	$E404	Pull this sector's track link off the stack and store it in TRACK ($80).
	$E407	If track link is $00, there are no more blocks in this file so branch to AR65
	$E409	Compare the side sector counter in R0 ($86) with the end count in SSNUM ($D5). If they are not equal, we haven't done enough new blocks yet so branch to AR45.
	$E40F	Almost done so JSR to GSSPNT ($DF45) to get the side sector pointer.
	$E412	Compare the pointer in .A with the end pointer in SSIND($D6). If SSIND>.A, we are almost done so branch to AR45. If SSIND=.A there is one more block left so branch to AR50.

NAME	ADDRESS	DESCRIPTION OF WHAT ROM ROUTINE DOES
AR65	$E418	All done. JSR to GSSPNT ($DF45) to get the side sector pointer. Save it onto the stack.
	$E41C	Load .A with a $00 and JSR to SSDIR ($DEDC) to set DIRBUF with the current SS pointer.
	$E421	Zero .A and .Y. Zero the track link of the side-sector sector in (DIRBUF),Y ($94),Y. Increment .Y.
	$E427	Pull the pointer into this sector off the stack, subtract $01, and store the result as the sector link of the side-sector sector in (DIRBUF),Y; ($94),Y.
	$E42D	JSR to WRTSS ($DE6C) to write out the current block of side sectors to disk.
	$E430	JSR to WATJOB ($D599) to wait for the write job to be completed.
	$E433	JSR to MAPOUT ($EEF4) to write the BAM.
	$E436	JSR to FNDREL ($CE0E) to find the relative file and calculate SSNUM and SSIND for the desired record.
	$E439	JSR to DBLBUF ($CF1E) to get back to the leading buffer.
	$E43C	JSR to SSPOS ($DEF8) to position SS and BUFTAB to SSNUM and SSIND.
	$E43F	On return, if V flag is set, the record is still beyond the end of the relative file so branch to AR70.
	$E441	All OK so exit from routine with a JMP to POSITN ($E275) to position to the record.
AR70	$E444	Still beyond end of file so: load .A with $80 (the last record flag), JSR to SETFLG ($DD97) to set the flag, load .A with $50 (no record error) and exit with a JSR to CMDERR ($C1C8).

		Create a new side sector and change the old side sectors to reflect it.
NEWSS	$E44E	JSR to NXTTS ($F11E) to find the next available track and sector.
	$E451	JSR to DBLBUF ($CF1E) to toggle to the inactive buffer.
	$E454	JSR to SCRUB ($DDF1) to write out the buffer if it is dirty (doesn't match copy on disk).
	$E457	JSR to GETACT ($DF93) to determine the active buffer number (returned in .A). Save the buffer number onto the stack.
	$E45B	JSR to CLRBUF ($DEC1) to zero the buffer
	$E45E	Load .X with the channel number from LINDX ($82).

NAME	ADDRESS	DESCRIPTION OF WHAT ROM ROUTINE DOES
	$E460	Load .A with the number of the buffer containing the side sectors from SS,X ($CD,X) and transfer this value into .Y.
	$E463	Pull the active buffer number off the stack and transfer it into .X.
	$E465	Load .A with $10, the side sector offset
	$E467	JSR to B0TOB0 ($DEA5) to move $10 (.A) bytes from buffer #(.X) to buffer #(.Y).
	$E46A	Load .A with $00 and JSR to SSDIR($DEDC) to set the pointer at DIRBUF ($94) to point to the start of the old SS buffer.
	$E46F	Load .Y with $02, and load .A with the side sector number from (DIRBUF),Y and save it onto the stack.
	$E474	Zero .A and JSR to SETPNT ($D4C8) to set the pointer at DIRBUF ($94) to point to the start of the new SS buffer.
	$E479	Pull the SS number off the stack, add 1, and store the result in the new side sector table at (DIRBUF),Y.
	$E47F	Multiply the SS number in .A by 2 (ASL), add 4, store the result (points to the new SS value in the buffer) in R3 ($89), and transfer this value into .Y.
	$E485	Subtract $02 from the result and store this pointer in R2 ($88).
	$E48A	Copy the current value of TRACK ($80) into R1 ($87) for use in SS update and into the new SS buffer at (DIRBUF),Y
	$E490	Increment .Y
	$E491	Copy the current value of SECTOR ($81) into R2 ($88) for use in SS update and into the new SS buffer at (DIRBUF),Y
	$E497	Set the track link at the start of the new SS block to $00.
	$E49C	Set the sector link at the start of the new SS block to $11 to indicate that the last non-zero character in the buffer is the one following the SS offset.
	$E4A1	Load .A with $10 (the SS offset) and JSR to SETPNT ($D4C8) to set the pointer to the new SS block.
	$E4A6	JSR to WRTAB ($DE50) to write out the new side sector block to disk.
	$E4A9	JSR to WATJOB ($D599) to wait for the write job to be completed.

Note: Finished creating new block. Now, revise old SS to reflect the new.

NAME	ADDRESS	DESCRIPTION OF WHAT ROM ROUTINE DOES
NS20	$E4AC	Load .X with the channel number from LINDX ($82).
	$E4AE	Load .A with the side sector buffer number from SS,X ($CD,X) and save this number onto the stack.
	$E4B1	JSR to GAFLGS ($DF9E) to get active buffer number and set flags.
	$E4B4	Load .X with the new channel number from LINDX ($82).
	$E4B6	Store the side sector buffer number from .A into SS,X ($CD,X). Note: this swaps the active buffer and the SS buffer.
	$E4B8	Pull the old side sector buffer number off the stack, load .X with the last buffer used from LBUSED ($0257), and store the old SS buffer # (in .A) into BUF0,X ($A7,X).
	$E4BE	Zero .A and JSR to SETPNT ($D4C8) to set the buffer pointer to the start of the buffer.
	$E4C3	Zero .Y and set the track link to point to the new SS block using the value from TRACK ($80). Increment .Y.
	$E4CA	Set the sector link to point to the new SS block using the value from SECTOR ($81).
	$E4CE	JMP to NS50 ($E4DE).
NS40	$E4D1	JSR to GETACT ($DF93) to get the active buffer number (returned in .A).
	$E4D4	Load .X with the channel number from LINDX ($82).
	$E4D6	JSR to IBRD ($DF1B) to read the next SS. buffer number (returned in .A).
	$E4DB	Zero .A and JSR to SETPNT ($D4C8) to set the buffer pointer to the start of the buffer.
NS50	$E4DE	Decrement the pointer in R4 ($8A) twice.
	$E4E2	Load .Y with the pointer into the buffer from R3 ($89).
	$E4E4	Load .A with the new SS track pointer from R1 ($87) and store this value into the data buffer at (DIRBUF),Y.
	$E4E8	Increment .Y.
	$E4E9	Load .A with the new SS sector pointer from R2 ($88) and store this value into the data buffer at (DIRBUF),Y.
	$E4ED	JSR to WRTOUT ($DE5E) to write out the revised side sector block.
	$E4F0	JSR to WATJOB ($D599) to wait for the write job to be completed.

NAME	ADDRESS	DESCRIPTION OF WHAT ROM ROUTINE DOES
	$E4F3	Load .Y with the pointer from $R4 ($8A) and compare it to $03. If .Y>$03, there are more side sectors to update so branch back to NS40.
	$E4F9	Terminate routine with a JMP to DBLBUF ($CF1E) to reset the active buffer.

ERROR MESSAGE TABLE $E4FC - $E5D4

Each entry consists of the applicable error numbers
followed by the message test with the first and last
characters OR'ed with $80. The key words in the text
are tokenized (values $80 - $8F). The tokenized word
list follows the main error message table.

Address	Error numbers	Error Message
$E4FC	$00	OK
$E500	$20,$21,$22,$23,$24,$27	READ ERROR
$E50B	$52	FILE TOO LARGE
$E517	$50	RECORD NOT PRESENT
$E522	$51	OVERFLOW IN RECORD
$E52F	$25,$28	WRITE ERROR
$E533	$26	WRITE PROTECT ON
$E540	$29	DISK ID MISMATCH
$E546	$30,$31,$32,$33,$34	SYNTAX ERROR
$E552	$60	WRITE FILE OPEN
$E556	$63	FILE EXISTS
$E55F	$64	FILE TYPE MISMATCH
$E567	$65	NO BLOCK
$E570	$66,$67	ILLEGAL TRACK OR SECTOR
$E589	$61	FILE NOT OPEN
$E58D	$39	FILE NOT FOUND
$E592	$01	FILES SCRATCHED
$E59F	$70	NO CHANNEL
$E5AA	$71	DIR ERROR
$E5AF	$72	DISK FULL
$E5B6	$73	CBM DOS V2.6 4030
$E5C8	$74	DRIVE NOT READY

TABLE OF TOKENIZED WORDS $E5D5 - $E609

Address				Address		
$E5D5	$09	ERROR		$E5F4	$06	NOT
$E5DB	$0A	WRITE		$E5F8	$07	FOUND
$E5E1	$03	FILE		$E5FE	$08	DISK
$E5E6	$04	OPEN		$E603	$0B	RECORD
$E5EB	$05	MISMATCH				

NAME	ADDRESS	DESCRIPTION OF WHAT ROM ROUTINE DOES
		Handle errors reported by controller:
		On entry: .A = error code number
		.X = job number
ERROR	$E60A	Save the error code onto the stack.
	$E60B	Store the job number into JOBNUM ($F9).
	$E60D	Transfer job number (from .X) to .A, multiply it by 2 (ASL), and transfer the result back into .X.
	$E610	Set TRACK ($80) and SECTOR ($81) using the values from the last header read in HDRS,X ($06,X) and HDRS+1,X ($07,X).
	$E618	Pull the disk controller error code off the stack and convert it into a DOS error code by:
	$E619	AND the error code in .A with $0F. If the result is $00, branch to ERR1 to handle error codes $10 - $14.
	$E61D	Compare the result to $0F (no drive). If the code is NOT $0F, branch to ERR2.
	$E621	Load .A with $74 (DOS no drive code) and branch to ERR3 (always).
ERR1	$E625	Load .A with $06.
ERR2	$E627	OR the code in .A with $20 and subtract 2 from the result.
ERR3	$E62D	Save the DOS error code onto the stack.
	$E62E	Compare the command number from CMDNUM ($022A) with $00 to see if this was a VALIDATE command. If not, branch to ERR4
	$E635	Set CMDNUM ($022A) to $FF.
	$E63A	Pull the DOS error code off the stack and JSR to ERRMSG ($E6C7) to transfer the error message to the error buffer.
	$E63E	JSR to INITDR ($D042) to initialize the drive and eliminate the bad BAM in RAM.
	$E641	JMP to CMDER3 ($E648) to complete the error handling.
ERR4	$E644	Pull the DOS error code off the stack.
CMDER2	$E645	JSR to ERRMSG ($E6C7) to transfer the the error message to the error buffer.
CMDER3	$E648	JSR to CLRCB ($C1BD) to clear out the command buffer.
	$E64B	Clear the write-BAM flag, WBAM ($02F9) so a bad copy of the BAM will not be written to disk.
	$E650	JSR to ERRON ($C12C) to start the error LED flashing.
	$E653	JSR to FREICH ($D4DA) to free the internal read or write channel.
	$E656	Zero BUFTAB+CBPTR ($A3) to clear the pointers.
	$E65A	Load .X with $45 (#TOPWRT) and transfer this value to the STACK POINTER to purge the stack

NAME	ADDRESS	DESCRIPTION OF WHAT ROM ROUTINE DOES
	$E65D	Load .A with the original secondary address from ORGSA ($84), AND it with $0F, and store the result as the current secondary address in SA ($83).
	$E663	Compare the secondary address (in .A) with $0F. If it is $0F (the command channel), branch to ERR10.
	$E667	Set the interrupt flag to prevent any interrupts!
	$E668	If the listener active flag in LSNACT ($79) is not $00, we are an active listener so branch to LSNERR.
	$E66C	If the talker active flag in TLKACT ($7A) is not $00, we are an active talker so branch to TLKERR.
	$E670	Load .X with the current secondary address from SA ($83).
	$E672	Load .A with the active channel number from LINTAB,X ($022B,X). If this channel number is $FF, the channel is inactive so branch to ERR10.
	$E679	AND the channel number (in .A) with $0F, store it as the current channel number in LINDX ($82) and JMP to TLERR ($E68E).
		--
		Talker error recovery: Release all bus lines and go idle.
TLKERR	$E680	JSR to FNDRCH ($D0EB) to find an unused read channel.
	$E683	JSR to ITERR ($EA4E) to release all bus lines and JMP to IDLE ($EBE7).
		Listener error recovery: Release all bus lines and go idle.
LSNERR	$E688	JSR to FNDRCH ($D0EB) to find an unused read channel.
	$E68B	JSR to ITERR ($EA4E) to release all bus lines and JMP to IDLE ($EBE7).
TLERR	$E68E	Unused on the 1541
ERR10	$E698	Terminate routine with a JMP to IDLE ($EBE7).
		--
		Convert hex to BCD: On entry: .A contains hex number On exit: .A contains BCD number
HEXDEC	$E69B	Transfer hex from .A to .X.
	$E69C	Zero .A and set decimal mode (SED).
HEX0	$E69F	Compare .X value to $00. If equal, branch to HEX5 to exit.
	$E6A3	Clear carry flag, add 1 to value in .A, decrement .X, and JMP back to HEX0.
HEX5	$E6AA	Clear decimal mode (CLD).

NAME	ADDRESS	DESCRIPTION OF WHAT ROM ROUTINE DOES
		Convert BCD to ASCII decimal digit.
		On exit: .X contains BCD number
		(CB+2)Y contains ASCII
BCDDEC	$E6AB	Transfer BCD from .A to .X.
	$E6AC	Divide BCD value in .X by 16 (4 x LSR)
	$E6B0	JSR to BCD2 ($E6B4) to convert the most significant digit to ASCII.
	$E6B3	Transfer original BCD byte from .X to .A
BCD2	$E6B4	AND the BCD value in .A with $0F to mask off the higher order nybble, OR the result with $30 (convert to ASCII), and store the ASCII value in (CB+2)Y; ($A5)Y
	$E6BA	Increment .Y
	$E6BB	Terminate routine with an RTS.
		--
OKERR	$E6BC	Transfer error message to error buffer: JSR to ERROFF ($C123) to turn off error LED.
	$E6BF	Load .A with $00 (no error).
ERRTS0	$E6C1	Set TRACK ($80) and SECTOR ($81) to $00.
ERRMSG	$E6C7	Load .Y with $00.
	$E6C9	Set pointer at CB+2/3 ($A5/6) to point to the error buffer ($02D5).
	$E6D1	JSR to BCDDEC ($E6AB) to convert the BCD number in .A to ASCII and store it at the start of the error buffer.
	$E6D4	Store $2C "," after the error code in the error buffer (CB+2),Y; ($A5),Y.
	$E6D8	Increment .Y (points into error buffer).
	$E6D9	Copy the first character of the error buffer from ERRBUF ($02D5) into the channel data area CHNDAT+ERRCHN ($0243).
	$E6DF	Transfer the error number from .X to .A and JSR to ERMOVE ($E706) to move the error message into the error buffer.
	$E6E3	Store $2C "," after the error message in the error buffer (CB+2),Y; ($A5),Y.
	$E6E7	Increment .Y (points into error buffer).
	$E6E8	Load .A with the track number from TRACK ($80).
	$E6EA	JSR to BCDDEC ($E6AB) to convert the track number in .A to ASCII and store it in the error buffer.
	$E6ED	Store $2C "," after the track number in the error buffer (CB+2),Y; ($A5),Y.
	$E6F1	Increment .Y (points into error buffer).
	$E6F2	Load .A with the sector number from SECTOR ($81).
	$E6F4	JSR to BCDDEC ($E6AB) to convert the sector number in .A to ASCII and store it in the error buffer.

NAME	ADDRESS	DESCRIPTION OF WHAT ROM ROUTINE DOES
	$E6F7	Decrement the .Y pointer by 1, transfer the result to .A, clear the carry flag, add $D5 (the start of the error buffer), and store the final result (points to the last character) into LSTCHR+ERRCHN ($0249).
	$E6FF	Increment the lo byte of the pointer in CB+2 ($A5) by 1 so it points to the second character of the message (we put the first character into the channel data area already.
	$E701	Set error channel status CHNRDY+ERRCHN ($F7) to $88 to indicate that it is ready-to-talk.
	$E705	Terminate routine with an RTS.
		--
		Move the error message from the error table to the error buffer. The tokens in the table are converted to words.
ERMOVE	$E706	Transfer the error message number from .A to .X.
	$E707	Save the current values of R0 ($86) and R0+1 ($87) onto the stack so we can use this as a temporary pointer.
	$E70D	Set up a pointer in R0/R0+1 to point to the error message table in ROM ($E4FC).
	$E715	Transfer the error number back into .A.
	$E716	Zero .X to use as an indirect pointer.
E10	$E718	Compare the error number (in .A) with the error number in the table (R0,X) ($86,X). If a match is found, branch to E50.
	$E71C	Save error number onto the stack.
	$E71D	JSR to EADV2 ($E775) to advance the pointer to the error table.
	$E720	If carry flag is clear, there are more messages to check so branch to E30
E20	$E722	No more messages so JSR to EADV2 ($E775) to advance the pointer.
	$E725	If carry flag is clear, we are not done with the message yet so branch to E20.
E30	$E727	Compare the hi byte of the pointer in R0+1 ($87) to $E6. If the pointer is less than $E6, there is more table left so branch to E40. If the pointer is greater than $E6, we are past the end of the table so branch to E45.
	$E72F	The hi bytes match so compare the lo bytes of the pointer in R0 ($86) with $0A (the end of the table). If we are past the end, branch to E45.
E40	$E735	Pull the error number off the stack and JMP to E10 to continue checking.

NAME	ADDRESS	DESCRIPTION OF WHAT ROM ROUTINE DOES
E45	$E739	Can't find error number in table so pop the error number off the stack and JMP to E90 ($E74D) to quit.
E50	$E73D	The error number has been located so JSR to EADV1 ($E767) to advance past the other error numbers.
	$E740	If carry flag is clear, we have not advanced far enough so branch to E50.
E55	$E742	JSR to E60 ($E754) to check for token and put character(s) into buffer.
	$E745	JSR to EADV1 ($E767) to advance pointer.
	$E748	If carry flag is clear, there is more to do so branch back to E55.
	$E74A	JSR to E60 ($E754) to check for token or last word.
E90	$E74D	All done! Pull original R0 and R0+1 values off the stack and replace them.
	$E753	Terminate routine with an RTS.

		Sub to check for token or word and put it into the buffer.
E60	$E754	Compare the character in .A with $20 (the maximum token number +1). If .A is greater, this is not a token so branch to E70.
	$E758	Save token (in .A) into .X.
	$E759	Store $20 (implied leading space) into the buffer at (CB+2),Y; ($A5),Y.
	$E75D	Increment .Y.
	$E75E	Move the token from .X back into .A.
	$E75F	JSR to ERMOVE ($E706) to add the token word to the message.
	$E762	Terminate routine with an RTS.
E70	$E763	Store character (in .A) into the buffer at (CB+2),Y; ($A5),Y.
	$E765	Increment .Y pointer into error buffer.
	$E766	Terminate routine with an RTS.

		Sub: Advance error pointer before move:
EADV1	$E767	Increment the lo byte of the pointer in R0 ($86). If the new value is not $00, branch to EA10.
	$E76B	Increment the hi byte of the pointer in R0+1 ($87).
EA10	$E76D	Load .A with the next character from the error message table (R0,X); ($A1,X).
	$E76F	Shift the byte in .A left to set the carry flag if this is the first or last character in the message.
	$E770	Load .A with the next character from the error message table (R0,X); ($A1,X).

NAME	ADDRESS	DESCRIPTION OF WHAT ROM ROUTINE DOES
	$E772	AND the character in .A with $7F to mask off bit 7.
	$E774	Terminate routine with an RTS.
EADV2	$E775	Sub: Advance error pointer after move: JSR to EA10 ($E76D) to get the next byte from the error message table.
	$E778	Increment the lo byte of the pointer in R0 ($86). If the new value is not $00, branch to EA20.
	$E77C	Increment the hi byte of the pointer in R0+1 ($87).
EA20	$E77E	Terminate routine with an RTS.

UTILITY LOADER PROGRAM

This utility is used to load and execute user programs
or system utilities from disk.
This utility may be used in two ways:
a) On power-up:
   If the data and clock lines are grounded at power up,
   the routine is entered. It waits until the ground clip
   is removed and then loads the first file found in the
   directory into disk RAM using the first two bytes of
   the file as the load address. Once the file is loaded,
   it is executed starting at the first byte.
b) Normal entry:
   The disk command "&:filename" will load and execute
   the file whose filename is specified. For example:
        PRINT#15,"&0:DISK TASK"

File structure:
   The utility or program must be of the following form.
   File type: USR
   Bytes 1/2: Load address in disk RAM (lo/hi).
   Byte 3:   Lo byte of the length of the routine
   Bytes 4/N: Disk routine machine code.
   Byte N+1: Checksum. Note that the checksum includes
              all bytes including the load address.
              formula: CHECKSUM = CHECKSUM + BYTE + CARRY

NOTE: Routines may be longer than 256 bytes. However,
      there MUST be a valid checksum byte after the
      number of bytes specified in byte #3 and after
      each subsequent 256 bytes!

BOOT2	$E77F	Exit routine with an RTS.
BOOT	$E780	Load .A with input port data from PB ($1800). Transfer data from .A to .X.
	$E784	AND the data byte (in .A) with $04 to see if clock is grounded. If not, branch to BOOT2 to exit.

362

NAME	ADDRESS	DESCRIPTION OF WHAT ROM ROUTINE DOES
	$E788	Transfer data byte from .X to .A.
	$E789	AND the data byte (in .A) with $01 to see if data line is grounded. If not, branch to BOOT2 to exit.
	$E78D	Clear interrupt flag so that background routines will run.
BOOT3	$E78F	BOOT CLIP MUST BE ON! Load .A with input port data from PB ($1800).
	$E791	AND the data byte (in .A) with $05 to see if clip has been removed. If not, branch to BOOT3 to wait until it is.
	$E795	Set the number of files to $01 by incrementing F2CNT ($0278).
	$E798	Set the command string length to $01 by incrementing CMDSIZ ($0274).
	$E79B	Set the first character in the command buffer, CMDBUF ($0200), to $2A ("*") to match any file name.
	$E7A0	JMP to BOOT4 ($E7A8) to continue.
UTLODR	$E7A3	NORMAL ENTRY POINT Load .A with $8D and JSR to PARSE ($C268) to parse the command string.
BOOT4	$E7A8	JSR to KILLP ($F258) to kill protect. Does nothing on the 1541!
	$E7AB	Load .A with the file count from F2CNT ($0278) and save it on the stack.
	$E7AF	Set file count in F2CNT ($0278) to $01.
	$E7B4	Set first-byte flag in R0 ($86) to $FF.
	$E7B8	JSR to LOOKUP ($C44F) to locate the file name on the disk.
	$E7BB	Check the track link for the file found in FILTRK ($0280). If it is $00, the file was not found so branch to UTLD00.
	$E7C0	Load .A with $39 to indicate a FILE NOT FOUND error and JSR to CMDERR ($C1C8) to exit.
UTLD00	$E7C5	Pull original file count off the stack and restore it into F2CNT ($0278).
	$E7C9	Set TRACK ($80) from the track link for the file from FILTRK ($0280).
	$E7CE	Set SECTOR ($81) from the sector link for the file from FILSEC ($0285).
	$E7D3	Load .A with $03 (USER FILE TYPE) and JSR to OPNTYP ($D477) to open the file.
UTLD10	$E7D8	Load .A with $00 and store it in R1($87) to initialize the checksum.
	$E7DC	JSR to GTABYT ($E839) to get the first byte from the file (lo of load address).
	$E7DF	Store the lo byte of the load address in R2 ($88).

NAME	ADDRESS	DESCRIPTION OF WHAT ROM ROUTINE DOES
	$E7E1	JSR to ADDSUM ($E84B) to add the byte into the checksum.
	$E7E4	JSR to GTABYT ($E839) to get the second byte from the file (hi of load address).
	$E7E7	Store the hi byte of the load address in R3 ($89).
	$E7E9	JSR to ADDSUM ($E84B) to add the byte into the checksum.
	$E7EC	Load .A with the flag from R0 ($86). If the flag is $00, this is not the load address so branch to UTLD20.
	$E7F0	Load lo byte of load address from R2 ($88) and save it onto the stack.
	$E7F3	Load hi byte of load address from R3 ($89) and save it onto the stack.
	$E7F6	Set first-byte flag in R0 ($86) to $00.
UTLD20	$E7FA	JSR to GTABYT ($E839) to get the data byte count from the file.
	$E7FD	Store the data byte count in R4 ($8A).
	$E7FF	JSR to ADDSUM ($E84B) to add the byte into the checksum.
UTLD30	$E802	JSR to GTABYT ($E839) to get a data byte from the file.
	$E805	Zero .Y and store the data byte (in .A) at desired address, (R2),Y; ($88),Y.
	$E809	JSR to ADDSUM ($E84B) to add the byte into the checksum.
	$E80C	Increment the lo byte of the pointer in R2 ($88) by $01. If the result is not $00, branch to UTLD35.
	$E813	Increment the hi byte of the pointer in R3 ($89) by $01.
UTLD35	$E817	Decrement the byte counter in R4 ($8A). If the result is not $00, there are more bytes to get so branch back to UTLD30.
	$E81B	JSR to GIBYTE ($CA35) to get a data byte from the file without an EOI check.
	$E81E	Load .A with the checksum from DATA($85) and compare it with the computed checksum in R1 ($87). If they match, all is OK so branch to UTLD50.
	$E824	Bad checksum so JSR to GETHDR ($DE3E) to set TRACK and SECTOR from the header.
	$E827	Load .A with $50 to indicate a NO RECORD error and JSR to CMDER2 ($E645).
UTLD50	$E82C	Load .A with the EOI flag from EIOFLG ($F8). If the flag is NOT $00, we are not done yet so branch back to UTLD10 to do another 256 bytes.

NAME	ADDRESS	DESCRIPTION OF WHAT ROM ROUTINE DOES
	$E830	Routine all loaded so pull load address off the stack (lo/hi), set up a jump vector in R2/3 ($88/9), and do an indirect JMP to the routine via (R2).
		Subroutines for UTLODR
		Get a byte from the file opened using the internal read channel. There is an end-of-file check done. If EOI occurs, a #51 DOS error is reported.
GTABYT	$E839	JSR to GIBYTE ($CA35) to fetch a byte and store it in DATA ($85).
	$E83C	Test the end of information flag, EOIFLG ($F8). If NOT $00, we have not come to the end so branch to GTABYE.
	$E840	We have an EOI condition. JSR to GETHDR ($DE3E) to set TRACK and SECTOR from the header.
	$E843	Load .A with $51 to indicate a RECORD SIZE error and JSR to CMDER2 ($E645).
GTABYE	$E848	Load .A with the byte from DATA ($85)
	$E84A	Terminate routine with an RTS.
		Compute the running checksum in R1: On entry: .A = new byte to add
ADDSUM	$E84B	Clear the carry flag.
	$E84C	Add the byte in R1 ($87) to the byte in .A and then add $00 to the result to add in the carry bit.
	$E850	Store the new checksum into R1.
	$E852	Terminate routine with an RTS.
		SERIAL BUS COMMUNICATION ROUTINES
		ENTRY POINT FOR IRQ ROUTINE TO SERVICE ATTENTION (ATN) SIGNALS FROM THE C-64.
ATNIRQ	$E853	Load .A with the contents of PA1 ($1801) to clear the interrupt (IRQ) flag (CA1).
	$E856	Store $01 in ATNPND ($7C) to indicate that an ATN request is pending.
	$E85A	Terminate routine with an RTS.
		Service the attention request from the C-64.
ATNSRV	$E85B	Set the interrupt flag (SEI) to prevent any interrupts.
	$E85C	Store $00 in ATNPND ($7C) to indicate that no ATN request is pending.
	$E860	Zero the listener and talker active flags LSNACT ($79) and TLKACT ($7A).

NAME	ADDRESS	DESCRIPTION OF WHAT ROM ROUTINE DOES
ATNS15	$E864	Load .X with $45 and transfer this value to the stack pointer to reset the stack.
	$E867	Store $80 in the EOI flag, EOIFLG ($F8) to indicate a non-EOI state.
	$E86B	Store $80 in the ATN mode flag, ATNMOD ($7D) to set ATN mode for ACPT routine
	$E86D	JSR to CLKHI ($E9B7) to wait for the clock line go high.
	$E870	JSR to DATLOW ($E9A5) to set the data line low as a response.
	$E873	To get hardware control of the data line acknowledge the attention signal by: loading .A with the contents of port B, PB ($1800), OR the byte with $10 to set the ACK ATN bit, and store the result back into port B, PB ($1800).
	$E87B	Check to see if the ATN signal is still present by: loading .A with the contents of port B, PB ($1800). If bit 7 is not set, the ATN signal is gone so branch to ATNS20 ($E8D7).
	$E880	AND the contents of .A with $04 to see if the clock line is still low. If bit 2 is set (result of AND is not $00), the clock line is still low so branch back to ATNS15 to wait.
	$E884	Clock line went high so there is a command byte waiting for us. JSR to ACPTR ($E9C9) to get the command byte.
	$E887	Compare the command byte (in .A) with $3F (unlisten). If this is not an unlisten command, branch to ATN35.
	$E88B	General unlisten command received. Zero the listener active flag, LSNACT ($7A) and branch to ATN122 ($E902).
ATN35	$E891	Compare the command byte (in .A) with $5F (untalk). If this is not an untalk command, branch to ATN40.
	$E895	General untalk command received. Zero the talker active flag, TLKACT ($7A) and branch to ATN122 ($E902).
ATN40	$E89B	Compare the command byte (in .A) with our talk address in TLKADR ($78). If this is not our talk address, branch to ATN45.

NAME	ADDRESS	DESCRIPTION OF WHAT ROM ROUTINE DOES
	$E89F	Talk command for us. Set the talker active flag, TLKACT ($7A) to $01, the listener active flag, LSNACT ($79) to $00, and branch to ATN95.
ATN45	$E8A9	Compare the command byte (in .A) with our listen address in LSNADR ($77). If this is not our listen address, branch to ATN50.
	$E8AD	Listen command for us. Set the listener active flag, LSNACT ($79) to $01, the talker active flag, TLKACT ($7A) to $00, and branch to ATN95
ATN50	$E8B7	Save the command byte by transferring it from .A to .X.
	$E8B8	Test if the command byte is a secondary address by AND'ing it with $60. If the result is not $60, this is not a secondary address so branch to ATN120. NOTE: SA = $60 + N
	$E8BE	A secondary address for the drive. Transfer the original command byte from .X back into .A.
	$E8BF	Store the original secondary address byte into ORGSA ($84).
	$E8C1	AND the secondary address (in .A) with $0F to strip off any junk and store the result as the current secondary address in SA ($83).
	$E8C5	Test if this is a CLOSE command for this secondary address. Load .A with the original secondary address from ORGSA ($84). AND this value with $F0 to mask off the low nybble. If the result is not $E0, this is not a CLOSE command so branch to ATN122.
	$E8CD	CLOSE the file with this SA. Clear the interrupt flag (CLI) to enable interrupts.
	$E8CE	JSR to CLOSE ($DAC0) to close the file. -- WARNING: CLOSE routine does not return in time to be handled by ATN122 --
	$E8D1	Set the interrupt flag (SEI) to prevent any interrupts.
ATN95	$E8D2	Test if the ATN signal is still present. If it is, branch back to ATN30.

NAME	ADDRESS	DESCRIPTION OF WHAT ROM ROUTINE DOES
ATSN20	$E8D7	ATN SIGNAL GONE - CARRY OUT COMMAND Store $00 in ATNMOD ($7D) to clear the attention mode.
	$E8DB	Release the ATN ACK line by loading the byte from port B, PB ($1800), AND'ing it with $EF ($FF-ATNA), and storing the result back into port B ($1800).
	$E8E3	Test the listener active flag, LSNACT ($79) to se if we are supposed to be a listener. If flag is $00, branch to ATN100.
	$E8E7	BE AN ACTIVE TALKER. JSR to DATHI ($E99C) to free data line. serial bus.
	$E8EA	JMP to IDLE ($EBE7).
ATN100	$E8ED	Test the talker active flag, TLKACT($7A) to see if we are supposed to talk. If flag is $00, branch to ATN110.
	$E8F1	BE AN ACTIVE TALKER. JSR to DATHI ($E99C) to free data line.
	$E8F4	JSR to CLKLOW ($E9AE) to pull clock low.
	$E8F7	JSR to TALK ($E909) to talk on the bus.
ATN110	$E8FA	JMP to ILERR ($EA4E) to release all the lines and shift to idle mode.
ATN120	$E8FD	FIX SO DEVICE NOT PRESENT IS REPORTED Store $10 in PB ($1800) to kill all the lines except ATN ACK (ATN ACKnowledge).
ATN122	$E902	Test if ATN signal is still present (bit 7 of PB set). If gone, branch to ATNS20. If still present, loop to ATN122.

SERIAL BUS TALK ROUTINES

NAME	ADDRESS	DESCRIPTION OF WHAT ROM ROUTINE DOES
TALK	$E909	Set the interrupt flag (SEI) to prevent any interrupts.
	$E90A	JSR to FNDRCH ($D0EB) to find an unused read channel. If no channel is available branch to NOTLK to exit.
TALK1	$E90F	Load .X with the current channel number from LINDX ($82).
	$E911	Load .A with the channel status from CHNRDY,X ($F2,X). If bit 7 is set, the status is OK so branch to TLK05.
NOTLK	$E905	Terminate routine with an RTS.
TLK05	$E906	NOTE: CODE ADDED TO FIX VERIFY ERROR JSR to TSTATN ($EA59) to test for an ATN signal.

NAME	ADDRESS	DESCRIPTION OF WHAT ROM ROUTINE DOES
	$E909	JSR to DEBNC ($E9C0) to test if the clock signal is gone. NOTE: this must be 80 microseconds or more from JMP TALK1.
	$E91C	AND the data byte in .A with $01 and save it on the stack.
	$E91F	JSR to CLKHI ($E9B7) to set the clock line high.
	$E922	Pull the test byte off the stack. If it is $00, this is a VERIFY ERROR so branch to TLK02 to send an EOI.
TALK2	$E925	JSR to TSTATN ($EA59) to test for an ATN signal.
	$E928	JSR to DEBNC ($E9C0) to test if the data line has been set low.
	$E92B	AND the test byte (in .A) with $01. If the result is not $00, the line has not been set hi (no response) so branch back to TALK2 to wait for response.
	$E92F	Load .X with the current channel number from LINDX ($82).
	$E931	Load .A with the channel status from CHNRDY,X ($F2,X), and AND it with $08 to test if we have an EOI condition. If the result is not $00, we do not have an EOI so branch to NOEOI ($E94B). Send an EOI signal to the C-64 by:
TLK02	$E937	JSR to TSTATN ($EA59) to test for an ATN signal.
	$E93A	JSR to DEBNC ($E9C0) to send an EOI and test if the data line has been set.
	$E93D	AND the test byte (in .A) with $01. If the result is not $00, the line has not been set hi (no response) so branch back to TLK02 to wait for hi response.
TLK03	$E941	JSR to TSTATN ($EA59) to test for an ATN signal.
	$E944	JSR to DEBNC ($E9C0) to test if the data line has been set.
	$E947	AND the test byte (in .A) with $01. If the result equals $00, the line has not been set lo (no response) so branch back to TLK02 to wait for lo response.
NOEOI	$E94B	JSR to CLKLOW ($E9AE) to set the clock line low.
	$E94E	JSR to TSTATN ($EA59) to test for an ATN signal.
	$E951	JSR to DEBNC ($E9C0) to test if the data line has been set.
	$E954	AND the test byte (in .A) with $01. If the result is not $00, the line has not been set hi (no response) so branch back to NOEOI to wait for hi response.

NAME	ADDRESS	DESCRIPTION OF WHAT ROM ROUTINE DOES
	$E958	Store $08 in CONT ($98) to set up the bit counter.
ISR01	$E95C	JSR to DEBNC ($E9C0) to let the port settle.
	$E95F	AND the test byte (in .A) with $01 to be sure the line is hi before we send. If the result is not $00, the line has not been set hi (no response) so branch to FRMFRX($E999) to wait for hi response
ISR02	$E963	Load .X with the current channel number from LINDX ($82).
	$E965	Load .A with the channel data byte from CHNDAT,X ($F2,X). Rotate the status byte one bit right (ROR) and store the result back into CHNDAT,X ($F2,X).
	$E96C	If the carry bit is set, branch to ISRHI to send a 1.
	$E96E	JSR to DATLOW ($E9A5) to send a 0.
	$E971	Branch to ISRCLK to clock it.
ISRHI	$E973	JSR to DATHI ($E99C) to send a 1.
ISRCLK	$E976	JSR to CLKHI ($E9B7) to set the clock line hi. (rising edge).
	$E979	Load .A with the speed flag from DRVTRK+1 ($23). If the flag is not $00, no slow down is required so branch to ISR03.
	$E97B	JSR to SLOWD ($FEF3) to slow down the data transmission.
ISR03	$E980	JSR to CLKDAT ($FEFB) to pull the clock low and release the data.
	$E983	Decrement the bit count in CONT ($98). If the count is not $00, there are more bits to send from this byte so branch back to ISR01.
ISR04	$E987	JSR to DEBNC ($E9C0) to test if the data line has been set.
	$E98A	AND the test byte (in .A) with $01. If the result equals $00, the line has not been set lo (no response) so branch back to ISR04 to wait for lo response.
	$E991	Clear the interrupt flag (CLI) to allow interrupts in preparation for sending the next byte.
	$E992	JSR to GET ($D3AA) to get the next data byte to send.
	$E995	Set the interrupt flag (SEI) to prevent any interrupts.
	$E996	JMP to TALK1 to keep on talking.

NAME	ADDRESS	DESCRIPTION OF WHAT ROM ROUTINE DOES
		TALK SUBROUTINES:
FRMERX	$E999	JMP to FRMERR ($EA4E) to release all lines and go to idle mode.
DATHI	$E99C	Set data out line high. Load .A with the byte from port B, PB ($1800), AND it with $FD ($FF-DATOUT), and store the result back in PB ($1800).
	$E9A4	Terminate routine with an RTS.
DATLOW	$E9A5	Set data out line lo. Load .A with the byte from port B, PB ($1800), OR it with $02 (DATOUT), and store the result back in PB ($1800).
	$E9AD	Terminate routine with an RTS.
CLKLOW	$E9AE	Set clock line lo. Load .A with the byte from port B, PB ($1800), OR it with $08 (CLKOUT), and store the result back in PB ($1800).
	$E9B6	Terminate routine with an RTS.
CLKHI	$E9B7	Set clock line hi. Load .A with the byte from port B, PB ($1800), AND it with $F7 ($FF-CLKOUT), and store the result back in PB ($1800).
	$E9BF	Terminate routine with an RTS.
DEBNC	$E9C0	Wait for response on bus. Load .A with the byte from port B, PB ($1800). Compare the old port value (.A) with the current value of PB ($1800). If there is no change, branch to DEBNC.
	$E9C8	Terminate routine with an RTS.
		SERIAL BUS LISTEN ROUTINES
ACPTR	$E9C9	Store $08 in CONT ($98) to set up the bit counter.
ACP00A	$E9CD	JSR to TSTATN ($EA59) to test for an ATN signal.
	$E9D0	JSR to DEBNC ($E9C0) to test if the clock line has been set.
	$E9D3	AND the test byte (in .A) with $04. If the result is not $00, the line has not been set hi (no response) so branch back to ACP00A to wait for hi response.
	$E9D7	JSR to DATHI ($E99C) to make data line high.
	$E9DA	Store $01 in T1HC1 ($1805) to set up for a 255 microsecond delay.
ACP00	$E9DF	JSR to TSTATN ($EA59) to test for an ATN signal.

NAME	ADDRESS	DESCRIPTION OF WHAT ROM ROUTINE DOES
	$E9E2	Load .A with the interrupt flag register from IFR1 ($180D) and AND the test byte with $40. If the result is NOT $00, the time has run out so it MUST be an EOI. Since it is an EOI, branch to ACP00B.
	$E9E9	JSR to DEBNC ($E9C0) to test if the clock line has been set.
	$E9EC	AND the test byte (in .A) with $04. If the result is $00, the clock line has not been set lo (no response) so branch back to ACP00 to wait for lo response. If the result is not $00, the line has been set lo so branch to ACP01 to go on.
ACP00B	$E9F2	JSR to DATLOW ($E9A5) to set data line low as a response.
	$E9F5	Load .X with $0A, and loop to count .X down to $00 to delay for talker turn around time.
	$E9FA	JSR to DATHI ($E99C) to make data line high.
ACP02A	$E9FD	JSR to TSTATN ($EA59) to test for an ATN signal.
	$EA00	JSR to DEBNC ($E9C0) to test if the clock line has been set.
	$EA03	AND the test byte (in .A) with $04. If the result is $00, the clock line has not been set lo (no response) so branch back to ACP02A to wait for lo response.
	$EA07	Store $00 in EOIFLG ($F8) to indicate that an EOI has been received.
ACP01 ACP03	$EA0B	Load .A with the data byte from port B, PB ($1800), EOR it with $01 to find the complement of the data bit, shift the data bit into the carry flag (LSR). AND the result in .A with $02 to test if the clock line has been set high to indicate valid data. If the result is NOT $00, the clock line has not been set hi yet so branch back to ACP03 and try again.
	$EA15	Three $EA (NOP) bytes to fill space left by speed-up to fix VC20 901229-02 ROM's.
	$EA18	We have valid data bit in the carry so do a rotate right (ROR) on DATA ($85) to store the bit into the data byte.
ACP03A	$EA1A	JSR to TSTATN ($EA59) to test for an ATN signal.
	$EA1D	JSR to DEBNC ($E9C0) to test if the clock line has been set.

NAME	ADDRESS	DESCRIPTION OF WHAT ROM ROUTINE DOES
	$EA20	AND the test byte (in .A) with $04. If the result is $00, the clock line has not been set lo (no response) so branch back to ACP03A to wait for lo response.
	$EA24	Decrement the bit counter in CONT ($98). If the count is not $00, there are more bits to get so branch back to ACP03.
	$EA28	JSR to DATLOW ($E9A5) to set data line low as a response.
	$EA2B	Load .A with the data byte from DATA ($85).
	$EA2D	Terminate routine with an RTS.

MAIN LISTEN ROUTINE

NAME	ADDRESS	DESCRIPTION OF WHAT ROM ROUTINE DOES
LISTEN	$EA2E	Set interrupt mask (SEI) to prevent any interrupts.
	$EA2F	JSR to FNDWCH ($D107) to find an unused write channel. If none available, branch to LSN15.
	$EA34	Load .A with the write channel status from CHNRDY,X ($F2,X).
	$EA36	Rotate the status byte right (ROR). If the carry bit is set, the write channel is inactive so branch to LSN30.
LSN15	$EA39	Test if this is an OPEN command by: loading .A with the original secondary address from ORGSA ($84) and AND'ing it with $F0. If the result is $F0, it is an OPEN command so branch to LSN30.
	$EA41	Not an active channel so JMP to ILERR ($EA4E) to abort.
LSN30	$EA44	JSR to ACPTR ($E9C9) to get a data byte.
	$EA47	Clear interrupt mask (CLI) to allow interrupts.
	$EA48	JSR to PUT ($CFB7) to put the data byte into its proper place (DATA, EOI, SA).
	$EA4B	JMP to LISTEN ($EA2E) to keep on listening.

NAME	ADDRESS	DESCRIPTION OF WHAT ROM ROUTINE DOES
FRMERR ITERR ILERR	$EA4E	Release all bus lines and go idle: Store $00 into port B, PB ($1800) and JMP to IDLE ($EBE7).

LISTEN SUBROUTINES

NAME	ADDRESS	DESCRIPTION OF WHAT ROM ROUTINE DOES
ATNLOW	$EA56	JMP to ATNSRV ($E85B) to service ATN request.

NAME	ADDRESS	DESCRIPTION OF WHAT ROM ROUTINE DOES
TSTATN	$EA59	Test if in ATN mode: Load .A with the attention mode flag from ATNMOD ($7D). If $00, we are not in attention mode so branch to TSTA50.

NAME	ADDRESS	DESCRIPTION OF WHAT ROM ROUTINE DOES
	$EA5D	We are in attention mode. Load .A with the byte from port B, PB ($1800). If bit 7 of this byte is clear, the ATN signal is gone so branch to TATN20 to do what we were told.
TSTRTN	$EA62	The ATN signal hasn't gone away yet so exit with an RTS.
TSTA50	$EA63	We are not in attention mode now. Load .A with the byte from port B, PB ($1800) If bit 7 of this byte is clear, there is no ATN signal present so branch to TSTRTN to exit. If bit 7 of this byte is set, there is an ATN signal present so JMP to ATNSRV ($E85B) to service the ATN request.
TATN20	$EA6B	JMP to ATNS20 ($E8D7) to carry out the attention command.

FLASH LED TO SIGNAL ERROR

NAME	ADDRESS	DESCRIPTION OF WHAT ROM ROUTINE DOES
PEZRO	$EA6E $EA70	No-error status: Load .X with $00. .BYTE $2C skips next two bytes.
PERR	$EA71 $EA73	Error status: Load .X with the error number from TEMP ($6F). Transfer the error number from .X into the stack pointer to use the stack as a storage register.
PE20	$EA74	Transfer the value of the stack pointer (the error number) into .X
PE30	$EA75	Load .A with $08 (the LED mask), OR it with the data port controlling the LED's LEDPRT ($1C00). and JMP to PEA7A ($FEEA) to turn on LED. NOTE: this is a patch to be sure the data direction register for the LED line is set to output.
REA7D	$EA7D	Transfer the byte in .Y to .A
PD10	$EA7E	Clear the carry flag.
PD20	$EA7F $EA83	Add $01 to the contents of .A. If the result is not $00, branch to PD20. Decrement .Y (the hi byte of the timer). If value of .Y is not $00, branch to PD10.
	$EA86	Turn off LED(s). Load .A with the byte from the data port controlling the LED, LEDPRT ($1C00). AND the byte with $F7 ($FF - LED mask) and store the result back into LEDPRT($1C00) to turn OFF the LED.

NAME	ADDRESS	DESCRIPTION OF WHAT ROM ROUTINE DOES
PE40	$EA8E	Transfer the byte in .Y to .A
PD11	$EA8F	Clear the carry flag.
PD21	$EA90	Add $01 to the contents of .A. If the result is not $00, branch to PD21.
	$EA94	Decrement .Y (the hi byte of the timer). If value of .Y is not $00, branch to PD11.
	$EA97	Decrement the count in .X. If the result is greater than or equal to $00, branch to PE30 to flash again.
	$EA9A	Compare .X to $FC to see if we have waited long enough between groups of flashes. If .X <> $FC branch to PE40 to wait some more. If .X = $FC, branch to PE20 to repeat the sequence.

INITIALIZATION OF DISK

NAME	ADDRESS	DESCRIPTION OF WHAT ROM ROUTINE DOES
DSKINT	$EAA0	Set the interrupt flag (SEI) to prevent interrupts.
	$EAA1	Clear the decimal mode flag (CLD).
	$EAA2	Store $FF into the data direction register DDRA1 ($1803).
	$EAA7	Load .X and .Y with $00.
		Fill zero page with ascending pattern
PV10	$EAAC	Transfer the byte from .X into .A.
	$EAAD	Store the byte from .A into $00,X.
	$EAAF	Increment .X. If .X is not $00, branch back to PV10.
		Check zero page bits.
PV20	$EAB2	Transfer the byte from .X into .A.
	$EAB3	Compare the byte in .A with $00,X. If no match, branch to PEZRO ($EA6E).
PV30	$EAB7	Increment the contents of $00,X by 1.
	$EAB9	Increment .Y. If .Y is not $00, branch back to PV30.
	$EABC	Check if $00,X equals byte in .A. If no match, something is wrong so branch to PEZRO ($EA6E).
	$EAC0	Store the $00 byte from .Y into $00,X.
	$EAC2	Check if $00,X equals $00. If it does not, something is wrong so branch to PEZRO ($EA6E).
	$EAC6	Increment the counter in .X. If the result is not $00, we have more of zero page to check so branch back to PV20.
		Test the two 64K bit ROM's.
RM10	$EAC9	Increment TEMP ($6F) to set the next error number ($01=$E/F;$02=$C/D ROM).

NAME	ADDRESS	DESCRIPTION OF WHAT ROM ROUTINE DOES
	$EACB	Store .X value (page number) into IP+1 ($76) as the hi byte of the pointer.
	$EACF	Set lo byte of pointer, IP ($75) to $00.
	$EAD1	Set .Y to $00 and .X to $20 (32 pages).
	$EAD4	Clear the carry flag.
RT10	$EAD5	Decrement the hi byte of the pointer in IP+1 ($76) and we'll do it backwards.
RT20	$EAD7	Add the ROM value from (IP),Y to the contents of .A, increment the Y pointer, and if .Y is not $00, branch back to RT20 to do another byte from this page.
	$EADC	Decrement .X (page count). If the page count is not zero, branch to RT10 to do the next page of the ROM.
	$EADF	Add $00 to .A to add in the last carry.
	$EAE1	Transfer the checksum from .A to .X.
	$EAE2	Compare the checksum in .A with the hi byte of the count in IP+1 ($76). If the bytes do not match, branch to PERR2 ($EB1F). $E/F ROM: checksum = $E0 $C/D ROM: checksum = $C0
	$EAE6	Compare checksum in .X with $C0 to check if we are done. If not, branch to RM10.
		Test the disk RAM.
CR20	$EAEA	Load .A with $01 (start of first block).
CR30	$EAEC	Save contents of .A (page number) into IP+1 ($76) as hi byte of pointer.
	$EAEE	Increment TEMP ($6F) to bump the error number ($03=RAM problem)
RAMTST	$EAF0	Load .X with $07 (number of RAM pages).
RA10	$EAF2	Transfer .Y value to .A and clear carry.
	$EAF4	Add the hi byte of the pointer, IP+1 ($76) to the accumulator and store the result in (IP,Y).
	$EAF8	Increment .Y and if .Y is not $00, branch to RA10 to fill RAM page.
	$EAFB	Increment the hi byte of the pointer in IP+1 ($76) and decrement the page count in .X. If .X is not $00, we have more pages to do so branch back to RA10.
	$EB00	Load .X with $07 (number of RAM pages).
RA30	$EB02	Decrement the hi byte of the pointer in IP+1 ($76). We'll check backwards.
RA40	$EB04	Decrement .Y, transfer the .Y value into .A and clear the carry.
	$EB07	Add the hi byte of the pointer, IP+1 ($76) to the accumulator and compare the result with (IP,Y). If they don't match, branch to PERR2 to report the error.
	$EB0D	EOR the contents of .A with $FF to flip the bits and store the result into the RAM at (IP),Y.

NAME	ADDRESS	DESCRIPTION OF WHAT ROM ROUTINE DOES
	$EB11	EOR the contents of .A with (IP),Y and store the result (should be $00) back into (IP),Y. If the result is not $00, branch to PERR2 to report the error.
	$EB17	Transfer the contents of .Y into .A. If .Y is not $00, we have more to do on this page so branch back to RA40.
	$EB1A	Decrement the page count in .X. If there are more pages to do, branch to RA30.
	$EB1D	Branch to DIAGOK.
PERR2	$EB1F	JMP to PERR ($EA71) to report error.
DIAGOK	$EB22	Load .X with $45 and transfer this value to the stack pointer to reset the stack.
	$EB25	Load .A with the byte from the LED control port, LEDPRT ($1C00), AND it with $F7 ($FF-LED mask) and store the result back in LEDPRT to turn off LED.
	$EB2D	Store $01 in PCR1 ($180C) to cause interrupt on the negative edge of ATN.
	$EB32	Store $82 (10000010) in IFR1 ($180D) and IER1 ($180E).

COMPUTE DEVICE # FROM BITS 5/6 OF PORT B

NAME	ADDRESS	DESCRIPTION OF WHAT ROM ROUTINE DOES
	$EB3A	Load .A with the data byte from Port B, PB ($1800). AND the byte with $60 (%01100000). Do one ASL and three ROL's to convert from bits 6/5 to bits 1/0. NOTE: 0XX00000 becomes 000000XX
	$EB43	OR .A with $48 (the talk address) and store the result in TLKADR ($78).
	$EB43	EOR .A with $60 (the listen address) and store the result in LSNADR ($77).

Initialize buffer pointer table

NAME	ADDRESS	DESCRIPTION OF WHAT ROM ROUTINE DOES
INTTAB	$EB4B	Zero .X and .Y
INTT1	$EB4F	Zero .A and store the $00 byte in .A in the buffer table at BUFTAB,X ($99,X).
	$EB53	Increment .X and load .A with the hi byte of the pointer to the buffer from BUFIND,Y ($FEE0) and store it into the buffer table at BUFTAB,X ($99,X).
	$EB59	Increment .X and .Y and compare the new value of .Y with $05 (the number of buffers). If there are more buffers to do, branch to INTT1.
	$EB5F	Store the lo byte of the pointer to the command buffer ($00) into the buffer table at BUFTAB,X ($99,X). Increment .X.

NAME	ADDRESS	DESCRIPTION OF WHAT ROM ROUTINE DOES
	$EB64	Store the hi byte of the pointer to the command buffer ($02) into the buffer table at BUFTAB,X ($99,X). Increment .X.
	$EB69	Store the lo byte of the pointer to the error buffer ($D5) into the buffer table table at BUFTAB,X ($99,X). Increment .X.
	$EB6E	Store the hi byte of the pointer to the error buffer ($02) into the buffer table table at BUFTAB,X ($99,X). Increment .X.
	$EB72	Load .A with $FF (inactive SA) and .X with $12 (the maximum secondary address)
DSKIN1	$EB76	Loop to set all LINTAB,X ($022B,X) values to $FF to indicate inactive.
	$EB7C	Load .X with $05 (the maximum number of channels − 1).
DSKIN2	$EB7E	Loop to set all BUF0,X ($A7,X), BUF1,X ($AE,X) and SS,X (CD,X) values to $FF to indicate that these buffers are unused.
	$EB87	Store $05 (the buffer count) into BUF0+CMDCHN ($AB)
	$EB8B	Store $05 (the buffer count + 1) into BUF0+ERRCHN ($AC)
	$EB8F	Store $FF into BUF0+BLINDX ($AD)
	$EB93	Store $FF into BUF1+BLINDX ($B4)
	$EB95	Store $05 (the error channel #) into LINTAB+ERRSA ($023B).
	$EB9A	Store $84 ($80 + the command channel #) into LINTAB+CMDSA ($023A).
	$EB9F	Store $0F (LINDX 0 to 5 free) into LINUSE ($0256).
	$EBA4	Store $01 (ready to listen) into CHNRDY+CMDCHN ($F6).
	$EBA8	Store $01 (ready to talk) into CHNRDY+ERRCHN ($F7).
	$EBAC	Store $E0 into BUFUSE ($024F) and $FF into BUFUSE+1 ($0250).
	$EBB6	Store $01 into WPSW ($1C) and WPSW+1 ($1D) to set up the write protect status
	$EBBC	JSR to USRINT ($CB63) to initialize the user jump table.
	$EBBF	JSR to LRUINT ($CEFA) to initialize the least recently used table.
	$EBC2	JSR to CNTINT ($F259) to initialize the disk controller.
	$EBC5	Set up the indirect NMI vector at VNMI ($65/6) to point to the diagnostic routine, DIAGOK ($EB22).
	$EBCD	Store $0A into SECINC ($69) as the normal next sector increment.
	$EBD1	Store $05 into REVCNT ($6A) as the normal recovery counter.

NAME	ADDRESS	DESCRIPTION OF WHAT ROM ROUTINE DOES
SETERR	$EBD5	Load .A with $73 and JSR to ERRTS0 ($E6C1) to set up power-on error message 73 CBM DOS V2.6 1541 0 0
	$EBDA	Load .A with $1A (%00011010) and store it in the data direction register DDRB1 ($1802). ATNA,CLKOUT,DATOUT are outputs.
	$EBDF	Store $00 in data port B, PB ($1800) to set DATA, CLOCK, & ATNA lines high.
	$EBE4	JSR to BOOT ($E780) to see if we need to boot a systems routine.
		--
		IDLE LOOP. WAIT FOR SOMETHING TO DO.
		--
IDLE	$EBE7	Clear interrupt mask (CLI) to allow interrupts. Release all the bus lines:
	$EBE8	Load .A with the byte from port B, PB ($1800), AND it with $E5 to set CLOCK, DATA, and ATNA lines high, and store the result back in PB ($1800).
	$EBF0	Check the value of CMDWAT ($0255) to see if there is a command waiting. If it is $00, there is none waiting so branch to IDL1.
	$EBF5	Store $00 in CMDWAT ($0255) to clear the command waiting flag.
	$EBFA	Store $00 in NMIFLG ($67) to clear the debounce.
	$EBFC	JSR to PARSXQ ($C146) to parse and then execute the command.
IDL1	$EBFF	Clear interrupt mask (CLI) to allow interrupts.
	$EC00	Check the value of ATNPND ($0255) to see if there is an attention pending. If it is $00, there is nothing pending (such as the drive running or an open file) so branch to IDL01.
	$EC04	JMP to ATNSRV ($E85B) to service the attention request.
IDL01	$EC07	Clear interrupt mask (CLI) to allow interrupts.
	$EC08	Store $0E (#14), the maximum secondary address for files in TEMP+3 ($72).
	$EC0C	Zero TEMP ($6F) and TEMP+1 ($70).
IDL02	$EC12	Load .X with the secondary address counter from TEMP+3 ($72).
	$EC14	Load .A with the channel number for this secondary address from LINTAB,X($022B,X) If it is $FF, there is no active file for this SA so branch to IDL3.

NAME	ADDRESS	DESCRIPTION OF WHAT ROM ROUTINE DOES
	$EC1B	We've found an active file so AND the channel number with $3F and store the result as the current channel number in LINDX ($82).
	$EC1F	JSR to GETACT ($DF93) to get the active buffer number (returned in .A).
	$EC22	Transfer the buffer number from .A to .X
	$EC23	Determine which drive is to be used by loading the old job number from LSTJOB,X ($025B,X), AND'ing it with $01, and transferring the result into .X.
	$EC29	Increment the count of the number of active files on drive X in TEMP,X($6F,X)
IDL3	$EC2B	Decrement the SA count in TEMP+3 ($72). If there are more secondary addresses left to check, branch back to IDL2.
	$EC2F	Load .Y with $04 (the number of buffers less 1).
IDL4	$EC31	Load .A with the current job code for this buffer from the job queue, JOBS,Y ($00,Y). If bit 7 is not set, no job is in progress so branch to IDL5.
	$EC36	There is a job in progress so AND the job code in .A with $01 to mask off the non-drive bits and transfer the result to .X.
	$EC39	Increment the count of the number of active files on drive X in TEMP,X($6F,X)
IDL5	$EC3B	Decrement the buffer counter in .Y. If there are more buffers to check, branch to IDL4.
	$EC3E	Set the interrupt mask (SEI) to prevent interrupts while reading LEDPRT ($1C00).
	$EC3F	Load .A with the data byte from the port controlling the LED, AND the byte with $F7 ($FF - LED mask), and save the result onto the stack.
	$EC45	Load .A with the current drive number from DRVNUM ($7F) and save it in R0($86)
	$EC49	Zero DRVNUM ($7F).
	$EC4D	Test the active file count for drive 0 in TEMP ($6F). If $00, branch to IDL7.
	$EC51	Load the write protect switch byte from WPSW ($1C). If it is $00 branch to IDL6.
	$EC55	JSR to CLDCHN ($D313) to close all files
IDL6	$EC58	Pull the LED data byte off the stack, OR it with $08 (LED mask) to turn on the LED since drive 0 is active, and save the byte back onto the stack.
IDL7	$EC5C	Increment the DRVNUM ($7F). (to $01)
	$EC5E	Test the active file count for drive 1 in TEMP+1 ($70). If $00, branch to IDL9.
	$EC62	Load the write protect switch byte from WPSW ($1C). If it is $00 branch to IDL8.

NAME	ADDRESS	DESCRIPTION OF WHAT ROM ROUTINE DOES
	$EC66	JSR to CLDCHN ($D313) to close all files
IDL8	$EC69	Pull the LED data byte off the stack, OR it with $00 (LED mask) to turn on the LED since drive 1 is active, and save the byte back onto the stack.
IDL9	$EC6D	Copy the original drive number from R0 ($86) back into DRVNUM ($7F).
	$EC71	Pull the LED data byte off the stack.
	$EC72	Load .X with the error status from ERWORD ($026C). If it is $00, the LED is not flashing so branch to IDL12.
	$EC77	Error light is flashing: Load .A with the LED data byte from LEDPRT ($1C00)
	$EC7A	Compare the error status in .X with $80. If it is not $80, this is not the first time we have seen this error so branch to IDL 10.
	$EC7E	We have just encountered a new error status so JMP to IDL11.
IDL10	$EC81	Load .X with the value of TIMER1 ($1805) If bit 7 is set, we are still timing so branch to IDL12.
	$EC86	Store $A0 into TIMER1 ($1805) to set the timer to a new 8 millisecond cycle.
IDL11	$EC8B	Decrement the count of 8 millisecond cycles in ERWORD ($026C). If the count is not $00 yet, branch to IDL12
	$EC90	Time is up. EOR the LED status in .A with the LED mask in ERLED ($026D) to toggle the LED.
	$EC93	Store $10 in ERWORD ($026C) to start a new timing cycle.
IDL12	$EC98	Store the current LED status (in .A) into the LED port, LEDPRT ($1C00).
	$EC9B	JMP to IDL1 ($EBFF) the top of the loop.
STDIR	$EC9E	Start loading the directory: Set current secondary address, SA ($83) to $00.
	$ECA2	Load .A with $01 and JSR to GETRCH ($D1E2) to allocate a channel and one buffer.
	$ECA7	Zero .A and JSR to SETPNT ($D4C8) to set the buffer pointer to the start of the buffer.
	$ECAC	Load .X with the channel number from LINDX ($82).
	$ECAE	Store $00 as the last character for this channel in LSTCHR,X ($0244).
	$ECB3	JSR to GETACT ($DF93) to get the active buffer number (returned in .A).

NAME	ADDRESS	DESCRIPTION OF WHAT ROM ROUTINE DOES
	$ECB6	Transfer the buffer number into .X
	$ECB7	Load .A with the current drive number from DRVNUM ($7F) and store this number as the last job number for this buffer in LSTJOB,X ($025B).
	$ECBC	Load .A with $01 and JSR to PUTBYT ($CFF1) to put the lo byte of the load address ($0401) into the buffer.
	$ECC1	Load .A with $04 and JSR to PUTBYT ($CFF1) to put the hi byte of the load address ($0401) into the buffer.
	$ECC6	Load .A with $01 and JSR to PUTBYT ($CFF1) twice to put a phony program line link ($0101) into the buffer.
	$ECCE	Load .A with the drive number for the directory from NBTEMP ($0272) and JSR to PUTBYT ($CFF1) to put this to the buffer as the lo byte of the first line number.
	$ECD4	Load .A with $00 and JSR to PUTBYT ($CFF1) to store this as the hi byte of the line number.
	$ECD9	JSR to MOVBUF ($ED59) to move the disk name into the buffer.
	$ECDC	JSR to GETACT ($DF93) to get the active buffer number (returned in .A).
	$ECDF	Multiply the buffer number by 2 (ASL) and transfer it into .X.
	$ECE1	Decrement the lo byte of the pointer in BUFTAB,X ($$99,X) twice.
	$ECE5	Load .A with $00 and JSR to PUTBYT ($CFF1) to store this as the end of program line null byte.
DIR1	$ECEA	Load .A with $01 and JSR to PUTBYT ($CFF1) twice to put a phony program line link ($0101) into the buffer.
	$ECF2	JSR to GETNAM ($C6CE) to get the buffer number and file name. If the carry flag is clear on return, this is the last entry so branch to DIR3.
	$ECF7	Load .A with the lo byte of the block count from NBTEMP ($0272) and JSR to PUTBYT ($CFF1) to put this to the buffer as the lo byte of the line number.
	$ECFD	Load .A with the hi byte of the block count from NBTEMP+1 ($0273) and JSR to PUTBYT ($CFF1) to put this to the buffer as the hi byte of the line number.
	$ED03	JSR to MOVBUF ($ED59) to move the file name and file type into the buffer.
	$ED06	Load .A with $00 and JSR to PUTBYT ($CFF1) to store this as the end of program line null byte.

NAME	ADDRESS	DESCRIPTION OF WHAT ROM ROUTINE DOES
	$ED0B	If the Z flag is not set on return, the buffer is not full so branch to DIR1 to do the next file entry.
DIR10	$ED0D	JSR to GETACT ($DF93) to get the active buffer number (returned in .A).
	$ED10	Multiply the buffer number by 2 (ASL) and transfer it into .X.
	$ED12	Store $00 as the lo byte of the pointer in BUFTAB,X ($$99,X).
	$ED16	Load .A with $88 (ready-to-talk).
	$ED18	Load .Y with the channel number from LINDX ($82).
	$ED1A	Store $88 (in .A) into the directory list flag DIRLST ($0254) to indicate that the directory list is full.
	$ED1D	Store $88 (in .A) as the channel status in CHNRDY,Y ($00F2,Y).
	$ED20	Load .A with the byte from DATA ($85).
	$ED22	Terminate routine with an RTS.
		--
		End directory loading:
DIR3	$ED23	Load .A with the lo byte of the block count from NBTEMP ($0272) and JSR to PUTBYT ($CFF1) to put this to the buffer as the lo byte of the line number.
	$ED29	Load .A with the hi byte of the block count from NBTEMP+1 ($0273) and JSR to PUTBYT ($CFF1) to put this to the buffer as the hi byte of the line number.
	$ED2F	JSR to MOVBUF ($ED59) to move the file name and file type into the buffer.
	$ED32	JSR to GETACT ($DF93) to get the active buffer number (returned in .A).
	$ED35	Multiply the buffer number by 2 (ASL) and transfer it into .X.
	$ED37	Decrement the lo byte of the pointer in BUFTAB,X ($$99,X) twice.
	$ED3B	Load .A with $00 and JSR to PUTBYT ($CFF1) three times to store the three null bytes at the end of a program.
	$ED46	JSR to GETACT ($DF93) to get the active buffer number (returned in .A).
	$ED49	Multiply the buffer number by 2 (ASL) and transfer it into .Y.
	$ED4B	Load .A with the lo byte of the pointer into the buffer from BUFTAB,Y ($0099,Y).
	$ED4E	Load .Y with the channel number from LINDX ($82).
	$ED50	Store the lo byte of the pointer (in .A) into the lo byte of the pointer to the last non-zero character in the buffer LSTCHR,X ($0244,X).

NAME	ADDRESS	DESCRIPTION OF WHAT ROM ROUTINE DOES
	$ED53	Decrement the pointer in LSTCHR,X ($0244,X) by 1 so it does actually point to the last character in the buffer.
	$ED56	JMP to DIR10 ($ED0D) to set the channel status and flags and exit.
		--
		Transfer file name to listing buffer
MOVBUF	$ED59	Zero .Y
MOVB1	$ED5B	Load .A with the character from NAMBUF,Y ($02B1,Y) and JSR to PUTBYT ($CFF1) to store it in the listing buffer.
	$ED61	Increment .Y. If .Y is not $1B (#27) yet, branch to MOVB1.
	$ED66	Terminate routine with an RTS.
		--
		Get character for directory load
GETDIR	$ED67	JSR to GETBYT ($D137) to get a byte from the data buffer (loads next block if necessary).
	$ED6A	On return, if the Z flag is set, we are at the end-of-file so branch to GETD3.
	$ED6C	Terminate routine with an RTS.
GETD3	$ED6D	Store the byte (in .A) into DATA ($85).
	$ED6F	Load .Y with the channel number from LINDX ($82).
	$ED71	Load .A with the lo byte of the pointer into the directory buffer from LSTCHR,Y ($0244,Y)
	$ED74	If the lo byte of the pointer is $00, we have exhausted the current buffer so branch to GD1.
	$ED76	We must be at the end-of-file so load .A with $80 (EOI) and store it as the channel status in CHNRDY,Y ($00F2,Y).
	$ED7B	Load .A with the byte from DATA ($85).
	$ED7D	Terminate routine with an RTS.
GD1	$ED7E	Save the null byte in .A onto the stack.
	$ED7F	JSR to DIR1 ($ECEA) to create pseudo program listing in the listing buffer.
	$ED82	Pull the null data byte off the stack.
	$ED83	Terminate routine with an RTS.
		--
		VALIDATE (COLLECT) DISK COMMAND
		--
		Create a new BAM to match the sectors used by the current directory entries.
VALDAT VERDIR	$ED84	JSR to SIMPRS ($C1D1) to parse the command string and extract the drive #.
	$ED87	JSR to INITDR ($D042) to initialize the drive specified.
	$ED8A	Store $40 in WBAM ($02F9) to mark BAM as dirty (needs to be written out).

NAME	ADDRESS	DESCRIPTION OF WHAT ROM ROUTINE DOES
	$ED8F	JSR to NEWMAP ($EEB7) to build a new blank BAM in RAM.
	$ED92	Store $00 in DELIND ($0292) to force a search for a valid directory entry and JSR to SRCHST ($C5AC) to search the directory for the first valid entry.
	$ED9A	If an entry is found (Z flag not set), branch to VD25 to process it.
VD10	$ED9C	No more entries so finish up. Set SECTOR ($81) to $00.
	$EDA0	Set TRACK ($80) with the value $12 (#18) from DIRTRK ($FE85).
	$EDA5	JSR to VMKBAM ($EDE5) to trace through the directory sectors and mark those in use in the BAM.
	$EDA8	Store $00 in WBAM ($02F9) to mark BAM as clean (BAM in RAM matches BAM on disk).
	$EDAD	JSR to SCRBAM ($EEFF) to write BAM out to disk.
	$EDB0	Terminate command with a JMP to ENDCMD ($C194).
VD15	$EDB3	Process directory entry for BAM Increment .Y (points to entry in buffer)
	$EDB4	Load the track link for the entry from (DIRBUF),Y; ($94),Y and save it onto the stack.
	$EDB7	Increment .Y (points to entry in buffer)
	$EDB8	Load the sector link for the entry from (DIRBUF),Y; ($94),Y and save it onto the stack.
	$EDBB	Load .Y with $13 so it points to the side sector track link of the entry.
	$EDBD	Load the SS track link for the entry from (DIRBUF),Y; ($94),Y. If the SS track link is $00, this isn't a relative file so branch to VD17.
	$EDC1	Store the SS track link in TRACK ($80).
	$EDC3	Increment .Y (points to entry in buffer)
	$EDC4	Load the SS sector link for the entry from (DIRBUF),Y; ($94),Y. Store the SS sector link in SECTOR ($81).
	$EDC8	JSR to VMKBAM ($EDE5) to trace through the SS file and mark the sectors used in the BAM.
VD17	$EDCB	Pull the main file's sector link off the stack and store it in SECTOR ($81).
	$EDCE	Pull the main file's track link off the stack and store it in TRACK ($80).
	$EDD1	JSR to VMKBAM ($EDE5) to trace through the main file and mark the sectors used in the BAM.

NAME	ADDRESS	DESCRIPTION OF WHAT ROM ROUTINE DOES
VD20	$EDD4	JSR to SRRE ($C604) to search for the next valid directory entry.
	$EDD7	If another entry is not found (Z flag is set) branch to VD10 to finish up.
VD25	$EDD9	Check if entry found is properly closed Zero .Y so it points to the first character in the entry, the file type.
	$EDDB	Load .A with the file type byte from (DIRBUF),Y; ($99),Y. If bit 7 is set, the file has been properly closed so branch to VD15 to process it.
	$EDDF	File was not properly closed so JSR to DELDIR ($C8B6) to delete it from the directory.
	$EDE2	JMP to VD20 ($EDD4) to find next entry.
VMKBAM	$EDE5	Trace file by links and mark BAM JSR to TSCHK ($D55F) to check that the TRACK and SECTOR values are legal.
	$EDE8	JSR to WUSED ($EF90) to mark the sector pointed to by TRACK and SECTOR as IN USE in the BAM.
	$EDEB	JSR to OPNIRD ($D475) to open the internal read channel and read in the first one or two file blocks.
MRK2	$EDEE	Load .A with $00 and JSR to SETPNT ($D4C8) to set the pointers to the first byte in the buffer (the track link).
	$EDF3	JSR to GETBYT ($D137) to read the track link (in .A). Store it into TRACK ($80).
	$EDF8	JSR to GETBYT ($D137) to read the sector link (in .A). Store it into SECTOR ($81)
	$EDFD	Load .A with the track link from TRACK ($80). If it is not $00, branch to MRK1.
	$EE01	Track link is $00. This must be the last block in the file so JMP to FRECHN ($D227) to free the channel and return.
MRK1	$EE04	JSR to WUSED ($EF90) to mark the sector pointed to by TRACK and SECTOR as IN USE in the BAM.
	$EE07	JSR to NXTBUF ($D44D) to read in the next block of the file.
	$EE0A	JMP to MRK2 ($EDEE) to do next block.

NEW (FORMAT) DISK COMMAND

A full, or long NEW marks off the tracks and sectors on a diskette, writes null data blocks in all sectors, and creates a new BAM and directory on track 18.
A short NEW merely creates a new BAM and directory on track 18.

NAME	ADDRESS	DESCRIPTION OF WHAT ROM ROUTINE DOES
NEW	$EE0D	JSR to ONEDRV ($C312) to set up drive and table pointers.
	$EE10	Load the number of the drive that was set up from FILDRV ($E2). If bit 7 is not set, a legal drive number was specified so branch to N101 to continue.
	$EE14	Load .A with $33 to indicate a BAD DRIVE NUMBER and JMP to CMDERR ($C1C8).
N101	$EE19	AND the drive number (in .A) with $01 to mask off the non drive bits and store the result as the current drive in DRVNUM ($7F).
	$EE1D	JSR to SETLDS ($C100) to turn on the drive active LED.
	$EE20	Load .A with the drive number from DRVNUM ($7F), multiply it by 2 (ASL), and transfer it into .X.
	$EE24	Load .Y with the pointer to the start of the new disk ID in the command buffer from FILTBL+1 ($027B).
	$EE27	Compare the ID pointer in .Y with the length of the command string in CMDSIZ ($0274). If these values are equal, there is no new disk ID. Therefore this must be a short new so branch to N108.
	$EE2C	Transfer new disk ID from the command buffer CMDBUF,Y ($0200,Y) and CMDBUF+1,Y ($0201,Y) to the master disk ID area DSKID,X ($12,X) and DSKID+1,X ($13,X).
	$EE36	JSR to CLRCHN ($D307) to clear all channels while formatting.
	$EE39	Store $01 into TRACK ($80) as first track to do.
	$EE3D	JSR to FORMAT ($C8C6) to set up JMP command in buffer that points to the formatting routine to be used by the disk controller.
	$EE40	JSR to CLRBAM ($F005) to clear the BAM.
	$EE43	JMP to N110 ($EE56) to continue.
N108	$EE46	Clear directory only. JSR to INITDR ($D042) to init. the drive
	$EE49	Load .X with the drive number from DRVNUM ($7F).
	$EE4B	Load .A with the DOS version number as given in the BAM, DSKVER,X ($0101,X) and compare it with the 1541 DOS version number ($41) from VERNUM ($FED5). If the version numbers match, branch to N110.

NAME	ADDRESS	DESCRIPTION OF WHAT ROM ROUTINE DOES
	$EE53	DOS versions do not match so JMP to VNERR ($D572) to abort.
N110	$EE56	JSR to NEWMAP ($EEB7) to create a new BAM.
	$EE59	Load .A with the current job code from JOBNUM ($F9) and transfer it to .Y.
	$EE5C	Multiply the job code in .A by 2 (ASL) and transfer the result to .X.
	$EE5E	Load .A with $90, the offset of the disk name in the BAM from DSKNAM ($FE88) and store this pointer in BUFTAB,X ($99,X).
	$EE63	Load .X with the buffer number from FILTBL ($027A), load .Y with $27 (the name length) and JSR to TRNAME ($C66E) to transfer the new disk name from the command buffer into the BAM area.
	$EE6B	Load .Y with $12 (position of disk ID).
	$EE6D	Load .X with the drive number from DRVNUM ($7F) and copy the DOS version number ($41) from VERNUM ($FED5) into DSKVER,X ($0101,X).
	$EE75	Transfer the drive number from .X to .A, multiply it by 2 (ASL), and transfer the result back into .X.
	$EE78	Transfer the first disk ID character from DSKID,X ($12,X) into (DIRBUF),Y ($94),Y. Increment .Y.
	$EE7D	Transfer the second disk ID character from DSKID+1,X ($13,X) into (DIRBUF),Y ($94),Y. Increment .Y twice.
	$EE83	Store the directory DOS version ($32; ASCII 2) into (DIRBUF),Y; ($94),Y.
	$EE87	Increment .Y.
	$EE88	Transfer the format type ($41; ASCII A) from VERNUM ($FED5) into (DIRBUF),Y ($94),Y.
	$EE8D	Load .Y with $02 so it points to the third byte in the BAM and store the format type ($41; in .A) into the BAM at (BMPNT),Y; ($6D),Y.
	$EE91	Transfer the directory track number, $12 from DIRTRK ($FE85) into TRACK ($80).
	$EE96	JSR to USEDTS ($EF93) to mark track 18 sector 0 as used in the BAM.
	$EE99	Set SECTOR ($81) to $01.
	$EE9D	JSR to USEDTS ($EF93) to mark track 18 sector 1 as used in the BAM.
	$EEA0	JSR to SCRBAM ($EEFF) to write out the new BAM to disk.
	$EEA3	JSR to CLRBAM ($F005) to set all of BAM area to $00.

NAME	ADDRESS	DESCRIPTION OF WHAT ROM ROUTINE DOES
	$EEA6	Load .Y with $01 and store $FF as the first directory block's sector link in (BMPNT),Y; ($6D),Y.
	$EEAC	JSR to DRTWRT ($D464) to write out the new directory block to disk.
	$EEAF	Decrement the sector number (from $01 to $00) in SECTOR ($81) and JSR to DRTRD ($D460) to read the BAM back into RAM.
	$EEB4	Terminate command with a JMP to ENDCMD ($C194).
NEWMPV NEWMAP		Create a new BAM map:
	$EEB7	JSR to CLNBAM ($F0D1) to set entire BAM area to $00's.
	$EEBA	Using .Y as a pointer, store $12 (#18) and $01 as the track and sector link in (BMPNT),Y; ($6D),Y; as the first two bytes of the new BAM.
	$EEC4	Increment .Y until it is $04.
NM10	$EEC7	Zero the area to be used to manipulate the BAM map bits, T0 ($6F), T1 ($70), and T2 ($71).
	$EECF	Transfer the byte from .Y into .A and divide it by 4 (2 * LSR) to find the track number.
	$EED2	JSR to MAXSEC ($F24B) to calculate the maximum sector number for this track and store this value as the number of sectors free on this track in (BMPNT),Y ($6D),Y.
	$EED7	Increment .Y. Transfer the maximum sector number from .A into .X.
NM20	$EED9	Set the carry flag (this 1 bit will indicate that this sector is free) and rotate this bit from the carry into the bit map area (T0/1/2) using ROL T0, ROL T1, and ROL T2.
		T2 ($71) T1 ($70) T0 ($6F) C before 00000000 11111111 11111111 1 after 00000001<-11111111<-11111111<-0
	$EEE0	Decrement the sector count in .X. If the resulting .X value is not $00, there are more to do so branch back to NM20.
NM30	$EEE3	Transfer the bit map for this track from T0,X ($6F,X) to the BAM area (BMPNT),Y; ($6D,Y). Increment .Y and .X. If the new .X value is not $03, we have more to transfer so branch back to NM30.
	$EEED	Compare the .Y value to $90. If it is less than $90, we have more tracks to do so branch back to NM10.

NAME	ADDRESS	DESCRIPTION OF WHAT ROM ROUTINE DOES
	$EEF1	JMP to NFCALC ($D075) to calculate the number of blocks free.

		Write out BAM to the drive specified in LSTJOB.
MAPOUT	$EEF4	JSR to GETACT ($DF93) to find the active buffer number (returned in .A).
	$EEF7	Transfer the buffer number to .X.
	$EEF8	Load .A with the job code for the last job from LSTJOB,X ($025B,X), AND it with $01 to mask off the non-drive bits, and store the result in DRVNUM ($7F).
		Write out BAM to the drive specified in DRVNUM.
SCRBAM	$EEFF	Load .Y with the drive number from DRVNUM ($7F).
	$EF01	Load .A with the BAM-dirty flag from MDIRTY,Y ($0251,Y). If the flag is not $00, the BAM is dirty (the copy in RAM does NOT match the copy on disk) so branch to SB10 to write it out to disk.
	$EF06	BAM is clean so there is no reason to write it out. Terminate routine with an RTS.
SB10	$EF07	Zero the BAM-dirty flag in MDIRTY,Y ($0251,Y).
	$EF0C	JSR to SETBPT ($EF3A) to set up the pointer to the BAM.
	$EF0F	Load .A with the drive number from DRVNUM ($7F), multiply it by 2 (ASL), and save the result onto the stack.
	$EF13	JSR to PUTBAM ($F0A5) to put the memory images to the BAM.
	$EF16	Pull the (drive number x 2) off the stack, clear the carry flag, add $01, and JSR to PUTBAM ($F0A5) to put the memory images to the BAM.
		Verify that the block count for the track matches the bit map for the track.
	$EF1D	Load .A from TRACK ($80) and push the track number onto the stack.
	$EF20	Load .A with $01 and store it in TRACK.
SB20	$EF24	Multiply the track number in .A by 4 (2 x ASL) and store the result as the lo byte of the buffer pointer in BMPNT ($6D).
	$EF28	JSR to AVCK ($F220) to check that the blocks free for the track agrees with the bit map.

NAME	ADDRESS	DESCRIPTION OF WHAT ROM ROUTINE DOES
	$EF2B	Increment the track count in TRACK ($80) If the new count is less than the the maximum track number (#36), branch back to SB20 to check the next track.
	$EF34	Pull the original track number off the stack and restore it into TRACK ($80).
	$EF37	JMP to DOWRIT ($D58A) to write out the BAM to disk.
		--
		Read in the BAM, if not already in RAM, and set the pointers to the BAM
SETBPT	$EF3A	JSR to BAM2A ($F10F) to get the BAM channel number in .A (dr0 = 6). Transfer the channel number into .X.
	$EF3E	JSR to REDBAM ($F0DF) to read in the BAM if not already in memory.
	$EF41	Load .X with the buffer number used for the read from JOBNUM ($F9).
	$EF43	Set the hi byte of the pointer to the BAM in BMPNT+1 ($6E) using the hi byte pointer value for the buffer from BUFIND,X ($FEE0,X).
	$EF48	Set the lo byte of the pointer to the BAM in BMPNT ($6D) to $00.
	$EF4C	Terminate routine with an RTS.
		--
		Get the number of blocks free on the drive specified in DRVNUM:
NUMFRE	$EF4D	Load .X with the drive number from DRVNUM ($7F).
	$EF4F	Transfer the lo byte of the number of blocks free from NDBL,X ($02FA,X) into NBTEMP ($0272).
	$EF55	Transfer the hi byte of the number of blocks free from NDBH,X ($02FC,X) into NBTEMP+1 ($0273).
	$EF5B	Terminate routine with an RTS.
		--
		Free the block specified in TRACK and SECTOR as free in the BAM:
WFREE	$EF5C	JSR to FIXBAM ($EFF1) to write out the BAM the value in WBAM indicates that it is needed.
FRETS	$EF5F	JSR to FREUSE ($EFCF) to calculate the index to the BAM entry that contains the desired TRACK and SECTOR. On return .Y points to the entry and .X points to the bit within the entry.
FRETS2	$EF62	Set the carry flag (the flag for no action required).
	$EF63	If Z flag is NOT set, the desired TRACK and SECTOR is already free in the BAM so branch to FRERTS to exit.

NAME	ADDRESS	DESCRIPTION OF WHAT ROM ROUTINE DOES
	$EF65	Load .A with BAM entry from (BMPNT),Y ($6D),Y, OR it with the bit map mask from BMASK,X ($EFE9,X) to turn on (free) the bit that corresponds to the desired block, and store the result back into (BMPNT),Y; ($6D),Y.
	$ED6C	JSR to DTYBAM ($EF88) to set the dirty BAM flag (BAM in RAM and BAM on disk do not match).
	$ED6F	Load .Y with the pointer to the number of blocks free for the track from TEMP ($6F) and clear the carry flag.
	$EF72	Load .A with the blocks free for the track from (BMPNT),Y; ($6D),Y, add 1, and store the result back into (BMPNT),Y
	$EF78	Load .A with the TRACK ($80) number of the block we just freed. If it is on the directory track (#18), branch to USE10 ($EFBA).
	$EF7F	Increment the lo byte of the count of the total number of blocks free on the disk, NDBL,X ($02FA,X) by 1. If the result is NOT $00, branch to FRERTS
	$EF84	Increment the hi byte of the count of the total number of blocks free on the disk, NDBH,X ($02FC,X) by 1.
FRERTS	$EF87	Terminate routine with an RTS.

		Set dirty-BAM flag: Indicates that the copy of the BAM in disk RAM does not match the disk copy.
DTYBAM	$EF88	Load .X with the current drive number from DRVNUM ($7F).
	$EF8A	Store a $01 into the dirty BAM flag in MDIRTY,X ($0251).
	$EF8F	Terminate routine with an RTS.

		Mark the block specified in TRACK and SECTOR as USED in the BAM:
WUSED	$EF90	JSR to FIXBAM ($EFF1) to write out the BAM the value in WBAM indicates that it is needed.
USEDTS	$EF93	JSR to FREUSE ($EFCF) to calculate the index to the BAM entry that contains the desired TRACK and SECTOR. On return .Y points to the entry and .X points to the bit within the entry.
	$EF96	If Z flag is set, the desired TRACK and SECTOR is already marked as USED in the BAM so branch to USERTS to exit.

NAME	ADDRESS	DESCRIPTION OF WHAT ROM ROUTINE DOES
	$EF98	Load .A with BAM entry from (BMPNT),Y ($6D),Y, EOR it with the bit map mask from BMASK,X ($EFE9,X) to zero (in use) the bit that corresponds to the desired block, and store the result back into (BMPNT),Y; ($6D),Y.
	$ED9F	JSR to DTYBAM ($EF88) to set the dirty BAM flag (BAM in RAM and BAM on disk do not match).
	$EDA2	Load .Y with the pointer to the number of blocks free for the track from TEMP ($6F).
	$EFA4	Load .A with the blocks free for the track from (BMPNT),Y; ($6D),Y, set the carry flag, subtract $01, and store the result back into (BMPNT),Y.
	$EFAB	Load .A with the TRACK ($80) number of the block we just freed. If it is on the directory track (#18), branch to USE20 ($EFBD).
	$EFB2	Load .A with the lo byte of the count of the total number of blocks free on the disk, NDBL,X ($02FA,X). If the lo byte is NOT $00, branch to USE10.
	$EFB7	Decrement the hi byte of the count of the total number of blocks free on the disk, NDBH,X ($02FC,X) by 1.
USE10	$EFBA	Decrement the lo byte of the count of the total number of blocks free on the disk, NDBL,X ($02FA,X) by 1.
USE20	$EFBD	Load .A with the hi byte of the count of the total number of blocks free on the disk, NDBH,X ($02FC,X). If the hi byte is NOT $00, branch to USERTS.
	$EFC2	Load .A with the lo byte of the count of the total number of blocks free on the disk, NDBL,X ($02FA,X). If the lo byte is greater than 2, branch to USERTS.
	$EFC9	Load .A with $72 to indicate a DISK FULL error and JSR to ERRMSG ($E6C7).
USERTS	$EFCE	Terminate routine with an RTS.
-----	------	--------------------------------------
		Calculate index into the BAM for FRETS and USEDTS. On exit: Z flag = 1 if used in BAM Z flag = 0 if free in BAM
FREUSE	$EFCF	JSR to SETBAM ($F011) to set BAM image in memory. On return .Y contains a pointer to the start of the bit map for the desired track.
	$EFD2	Transfer the pointer from .Y to .A.
FREUS2	$EFD3	Store the pointer from .A into TEMP ($6F).

NAME	ADDRESS	DESCRIPTION OF WHAT ROM ROUTINE DOES
FREUS3	$EFD5	Load .A with the desired sector number from SECTOR ($81) and do three LSR's to divide the sector number by 8 to find out which of the three bytes for this track the sector is in.
	$EFDA	Set the carry flag, add the pointer to the start of the track from TEMP ($6F) to the sector index (0/1/2) in .A, and transfer the result to .Y.
	$EFDE	Load .A with the desired sector number from SECTOR ($81), AND the sector number with $07 to find the bit position that corresponds to that sector, and transfer the result into .X.
	$EFE3	Load .A with the BAM byte that contains the bit for the desired block from (BMPNT),Y; ($6D),Y, and AND it with the bit map for the appropriate bit from BMASK,X ($EFE9,X) to set the Z flag.
	$EFE8	Terminate routine with an RTS.
		Bit mask table $EFE9-EFF0
BMASK	$EFE9	.BYTE $01 1
	$EFEA	.BYTE $02 2
	$EFEB	.BYTE $04 4
	$EFEC	.BYTE $08 8
	$EFED	.BYTE $10 16
	$EFEE	.BYTE $20 32
	$EFEF	.BYTE $40 64
	$EFF0	.BYTE $80 128
		Write out BAM to disk if value in WBAM indicates that it is necessary.
FIXBAM	$EFF1	Load .A with $FF and BIT this value with the value in WBAM ($02F9).
	$EFF6	If Z flag set (WBAM was $00) branch to FBAM10 to exit.
	$EFF8	If N flag clear (bit 7 of WBAM was 0) branch to FBAM10 to exit.
	$EFFA	If V flag set (bit 6 of WBAM was 0) branch to FBAM10 to exit.
	$EFFC	Set WBAM ($02F9) to $00 and JSR to DOWRIT ($D58A) to write BAM to disk.
FBAM10	$F004	Terminate routine with an RTS.
		Zero the BAM area:
CLRBAM	$F005	JSR to SETBPT ($EF3A) to set the pointers to the BAM.
	$F008	Zero .Y and .A.
CLB1	$F00B	Loop, using .Y as an index, to store $00's in all 256 locations in the BAM buffer.
	$F010	Terminate routine with an RTS.

NAME	ADDRESS	DESCRIPTION OF WHAT ROM ROUTINE DOES
SETBAM	$F011	Set BAM image in memory: Save the values of T0 ($6F) and T1 ($70) onto the stack so we can use this as a work area.
	$F017	Load .X with the current drive number from DRVNUM ($7F). Load .A with the drive status for this drive from NODRV,X ($FF,X). If the drive status is $00, we have a functioning drive so branch to SBM10 to continue.
	$F019	Load .A with $74 to indicate a DRIVE NOT READY error and JSR to CMDER3 ($E648).
SBM10	$F022	JSR to BAM2A ($F10F) to load .A with the channel number and .X with the drive #.
	$F025	Transfer the channel number (in .A) into T0 ($6F).
	$F027	Transfer the drive number from .X into .A, multiply it by 2 (ASL), store the result in T1 ($70) and in .X.
	$F02E	Load .A with the current track number from TRACK ($80) and compare it with the track value given in the BAM track table, TBAM,X ($029D,X). If the values match, the BAM is in the correct area of memory so branch to SBM30.
	$F033	Increment .X by 1 and store the result in T1 ($70). Note that .X now points to the alternate BAM channel.
	$F036	Compare the current track value (in .A) with the contents of the BAM track table TBAM,X ($029D,X) for the alternate BAM location. If the value match, the BAM is in an appropriate location so branch to SBM30.
	$F03B	JSR to SWAP ($F05B) to read in the BAM if necessary and move it to the correct area of the disk RAM.
SBM30	$F03E	Load .A with the BAM channel number from T1 ($70).
	$F040	Load .X with the current drive number from DRVNUM ($7F).
	$F042	Store the channel number (in .A) into UBAM,X ($029B,X) to set the last channel used pointer.
	$F045	Multiply the channel number (in .A) by four (2 x ASL), clear the carry, and add $A1, the lo byte of the pointer, to the start of the BAM ($02A1). Store the result into the lo byte of the BAM pointer, BMPNT ($6D).

NAME	ADDRESS	DESCRIPTION OF WHAT ROM ROUTINE DOES
	$F04C	Load .A with $02, the hi byte of the pointer to the start of the BAM, add $00 to add in the carry (if any) from the previous addition, and store the result as the hi byte of the BAM pointer, BMPNT+1 ($6E).
	$F052	Zero .Y.
	$F054	Pull the original values of T1 ($70) and T0 ($6F) off the stack and store them back in their original locations.
	$F05A	Terminate routine with an RTS.
		--
		Swap images of the BAM:
SWAP	$F05B	Load .X with the index into the buffer from T0 ($6F) and JSR to REDBAM ($F0DF) to read the BAM if not already in RAM.
	$F060	Load .A with the current drive number from DRVNUM ($7F) and transfer the drive number into .X.
	$F063	Multiply the drive number in .A by two (ASL), OR it with the least used BAM pointer in UBAM,X ($029B,X), EOR it with $01, and AND it with $03. Store the result into T1 ($70) and JSR to PUTBAM ($F0A5) to put the memory image into the BAM.
	$F070	Load .A with the buffer number from JOBNUM ($F9), multiply it by two (ASL), and transfer the result into .X.
	$F074	Load .A with the track number from TRACK ($80), multiply it by four (2 x ASL), and store the result as the lo byte of the pointer in BUFTAB,X ($99,X).
	$F07A	Load .A with the value from T1 ($70), multiply it by four (2 x ASL), and transfer the result into .Y.
SWAP3	$F07F	Transfer one byte of the BAM from its position in RAM, (BUFTAB,X) ($99,X), to its proper position BAM,Y ($02A1,Y).
	$F084	Zero the memory location that held the BAM byte (BUFTAB,X); ($99,X).
	$F088	Increment the lo byte of the pointer to the original BAM image BUFTAB,X ($99,X).
	$F08A	Increment .Y, the pointer to the new BAM image. Transfer this value into .A, AND it with $03 to mask off the high order bits, and if the result is not $00, branch back to SWAP3 to move the next byte.
	$F090	Load .X with the drive number from T1 ($70). Load .A with the current track number from TRACK ($80) and store the track number into TBAM,X ($029D,X) to set the track number for the image.

NAME	ADDRESS	DESCRIPTION OF WHAT ROM ROUTINE DOES
	$F097	Load .A with the write-BAM flag from WBAM ($02F9). If the flag is non-zero, branch to SWAP4 so we don't write out the BAM now.
	$F09C	JMP to DOWRIT ($D58A) to write out the BAM to disk and terminate the routine.
SWAP4	$F09F	OR the write-BAM flag (in .A) with $80 to indicate that a write of the BAM is pending and store the result back into WBAM ($02F9).
	$F0A4	Terminate routine with an RTS.

		Transfer memory image of BAM into the correct position in disk RAM:
PUTBAM	$F0A5	Transfer the pointer in .A into .Y.
	$F0A6	Load .A with the track number of the BAM from TBAM,Y ($029D,Y). If the track number is $00, there is no BAM image in RAM so branch to SWAP2.
	$F0AB	Save the track number onto the stack.
	$F0AC	Zero the track flag in TBAM,Y ($029D,Y).
	$F0B1	Load .A with the buffer number from JOBNUM ($F9), multiply it by two (ASL), and transfer the result into .X.
	$F0B5	Pull the track number off the stack, multiply it by four (2 x ASL), and store the result as the lo byte of the pointer in BUFTAB,X ($99,X).
	$F0BA	Transfer the pointer in .Y into .A, multiply it by four (2 x ASL), and transfer the result back into .Y.
SWAP1	$F0BE	Transfer one byte of the BAM image from BAM,Y ($02A1) to (BUFTAB,X); ($99,X).
	$F0C3	Zero the memory location that held the BAM byte BAM,X ($02A1,X).
	$F0C8	Increment the lo byte of the pointer to the original BAM image BUFTAB,X ($99,X).
	$F0CA	Increment .Y, the pointer to the new BAM image. Transfer this value into .A, AND it with $03 to mask off the high order bits, and if the result is not $00, branch back to SWAP1 to move the next byte.
SWAP2	$F0D0	Terminate the routine with an RTS.

		Zero the track number for BAM images:
CLNBAM	$F0D1	Load .A with the drive number from TRACK ($80), multiply it by two (ASL), and transfer the result into .X.
	$F0D5	Zero .A and store $00 as the track # for the BAM image in TBAM,X ($029D,X).
	$F0DA	Increment .X and store $00 as the track # for the BAM image in TBAM,X ($029D,X).

NAME	ADDRESS	DESCRIPTION OF WHAT ROM ROUTINE DOES
	$F0DE	Terminate the routine with an RTS.

REDBAM	$F0DF	Read BAM from disk if not already in RAM Load .A with the value from BUF0,X and compare it with $FF. If it is not $FF, the BAM is in memory so branch to RBM20.
	$F0E5	Transfer the channel number from .X into .A and save it onto the stack.
	$F0E7	JSR to GETBUF ($D28E) to find a free buffer. On return transfer the buffer number from .A into .X.
	$F0EB	If a buffer was found (bit 7 of buffer number not set), branch to RBM10.
	$F0ED	Load .A with $70 to indicate a NO CHANNEL ERROR and JSR to CMDERR ($C1C8).
RBM10	$F0F2	Store the buffer number assigned (in .X) into JOBNUM ($F9).
	$F0F4	Pull the channel number off the stack and transfer it into .Y.
	$F0F6	Transfer the buffer number from .X to .A, OR it with $80 to set it as inactive for stealing, and store the result into BUF0,Y ($00A7,Y).
	$F0FC	Multiply the buffer number (in .A) by two (ASL) and transfer the result into .X.
	$F0FE	Load .A with the directory track number (#18) from DIRTRK ($FE85) and store it in the header table at HDRS,X ($06,X).
	$F103	Store $00 as the BAM sector number in the header table at HDRS+1,X ($07,X).
	$F107	JMP to DOREAD ($D586) to read in the BAM and terminate routine.
RBM20	$F10A	AND the channel number (in .A) with $0F and store the result in JOBNUM ($F9) to set the BAM's job number.
	$F10E	Terminate routine with an RTS.

BAM2A	$F10F	Load .A with the channel # for the BAM Load .A with $06, the BAM's channel #
	$F111	Load .X with the current drive number from DRVNUM ($7F). If the drive number is not $00, branch to B2X10.
	$F115	Clear the carry flag and add $07 to find the BAM channel number for drive #1.
B2X10	$F118	Terminate routine with an RTS.

BAAM2X	$F119	Load .X with the channel # for the BAM JSR TO BAM2A ($F10F) to load .A with the BAM's channel number.
	$F11C	Transfer the channel # from .A to .X.

398

NAME	ADDRESS	DESCRIPTION OF WHAT ROM ROUTINE DOES
	$F11D	Terminate routine with an RTS.
		--
		Next available track and sector: Given current track and sector, this routine returns the next available track and sector.
NXTTS	$F11E	JSR to GETHDR ($DE3E) to set TRACK and SECTOR from the most recent header.
	$F121	Store $03 into TEMP ($6F).
	$F125	Load .A with $01, OR it with the value of the write-BAM flag, WBAM ($02F9), and store the result back into WBAM to prevent a write of the BAM.
NXTDS NXT1	$F12D	Load .A with the value from TEMP ($6F) and save it onto the stack.
	$F130	JSR to SETBAM ($F011) to set the BAM image into memory.
	$F133	Pull the original value of TEMP off the stack and store it back in TEMP ($6F).
	$F136	Load .A with the BAM value from (BMPNT),Y; ($6D,Y). If the value is not $00 (no sectors free), branch to FNDNXT ($F173).
	$F13A	Load .A with the current track number from TRACK ($80). If the track number is #18 (directory track), branch to NXTERR to abort.
	$F141	If the current track is less than #18, branch to NXT2.
	$F143	Increment the track number in TRACK ($80)
	$F145	Compare the value of TRACK to $24 (#36), the maximum track value. If they are not equal, branch to NXT1 to check out this track.
	$F14C	Load .X with $12 (#18), the directory track number from DIRTRK ($FE85).
	$F14F	Decrement the track number in .X.
	$F150	Store the track number (in .X) into TRACK ($80).
	$F152	Store $00 as the sector number into SECTOR ($81).
	$F156	Decrement the counter in TEMP ($6F).
	$F158	If the count is not $00 yet, branch to NXT1.
NXTERR	$F15A	Load .A with $72 to indicate a DISK FULL error and JSR to CMDERR ($C1C8).
NXT2	$F15F	Decrement the track number in TRACK ($80)
	$F161	If the value in TRACK is not $00, branch to NXT1 to check out this track.
	$F163	Load .X with $12 (#18), the directory track number from DIRTRK ($FE85).
	$F166	Increment the track number in .X.

NAME	ADDRESS	DESCRIPTION OF WHAT ROM ROUTINE DOES
	$F167	Store the track number (in .X) into TRACK ($80).
	$F169	Store $00 as the sector number into SECTOR ($81).
	$F16D	Decrement the counter in TEMP ($6F).
	$F16F	If the count is not $00 yet, branch to NXT1.
	$F171	If the count is $00, branch to NXTERR.
		--
		Find the optimum next sector on this track. Next sector=Current+change (#10)
FNDNXT	$F173	Load .A with the sector number from SECTOR ($81).
	$F175	Clear the carry flag and add the sector increment from SECINC ($69). The normal increment is $0A (#10). It is $03 for the directory track.
	$F178	Store the new sector number into SECTOR.
	$F17A	Load .A with the current track number from TRACK ($80) and JSR to MAXSEC ($F24B) to find the maximum sector number on this track (returned in .A).
	$F17F	Store the maximum sector number into LSTSEC ($024E) and CMD ($024D).
	$F185	Compare the maximum sector number (in .A) with the new sector value in SECTOR ($81). If the new sector value is less than the maximum, branch to FNDN0.
		New sector number too big so subtract away the maximum sector number on track.
	$F189	Set the carry flag.
	$F18A	Load .A with the new sector number from SECTOR ($80).
	$F18C	Subtract the maximum sector number on this track from LSTSEC ($024E) and store the result into SECTOR ($81).
	$F191	If the revised sector number is $00, branch to FNDN0.
	$F193	Decrement the revised sector number in SECTOR ($81) by 1.
FNDN0	$F195	JSR to GETSEC ($F1FA) to set the BAM into memory and find the first available sector following the revised sector #.
	$F198	If no sector is available on this track (Z flag = 1), branch to FNDN2.
FNDN1	$F19A	Exit with a JMP to WUSED ($EF90) to set this new sector as in use.
FNDN2	$F19D	Set the sector number in SECTOR ($81) to $00.

NAME	ADDRESS	DESCRIPTION OF WHAT ROM ROUTINE DOES
	$F1A1	JSR to GETSEC ($F1FA) to set the BAM into memory and find the first available sector following the revised sector #.
	$F198	If a sector is available on this track (Z flag = 0), branch to FNDN1.
	$F1A6	JMP to DERR ($F1F5) to abort.
		--
		Find optimum initial track and sector:
INTTS	$F1A9	Load .A with $01, OR it with the write-BAM flag, WBAM ($02F9), and store the result back in WBAM to indicate a write of BAM is pending.
	$F1B1	Load .A with the value from R0 ($86) and save it onto the stack.
	$F1B4	Store $01 into R0 ($86). NOTE: TRACK = DIRECTORY TRACK - R0
	$F1B8	Load .A with the directory track number ($12) from DIRTRK ($FE85).
	$F1BB	Set the carry flag, subtract the counter in R0 and store the result into TRACK ($80).
	$F1C0	If the value in TRACK is less than or equal to 0, branch to ITS2.
		Do tracks 17 -> 1
	$F1C4	JSR to SETBAM ($F011) to set the pointer to the BAM.
	$F1C7	Load .A with the number of blocks free on this track from (BMPNT),Y; ($6D,Y).
	$F1C9	If some sectors are free on this track (Z flag not set), branch to FNDSEC ($F1E6). None free on lower track so try a higher one:
ITS2	$F1CB	Load .A with the directory track number ($12) from DIRTRK ($FE85).
	$F1CE	Clear the carry flag, add the counter in R0 and store the result into TRACK ($80)
	$F1D3	Increment the track counter in R0 ($86).
	$F1D5	If the value in TRACK is greater than or equal to the maximum track number (#36), branch to ITS3.
	$F1DA	Load .A with $67 to indicate a SYSTEM TRACK & SECTOR error and JSR to CMDER2 ($E645).
		Do tracks 19 -> 35
ITS3	$F1DF	JSR to SETBAM ($F011) to set the pointer to the BAM.
	$F1E2	Load .A with the number of blocks free on this track from (BMPNT),Y; ($6D,Y).

NAME	ADDRESS	DESCRIPTION OF WHAT ROM ROUTINE DOES
	$F1E4	If no sectors are free on this track (Z flag is set), branch to ITS1 to try a lower numbered track.
FNDSEC	$F1E6	Pull the original value of R0 off the stack and store it back in R0 ($86).
	$F1E9	Store $00 as the sector number in SECTOR ($81).
	$F1ED	JSR to GETSEC ($F1FA) to set the BAM and find first available sector.
	$F1F0	If no sector available, branch to DERR.
	$F1F2	Terminate routine with a JMP to WUSED ($EF90) to mark sector as used in BAM.
DERR	$F1F5	Error in BAM: Load .A with $71 to indicate an error in the BAM and JSR to CMDER2 ($E645).
GETSEC	$F1FA	Set the BAM and find the first available sector starting at SECTOR: JSR to SETBAM ($F011) to set the pointer to the BAM.
	$F1FD	Transfer the .Y value into .A and save it onto the stack.
	$F1FF	JSR to AVCK ($F220) to check the bit map validity.
	$F202	Load .A with the current track number from TRACK ($80) and JSR to MAXSEC ($F24B) to find the maximum sector number allowed on this track. On return, store the maximum sector number (in .A) into LSTSEC ($024E).
	$F20A	Pull the original .Y value off the stack and store it in TEMP ($6F).
GS10	$F20D	Compare the current sector number from SECTOR ($81) with the maximum sector count in LSTSEC ($024E). If the current sector number is too large, branch to GS20.
	$F214	JSR to FREUS3 ($EFD5) to calculate index into the BAM. On return, if the Z flag is not set, the sector is free so branch to GS30.
	$F219	Sector was not free: Increment the sector number in SECTOR ($81) and branch (always) to GS10.
GS20	$F21D	Load .A with $00. Note that this sets the Z flag to indicate that a free sector was not found.
GS30	$F21F	Terminate routine with an RTS.
AVCK	$F220	Check the validity of the bit map: Load .A with the value of TEMP ($6F) and save it onto the stack.

NAME	ADDRESS	DESCRIPTION OF WHAT ROM ROUTINE DOES
	$F223	Store $00 into TEMP ($6F).
	$F227	Load .Y with $04, the number of bytes per track in the BAM from BAMSIZ ($FE86)
	$F22A	Decrement .Y by 1 (now $03).
AC10	$F22B	Load .X with $07 (bit counter).
AC20	$F22D	Load .A with the BAM byte for this track from (BMPNT),Y; ($6D,Y), and AND the BAM byte with the bit mask from BMASK,X ($EFE9,X) to isolate the bit for this sector. If the result is $00, the sector is allocated so branch to AC30.
	$F234	Since the sector is free, increment the count of free sectors in TEMP ($6F).
AC30	$F236	Decrement the bit counter (1 bit/sector) in .X. If the count is greater than or equal to $00, branch to AC20.
	$F239	Decrement the byte counter (8 sectors/ byte) in .Y. If the count is not $00, branch to AC10.
	$F23C	Compare the number of bytes free on the track as given in the BAM at (BMPNT),Y ($6D,Y) with the count we did in TEMP ($6F). If the counts DO NOT MATCH, branch to AC40 to abort.
	$F242	Pull the original value of TEMP off the stack and restore it into TEMP ($6F).
	$F245	Terminate routine with an RTS.

NAME	ADDRESS	DESCRIPTION OF WHAT ROM ROUTINE DOES
AC40	$F246	Error in BAM: Load .A with $71 to indicate an error in the BAM and JSR to CMDER2 ($E645).

NAME	ADDRESS	DESCRIPTION OF WHAT ROM ROUTINE DOES
MAXSEC	$F24B	Returns the number of sectors allowed on this track. Track number in .A. Load .X with the number of zones ($04) from NZONES ($FED6).
MAX1	$F24E	Compare the track number (in .A) with the zone boundary value from TRKNUM-1,X ($FED6,X).
	$F251	Decrement the zone count in .X.
	$F252	If the track number in .A is less than the boundary value, branch to MAX1.
	$F254	Load .A with the number of sectors/track for this zone from NUMSEC,X ($FED1,X).
	$F257	Terminate routine with an RTS.

NAME	ADDRESS	DESCRIPTION OF WHAT ROM ROUTINE DOES
KILLP	$F258	Kill protection: Does NOTHING on 1541! Terminate routine with an RTS.

NAME	ADDRESS	DESCRIPTION OF WHAT ROM ROUTINE DOES
		DISK CONTOLLER ROUTINES
		=========================
CNTINT	$F259	Controller initialization
	$F25B	Store %01101111 in DDRB2 ($1C02) to set the data direction for Port B.
	$F25E	Store %01100000 in DSKCNT ($1C00) to turn off the motor & LED and set phase A
	$F26C	Set the peripheral control register ($1C0C) for neg edge latch mode, CA2 hi to disable the SO line to the 6502, CB1 is input, and CB2 is R/W mode control.
	$F27B	set T1HL2($1C07) to $3A and T1LL2($1C06) to $00 so there is 20ms between IRQ's
	$F281	store $7F in IER2 ($1C0E) to clear all IRQ sources.
	$F286	store $C0 in IFR2 ($1C0D) to clear the bit and then into IER2 ($1C0E) to enable the timer IRQ.
	$F28E	store $FF as the current drive, CDRIVE ($3E) and as init flag, FTNUM ($51).
	$F294	set header block ID, HBID ($39) to $08
	$F298	set data block ID, DBID ($47) to $07
	$F29C	set NXTST ($62/3) to point to INACT ($FA05).
	$F2A4	set MINSTP ($64) to 200 to indicate the minimum number of steps required to invoke the fast stepping mode.
	$F2A8	store 4 into AS ($5E) to indicate the number of steps needed to accelerate and decelerate the head.
	$F2AC	store 4 into AF ($5F) as the acceleration/deceleration factor.
LCC		Main controller loop: Scans the job queue for job requests Finds job on current track if it exists
	$F2B0	Save stack pointer in SAVSP ($49).
	$F2B3	reset IRQ flag
	$F2B6	set bits 3,2,& 1 of PCR2 ($1C0C) to enable S.O. to 6502, hi output
TOP	$F2BE	top of loop to scan job queue. Load .Y with #$05 as pointer to top of queue.
CONT10	$F2C3	Load .A with byte from queue, JOBS,Y ($0000,Y). Test if bit 7 is set. If not, branch to CONT20 since no job here.
	$F2C5	Check if job is a jump code ($D0). If not, branch to CONT30.
	$F2CA	Transfer queue position from .Y to .A and JMP to EX2 ($F370) to do jump job.
CONT30	$F2CD	AND job code with $01. If result is 0, the drive # is valid so branch to CONT35
	$F2D1	Load .A with $0F to indicate a bad drive number and JMP to ERRR ($F969)

NAME	ADDRESS	DESCRIPTION OF WHAT ROM ROUTINE DOES
CONT35	$F2D8	Store job drive # in DRIVE ($3D).
	$F2DB	Compare job drive # with current drive number in CDRIVE ($3E). (CDRIVE is $FF if the drive is not turned on.) If they are equal, branch to CONT40
	$F2DF	JSR to TURNON ($F97E) to turn on drive.
	$F2E2	Set CDRIVE to job drive # and exit for now with a JMP to END ($F99C).
CONT40	$F2E9	Check the value in DRVST ($20) to see if the drive is up to speed. If bit 7 is set, it isn't so JMP to END ($F99C).
	$F2ED	Check if the head is stepping. If it is, exit with a JMP to END ($F99C). If it is not stepping, branch to QUE.
CONT20	$F2F3	Decrement .Y pointer into queue. If more locations in queue, branch back to CONT10. If none left JMP to END ($F99C).
QUE	$F2F9	Store $20 in DRVST ($20) to set drive status to running.
	$F2FD	Check if head needs to be stepped for this job. If not, branch to QUE20.
QUE05	$F306	Check other jobs to see if one for this track. If not, calculate steps needed.
	$F315	Store $60 in DRVST ($20) to set drive status to stepping, store destination track in DRVTRK ($22) and exit for now with a JMP to END ($F99C).
QUE20	$F320	check if job is on current drive. If not, branch back to QUE05.
	$F32A	calculate distance to track
	$F32D	are we on track already? if so, branch to GOTU.
	$F32F	store number of steps to the desired track in NXTRK ($42)
	$F339	JMP back to QUE05 to check if another job is closer.
GOTU	$F33C	Calculate zone (1-4) of the desired track and store the number of sectors on the track in SECTR ($43).
	$F34D	Calculate recording density and set the divide by N counter by storing a value in DSKCNT ($1C00).
	$F35F	Load .x with drive number and .A with the job code.
	$F363	Compare job code with $40. If equal, branch to BMP to do bump job.
EXE	$F367	Compare job code with $60. If equal, branch to EX to do execute job.
	$F36B	Not Bump or Execute, JMP to SEAK ($F3B1)

EX		Do an execute job
	$F367	set pointer to buffer in BUFPNT ($30/1)
	$F379	do indirect JMP via BUFPNT to the code that starts at the start of the buffer.

NAME	ADDRESS	DESCRIPTION OF WHAT ROM ROUTINE DOES
BMP		Do a bump to track #1
	$F37C	Store $60 as the drive status, DRVST (20) to indicate head is stepping.
	$F380	Set track phase to phase A
	$F388	Store -45 ($A4) as the number of tracks to move head in STEPS ($4A).
	$F38C	Set DRVTRK ($22) to 1 as new track#
	$F390	Job done so JMP to ERRR ($F969).
SETJB	$F393	Sub to set pointer to buffer, BUFPNT ($30/31) and into header table, HDRPNT ($32) for this position in job queue.

NAME	ADDRESS	DESCRIPTION OF WHAT ROM ROUTINE DOES
SEAK	$F3B1	Search for a valid header block on this track. Up to 90 header and data blocks are scanned while looking for a valid header block before this routine gives up. A valid header block must have:

  1) a SYNC mark
  2) a header block ID ($08)
  3) a valid checksum (EOR of sector, track, ID1, and ID2)
  4) the sector number
  5) the track number
  6) the second disk ID character given when the disk was formatted
  7) the first disk ID character given when the disk was formatted

  NOTE: The actual order of these bytes is as given above. Not as listed in the 1541 manual!

NAME	ADDRESS	DESCRIPTION OF WHAT ROM ROUTINE DOES
SEAK	$F3B1	Store $5A (90) in TMP ($4B) as the sync mark counter (quit if counts down to 0)
	$F3B7	Store $52 into STAB ($24) as the header block ID code to wait for (GCR for $08).
	$F3BB	JSR to SYNC ($F556) to wait for sync
	$F3BE	Read first character after sync
	$F3C4	Compare it to character in STAB ($24)
	$F3C6	If no match, this is not a header block so branch to SEEK20.
SEEK15	$F3C8	Loop to read in the next 7 characters and store in STAB+1,X ($25,X).
	$F3D5	JSR to CNVBIN ($F497) to convert the header bytes from GCR form to normal.
SEEK30	$F3D8	Loop to compute checksum of header read EOR checksum, sector, track, ID1 & ID2.
	$F3E2	If computed checksum is not 0, branch to CSERR ($F41E) to report error.
	$F3E6	Update current track from header data
	$F3EC	Compare job code in JOB ($45) with $30 to see if it is a seek job. If it is, branch to ESEEK ($F410) to do it.

NAME	ADDRESS	DESCRIPTION OF WHAT ROM ROUTINE DOES
	$F3F2	Compare master disk ID in $12/13 to the disk ID from the header in $16/17. If they don't match, branch to BADID($F41B) to report a disk ID mismatch error.
	$F404	JMP to WSWCT ($F423) to find the best sector on this track to service (usually the current sector + 2)
SEEK20	$F407	Decrement SYNC counter in TMP($4B) by 1 to see if we should check more syncs. If not 0 yet, branch back to SEEK10. If 0, load .A with a $02 (to indicate header block not found) and JMP to ERRR ($F969)
ESEEK	$F410	Change master disk ID in $12/$13 to match the ID read in from $16/17
DONE	$F418	Load .A with a $01 (to indicate job completed OK) and exit to error handler
		--
BADID	$F41B	Load .A with a $0B (to indicate disk ID mismatch) and exit to error handler
CSERR	$F41E	Load .A with a $09 (to indicate a bad checksum) and exit to error handler
		--
WSECT		Determine best sector on this track to service (optimum is current sector + 2)
	$F423	Store $7F as the current sector in $4C
	$F427	Load .A with the sector number from the header just read from HEADER+3 ($19).
	$F429	Add 2
	$F42C	Compare sum to the number of sectors on this track in SECTR ($43). If sum is too big, subtract the number of sectors.
L460	$F432	Store sum as next sector to be serviced in NEXTS ($4D).
L480	$F43A	JSR to SETJB ($F393) to set pointers.
	$F443	Check to be sure job is for this drive. If not, branch to L470 ($F483).
	$F447	Check to be sure job is for this track. If not, branch to L470 ($F483).
	$F44F	Compare job code in JOB ($45) with $60 to see if it is an execute job. If it is, branch to L465.
	$F455	Load .A with job's sector, (HDRPNT),Y and subtract the upcoming sector from NEXTS ($4D). If result is positive, branch to L465 since sector coming up.
	$F45E	Add value from NEXTS ($4D) back in.
L465	$F461	Compare to distance to other sector request. If further away, branch to L470 since other job is closer.
	$F465	Save distance to sector on the stack. Check job code in JOB ($45). If a read job, branch to TSTRDJ.

NAME	ADDRESS	DESCRIPTION OF WHAT ROM ROUTINE DOES
	$F46A	This is a write job. Pull distance to sector off the stack. Since a write job requires set up time, if sector is less than 9 ahead or more than 12 ahead, we are better off doing another job so branch to L470.
DOITT	$F473	This job is closer than others so set up by storing distance in CSECT ($4C) and setting BUFPNT to point to the buffer. Branch always to L470
TSTRDJ	$F47E	This is a read job. Pull distance to sector off the stack. Since a read job doesn't need much set up time, if sector is less than 6 ahead, we better do it so branch to DOITT.
L470	$F483	Decrement queue position in JOBN ($3F) by 1. If more to check branch to L480.
	$F487	No more to check. Test if any jobs were found. If none, JMP to END ($F99C). If yes, set up job and JMP to REED ($F4CA)
CNVBIN	$F497	Convert GCR image of header into the normal 8 bit binary and move the values into $16/7/8/9/A. The characters decoded include: -Header block ID code (usually $08) -Hdr block checksum (EOR of T/S/ID1/ID2) -Sector number -Track number -ID2 (2nd ID chr given when formatted) -ID1 (1st ID chr given when formatted) -The remaining characters are junk!
REED		Read in the track and sector that is specified in the header table
	$F4CA	Check if this is a read job. If not, JMP to WRIGHT ($F4CE)
READ01	$F4D1	JSR to DSTRT ($F50A) find header and set up to the start of the data block
READ11	$F4D4	Loop to read first 256 data bytes and store them in the data buffer.
READ20	$F4DF	Loop to read the last 70 data bytes and store them in the overflow buffer from $01BA to $01FF.
	$F4ED	JSR to GCRBIN ($F8E0) to convert the 326 GCR data bytes into 256 normal bytes
	$F4F0	Compare the first byte in the data block from BID ($38) with the header block ID character (normally $07) in HDIB ($47) to check if this is a legal data block.
	$F4F4	If they match, branch to READ28.

NAME	ADDRESS	DESCRIPTION OF WHAT ROM ROUTINE DOES
	$F5F6	No match, so load .A with a 4 to flag a DATA BLOCK NOT FOUND error and JMP to ERRR ($F969).
READ28	$F4FB	JSR to CHKBLK ($F5E9) to compute the checksum for the data block by EORing all the 256 data bytes.
	$F4FE	Compare the computed checksum in .A with with the checksum read from the disk in CHKSUM ($3A). If equal, branch to READ40
	$F502	No match, so load .A with a 5 to flag a DATA BLOCK CHECKSUM error
	$F504	Byte $2C to skip over next LDA
	$F5F6	Load .A with a 1 to indicate a good read
	$F507	JMP to ERRR ($F969).
DSTRT	$F50A	JSR to SRCH ($F510) to find the desired header block. JMP to SYNC ($F556) to wait for the data block sync character.
SRCH		Find a specific header. The track and sector desired must be stored in the header table
	$F510	Use values from the header table and the master disk ID ($12/3) to set up an image of the desired header $16-$19
	$F529	EOR the track, sector, and ID characters to calculate the header checksum and store it in $1A.
	$F533	JSR to CONHDR ($F934) to convert the header image into its GCR image.
	$F536	Load .X with $5A as a counter of the number of sync marks checked.
SRCH20	$F538	JSR to SYNC ($F556) to wait for the next sync mark.
SRCH25	$F53D	Loop to scan the 8 bytes following the sync mark to attempt to find a match to the GCR image of the desired header. If any character does not match the image, branch to SRCH30.
	$F54D	All characters match so exit with an RTS
SRCH30	$F54E	Decrement the sync mark counter in .X If counter is not 0 yet, branch back to SRCH20 to wait for next sync.
	$F551	No match, so load .A with a 2 to flag a BLOCK HEADER NOT FOUND error.
ERR	$F553	JMP to ERRR ($F969).
SYNC	$F556	Wait for SYNC mark A SYNC mark is 10 or more consecutive 1's bits written onto the disk. It is used to identify the start of a block of information recorded on disk. The

NAME	ADDRESS	DESCRIPTION OF WHAT ROM ROUTINE DOES
		first character following a SYNC mark is used to determine whether this is a header block ($08) or a data block ($07).
	$F556	Store $D0 in TIMER1 ($1805) to allow a maximum wait of 20 milliseconds for a sync before timing out.
	$F55B	Load .A with $03 (the error code for a NO SYNC FOUND error)
SYNC10	$F55D	Test bit 7 of TIMER1 ($1805) to check for a time-out. If time is up, branch to ERR ($F553) to exit.
	$F562	Test bit 7 of DSKCNT ($1C00) to check for a sync. If no sync, branch back to SYNC10 to wait some more.
	$F567	Load .A from DATA2 to reset the PA latch clear the 6502's overflow flag, and RTS
WRIGHT		Write contents of data buffer to disk
	$F56E	Compare job code in .A with $10 to check if this is write job. If not, JMP to VERIFY ($F691).
	$F575	JSR to CHKBLK ($F5E9) to compute the checksum for the data block. Store the checksum in CHKSUM ($3A).
	$F57A	Load .A from DSKCNT and AND it with $10 to check for write protect tab. If the result is not $00, OK to write so branch to WRT10.
		Load .A with $08 to flag a WRITE PROTECT error and JMP to ERRR ($F969)
WRT10	$F586	JSR to BINGCR ($F78F) to convert data in the buffer into GCR form.
	$F589	JSR to SRCH ($F510) to find the correct header block
	$F58C	Wait for 8 more bytes to go by. This is the header gap.
		NOTE: The header gap on the 1541 is 8 bytes long. The gap on the 4040 is 9 bytes long. This is the main reason why the drives are write incompatible!
	$F594	Store $FF in DDRA2 ($1C03) to make Port A an output port
	$F599	Load .A from PCR2 ($1C0C), AND the value with $1F, OR it with $C0, and store the result in PCR2 to turn on write mode.
	$F5A3	Store $FF in DATA2 ($1C01) as the SYNC mark character
WRTSNC	$F5AB	Loop to write out 5 consecutive $FF bytes (5x8 = 40 1's).

NAME	ADDRESS	DESCRIPTION OF WHAT ROM ROUTINE DOES
	$F5B1	Load .Y with $BB to point into the overflow buffer ($01BB-01FF).
WRT30	$F5B3	Load .A with byte from overflow buffer, wait till last byte is out, store new byte into DATA2 ($1C01), increment .Y pointer, and if more characters to do, branch back to WRT30.
WRT40	$F5BF	Load .A with byte from data buffer, wait till last byte is out, store new byte into DATA2 ($1C01), increment .Y pointer, and if more characters to do, branch back to WRT40.
	$F5CA	Wait for final byte to clear
	$F5CC	Load .A from PCR2 ($1C0C), OR the value with $E0, and store the result back in PCR2 to shift to read mode.
	$F5D4	Store $00 in data direction register DDRA2 to make port A an input port.
	$F5D9	JSR to WTOBIN ($F5F2) to convert GCR data in buffer back into its normal 8 bit form to prepare to verify it.
	$F5DC	Convert the write job number in the job queue into a verify job.
	$F5E6	JMP to SEAK ($F3B1) to scan the queue for the next job.
CHKBLK	$F5E9	Calculate data block checksum EOR the 256 data bytes. Return with the checksum in .A
WTOBIN	$F5F2	Convert the 10 bit image of the data to normal 8 bit binary. Since 5 encoded bytes (40 bits) are converted into 4 normal bytes (32 bits), the encoded form of 256 data bytes takes up 320 bytes. At the start of this routine the first 64 encoded bytes that were read are stored in the overflow buffer ($01BA-FF) and the remaining 256 bytes are in the normal data buffer. At the end of the routine the decoded bytes are stored in the normal data buffer.
	$F5F2	Set up pointers to the buffers
	$F5FE	Do the overflow buffer ($01BA-FF) first.
	$F604	Store $BB in GCRPNT ($34) so it points to the first byte in the overflow buffer ($01BB) that is to be processed by the routine GET4GB.
	$F608	Store $BB in BYTCNT ($52) so it points to the location where the first decoded data byte is to be stored.
	$F60A	JSR to GET4GB ($F7E6) to convert the

411

NAME	ADDRESS	DESCRIPTION OF WHAT ROM ROUTINE DOES
		first five GCR bytes into 4 normal bytes (the data block ID + 3 data bytes). The decoded bytes appear in $52-5
	$F60D	Store data block ID chr in BID ($38).
	$F611	Move decoded data bytes from $53-$55 to the buffer ($01BB-D). Note that the decoded bytes are put back into the overflow buffer.
WTOB14	$F624	JSR to GET4BG ($F7E6) to convert the next 5 GCR bytes to 4 normal bytes and store them in $52-5.
	$F629	Move decoded data bytes from $53-$55 to the buffer ($01BB-D). Note that the decoded bytes are put back into the overflow buffer.
	$F641	If more in overflow, branch to WTOB14
WTOB50	$F643	Move last two data bytes into buffer
WTOB53	$F64F	Loop to convert the 256 bytes in data buffer. JSR to GET4BG ($F7E6) to convert the next 5 GCR bytes to 4 normal bytes and store them in $52-5.
	$F629	Move decoded data bytes from $53-$55 to the data buffer. Note that the decoded bytes are put back in the data buffer.
		At this point the data bytes have all been decoded. Some bytes are in the overflow buffer and some are in the lower part of the data buffer. The following routines shift the bytes in the buffer up and then fill the lower part of the buffer with the bytes from the overflow buffer.
WTOB52	$F66E	Move decoded bytes in lower part of the data buffer up into their proper places in the buffer.
WTOB57	$F683	Move decoded bytes from the overflow buffer to the bottom of the data buffer.
	$F68E	Set GCRFLG ($50) to 0 to indicate that the data in buffer is in normal form.
	$F690	Exit with an RTS.
VRFY		Verify a data block This routine converts the data in the data buffer into its 10 bit encoded form (GCR). It then compares the GCR image with what is recorded on the disk. The encoded data is then changed back into normal 8 bit binary form.
	$F691	Compare job code in .A with $20 to check that this is a verify job. If not, JMP to SECTSK (F6CA) to do a sector seek.

NAME	ADDRESS	DESCRIPTION OF WHAT ROM ROUTINE DOES
	$F698	JSR to CHKBLK ($F5E9) to compute the checksum for the data block. Store the checksum in CHKSUM ($3A).
	$F69D	JSR to BINGCR ($F78F) to convert the data to its GCR image.
	$F6A0	JSR to DSTRT ($F50A) to find the right sector and wait for data.
VRF15	$F6A3	Loop to read 64 data bytes from disk and compare them to those in the overflow buffer. If any bytes do not match, branch to VRF20 to report error.
VRF30	$F6B3	Loop to read 254 data bytes from disk and compare them to those in the data buffer. If any bytes do not match, branch to VRF20 to report error.
	$F6C2	All bytes match so JMP to DONE ($F418)

| VRF20 | $F6C5 | Bad byte, so load .A with $07 to flag a WRITE-VERIFY error & JMP to ERRR ($F969) |

| SECTSK | $F6CA | JSR to SRCH to do a sector search JMP to DONE ($F418) |

| PUT4GB | $F6D0 | Convert binary to GCR This routine is used to convert 4 normal 8 bit bytes into the 10 bit encoded form used for recording onto disk. Encoding involves breaking up each 8 bit normal byte into two 4-bit nybbles. The 5-bit equivalent for each nybble is found by looking in a table. The 10 bits that result are stored in two consecutive memory locations. When four 8-bit bytes are encoded, the resulting 40 bits are stored like this: |

Four normal 8 bit bytes stored in $52/3/4/5
AAAABBBB CCCCDDDD EEEEFFFF GGGGHHHH

Four 10 bit encoded bytes stored in buffer
aaaaabbb bbcccccd ddddeeee effffgg ggghhhhh

| | $F6D0 | Clear critical areas of the buffer where the encoded bytes are to be stored. GTAB to GTAB+4 ($56-5A) |
| | $F6D8 | Load first 8-bit byte ($52), AND it with $F0 (11110000) to mask off the low nybble (AAAA0000), do four LSR's to convert the hi nybble to a low nybble (0000AAAA), look up the corresponding five bit GCR value (000aaaaa) in BGTAB BGTAB ($F77F+), do three ASL's on it (aaaaa000), and store it in the first position in the encoded data area ($56) |

413

NAME	ADDRESS	DESCRIPTION OF WHAT ROM ROUTINE DOES
	$F6E9	Load first 8-bit byte ($52), AND it with $0F (00001111) to mask off the high nybble (0000BBBB), find the five bit GCR equivalent (000bbbbb) in BGTAB ($F77F+), do two ROR's on it alternated with ROR's on $57 .A=(0000Cbbb) $57=bb000000, AND the value in .A with $07 (00000111), OR the value in .A with the value in $52 (aaaaa000), and store the result (aaaaabbb) in the first position of the GCR data buffer (BUFPNT),Y ($30,Y).
	$F6FE	Load second 8-bit byte ($53), AND it with $F0 (11110000) to mask off the low nybble (CCCC0000), do four LSR's to convert the hi nybble to a low nybble (0000CCCC), look up the five bit GCR equivalent (000ccccc) in BGTAB ($F77F+), do one ASL on it (00ccccc0), OR it with the contents of $57 (bb000000), and put the result (bbccccc0) in $57.
	$F70F	Load second 8-bit byte ($53), AND it with $0F (00001111) to mask off the high nybble (0000DDDD), find the five bit GCR equivalent (000ddddd) in BGTAB ($F77F+), do four ROL's on it (dddd0000 C=d), store it in $58(dddd0000), do one more ROL (ddd0000d C=d), AND it with $01, OR it with the value in $57(bbccccc0) and store the result (bbccccd) into the second byte of the GCR buffer
	$F725	Load third 8-bit byte ($54), AND it with $F0 (11110000) to mask off the low nybble (EEEE0000), do four LSR's to convert the hi nybble to a low nybble (0000EEEE), look up the five bit GCR equivalent (000eeeee) in BGTAB ($F77F+), do one FOR on it (0000eeee C=e), OR it with the contents of $58 (dddd0000), store the result (ddddeeee) in the third byte of the GCR buffer, do another ROR (eC000eee)C=e, AND it with $80(10000000) and store the result (e0000000) in $59.
	$F73D	Load third 8-bit byte ($54), AND it with $0F (00001111) to mask off the high nybble (0000FFFF), find the five bit GCR equivalent (000fffff) in BGTAB ($F77F+), do two ASL's on it (0fffff00), AND it with $7C (01111100), OR it with the value in $59 (e0000000), and store the result (efffff00) in $59
	$F74D	Load the fourth 8-bit byte ($55), AND it with $F0 (11110000) to mask off the low nybble (GGGG0000), do four LSR's to

NAME	ADDRESS	DESCRIPTION OF WHAT ROM ROUTINE DOES
		convert the hi nybble to a low nybble (0000GGGG), look up the five bit GCR equivalent (000ggggg) in BGTAB ($F77F+), do three ROR's on .A alternated with ROR's on $5A .A=(00000gg) $5A=(ggg00000) AND .A with $03 (00000011), OR .A with the contents of $59 (efffff00), & store result (efffffgg) in the fourth byte of the GCR buffer.
	$F76F	Load the fourth 8-bit byte ($55), AND it with $0F (00001111) to mask off the high nybble (0000HHHH), find the five bit GCR equivalent (000hhhhh) in BGTAB ($F77F+), OR it with the value in $59 (ggg00000), and store the result (ggghhhhh) in the fifth position of the GCR buffer.

NAME	ADDRESS	DESCRIPTION OF WHAT ROM ROUTINE DOES
BGTAB	$F77F	Table of 5 bit GCR equivalents

---

4 bit nybble		5 bit GCR code	
$00	0000	$0A	01010
$01	0001	$0B	01011
$02	0010	$12	10010
$03	0011	$13	10011
$04	0100	$0E	01110
$05	0101	$0F	01111
$06	0110	$16	10110
$07	0111	$17	10111
$08	1000	$09	01001
$09	1001	$19	11001
$0A	1010	$1A	11010
$0B	1011	$1B	11011
$0C	1100	$0D	01101
$0D	1101	$1D	11101
$0E	1110	$1E	11110
$0F	1111	$15	10101

Note: 5 bits are used to ensure that not more than 2 consecutive 0's are recorded on disk.

NAME	ADDRESS	DESCRIPTION OF WHAT ROM ROUTINE DOES
BINGCR		Create write image of data This routine converts 260 normal 8-bit bytes into their 10-bit equivalents to produce an image for writing to disk. A total of 325 GCR bytes are produced.

NAME	ADDRESS	DESCRIPTION OF WHAT ROM ROUTINE DOES
		The original 8-bit bytes are:
		1 data block ID character ($07)
		256 data bytes (stored in buffer X)
		1 data checksum
		2 off bytes ($00)
		---
		260 8-bit binary bytes
		The first 69 GCR bytes are stored in the overflow buffer ($10BB-FF). The rest of the GCR bytes are stored in buffer X and replace the original data bytes
	$F78F	Initialize pointers to buffers
	$F797	Set pointer to start of overflow $01bb
	$F7A5	Move data block ID code from DBID ($47) and first 3 data characters into a work area ($52/3/4/5) for input by the PUT4GB routine ($F6D0)
BING07	$F7BA	Store pointer to next byte to convert (in .Y) into BYTCNT ($36).
	$F7BC	JSR to PUT4GB ($F6D0) to convert the four bytes in $52/3/4/5 into their five GCR equivalents and store in buffer. Use the overflow buffer first and then use the data buffer.
	$F7BF	Move next four bytes into the work area ($52/3/4/5).
	$F7D7	If more bytes to convert (.Y is count) branch back to BING07.
	$F7D9	Move data block checksum from DBID ($3A) and two off bytes ($00) into the work area ($53/4/5) NOTE: THE LAST DATA BYTE IS IN $52.
	$F7E3	JSR to PUT4GB ($F6D0) to convert the four bytes in $52/3/4/5 into their five GCR equivalents and store in buffer.
GET4GB		Convert GCR to binary This routine is used to decode 5 GCR bytes (used for recording on disk) into 4 normal 8-bit binary bytes. Decoding involves extracting 5 bits from one or two GCR bytes. The 4-bit nybble that is equivalent to it is found by looking in a table. The pattern of 5-bit segments in the 5 GCR bytes and the equivalent 4-bit nybbles in the four binary bytes are indicated below:

```
Four 10 bit encoded bytes stored in buffer
  aaaaabbb bbcccccd ddddeeee efffffgg ggghhhhh
```

NAME	ADDRESS	DESCRIPTION OF WHAT ROM ROUTINE DOES

Four normal 8 bit bytes stored in $56/7/8/9
AAAABBBB CCCCDDDD EEEEFFFF GGGGHHHH

	$F7E6	Load the first GCR byte (aaaaabbb) from (BUFPNT),Y, AND it with $F8 (11111000) to mask off the low bits (aaaa000), do three LSR's and store the result (000aaaaa) in GTAB ($56)
	$F7F1	Load the first GCR byte (aaaaabbb) from (BUFPNT),Y, AND it with $07 (00000111) to mask off the high bits (00000bbb), do two ASL's and store the result(000bbb00) in $57.
	$F7F9	Increment Y and check if Y=0. If so, change BUFPNT so it points to the data buffer rather than the overflow buffer.
	$F802	Load the second GCR byte (bbcccccd) from (BUFPNT),Y, AND it with $C0 (11000000) to mask off the low bits (bb000000), do three ROL's (000000bb), OR it with the value in $57 (000bbb00), and store the result (000bbbbb) back in $57.
	$F80D	Load the second GCR byte(bbcccccd) from (BUFPNT),Y, AND it with $3E (00111110) to mask off unwanted bits (00ccccc0), do one LSR and store the result (000ccccc) in $58.
	$F814	Load the second GCR byte (bbcccccd) from (BUFPNT),Y, AND it with $01 (00000001) to mask off unwanted bits (0000000d), do four ASL's and store the result (000d0000) in $58.
	$F81F	Load the third GCR byte (ddddeeee) from (BUFPNT),Y, AND it with $F0 (11110000) to mask off the low bits (dddd0000), do four LSR's (0000dddd), OR it with the value in $59 (000d0000), and store the result (000ddddd) back in $59.
	$F82B	Load the third GCR byte (ddddeeee) from (BUFPNT),Y, AND it with $0F(00001111) to mask off hi bits (0000eeee), do one ASL and store the result (000eeee0) in $5A.
	$F833	Load the fourth GCR byte (effffgg) from (BUFPNT),Y, AND it with $80 (10000000) to mask off the low bits (e0000000), do two ROL's (000e0000), OR it with the value in $5A (0000eeee), and store the result (000eeeee) back in $5A.
	$F840	Load the fourth GCR byte (effffgg) from (BUFPNT),Y, AND it with $7C (01111100) to mask off unwanted bits (0fffff00), do two LSR's and store the result(000fffff) in $5B.

NAME	ADDRESS	DESCRIPTION OF WHAT ROM ROUTINE DOES
	$F848	Load the fourth GCR byte (effffgg) from (BUFPNT),Y, AND it with $03 (00000011) to mask off unwanted bits (000000gg), do three LSR's and store the result (000gg000) in $5C.
	$F854	Increment Y. If Y=0 change BUFPNT to point to the next buffer.
	$F85A	Load the fifth GCR byte (ggghhhhh) from (BUFPNT),Y, AND it with $E0 (11100000) to mask off the low bits (ggg00000), do four ROL's (00000ggg), OR it with the value in $5C (000gg000), and store the result (000ggggg) back in $5C.
	$F866	Load the fifth GCR byte(ggghhhhh) from (BUFPNT),Y, AND it with $1F (00011111) to mask off the high bits (000hhhhh), and store in $5D
		At this point the 40 bits that made up the 5 GCR bytes have been separated into eight 5-bit values that correspond to the eight 4-bit nybbles that will make up the four normal binary bytes. The 8 5-bit values are stored in $56-D. The following routines look up the 4-bit hi nybbles in GCRHI ($F8A0) and the low nybbles in GCRLO (starts at $F8C0)
	$F86D	Load .X with the first 5-bit value from $56, load .A with 4-bit high nybble from GCRHI,X, load X with a second five bit value from $57, OR .A with the four bit low nybble from GCRLO,X, and store the result in $52.
	$F87B	Load X with the third 5-bit value from $58, load .A with 4-bit high nybble from GCRHI,X, load X with the fourth 5-bit value from $59, OR .A with the 4-bit low nybble from GCRLO,X and store the result in $53.
	$F887	Load X with the fifth 5-bit value from $5A, load .A with 4-bit high nybble from from GCRHI,X, load X with the second five bit value from $5B, OR .A with the four bit low nybble from GCRLO,X, and store the result in $54.
	$F893	Load .X with the seventh 5 value from $5C, load .A with 4-bit high nybble from GCRHI,X, load X with the second 5-bit value from $5D, OR .A with the four bit low nybble from GCRLO,X, and store the result in $55.

NAME	ADDRESS	DESCRIPTION OF WHAT ROM ROUTINE DOES

NOTE: The five bit to four bit tables below have many $FF
entries. These are the five bit codes that are not used.
If one of these is found, it causes a byte decoding error

GCRHI($F8A0) & GCRLO($F8C0) Tables of 5 bit GCR to binary
----

5 bit GCR code		High nybble ($F8A0+)			Low nybble ($F8C0+)		
$00	00000	$FF	11111111	ERROR	$FF	11111111	ERROR
$01	00001	$FF	11111111	ERROR	$FF	11111111	ERROR
$02	00010	$FF	11111111	ERROR	$FF	11111111	ERROR
$03	00011	$FF	11111111	ERROR	$FF	11111111	ERROR
$04	00100	$FF	11111111	ERROR	$FF	11111111	ERROR
$05	00101	$FF	11111111	ERROR	$FF	11111111	ERROR
$06	00110	$FF	11111111	ERROR	$FF	11111111	ERROR
$07	00111	$FF	11111111	ERROR	$FF	11111111	ERROR
$08	01000	$FF	11111111	ERROR	$FF	11111111	ERROR
$09	01001	$80	1000----		$08	----1000	
$0A	01010	$00	--------		$00	----0000	
$0B	01011	$10	0001----		$01	----0001	
$0C	01100	$FF	11111111	ERROR	$FF	11111111	ERROR
$0D	01101	$C0	1100----		$0C	----1100	
$0E	01110	$40	0100----		$04	----0100	
$0F	01111	$50	0101----		$05	----0101	
$10	10000	$FF	11111111	ERROR	$FF	11111111	ERROR
$11	10001	$FF	11111111	ERROR	$FF	11111111	ERROR
$12	10010	$20	0010----		$02	----0010	
$13	10011	$30	0011----		$03	----0011	
$14	10100	$FF	11111111	ERROR	$FF	11111111	ERROR
$15	10101	$F0	1111----		$0F	----1111	
$16	10110	$60	0110----		$06	----0110	
$17	10111	$70	0111----		$07	----0111	
$18	11000	$FF	11111111	ERROR	$FF	11111111	ERROR
$19	11001	$90	1001----		$09	----1001	
$1A	11010	$A0	1010----		$0A	----1010	
$1B	11011	$B0	1011----		$0B	----1011	
$1C	11100	$FF	11111111	ERROR	$FF	11111111	ERROR
$1D	11101	$D0	1101----		$0D	----1101	
$1E	11110	$E0	1110----		$0E	----1110	
$1F	11111	$FF	11111111	ERROR	$FF	11111111	ERROR

GCRBIN		Decode GCR data image
		This routine decoded the 69 GCR bytes stored in the overflow buffer ($10BB-FF) into normal 8-bit bytes. The decoded bytes are stored in a data buffer.
	$F8E0	Zero byte counter & lo bit of pointers
	$F8E8	Set lo byte of pointer, NXTBF ($4E) to $BA and set the hi byte NXTPNT ($4F) to $01 so they point to the first byte of the GCR image in the overflow buffer.

NAME	ADDRESS	DESCRIPTION OF WHAT ROM ROUTINE DOES
	$F8F0	Set SAVPNT+1 ($2F) to point to the data buffer where the 8-bit bytes are to be stored.
	$F8F4	JSR to GET4GB ($F7E6) to convert the first five GCR bytes into binary, the header block ID, the header checksum, the sector #, and the track #. The decoded bytes appear in $52-5.
	$F8F7	Store header block ID code in BID ($38)
	$F8FB	Move the three decoded bytes from $53-55 into the buffer. Note that these bytes are NOT stored in the overflow buffer where the GCR image is stored.
GCRB10	$F90C	Transfer byte pointer from .Y into BYTCNT ($36).
	$F90E	JSR to GET4GB ($F7E6) to convert the next five GCR bytes to normal and store them in $52-5.
	$F913	Move decoded data byte from $52 into the data buffer.
	$F918	Test .Y to see if entire overflow buffer has been done. If done, branch to GCRB20
	$F91A	Move decoded data bytes from $53-5 into the data buffer.
	$F929	If .Y is not $00, there is more to do so branch back to GCRB10.
GCRB20	$F92B	Move header block checksum from $53 to CHKSUM ($3A)
	$F92F	Restore buffer pointer and RTS.
CONHDR		Convert header to write image This routine creates a GCR image of a header block. It uses the header block ID code from HBID ($39) and the header information stored in $1A (checksum), $19 (sector), $18 (track), $17 (ID2), and $16 (ID1). A final $00 byte is used as a final off byte. Four of the binary bytes are moved into a staging area and the subroutine PUT4GB ($F6D0) is used to convert these bytes to their GCR image and store them in the STAB buffer($24-D)
	$F934	Save current value of the buffer pointer BUFPNT+1 ($31) in SAVPNT+1 ($2F).
	$F938	Make BUFPNT+1 ($31) point to >STAB ($00)
	$F93C	Make GCRPNT ($34) point to <STAB ($24)
	$F940	Move hdr blk ID from HBID ($39) to $52
	$F944	Move checksum from $1A to $53
	$F948	Move sector from $19 to $54
	$F94C	Move track from $18 to $55
	$F950	JSR to PUT4GB ($F6D0) to convert the four bytes in $52-5 to 5 GCR bytes and store them at the start of STAB ($24-8).

NAME	ADDRESS	DESCRIPTION OF WHAT ROM ROUTINE DOES
	$F953	Move 2nd ID chr from $17 to $52
	$F957	Move 1st ID chr from $16 to $53
	$F95B	Store $00 off bytes into $54 & $55
	$F961	JSR to PUT4GB ($F6D0) to convert the four bytes in $52-5 to 5 GCR bytes and store them in STAB ($29-D).
	$F964	Restore the buffer pointer BUFPNT+1($31) to its previous value and RTS.

UTILITY ROUTINES

NAME	ADDRESS	DESCRIPTION OF WHAT ROM ROUTINE DOES
ERRR		Disk controller error handling This routine is used to terminate all of the major disk controller routines. The inputs to this routine are: the error code (see table) in .A, the job buffer number in JOBN ($3F), and the GCRFLG ($50) (tells if the data in the buffer has been left in write image (1) or binary (0) form). The routine stuffs the error code into the job queue, converts the data back to binary (if necessary), starts time-out to turn off the drive motor, resets the stack pointer, and exits to $F2BE to begin scanning the job queue again.
	$F969	Store error code in .A into job queue
	$F96E	Check GCRFLG ($50) to see if data left in GCR format. If not, branch to ERRR10.
	$F972	JSR to WTOBIN ($F5F2) to convert data from GCR to normal.
ERRR10	$F96E	JSR to TRNOFF ($F98F) to start the time-out to turn off the drive motor.
	$F978	Use value from SAVSP ($49) to reset the stack pointer.
	$F97B	JMP to TOP ($F2BE) to scan job queue.

NAME	ADDRESS	DESCRIPTION OF WHAT ROM ROUTINE DOES
TURNON		Turn on disk drive motor
	$F97E	Store $A0 into drive status, DRVST ($20) to indicate that the drive is ON but not yet up to speed (accelerating).
	$F982	Set bit 2 (00000100) of DSKCNT ($1C00) to turn ON the drive motor.
	$F98A	Store $3C into acceleration timer,ACLTIM ($48) to cause drive status to be set to up-to-speed after 1.5 seconds. (60 interrupts at .025 seconds each)

NAME	ADDRESS	DESCRIPTION OF WHAT ROM ROUTINE DOES
TRNOFF		Turn off disk drive motor
	$F98F	Load .X with current drive # (0)
	$F991	Set bit 4 (00010000) of the drive status DRVST ($20) to indicate DRIVE IS OFF!

NAME	ADDRESS	DESCRIPTION OF WHAT ROM ROUTINE DOES
	$F997	Store $FF into acceleration timer to cause the drive to be turned OFF after 6.4 seconds. (255 interrupts x .025 sec)
END		Drive motor and head stepper control This routine is the last part of the main IRQ routine. As a result, it is executed every 10 milliseconds. Control is transferred to the routine by JMP instructions at the conclusion of the main disk controller routines. The RTS at the end of the routine transfers control to master IRQ routine at $FE7C.
	$F99C	Move value in the 6522's timer #1 high latch ($1C07) into timer #1's high bit counter ($1C05)
	$F9A5	Test if write protect status has changed by loading the value from the 6522's data PORT B($1C00), ANDing it with $10 and comparing it to the value in LWPT ($1E). If not equal, set flag for change in status, WPSW ($1C) to $01.
	$F9B1	Test whether the head stepper is in (0 or 2) or out (1) of phase. The head's stepper motor moves half a track at a time. If the head is halfway between two tracks, the value stored in PHASE($02FE) is 1. If the value in PHASE is 0, branch to END40 ($F9CB). If PHASE is 2, set it to $00 and branch to END40. If it is $01 set it to $02 & branch to DOSTEP ($FA2E) to move head half a track.
	$F9CB	Check CDRIVE ($3E) to see if the drive is active. If not active, branch to END33X to end the IRQ routine.
	$F9CF	Load DRVST ($20) to see if the motor is ON and compare value with $20. If there is anything to do (result not equal), then branch to END10.
END33X	$F9D6	JMP to END33 ($FABE) to end IRQ.
END10	$F9D9	Something doing, so decrement the acceleration timer, ACLTIM ($48), and if drive is not yet up to speed, branch to END30. Since drive is up to speed, clear the not-up-to-speed bit (bit 7) of the drive status, DRVST ($20).
END20	$F9E4	AND the value of DRVST ($20) with $10 to test whether a time-out has occurred and it is time to turn off the drive motor. If not, branch to END30 ($F9FA).

NAME	ADDRESS	DESCRIPTION OF WHAT ROM ROUTINE DOES
	$F9E8	Turn off drive motor by loading .A with the value of DRVCNT($1C00), ANDing it with $FB (to clear bit 2) and storing the result back in DRVCNT.
	$F9F0	Store $FF in CDRIVE ($3E) to indicate there is no currently active drive.
	$F9F4	Set DRVST ($20) to $0 to indicate that the drive is switched OFF. Then branch to END33X ($F9D6) to end IRQ routine.
END30	$F9FA	AND .A (contains drive status) with $40 to test if head must be moved. If the result is 0 (no stepping needed) JMP to END33 ($FABE) to end the IRQ routine. If stepping is required, do an indirect JMP via NXTST ($0062) to the proper head stepping routine: SHORT - $FA3B - short step mode SETLE - $FA4E - settle head mode SSACL - $FA7B - accelerate mode SSRUN - $FA97 - fast stepping mode SSDEC - $FAA5 - decelerate mode
INACT	$FA05	Set up to step the head: Load .A with the number of steps to move the head from STEPS ($4A). If negative (>127), find the absolute value using the 2's complement.
INAC10	$FA0E	Compare the number of steps to the value (usually $C8)in MINSTP ($64) to see if the distance is big enough to use the fast stepping mode. If the distance is large enough, branch to INA20 ($FA1C).
	$FA12	Not big enough so set up the pointer in NXTST ($62/3) to point to the short step routine, SHORT ($FA3B) and branch to DOSTEP ($FA2E).
INAC20	$FA1C	Calculate the number of steps to do in fast stepping mode by subtracting the value in AS ($5E) from .A twice (for acceleration and deceleration). Store the result in RSTEPS ($61). Then move the number of steps needed for the head to accelerate from AS ($5E) to ACLSTP ($60). Finally set pointer in NXTST ($62/3) to point to the acceleration mode routine SSACL ($FA7B)
DOSTEP	$FA2E	Load value from STEPS ($4A). If positive (<127), branch to STPIN ($FA63) to step the head inwards.
STPOUT	$FA32	Increment STEPS ($4A) to reduce number left to do by 1, load .X with the value from DSKCNT ($1C00) decrement it by 1, and branch to STP ($FA69).

NAME	ADDRESS	DESCRIPTION OF WHAT ROM ROUTINE DOES
SHORT	$FA3B	Short distance head stepping. Load the number of steps left to do from STEPS ($4A). If any left, branch to DOSTEP ($FA2E). If not, set NXTST pointer($62/3) to point to the settle head routine SETLE ($FA4E) and store $05 in ACLSTP ($60) to set the settle time. Branch to END33 ($FABE) to end IRQ.
SETLE	$FA4E	Settle head routine. Decrement ACLSTP ($60) and if non-zero, brach to END33 ($FABE) to end IRQ. If zero, set drive status, DRVST ($20), to indicate that the drive is available for use by clearing bit 6. Set NXTST pointer($62/3) to point to the head inactive routine ($FA05) and branch to END33 ($FABE).
STPIN	$FA63	Decrement STEPS ($4A) to reduce number left to do by 1, load .X with the value from DSKCNT($1C00) and increment it by 1
STP	$FA69	Transfer the value in .X to .A (this is DSKCNT+1 for a step in and DSKCNT-1 for a step out), AND the value with $03, and store it in TMP ($4B). Load DSKCNT, AND it with $FC to mask off bits 0 & 1, OR it with TMP to set the new values for these bits, and store the result back in DSKCNT. JMP to END33 ($FABE) to end IRQ.

NOTE: cycling bits 0 & 1 of DSKCNT
       ($1C00) will move the head.
       00/01/10/11/00 will move head in
       00/11/10/01/00 will move head out

NAME	ADDRESS	DESCRIPTION OF WHAT ROM ROUTINE DOES
SSACL	$FA7B	Accelerate head routine. Set carry flag, load the 6522 Timer1 hi latch T1HL2 ($1C07), subtract the value in AF ($5F; acceleration factor), and store the result in T1HC2 ($1C05; timer1 hi counter). Decrement the number of acceleration steps left in ACLSTP ($60) and if any steps left, branch to SSA10.
	$FA88	No steps left, so reset the number of acceleration steps left ACLSTP ($60) using the value in AS ($5E) and set the NXTST pointer ($62/3) to point to the fast stepping routine, SSRUN ($FA97).
SSA10	$FA94	JMP to DOSTEP ($FA2E)

NAME	ADDRESS	DESCRIPTION OF WHAT ROM ROUTINE DOES
SSRUN	$FA97	Fast stepping mode routine. Decrement number of steps left to do in RSTEPS ($61). If any left, branch to DOSTEP ($FA2E). Since none left, set the NXTST pointer ($62/3) to point to the

NAME	ADDRESS	DESCRIPTION OF WHAT ROM ROUTINE DOES
		decelerate routine SSDEC ($FAA5) and branch to DOSTEP ($FA2E).
SSDEC	$FAA5	Decelerate head routine. Load .A from the 6522 Timer1 hi latch T1HL2 ($1C07), clear the carry flag, add the acceleration factor AF ($5F), and store the result in T1HC2 ($1C05; timer1 hi counter). Decrement the number of deceleration steps left ACLSTP ($60) and if any steps left, branch to SSA10. Since no steps left, set the NXTST pointer ($62/3) to point to the settle routine, SETLE ($FA4E). Set the number of acceleration steps left to $03 to allow settling time.
END33	$FABE	Terminate the motor and stepper control routine by clearing bit 1 of the 6522's peripheral control register, PCR2($1C0C) This force CA2 low which disables the SO line to the 6502. Finally, do an RTS to transfer control back to the main IRQ routine at $FE7C.
FORMT	$FAC7	This routine is used to format (NEW) a diskette. The code is executed in place (rather than moved into RAM and then executed as in the 4040). The IP FORMAT routine ($C8C6) sets up a JMP $FAC7 at the start of buffer #0, puts an EXECUTE ($E0) job into the job queue at $03, and then waits for the job to be completed.
FORMT	$FAC7	Load .A from FTNUM ($51) to check if formatting has begun. If FTNUM>0, the formatting has begun so branch to L213 ($FAF5). If not, begin formatting by: Setting DRVST($20) to $60 (head is now stepping), storing $01 into DRVTRK ($22) to set the current track and into FTNUM ($51; format begun flag).
	$FAD7	Do BUMP to track 1 by stepping head out 46 tracks. Store -92 (256-2*46) into STEPS ($4A) and clear bits 0 & 1 of DSKCNT ($1C00) to set head phase to 00.
	$FAE3	Set CNT ($0620) to $0A to allow up to 10 errors before abort.
	$FAE8	Set NUM($0621/2) to 4000 ($0FA0) as a first guess at number of bytes that can be recorded on half a track. Exit with a JMP to END ($F99C)

NAME	ADDRESS	DESCRIPTION OF WHAT ROM ROUTINE DOES
L213	$FAF5	On re-entry .A holds the track number (loaded from FTNUM). Compare it to the track in HDRPNT($32). If they match, we are on the correct track so branch to L214 ($FB00). If different, put the .A value (track we want) into HDRPNT ($32) and exit with a JMP to END ($F99C).
L214	$FB00	Test bit 4 of DSKCNT ($1C00) to see if write protect is on. If 1, protect is not on so branch to TOPP ($FB0C). If 0, load .A with $08 to indicate a WRITE PROTECT error & JMP to FMTERR ($FDD3).
TOPP	$FB0C	JSR to SYNCLR ($FDA3) to erase the track by writing 28*256 SYNC marks.
	$FB0F	JSR to WRTNUM ($FDC3) to write out NUM ($0621/22; value = 4000) SYNC marks.
	$FB12	Store a non-sync character ($55) into the output port DATA2 ($1C01) and JSR to WRTNUM ($FDC3) to write NUM ($0621/2; value = 4000) non-sync bytes.

At this point the track will have one
area that contains SYNC and another area
that has non-sync characters like this:
11111111001100110011001100111111
  SYNC   4000 non-sync bytes   SYNC
The following routines time the SYNC and
non-sync segments to determine how many
characters can be written on the track.
This is used to calculate the length of
the gap between sectors (inter-sector).

NAME	ADDRESS	DESCRIPTION OF WHAT ROM ROUTINE DOES
	$FB1A	JSR to KILL ($FE00) to kill write mode.
	$FB1D	JSR to SYNC ($F556) to wait for the start of the SYNC section.
	$FB20	Set bit 6 of the 6522's ACR1 ($180B) to set it up as a free running 100 micro-second timer.
	$FB35	Set .X and .Y to $00. They will hold the timer count. .X=least significant byte .Y=most significant bit
FWAIT	$FB39	Loop to wait for SYNC area
FWAIT2	$FB3E	Loop to wait for not-sync area
F000	$FB43	Reset interrupt flags to start the timer
F001	$FB46	Loop to time the non-sync area. Check if SYNC here yet. If here, branch to F005 ($FB5C). If no SYNC yet, check IFR1 ($1804) to see if timer has timed out. If time not up yet, branch back to F001 ($FB46). If time is up, increment .X by 1 (and .Y if .X=0) and branch back to F000 ($FB43) to reset the timer. If .Y is 0, we have a count of 65535 which

NAME	ADDRESS	DESCRIPTION OF WHAT ROM ROUTINE DOES
F005	$FB5C	means we can't find a sync mark so abort by loading .A with $02 and JMP to FMTERR Found a SYNC so store the non-sync times in T2 ($71/2). Reset .X and .Y to $00 and begin timing the SYNC area.
F006	$FB64	Reset interrupt flags to start the timer
F007	$FB67	Loop to time the SYNC area: Check if not-sync here yet. If here, go to F009 ($FB7D). If still have a SYNC, check IFR1 ($1804) to see if timer has timed out. If not time yet, branch back to F007 ($FB67). If time up, increment .X by 1 (and .Y if .X=0) and loop back to F006 ($FB64) to reset the timer. If .Y is 0, we have a count of 65535 which means we can't find no-SYNC. So abort: load .A with a $02 and JMP to FMTERR
F009	$FB7D	Found non-sync. Calculate the difference between the SYNC and non-sync times. If the difference is less than 4, branch to COUNT ($FBB6). If the difference is more than 4, make NUM ($0261/2) the average of the two times and branch to TOPP ($FB0C) to try again.
COUNT	$FBB6	Set .X and .Y to $00 to prepare to count the number of characters in the non-sync area.
CNT10	$FBBB	Test bit 7 of DSKCNT ($1C00) to see if SYNC is here yet. If SYNC here, branch to CNT20 ($FBCE). If not, test the timer If not time, branch back to CNT10. If time for one character is up, increment .X (and .Y if needed), clear the timer flag (.V) and branch back to CNT10. If .Y=0 we have a count of 65535 so abort: load .A with $03 & JMP to FMTERR ($FDD3)
CNT20	$FBCE	Store the byte count (count*2) in TRAL ($0624/5) and turn off the 6522's timer
DS08	$FBE0	Calculate the total number of bytes we need to record on this track: (282 chr/sect x 5/4 x #sect) Subtract this from the total we found and divide by the number of sectors to get the size of the gap between sectors. If the calculated gap is less than 4, it is too small so load .A with $05 and JMP to FMTERR ($FDD3). If it is big enough, store inter-sector gap in DTRCK ($0626).
	$FC36	Set sector counter SECT ($0628) to $00.
MAK10	$FC3F	Loop to create sector header images in buffer 0 ($0300+) .Y is the pointer into the buffer (0 for sect #1).

NAME	ADDRESS	DESCRIPTION OF WHAT ROM ROUTINE DOES
	$FC3F	Move sector ID code from HBID ($39) to $0300+Y ($0300 for #1).
	$FC44	Increment .Y twice to skip the checksum and move sector number from SECT ($0628) to $0300+Y ($0302 for sector #1).
	$FC4C	Increment .Y and move the track number from FTNUM ($51) to $0300+Y ($0303 for sector #1)
	$FC52	Increment .Y and move ID2 from DSKID+1 ($13) to $0300+Y ($0304 for sector #1).
	$FC58	Increment .Y and move ID1 from DSKID ($12) to $0300+Y ($0305 for sector #1).
	$FC5E	Increment .Y and store $0F in $0300+Y ($0306 for #1) as off byte.
	$FC64	Increment .Y and store $0F in $0300+Y ($0307 for #1) as off byte.
	$FC68	Increment .Y, calculate the header blk checksum and store it in $02F9+Y ($0302 for sector #1)
	$FC7A	Increment SECT ($0628) and compare it to number of sectors on track SECTR ($43)
	$FC84	If done all images, save the number of sectors on this track onto the stack. Increment .X (becomes $01) and transfer it to .A (dummy data character).
		NOTE: .X should really be $00. Since it is $01, all the data blocks on a diskette formatted on a 1541 drive have 1 garbage character followed by 255 $01's rather than 256 $00's
CRTDAT	$FC86	Loop to put 255 dummy data bytes ($01's) into data buffer #2 ($0500+)
	$FC8E	Set the buffer pointer BUFPNT ($30/1) to point to the header block images ($0300) and JSR to FBTOG($FE30) to convert the header images to a GCR write image with no header block ID code.
	$FC95	Pull # of sectors from stack, transfer the value to .Y, and JSR to MOVUP($FDE5) to move the GCR header image stored in in buffer #0 69 bytes up in memory. Then JSR to MOVOVR ($FDF5) to move the 69 header image bytes from the overflow buffer into the low end of buffer #0.
	$FC9E	Set the buffer pointer BUFPNT ($30/1) to point to the dummy data block, JSR to CHKBLK($F5E9) to calculate the data blk checksum, store it in CHKSUM, and JSR to BINGCR($F78F) to convert the dummy data block into its GCR write image.

NAME	ADDRESS	DESCRIPTION OF WHAT ROM ROUTINE DOES
		Begin formatting the track now!
		--
	$FCAA	Set the pointer to the header GCR image HDRPNT ($32) to $00 so it points to the start of the first header image.
	$FCAE	JSR to CLEAR ($FE0E) to wipe the track.
WRTSYN	$FCB1	Store $FF in PORT2 ($1C01) to be ready to write a sync character. Load .X with $05 (5 SYNC's coming up!)
WRTS10	$FCB8	Write out 5 sync marks
	$FCBE	Initialize .X to $0A (output 10 bytes) and set .Y with the value from HDRPNT ($32) so it points to the start of the header GCR image.
WRTS20	$FCC2	Write out the 10 header characters
	$FCCF	Load .X with $08 (HARD SET VALUE!) NOTE: This means you can not easily change the header gap size!
WRTS30	$FCD1	Loop to output eight $55 bytes to form the header gap (gap1).
	$FCDC	Store $FF in PORT2 ($1C01) to be ready to write a sync mark. Load .X with $05 (5 SYNC's coming up!)
DBSYNC	$FCE0	Write out 5 sync marks
	$FCE9	Initialize .X to $BB to point to the first byte of the overflow buffer (the start of the dummy data block)
WRTS40	$FCEB	Loop to write out the 69 GCR bytes in the overflow buffer
WRTS50	$FCF9	Loop to write out the 256 GCR bytes in data buffer #2 ($0500+)
	$FD04	Load .A with $55 and .X with the tail (inter-sector) gap from DTRCK ($0626)
WGP2	$FD09	Loop to write .X $55 characters to form the tail (inter-sector) gap.
	$FD12	Advance the header pointer HDRPNT($32/3) by 10 so it points to the start of the next header image.
	$FD19	Decrement the sector counter SECT($0628) by 1 and test to see if any more sectors to do. If more, branch back to WRTSYN to do the next sector. If no more, wait for the last byte to be written out and then JSR to KILL ($FE00) to switch to read mode.
		--
		Formatting done. Verify it!
		--
	$FD27	Set TRYS ($0623) to $C8 to limit the number of attempts to verify to 200.
COMP	$FD2C	Set BUFPNT ($30/1) to point to the start of the headers in buffer #0 ($0300) and set SECT ($0628) with the # of sectors on this track from SECTR ($43).

NAME	ADDRESS	DESCRIPTION OF WHAT ROM ROUTINE DOES
CMPR10	$FD39	JSR to SYNC($F556) to wait for a SYNC mark. Once found, set .X to $0A (there are 9 header characters to read) and .Y $00 (point to character in header image)
CMPR15	$FD40	Loop to read header bytes and compare them to the image in the buffer. If any byte doesn't match, branch to CMPR20.
	$FD4E	Header reads back OK so add 10 to BUFPNT ($30) so it points to next header image.
	$FD55	JMP to TSTDAT ($FD62)
CMPR20	$FD58	Bad verify. Decrement TRYS ($0623). If more attempts left, branch back to COMP ($FD2C) to try again. If we have tried 200 times, abort: load .A with $06 and JMP to FMTERR ($FDD3)
TSTDAT	$FD62	Header OK so check the data block. JSR to SYNC ($F556) to wait for the data block SYNC mark. Once found, set .Y to $BB to point to the start of the data block image in the overflow buffer
TST05	$FD67	Loop to read and verify the 69 GCR bytes in the overflow buffer. If no match, branch to CMPR20 ($FD58) and try again.
	$FD75	Overflow buffer OK so set .X to $FC (255-3; don't bother checking the OFF bytes at the end).
TST10	$FD77	Loop to read and verify the 253 GCR bytes in data buffer #3. If no match, branch to CMPR20 ($FD58) and try again.
	$FD86	Decrement the sector counter in SECT ($0628) by 1 and test to see if any more to do. If more, branch back to CMPR10 to do next sector. If no more, increment the track counter FTNUM ($51) and test if there are any more tracks to do. If all done, branch to FMTEND ($FD96). If more to do, JMP to END ($F99C) to step the head to the next track.
FMTEND	$FD96	Set the track counter, FTNUM ($51) to $FF and the GCRFLG ($50) to 0. To flag a successful completion load .A with $01 and JMP to ERRR ($F969).
		Formatting and Verification Completed!
		Formatting Subroutines
SYNCLR	$FDA3	Wipe track by writing 40*256 SYNC marks Set bits 6 & 7 of the 6522's peripheral control register PCR2 ($1C0C). This latches the signal on the CB2 line.

NAME	ADDRESS	DESCRIPTION OF WHAT ROM ROUTINE DOES
	$FDAD	Store $FF in the data direction register DDRA2 ($1C03) to make PORT A an output port and put $FF in the data port DATA2 ($1C01) to produce SYNC characters.
	$FDB5	Initialize .X to $28 (hi counter) and .Y to $00 (lo counter).
SYC10	$FDB9	Loop to write out 40*256 SYNC marks using .X & .Y as counters
	$FDC2	RTS -*- WARNING WRITE MODE LEFT ON -*-
WRTNUM		Write out NUM ($0621/2) bytes
	$FDC3	Load .X with the LSB and .Y with the MSB of NUM ($0621/2).
WRTN10	$FDC9	Loop to write out what ever is in the data port DATA2 ($1C03) NUM times using .X and .Y as counters
	$FDD2	RTS
FMTERR		Handles format errors
	$FDD3	Decrement the retry counter CNT ($0620) and, if no tries left, branch to FMTE10. If any left, JMP to END($F99C) to do any stepping required and try again.
FMTE10	$FDDB	Set the track counter FTNUM ($51) to $FF and the GCRFLG ($50) to 0 and JMP to ERRR ($F969).
MOVUP		Move .Y bytes in buffer #0 up 69 bytes
	$FDE5	Loop to move .Y characters in buffer #0 ($0300+) up 69 memory locations in RAM.
	$FDEE	Move byte from $0300 to $0345. RTS
MOVOVR		Move 69 bytes from overflow buffer into the bottom of the data buffer pointed to by BUFPNT ($30/1)
	$FDF5	Load .Y with $44 (68)
	$FDF7	Loop to move 69 bytes from $01BB+ into the data buffer. RTS
KILL		Disable write mode
	$FE00	Set bits 5, 6 and 7 of the 6522's PCR2 ($1C0C) to set CB2 high. Store 0 in the data direction register DDRA2 ($1C03) to make PORT A an input port. RTS
CLEAR		Wipe track with non-sync characters
	$FE0E	Clear (zero) bit 5 of the 6522's PCR2 ($1C0C). This forces CB2 low.
	$FE18	Store $FF in the data direction register DDRA2 ($1C03) to set output mode and put $55 in the data port DATA2 ($1C01) to write non-sync characters.
	$FE22	Initialize .X to $28 (hi counter) and .Y to $00 (lo counter).

NAME	ADDRESS	DESCRIPTION OF WHAT ROM ROUTINE DOES
CLER10	$FE26	Loop to write out 40*256 non-sync characters using .X & .Y as counters.
	$FE2F	RTS -*- WARNING WRITE MODE LEFT ON -*-
FBTOG	$FE30	Convert header images in buffer #0 into GCR form without the header ID code.
	$FE30	Zero the low byte of the buffer pointers pointers BUFPNT($31) and SAVPNT ($2E) and the byte counter BYTCNT ($36).
	$FE38	Set the GCR pointer GCRPNT ($34) to $BB so it points to the first character in the overflow buffer ($01BB+).
	$FE3C	Save the hi byte of the buffer pointer BUFPNT ($31) into SAVPNT ($2F) and then set BUFPNT to $01 to point to the overflow buffer.
FBG10	$FE44	Loop to move 4 bytes at a time into the staging area $52-55 and then do a JSR to PUT4BG ($F6D0) to convert them into five GCR bytes and store them in the overflow or data buffer. Terminate the routine with a JMP to PUT4BG to convert and store the last four.

MAIN SYSTEM IRQ ROUTINE (IRQ VECTOR POINTS HERE)

NAME	ADDRESS	DESCRIPTION OF WHAT ROM ROUTINE DOES
SYSIRQ	$FE67	IRQ's are generated in two ways: 1) by an ATN signal from the VIC-20 or the C-64 on the serial bus, or 2) by a time out of the 6522's timer This happens every 10 milliseconds This routine tests for the source of the IRQ signal and branches to the correct ROM routine.

NAME	ADDRESS	DESCRIPTION OF WHAT ROM ROUTINE DOES
	$FE67	Save .A, .X, and .Y on the stack
	$FE6C	Test if IRQ caused by an ATN signal on the serial bus by checking bit 1 of the interrupt flag register of the 6522 that handles the bus IFR1 ($180D). If this bit is not set (1), there was no ATN signal so branch to IRQ10 ($FE76). If it is set, JMP to the bus handling routine ATNIRQ ($E85F).
IRQ10	$FE76	Test if the 6522 timer has timed out by testing bit 7 of the interrupt flag register of the 6522 that serves as a disk controller IFR2 ($1C0D). If the bit is not set, branch to IRQ20 ($FE7F). If it is set, do a JSR to the floppy disk controller routines, LCC($F2B0).
IRQ20	$FE7F	Pull .A, .X, and .Y from the stack and do an RTI.

ADDRESS	VALUE	MISCELLANEOUS CONSTANTS & TABLES IN ROM
$FE85	$12	Directory track number (18)
$FE86	$04	Number of bytes/track in BAM
$FE87	$04	Offset of BAM in the sector
$FE88	$90	Offset of disk name in BAM sector

Command Search Table

ADDRESS	VALUE	
$FE89	$56	V = Validate or collect disk
$FE8A	$49	I = Initialize BAM & directory
$FE8B	$44	D = Duplicate or backup disk (N.A.)
$FE8C	$4D	M = Memory operation (M-R,M-W,M-E)
$FE8D	$42	B = Block operation (B-R,B-A,B-W,etc)
$FE8E	$55	U = User jump commands (except U+ & U-)
$FE8F	$50	P = Position (for REL files)
$FE90	$26	& = Utility loader
$FE91	$43	C = Copy file (copy disk N.A. on 1541)
$FE92	$52	R = Rename file
$FE93	$53	S = Scratch file
$FE94	$4E	N = New or format a diskette

(Lo Byte)		(Hi Byte)		Command Jump Table
$FE95	$84	$FEA1	$ED	V = Validate
$FE96	$05	$FEA2	$D0	I = Initialize BAM
$FE97	$C1	$FEA3	$C8	D = Duplicate (N.A.)
$FE98	$F8	$FEA4	$CA	M = Memory operation
$FE99	$1B	$FEA5	$CC	B = Block operation
$FE9A	$5C	$FEA6	$CB	U = User jump commands
$FE9B	$07	$FEA7	$E2	P = Position (for REL)
$FE9C	$A3	$FEA8	$E7	& = Utility loader
$FE9D	$F0	$FEA9	$C8	C = Copy file
$FE9E	$88	$FEAA	$CA	R = Rename file
$FE9F	$23	$FEAB	$C8	S = Scratch file
$FEA0	$0D	$FEAC	$EE	N = New a diskette

STRUCTURE IMAGES FOR COMMANDS

ADDRESS	VALUE		
$FEAD	$51	%01010001	disk copy
$FEAE	$DD	%11011101	rename a file (not parsed)
$FEAF	$1C	%00011100	scratch a file (not parsed)
$FEB0	$9E	%10011110	new a diskette (not parsed)
$FEB1	$1C	%00011100	load a file
		PGDRPGDR	Not greater than one file
		FS1 FS2	Not default drive(s)
			Required filename

MODE TABLE   (R/W/A/M)

ADDRESS	VALUE	
$FEB2	$52	R = Read mode
$FEB3	$57	W = Write mode
$FEB4	$41	A = Append
$FEB5	$4D	M = Modify (read improperly closed file)

ADDRESS	VALUE	MISCELLANEOUS CONSTANTS & TABLES IN ROM

(1st Byte)   (Hi Byte)   File type table

$FEB6	$44 D	$FEBB	$44 D	$FEC0	$45 E	$FEC5	$4C L	DEL
$FEB7	$53 S	$FEBC	$53 S	$FEC1	$45 E	$FEC6	$51 Q	SEQ
$FEB8	$50 P	$FEBD	$50 P	$FEC2	$52 R	$FEC7	$47 G	PRG
$FEB9	$55 U	$FEBE	$55 U	$FEC3	$53 S	$FEC8	$52 R	USR
$FEBA	$4C L	$FEBF	$52 R	$FEC4	$45 E	$FEC9	$4C L	REL

$FECA	$08	LED mask for drive 0
$FECB	$00	LED mask for drive 1 (N.A. on 1541)

ERROR FLAG VARIABLES FOR USE BY BIT

$FECC	$00	ER00
$FECD	$3F	ER0
$FECE	$7F	ER1
$FECF	$BF	ER2
$FED0	$FF	ER3

NUMBER OF SECTORS/TRACK IN EACH ZONE

$FED1	$11	17 sectors/track in zone 4 (31-35)
$FED2	$12	18 sectors/track in zone 3 (25-30)
$FED3	$13	19 sectors/track in zone 2 (18-24)
$FED4	$15	21 sectors/track in zone 1 (01-17)

$FED5	$41	DOS version number (65)
$FED6	$04	Number of different zones

ZONE BOUNDARIES (HIGHEST TRACK # + 1)

$FED7	$24	Track #36 - end of zone 4 (31-35)
$FED8	$1F	Track #31 - end of zone 3 (25-30)
$FED9	$19	Track #25 - end of zone 2 (18-24)
$FEDA	$12	Track #18 - end of zone 1 (01-17)

OFFSETS FOR ERROR RECOVERY

$FEDB	$01	
$FEDC	$FF	
$FEDD	$FF	
$FEDE	$01	
$FEDF	$00	

HI BYTE OF POINTERS TO DATA BUFFERS

$FEE0	$03	Data buffer #0 ($0300-03FF)
$FEE1	$04	Data buffer #1 ($0400-04FF)
$FEE2	$05	Data buffer #2 ($0500-05FF)
$FEE3	$06	Data buffer #3 ($0600-06FF)
$FEE4	$07	Data buffer #4 ($0700-07FF)
$FEE5	$07	Data buffer #5 ($0700-07FF)

$FEE6	$FD	Checksum for $E and $F ROMs

ADDRESS	VALUE	MISCELLANEOUS CONSTANTS & TABLES IN ROM

NMI VECTOR POINTS HERE

ADDRESS	VALUE	
$FEE7	NMI	Do indirect jump to the address stored in VNMI ($0065). This vector points to XXXXXX ($XXXX)

PATCH FOR POWER-ON ERRORS

$FEEA	PEA7A	Store the value that is in .A on entry into the 6522's data port 2, LEDPRT ($1C00; also called DSKCNT) and in the data direction register, LEDOUT ($1C02; also called DDRB2). Exit with a JMP to REA7D ($EA7D) to return to the LED blink routine.

PATCH FOR 1541 DISK WITH SLOW SERIAL RECEIVE

$FEF3	SLOWD	Produce a 40 microseconds delay with a loop that counts .X down from 5 to 1. Exit with an RTS.

$FEFB		JSR $E9AE	unused junk
$FEFE		JMP $E99C	unused junk

PATCH TO NMI ROUTINE TO CHECK FOR U+ AND U- COMMANDS

$FF01	NNMI	Load .A with the second character in the command buffer CMDBUF+2 ($0202). Compare it with "-" and, if equal, branch to NNMI10 ($FF0D). If not a "-", subtract a "+" from it. If not zero, command must be a real UI command so branch back to NMI ($FEE7) to do normal NMI.
$FF0D	NNMI10	Store .A (contains zero or a "-") into DRVTRK+1 ($23) and do an RTS to continue

$FF10 - $FFE6	UNUSED GARBAGE

TABLE OF JUMP VECTORS TO ROUTINES (LO BYTE/HI BYTE)

ADDRESS	VALUE		
$FFE6	$C6/$C8	FORMAT ROM routine	$C8C6
$FFE8	$8F/$F9	TRNOFF ROM routine	$F98F
$FFEA	$5F/$CD	UBLKRD ROM routine	$CD5F
$FFEC	$97/$CD	UBLKWT ROM routine	$CD97
$FFEE	$00/$05	Link to buffer #2	$0500
$FFF0	$03/$05	Link to buffer #2	$0503
$FFF2	$06/$05	Link to buffer #2	$0506
$FFF4	$09/$05	Link to buffer #2	$0509
$FFF6	$0C/$05	Link to buffer #2	$050C
$FFF8	$0F/$05	Link to buffer #2	$050F
$FFFA	$01/$FF	NNMI ROM routine	$FF01
$FFFC	$A0/$EA	DSKINT ROM routine	$EAA0
$FFFE	$67/$FE	SYSIRQ ROM routine	$FE67

APPENDIX C
PROGRAM LISTINGS

NOTE: Lines 830 and 930 contain a special character #166. This character can be typed by holding down the Commodore logo key in the lower left corner and pressing the + key.

```
100 REM DISPLAY A BLOCK AVAILABILITY MAP
    - 1541
110 DIMN$(16)
120 DEFFNS(I)=2^(S-INT(S/8)*8)AND(B(INT(
S/8)))
130 PRINT"{CLR}DISPLAY A BAM - 1541"
140 PRINT"{DOWN}INSERT DISKETTE IN DRIVE
"
150 PRINT"{DOWN}PRESS {RVS}RETURN{ROFF}
TO CONTINUE"
160 GETC$:IFC$=""THEN160
170 IFC$<>CHR$(13)GOTO160
180 PRINT"OK"
190 OPEN15,8,15
200 PRINT#15,"IO"
210 INPUT#15,EN$,EM$,ET$,ES$
220 IFEN$="00"OREN$="22"OREN$="23"GOTO26
0
230 PRINT"{DOWN}"EN$,  "EM$","ET$","ES$
240 CLOSE15
250 END
260 OPEN2,8,2,"#"
270 PRINT#15,"U1";2;0;18;0
280 INPUT#15,EN$,EM$,ET$,ES$
290 REM GET DOS
300 PRINT#15,"B-P";2;2
310 GET#2,B$
320 IFB$=""THENB$=CHR$(0)
330 DOS=ASC(B$)
340 IFDOS=65THENDOS$="V2.6":GOTO380
350 IFDOS=1THENDOS$="V1.2":GOTO380
360 DOS$="V?.?"
370 REM GET BLOCKS FREE
380 BF=0
390 B=4
400 FORI=1TO35
410 IFI=18THENI=I+1:B=B+4
420 PRINT#15,"B-P";2;B
430 GET#2,B$
440 IFB$=""THENB$=CHR$(0)
450 A=ASC(B$)
460 BF=BF+A
470 B=B+4
480 NEXTI
490 REM GET DISK NAME
```

```
500 PRINT#15,"B-P";2;144
510 FORI=1TO16
520 GOSUB1140
530 N$(I)=CHR$(A)
540 NEXTI
550 REM GET COSMETIC ID
560 ID$=""
570 PRINT#15,"B-P";2;162
580 FORI=1TO2
590 GOSUB1140
600 ID$=ID$+CHR$(A)
610 NEXTI
620 PRINT"{CLR}    {RVS}TRACK{ROFF}      11
1111111122222222223333333"
630 PRINT"     12345678901234567890123456
789012345"
640 PRINT"{RVS}S{ROFF}0
                        "N$(1);
650 PRINT"{RVS}E{ROFF}1
                        "N$(2);
660 PRINT"{RVS}C{ROFF}2
                        "N$(3);
670 PRINT"{RVS}T{ROFF}3
                        "N$(4);
680 PRINT"{RVS}O{ROFF}4
                        "N$(5);
690 PRINT"{RVS}R{ROFF}5
                        "N$(6);
700 PRINT" 6
          "N$(7);
710 PRINT" 7
          "N$(8);
720 PRINT" 8
          "N$(9);
730 PRINT" 9
          "N$(10);
740 PRINT"10
          "N$(11);
750 PRINT"11
          "N$(12);
760 PRINT"12
          "N$(13);
770 PRINT"13
          "N$(14);
780 PRINT"14
          "N$(15);
790 PRINT"15
          "N$(16);
800 PRINT"16"
810 PRINT"17"
```

```
820 PRINT"18
    ";DOS$;" ";LEFT$(ID$,1);
830 PRINT"19                              {R
VS} {ROFF}OR{#166}=EMPTY ";RIGHT$(ID$,1)
;
840 PRINT"20                            ";
850 BF$=RIGHT$("   "+RIGHT$(STR$(BF),LEN(
STR$(BF))-1),3)
860 IFBF=1THENPRINT" ";BF$;" BLOCK FREE"
:GOTO880
870 PRINTBF$;" BLOCKS FREE"
880 A$="."
890 CR$="{RIGHT 35}"
900 PRINT#15,"B-P";2;4
910 FORT=1TO35
920 IFT/2<>INT(T/2)THENF$="{RVS} {ROFF}"
:GOTO940
930 F$="{#166}"
940 GET#2,B$
950 FORI=0TO2
960 GET#2,B$
970 IFB$=""THENB$=CHR$(0)
980 B(I)=ASC(B$)
990 NEXTI
1000 PRINT"{HOME}{DOWN 2}{RIGHT 2}";LEFT
$(CR$,T);
1010 NS=20+2*(T>17)+(T>24)+(T>30)
1020 FORS=0TONS
1030 IFFNS(S)=0THENPRINTA$;:GOTO1050
1040 PRINTF$;
1050 PRINT"{DOWN}{LEFT}";
1060 NEXTS
1070 NEXTT
1080 PRINT"{HOME}{DOWN 22}";
1090 CLOSE2
1100 INPUT#15,EN$,EM$,ET$,ES$
1110 CLOSE15
1120 END
1130 REM GET A BYTE
1140 GET#2,B$
1150 IFB$=""THENB$=CHR$(0)
1160 A=ASC(B$)
1170 IFA>127THENA=A-128
1180 IFA<32ORA>95THENA=63
1190 IFA=34THENA=63
1200 RETURN
```

```basic
820 PRINT"18
:"DOS$";"(LEFT$(ID$,1);"
830 PRINT"19                        (R
V5) (RQRF)OR(&166)=EMPTY";(RIGHT$(ID$,1)

840 PRINT"20                      "
850 BF$=RIGHT$("    "+RIGHT$(STR$(BF),LEN(
STR$(BF))-1),3)
860 IFBF=1THENPRINT"(BF$;" BLOCK FREE"
:GOTO880
870 PRINTBF$;" BLOCKS FREE"
880 A$=","
890 CR$=(RIGHT 33)"
900 PRINT#15,"B-F";I;4
910 FORT=1TO25
920 IFT/2<>INT(T/2)THENB$=XRV$:(RQFF)X
:GOTO940
930 F$="(#166)"
940 GET#2,B$
950 FORI=0TO2
960 GET#2,B$
970 IFB$=""THENB$=CHR$(0)
980 B(I)=ASC(B$)
990 NEXTI
1000 PRINT"(HOME)(DOWN 2)(RIGHT 2)(LEFT 23)"
&(CR$,T);
1010 NB=20+2*(T<17)+(T<24)+(T>20)
1020 FORS=0TONB
1030 IFNS(S)=0THENPRINTNA$;:GOTO1050
1040 PRINTBF$
1050 PRINT"(DOWN)(LEFT)";
1060 NEXTS
1070 NEXTT
1080 PRINT"(HOME)(DOWN 22)"
1090 CLOSE2
1100 INPUT#15,EN$,EM$,ET$,ES$
1110 CLOSE15
1120 END
1130 REM GET A BYTE
1140 GET#2,B$
1150 IFB$=""THENB$=CHR$(0)
1160 A=ASC(B$)
1170 IFA>127THENA=A-128
1180 IFA<32ORA>95THENA=42
1190 IFA=34THENA=42
1200 RETURN
```

```
100 REM VIRTUAL DIRECTORY - 1541
110 CLR
120 H$="0123456789ABCDEF"
130 FORI=0TO5
140 READFT$(I)
150 NEXTI
160 PRINT"{CLR}VIRTUAL DIRECTORY - 1541"

170 PRINT"{DOWN}INSERT DISKETTE IN DRIVE
"
180 PRINT"{DOWN}PRESS {RVS}RETURN{ROFF}
TO CONTINUE"
190 GETC$:IFC$=""THEN190
200 IFC$<>CHR$(13)GOTO190
210 PRINT"OK"
220 OPEN15,8,15
230 PRINT#15,"IO"
240 INPUT#15,EN$,EM$,ET$,ES$
250 IFEN$="00"GOTO300
260 PRINT"{DOWN}"EN$,  "EM$",  "ET$",  "ES$
270 CLOSE15
280 END
290 REM FORMATTING ID
300 PRINT#15,"M-R"CHR$(22)CHR$(0)CHR$(2)

310 GET#15,B$
320 GOSUB1370
330 FI$=FI$+CHR$(A)
340 GET#15,B$
350 GOSUB1370
360 FI$=FI$+CHR$(A)
370 REM BLOCKS FREE
380 PRINT#15,"M-R"CHR$(250)CHR$(2)CHR$(3
)
390 GET#15,B$
400 L=ASC(B$+CHR$(0))
410 GET#15,B$
420 GET#15,B$
430 H=ASC(B$+CHR$(0))
440 BF=L+(H*256)
450 BA=664-BF
460 OPEN4,3
470 OPEN2,8,2,"#"
480 OPEN3,8,3,"$0,P,R"
490 GET#3,B$
500 DOS=ASC(B$+CHR$(0))
510 FORI=3TO143
520 GET#3,B$
530 NEXTI
540 FORI=144TO159
```

```
550 GOSUB1360
560 DN$=DN$+CHR$(A)
570 NEXTI
580 GET#3,B$
590 GET#3,B$
600 FORI=162TO163
610 GOSUB1360
620 ID$=ID$+CHR$(A)
630 NEXTI
640 FORI=164TO255
650 GET#3,B$
660 NEXTI
670 FORI=1TO6
680 PRINT#4
690 NEXTI
700 PRINT#4,"DISK NAME:        "DN$
710 PRINT#4,"DISK ID:          "ID$
720 PRINT#4,"FORMATTING ID:    "FI$
730 PRINT#4,"DOS TYPE:         "DOS
740 PRINT#4,"BLOCKS ALLOCATED:"BA
750 PRINT#4,"BLOCKS FREE:      "BF
760 PRINT#4
770 PRINT#4,"BLOCKS      FILE NAME        TYP
E   T-S   LOAD"
780 IFF/8=INT(F/8)THENPRINT#4
790 GET#3,B$
800 FT=ASC(B$+CHR$(0))
810 FT$=FT$(7ANDFT)
820 GET#3,B$
830 T=ASC(B$+CHR$(0))
840 T$=RIGHT$("0"+RIGHT$(STR$(T),LEN(STR
$(T))-1),2)
850 GET#3,B$
860 S=ASC(B$+CHR$(0))
870 S$=RIGHT$("0"+RIGHT$(STR$(S),LEN(STR
$(S))-1),2)
880 LA$=""
890 IF(7ANDFT)<>0AND(7ANDFT)<>2GOTO1020
900 PRINT#15,"U1";2;0;T;S
910 PRINT#15,"B-P";2;2
920 GET#2,B$
930 A=ASC(B$+CHR$(0))
940 H=INT(A/16)
950 L=A-16*H
960 LA$=MID$(H$,H+1,1)+MID$(H$,L+1,1)
970 GET#2,B$
980 A=ASC(B$+CHR$(0))
990 H=INT(A/16)
1000 L=A-16*H
1010 LA$=MID$(H$,H+1,1)+MID$(H$,L+1,1)+L
```

444

```
A$
1020 F$=""
1030 NULL=0
1040 FORI=1TO16
1050 GOSUB1360
1060 IFB$=CHR$(0)THENNULL=NULL+1
1070 F$=F$+CHR$(A)
1080 NEXTI
1090 IFNULL=16GOTO1270
1100 FORI=1TO9
1110 GET#3,B$
1120 NEXTI
1130 GET#3,B$
1140 B=ASC(B$+CHR$(0))
1150 GET#3,B$
1160 B=B+256*ASC(B$+CHR$(0))
1170 B$=RIGHT$("    "+RIGHT$(STR$(B),LEN(S
TR$(B))-1),3)
1180 IFST=64THENEOI=1
1190 IFFT<128THENPRINT#4,"{RVS}";
1200 PRINT#4," "B$"    "F$"   "FT$" "T$"-"
S$" "LA$
1210 F=F+1
1220 IFF/8<>INT(F/8)THENGET#3,B$:GET#3,B
$
1230 GETC$:IFC$=""GOTO1250
1240 GETC$:IFC$=""THEN1240
1250 IFEOI=1GOTO1270
1260 GOTO780
1270 CLOSE4
1280 CLOSE3
1290 CLOSE2
1300 INPUT#15,EN$,EM$,ET$,ES$
1310 CLOSE15
1320 END
1330 REM FILE TYPES
1340 DATA DEL,SEQ,PRG,USR,REL,???
1350 REM GET A BYTE
1360 GET#3,B$
1370 IFB$=""THENB$=CHR$(0)
1380 A=ASC(B$)
1390 IFA>127THENA=A-128
1400 IFA<32ORA>95THENA=63
1410 IFA=34THENA=63
1420 RETURN
```

```
100 REM FIND A FILE
110 PRINT"{CLR}FIND A FILE - 1541"
120 PRINT"{DOWN}INSERT DISKETTE IN DRIVE
"
130 PRINT"{DOWN}PRESS {RVS}RETURN{ROFF}
TO CONTINUE"
140 GETC$:IFC$=""THEN140
150 IFC$<>CHR$(13)GOTO140
160 PRINT"OK"
170 OPEN15,8,15
180 PRINT#15,"IO"
190 INPUT#15,EN$,EM$,ET$,ES$
200 IFEN$="00"GOTO240
210 PRINT"{DOWN}"EN$,"EM$","ET$","ES$
220 CLOSE15
230 END
240 INPUT"{DOWN}FILENAME";F$
250 IFLEN(F$)<>0ANDLEN(F$)<17GOTO280
260 CLOSE15
270 END
280 OPEN2,8,2,"0:"+F$+",?,R"
290 INPUT#15,EN$,EM$,ET$,ES$
300 IFEN$="00"GOTO320
310 GOTO530
320 PRINT#15,"M-R"CHR$(97)CHR$(2)
330 GET#15,D$
340 D=ASC(D$+CHR$(0))
350 PRINT#15,"M-R"CHR$(24)CHR$(0)CHR$(2)

360 GET#15,T$
370 T=ASC(T$+CHR$(0))
380 GET#15,S$
390 S=ASC(S$+CHR$(0))
400 D$=RIGHT$(STR$(D),LEN(STR$(D))-1)
410 IFD<10THEND$="0"+D$
420 T$=RIGHT$(STR$(T),LEN(STR$(T))-1)
430 IFT<10THENT$="0"+T$
440 S$=RIGHT$(STR$(S),LEN(STR$(S))-1)
450 IFS<10THENS$="0"+S$
460 PRINT"{DOWN}TRACK 18 - SECTOR "D$
470 PRINT"{DOWN}TRACK "T$" - SECTOR "S$
480 CLOSE2
490 INPUT#15,EN$,EM$,ET$,ES$
500 CLOSE15
510 PRINT"{DOWN}DONE!"
520 END
530 PRINT"{DOWN}"EN$,"EM$","ET$","ES$
540 CLOSE2
550 INPUT#15,EN$,EM$,ET$,ES$
560 CLOSE15
570 PRINT"{DOWN}{RVS}FAILED{ROFF}"
580 END
```

447

```
100 REM DISPLAY TRACK & SECTOR - 1541
110 CLR
120 HD$="0123456789ABCDEF"
130 PRINT"{CLR}DISPLAY TRACK & SECTOR -
1541"
140 PRINT"{DOWN}INSERT DISKETTE IN DRIVE
"
150 INPUT"{DOWN}DISPLAY TRACK & SECTOR (
T,S)";T,S
160 IFT<1ORT>35THENEND
170 NS=20+2*(T>17)+(T>24)+(T>30)
180 IFS<0ORS>NSTHENEND
190 INPUT"{DOWN}OUTPUT TO SCREEN OR PRIN
TER (S/P)    S{LEFT 3}";O$
200 IFO$<>"S"ANDO$<>"P"THENEND
210 INPUT"{DOWN}ARE YOU SURE   Y{LEFT 3}"
;Q$
220 IFQ$<>"Y"THENEND
230 OPEN15,8,15
240 T$=RIGHT$(STR$(T),LEN(STR$(T))-1)
250 IFT<10THENT$="0"+T$
260 S$=RIGHT$(STR$(S),LEN(STR$(S))-1)
270 IFS<10THENS$="0"+S$
280 REM SEEK
290 JOB=176
300 GOSUB850
310 IFE<>1GOTO360
320 REM READ
330 JOB=128
340 GOSUB850
350 IFE=1GOTO470
360 IFE>1ANDE<12THENEN$=RIGHT$(STR$(E+18
),2):GOTO380
370 EN$="02":EM$="?TIMEOUT":GOTO390
380 EM$="READ ERROR"
390 ET$=T$
400 ES$=S$
410 PRINT"{DOWN}"EN$,  "EM$","ET$","ES$
420 IFE<>4ANDE<>5GOTO450
430 GOSUB1020
440 GOTO470
450 CLOSE15
460 END
470 IFO$="S"GOTO550
480 OPEN4,4
490 FORI=1TO6
500 PRINT#4
510 NEXTI
520 PRINT#4,"              DISPLAY TRACK & SE
CTOR"
```

```
530 PRINT#4,"                TRACK "T$" - SECT
OR "S$
540 PRINT#4
550 FORK=0TO1
560 PRINT"{CLR}{RVS}            DISPLAY TRA
CK & SECTOR            {ROFF}"
570 PRINT"{HOME}{DOWN}{RVS}            TRA
CK "T$" - SECTOR "S$"            {ROFF}"
580 PRINT"{HOME}{DOWN 2}"
590 FORJ=0TO15
600 D=K*128+J*8
610 GOSUB970
620 BP$=" . "+DH$+": "
630 H$=""
640 A$=""
650 FORI=0TO7
660 PRINT#15,"M-R"CHR$(K*128+J*8+I)CHR$(
4)
670 GET#15,B$
680 D=ASC(B$+CHR$(0))
690 GOSUB970
700 H$=H$+DH$+" "
710 IFD>127THEND=D-128
720 IFD<32ORD>90THEND=46
730 A$=A$+CHR$(D)
740 NEXTI
750 PRINTBP$;H$;A$
760 IFO$="P"THENPRINT#4,BP$;H$;A$
770 NEXTJ
780 IFO$="P"GOTO800
790 GOSUB1020
800 NEXTK
810 IFO$="P"THENCLOSE4
820 CLOSE15
830 GOTO110
840 REM JOB QUEUE
850 TRY=0
860 PRINT#15,"M-W"CHR$(8)CHR$(0)CHR$(2)C
HR$(T)CHR$(S)
870 PRINT#15,"M-W"CHR$(1)CHR$(0)CHR$(1)C
HR$(JOB)
880 TRY=TRY+1
890 PRINT#15,"M-R"CHR$(1)CHR$(0)
900 GET#15,E$
910 IFE$=""THENE$=CHR$(0)
920 E=ASC(E$)
930 IFTRY=500GOTO950
940 IFE>127GOTO880
950 RETURN
960 REM DECIMAL TO HEXADECIMAL
```

```
970 H=INT(D/16)+1
980 L=D-(H-1)*16+1
990 DH$=MID$(HD$,H,1)+MID$(HD$,L,1)
1000 RETURN
1010 REM DELAY
1020 PRINT"{DOWN}PRESS {RVS}RETURN{ROFF}
 TO CONTINUE"
1030 GETC$:IFC$=""THEN1030
1040 IFC$<>CHR$(13)GOTO1030
1050 PRINT"OK"
1060 RETURN
```

```
100 REM DISPLAY A CHAIN - 1541
110 CLR
120 PRINT"{CLR}DISPLAY A CHAIN - 1541"
130 PRINT"{DOWN}INSERT DISKETTE IN DRIVE
"
140 INPUT"{DOWN}TRACK & SECTOR (T,S)";T,
S
150 IFT<1ORT>35THENEND
160 NS=20+2*(T>17)+(T>24)+(T>30)
170 IFS<0ORS>NSTHENEND
180 INPUT"{DOWN}OUTPUT TO SCREEN OR PRIN
TER (S/P)   S{LEFT 3}";O$
190 IFO$<>"S"ANDO$<>"P"THENEND
200 INPUT"{DOWN}ARE YOU SURE   Y{LEFT 3}"
;Q$
210 IFQ$<>"Y"THENEND
220 OPEN15,8,15
230 PRINT#15,"IO"
240 INPUT#15,EN$,EM$,ET$,ES$
250 IFEN$="00"GOTO290
260 PRINT"{DOWN}"EN$", "EM$", "ET$", "ES$
270 CLOSE15
280 END
290 IFO$="S"GOTO390
300 PRINT"{DOWN}{RVS}PRINTING{ROFF} A CH
AIN"
310 OPEN4,4
320 FORI=1TO6
330 PRINT#4
340 NEXTI
350 PRINT#4,"                DISPLAY A CHAI
N"
360 PRINT#4,"          BLOCK    TRACK - SE
CTOR"
370 PRINT#4
380 GOTO420
390 PRINT"{CLR}{RVS}                DISPLAY
 A CHAIN              {ROFF}"
400 PRINT"{HOME}{DOWN}{RVS}          BLOC
K    TRACK - SECTOR           {ROFF}"
410 PRINT"{HOME}{DOWN 2}"
420 B=B+1
430 GOSUB1030
440 REM SEEK
450 JOB=176
460 GOSUB910
470 IFE<>1GOTO520
480 REM READ
490 JOB=128
500 GOSUB910
```

```
510 IFE=1GOTO630
520 IFE>1ANDE<12THENEN$=RIGHT$(STR$(E+18
),2):GOTO540
530 EN$="02":EM$="?TIMEOUT":GOTO550
540 EM$="READ ERROR"
550 ET$=T$
560 ES$=S$
570 IFO$="P"THENPRINT#4,"            "EN$"
, "EM$", "ET$", "ES$:GOTO590
580 PRINT"           "EN$",   "EM$",  "ET$", "
ES$
590 IFE=40RE=5GOTO630
600 IFO$="P"GOTO810
610 GOSUB1090
620 GOTO820
630 B$=RIGHT$(STR$(B),LEN(STR$(B))-1)
640 IFB<10THENB$="  "+B$
650 IFB<100THENB$=" "+B$
660 IFO$="P"THENPRINT#4,"          "B$"
      "T$" - "S$:GOTO680
670 PRINT"           "B$"         "T$" - "S
$
680 PRINT#15,"M-R"CHR$(0)CHR$(4)CHR$(2)
690 GET#15,T$
700 T=ASC(T$+CHR$(0))
710 IFT=0GOTO760
720 GET#15,S$
730 S=ASC(S$+CHR$(0))
740 IFT>350RS>20+2*(T>17)+(T>24)+(T>30)G
OTO850
750 IFO$="S"ANDB/16<>INT(B/16)GOTO420
760 IFO$="P"GOTO780
770 GOSUB1090
780 IFT=0GOTO810
790 IFO$="S"GOTO390
800 GOTO420
810 IFO$="P"THENCLOSE4
820 CLOSE15
830 GOTO110
840 REM ILLEGAL TRACK OR SECTOR
850 GOSUB1030
860 IFO$="P"THENPRINT#4,"          66, IL
LEGAL TRACK OR SECTOR,"T$","S$:GOTO810
870 PRINT"{DOWN}66, ILLEGAL TRACK OR SEC
TOR,"T$","S$
880 GOSUB1090
890 GOTO820
900 REM JOB QUEUE
910 TRY=0
920 PRINT#15,"M-W"CHR$(8)CHR$(0)CHR$(2)C
```

```
HR$(T)CHR$(S)
930 PRINT#15,"M-W"CHR$(1)CHR$(0)CHR$(1)C
HR$(JOB)
940 TRY=TRY+1
950 PRINT#15,"M-R"CHR$(1)CHR$(0)
960 GET#15,E$
970 IFE$=""THENE$=CHR$(0)
980 E=ASC(E$)
990 IFTRY=500GOTO1010
1000 IFE>127GOTO940
1010 RETURN
1020 REM STR$(T,S)
1030 T$=RIGHT$(STR$(T),LEN(STR$(T))-1)
1040 IFT<10THENT$="0"+T$
1050 S$=RIGHT$(STR$(S),LEN(STR$(S))-1)
1060 IFS<10THENS$="0"+S$
1070 RETURN
1080 REM DELAY
1090 PRINT"{DOWN}PRESS {RVS}RETURN{ROFF}
 TO CONTINUE"
1100 GETC$:IFC$=""THEN1100
1110 IFC$<>CHR$(13)GOTO1100
1120 RETURN
```

```
100 REM EDIT TRACK & SECTOR - 1541
110 POKE56,159
120 CLR
130 HD$="0123456789ABCDEF"
140 CD$="{HOME}{DOWN 20}"
150 PRINT"{CLR}EDIT A SECTOR - 1541"
160 PRINT"{DOWN}REMOVE {RVS}WRITE PROTEC
T TAB{ROFF}"
170 PRINT"{DOWN}INSERT DISKETTE IN DRIVE
"
180 INPUT"{DOWN}EDIT TRACK & SECTOR (T,S
)";T,S
190 IFT<1ORT>35GOTO1580
200 NS=20+2*(T>17)+(T>24)+(T>30)
210 IFS<0ORS>NSGOTO1580
220 INPUT"{DOWN}STARTING BYTE (00/80)";S
B$
230 IFLEN(SB$)=0GOTO1580
240 SB=VAL(SB$)
250 IFSB<>0ANDSB<>80GOTO1580
260 IFSB=0THENBP=0:GOTO280
270 BP=128
280 INPUT"{DOWN}ARE YOU SURE   Y{LEFT 3}"
;Q$
290 IFQ$<>"Y"GOTO1580
300 OPEN15,8,15
310 T$=RIGHT$(STR$(T),LEN(STR$(T))-1)
320 IFT<10THENT$="0"+T$
330 S$=RIGHT$(STR$(S),LEN(STR$(S))-1)
340 IFS<10THENS$="0"+S$
350 REM SEEK
360 JOB=176
370 GOSUB1620
380 IFE<>1GOTO430
390 REM READ
400 JOB=128
410 GOSUB1620
420 IFE=1GOTO520
430 IFE>1ANDE<12THENEN$=RIGHT$(STR$(E+18
),2):GOTO450
440 EN$="02":EM$="?TIMEOUT":GOTO470
450 IFE=7ORE=8THENEM$="WRITE ERROR":GOTO
470
460 EM$="READ ERROR"
470 ET$=T$
480 ES$=S$
490 PRINT"{DOWN}"EN$,  "EM$","ET$","ES$
500 CLOSE15
510 GOTO1580
520 PRINT"{CLR}{RVS}                EDIT TRACK
```

```
                    & SECTOR                {ROFF}"
530 PRINT"{HOME}{DOWN}{RVS}                    TRA
CK "T$" - SECTOR "S$"                {ROFF}"
540 PRINT"{HOME}{DOWN 2}"
550 FORJ=0TO15
560 D=J*8+BP
570 GOSUB1740
580 BP$=" . "+DH$+": "
590 H$=""
600 A$=""
610 FORI=0TO7
620 PRINT#15,"M-R"CHR$(J*8+I+BP)CHR$(4)
630 GET#15,B$
640 D=ASC(B$+CHR$(0))
650 POKE(40704+J*8+I),D
660 GOSUB1740
670 H$=H$+DH$+" "
680 IFD>127THEND=D-128
690 IFD<32ORD>95THEND=46
700 IFD=34THEND=46
710 A$=A$+CHR$(D)
720 NEXTI
730 PRINTBP$H$" {RVS}"A$"{ROFF}"
740 NEXTJ
750 PRINT"{DOWN}{RVS}EDIT{ROFF} TRACK "T
$" - SECTOR "S$" (Y/N)?"
760 GOSUB1790
770 IFQ$<>"Y"GOTO1390
780 PRINTCD$"PRESS {RVS}CLR{ROFF} TO EXI
T                    "
790 PRINT"{HOME}{DOWN 3}{RIGHT 7}";
800 S=1151
810 C=1
820 A=PEEK(S):IFA>127THENA=A-128
830 M=S
840 POKEM,A+128
850 GETI$:IFI$=""THEN850
860 I=ASC(I$)
870 IFI=147THENPOKEM,A:GOTO1360
880 IFI=19THENPOKEM,A:GOTO790
890 IFI=141THENI=13
900 IFI<>13GOTO930
910 IFC=23ANDS<>1773THENPRINT"{RIGHT}";:
GOTO1230
920 IFS<1751THENPOKEM,A:FORI=CTO23:PRINT
"{RIGHT}";:S=S+1:NEXTI:S=S-1:C=23:GOTO12
30
930 IFI=32THENI=29:I$=CHR$(29)
940 IFI<>29GOTO970
950 IFC<>23THENC=C+1:S=S+1:GOTO1290
```

456

```
960 IFS<>1773THENPRINT"{RIGHT}";:GOTO123
0
970 IFI<>157GOTO1000
980 IFC<>1THENC=C-1:S=S-1:GOTO1290
990 IFC=1ANDS<>1151THENFORI=1TO18:PRINT"
{LEFT}";:NEXTI:C=23:S=S-18:GOTO1300
1000 IFI<>17GOTO1020
1010 IFS+40<1774THENS=S+40:GOTO1290
1020 IFI<>145GOTO1040
1030 IFS-40>1150THENS=S-40:GOTO1290
1040 IFA=320RA=160GOTO850
1050 IFI<480RI>57ANDI<650RI>70GOTO820
1060 PRINTI$;
1070 A=I:IFI>64THENA=A-64
1080 IFA<7THENL=A+9
1090 IFA>47THENL=A-48
1100 IFINT((C+1)/3)=(C+1)/3THENR=PEEK(S-
1):GOTO1120
1110 R=PEEK(S+1)
1120 IFR>127THENR=R-128
1130 IFR<7THENR=R+9
1140 IFR>47THENR=R-48
1150 IFINT((C+1)/3)<>(C+1)/3THENI=L*16+R
:GOTO1170
1160 I=R*16+L
1170 POKE40704+8*INT((M-1151)/40)+INT(C/
3),I
1180 IFI>127THENI=I-128
1190 IFI<320RI>95THENI=46
1200 IFI=34THENI=46
1210 IFI>64THENPOKEM+25-C+INT(C/3),I-64+
128:GOTO1230
1220 POKEM+25-C+INT(C/3),I+128
1230 IFC=23ANDS<>1773THENFORI=1TO17:PRIN
T"{RIGHT}";:NEXTI:C=1:S=S+18:GOTO1300
1240 IFS=1773THENPRINT"{LEFT}";:GOTO1300

1250 S=S+1
1260 C=C+1
1270 POKEM,A
1280 GOTO820
1290 PRINTI$;
1300 A=PEEK(M):IFA>127THENA=A-128
1310 POKEM,A
1320 GOTO820
1330 PRINTCD$"EXIT (Y/N)?"
1340 GOSUB1790
1350 IFQ$="N"GOTO780
1360 PRINTCD$"{RVS}REWRITE{ROFF} TRACK "
T$" - SECTOR "S$" (Y/N)?"
1370 GOSUB1790
```

```
1380 IFQ$="Y"GOTO1450
1390 CLOSE15
1400 PRINTCD$"ATTEMPT TO EDIT A SECTOR {
RVS}FAILED{ROFF}        "
1410 PRINT"{DOWN}PRESS {RVS}RETURN{ROFF}
 TO CONTINUE"
1420 GETC$:IFC$=""THEN1420
1430 IFC$<>CHR$(13)GOTO1420
1440 GOTO120
1450 PRINTCD$"{RVS}REWRITING{ROFF} TRACK
 "T$" - SECTOR "S$"            "
1460 FORI=0TO127
1470 PRINT#15,"M-W"CHR$(I+BP)CHR$(4)CHR$
(1)CHR$(PEEK(40704+I))
1480 NEXTI
1490 REM WRITE
1500 T=VAL(T$)
1510 S=VAL(S$)
1520 JOB=144
1530 GOSUB1620
1540 CLOSE15
1550 IFE<>1GOTO1400
1560 PRINTCD$"ATTEMPT TO EDIT A SECTOR C
OMPLETE"
1570 GOTO1410
1580 POKE56,160
1590 CLR
1600 END
1610 REM JOB QUEUE
1620 TRY=0
1630 PRINT#15,"M-W"CHR$(8)CHR$(0)CHR$(2)
CHR$(T)CHR$(S)
1640 PRINT#15,"M-W"CHR$(1)CHR$(0)CHR$(1)
CHR$(JOB)
1650 TRY=TRY+1
1660 PRINT#15,"M-R"CHR$(1)CHR$(0)
1670 GET#15,E$
1680 IFE$=""THENE$=CHR$(0)
1690 E=ASC(E$)
1700 IFTRY=500GOTO1720
1710 IFE>127GOTO1650
1720 RETURN
1730 REM DECIMAL TO HEXADECIMAL
1740 H=INT(D/16)+1
1750 L=D-(H-1)*16+1
1760 DH$=MID$(HD$,H,1)+MID$(HD$,L,1)
1770 RETURN
1780 REM QUERY
1790 GETQ$:IFQ$=""THEN1790
1800 IFQ$<>"Y"ANDQ$<>"N"GOTO1790
1810 RETURN
```

```
100 REM EDIT DOS VERSION
110 PRINT"{CLR}EDIT DOS VERSION - 1541"
120 PRINT"{DOWN}REMOVE {RVS}WRITE PROTEC
T TAB{ROFF}"
130 PRINT"{DOWN}INSERT DISKETTE IN DRIVE
"
140 PRINT"{DOWN}PRESS {RVS}RETURN{ROFF}
TO CONTINUE"
150 GETC$:IFC$=""THEN150
160 IFC$<>CHR$(13)GOTO150
170 PRINT"OK"
180 OPEN15,8,15
190 PRINT#15,"IO"
200 INPUT#15,EN$,EM$,ET$,ES$
210 IFEN$="00"GOTO250
220 PRINT"{DOWN}"EN$","EM$","ET$","ES$
230 CLOSE15
240 END
250 PRINT#15,"M-R"CHR$(1)CHR$(1)
260 GET#15,DOS$
270 IFDOS$=""THENDOS$=CHR$(0)
280 ODV=ASC(DOS$)
290 PRINT"{DOWN}OLD DOS VERSION:";ODV
300 NDV=-1
310 INPUT"{DOWN}NEW DOS VERSION";NDV
320 IFNDV<0ORNDV>255GOTO500
330 INPUT"{DOWN}ARE YOU SURE (Y/N)  Y{LE
FT 3}";Q$
340 IFQ$<>"Y"GOTO500
350 T=18
360 S=0
370 REM SEEK
380 JOB=176
390 GOSUB530
400 REM READ
410 JOB=128
420 GOSUB530
430 PRINT#15,"M-W"CHR$(2)CHR$(4)CHR$(1)C
HR$(NDV)
440 REM WRITE
450 JOB=144
460 GOSUB530
470 CLOSE15
480 PRINT"{DOWN}DONE!"
490 END
500 CLOSE15
510 END
520 REM JOB QUEUE
530 TRY=0
540 PRINT#15,"M-W"CHR$(8)CHR$(0)CHR$(2)C
```

```
HR$(T)CHR$(S)
550 PRINT#15,"M-W"CHR$(1)CHR$(0)CHR$(1)C
HR$(JOB)
560 TRY=TRY+1
570 PRINT#15,"M-R"CHR$(1)CHR$(0)
580 GET#15,E$
590 IFE$=""THENE$=CHR$(0)
600 E=ASC(E$)
610 IFTRY=500GOTO630
620 IFE>127GOTO560
630 IFE=1THENRETURN
640 CLOSE15
650 PRINT"{DOWN}{RVS}FAILED{ROFF}"
660 END
```

```
100 REM VALIDATE A DISKETTE - 1541
110 CLR
120 CD$="{DOWN 21}"
130 DIMF$(143),T%(143),S%(143)
140 PRINT"{CLR}VALIDATE A DISKETTE - 154
1"
150 PRINT"{DOWN}INSERT DISKETTE IN DRIVE
"
160 PRINT"{DOWN}PRESS {RVS}RETURN{ROFF}
TO CONTINUE"
170 GETC$:IFC$=""THEN170
180 IFC$<>CHR$(13)GOTO170
190 PRINT"OK"
200 OPEN15,8,15
210 PRINT#15,"IO"
220 INPUT#15,EN$,EM$,ET$,ES$
230 IFEN$="00"GOTO270
240 PRINT"{DOWN}"EN$", "EM$","ET$","ES$
250 CLOSE15
260 END
270 PRINT"{DOWN}{RVS}FETCHING{ROFF} DIRE
CTORY"
280 OPEN2,8,2,"$0,S,R"
290 INPUT#15,EN$,EM$,ET$,ES$
300 IFEN$="00"GOTO320
310 GOTO240
320 FORI=0TO253
330 GET#2,B$
340 NEXTI
350 N=0
360 FORJ=0TO7
370 GET#2,B$
380 IFB$=""THENB$=CHR$(0)
390 A=ASC(B$)
400 IFA>127ANDA<133GOTO510
410 FORI=0TO2
420 GET#2,B$
430 NEXTI
440 IFB$=""THENB$=CHR$(0)
450 A=ASC(B$)
460 IFA=0THENJ=7:NEXTJ:GOTO820
470 FORI=0TO25
480 GET#2,B$
490 NEXTI
500 GOTO750
510 GET#2,B$
520 IFB$=""THENB$=CHR$(0)
530 T%(N)=ASC(B$)
540 GET#2,B$
550 IFB$=""THENB$=CHR$(0)
```

```
560 S%(N)=ASC(B$)
570 F$=""
580 NULL=0
590 FORI=0TO15
600 GET#2,B$
610 IFB$=""THENB$=CHR$(0)
620 A=ASC(B$)
630 IFA=0THENNULL=NULL+1
640 IFA>127THENA=A-128
650 IFA<320RA>95THENA=63
660 IFA=34THENA=63
670 F$=F$+CHR$(A)
680 NEXTI
690 IFNULL=16THENJ=7:NEXTJ:GOTO820
700 F$(N)=F$
710 N=N+1
720 FORI=0TO10
730 GET#2,B$
740 NEXTI
750 IFJ=7GOTO790
760 FORI=0TO1
770 GET#2,B$
780 NEXTI
790 NEXTJ
800 IFST=64GOTO820
810 GOTO360
820 CLOSE2
830 INPUT#15,EN$,EM$,ET$,ES$
840 IFN>0GOTO880
850 PRINT"{DOWN}NO CLOSED FILES ARE IN T
HE DIRECTORY"
860 CLOSE15
870 END
880 I=0
890 PRINT"{CLR}"
900 N$=RIGHT$("00"+RIGHT$(STR$(N),LEN(ST
R$(N))-1),3)
910 FORJ=0TON-1
920 J$=RIGHT$("00"+RIGHT$(STR$(J+1),LEN(
STR$(J+1))-1),3)
930 PRINT"{HOME}{RVS}VALIDATING{ROFF} #"
J$"/"N$:    "F$(J)
940 PRINT"{HOME}";LEFT$(CD$,I+2);F$(J);"
";
950 NB=1
960 T=T%(J)
970 S=S%(J)
980 GOSUB1640
990 PRINT"{HOME}"LEFT$(CD$,I+2)F$(J)NB
1000 JOB=176
```

462

```
1010 GOSUB1520
1020 IFE=1GOTO1040
1030 GOTO1170
1040 JOB=128
1050 GOSUB1520
1060 IFE=1GOTO1080
1070 GOTO1170
1080 PRINT#15,"M-R"CHR$(0)CHR$(4)CHR$(2)

1090 GET#15,B$
1100 T=ASC(B$+CHR$(0))
1110 IFT=0GOTO1170
1120 GET#15,B$
1130 S=ASC(B$+CHR$(0))
1140 IFT>350RS>20+2*(T>17)+(T>24)+(T>30)
THENI=I+2:R$="{RVS}":GOTO1230
1150 NB=NB+1
1160 GOTO980
1170 I=I+2
1180 R$="{ROFF}"
1190 IFE=1GOTO1240
1200 R$="{RVS}"
1210 GOSUB1700
1220 GOTO1250
1230 E$="ILLEGAL TRACK OR SECTOR{LEFT}":
GOTO1250
1240 E$="00, OK,00,00"
1250 PRINT"{HOME}"R$;LEFT$(CD$,I);F$(J)"
 "E$"{ROFF}"
1260 F$(J)="{HOME}{RVS}"+J$+"{ROFF}"+R$+
LEFT$(CD$,I)+"{LEFT 3}"+F$(J)+" "+E$+"{R
OFF}"
1270 IFI=20ANDJ<>N-1THENFORD=1TO1000:NEX
TD:PRINT"{CLR}":I=0
1280 NEXTJ
1290 CLOSE15
1300 IFN<11THENS=N:GOTO1500
1310 INPUT"{DOWN}SUMMARY INFORMATION (Y/
N)   Y{LEFT 3}";Q$
1320 IFQ$<>"Y"GOTO110
1330 SI$="{CLR}{RVS}      /"+N$+"       SUMMAR
Y INFORMATION          {ROFF}"
1340 S=0
1350 PRINTSI$
1360 FORI=0TO9
1370 PRINTF$(S)
1380 S=S+1
1390 IFS=NTHENI=9
1400 NEXTI
1410 IFS<>NGOTO1460
```

```
1420 IFS=NTHENPRINT"{DOWN}{RVS}
 TYPE 'C' TO CONTINUE          {ROFF}"
1430 GETC$:IFC$=""THEN1430
1440 IFC$<>"C"GOTO1430
1450 GOTO110
1460 PRINT"{DOWN}{RVS}  TYPE 'C' TO CONT
INUE OR 'S' TO STOP    {ROFF}"
1470 GETC$:IFC$=""THEN1470
1480 IFC$<>"C"ANDC$<>"S"GOTO1470
1490 IFC$="C"GOTO1350
1500 GOTO110
1510 REM JOB QUEUE
1520 TRY=0
1530 PRINT#15,"M-W"CHR$(8)CHR$(0)CHR$(2)
CHR$(T)CHR$(S)
1540 PRINT#15,"M-W"CHR$(1)CHR$(0)CHR$(1)
CHR$(JOB)
1550 TRY=TRY+1
1560 PRINT#15,"M-R"CHR$(1)CHR$(0)
1570 GET#15,E$
1580 IFE$=""THENE$=CHR$(0)
1590 E=ASC(E$)
1600 IFTRY=500GOTO1620
1610 IFE>127GOTO1550
1620 RETURN
1630 REM STR$(T,S)
1640 T$=RIGHT$(STR$(T),LEN(STR$(T))-1)
1650 IFT<10THENT$="0"+T$
1660 S$=RIGHT$(STR$(S),LEN(STR$(S))-1)
1670 IFS<10THENS$="0"+S$
1680 RETURN
1690 REM EN$,EM$,ET$,ES$
1700 IFE>1ANDE<12THENEN$=RIGHT$(STR$(E+1
8),2):GOTO1720
1710 EN$="02":EM$="?TIME OUT":GOTO1730
1720 EM$="READ ERROR"
1730 ET$=T$
1740 ES$=S$
1750 E$=EN$+",  "+EM$+", "+ET$+", "+ES$
1760 RETURN
```

```
100 REM DUPLICATE TRACK & SECTOR - 1541
110 PRINT"{CLR}DUPLICATE TRACK & SECTOR
- 1541"
120 PRINT"{DOWN}INSERT DISKETTE IN DRIVE
"
130 INPUT"{DOWN}SOURCE TRACK AND SECTOR
(T,S)";T,S
140 GOSUB580
150 TR=T:T=0
160 SR=S:S=0
170 INPUT"{DOWN}TARGET TRACK AND SECTOR
(T,S)";T,S
180 GOSUB580
190 TW=T
200 SW=S
210 INPUT"{DOWN}ARE YOU SURE   Y{LEFT 3}"
;Q$
220 IFQ$<>"Y"THENEND
230 OPEN15,8,15
240 PRINT#15,"I0"
250 INPUT#15,EN$,EM$,ET$,ES$
260 IFEN$="00"GOTO310
270 PRINT"{DOWN}"EN$", "EM$", "ET$", "ES$
280 CLOSE15
290 END
300 REM SEEK
310 T=TR
320 S=SR
330 JOB=176
340 GOSUB630
350 IFE=1GOTO380
360 GOTO750
370 REM READ
380 JOB=128
390 GOSUB630
400 IFE=1GOTO430
410 GOTO750
420 REM SEEK
430 T=TW
440 S=SW
450 JOB=176
460 GOSUB630
470 IFE=1GOTO500
480 GOTO750
490 REM WRITE
500 JOB=144
510 GOSUB630
520 IFE=1GOTO540
530 GOTO750
540 CLOSE15
```

```
550 PRINT"{DOWN}DONE!"
560 END
570 REM ILLEGAL TRACK OR SECTOR
580 IFT<10RT>35THENEND
590 NS=20+2*(T>17)+(T>24)+(T>30)
600 IFS<00RS>NSTHENEND
610 RETURN
620 REM JOB QUEUE
630 TRY=0
640 PRINT#15,"M-W"CHR$(8)CHR$(0)CHR$(2)C
HR$(T)CHR$(S)
650 PRINT#15,"M-W"CHR$(1)CHR$(0)CHR$(1)C
HR$(JOB)
660 TRY=TRY+1
670 PRINT#15,"M-R"CHR$(1)CHR$(0)
680 GET#15,E$
690 IFE$=""THENE$=CHR$(0)
700 E=ASC(E$)
710 IFTRY=500GOTO750
720 IFE>127GOTO660
730 RETURN
740 REM ERROR HANDLER
750 ET$=RIGHT$(STR$(T),LEN(STR$(T))-1)
760 IFT<10THENET$="0"+ET$
770 ES$=RIGHT$(STR$(S),LEN(STR$(S))-1)
780 IFS<10THENES$="0"+ES$
790 IFE>1ANDE<12THENEN$=RIGHT$(STR$(E+18
),2):GOTO810
800 EN$="02":EM$="?TIME OUT":GOTO830
810 IFE=70RE=8THENEM$="WRITE ERROR":GOTO
830
820 EM$="READ ERROR"
830 PRINT"{DOWN}"EN$,  "EM$","ET$","ES$
840 PRINT"{DOWN}{RVS}FAILED{ROFF}"
850 CLOSE15
860 END
```

```
100 REM COPY TRACK & SECTOR - 1541
110 PRINT"{CLR}COPY TRACK & SECTOR - 154
1"
120 PRINT"{DOWN}INSERT MASTER IN DRIVE"
130 INPUT"{DOWN}TRACK AND SECTOR (T,S)";
T,S
140 IFT<1ORT>35THENEND
150 NS=20+2*(T>17)+(T>24)+(T>30)
160 IFS<0ORS>NSTHENEND
170 INPUT"{DOWN}ARE YOU SURE  Y{LEFT 3}"
;Q$
180 IFQ$<>"Y"THENEND
190 OPEN15,8,15
200 PRINT#15,"IO"
210 INPUT#15,EN$,EM$,ET$,ES$
220 IFEN$="00"GOTO270
230 PRINT"{DOWN}"EN$,  "EM$", "ET$", "ES$
240 CLOSE15
250 END
260 REM SEEK
270 JOB=176
280 GOSUB570
290 IFE=1GOTO320
300 GOTO690
310 REM READ
320 JOB=128
330 GOSUB570
340 IFE=1GOTO360
350 GOTO690
360 CLOSE15
370 PRINT"{DOWN}INSERT CLONE IN DRIVE"
380 PRINT"PRESS {RVS}RETURN{ROFF} TO CON
TINUE"
390 GETC$:IFC$=""THEN390
400 IFC$<>CHR$(13)GOTO390
410 PRINT"OK"
420 OPEN15,8,15
430 REM SEEK
440 JOB=176
450 GOSUB570
460 IFE=1GOTO490
470 GOTO690
480 REM WRITE
490 JOB=144
500 GOSUB570
510 IFE=1GOTO530
520 GOTO690
530 CLOSE15
540 PRINT"{DOWN}DONE!"
550 END
```

```
560 REM JOB QUEUE
570 TRY=0
580 PRINT#15,"M-W"CHR$(8)CHR$(0)CHR$(2)C
HR$(T)CHR$(S)
590 PRINT#15,"M-W"CHR$(1)CHR$(0)CHR$(1)C
HR$(JOB)
600 TRY=TRY+1
610 PRINT#15,"M-R"CHR$(1)CHR$(0)
620 GET#15,E$
630 IFE$=""THENE$=CHR$(0)
640 E=ASC(E$)
650 IFTRY=500GOTO690
660 IFE>127GOTO600
670 RETURN
680 REM ERROR HANDLER
690 ET$=RIGHT$(STR$(T),LEN(STR$(T))-1)
700 IFT<10THENET$="0"+ET$
710 ES$=RIGHT$(STR$(S),LEN(STR$(S))-1)
720 IFS<10THENES$="0"+ES$
730 IFE>1ANDE<12THENEN$=RIGHT$(STR$(E+18
),2):GOTO750
740 EN$="02":EM$="?TIME OUT":GOTO770
750 IFE=7ORE=8THENEM$="WRITE ERROR":GOTO
770
760 EM$="READ ERROR"
770 PRINT"{DOWN}"EN$,  "EM$","ET$","ES$
780 PRINT"{DOWN}{RVS}FAILED{ROFF}"
790 CLOSE15
800 END
```

```
100 REM RECOVER TRACK & SECTOR - 1541
110 PRINT"{CLR}RECOVER TRACK & SECTOR -
1541"
120 PRINT"{DOWN}INSERT DISKETTE IN DRIVE
"
130 INPUT"{DOWN}RECOVER TRACK AND SECTOR
 (T,S)";T,S
140 IFT<1ORT>35THENEND
150 NS=20+2*(T>17)+(T>24)+(T>30)
160 IFS<0ORS>NSTHENEND
170 INPUT"{DOWN}ARE YOU SURE  Y{LEFT 3}"
;Q$
180 IFQ$<>"Y"THENEND
190 OPEN15,8,15
200 PRINT#15,"IO"
210 INPUT#15,EN$,EM$,ET$,ES$
220 IFEN$="00"GOTO290
230 PRINT"{DOWN}"EN$, "EM$","ET$","ES$
240 PRINT"{DOWN}PRESS {RVS}RETURN{ROFF}
TO CONTINUE"
250 GETC$: IFC$=""THEN250
260 IFC$<>CHR$(13)GOTO250
270 PRINT"OK"
280 REM SEEK
290 JOB=176
300 GOSUB520
310 IFE=1GOTO340
320 GOTO640
330 REM READ
340 JOB=128
350 GOSUB520
360 IFE=4GOTO420
370 IFE=5GOTO440
380 IFE<>1GOTO640
390 PRINT"{DOWN}00, OK,00,00"
400 CLOSE15
410 END
420 PRINT#15,"M-W"CHR$(71)CHR$(0)CHR$(1)
CHR$(7)
430 REM WRITE
440 JOB=144
450 GOSUB520
460 IFE=1GOTO480
470 GOTO640
480 CLOSE15
490 PRINT"{DOWN}DONE!"
500 END
510 REM JOB QUEUE
520 TRY=0
530 PRINT#15,"M-W"CHR$(8)CHR$(0)CHR$(2)C
```

```
HR$(T)CHR$(S)
540 PRINT#15,"M-W"CHR$(1)CHR$(0)CHR$(1)C
HR$(JOB)
550 TRY=TRY+1
560 PRINT#15,"M-R"CHR$(1)CHR$(0)
570 GET#15,E$
580 IFE$=""THENE$=CHR$(0)
590 E=ASC(E$)
600 IFTRY=500GOTO640
610 IFE>127GOTO550
620 RETURN
630 REM ERROR HANDLER
640 ET$=RIGHT$(STR$(T),LEN(STR$(T))-1)
650 IFT<10THENET$="0"+ET$
660 ES$=RIGHT$(STR$(S),LEN(STR$(S))-1)
670 IFS<10THENES$="0"+ES$
680 IFE>1ANDE<12THENEN$=RIGHT$(STR$(E+18
),2):GOTO700
690 EN$="02":EM$="?TIME OUT":GOTO720
700 IFE=7ORE=8THENEM$="WRITE ERROR":GOTO
720
710 EM$="READ ERROR"
720 PRINT"{DOWN}"EN$",  "EM$","ET$","ES$
730 PRINT"{DOWN}{RVS}FAILED{ROFF}"
740 CLOSE15
750 END
```

```
100 REM LAZARUS - 1541
110 PRINT"{CLR}LAZARUS - 1541"
120 PRINT"{DOWN}INSERT DISKETTE IN DRIVE
"
130 INPUT"{HOME}{DOWN 4}ATTEMPT A RESURR
ECTION (Y/N)   Y{LEFT 3}";Q$
140 IFQ$<>"Y"THENEND
150 OPEN15,8,15
160 REM SEEK
170 FORT=1TO35
180 NS=20+2*(T>17)+(T>24)+(T>30)
190 T$=RIGHT$(STR$(T),LEN(STR$(T))-1)
200 IFT<10THENT$="0"+T$
210 JOB=176
220 GOSUB510
230 IFE=1GOTO250
240 BD=BD+1:R=R+NS:GOTO420
250 REM READ
260 FORS=0TONS
270 S$=RIGHT$(STR$(S),LEN(STR$(S))-1)
280 IFS<10THENS$="0"+S$
290 PRINT"{HOME}{DOWN 6}{RVS}RESURRECTIN
G{ROFF} TRACK "T$" - SECTOR "S$
300 JOB=128
310 GOSUB510
320 IFE=1GOTO410
330 R=R+1
340 IFE<>4ANDE<>5GOTO410
350 IFE=5GOTO380
360 PRINT#15,"M-W"CHR$(71)CHR$(0)CHR$(1)
CHR$(7)
370 REM WRITE
380 JOB=144
390 GOSUB510
400 IFE<>1THENW=W+1
410 NEXTS
420 NEXTT
430 CLOSE15
440 PRINT"{HOME}{DOWN 6}
                         "
450 IFBD=35THENPRINT"{HOME}{DOWN 6}?BAD
DISK":END
460 PRINT"{HOME}{DOWN 6}READ ERRORS :"R
470 PRINT"{DOWN}WRITE ERRORS:"W
480 PRINT"{DOWN}DONE!"
490 END
500 REM JOB QUEUE
510 TRY=0
520 PRINT#15,"M-W"CHR$(8)CHR$(0)CHR$(2)C
HR$(T)CHR$(S)
```

```
530 PRINT#15,"M-W"CHR$(1)CHR$(0)CHR$(1)C
HR$(JOB)
540 TRY=TRY+1
550 PRINT#15,"M-R"CHR$(1)CHR$(0)
560 GET#15,E$
570 IFE$=""THENE$=CHR$(0)
580 E=ASC(E$)
590 IFTRY=500GOTO610
600 IFE>127GOTO540
610 RETURN
```

```
100 REM INTERROGATE FORMATTING ID'S - 15
41
110 DIMT(35)
120 FORI=1TO35
130 T(I)=1
140 NEXTI
150 PRINT"{CLR}INTERROGATE FORMATTING ID
'S - 1541"
160 PRINT"{DOWN}INSERT MASTER IN DRIVE"
170 PRINT"{DOWN}PRESS {RVS}RETURN{ROFF}
TO CONTINUE"
180 GETC$:IFC$=""THEN180
190 IFC$<>CHR$(13)GOTO180
200 OPEN15,8,15
210 PRINT"{CLR}"
220 REM SEEK
230 FORT=1TO35
240 IFT(T)=0GOTO440
250 GOSUB550
260 IFE<>1GOTO410
270 PRINT#15,"M-R"CHR$(22)CHR$(0)
280 GET#15,I$
290 IFI$=""THENI$=CHR$(0)
300 I=ASC(I$)
310 I$=RIGHT$(STR$(I),LEN(STR$(I))-1)
320 PRINT#15,"M-R"CHR$(23)CHR$(0)
330 GET#15,D$
340 IFD$=""THEND$=CHR$(0)
350 D=ASC(D$)
360 D$=RIGHT$(STR$(D),LEN(STR$(D))-1)
370 I$="CHR$("+I$+")"
380 D$="CHR$("+D$+")"
390 ID$=I$+" + "+D$
400 GOTO450
410 IFE=3THENID$="?NO SYNC MARKS":GOTO45
0
420 IFE=2THENID$="?HEADER BLOCKS NOT PRE
SENT":GOTO450
430 IFE=9THENID$="?CHECKSUM ERROR IN HEA
DERS":GOTO450
440 ID$="?TIME OUT"
450 T$=RIGHT$(STR$(T),LEN(STR$(T))-1)
460 IFT<10THENT$=" "+T$
470 PRINT"TRACK "T$" = "ID$
480 REM PAUSE
490 GETC$:IFC$=""GOTO510
500 GETC$:IFC$=""THEN500
510 NEXTT
520 CLOSE15
530 END
```

```
540 REM JOB QUEUE
550 TRY=0
560 PRINT#15,"M-W"CHR$(8)CHR$(0)CHR$(2)C
HR$(T)CHR$(0)
570 PRINT#15,"M-W"CHR$(1)CHR$(0)CHR$(1)C
HR$(176)
580 TRY=TRY+1
590 PRINT#15,"M-R"CHR$(1)CHR$(0)
600 GET#15,E$
610 IFE$=""THENE$=CHR$(0)
620 E=ASC(E$)
630 IFTRY=500GOTO650
640 IFE>127GOTO580
650 RETURN
```

```
100 REM INTERROGATE A TRACK - 1541
110 PRINT"{CLR}INTERROGATE A TRACK - 154
1"
120 PRINT"{DOWN}INSERT MASTER IN DRIVE"
130 INPUT"{DOWN}INTERROGATE TRACK";T
140 IFT<10RT>35THENEND
150 INPUT"{DOWN}ARE YOU SURE  Y{LEFT 3}"
;Q$
160 IFQ$<>"Y"THENEND
170 OPEN15,8,15
180 NS=20+2*(T>17)+(T>24)+(T>30)
190 REM SEEK
200 JOB=176
210 GOSUB370
220 REM READ
230 PRINT"{CLR}"
240 FORS=0TONS
250 JOB=128
260 GOSUB370
270 S$=RIGHT$(STR$(S),LEN(STR$(S))-1)
280 IFS<10THENS$=" "+S$
290 PRINT"TRACK";T;"- ";
300 IFE=1THENPRINT"SECTOR "S$" = OK":GOT
O330
310 IFE>1ANDE<12THENEM$=STR$(E+18)+" REA
D ERROR"
320 PRINT"SECTOR "S$" ="EM$
330 NEXTS
340 CLOSE15
350 END
360 REM JOB QUEUE
370 TRY=0
380 PRINT#15,"M-W"CHR$(8)CHR$(0)CHR$(2)C
HR$(T)CHR$(S)
390 PRINT#15,"M-W"CHR$(1)CHR$(0)CHR$(1)C
HR$(JOB)
400 TRY=TRY+1
410 PRINT#15,"M-R"CHR$(1)CHR$(0)
420 GET#15,E$
430 IFE$=""THENE$=CHR$(0)
440 E=ASC(E$)
450 IFTRY=500GOTO480
460 IFE>127GOTO400
470 RETURN
480 EM$="?TIME OUT"
490 RETURN
```

```
100 REM SHAKE, RATTLE, & ROLL - 1541
110 PRINT"{CLR}SHAKE, RATTLE, & ROLL - 1
541"
120 PRINT"{DOWN}INSERT DISKETTE IN DRIVE
"
130 INPUT"{DOWN}CLATTER TRACK";T
140 IFT<1ORT>35THENEND
150 INPUT"{DOWN}ARE YOU SURE  Y{LEFT 3}"
;Q$
160 IFQ$<>"Y"THENEND
170 OPEN15,8,15
180 OPEN2,8,2,"#"
190 PRINT"{CLR}"
200 REM SEEK
210 GOSUB360
220 NS=20+2*(T>17)+(T>24)+(T>30)
230 FORS=0TONS
240 REM READ
250 PRINT#15,"U1";2;0;T;S
260 INPUT#15,EN$,EM$,ET$,ES$
270 PRINT"TRACK";T;"- ";
280 IFEN$="00"THENPRINT"SECTOR";S;"= OK"
:GOTO300
290 PRINT"SECTOR "ES$" = "EN$" "EM$
300 NEXTS
310 CLOSE2
320 INPUT#15,EN$,EM$,ET$,ES$
330 CLOSE15
340 END
350 REM JOB QUEUE
360 TRY=0
370 PRINT#15,"M-W"CHR$(8)CHR$(0)CHR$(2)C
HR$(T)CHR$(S)
380 PRINT#15,"M-W"CHR$(1)CHR$(0)CHR$(1)C
HR$(176)
390 TRY=TRY+1
400 PRINT#15,"M-R"CHR$(1)CHR$(0)
410 GET#15,E$
420 IFE$=""THENE$=CHR$(0)
430 IFTRY=500GOTO460
440 IFASC(E$)>127GOTO390
450 RETURN
460 CLOSE2
470 INPUT#15,EN$,EM$,ET$,ES$
480 CLOSE15
490 PRINT"{DOWN}{RVS}FAILED{ROFF}"
500 END
```

```
100 REM INTERROGATE A DISKETTE - 1541
110 DIMT(35)
120 FORI=1TO35
130 T(I)=1
140 NEXTI
150 PRINT"{CLR}INTERROGATE A DISKETTE -
1541"
160 PRINT"{DOWN}INSERT MASTER IN DRIVE"
170 PRINT"{DOWN}PRESS {RVS}RETURN{ROFF}
TO CONTINUE"
180 GETC$:IFC$=""THEN180
190 IFC$<>CHR$(13)GOTO180
200 PRINT"OK"
210 PRINT
220 OPEN15,8,15
230 FORT=1TO35
240 IFT(T)=0GOTO390
250 NS=20+2*(T>17)+(T>24)+(T>30)
260 REM SEEK
270 JOB=176
280 GOSUB430
290 REM READ
300 FORS=0TONS
310 JOB=128
320 GOSUB430
330 IFE=1GOTO380
340 S$=RIGHT$(STR$(S),LEN(STR$(S))-1)
350 IFS<10THENS$=" "+S$
360 IFE>1ANDE<12THENEM$=STR$(E+18)+" REA
D ERROR"
370 PRINT"TRACK";T;"- SECTOR "S$" ="EM$
380 NEXTS
390 NEXTT
400 CLOSE15
410 END
420 REM JOB QUEUE
430 TRY=0
440 PRINT#15,"M-W"CHR$(8)CHR$(0)CHR$(2)C
HR$(T)CHR$(S)
450 PRINT#15,"M-W"CHR$(1)CHR$(0)CHR$(1)C
HR$(JOB)
460 TRY=TRY+1
470 PRINT#15,"M-R"CHR$(1)CHR$(0)
480 GET#15,E$
490 IFE$=""THENE$=CHR$(0)
500 E=ASC(E$)
510 IFTRY=500GOTO540
520 IFE>127GOTO460
530 RETURN
540 EM$="?TIME OUT"
550 RETURN
```

```
100 REM DUMP TRACK & SECTOR - 1541
110 POKE56,159
120 CLR
130 PRINT"{CLR}DUMP TRACK & SECTOR - 154
1"
140 PRINT"{DOWN}INSERT DISKETTE IN DRIVE
"
150 INPUT"{DOWN}TRACK & SECTOR (T,S)";T,
S
160 IFT<1ORT>35GOTO630
170 NS=20+2*(T>17)+(T>24)+(T>30)
180 IFS<0ORS>NSGOTO630
190 INPUT"{DOWN}ARE YOU SURE  Y{LEFT 3}"
;Q$
200 IFQ$<>"Y"GOTO630
210 OPEN15,8,15
220 PRINT#15,"IO"
230 INPUT#15,EN$,EM$,ET$,ES$
240 IFEN$="00"GOTO290
250 PRINT"{DOWN}"EN$","EM$","ET$","ES$
260 PRINT"{DOWN}PRESS {RVS}RETURN{ROFF}
TO CONTINUE"
270 GETC$:IFC$=""THEN270
280 IFC$<>CHR$(13)GOTO270
290 T$=RIGHT$(STR$(T),LEN(STR$(T))-1)
300 IFT<10THENT$="0"+T$
310 S$=RIGHT$(STR$(S),LEN(STR$(S))-1)
320 IFS<10THENS$="0"+S$
330 REM SEEK
340 JOB=176
350 GOSUB670
360 IFE=<>1GOTO410
370 REM READ
380 JOB=128
390 GOSUB670
400 IFE=10RE=40RE=5GOTO510
410 IFE>1ANDE<12THENEN$=RIGHT$(STR$(E+18
),2):GOTO430
420 EN$="02":EM$="?TIME OUT":GOTO440
430 EM$="READ ERROR"
440 ET$=T$
450 ES$=S$
460 PRINT"{DOWN}"EN$","EM$","ET$","ES$
470 CLOSE15
480 POKE56,160
490 CLR
500 END
510 FORJ=0TO31
520 FORI=0TO7
530 PRINT#15,"M-R"CHR$(J*8+I)CHR$(4)
```

```
540 GET#15,D$
550 D=ASC(D$+CHR$(0))
560 POKE(40704+J*8+I),D
570 NEXTI
580 NEXTJ
590 CLOSE15
600 PRINT"{DOWN}DONE!"
610 PRINT"{DOWN}POKE56,160:CLR"
620 END
630 POKE56,160
640 CLR
650 END
660 REM JOB QUEUE
670 TRY=0
680 PRINT#15,"M-W"CHR$(8)CHR$(0)CHR$(2)C
HR$(T)CHR$(S)
690 PRINT#15,"M-W"CHR$(1)CHR$(0)CHR$(1)C
HR$(JOB)
700 TRY=TRY+1
710 PRINT#15,"M-R"CHR$(1)CHR$(0)
720 GET#15,E$
730 IFE$=""THENE$=CHR$(0)
740 E=ASC(E$)
750 IFTRY=500GOTO770
760 IFE>127GOTO700
770 RETURN
```

```
100 REM BULK ERASER - 1541
110 PRINT"{CLR}BULK ERASER - 1541"
120 PRINT"{DOWN}INSERT DISKETTE IN DRIVE
"
130 INPUT"{DOWN}{RVS}ERASE{ROFF} THIS DI
SKETTE   Y{LEFT 3}";Q$
140 IFQ$<>"Y"THENEND
150 INPUT"{DOWN}ARE YOU SURE   Y{LEFT 3}"
;Q$
160 IFQ$<>"Y"THENEND
170 OPEN15,8,15
180 FORI=0TO23
190 READD
200 D$=D$+CHR$(D)
210 NEXTI
220 PRINT#15,"M-W"CHR$(0)CHR$(4)CHR$(24)
D$
230 FORT=1TO35
240 PRINT"{HOME}{DOWN 8}{RVS}ERASING{ROF
F} TRACK"T
250 REM SEEK
260 JOB=176
270 GOSUB360
280 REM EXECUTE
290 JOB=224
300 GOSUB360
310 NEXTT
320 PRINT"{HOME}{DOWN 8}DONE!
"
330 CLOSE15
340 END
350 REM JOB QUEUE
360 TRY=0
370 PRINT#15,"M-W"CHR$(8)CHR$(0)CHR$(2)C
HR$(T)CHR$(0)
380 PRINT#15,"M-W"CHR$(1)CHR$(0)CHR$(1)C
HR$(JOB)
390 TRY=TRY+1
400 PRINT#15,"M-R"CHR$(1)CHR$(0)
410 GET#15,E$
420 IFE$=""THENE$=CHR$(0)
430 E=ASC(E$)
440 IFTRY=500GOTO470
450 IFE>127GOTO390
460 RETURN
470 CLOSE15
480 PRINT"{DOWN}{RVS}FAILED{ROFF}"
490 END
500 REM 21 ERROR
```

```
510 DATA   32,163,253,169, 85,141,  1, 28
520 DATA  162,255,160, 48, 32,201,253, 32
530 DATA    0,254,169,  1, 76,105,249,234
```

APPENDIX D
MATHEMATICAL CONVERSION ROUTINES

```
100  REM DECIMAL TO HEXADECIMAL
110  H$="0123456789ABCDEF"
120  PRINT"{CLR}DECIMAL TO HEXADECIMAL"
130  D=-1
140  INPUT"{DOWN}DECIMAL        ";D
150  IFD<0ORD>255THENEND
160  H=INT(D/16)
170  L=D-(H*16)
180  HD$=MID$(H$,H+1,1)+MID$(H$,L+1,1)
190  PRINT"{DOWN}HEXADECIMAL: "HD$
200  GOTO130
```

```
100 REM HEXADECIMAL TO DECIMAL
110 H$="0123456789ABCDEF"
120 PRINT"{CLR}HEXADECIMAL TO DECIMAL"
130 HD$=""
140 INPUT"{DOWN}HEXADECIMAL";HD$
150 IFLEN(HD$)=OTHENEND
160 IFLEN(HD$)<>2THENEND
170 H=0
180 FORI=1TO16
190 IFLEFT$(HD$,1)=MID$(H$,I,1)THENH=I:I
=16
200 NEXTI
210 IFH=OGOTO130
220 H=H-1
230 L=0
240 FORI=1TO16
250 IFRIGHT$(HD$,1)=MID$(H$,I,1)THENL=I:
I=16
260 NEXTI
270 IFL=OGOTO130
280 L=L-1
290 D=H*16+L
300 PRINT"{DOWN}DECIMAL      :"D
310 GOTO130
```

```
100 REM HEXADECIMAL TO DECIMAL
110 H$="0123456789ABCDEF"
130 PRINT"CONVERT HEXADECIMAL TO DECIMAL"
150 HD$=""
140 INPUT"ENTER HEXADECIMAL";HD$
150 IF LEN(HD$)=0 THEN END
160 IF LEN(HD$)<>2 THEN END
170 H=0
180 FOR I=1 TO 15
190 IF LEFT$(HD$,1)=MID$(H$,I,1) THEN H=H+I-1
    =16
200 NEXT I
210 IF H=0 GOTO 130
220 H=H-1
230 L=0
240 FOR J=1 TO 16
250 IF RIGHT$(HD$,1)=MID$(H$,J,1) THEN L=J-1
    L=16
260 NEXT J
270 IF J=0 GOTO 130
280 L=L-1
290 D=H*16+L
300 PRINT" CONVERT DECIMAL   =";D
310 GOTO 130
```

```
100 REM DECIMAL TO BINARY
110 DEFFNB(B)=2^(B-INT(B/8)*8)ANDD
120 PRINT"{CLR}DECIMAL TO BINARY"
130 D=-1
140 INPUT"{DOWN}DECIMAL";D
150 IFD<0ORD>255THENEND
160 PRINT"{DOWN}BINARY : ";
170 FORB=7TO0 STEP-1
180 IFFNB(B)=0THENPRINT"0";:GOTO200
190 PRINT"1";
200 NEXTB
210 PRINT
220 GOTO130
```

```
100 REM BINARY TO DECIMAL
110 PRINT"{CLR}BINARY TO DECIMAL"
120 B$=""
130 INPUT"{DOWN}BINARY (E.G., 10101010)"
;B$
140 IFLEN(B$)=0THENEND
150 IFLEN(B$)<>8THENEND
160 B=0
170 D=0
180 FORI=1TO8
190 IFMID$(B$,I,1)="1"THENB=B+1:D=D+2^(8
-I):GOTO210
200 IFMID$(B$,I,1)="0"THENB=B+1
210 NEXTI
220 IFB<>8GOTO120
230 PRINT"{DOWN}DECIMAL              :
"D
240 GOTO120
```

```
100 REM HEXADECIMAL TO GCR
110 H$="0123456789ABCDEF"
120 DIMB$(15)
130 B$(0)="01010"
140 B$(1)="01011"
150 B$(2)="10010"
160 B$(3)="10011"
170 B$(4)="01110"
180 B$(5)="01111"
190 B$(6)="10110"
200 B$(7)="10111"
210 B$(8)="01001"
220 B$(9)="11001"
230 B$(10)="11010"
240 B$(11)="11011"
250 B$(12)="01101"
260 B$(13)="11101"
270 B$(14)="11110"
280 B$(15)="10101"
290 PRINT"{CLR}HEXADECIMAL TO GCR"
300 HG$=""
310 INPUT"{DOWN}HEXADECIMAL (E.G., 084A0
023)";HG$
320 IFLEN(HG$)=0THENEND
330 IFLEN(HG$)<>8THENEND
340 FORI=1TO4
350 HG$(I)=MID$(HG$,I*2-1,2)
360 NEXTI
370 FORJ=1TO4
380 H(J)=0
390 FORI=1TO16
400 IFLEFT$(HG$(J),1)=MID$(H$,I,1)THENH(
J)=I:I=16
410 NEXTI
420 IFH(J)=0GOTO300
430 H(J)=H(J)-1
440 L(J)=0
450 FORI=1TO16
460 IFRIGHT$(HG$(J),1)=MID$(H$,I,1)THENL
(J)=I:I=16
470 NEXTI
480 IFL(J)=0GOTO300
490 L(J)=L(J)-1
500 NEXTJ
510 FORI=1TO4
520 IMAGE$=IMAGE$+B$(H(I))
530 IMAGE$=IMAGE$+B$(L(I))
540 NEXTI
550 PRINT"{DOWN}"IMAGE$
560 PRINT"{UP}";
```

```
570 FORI=1TO8
580 PRINT"^      ";
590 NEXTI
600 PRINT"{UP}"
610 FORI=1TO5
620 BD$(I)=MID$(IMAGE$,I*8-7,8)
630 NEXTI
640 FORJ=1TO5
650 FORI=1TO8
660 IFMID$(BD$(J),I,1)="1"THEND(J)=D(J)+
2^(8-I)
670 NEXTI
680 NEXTJ
690 FORI=1TO5
700 H=INT(D(I)/16)+1
710 L=D(I)-(H-1)*16+1
720 DH$(I)=MID$(H$,H,1)+MID$(H$,L,1)
730 NEXTI
740 PRINT"{DOWN}HEXADECIMAL: ";
750 FORI=1TO4
760 PRINTHG$(I);" ";
770 NEXTI
780 PRINT
790 PRINT"{DOWN}GCR          : ";
800 FORI=1TO5
810 PRINTDH$(I);" ";
820 NEXTI
830 PRINT
840 PRINT"{DOWN}DONE!"
850 END
```

```
100 REM GCR TO HEXADECIMAL
110 H$="0123456789ABCDEF"
120 DEFFNB(B)=2^(B-INT(B/8)*8)ANDD
130 DIMB$(15)
140 B$(0)="01010"
150 B$(1)="01011"
160 B$(2)="10010"
170 B$(3)="10011"
180 B$(4)="01110"
190 B$(5)="01111"
200 B$(6)="10110"
210 B$(7)="10111"
220 B$(8)="01001"
230 B$(9)="11001"
240 B$(10)="11010"
250 B$(11)="11011"
260 B$(12)="01101"
270 B$(13)="11101"
280 B$(14)="11110"
290 B$(15)="10101"
300 PRINT"{CLR}GCR TO HEXADECIMAL"
310 GH$=""
320 INPUT"{DOWN}GCR (E.G., 525DA52A53)";
GH$
330 IFLEN(GH$)=0THENEND
340 IFLEN(GH$)<>10THENEND
350 FORI=1TO5
360 GH$(I)=MID$(GH$,I*2-1,2)
370 NEXTI
380 FORJ=1TO5
390 H(J)=0
400 FORI=1TO16
410 IFLEFT$(GH$(J),1)=MID$(H$,I,1)THENH(
J)=I:I=16
420 NEXTI
430 IFH(J)=0GOTO310
440 H(J)=H(J)-1
450 L(J)=0
460 FORI=1TO16
470 IFRIGHT$(GH$(J),1)=MID$(H$,I,1)THENL
(J)=I:I=16
480 NEXTI
490 IFL(J)=0GOTO310
500 L(J)=L(J)-1
510 NEXTJ
520 FORI=1TO5
530 HD(I)=H(I)*16+L(I)
540 NEXTI
550 IMAGE$=""
560 FORI=1TO5
```

```
570 D=HD(I)
580 FORB=7TOO STEP-1
590 IFFNB(B)=OTHENIMAGE$=IMAGE$+"O":GOTO
610
600 IMAGE$=IMAGE$+"1"
610 NEXTB
620 NEXTI
630 PRINT"{DOWN}"IMAGE$
640 PRINT"{UP}";
650 FORI=1TO5
660 PRINT"^          ";
670 NEXTI
680 PRINT"{UP}"
690 FORI=1TO8
700 H$(I)=MID$(IMAGE$,I*5-4,5)
710 NEXTI
720 FORJ=1TO8
730 FORI=0TO15
740 IFH$(J)=B$(I)THEND(J)=I+1:I=15
750 NEXTI
760 NEXTJ
770 FORI=1TO8
780 IFD(I)=OTHENBDE=1
790 NEXTI
800 IFBDE=1GOTO940
810 PRINT"{DOWN}GCR        : ";
820 FORI=1TO5
830 PRINTGH$(I)" ";
840 NEXTI
850 PRINT
860 PRINT"{DOWN}HEXADECIMAL: ";
870 FORI=1TO8
880 PRINTMID$(H$,D(I),1);
890 IFI/2=INT(I/2)THENPRINT" ";
900 NEXTI
910 PRINT
920 PRINT"{DOWN}DONE!"
930 END
940 FORI=1TO8
950 IFD(I)=OTHENPRINT"{RVS}"H$(I)"{ROFF}
";:GOTO970
960 PRINTH$(I);
970 NEXTI
980 PRINT"{DOWN}{RVS}BYTE DECODING ERROR
{ROFF}"
990 END
```

INDEX

INDEX

O

P

Q

R

V

W